Psychological Problems
in Mental Deficiency

UNDER THE EDITORSHIP OF
Wayne H. Holtzman and Gardner Murphy

Psychological Problems

HARPER & ROW, *Publishers*   *New York, Evanston, and London*

FOURTH EDITION

in *Mental Deficiency*

SEYMOUR B. SARASON
Yale University

JOHN DORIS
Cornell University

with chapters by
FRANCES KAPLAN
and
M. MICHAEL KLABER

Contents

Preface

This fourth edition is in most respects a new book. The fact that there are now two authors reflects several things: mental subnormality is no longer a field which can be adequately grasped, digested, and communicated by one person; we, the authors, are long-time friends and colleagues who share common interests and orientations, while at the same time differing as to the aspects of the field which interest us most; and, finally, we have both struggled with the problem of how to present subject matter so that the student can see that the way *he* thinks is as important as the facts he learns. It is this last consideration which probably was most influential in determining the style and content of this book.

In collaborating we learned from each other, and it is our hope that the reader will have similarly benefited from this collaboration.

We wish to express our profound thanks to Dr. Frances Kaplan and Dr. Michael Klaber who were willing to contribute chapters describing and summarizing their research before it has been published elsewhere. Their research programs concern problems and issues which for too long have escaped systematic study. We consider their chapters to be a distinctive feature of this book.

As usual, Anita Miller's help and patience in the typing of this manuscript were as crucial for our emotional stability as they were for the mechanics of execution and completion.

It is also appropriate that we express our thanks to two of our graduate students, Myra Casper and Margaret Thomas, who gave much help at various stages in our work on this book, from tracking down some most elusive references to the preparation of the index.

Seymour B. Sarason
John Doris

Psychological Problems
in Mental Deficiency

Goals and organization of the book

It is a truism among researchers that the way in which a problem is formulated determines in large measure the methodology to be used. Similarly, the design or organization of a book is determined by the goals of the writer. Unfortunately, both for researchers and writers, a clear statement of goals is not always easy to come by; and, when it is, one sometimes finds that goals may be in conflict with each other in the sense that they give rise to competing modes of study and organization —which is why researchers will often "break up" a problem into several discrete studies. This solution is far less available to writers of books, i.e., except under unusual circumstances writers have to accomplish their goals in a single volume.

The above is by way of saying that the writers of this book struggled with a problem of which all teachers are aware. Indeed, it is a problem which at the same time that it is challenging and fascinating—and guarantees that the teacher will be ever vigilant and responsive—is also a major source of despair and worry. Simply stated, the problem is: Assuming clarity of purpose, how does one vary one's methods in harmony with the knowledge that the class is (or may be) extremely heterogeneous? As one elementary school teacher put it: "I have no doubt that one of the rewards teachers receive in the hereafter is that their classes are truly homogeneous." To which another teacher replied, "So what do we do here and now?"

Let us concretize the problem we faced. One of the goals we hoped to accomplish was to help the reader gain some historical perspective on the problems we discuss. We do not mean by historical perspective a list of names, or a chronological sequence of dates, events, or studies, but rather a number of generalizations which would give the reader some sense of personal continuity with the past, the need for tentativeness in regard to the current scene, and the feeling that both he and the field will change in the future. In short, we wished that the reader would not undersell the past, oversell the present, or overlook that the outlines of a "different" future are already in the process of development. Given this as one of our aims it might seem self-evident that one should proceed in a straightforward historical fashion, i.e., start at the beginning (which is far from easy to define) and trace the history of the field or particular problem. Our experience in teaching courses in mental subnormality forced on us an awareness of two reasons for hesitating to proceed in this fashion. The first stemmed from our impression that people who become interested in mental subnormality—at least to the extent of reading a book or taking a course—do so because of some interest in the current scene and not because of an historical concern. When beginning with a detailed historical presentation there is a tendency not to capitalize on interest in the current scene, and the concomitant risk of having historical factors viewed in the category of "the past" and not as part of the living present. This need not happen but in our experience it happens frequently. The second reason, and one implied in the first, is our belief that in looking back on history, the generalizations one can develop will be determined by the knowledge of the ground one is standing on, i.e., the present or relatively near past.

Because of these considerations we decided that the first part of this book would deal with issues and problems which in the past three decades or so seem to have dominated this field in terms of practice, research, and program development. If our experience as teachers is any guide, these issues and problems have in one way or another attracted individuals to the field. The marked changes which have relatively recently made mental subnormality a popular area; the styles of thinking about the behavior of subnormal individuals; the ever-present problems of criteria, grouping, and diagnosis; the ambiguities and significances of "cultural deprivation"; modes of educational and institutional intervention and their consequences; the difficulties of squaring practices with theories—these are the issues and problems we take up in the first half of this book. Special mention should be made here of two chapters each of which addresses itself to a problem which, in our opinion, will in the near future receive far more attention than it has in the past. The first of these chapters was written by Dr. Michael Klaber and describes what may be the most systematic and comprehensive comparative study yet done on the "climates" of institutions for mentally subnormal individuals. When one considers that institutionalization has been one of society's major ways of responding to the problem, it is indeed surprising that this area has been so little studied. The second of these special chapters was written by Dr. Frances Kaplan and describes exploratory clinical and research work on how the retarded child seems to affect family organization, with a special focus on the normal siblings. Dr. Kaplan's work presents us squarely with the limitations of a clinical approach which absorbs itself with the subnormal individual and neglects what can be done to prevent unfortunate consequences to those around him. The chapters by Drs. Klaber and Kaplan underline a central theme running through the preceding chapters (as well as the rest of the book), i.e., we must not be blinded to new ways of thinking and doing but must ever be alert to the necessity of examining with a critical eye that which we do so that we may assess the validity of what we do and what we think.

It is easy, of course, to say that one should be objective and critical; at the same time that such a statement is necessary it is not very helpful. We are firmly of the opinion that heightened awareness of three related factors does help in attaining a dispassionate criticalness, and it is these factors which receive extended discussion in the second part of this book. The first of these involves being able to see the historical continuity between present and past. Consequently, when we discuss in detail the heredity–environment controversy it is with the aim of demonstrating that past controversies are very much related to issues discussed in the earlier chapters of this book, e.g., the current interest in cultural deprivation does not reflect a new discovery but is rather a modern version of some old ideas. To the extent that the reader becomes aware of this continuity and the factors which in the past have contributed to the generation of more heat than light, he may be able to take critical distance from his own passionate convictions. At the least, he may more sharply distinguish between an opinion and a fact. It is this reason—and not because of some abstract interest in social and intellectual history—that we present and discuss in some detail the not always glorious history of the eugenics movement and its consequences for mental subnormality. Failure to distinguish between opinion and fact is bad enough; but when, in addition, facts are used to justify social action as if the two are not separated by a particular set of values, we have a situation in which great, unintended harm can occur. As we say in different parts of this book:

Expertise itself, a knowledge of facts and theories never leads to a social action program. It is only when the expertise interacts with a value system that social action programs arise. It is easier to see the interaction when one deals with the more remote past than it is for the time in which we live. That it is more difficult places a special obligation on us, *particularly those of us whose activities and practices are intended to change the lives of other people.* We have strenuously to resist assuming, implicitly or explicitly, that our practices are the result of cold logic and scientific facts unmediated by the knotty problems of value.

The second factor discussed at length in the later parts of this book—and discussed briefly in Chapter 2—is that the theories and practices which characterize a field at a particular point in time reflect the nature of that society at that time. That is to say, as professionals as well as citizens we reflect the different forces operative in the society at the time. When we lose sight of this we unwittingly erect a barrier against recognizing patterns of social change which ultimately, in varying degrees and ways, will change us and our fields. The third factor elaborated upon in the later pages of this book—and briefly discussed in Chapter 3 when we discuss brain injury as an etiological scapegoat—concerns biological factors and their inextricable relation to psychological and social ones. We there try to deal with the tendency, so strong in all of us, to view problems in an either-or, black-white, dichotomous fashion, e.g., it is heredity *or* environment, it is biological *or* psychological. Reality stubbornly resists conforming to this oversimplified style of thinking. The final chapter in this book, which concerns infantile autism, is a sobering example of how this kind of thinking can generate and continue controversy until the point where the combatants begin to recognize that either-or explanations are getting in the way of obtaining new insights and knowledge.

We recognize that this book might have been organized differently. But perhaps more important than organization is whether we have communicated to the reader a way of thinking about problems, and not only problems in mental subnormality. What fascinates us about this field is how it overflows into so many other areas in ways that make a mockery of boundaries which traditionally separate people and fields. Psychology, education, biology, sociology, anthropology, social history—these are but some of the areas into which increasing numbers of those interested in mental subnormality must enter, not because it is good to have broad knowledge but because in reality the problem encompasses aspects of all of these fields. As our horizons are enlarged we may better be able to see that ways of thinking—the role of passion and bias, the necessity and difficulty of adhering to rules of evidence, the importance of perspective, the distinction between facts and values—are amazingly similar as one goes from problem to problem and field to field.

$\mathcal{M}$ental deficiency and the larger society

$\mathbf{M}$ental deficiency is a particularly clear instance of the contention that no field of scientific investigation is independent of the larger society in which it is embedded. In the twentieth century this is most clearly demonstrated, of course, by the developments which have taken place, and are taking place, in atomic physics. The direction of research, its content and scope, the sources of its support, its applications, the nature and locale of training and research laboratories—these and other characteristics of atomic physics in one or another way bear the imprint of our larger society. Earlier in the century very few individuals could have anticipated that as small and as pure a field as atomic physics would become involved in matters of public policy and the general welfare. The developments in atomic physics have not been without significance for the field of mental deficiency if only because of the possibility that an increased radiation level of the atmosphere can so affect human genetics that subsequent generations may suffer an increase in the number of mentally defective individuals.

It is beyond the scope of this book to go into detail about the factors which in the course of two or three decades contributed to changing the face of the field of mental deficiency. In this chapter we shall briefly discuss some of the more important and relatively recent factors in order to give the reader some basis for developing an historical perspective that may serve as a control over undue pessimism, unwarranted optimism, and narrowness of view. Particularly when a field is expanding and changing rapidly by virtue of events external to it—for example, in the form of available governmental support for facilities, training, and research—it frequently happens that increased activity is confused with progress, publications with enlightenment, and past efforts and thoughts with obvious irrelevance.

The Pre-World War II Period

Although nearly all of the important problems with which we now deal in mental deficiency confronted us several decades ago, they were of concern and interest to far fewer people than is now the case. It would be a mistake to conclude, however, that because few people were interested there was an absence of strong controversy. As Blatt and Garfunkel (1965) have indicated, it is precisely because the problem with which the mentally deficient individual has always confronted us concerns the limits of the "educability of intelligence" that "it involves one immediately in conceptions of the nature of man, an involvement which lends fascination to the problem at the same time that it touches off strong feeling and inevitable controversy. It should not be surprising, therefore, that even in the research literature cold data and hot controversy have existed side by side." As these and other writers have shown, differing conceptions about the relation between heredity and environment have influenced individual attitudes toward the development, management, and education of the mentally subnormal individual. Later in this book we shall go into this matter in greater detail. Suffice it to say here that it has long been recognized that problems in mental subnormality are of central significance to such fields as psychology, genetics, and education.

Restricting ourselves to the decades immediately preceding World War II, we are still left with the question of why mental subnormality—as an area of professional practice as well as an area of basic and applied research—involved relatively few people and was barely represented in university centers of training and research. A partial but significant aspect of the answer to this question—and an answer which has relevance for fields other than mental subnormality—is that concern and responsibility for the mentally subnormal individual were not part of our national policy. The lack of any national concern with the problem derived in part from the indifference or inaction reflected by absence of policy on the community level and, in some instances, the state level as well. Where a policy did exist, it tended to have one implicit and one explicit characteristic. The implicit characteristic was the belief that not very much could be done for the mentally subnormal individual. The explicit characteristic was that it was in his and, therefore, society's best interest to remove and segregate him from family and community. Institutionalization—usually to large, inaccessible, or hard-to-reach institutions—was society's major reaction to the problems of the mentally subnormal individual.

In our larger urban centers there were special classes for the subnormal child. But these were grossly inadequate in terms of the numbers considered eligible, and in many instances were developed because existing state institutions had long and slow-moving waiting lists. To a much greater degree than is now the case the special class within a school tended to be viewed as an alien body in the educational culture—an attitude that extended to the teachers as well as the children in these classrooms. It was both consistent and ironic that just as state institutions were built in inaccessible places the special class in the public school was often badly placed, e.g., in the basement, next to the boiler room. In the larger society as well as in the educational culture the problem was handled when it was handled at all, by physical, psychological, and social segregation.[1]

It would indeed be erroneous if one were to conclude that the situation as we have described it reflected some kind of human perversity or a motivated indifference or callousness. It would be nearer correct to view the situation as reflecting two things: the absence of any national policy or feeling of public responsibility, and the presence of the view that very little could be done to adapt the mentally subnormal individual to existing community settings. It was the latter view that was crucial if only because actions and programs— and the possibilities of changes in either—are largely determined by conceptions of what an individual or a group *is* and, therefore, capable of. The relationship between conceptions and programs is so crucial in this area that we will attempt to emphasize the point by an example from another area of social problems.

---

[1] One of the most interesting personal accounts of the early history of special education and clinical psychology in this country is Wallin's *The Odyssey of a Psychologist* (1955). Dr. Wallin was truly a pioneer in these fields and his descriptions of experiences and conditions vividly convey the nature of the obstacle course which the retarded child and the special educator had to run to gain recognition within the educational settings and in the larger society. We quite agree with Dr. Laurance Shaffer's comments about Dr. Wallin's book: "I was entranced by your story, and found it one of the most interesting documents I have ever read. It is a lively, warm, human story, and moreover is excellently written. I would not want you to change a word of it. . . . your manuscript is a genuine contribution to the history of clinical psychology and the profession is indeed fortunate that you have taken the time to record the details of your career so effectively. . . . By all means, your manuscript should be available to the future generations of clinical psychologists, as an important source book of the history of our profession." Dr. Wallin's book was completed in 1954—his first of scores of publications was in 1902—and he was unable to secure a publisher. It was published personally by Dr. Wallin and, therefore, has received far less circulation than it deserves. The fact that this book was rejected by commercial publishers and university presses in the fifth decade of this century should temper our optimism about how far the field has come.

It has long been the practice in criminal courts to require the vast bulk of arrested individuals to post bond in order to insure their appearance in court when they come to trial. The reasons for this procedure need not occupy us here except to say that they all reflect the assumption that the "psychology" of most of these arrested individuals clearly indicated that they could not be trusted to show up in court unless the bond system was utilized. In recent years in some of our big cities a procedure was tried in which each arrested individual was interviewed by an outside individual or panel who then recommended to the court whether or not the individual should be required to post. The results clearly indicate that with this new procedure the number of individuals who fail to appear for trial is amazingly small. In short, different "psychologies" give rise to different actions and results.

There were individuals in the pre-World War II period who did not share the prevailing conceptions about mental subnormality, but they were few in number and their influence was small. Although pioneers and innovators can accelerate the pace of "readiness" of the larger society to new ideas and conceptions, the most potent sources of acceleration reside in factors and conditions beyond the control of any one individual.

In contrast to today, the field of mental subnormality was hardly represented in the teaching and research of university departments. Psychology, psychiatry, sociology, anthropology—in these traditional university departments it was indeed rare to find any interest in mental subnormality. It is true that textbooks in abnormal psychology and psychiatry contained pictures of some mentally deficient children but this was almost always to demonstrate bodily curiosities and deformities, a practice not conducive to engendering enthusiasm in students with an interest in the complexity we call a person. It is fair to say that it was only in departments and schools of education that one could learn about mental subnormality, and this possibility existed largely in state universities as a response to the need for teachers in state institutions and those local communities having special classes. Even in schools of education mental subnormality was not a highly regarded area, as such regard is reflected in numbers of faculty and students as well as laboratory facilities (e.g., demonstration classes). Before World War II mental subnormality was far from a welcome guest in halls of learning.

An Emerging National Policy. However ignored mental subnormality was by the larger society, events were taking place in the decade before World War II which were to culminate in attitudes or policies of fateful significance for the future of the field. Put most succinctly: the dominating and even overwhelming event of the 1930s was a prolonged economic depression which threatened to destroy the fabric of American society. That our society came through this catastrophe cannot erase the fact that it disrupted the lives, livelihood, and hopes of millions of people to an extent so as to bring about a fundamental change in the relation between government and the individual. The nature and significance of this change have been well stated by Rae-

Grant, Gladwin, and Bower.[2] Although their discussion is in the context of current developments in the mental health field (and its relation to the war on poverty), it has obvious relevance for the field of mental subnormality.

The central theme of the New Deal was an insistence that private ownership of property carried with it a responsibility to use this property in the public interest as well as in the interest of the owner. In particular, emphasis was placed upon making available, to any person willing to strive for it, an opportunity to be decently and gainfully employed, even though this meant cutting into the profits of employers in order to create the necessary jobs for all those deserving of employment. This was done both through taxation and through encouragement of collective bargaining agreements which gave to labor more and more elements of job security. Put in the more general terms fashionable today, the goal of the New Deal was to provide a satisfactory and relatively secure place in our society for anyone who was willing to strive for his own betterment and in other ways to act in accordance with middle class standards of behavior.

President Roosevelt was extraordinarily successful in achieving these goals. In doing so he had to bring about two major innovations in the social and economic structure of the United States. One of these was a redefinition of the mutual obligations existing between the Nation and its citizens—the establishment of a contract, if you will, which states that anyone who strives will be rewarded for striving. This was accomplished through presidential and other pronouncements, plus the proliferation of a great array of programs and agencies all committed to operating within the terms of the new contract. These were the days when Washington was referred to as alphabet soup. Some agencies, however, were more vulnerable than others. The NRA was declared unconstitutional and the NYA was allegedly communist infiltrated. Others, like the WPA, reached new high-water marks in their commitment to the furtherance of human dignity. Some remain to this day—the SEC, NLRB, and Social Security are examples. Good, bad, or indifferent, however, the net effect of the activities of these many agencies was the repetition thousands of times over, all over the country, of social transactions based upon the new responsibilities of the Nation to its citizens. Very soon it became inconceivable that any other basis could have been tolerated. The Bonus March of only a short time before seemed like a bad dream which could never really have happened.

The other innovation was of course the development of new mechanisms which would create and maintain the opportunities and security which were now guaranteed to those willing to demonstrate that they were deserving of them. Many of the necessary mechanisms were established by the alphabet soup agencies, but many others came into being through changes in the strategy and procedure of other agencies, both public and private. New bodies of knowledge and theory came into being, designed to understand and to safeguard the new responsibilities and the new opportunities. . . .

The new contract calls for an additional shift in rights and responsibilities. Not only must the obligations of the owners of private property be broadened still farther, but the ranks of those toward whom our society extends its opportunities

---

2 At the same time as the present book was completed, Dr. Gladwin (1967) published a book which describes in greater detail the ways in which the relation between government and certain social problems has changed since the third decade of this century. His book, involving as it does the issue of "poverty," has important implications for anyone concerned with the possible relationships between conditions of poverty, on the one hand, and social competence, on the other hand.

must be expanded to include this time *all* persons who are citizens of our land, simply because as human beings they are worthy of respect and deserving of any opportunities afforded the rest of us. The rationale for this obligation derives from a realization, relatively recent but already well established, that significant numbers of people, including for example very large numbers of Negroes, Puerto Ricans, Mexican-Americans, and white Appalachian mountaineers, live in circumstances which are incapacitating for those who grow up in them, and that these circumstances are created and sustained by the dominant institutions of the larger society. (Rae-Grant, Gladwin, and Bower, 1966)

The slow but continuous change in the conception of society's responsibilities to the individual was one of several crucial developments which set the stage for a future *national* awareness of and responsiveness to the complexities and size of the problem of mental subnormality.

WORLD WAR II

If the consequences of the economic depression of the 1930s were to have a delayed but potent effect on the future of the field of mental subnormality, the approach and beginning of World War II accelerated the emergence of mental subnormality as a major problem in our society. There is apparently (and unfortunately) nothing like a war to force a society to look at its human resources. Ginzberg and Bray succinctly illustrate how wars force the attention of a society to problems heretofore ignored or glossed over:

During World War II more than 5 million men liable for military service were rejected as unsuitable because of a physical, emotional, mental, or moral disability. Since about 18 million men were examined, this implies that approximately one out of every three young men was considered so handicapped that he could not serve his country in uniform during a major war. In the year following the outbreak of hostilities in Korea about 500,000 of the million and a half men examined were rejected. Once again, the number and proportion of handicapped men were very large.

Hidden within these startling figures is the still more startling fact that during World War II, 716,000 men were rejected on the grounds that they were "mentally deficient." At the peak of mobilization the Army had eighty-nine divisions. Those rejected for mental disabilities were the equivalent in manpower of more than fifty divisions. In the year following the outbreak of fighting in Korea more than 300,000 were rejected on this same ground of "mental deficiency." Some were truly mentally deficient; many more were educationally deprived. (Ginzberg and Bray, 1953, p. 3)

In a later chapter we shall discuss in detail Ginzberg and Bray's analysis and discussion of "the uneducated" in World War II. At this point it is important to note that the war brought to the attention of a wide variety of individuals and groups the fact that mental subnormality was a big problem in terms of numbers involved and—just as important—was related to and reflected educational and social conditions peculiar to our society. It was no longer possible to escape recognition of the fact that diagnostic labels such as "mental deficiency" or "mental subnormality" or "feeblemindedness" or "mental retardation" referred to a heterogeneous collection of individuals and problems.

The Post-World War II Period

The changed relationship between government and the individual which emerged from the economic depression was reinforced by virtue of the obligations to its citizens explicitly taken on by government as a result of World War II, and resulted, after the war, in a national policy which was surprising only because it took place in a short period of time and with hardly any debate. What had been implicit became explicit policy: It was the obligation of our society to help in tangible ways individuals and groups who for reasons beyond their control required external help in one or another way. Mental illness, physical disease, mental subnormality, juvenile delinquency—these were some of the problem areas about which it was now felt the federal government must take responsibility. The human values reflected in such a policy were but one consideration in its easy acceptance. Other factors were the financial inability of many local and state governments to mount adequate programs of service and to stimulate and initiate research programs which hopefully would contribute to new knowledge and better ways of providing help.

There can be little doubt that in the post-World War II period the emergence of mental retardation as a national problem was markedly accelerated by two related developments: the civil rights movement and the "war on poverty." These two intertwined developments forced on public consciousness what had long been relatively ignored, i.e., in our society there were millions of people who by virtue of their inability to partake fully of their rights as citizens were poorly educated, were vocationally unskilled in a world of increasing automation, and were disproportionate contributors to a variety of social problems. The relationships among minority status, education, regional–cultural factors, and "mental deficiency" had been demonstrated a number of times but Ginzberg and Bray's studies of World War II rejectees suffice for our present purposes. As we indicated earlier, Ginzberg and Bray found that in World War II 716,000 individuals who were between 18 and 37 years of age were rejected on the grounds of mental deficiency. The problems associated with the interpretation of this figure may be seen from the following quotation.

Relatively little research has been devoted to ascertaining the number of individuals in the population who cannot meet a minimum performance criterion as workers and citizens. Some authorities estimate that approximately one per cent of the population can perform even unskilled work only under close supervision in a protective environment. It is believed that another one per cent of the population are able to work effectively only if they have some type of special supervision. According to these estimates the percentage of persons who would not meet a minimum performance standard because of intellectual deficiency would be 2 per cent. The more than 700,000 men rejected for military service under the general heading of "mental deficiency" amounted to about 4 per cent of the men examined. On the surface this might be taken to mean that the screening standards used were somewhat tight but approximately correct. Again, however, a national average obscures the truth, for nearly 14 per cent were rejected in some states and only one-half of one per cent in others. The fact that the national rejection rate was only a little higher than the theoretical rate of true mental deficiency cannot be taken as an indication that the screening validly assessed either mental deficiency or ability to give satisfactory performance. The regional patterning of the rejections indicates that the screening assessed primarily the individual's educational background. (Ginzberg and Bray, 1953, p. 41)

The regional patterning of rejections is indeed striking as can be seen in Table 2.1.

T A B L E   2 . 1   Rejection Rates per Thousand Registrants, by Region and Race (From Ginzberg and Bray, 1953)

Region	Total	White	Negro
Total U.S.	40	25	152
New England	17	16	65
Middle Atlantic	15	11	67
Southeast	97	52	202
Southwest	60	54	107
Central	14	12	61
Northwest	14	13	40
Far West	10	9	50

Several striking facts are revealed by this table. First, the rate of rejection in the Southeast is almost ten times as large as that in the Far West. All of the regions of the country except two have a total rejection rate between 10 and 17 per 1,000 examined; the Southeast and the Southwest have rates of 97 and 60, respectively. Although the range is less for the white population, it is still striking. The Far West has a rejection rate of 9 while the Southeast and the Southwest each have a rate of more than 50. The Negro rate is so much larger in every region that it might appear to be a different population; the over-all Negro rate is just over six times the white rate. However, there is evidence within the Negro distribution to suggest that the population is basically parallel. One finds, for instance, that the rate of rejection for Negroes in the Northwest and the Far West is actually below the white rate in the Southeast and the Southwest. Even in the other three regions—New England, Middle Atlantic, and Central, the Negro rate is only slightly above the white rate in the South. The sixfold difference in total rates between Negroes and whites results from the exceptionally high rejection rate for Negroes in the Southeast and the lower but still high rate in the Southwest. The most extreme regional and racial differences are between the rejection rate for whites in the Far West of 9 per 1,000, or less than one per cent, and the rate of 202 per 1,000, or more than 20 per cent, for Negroes in the Southeast. Unless there were evidence that there are gross differences in mental capacity among various racial and ethnic groups, here is an overwhelming demonstration that the results of the screening examination reflected primarily differences in the educational and environmental opportunities in different regions.

Although similar rejection rates have been tabulated and analyzed by various experts, all of the analyses to date have been limited either to national totals, regional comparisons, or state comparisons. These comparisons shed considerable light upon the problem of the illiterate and the poorly educated youth of the country, but a more thorough understanding of the problem awaits an analysis of smaller geographic units which might bring out the range of specific factors likely to contribute to high or low rejection rates.

On the basis of Selective Service sample data, we prepared two detailed maps. The first presents the rate of rejection for mental deficiency for white registrants in each of the more than 3,000 counties throughout the United States. The second map is necessarily less extensive; it shows the Negro rejection rates for Eastern counties having at least 100 Negroes in our sample. Nearly all other counties in the nation had too few Negroes examined to compute a rate. Exceptions were a few large urban counties.

The most general finding that emerges from the study of rejection rates on a county basis is the general gradation from low to high rates rather than abrupt changes. In a large number of cases this gradualness ignores state boundaries, suggesting that local factors play the predominant part in determining the differential rates. There is, however, contrary evidence which suggests that in some instances state policies are determining. Sharp differences are conspicuous between Mississippi and the bordering states, and between the western and northwestern counties of Texas and the much higher rates in the neighboring states. Much the same contrast is observed between the higher rates in West Virginia and those in the border counties of Ohio and Pennsylvania, and in the border counties of Kentucky and Virginia.

The map of county rejection rates for Negro registrants in the Southeast helps to bring certain generalizations to the surface. An outstanding fact is that every county in South Carolina, without exception, had a Negro rejection rate of 175 per 1,000 or more. The situation in Alabama was a little better. The counties in which the cities of Birmingham and Mobile are located show, however, relatively low rates. The other states show greater variation between high, medium, and low county rejection rates. There is no doubt that the degree of urbanization is a major factor related to lower rejection rates of Negroes, just as for whites. On the basis of sample studies, the other two factors which seem frequently to be connected with relatively low rejection rates for Negroes are the economic prosperity of the county and a relatively low proportion of Negroes in the total population. There are, however, a considerable number of counties where such specific factors as local white or Negro leadership, or special efforts by outside groups, such as foundations interested in Negro education, apparently are important. Such factors may be at work where the rejection rate for a particular county or group of counties is low in comparison to others which are broadly similar on an economic and demographic basis. (Ginzberg and Bray, 1953, pp. 43–48)

The above findings highlight regional differences but they also make more understandable why in the post-war years there was an enormous migration from one part of the country to another, particularly to our large urban centers where during and after the war there were greater vocational opportunities as well as fewer obvious restrictions on the exercise of one's rights as a citizen. That this migration and urbanization would and did create many problems needs no special documentation.

Public recognition of the thorny and complicated interrelationships between mental retardation and poverty was guaranteed by the report of the President's Panel on Mental Retardation, *National Action to Combat Mental Retardation* (1962), as the following statements from that report will indicate:[3]

The majority of the mentally retarded are the children of the more disadvantaged classes of our society. This extraordinarily heavy prevalence in certain deprived population groups suggests a major causative role, in some way not yet fully delineated, for adverse social, economic, and cultural factors. These conditions may not only mean absence of the physical necessities of life, but the lack of opportunity and motivation. A number of experiments with the education of presumably retarded children from slum neighborhoods strongly suggests that a predominant cause of mental retardation may be the lack of learning opportunities or absence of "intellectual vitamins" under these adverse environmental conditions. Deprivation in childhood of opportunities for learning intellectual skills, childhood emotional disorders which interfere with learning, or obscure motivational factors appear somehow to stunt young people intellectually during their developmental period. Whether the causes of retardation in a specific individual may turn out to be biomedical or environmental in character, there is highly suggestive evidence that the root causes of a great part of the problem of mental retardation are to be found in bad social economic conditions as they affect individuals and families, and that correction of these fundamental conditions is necessary to prevent mental retardation successfully on a truly significant scale. (pp. 8–9)

Research in the behavioral sciences is at present primarily addressed to thera-

---

[3] One indication of how the field of mental subnormality changed after World War II can be seen in the rate of publication of books dealing with the social and psychological aspects of the problem. When the first edition of this book was published in 1949 there were only a handful of other books in roughly the same content area. Approximately twenty years later dozens of books are available dealing with one or another aspect of mental subnormality. Whereas twenty years ago one might have been able to write a book covering in some depth the major problems, theoretical statements, and relevant research studies, such a task is today a near impossible one. For example, if the reader were to consult the books edited by Ellis (1963, 1966)—books devoted primarily to different psychological theories as they bear on mental subnormality—he will obtain a good idea of the variety and vigorousness of the thinking and writing going on. When one considers that these three excellent volumes do not cover all theoretical approaches, and that many of the presented approaches address themselves to limited aspects of problems, it becomes obvious that specialization has occurred and that the job of the general scholar has become extraordinarily difficult. When one remembers that there can be unfortunate consequences to increased specialization—such as missing the forest of problems because of the theoretical trees—the enormous growth of publications cannot be viewed as an unmixed blessing.

peutic and rehabilitative possibilities. The most fertile unploughed area for further behavioral and social science research is indicated by the accumulating evidence that a host of social, economic, and environmental factors—often categorized as cultural deprivation—are correlated or associated to a high degree with the incidence of mental retardation, especially in its milder manifestations of low intellectual and social performance. (p. 24)

Mental subnormality has come into national focus in a way that emphasizes how much of a community is involved in one way or another with this problem area. The enormity of the problem in the inner-city population, the significance of it in racial issues, the basis it has provided for many school and preschool programs, the popular use of terms such as "cultural deprivation" or "war on poverty"—all of these in one way or another, directly or indirectly, reflect an increasing awareness of the degree to which subnormality is a community problem. There is now scarcely a community agency that does not cope with some aspect of mental subnormality.

THE "PERSONAL" FACTOR

There can be little doubt that the current recognition afforded mental subnormality stems to an important degree from the activities of the National Association for Retarded Children. Rarely has a small group of parents developed an organization which not only had fantastic growth but played a pioneering role in legislation, facilities, and research activity.

Across the United States as early as 1930, voices began to unite in the cause of mental retardation. They were raised by parents banding together in local groups to share problems, to seek answers to questions about their retarded children.

After World War II the voices grew more audible, more insistent. But even then few of the groups knew of the others.

In 1950, however, 42 parents met in Minneapolis, determined to unite their efforts. Motivated by personal sorrows, disappointments and frustrations, they became spokesmen for a better life for all retarded children. To this charge they dedicated their energies and resources.

The struggle they faced was formidable.

The whole country needed awakening to the huge problem. The mistaken beliefs about the mentally retarded, imbedded for centuries in man's thinking, needed to be replaced by knowledge and acceptance—gaps in desperately needed services filled with programs of diagnosis, education, and care. These new programs were not to come easily; for two decades of depression and war had blighted creative approaches and had drastically curtailed the recruitment of young professionals to serve retarded persons.

With the inspiration reinforced in Minneapolis, the organization, originally called the National Association of Parents and Friends of Mentally Retarded Children, began to grow. Letters from isolated, despairing parents poured in and were answered with advice on how to help themselves and their children through cooperative effort.

Independent groups all over the nation, learning of the Association, joined the growing forces. By 1955 there were 363 organized Local Associations; by 1960, 750.

The first years saw great achievements, with the business of the Association carried on solely by volunteers and mostly by mail. Then the resources, though meagre, were found for a national office and it was opened in 1954 in New York City with a small staff.

In the next decade the National Association for Retarded Children grew into one of America's most dynamic voluntary organizations. By 1965 its membership exceeded 100,000. There were over 1,000 Local and State Associations. Provisions had been made for a growing component of professional employees to assist officers, boards and committees—nationally, in the states, and in the communities.

Monumental accomplishments were recorded during the first fifteen years. New classes, clinics, workshops, activity centers, camps and other programs were established in large numbers. Manpower training programs were generated. Creative ideas began to emerge from government, private agencies, and the professions.

The groundwork was laid, furthermore, for the realization in the decade ahead of the early visions of truly adequate services and effective programs of prevention—to achieve, indeed, comprehensive programs for all mentally retarded persons. (National Association for Retarded Children, 1962)

It was the NARC which sponsored the surveys of research by Masland (1958) and Sarason and Gladwin (1958)—brought together in the publication *Mental Subnormality* (Masland, Sarason, and Gladwin, 1958).

The fact that the growth of the NARC took place at the same time that Senator, and later, President John F. Kennedy—whose family had a personal interest in mental subnormality and whose father had established a foundation to support activities in this field—became a dominant figure in American life reflects a fortuitous combination of events which insured that mental subnormality would be a concern of government which had already become the prime support of research, training, and service programs.

In this chapter we have attempted to give the reader in brief fashion some perspective in the recent history of the field of mental subnormality, if only to indicate that its current popularity is a relatively new development very much reflecting characteristics of and developments in our larger society. The significance of perspective resides not only in organizing past developments and understanding the present but in grasping the principle that our current theorizing, research, and practices will be viewed and interpreted at some future time in different, and probably surprising, ways. It is understandable, but nevertheless a source of ultimate disappointment, to view current knowledge and practices as immune either to changes in the larger society or to the shattering effects of new theories and findings. This point will be treated in much greater detail and will cover a larger span of history in later chapters where we trace aspects of the history of attempts to "explain" the mentally defective individual in terms of biological and genetic factors. As we shall see in those chapters, and as we have attempted to suggest in the present chapter, at any time in history, theories and facts, no less than people, have to be viewed in the context of the society at that time. This is particularly the case when one bears in mind that facts and theories do not directly give rise to social action without first filtering through and reflecting a set of values, and it is this set of values which will mirror important aspects of the society.

But one does not need history to begin, as we shall in the next chapter, discussion of certain ways of thinking which can be found in so much of the present as well as of the past approach to problems of mental subnormality. It is our view that focusing in early chapters of this book on current problems and modes of thinking—which may be most familiar too, or more readily identifiable by, those individuals relatively new to this field—will in later chapters facilitate a feeling of kinship with those who labored in earlier times.

The use and misuse of labels

In Chapter 2 the reader may have noted that a variety of terms or labels (e.g., mental deficiency, mental subnormality, mental retardation) were used, raising the question as to their meaning and interchangeability. We shall postpone until the next chapter discussion of the past and present usage of these terms and the criteria governing their applicability. At this point, it is important that the reader become aware of some problems in attitude and thinking which can be as fateful for the diagnostic process as the way in which labels and criteria are formulated. One such problem concerns our attitude toward test scores, i.e., the tendency to view such scores as explanations of behavior. It cannot be emphasized too strongly that a low IQ score provides no basis for statements about the ways one particular individual differs from others with an identical score; nor does it reveal the individual's differential reactions to a variety of situations, his attitudes toward himself and others, or what effects he will produce on what kinds of people in what kinds of situations. Nor does it give any indication of the relation of the foregoing to the presence or absence of central nervous system impairment or to the familial–cultural background in which the individual developed. It is extremely simple, although logically naive, to explain a defective child's behavior on the basis of his low IQ—as if there were in the child a force varying inversely with the IQ, causing him to behave as he does. For example, it is not unusual for people who know that a particular child has a low IQ to say in regard to a "stupid" act of his: "What can you expect from someone as low as that? If he had more brains he wouldn't have done it." It does not seem to occur to these people to ask why *this* child and not others with identical IQ scores behaved in the particular way, why this situation and not others elicited the "stupid" response, and why when superior children behave in the same way (running away, committing a crime, killing animals, etc.) the fact of their superior intelligence is not blamed for their behavior. Let us illustrate the problem we are discussing by a concrete case.

〰 A Regional Center for the Mentally Retarded was requested by the juvenile court to become involved in a case in which the question of primary concern was whether or not a mother of six children was mentally retarded. The referral question was specific and quite clear, if the mother was found to be mentally subnormal the state could act quickly to separate her from her children. The reason for the referral was equally clear. The juvenile court had a good deal of evidence leading them to question the mother's intellectual functioning with respect to her capacity to deal effectively with her six children.

The mother, a Negro woman, 27 years of age, had long ago become known to both the welfare department and the juvenile court. For some time the family had been on state aid (Aid to Dependent Children) and, consequently, had been the responsibility of the welfare department. Similarly, the two oldest of the six children (ages 10, 9, 7, 4, 2, and 1) already had been involved in difficulties with the law, and so had come in contact with the juvenile court.

The family situation had been, for some time, a difficult one, and recently had deteriorated to a point that the juvenile court felt to be perilous in terms of the health, safety, and welfare of the children. The father recently had been arrested for stealing a car and currently was in jail. During the routine interrogation following his arrest it was discovered that he was a fugitive from justice, that he had escaped from a prison in Florida where he was serving another sentence for robbery. Following his escape he had come north and had married the woman for whom an intellectual evaluation was being requested. He never informed her of his past, and she had no knowledge of the situation until the police explained it to her. It appeared that, in all probability, the husband would have to return to Florida to complete his previous sentence after he finished serving his current sentence. In any event, it appeared that the father—who had been unemployed for several years before his arrest—would be unavailable to the family for quite some time to come.

Although the father never had been able to secure and hold down a job for any period of time he was of some help to the mother in terms of caring for the children. During the period following his arrest the family situation had deteriorated significantly. The children were not attending school with any regularity; visits to the home had resulted in observations of general chaos and disorganization; the younger children were not being fed or clothed properly; and the older children were running wild, disobeying the mother, and staying away from the home for long periods of time.

Under these conditions the juvenile authorities felt that they had to step into the situation. They were concerned over the health and welfare of the children and the mother, and felt that only by removing the children from the home could they begin to provide for their needs and at the same time alleviate the pressures under which the mother was functioning. When they approached the mother with this suggestion she became almost hysterical and threatened to run away with her children before she would allow anyone to separate them from her.

Because psychological examination was being requested it was decided that the Psycho-Educational Clinic would take primary responsibility for the case.[1] Before scheduling the client for testing, however, we were able to meet with the case worker from the juvenile court. The case worker, a competent, sensitive, and dedicated woman, was quite concerned about the prospects that the mother and her children would be separated. She felt that this "solution" was not a solution at all, but that it would create more problems than it would solve. She clearly indicated her desire that our evaluation concern itself with much more than just "an I.Q. number," and that we utilize our time with the client to evolve as comprehensive an impression of the case as possible. We agreed with her feelings and informed her of our intention to do just that, and of our desire to work closely with the juvenile court in developing as helpful a plan as possible. We arranged to see the client the following day.

The next day, when the case worker brought the client to the Clinic, the mother appeared to be a frail and petrified woman who looked and dressed much younger than her stated age. She approached the testing situation in a markedly frightened, tense, and bewildered fashion, but was acutely aware of the fact that she was in a "head clinic." Before we could begin testing she anxiously informed us that her "mind is OK and I don't need a mental test." Every word she said was spoken in an apprehensive and tremulous manner. Throughout the period of evaluation she remained extremely frightened and obviously intimidated. She never was able to relax, and her nervousness was manifested in an almost continuous eye tic. Our written observations stated that we "rarely had seen such an obviously frightened and anxious person, a person who is so obviously alone and intimidated by the world around her."

The formal testing results failed to establish whether or not the woman was mentally subnormal. In view of the client's emotional state at and during the time of testing, it was almost surprising that she performed as well as she did. Her performance itself was marked by a great intra- and intertest variability—the type of scattered, sporadic, and uneven performance often associated with an extreme degree of anxiety. With this in mind it was our feeling that, were it not for the almost debilitating effects of anxiety and tension, the client might have performed at a higher level.

---

[1] This case is taken from a book describing the origins and activities of the Psycho-Educational Clinic of the Department of Psychology at Yale. One section of that book is devoted to the clinical and research relationships between the Psycho-Educational Clinic and the New Haven Regional Center for the Mentally Retarded.

More than anything else, we were struck by the fact that we were confronted by a woman who appeared to be so totally alone and isolated, who was being called on to maintain a home and children during a period in her life when she was most vulnerable to the interfering effects of prolonged and realistic anxiety. This fact, coupled with her obvious devotion to her children, led us to feel it was necessary to explore ways, other than removal and separation, in which the situation could be handled.

We shared our findings and our feelings about the case with the juvenile court case worker. She concurred with much that we had observed and described to us just how alone the client and her children really were. From her information it appeared that the woman had no family or friends in the housing project in which she lived, or indeed, in the entire New Haven area. She was alone and friendless, separated from her husband, and isolated from any meaningful contact with the community of which she was, nominally, a part. Whatever homemaking and child-rearing skills and talents she possessed were being undermined and rendered useless by the loneliness and anxiety that engulfed her.

The more we discussed the situation the more we found ourselves emphasizing the psychological, emotional, and social variables that had become predominant factors in the situation. No longer were we talking about "intelligence" or "mental subnormality" as the prepotent variables to be considered in deciding what to do or what to suggest.

Pursuing this line of inquiry we soon found ourselves thinking in terms of what we could put into rather than take away from the situation in order to help both the mother and the children. We began thinking about the possibility of placing someone in the home on a continuous and regular basis, to assist the mother in the day-to-day management of the house and the children. In considering this possibility we were fully aware that the most important factor was not selecting someone who was merely an efficient and competent homemaker, but choosing the kind of person (a mature, stable, and accepting woman) who was willing and able to develop a relationship with the client; who could be a friend; and who could be supportive as well as function in an instructive manner. In short, we were looking for someone capable of reducing the client's apparent loneliness, of being her friend as well as her helper.

The case worker quickly thought of a person she felt would be "perfect for the job." The woman the case worker had in mind was someone she had met when the woman and her children were themselves the case worker's clients. She described the woman as a mature, gracious, and extremely giving person, capable of exhibiting great strength as well as great gentleness. She lived in the same housing project as the client, and was anxious to "get off relief" and become financially independent of the welfare department. The case worker felt this woman would be the most appropriate person to go into the home as a homemaker.

The case worker contacted the potential homemaker and explained the entire situation to her. The woman was extremely anxious to become involved in the situation and saw it both as a chance to help another human being in distress and as a way of getting off the relief rolls herself. Because of the urgency of the situation the woman, rather than waiting for the city welfare department's red tape to evaluate and process her into the homemakers' program, immediately began to visit the home and to establish a relationship with the client.

In a relatively short time (approximately three weeks) the situation began to change, and to change in a dramatic fashion. The client began to relax a bit, and became much more communicative. The house began shaping up again, and the children were attending school and eating regularly. The homemaker began taking the client out of the home, introducing her to some of the other tenants, and showing her the best places in town to obtain bargains. Between the two of them they worked out a budget for the home and began redecorating parts of the apartment. The client began looking forward to the almost daily visits of the homemaker and started to assert herself more strongly in the home. More than anything else the client had—perhaps for the first time—a real friend, another person in the world with whom she could talk, laugh, trade stories, and share problems. The client began to "live" and her children began "living" with her. The entire home situation, although by no means completely transformed, began to get better.

After a few weeks the homemaker contacted the juvenile case worker and informed her that the welfare department had turned down her application to become a paid homemaker. She was angry, hurt; she could not understand why she should have been turned down. We investigated the situation and found, to our dismay, that the welfare department—at least in terms of the homemaker's service—had a policy of not hiring onto their staff people who were their clients. It appeared to be a curious and cruel paradox. On the one hand, the welfare department was working toward the goal of getting their clients off the relief rolls and into gainful employment. On the other hand, they could not bring themselves to hire their own clients and thereby hasten the process whereby they could become self-sufficient. Although we tried to work out an arrangement with the welfare department our efforts were of no avail.

We then visited the homemaker and discussed the situation with her. We could understand her anger and disappointment and told her so. We also investigated and reviewed with her the changes that had occurred in the client's home and life ever since she had entered the household and had become a factor in the situation. We asked her, as a personal favor to us while we investigated other possible sources of income for her, to continue her association with the client and her family. Being the kind of person she was, she agreed to maintain the relationship with the client.

At approximately this time one of the projects connected with Community Progress Incorporated was initiating a homemaker's service that would divide the city into areas requiring a homemaker's service and would then assign a home-maker to that region.[2] We contacted the director of the program and clearly informed him of the situation and described the qualities of the woman who currently was volunteering her services in the client's home. He was quite impressed with her credentials and arranged an immediate interview. His feeling at

---

[2] Community Progress Incorporated (CPI) was one of the first community action programs in the country and the relation of the Psycho-Educational Clinic to it is described by Sarason et al., 1966.

the conclusion of the interview was that the woman would be perfect for the program. He promised to contact her as soon as the program started and guaranteed a staff position for her. The program was scheduled to start in approximately three months.

The volunteer homemaker was delighted with the results of the interview. She said that during the period between then and the initiation of the program she still would investigate other job opportunities. She also promised, however, to maintain her contact with the client and the client's children. She felt that the client had benefitted from their relationship and would continue to benefit from the friendship that had developed between them. There was little to do but agree with her, and add our thanks. (Sarason, Levine, Goldenberg, Cherlin, and Bennett, 1966)

What was quite clear in this case was that from the standpoint of the referring agency the present and past behavior of the mother would be *explained* if the diagnostic label of mental retardation was considered to be appropriate. Why she married her husband, why she had so many children, why the family situation was deteriorating, why she did not want to be separated from her children, why she responded to the pressures of her life in the way she did—these and other forms of behavior would be understandable if she were found mentally retarded even though the same referring agency had experience with scores of cases in which there was a similar or even greater degree of retardation not associated with the behavior and family conditions described above. We are not maintaining that test scores and diagnoses are without significance but rather that it is all too frequent to attribute to them a degree of explanatory value that neither reality nor theory nor common sense justify.

What would have been the reaction of the referring agency if the psychologist had found that this woman had an IQ of 120? It requires no special wisdom or knowledge to say that they would *think* differently about her and *explore* different possibilities of action. They would not maintain that her present and past behavior were explainable by her high test score.

Brain Injury as Etiological Scapegoat

The nature and consequences of brain injury or central nervous system impairment are frequent and vital matters of concern to anyone in the field of mental subnormality, as later chapters will attempt to indicate. Because of the increasing frequency with which one or another form of the diagnostic label "brain injury" is being applied, it is necessary for the reader to be sensitive to the tendency to use such a label in a way which grossly oversimplifies the complex problem of understanding behavior.

It very frequently happens that when this diagnosis is made the assumption is also made that we now can explain the behavior of the child. That is to say, the behavior of the child is a consequence of the brain injury. Put in another way, in the past as well as in the future the brain injury limits the potentialities of the child. We look back over the history of the child's development with an altered perception which allows us to understand why he experienced the difficulties he did. Unfortunately, there are neither logical nor theoretical grounds on which to justify such use of the brain-injury type of diagnosis. *The fact that both brain injury and certain types of behavior exist is in itself no basis for concluding that one is the cause of the other.* In addition, there is no theory of child development which states or even implies that a brain injury can give rise to certain behavioral characteristics *regardless of the social-cultural–psychological matrix in which development has taken place.* On theoretical grounds, one is never justified in drawing the conclusion that behavioral characteristics directly reflect the brain injury.[3] To the extent that we imply or infer such a conclusion we obscure the complexity of the brain–behavior relationship at the possible expense of knowledge which would alter our perception of the potentialities of these children. Sarason illustrates the point with the following case and discussion.

◦◡◦   In the spring of 1959 a colleague asked me if I would see the grand-daughter of a friend of his. The child, who was 4½ years of age had been in a private nursery since the age of two. The question to which I was to address myself was whether the child should remain in this nursery or be placed elsewhere.

Although the grandparent was requesting the evaluation, she had not seen the child since the time of the child's placement in the nursery. The child's mother and father had been divorced shortly after the girl's placement; they visited the child very infrequently.

Before seeing the child (Cynthia) I had a meeting with the pediatrician who had regularly visited and examined her, such services being paid for by the grandmother. According to the pediatrician, Cynthia's development up until placement in the nursery was slow and atypical. There were no gross neurological signs, the head was of the sugar-loaf variety, and motor movements were markedly awkward. He felt there was some kind of brain injury and there was no doubt that the child was now operating at a subnormal level. However, he felt that Cynthia had gained whatever she could gain in this nursery and some other placement should be considered. He made it quite clear that she could not be placed with either parent. I learned from the pediatrician that the nursery contained almost exclusively severely subnormal bed-patients. It turned out, in fact, that she was the only truly ambulatory child in the nursery.

When I arrived at the nursery, I was greeted at the door by Cynthia. She did

---

[3] Brain injury certainly can directly affect the functioning of an organ or organ system but the psychological behavior which ensues is not directly a function of the injury. For example, brain injury can produce convulsions but the organization of behavior following convulsion is not an inevitable consequence of the injury and its somatic sequelae. Similarly, brain injury can result in blindness but the style and content of the psychological adaptation to the blindness is not an inevitable consequence of the brain injury or of blindness.

indeed have a peculiarly shaped head, her arms seemed abnormally big for her body size, and her body movements were certainly not graceful. She did have an animated facial expression. She made speech sounds but I had difficulty comprehending what she was trying to say.

We were soon joined by the nurse who pretty much managed the nursery by herself during the day. The nurse sent Cynthia out to play so that we could talk without interruption. She then related to me how strongly she felt that Cynthia should no longer stay in this nursery where there was no stimulation. She clearly felt very positively toward Cynthia and indicated that she would miss the child keenly. The child had been out of the nursery only a handful of times and, with one exception, these visits were to the nurse's home. The one exception had occurred two weeks before when the nurse had to go to a local drug store and decided to take Cynthia along. As they walked into the store the nurse was momentarily unaware that Cynthia was trailing behind her. When she turned around she saw that Cynthia had become white as a sheet and was standing transfixed as if beginning to panic. The nurse instantly realized that the store was an overwhelming strange experience for Cynthia. She immediately took the child out of the store and returned to the nursery.

When Cynthia returned to the room, I attempted to carry on a conversation with her, but I had great difficulty comprehending her speech and I was not sure how much she understood what I was saying. The nurse seemed to understand her somewhat better and when I felt it appropriate to begin the testing, I requested that the nurse remain in the room. However, shortly after the testing began (I attempted to make the relationship as game-like as possible), Cynthia became tearful and distractible. I had the feeling that she sensed she was being evaluated. She returned several times to the arms of the nurse. I gave up any attempt at formal evaluation when her tearfulness changed to a pathetic kind of crying.

I will now briefly describe the conclusions I arrived at and the recommendations made. First, on the basis of what I observed there was not the faintest doubt in my mind that this child, compared to her peers, was markedly subnormal. Her speech, her inadequate comprehension of whatever instructions and tasks I was able to give to her, her motor clumsiness, and a tendency to hyperactivity—in combination those characteristics indicated a severe degree of subnormality. Second, the relationship between Cynthia and the nurse was that between mother and child. In fact, this nurse was the only human being with whom Cynthia had a relationship. Third, it was impossible for me to determine to what extent the degree of subnormality was a function of having lived for the past two-and-a-half years in this nursery, to what extent it reflected a non-specific form of brain-damage, and to what extent it reflected pre-nursery experiences. What interests me now about this case is that I implicitly assumed that there was a necessary relationship of some kind and degree between the brain-injury and behavioral characteristics. I perceived Cynthia as having a brain-injury which seriously affected what may have been excellent potential for development. It did not then occur to me, as it should have, that the psychological effects of a brain-injury cannot reflect the injury directly but rather the interaction between an organism, which has certain characteristics, and a psychological environment which has its characteristics. As soon as one adopts this viewpoint—which is certainly not novel and is derivable from any systematic psychological theory except that we tend not to take theory seriously—it becomes clear that we have not been justified in "explaining" psychological behavior by the presence of a brain-injury. In addition, such a viewpoint shifts our attention to the different ways in which the environment reacts to the organism and how these ways differ in the degree to which they exacerbate or minimize one of the organism's characteristics. It is such a focus which presents us with the possibility of having to change our conceptions of the brain–behavior relationship because it suggests that as fateful as the brain-injury is the manner in which patterns of stimulation impinge on the organism.

But now to return to Cynthia. Although I was aware that her behavior was a function of a number of factors, I assumed that this behavior reflected rather directly, to some degree at least, brain disfunction. I did not raise or pursue these questions: Is it possible that Cynthia does have a brain-injury but that the symptomatic behavior I have observed is not intrinsically a characteristic of that brain-injury but rather the product of a complex, mutually interacting relationship between organism and environment? If this relationship had been different, would one still see a similar behavioral picture which we tend to think as being intrinsically characteristic of the injury? In connection with this last question I recommended that Cynthia be transferred to another institutional placement, but under no circumstances should this be attempted unless the nurse accompanied her and remained with her until a satisfactory relationship with another adult had been established. I obviously feared the consequences of placing Cynthia in a strange environment after separating her from the only human being with whom she had a relationship.

In discussing possible transfer I suggested two places with special interest in brain-injured children. Let us assume that Cynthia was sent to one of these places and that after a year or so her level of function markedly improved. What light would this shed on brain-injury? One would obviously not conclude that the brain-injury had been diminished or cured. One might conclude that the specific training procedures employed produced the behavioral changes, except that we know that this child was experiencing far more in the institution than is subsumed under the term "training procedures." It is my contention that an obvious but important conclusion to be drawn is that there was no necessary relation between Cynthia's brain-injury and behavioral characteristics, i.e., during the interval of a year the same brain-injury is associated with different behavioral pictures. Does this not suggest that under different conditions of training and stimulation the intellectual and personality picture I observed in the nursery need not have occurred? In cases like this are we not taking the easy way out when we make the brain-injury the etiological scapegoat?

But Cynthia did not go into another institution. Somewhat more than a year after I first saw Cynthia I received a letter from the grandmother informing me that for the past year Cynthia had gone to live with the nurse who had been prevailed upon to resign her job and devote all her time to Cynthia. The nurse had placed Cynthia in a nursery school where she had done very well. In fact, the nursery school felt that Cynthia was ready for first grade but there was a question whether this was a desirable promotion from the standpoint of personality maturity. I was asked if I would make another visit and evaluation.

I read the letter with dismay because I assumed that someone was selling the grandmother a bill of goods. I could not believe that the Cynthia I had seen somewhat more than a year ago—the child who had such a history of atypical development—was the girl being described in the letter.

When I arrived at the garden apartment to which the nurse had moved with Cynthia, I was greeted by the child who spoke as clearly as one could wish, comprehended all that I said and carried on a clear conversation with me. I took a walk with her through the development during which she greeted and was greeted by what seemed to be hundreds of children. When we returned to the apartment we talked about school. I determined that she knew all the letters of the alphabet by sight regardless of the order in which they were presented. She also had a grasp of simple number concepts. When I began some formal testing she, as on my previous visit, became visibly uncomfortable and indicated that she would prefer doing something else. I persisted with enough Wechsler performance tasks to determine that she could function within normal limits.

I do not want to give the impression that Cynthia had changed markedly in all respects. She certainly was not a graceful child, and one was still struck by her peculiarly shaped head. Although she spoke clearly and carried on meaningful conversations, affective expression seemed on the flat side. For the purposes of the present discussion the important thing is that a dramatic change in psychological behavior had occurred over a period somewhat longer than a year. (Sarason, 1964)[4]

Diagnostic labels and test scores can and certainly do have value. But, in using them, one must constantly guard against sloppy thinking and, more important, oversimplifications which obscure the alternative actions one might take in a given case.

Consequences of the Diagnostic Process

It cannot be overemphasized that diagnoses give rise to actions, which is but another way of saying that they influence the lives of individuals. The fact that the diagnostic process is taking or has taken place bespeaks the existence of questions pertaining to an individual's present and past behavior, i.e., the process is a form of problem solving the immediate aim of which is to understand the ways in which the questions may be related to each other. The diagnostic process is never directed to a simple question (e.g., Is the individual retarded?) to which there is a simple answer, but it is rather directed to a

---

[4] We should remind the reader that we have presented this case not with the intention of making generalizations about the capabilities of brain-injured children but to emphasize the dangers of oversimplified thinking about and use of diagnostic labels. Behavior is a function of a variety of current and past variables and conditions and we do an injustice to this complexity by resorting to oversimplifications. As we shall discuss in greater detail in Chapter 20, the relation between degree, locus, and type of brain injury, on the one hand, and development, performance, and behavior, on the other hand, is far from proportional or clear.

series of questions about an individual's behavior and performance.[5] But the diagnostic process is not an intellectual exercise devoted to questions about present and past behavior. It is a process undertaken with the explicit aim of providing a basis for recommended actions and this aspect of the process should never be handled lightly precisely because the recommended actions can forever affect the life of another person. This statement, we hope, will not be viewed as an expression of mere sentiment or undue concern but rather as a statement of what truly occurs in real life. When one removes a child from a regular classroom, when one decides not to recommend a child for a preschool program, when one suggests institutionalization, when one concludes that a child cannot benefit from certain interpersonal or group experiences—when these and other kinds of decisions follow upon the diagnostic process it is obvious that one is influencing decisively the lives of other people. We are not concerned here with the rightness or wrongness of such recommendations but with the fact that decisions to act or not to act in certain ways are fateful for the lives of those whom we are trying to help.

It is easy to overlook that one of the most frequent consequences of the diagnostic process is that it presents one with alternatives for action. In the field of psychological diagnosis, at least, the clarity and validity of diagnostic formulations are not of a degree so as to reduce markedly the number of possible alternatives one must consider before deciding on *a* course of action. It must also be recognized that there are frequently time pressures (i.e., present and emergent stress conditions) which do not permit the clinician the luxury of tranquil reflection, pressures which by their very nature can unduly affect the objectivity and comprehensiveness of the clinician's thinking. Just as pressure to perform can adversely affect the patient, the pressure to formulate a course of action can adversely affect the clinician's thinking. When one is dealing with serious human problems it is unrealistic to view the diagnostic process and recommended actions as always taking place in the arena of calm objectivity. It is precisely in these stress or emergency situations that the diagnostic–action process can have serious untoward consequences. We are stressing this point because we feel it important for the reader to understand that the statement and examination of alternative actions is, under the best of conditions, an extremely difficult form of clinical problem solving and, under far less ideal circumstances, a near-impossible task. Our concern, of course, is less for the clinician than for the individual whose life is being influenced.[6]

---

[5] It is unfortunately true that in the area of mental subnormality one will too frequently find simple diagnostic answers to what appear to be simple diagnostic questions. In each of these instances it is not difficult to demonstrate that the simple diagnostic answer does not provide an adequate understanding of the questions about behavior and performance which made the diagnostic process necessary.

[6] We are saying here something quite familiar to the astute parent or classroom teacher, i.e., responding to a child's behavior sensitively and appropriately is far from a routine task and under the best of circumstances one's "diagnosis and actions" can

Our discussion thus far is incomplete in one important respect. We have been discussing the consequences of the diagnostic process as if they concerned *one* individual. This is rarely, if ever, the case. The following will illustrate the point.

ᔕ The Regional Center received a letter requesting it to consider placement for a nine-year-old mongoloid girl. The letter, written by the child's mother, was clear, concise, and very specific with respect to the nature and content of the service being requested. The letter stated that the child had been placed at birth in a nursery school some distance from New Haven. Because of the child's current age (she was now older than the other children at the nursery) and the lack of adequate training facilities (the nursery was not equipped to deal with mentally subnormal children) the nursery had suggested that the parents seek placement in a different setting, one that had the necessary facilities and programs to meet the training and educational needs of the child. The letter went on to state that the child was thought to be "trainable," and ended with the hope that the new Regional Center would be able to "do a great deal for her progress."

The referral was by no means atypical: a parent was asking for a particular type of service (in this case, institutionalization), and had furnished the type of information she felt would facilitate the Regional Center's deliberation and planning. The staff of the Regional Center set about its business by having the parents sign the customary release forms so that the staff could secure the appropriate records concerning the situation and begin its preliminary investigation.

The preliminary investigation yielded a picture of the situation that was somewhat at variance with, and certainly more complicated than, the picture communicated by the parents in their letter of referral. What emerged was the picture of a situation that for nine years had been filled with great personal and familial anxiety, doubt, guilt, fear, and all those variables that interact to produce a conflict-ridden family. What follows is a summary of the situation in terms of its history or development, and a description of the situation as we experienced it.

The parents, a couple who had known each other for many years before their marriage relatively late in life, felt that they would like to start a family as soon as possible. The wife's subsequent pregnancy was marked by a great deal of physical and emotional difficulty. After a long and arduous period of time in delivery the wife gave birth to a female child who immediately was diagnosed as mongoloid. Because of the difficulty delivery and the mother's weakened condition she was not conscious that she had given birth to a defective child. The father, himself quite shaken by the knowledge, did not wish the mother to be informed of the situation until she was physically strong enough to handle it. He therefore requested that the doctor not inform his wife of the situation "for a few more days." Through some misunderstanding the father's wishes were ignored and the mother was made aware of the circumstances surrounding her newborn child that same day. Her reaction was almost catastrophic. Her extreme disappointment and emotional upheaval resulted in an intense period of despair, anguish, and feelings of

---

misfire. It is when the behavior is surrounded by the characteristics of stress and emergency that the consequences of one's formulations and actions are apt to take the form of "problem creation through problem solution."

inadequacy. The mother suffered what was described as a nervous breakdown, characterized by suicidal preoccupations and a complete rejection of her child. Arrangements quickly were made to place the child in a nursery, the same nursery in which the child was residing at the time the Regional Center received the parents' request for institutionalization.

Because of the mother's emotional condition and frame of mind following the birth of the child, the family doctor (not the doctor who had ignored the father's wishes at the hospital) suggested that the couple try to have another child as quickly as possible. He made this suggestion with the idea that it would help the wife to overcome her feelings of inadequacy and despair, and—at the same time—would prove to her that she could have a normal baby. The wife became pregnant shortly thereafter and delivered a normal baby boy less than a year after the birth of her mongoloid child.

Despite the birth of the new child the mother's feelings about her mongoloid child remained essentially unchanged. She would not allow the mongoloid child (then about a year old) to be brought into the home under any conditions, and she devoted all her available time to the rearing of her newborn son.

During the succeeding years a family pattern was established. On the average of once a month the parents would take a trip to the nursery where they had placed their daughter. On these days (usually a Sunday) they would leave their son with a trusted relative, one of the very few people aware of the situation. They would visit their daughter at school, bring her additional clothes and sweets, often take her for a ride in the car, and then return to New Haven, pick up their son, and take him home. The son was never told of the existence of his sister and she was never brought to the home. When the son became old enough to begin asking questions regarding his parents' periodic trips he was told that they were "going for a ride and would be back in a few hours." Throughout these years the family doctor—possibly because he was aware of the mother's emotional difficulties and past history with respect to her mongoloid daughter—kept reinforcing the mother's feeling that the son should be kept unaware and uninformed of his sister's existence. Whenever the problem came up it was resolved in terms of waiting "until he is old enough" to understand before making him aware of the facts.

Although the parents maintained contact with their daughter and made no attempt to sever their relationship or abrogate their formal responsibilities toward her, they had very little information concerning her growth and development. They did not know if she could dress herself, were unaware that she was toilet trained, and had no knowledge of the degree of speech development or learning that had taken place since the time of her placement at the nursery. Their contact with the child was confined to periodic visits and phone calls to find out "if there is any improvement since the last visit."

The regular intake conference of the Regional Center took place with the benefit of the additional information that had been gathered during the preliminary investigation. After a review of the essential material now available, several variables emerged that appeared to be particularly salient. First, there was the variable involving the attitudes and behavior of the mother. We found ourselves most impressed with the degree and duration of the mother's conflicts concerning her mongoloid daughter, and the amount of anxiety and guilt she must have experienced about her feelings toward the child. Second, there was the factor involving the "normal" sibling in the family. What concerned us here were not only the kinds of questions (both verbalized and unspoken) he might have about the situation, but also the degree to which his parents' conflicts had affected his own growth and development. Because of the kinds of questions these variables raised, it was the group consensus that the case might be handled best by one of the psychologists working with the Regional Center. It was decided, therefore, that he should assume the primary responsibility for handling the case.

The day after the intake conference we telephoned the family in the hope of arranging a home visit, through which we could establish contact with the family and begin to explore the problems and possibilities of the situation. The telephone conversation (with the mother) began on a discordant note. She failed to see the reason for our call, and felt that the entire situation was outlined clearly in her letter to the Regional Center and in the information to which she had given us access by signing the release form. From her point of view the request for institutionalization was clear and would be the only plan of action she would accept. She was quite suspicious of our reasons for calling her and felt that we might be utilizing her and her husband's difficulties as a sort of teaching situation or trial case for interns in psychology. She reiterated her physician's advice that her eight-year-old son be kept out of the situation, and she used this reasoning as a basis for her refusal to allow us to visit the home. She did not want her son around whenever there was the slightest possibility that mention would be made of her mongoloid child. On our part, we explained to the mother that our request to visit the home was a standard procedure which the Regional Center had adopted with respect to most of its cases, and that it had nothing to do with a trial case or any purpose other than making it easier for the Regional Center to work more closely with the family in developing and implementing the most appropriate program for everyone concerned. We told her that we understood her feelings about not wanting to involve her son and that we would be happy to schedule our visit at a time when both she and her husband were at home and their son was either away at school or involved in some other activity that kept him away from the home. At this point the mother's anger and suspiciousness appeared to wane, and soon were replaced by a feeling closely akin to relief, relief that we were indeed interested sufficiently in her problem to make available to her a staff member who was willing to come to the home at a time and in a manner that would make the situation as comfortable as possible. We then arranged to visit the home at a time (8:30 A.M.) after the son had left for school and before the husband left for work.

At the appointed time and day we arrived at the home just in time to join the parents over a cup of coffee and to discuss the situation around the kitchen table. The home was a modest but extremely pleasant one, located in one of the better sections of town.

Even before we began to discuss the case itself the mother felt compelled to apologize for her behavior over the phone. In her apology she conveyed very many of her anguished and guilt-ridden feelings concerning her daughter in a direct manner. In the process she quickly became very tearful and hardly could speak. Her husband, a mild-mannered but extremely strong and supportive person, immediately comforted her and continued the discussion while his wife regained control of herself.

We then became more involved in a discussion about the parents' request and the ways in which the Regional Center could be of help. We indicated our understanding of the situation, but also pointed out that the philosophy of the Regional Center is such that we could not guarantee anonymity to the parents because we could not promise to keep the daughter removed from the resources of the area (schools, recreation centers) or from the facilities (religious and social institutions) that existed in the community. We also discussed the fact that there had never been an adequate developmental and psychological assessment of their daughter so that we were unable at this point to state that she was trainable or educable (a distinction of which the parents were unaware). At this point we indicated the variety of things mongoloid children could learn (reading, vocational skills, etc.) under appropriate conditions and with the help of trained personnel and specialized programming. The longer we discussed the situation the more attentive the parents became and the less prone they were to chronicle the years of torment and anguish they had been through.

The discussion then turned to their concern about when and how their son would be informed of the existence of his sister, the conditions under which he would find out, and the possible consequences and effects it would have on him. In discussing their son the parents were remarkably frank and concerned about his current status independent of the situation concerning his sister. What quickly emerged was a picture of an eight-year-old boy who was not as normal and healthy as we might have believed. Although describing her love and devotion ("My whole life is concerned with him.") for her son the mother was quick to point out that he was a "very troubled boy" who kept to himself a good deal of the time and had very few friends. The father saw his son as a somewhat effeminate youngster who spent too much of his time reading and talking with adults and elderly relatives. The mother agreed with much that the father said and added that the young boy was asking more and more questions concerning their "Sunday afternoon trips" and recently had asked her whether or not he was an adopted child. They were, in short, extremely concerned about their son and his development. All we felt we should do was to point out the fact that children are extremely sensitive to these things, that they do have questions, and that these questions do not appear to become less potent with the passage of time.

Turning once more to their daughter the parents made it clear that even if she were placed at the Regional Center they would not want to bring her home until she had become "more of a person" and until they had been able to inform their son of her existence and prepare him for the situation. We agreed with the parents and told them that the Regional Center was acutely aware of the difficulties involved in the situation and was prepared to offer whatever help was possible both in terms of preparing their daughter for a more active involvement in the community and in helping them deal with the issue of how and when to prepare their son for the situation. At this point we attempted to be as concrete as possible in terms of the variety of programs that were and would be available at the Regional Center to help them with their problem. We described the development of the sibling groups, parent groups, and other programs whose aim it was to help the parents and siblings of mentally subnormal individuals deal with the problems that confronted them and their families. We also indicated our intention of involving them in whatever plans and programs might be developed with respect to their child and her education and training.

Toward the end of our meeting the parents appeared genuinely interested with the possibilities and programs we described. Although still quite frightened and skeptical, they agreed to think about the things we had discussed. They wanted to know if our presence in their home was a "one-shot affair" or if we were prepared to see them again or as often as they felt necessary. We told them that we would work with them for the entire period of time during which they felt it necessary and helpful. Before leaving we set up a second appointment with them and left the phone number where they could get in touch with us if there was anything they wanted to talk about before our next meeting. The next meeting was set up for the next week at the same time.

A day before our next scheduled meeting we received a phone call from the mother. In a very hesitant and apologetic manner she informed us of her and her husband's decision to put off their request for institutionalizing their daughter at the Regional Center. She told us they had discussed the situation and had decided to investigate other placement possibilities. Although she did not sound confident about their decision and was extremely thankful for our concern and attention, she nevertheless felt it would be wiser to seek a different placement. After informing us of their decision the mother seemed hesitant about terminating the conversation, so we asked her what factors had influenced their decision. Almost as if she were betraying a confidence she told us that after speaking with us she and her husband had felt it important that they consult their family doctor, the man who "has done so much for us through the years." The doctor was quite opposed to the ideas we had discussed and the suggestions we had made. He felt it was not the appropriate time to involve their son in the situation; that the wife was still too emotionally weak to become involved again in a potentially traumatic situation; and that it was best to postpone the type of program and planning that we had discussed. The mother felt he was correct in his judgment and was withdrawing her application for immediate placement. Before hanging up she asked us if she could contact us again if she and her husband were to change their minds. We told her that we would be available whenever she wished to discuss the matter again.

At our next intake conference we informed our colleagues at the Regional Center of the results of our home visit and of the ensuing telephone conversation with the mother. We all were concerned about the situation, not only because of the results and consequences for the mongoloid child (her future treatment, education, and training), but because of our findings with respect to the parents and the "normal" child. It appeared that the family doctor was the primary agent in influencing the parents to seek placement elsewhere, so we discussed the appropriateness of exploring with him the reasons and bases for his feelings and decisions. Our concern was not solely one of attempting to influence him in the situation, but to apprise him of our findings and perceptions of the situation with respect to the parents and sibling as well as the institutionalized child. We felt it appropriate to involve our own medical staff member in whatever liaison and discussions we could establish with the family doctor.

Although the parents have currently withdrawn their request for institutionalization at the Regional Center, we do not consider the case closed. At the time of this writing we are in the process of establishing a meeting between ourselves (and our medical staff member) and the family doctor—a meeting we hope will lead to a fuller exploration of the variables, problems, and possibilities of the situation.[7]

In this example the diagnosis of the newborn child had, in the mind of the physician, obviously important consequences for the family. Later in this book we shall discuss in greater detail the appropriateness of a way of thinking which can give rise to more problems than it resolves, if it resolves any. What is relevant here is the fact that diagnostic formulations and derived actions very much involve and affect the family. It is our contention that a real question may be raised about the appropriateness of viewing *an* individual as the *object* of the diagnostic process, not only because his behavior and performance reflect to some degree relationships within the family—it is a relationship of mutual influences—but also because any action in regards to the individual inevitably influences other members of the family. We tend to regard those inevitable influences as not requiring their own diagnostic assessment, although they can be as important and as fateful as the diagnosis of the individual.

In this chapter we have attempted to indicate that the utilization of diagnostic labels is an extremely serious matter frequently involving implicit and unverbalized assumptions about behavior which are hardly justifiable. Arriving at a diagnostic formulation with recommended actions is, at this stage of our knowledge, not a process to be carried out in cookbook style. It is a process which is very much influenced by theoretical conceptions, value judgments, experience, and habits of thinking which can expand or limit awareness of alternatives or which can facilitate or inhibit recognition of tested and untested assumptions. The diagnostic process is a form both of problem solving and decision making which has (as it should) consequences for other individuals. It is this last point that must be constantly kept in mind if only as a reminder that these consequences should always be preceded by careful scrutiny of external knowledge *and* one's own way of thinking.

We might have characterized the contents of this chapter by saying that *what* one is dealing with in the diagnostic process is in part a function of *how* one thinks and that different styles of thinking about the same case can result in markedly different diagnoses and actions. This statement, as will become clear in Chapters 15, 16, and 17, certainly holds when one contrasts one era with another in the history of mental subnormality, but what we have tried to emphasize in the present chapter is that it also holds for a particular time period, i.e., the present one.

---

[7] Two of the major issues raised by this (and the previous) case concern the effects of a retarded child on the normal siblings in the family and the problem of the effects of institutionalization. The first of these issues is taken up in Chapter 10 by Dr. Frances Kaplan, and the second in Chapter 9 by Dr. Michael Klaber in the present volume.

Any formal or systematic psychological diagnostic process is governed by or concerned with criteria of behavior and performance according to which the diagnostician can study the nature of the problem and a course of action. In the next chapter we shall discuss the problem of criteria and the thorny issues it poses to those not satisfied with oversimplified concepts and overevaluation of current knowledge.

The problem of criteria

However much different writers may disagree about matters of causation and action, there has long been agreement that on a purely descriptive level there are two broad categories of subnormal individuals. The first category contains those individuals for whom there are compelling grounds for stating that they have a defective central nervous system, that this organic, or brain, defect existed at or shortly after birth, and that it is related to the fact that the individual is indisputably intellectually retarded as compared to his age peers. As we shall see in later chapters there are a wide variety of etiological factors (e.g., traumatic, genetic, metabolic) which may result in an impaired central nervous system, of which the brain is an integral part. We have already expressed the opinion that the relations between behavior and brain damage are by no means simple and clear. These kinds of knotty etiological problems should not obscure for the reader that this one broad category contains a truly heterogeneous collection of individuals who may be characterized as brain damaged and intellectually retarded. These individuals may be found in any class of society and in most parts of the world. The individual comprising this category vary considerably on a host of factors: degree of central nervous system involvement, motor defect, size, appearance, longevity, and degree of personal care required. Over the decades this category has been given such labels as feeble-minded or mentally deficient, labels meant to communicate that there was something awry with the brain not only in a functional but in a neuro-physiological sense as well.[1]

The second broad descriptive category of retarded individuals comprises a very large number in whom there is no discernible central nervous system impairment, who are found in the lowest social classes in our society, who are intellectually retarded according to conventional tests of intelligence and who do not progress normally through the grades. Over the years there have been a number of outstanding workers who have emphasized the necessity of differentiating these individuals from those categorized as mentally deficient, primarily because they clearly saw the obvious: Cultural or sociological factors were implicated in the development and performance of these individuals. The role of other factors, e.g., genetic, was variously viewed by these workers. For example, in 1908, Binet and Simon had the following to say about the relation of cultural background and test scores:

. . . retardation is a term relative to a number of circumstances which must be taken into account in order to judge each particular case. We can make the boundary between moronity and the normal state more definite by considering a special category of subjects. We wish to speak of defective adults whom we have had occasion to observe in the Parisian hospitals who were subjects for custodial care. This forms a special category for many reasons: first on account of nationality and race, it is a question as to whether they are Parisians or persons living in the regions of Paris; second, on account of social conditions; all belong to the laboring class. *The limit that we place for them would not be correct for any others; we express complete reserve for the application of it which one would wish to make for subjects of different environments.*" (Binet 1916a. Italics ours.)

It is interesting, if only from the standpoint of historical perspective, that in a recent major study of the relation between cultural and educational factors, on the one hand, and intellectual and educational performance, on the other hand—a study of what today is called cultural deprivation—Blatt and Garfunkel (1965) explicitly view themselves as intellectual descendants of Binet's views.

---

[1] In earlier decades of this century the terms "mental deficiency" and "feeblemindedness" were used synonymously in the American literature. In recent decades, however, the term feeblemindedness tends no longer to be used, perhaps, we think, because it was long responded to by parents as a term of derogation (which indeed it was). It is a necessary complication for the reader to be informed that in the British literature the term mental deficiency is usually used as a substitute for feeblemindedness in the generic sense, the label feeblemindedness being applied by British workers to what American workers call the moron, although "moron" is being decreasingly used in the literature again because of its derogatory implications, e.g., the "moron" jokes which seem to have cyclical popularity. It is, in our opinion, a tribute to parent groups that they have made the public and professional groups aware that certain terms were not only offensive but, in fact, reflected a derogation of the defective individual as a human being worthy of as much attention, help, and scrutiny as any other human being.

Doll (1947) in this country and Lewis (1933) in England long recognized and advocated the importance of differentiating the mentally deficient from the mentally retarded (Doll) and the "subcultural" type (Lewis). Lewis maintained that classifying the subcultural type of subnormality with the pathological types obscures the pressing social problems presented by and the remedial measures required for the former. Kanner also emphasized the significance of the differentiation:

1. *Absolute feeblemindedness.* One variety consists of individuals so markedly deficient in their cognitive, affective, and constructively conative potentialities that they would stand out as defectives in any existing civilization. They are designated as idiots and imbeciles. They would be equally helpless and ill-adapted in a society of savants and in a society of savages. They are not only deficient intellectually but deficient in every sphere of mentation. They are truly, absolutely, irreversibly feebleminded or mentally deficient in every sense of the word. The most carefully planned therapeutic and education efforts will not succeed in helping them to function self-dependently, without the need for protecting supervision. They continue throughout their lives in need of custodial care, the custody being carried on by relatives or in appropriate institutions.

    Even in this group, the assumption of irreversibility has recently been challenged. Disregarding the sensational claims made in newspaper reports and popular magazine articles, one must still await further and more conclusive results of experiments with glutamic acid. So far, sporadic additions of a few points to the intelligence quotient have not managed to lift even the most responsive patients out of the absoluteness of their defects. At least for the time being, the enthusiasm about glutamic acid is a little too reminiscent of the promises made not too long ago with regard to the "brightening" effects of cortin in mongolians.

2. *Relative feeblemindedness.* Another, larger variety is made up of individuals whose limitations are definitely related to the standards of the particular society which surrounds them. In less complex, less intellectually centered societies, they would have no trouble in attaining and retaining equality of realizable ambitions. Some might even be capable of gaining superiority by virtue of assets other than those measured by the intelligence tests. They could make successful peasants, hunters, fishermen, tribal dancers. They can, in our own society, achieve proficiency as farm hands, factory workers, miners, waitresses, charwomen . . .

    The members of this group are not truly and absolutely feebleminded or *mentally* deficient. Their principal shortcoming is a greater or lesser degree of inability to comply with the *intellectual* requirements of their society. In other respects, they may be as mature or immature, stable or unstable, secure or insecure, placid or moody, aggressive or submissive as any other member of the human species. Their "deficiency" is an *ethnologically determined phenomenon* relative to the local stardards and, even within those standards, relative to educational postulates, vocational ambitions, and family expectations. They are "subcultural" in our society but may not be even that in a different, less sophisticated setting.

    It is for this group that the suggested designation of intellectual inadequacy seems more appropriate than any other existing term. (Kanner, 1949)

When one truly familiarizes himself with the work or writings of people like Binet, Doll, Lewis, and Kanner (among others) it becomes abundantly clear that it has long been recognized that failure to distinguish between the mentally deficient, on the one hand, and the mentally retarded or subcultural subnormality on the other hand, can only contribute to fuzzy thinking, public confusion, and misguided social action.

For the purposes of this book it is our preference to distinguish between mental deficiency and mental retardation, reserving the latter label for that large group of individuals whose intellectual and educational deficits appear, to an undetermined but important extent, to be related to a constellation of social, familial, and cultural factors to be described shortly.[2] Our preference for the term "mental retardation" rather than "subcultural" reflects two considerations. First, the term subcultural is not strictly in accord with anthropological usage, i.e., the mentally retarded for whom the term would be used are found in places varying both geographically and culturally and, therefore, do not and cannot share common cultural experiences. Second, although reference to mentally retarded as "subcultural" does at least direct attention to a most important aspect of the problem, one sometimes gets the impression that a value judgment is implied in the use of the term, i.e., the subculture is inferior to our own. The danger in such a value judgment is that by branding the subculture as inferior, one is likely to misperceive or misinterpret the behavior of individuals in the subculture, that is, it becomes difficult to understand the subculture in its own terms.

ILLUSTRATIVE CASES

For a description of mental retardation in a family in a city slum at the turn of the century one cannot do better than Goddard's description of a Kallikak family.[3]

---

[2] This distinction between mental deficiency and mental retardation—with the term mental subnormality embracing both—is not by any means universally recognized. If anything, the tendency is to use the term mental retardation in the most general or encompassing way, a degree of coverage which defeats the aim of communication. The distinction we prefer conforms essentially to usage suggested by the World Health Organization (1954). We are quite aware that the use of the term mental retardation in an encompassing way may be so general and overlearned that it is asking too much to expect that the distinctions we and others prefer will gain acceptance. In all candor the writers must confess that in our professional activities we have not always been able to be consistent with our position if only because of the communication problem it may present to others. The problem is not made any easier in later chapters when we discuss the work and writings of earlier workers whose use of terms may be quite different than what we are accustomed to today.

[3] "Garden-variety" and "Kallikak" are two other terms which have been used to designate what in this book we shall call the mentally retarded. These terms also seem to contain a pejorative connotation, as a reading of Goddard's (1912) book on the Kallikak family would indicate. The work and role of Goddard, particularly as they relate to the development of the eugenics movement and the heredity–environment controversy, are discussed in detail in Chapters 13, 15 and 16.

෨෴   On one of the coldest days in winter the field worker visited the street in a city slum where three sons of Joseph live. She had previously tested several of the children of these families in the public school and found them, in amiability of character and general mentality, strikingly like our own Deborah, lacking, however, her vitality. There was no fire in their eyes, but a languid dreamy look, which was partly due, no doubt, to unwholesome city environment. In one house she found the family group—six human beings, two cats, and two dogs—huddled in a small back room around a cook stove, the only fire in the house. In this room were accumulated all the paraphernalia of living. A boy of eleven, who had been tested in the school previously, was standing by the fire with a swollen face. He had been kept home on this account. In a rocking-chair, a little girl of twelve was holding a pale-faced, emaciated baby. In the corner two boys were openly exposing themselves. The mother was making her toilet by the aid of a comb and basin of water, set on the hearth of the stove; a pot and kettle were on top. The entrance of the field worker caused no commotion of any kind. The boy with the swollen face looked up and smiled, the mother smiled and went on with her toilet, the girl with the baby smiled, the boys in the corner paid no attention. A chair was finally cleared off and she sat down, while everybody smiled. She learned that the husband made a dollar a day and that the girl next older than the child of twelve was married and had a baby. Another younger girl was at school, the family having been at last able to provide her with shoes. The girl of twelve should have been at school, according to the law, but when one saw her face, one realized it made no difference. She was pretty, with olive complexion and dark, languid eyes, but there was no mind there. Stagnation was the word written in large characters over everything. Benumbed by this display of human degeneracy, the field worker went out into the icy street.

A short distance farther on, she came to the home of another brother. The hideous picture that presented itself as the door opened to her knock was one never to be forgotten. In the first home, the type was no lower than moron. One felt that when winter was over and spring had come, the family would expand into a certain expression of life—but here, no such outlook was possible, for the woman at the head of this house was an imbecile. In one arm she held a frightful looking baby, while she had another by the hand. Vermin were visible all over her. In the room were a few chairs and a bed, the latter without any washable covering and filthy beyond description. There was no fire, and both mother and babies were thinly clad. They did not shiver, however, nor seem to mind. The oldest girl, a vulgar, repulsive creature of fifteen, came into the room and stood looking at the stranger. She had somehow managed to live. All the rest of the children, except the two that the mother was carrying had died in infancy.[4]

McPherson's description of defective families, published in 1937, indicates that Goddard's observations made at the beginning of the century are not dated. The following are descriptions of the H——y and H——n families.

---

[4] From H. H. Goddard, *The Kallikak family*. Macmillan, 1912. By permission of Henry H. Goddard.

The H_____y Family

The father of this family was a laborer, very deaf. Accused by wife of having relations with daughter. He was said to be alcoholic. The mother, 48, admitted to Belchertown in 1932, with an I.Q. of .68. Attempts were made to improve her care of the family under the supervision of the S.P.C.C. for eleven years but she did not improve. She kept a filthy home, was sexually promiscuous, and had incestuous relations with son, who may be father of twins born in 1930. Her own husband requested her commitment to this institution following her arrest for neglect of home. This family has been known to welfare departments for years. Children of this family, Louise, Harry, and Ruby, were committed in 1930 to the Division of Child Guardianship. Louis, age 23, I.Q. .70. Was committed to Belchertown State School in 1934. In 1930, he was in court charged with incest with mother and sister, charge later changed to assault and battery. In court in 1933 for abuse of a female child, committed to County Jail and then to Belchertown. He escaped in 1934. Louise, 20, I.Q. .69. Was committed to Belchertown in 1934. She was in Juvenile Court as delinquent child, admitted having relations with father and brother. Had been in care of Social Service Division of Department of Mental Diseases where she was found to be childish and incompetent and she was returned to aunt who found her unmanageable and requested her removal. Harry, age 18, I.Q. .47. Sent to this school in 1930. He was suspected of imitating incestuous acts he had seen at home. Has defective speech. Ruby—no information. Earl, 14, I.Q. .52, speech defect. Admitted to State School in 1931. Margaret, 9 years old, in care of Division of Child Guardianship. Said to be very backward. Her paternity is denied by father of this family. Winifred, age 7, I.Q. .63. Admitted in 1933. It is suspected that her own brother is the father.

The H——n Family

The father was said to be feeble-minded and lacking in responsibility. Never able to make a living for family. He was related through his mother with two other families at the state school. The mother was suspected of being immoral with star boarder in the home, whom she permitted to have relations with daughters for the sake of money. The home was kept in terrible shape. Mother and children caked with dirt and covered with vermin. Younger children said to have sores where rats nibbled fingers and toes. The children, as we know them at this school, consisted of Henry, age 41, said to be simple. He married and his wife was said to be not much brighter. Mentally incapable of earning a living and providing a home for family. Robert, 48, said to be feeble-minded. Sexually abused his sister. Emma May, 36, I.Q. .55. Had been sexually abused by boarder in home. Was committed to Wrentham State School in 1915, transferred to this school in 1923. Hattie, 33. Was in the care of Children's Aid Association from 1915–1919. Placed in many foster homes but did not do well. She was sent to Lancaster as a stubborn child because of instruction of younger children in sex matters and experiences with boys. Was paroled and again returned. Released in 1924 and became pregnant. She was committed to this school in 1926 with an

I.Q. of .85. Discharged as not feeble-minded but she has never gotten along well in the community. Married and deserted her husband for another man. She was diagnosed at the Psychopathic Hospital as a psychopathic personality without psychosis. Martha, 31, I.Q. .47. Admitted to this school in 1923. Sexually abused by brother. Rosie Ella, 28, said to be feeble-minded. Under guardianship of Children's Aid Association of Hampshire County. Laura Ellen, 26, I.Q. .76. Admitted to this school in 1923. Tried parole in 1937 but she did not adjust well and wanted to return. Alice, 25, I.Q. .49. Admitted to this school in 1923 and can do first and second grade work. Lena May, 22, supposed to be the illegitimate child of a boarder in the parents' home. She has since died. (McPherson, 1937)

The following is a partial description of a family reported by Bice in 1947:

The Nineveh Family

The father, whose date of birth is unknown, was the son of American-born parents of German extraction. He was a Protestant. At maturity he was estimated to be of borderline mentality, one report indicating a mental age of 10 years 6 months. The father informed a social case worker that he was a printer by trade; however, during the time he was known to social agencies he did not work as a printer. He was a junk dealer and reported earnings as much as $100.00 a month. His conception of the occupation of a junk dealer may be reflected in the fact that he was at one time arrested for receiving stolen goods and was given a suspended sentence. Sentence was also suspended on another occasion when he was found guilty of abandoning his children. From 1936 to 1940 the family was on relief. One worker who investigated the case reported that the father saw no harm in permitting the children to roam the streets at any time they chose and he encouraged them to beg. When he died a neighbor expressed the consensus in the community: "It was sad, but it was a blessing to the county."

The mother was also the child of American-born parents; their ancestry was Irish. She was a Roman Catholic. She was married at the age of 15 and had not reached her 16th birthday when her first child was born. In the 29 years which followed, there were 19 additional children born of this union, 10 of whom died in infancy. A social case worker stated in her reports that the mother was "careless" and "gave the impression of being mentally defective." At maturity her mental age was reported to be 8 years and 8 months. Harriet's mother considered herself a nervous person whose health had been ruined by worry over the health of her children.

Charles, the oldest child, was found to have but little academic ability; the only activity in which he did well was drawing, a talent also possessed by some siblings. He, as well as all the other children who did not die in infancy, was committed to the care of the state board of children's guardians. Later he spent one year at a training school for the feeble-minded. He has been arrested on numerous occasions. He later married and, by the time he was 39 years of age he had seven children. During the war he sold soft drinks at a small stand in a shipyard. He had little interest in the education of his children. When the authorities insisted on school attendance, he said that the members of the family were so attached to each other that they could not bear to be separated long enough for the children to be in school.

Doris, second child of the Ninevehs, married a man whose brother was in an institution for the feeble-minded. By the time she was 33 she had had five children, all of whom were wards of the state.

Eric had a school record much like that of his siblings. Though crippled by poliomyelitis, he used to do acrobatic stunts and make chalk drawings on city sidewalks, in order to solicit funds from onlookers. He was arrested twice for disorderly conduct. He was found at the age of 27 to have a mental age of 7 years 3 months, and was committed to a state institution for the feeble-minded.

Frances entered public school at the age of six and left ten years later when she was in the sixth grade. Later, when the girl was in conflict with the law, her mother said: "I don't know what has become of all the education the children had." While she was attending school, Frances earned from three to four dollars a week selling matches, wax paper, and notions on the street.

The first report of Frances' delinquency was made when she was 17 and was arrested for soliciting in a nearby city. Thereafter she continued to be known to social agencies as a prostitute. The records contain such entries as: "girl is known prostitute"; "was arrested in a disorderly house"; "her earnings were three or four dollars a night." Frances had two children, both of whom were given the same first and middle names. The father of the first child was a neighbor. The second child was born when Frances was 20. Her experiences had by that time been so varied and extensive that the child's paternity could not be established. Frances was committed to an institution for delinquent women. At that time she had syphilis and gonorrhea.

At the age of 24, she was committed to a training school for the feeble-minded. Psychologists indicated that she had a mental age sufficiently high so that, if one were to judge on that basis alone, she might be considered a borderline case; however, her judgment was poor, her reasoning inferior, and her comprehension limited. Her total functioning was considered to be on a feeble-minded level."[5]

Town's study (1939) of 141 defective families rounds out somewhat the above descriptions:

1. The mortality rate among such families is larger than that of the general population. One hundred and fifteen children in 56 families died in infancy or before 14 years of age, prompting Town to comment that "this great mortality is doubtless accounted for largely by the low mentality of the mothers which prevented the proper care of the children."
2. In 28 families marriages were broken by desertion, abandonment, separation, annulment, or divorce.

---

[5] Harry V. Bice, "Mental deficiency, moron level." In Arthur Burton and Robert E. Harris (eds.), *Case histories in clinical and abnormal psychology.* Harper, 1947, pp. 383–385. Reprinted by permission of the author and the publisher, and through the courtesy of the North Jersey Training School, the New Jersey State Board of Child Welfare, and the State Home for Boys at Jamesburg.

3. In 37 percent of the families housekeeping conditions were recorded as "flagrantly" bad. "Keeping a house in order, preparing regular meals and caring for a family of children is a task much too great for the feeble wits of the mothers of these families."
4. Malnutrition was found in 21 families.
5. Illegitimate maternity was found in 51 families. Incest occurred in 7 families, and prostitution in 14 families.
6. Reformatory, penitentiary, jail, or prison terms were recorded in 38 families.
7. In 20 families at least one child was removed from the custody of the parents. "Each transfer of custody implies parental neglect serious enough to be classified by a court as constituting improper guardianship."
8. In 20 families habitual practice of physical violence toward other members of the household was noted.

In 1965 Blatt and Garfunkel studied a number of families living in a section of approximately one square mile in Cambridge, Massachusetts. This area had previously been found by Sweetser (1962a,b) to be one of the most socially and economically deprived areas in Metropolitan Boston. As Blatt and Garfunkel state:

This area had a high percentage of nonwhite population, working mothers, residential instability, crowded housing, low family income, male unemployment, low occupational status, and inferior educational opportunities. For several generations it had been the highest "delinquency area" of Cambridge. Two federally supported low-income housing projects formed the central core of this community and the majority of families eventually selected for the study resided in these projects. Other families lived in tenement houses in varying degrees of disrepair, some in better condition than project apartments and others in poorer condition. The vast majority of families in the area were marginally economically independent or were on Aid to Dependent Children or other public welfare.

Blatt and Garfunkel present the following cases *not* because they are the clearest instances of cultural–familial retardation but because in each instance a question could be raised about the psychological diagnosis of the intellectual and educational performance of some of the parents and siblings of their subject population. These are not their worst cases and they are given here only to indicate to the reader the types of environments from which the mentally retarded come.

   The family of Subject 2 lives in a section of Cambridge known as "red block." This block consists of four, four-story apartment houses, all connected. Family 2 lives in a building that was condemned several years ago but never demolished. Many families go to live on "red block" when they are evicted from the project or as a last resort. In this neighborhood, it is considered degrading to have to live on this block. The particular building under discussion is in a deplorable physical condition, dirty, and an apparent fire trap. Stairways are broken and garbage strewn on all floors. Stairways and hallways are dark, with light coming through a skylight during the day. Obscene words are written on the walls of the hallways; the entire house smells of kerosene which is the only type of fuel used; ceilings are cracked and plaster is falling down. The house is infested with rats and this seems to a continuous problem tenants are faced with. No door has a name or number on it and mailboxes do not give indication as to which apartment contains which family. Most people in the house pick up their mail at the post office, as most mail is in the form of relief or other dependency checks, easily stolen from broken central mailboxes. It was pointed out that this obscurity helps in avoiding creditors as well as other unwanted visitors.

The family is known to 11 social agencies in the Greater Boston Area, including Public Welfare, Catholic Charities, and Family Service.

The father is 40 years old, reports having completed seven grades of school, not working, and presently a patient at the Veterans Administration Hospital, suffering with asthma. Previous to his hospital confinement, he was an odd-job worker. He is said to be an alcoholic.

The mother is 37 years old, reported that she stayed back a lot in school and did not like school but completed seven grades.

There are eight children in this family, six of school age, none in the special class. However, the 14-year-old son is in the fifth grade; the 12-year-old daughter is in the sixth grade; the 11-year-old daughter is in the third grade; the eight-year-old daughter is in the first grade; the seven-year-old daughter is in kindergarten; and the six-year-old son is in kindergarten. There is evidence here of general and multiple grade repetition of siblings.

Subject 2, a three-and-a-half-year-old boy, one of two preschoolers in the family, was delivered after a normal pregnancy. The mother reports an uneventful early life, he ate well, was weaned without difficulty, walked at about a year and talked at about a year. His toilet-training began at about six months of age and by one year he was trained.

⁓ Family 3 lives in a duplex four-room apartment in Cambridge. The interior of the apartment is in dire need of repairs, very dark and poorly furnished. During the winter months it is poorly heated and very cold. In general the apartment is very dirty with heaps of garbage on the floors of each room. The toilet and kitchen are unhygienic and neglected. Mattresses on the floor serve as beds and, in summary, it would be difficult to imagine more depressing physical surroundings.

The father is 42 years old and reportedly a graduate of Technical High School. He is a veteran and has always been employed as a welder. He is reputed to be a heavy drinker and to consider his own needs and desires above those of his family. His wife reports that he has not shown any interest in caring for his children or his wife for several years. He has separated many times from his wife, legally during the past year.

The mother is 36 years old and attended school as far as the eighth grade. She reports never to have repeated any grades and considers herself bright, in fact much brighter than her children whom she refers to as "stupid." She has always assumed full responsibility for her family and presently works nights to add to the 30 dollars a week that her husband is required to pay for support of the family.

The oldest sibling, 15 years of age, in good health, just completed the eighth grade at school. In the past, he repeated grades 3, 4, and 6. He dislikes school and is a poor student. The 14-year-old daughter is in good health and considered to be "smartest" of all the children. She began at a parochial school but was removed for school failure. She now attends public school and has repeated the eighth grade. She assumes major responsibility for the care of Subject 3. The 12-year-old son is in good health and considered by the mother to be "lazy." He attends the sixth grade and has repeated the fourth grade. He dislikes school very much. The second youngest child is five years of age and began school in the fall. He is in good health.

Subject 3 was three years old when he entered the project. Although he was an RH-negative baby, he received a clean bill of health during a very closely supervised nine month post-natal period. He has never been hospitalized nor has he had any childhood illnesses. He walked at about eleven months, was able to understand words at about two years of age, and is just now beginning to speak. He completed toilet-training quite recently, gets along very well with peers and family, is considered friendly and easily manageable by the family, and is considered to be brighter than other children in the family.

⌢⌣ The family of Subject 4 lives in a six-room apartment on the second and third floors above a dental equipment firm. Both the interior and exterior of the building are in need of extensive repair. The inside is furnished with only the barest essentials. It is very dirty, windows are broken, and most of the walls are broken away.

The family is known to ten social agencies in the Greater Boston Area, including Public Welfare, Society for the Prevention of Cruelty to Children, State Division of Child Guardianship, Family Society, and Legal Aid Society.

The father is 36 years old, attended but did not graduate from vocational school, and had repeated several grades. He is rarely at home, is said to be of little help to the mother, and spends whatever money is available on "drinking or running about."

The mother is 28 years old, completed the ninth grade of junior high school, while repeating two grades. She quit school at 16 to go to work, married at that time, with frequent separations terminating in divorce in 1959. Since her divorce, she has been receiving Aid to Dependent Children assistance. She appears unable to keep up with rearing her seven children. They are physically unclean and unmanageable.

The oldest sibling is ten years old, recently completed the fourth grade, and has repeated the first grade. The nine-year-old daughter has just completed the third grade and has not repeated any grades. The seven-year-old daughter has repeated the first grade. The six-year-old son has just completed the first grade and is going to repeat it this year. The five-year-old son completed kindergarten this year but will repeat it again next year.

Subject 4, three-and-a-half years old on entrance to the project, is one of two preschool children in the family. His early history was normal and unremarkable.

He reportedly said words at about one year of age, walked at 11 months, and has been toilet-trained since his second birthday. He gets along well with other children in the neighborhood although he does not get along with his brother, one year older than he. His mother reports him as being "spoiled." He is the baby in the family and apparently both mother and siblings "spoil him."

⌒⌒⌒ The family of Subject 5 lives in a five-room project apartment. The interior of the apartment is neat and clean, although sparsely and poorly furnished. There is some attempt to keep the apartment in good order.

The family is known to nine social agencies, including Public Welfare, Family Service, State Division of Child Guardianship, and the Society for the Prevention of Cruelty to Children.

The father is 38 years old, completed six grades of school and repeated at least three grades prior to his leaving school at age 16. He has always worked as a fisherman. During the fishing season he leaves his family for long periods of time and when he is home he spends his evenings drinking, gambling, and "running around." He is reported to be an ill-tempered person, easily angered and unconcerned with the financial or emotional support of his family.

The mother is 30 years old and attended part of the second year of high school. She left school at age 16 in order to get out of an unhappy home situation, married at that time, and is presently suing for divorce. Since her separation she has been receiving Aid to Dependent Children funds. Because her husband is frequently away from home, child rearing is left almost entirely to her. She feels she is too easy on the children, not strict enough and, as a result, the children get what they want.

The oldest sibling, a daughter, has just completed the eighth grade and has never repeated any grades. A son, age nine, repeated the first grade and is now attending special class. He is a "fire setter" who was sent by the courts to a child guidance clinic and is presently awaiting treatment. A son, age eight, has completed the second grade and has not repeated any grades. A daughter, age five, just completed kindergarten and is going into the first grade.

Subject 5, one of two preschool children in the family had an uneventful early childhood, talking about the same age as the other children, and walking by the time he was one year old. He was toilet-trained by the time he was two and one-half, although he still has accidents at night. He is a pleasant little boy, minds his mother well, responds to her discipline, rarely has to be spanked, is good natured, and mixes well with other children in the neighborhood and his siblings.

⌒⌒⌒ The family of Subject 6 lives in a wooden house outside the project area. The house has broken windows, broken wallboards, paint cracked and peeling, and garbage, glass, and other debris strewn around the yard. Torn shades and broken windows can be seen from the outside of the house. The front entrance reveals a garbage cluttered portal and narrow dark steps, unlighted and smelling of gasoline. Inside, rooms are extremely small, furnishings are bare and in disrepair, and at various places there are barrels of garbage, old rags, and other debris. Beds are not made, four in some rooms, some without blankets, others with clothes or other articles piled upon them.

The father is 38 years old, said by the mother to be a graduate of a technical high school, and is currently working as an unskilled laborer at an automobile agency. He recently was released from jail where he spent one week for contempt of court for failure to pay a bill.

The mother is 40 years old, completed eight grades of school and went a few weeks to trade high school. At the time of her initial interview, she was in her seventh month of pregnancy, expecting her sixth child by Caesarean section. She appears to be a rambling, tangential woman who either has a good sense of humor or extremely inappropriate affect. She appears to have difficulty caring for her children and her stated motive for entering her child in the research project is "to get him off my back for three or four hours a day."

The oldest sibling is 12 years old, mentally retarded and excluded from public school for a period of five years. He is presently in a special class. The ten-year-old daughter is in the second grade. The nine-year-old daughter is presently repeating the first grade and the six-year-old daughter is repeating kindergarten.

Subject 6 was born by Caesarean section, exhibiting a slow developmental history. Although he walked at an average age, at age three and a half when he entered the project class, he was just beginning to talk. He eats poorly and had been hospitalized where a diagnosis of anemia on the basis of malnutrition was made.

〜 The family of Subject 7 lives in one of the two aforementioned housing projects. The apartment is dirty, barren of furniture, extremely crowded (although this is a five-room apartment), and, in general quite dilapidated.

The family is known to 11 social agencies in the Greater Boston Area, including Public Welfare, Family Society, and Legal Aid Society.

The father, age unknown, is rarely home and the mother has little idea what his educational attainment was. Mother describes him as "drunk all the time and there's no point interviewing him."

The mother is 39 years old, toothless, and just returned from the hospital where she gave birth to her eighth child. She completed three years of high school.

The oldest sibling, 18 years of age, is a special class graduate, went one year to vocational school and is now "away." A 17-year-old son is in the first year of trade school. A 13-year-old daughter is in the special class. A nine-year-old son is in the first grade. A six-year-old daughter is in kindergarten.

Subject 7, one of three preschool children in the family, was approximately four years of age on entrance to the project class. He appears to be an appealing child, inhibited and largely non-verbal. He is of average size and does not have any noticeable physical disorders. (Blatt and Garfunkel, 1965)

It should be emphasized that the primary purpose in presenting the case material was not to describe mentally retarded individuals but rather to describe that complex matrix of sociological, cultural, educational, economic, and familial variables which are associated with mental retardation. As we shall see in the following section, describing this matrix of variables is a necessary but far from sufficient basis for individual diagnosis.

The Diagnostic Problem

In its 1957 *Etiological Classification Manual* the American Association on Mental Deficiency states the following about what we have termed the mentally retarded:

This category depends on multiple causative mechanisms of which the most distinctive is an inherited sub-average intellectual status or inadequacy. All the evidence tends to indicate that the genetic mechanism is polygenic, and represents, either in a qualitative or quantitative sense, an accumulation of those items of the polygenic "intelligence" transmitting factor which determines the lower part of the normal distribution curve for intellectual capacity. In other words, we are dealing here with "normal" or physiological genes involved in the inheritance of intelligence. It differs from other hereditary conditions associated with mental retardation in that the latter represents, as a rule, clearly abnormal or pathological genetic factors, arising originally through mutations, and not present in the normal population, genetically speaking. (p. 14)

In its 1959 *Manual* what had previously been referred to as cultural–familial mental retardation was now categorized under the heading "Mental Retardation Due to Uncertain (or Presumed Psychologic) Cause with the Functional Reaction Alone Manifest":

In addition to absence of reasonable indication of cerebral pathology, classification in this category requires that there be evidence of retardation in intellectual functioning in at least one of the parents and in one or more of the siblings where there are such.

Because of the parental inadequacy in these cases there is usually some degree of cultural deprivation present. This deprivation is not generally of such a severe nature as to warrant classification under *psychogenic mental retardation associated with deprivation of stimulation*. In those cases where the cultural deprivation is of severe degree, classification under *cultural-familial mental retardation* takes precedence where there is a familial history of intellectual subnormality.

There is no intent in this category to specify either the independent action of, or the relationship between, genetic and cultural factors in the etiology of cultural-familial mental retardation. The exact role of genetic factors cannot be specified since the nature and mode of transmission of genetic aspects of intelligence is not yet understood. Similarly, there is no clear understanding of the specific manner in which environmental factors operate to modify intellectual functioning.

Cultural-familial mental retardates invariably exhibit a mild degree of retardation in measured intelligence and adaptive behavior. (Heber, 1959, pp. 39–40)

The differences in the 1957 and 1959 statements are marked. Whereas in the 1957 statement a genetic etiology is emphasized, in 1959 the role of genetic factors is not denied but ignorance of how they operate and interact with other variables is stressed.[6] In 1957 the causative role of cultural deprivation

---

[6] The role of genetic mechanisms in the etiology of mental retardation and the mental deficiencies is taken up in Chapters 11 through 19. It is one of the major aims of those chapters to suggest that controversies about the role of genetic mechanisms reflect not

is not mentioned, while in 1959 it is clearly raised as a possible but not well understood complex of variables. In general, the 1959 statement is a much more cautious one. We would agree with Blatt and Garfunkel's assessment of the change in statements.

From the above it appears that the more or less accepted viewpoint had been altered and the condition was now predicated upon the following: (1) an absence of demonstrable central nervous system pathology, or a type of minimal pathology not considered of etiological significance as far as mental retardation is concerned; (2) intellectual functioning within the retarded range in at least one of the parents and one or more siblings where there are such; (3) retardation of a mild degree; (4) usually of a lower socio-economic class; (5) the use of the term, cultural–familial mental retardation, does not presuppose that the condition is inherited through some multiple or other genetic phenomena; nor does it presuppose that it is not. At this point, the question appears to be regarded as an open one, a position which we fully share.

The fact that the question of etiology may be regarded as an open one should not obscure what appears to be near unanimity of opinion that the biological substratum of intelligence ultimately will be found to reflect genetic mechanisms and processes. There is no reason to assume that the human brain is exempt from the influences contained within the genetic material from which the human individual develops. However, the relationships between brain and intelligence are so little understood, and so poorly studied, that many investigators consider it unwarranted to implicate genetic mechanisms at this time. (Blatt and Garfunkel, 1965)

One thing, however, is clear from this discussion: The diagnosis requires an assessment not only of an individual child but of his parents and siblings where there are such. In a later chapter we shall take up in detail the problems of psychological diagnosis. What is important at this point in our discussion is that the reader be acquainted with certain issues and problems arising from attempts to meet the requirements stated or implied in the 1959 statement.

The assessment of intellectual functioning can be made only through tests or procedures that reflect a comprehensive theory of intelligence—a condition not met by the most frequently used tests today, as Guilford has well shown. It cannot be too strongly stated that most of our tests are woefully inadequate for the evaluation of various human aptitudes. To give the reader some idea of the complexity of the problem as well as an indication of the progress which has been made we present below a portion of Guilford's discussion of but one

---

only the facts of research and the development of theories but two other factors rarely made explicit: the value systems of individuals, and the dominant characteristics of the society in which they live. Put in another way, marked changes in a society—such as those which have characterized our own society in recent decades—tend to be reflected in scientific controversy because of the increasing awareness of the social implications of research findings. We shall endeavor to demonstrate that we are far more aware of the social implications of research than we are of the ways in which differing types of social consciousness or concerns or values affect the interpretations and uses of research findings.

(the cognition or discovery factors) of the three groups of factors which seem to fall under the general heading of thinking:[7]

The cognition factors have to do with becoming aware of mental items or constructs of one kind or another. In the tests of these factors, something must be comprehended, recognized, or discovered by the examinee. They represent functions on the receiving side of behavior sequences.

The cognition abilities can be differentiated along the lines of two major principles. For some time we have been aware that thinking factors tend to pair off according to the material or content used in the tests. For each factor of a certain kind found in verbal tests there seemed to be a mate found in tests composed of figures or designs. We found, for example, a factor called *eduction of perceptual relations,* parallel with a factor called *education of conceptual relations;* a factor called *perceptual foresight,* parallel to one called *conceptual foresight;* and a factor of *perceptual classification,* parallel with one of *conceptual classification.* Only recently there has been increasing evidence for a third content category. Factors were found in tests whose contents are letters, or equivalent symbols, where neither perceived form or figure nor verbal meaning is the basis of operation. Factors based upon this type of material have been found, parallel to other factors where the test content is figural or verbal. Thus a third content category seems necessary.

A second major principle by which cognition factors may be differentiated psychologically depends upon the kind of things discovered; whether it is a relation, a class, or a pattern, and so on. Thus, for each combination of content and thing discovered, we have a potential factor. The cognition factors can therefore be arranged in a matrix as shown in Table 4.1. The third and fourth rows seem to be complete at the present time. There are vacancies in the other four rows. With each factor name are usually given two representative tests by name to help give the factor operational meaning. A word or two will be said in addition regarding the less familiar tests.

It should not be surprising to find the factor of *verbal* comprehension, the best known, and the dominant one in verbal-intelligence tests generally, in the first row of the cognition factors and in the conceptual column. The fact that the cognition factors sometimes come in threes leads us to look for parallel factors for the

---

[7] We quote a fair amount from Guilford's article in order to give the reader, particularly those not acquainted with discussions of theories and measurement of intelligence, some basis for understanding why a number of psychologists consider existing tests inadequate as "samplers" of the complexity we label intelligence. To the applied psychologist—be he clinician or teacher—the theoretical issues involved in conceptualizing and measuring intelligence are not matters to which he can be indifferent because how these issues are resolved have very practical significances for both his work and those he serves. In recent years these issues have received recognition by researchers in mental subnormality, best illustrated in the work of Meyers and Dingman (1966). (See Foot note on page 75.)

With all their limitations, it should not be concluded that our most widely used tests of intelligence are without value. Such a conclusion would indeed be unfortunate on several grounds, as McNemar (1964) has made clear. At the very least, McNemar's *acidic critique of those who would throw out the concept of general intelligence as well as existing tests of intelligence will prevent the reader from oversimplifying the nature of the problem and jumping to conclusions. The one thing about which everybody is in agreement is that the nature and measurement of intelligence are extraordinarily difficult problems for which definitive answers are yet to make an appearance.*

TABLE 4.1 Cognition (Discovery) Factors (Guilford, 1956)

Type of Thing Known or Discovered	Type of Content		
	Figural	Structural	Conceptual
Fundamentals	*Figural closure*		*Verbal comprehension*
	Street Gestalt Completion		Vocabulary
	Mutilated words		
Classes	*Perceptual classification*		*Verbal classification*
	Figure classification		Word classification
	Picture classification		Verbal classification
Relations	*Eduction of perceptual relations*	*Eduction of structural relations*	*Eduction of conceptual relations*
	Figure analogies	Seeing trends II	Verbal analogies
	Figure matrix	Correlate completion II	Word matrix
Patterns or systems	*Spatial orientation*	*Eduction of patterns*	*General reasoning*
	Spatial orientation	Circle Reasoning	Arithmetic reasoning
	Flags, figures, cards	Letter triangle	Ship destination
Problems			*Sensitivity to problems*
			Seeing problems
			Seeing deficiencies
Implications	*Perceptual foresight*		*Conceptual foresight*
	Competitive planning		Pertinent questions
	Route planning		Alternate methods
			Penetration
			Social institutions
			Similarities

perceptual and structural columns. One candidate for the perceptual cell in this row would be the well-known factor of *perceptual speed*. This factor has to do with discriminations of small differences in form rather than in awareness of total figures, hence it does not quite fill the requirement of parallel properties with *verbal comprehension*. A better factor for this purpose is the one Thurstone called "speed and strength of closure," called *figural closure* in Table 4.1. For this factor, awareness of perceived objects from limited cues is the key property. The limitation of cues is necessary to make the test sufficiently difficult for testing purposes. . . .

Two factors involving ability to recognize classes are known, one in which the class is formed on the basis of figural properties and the other on the basis of meanings. It was interesting that the Picture Classification test had more relation to the *perceptual-classification* factor than to the *conceptual-classification* factor in spite of the fact that the things to be classified were common objects, the basis for whose classification was intended to be their meaning. This might mean that the perceptual–conceptual distinction is a somewhat superficial matter, pertaining only to how the material is presented. It is possible, however, that in many of the items in this test the general shapes and sizes and other figural properties are an aid in classification. For example, there are cleaning implements, containers, etc., in some items, where similarities of appearance may serve as clues. (pp. 268–270)

. . . For the discovery of problems, there is only one factor—*sensitivity to problems,* which is in the conceptual column. The appearance of this factor parallel to *general reasoning* in the row preceding, emphasizes the well-known observation that it is one thing to be aware that a problem exists and another thing to be aware of the nature of the problem. The titles of the tests are quite descriptive. A sample item from the test Seeing Problems asks the examinee to list as many as five problems in connection with a common object like a candle. The test Seeing Deficiencies presents in each item the general plan for solving a given problem, but the plan raises some new problems. What are those problems?

Whether we shall ever find parallel factors for seeing problems or deficiencies of figural and structural types remains to be seen. Problems of a figural type are faced in aesthetic pursuits such as painting and architecture. Problems of a structural type might be faced in connection with spelling or the development of language. Tests pertaining to the seeing of problems have thus far provided no figural or structural bases for problems. It should be relatively easy to test the hypothesis that such factors exist. If they do exist, their possible implications for everyday performance need further study. . . .

Porteus has maintained that his series of maze tests measure foresight. He can well claim support from the factor-analysis results just mentioned. The type of foresight measured by maze tests, however, is of a concrete variety. This ability may be important for the architect, the engineer, and the industrial-lay-out planner. It may not be found related to the abstract type of planning that we find in the political strategist and the policy maker. So far as our results go, the maze test should by no means be offered as a test of general intelligence. This statement might need modification, however, after the maze test is factor analyzed in a population of lower general intellectual level (where general intelligence is defined operationally as an average of all intellectual abilities). In a population of "high-level personnel," we can say that a maze test measures most strongly the factor of *perceptual foresight* and, incidentally, to some degree the factors of *visualization* and *adaptive flexibility.*

The appearance of a factor called *penetration,* in the last column of Table 4.1, along with *conceptual foresight,* calls for comment. A factor of penetration was hypothesized in the first analysis of creative abilities and was not found. An unidentified factor found there might well have been *penetration.* A factor has been so identified in a more recent analysis that emphasized creative ability tests. It is strongly loaded on a test called Social Institutions, which asks what is wrong with well-known institutions such as tipping. It was designed as a test of *sensitivity to problems,* and it has consistently had a loading on that factor. In the first creativity analysis, two scores were based upon this test; one being the total number of low-quality or obvious defects and the other was the total number of high-quality or "penetrating" defects—defects that can be seen only by the far-sighted person. As a matter of fact, the two scores had much to do with effecting a separation of the seeing-problems tests into two groups, one of which might have been identified as the *penetration* factor. (Guilford, 1956, pp. 272–273)

Despite the work and writings of Guilford and others (Sarason and Gladwin, 1958) it is still unfortunately the case that assessment of intellectual functioning and the diagnosis of mental subnormality are based on conventional tests which tap a very restricted sample of intellectual functions or processes. "In addition to absence of reasonable indication of cerebral pathology, classification in this category requires that there be evidence of retardation in intellectual functioning in at least one of the parents and in one or more of the siblings where there are such"—we are far from having the tools which are adequate to meeting this task. It is not that conventional tests are invalid but rather that they are incomplete. It is not that they are diagnostically useless—this is clearly not the case—but rather that we use them without explicit recognition that they give us only part of the picture of "human intellect." Since, as we indicated in Chapter 3, diagnostic decisions give rise to actions which influence the lives of others, it is both scientifically and clinically necessary that we constantly and critically scrutinize the bases for our actions.[8]

Fulfilling the criteria for the diagnosis of mental retardation (or what others have termed cultural–familial mental retardation) encounters more than the obstacle of inadequate tests or the inadequate use of conventional tests. An equally thorny obstacle is, as Sarason and Gladwin (1958) pointed out, our failure and inability to focus on and assess the level and quality of problem-solving behavior *outside the test situation*.[9] The discerning clinician has long

---

[8] Several years ago a psychologist asked one of the writers why he frequently voiced criticisms of the use of the IQ and psychological tests in the diagnosis of mental subnormality. It was this person's explicit position that "everyone" now knew about the inconstancy of the IQ, the theoretical narrowness of conventional intelligence tests, and the inadvisability of diagnoses based on test scores. Following this description of reality one of the writers read the case folders of every child in a dozen classes for the mentally retarded, the classes being divided among three different school systems. Aside from a handful of cases, in every instance the "official" diagnosis was based on the administration of a conventional intelligence test. In a few of these instances a special school achievement test had also been given. It was abundantly clear that obtaining a low test score on a conventional intelligence test fulfilled criteria for a particular psychological diagnosis and was the major basis for special class placement. It will come as no surprise to the reader familiar with urban education to learn that the other major basis for special class placement was misbehavior in the regular class. It is important to note that the data of Garfield and Affleck (1960) on the use of tests for purposes of institutionalization confirm our own observations on placement in special classes.

[9] In this connection the reader is urged to consult the study by Jastak, MacPhee, and Whiteman (1963) in which they secured a random sampling (ages 10 through 64) of the State of Delaware. Their final sample consisted of 1442 households containing 1907 individuals who were intensively studied. Four indices of retardation were used: the psychometric average, the highest single test score obtained (Psychometric Altitude), an index of schooling completed, and an index of occupational achievement. What is

been aware that intelligence tests may be excellent indications of educational achievement and poor indicators of nontest or nonacademic intellectual activity. Some examples follow:

Case 1

Ginzberg and Bray describe the case of a man who was either a low scorer on the Army General Classification Test or illiterate—or both. In any event, he was one of the many who after induction was sent to one of the Special Training Units. This man subsequently received the Silver Star, one of the infrequently given medals during war. This man's behavior during combat is given in the following citation:

∽ At this time PFC E.S.M. was a member of a squad whose mission was to clear an enemy position of a delaying force of Germans in order to permit the remainder of the platoon to advance. PFC E.S.M., by his intrepid action, quick thinking, and deliberate coolness under fire, killed three and wounded three of the enemy, led to the capture of 20 prisoners, and paved the way for the balance of his platoon to attain their immediate objective. Suddenly he came upon a group of three Germans and quickly fired three shots. The result was two enemy killed and one wounded. Although it was daylight and there was no cover whatsoever, and the Germans in the area had opened fire upon him from all directions, he deliberately exposed himself to those dangers and with determination and boldness moved forward. Three more Germans tried to stem this individual advance, but PFC E.S.M. fired three more well aimed shots and three enemy met the same fate as their comrades. Still under fire of enemy riflemen and machine guns, he surged forward never losing sight of the fact that he had a squad in back of him. PFC E.S.M. encouraged them to move forward as he personally removed each obstacle from their path. This unusual display of outstanding individual initiative and courage so startled the surprised Germans, that the 20 remaining enemy defending this particular terrain threw up their hands and surrendered. PFC E.S.M.'s heroic and courageous action on this occasion reflect great credit on himself and become the highest traditions of the American soldier. (Ginzberg and Bray, 1953, p. 89)

If one views the described instance as a sample of probem-solving behavior, it seems not unreasonable to conclude that this soldier was capable of a completely adequate degree of sustained problem-solving activity, his previous level of performance on intelligence or achievement tests notwithstanding.

---

important here is that two of the indices reflected behavior and performance outside the test situation. Three levels of retardation were employed: 25 percent, 9 percent, and 2 percent, e.g., individuals retarded by "the 25 percent criterion fell in the lowest 25 percent of their age group on Average, *and* Altitude, *and* Index of Schooling Completed, *and* Index of Occupational Achievement, where applicable." It is clear from their data that using indices of behavior and performance significantly reduces the number of individuals designated as retarded in contrast to when test indices only are used. This important study is discussed in Chapter 5.

That this soldier's behavior suggests that personality factors were probably not irrelevant to his problem-solving behavior, as indeed they never are, goes without saying.

Case 2

The second case is also from Ginzberg and Bray:

E.H., a white soldier, born and still living in rural Kentucky when inducted, represents perhaps the clearest case of a man who should be classified as a very good soldier. He was inducted at the age of 19 in the summer of 1943. While being examined for registration a year previously, he fainted and fell and suffered a simple fracture and a lacerated wound, for which he was hospitalized at the local Air Force Station Hospital. Shortly after induction, he was sent to the Special Training Unit at Camp Atterbury, Indiana, where he spent two months. He had attended school for four years. The date is not given, but when E.H. took the Army General Classification Test, probably prior to his assignment to the Special Training Unit, he received the very low score of 42. After completing the special training, he was sent to the Infantry Replacement Training Center at Camp Blanding, Florida. Although many men received ratings of excellent for character and efficiency during basic training, E.H. was graded very good in character and only satisfactory in efficiency. He was trained as a rifleman. Immediately after "D Day" he was en route to the European Theater as a member of the 8th Infantry Division. He received the Combat Infantry Badge, which made him automatically eligible for the Bronze Star Medal. Moreover, he earned three Bronze Service Stars for the Campaigns in Northern France, the Rhineland, and Central Europe. But his most important achievement was the award of the Silver Star for gallantry in action, which carried the following citation:

"Sgt. H., a squad leader, exposed himself to enemy small arms, mortar and artillery fire to work his way within 25 yards of an enemy machine gun position which was holding up their advance. He threw two hand grenades and then overran the positions, killing one of the enemy and wounding two others. Later, during the attack, his squad accounted for more than 30 Germans. Sgt. H.'s great courage, coolness under fire, and devotion to duty were an inspiration to his men." (Ginzberg and Bray, 1953, p. 122)

Although we do not know the kinds of intellectual activities or problem-solving behaviors involved in being a squad leader, more particularly, a successful squad leader under conditions of stress, it again seems not unreasonable to conclude that this man's intellectual activity is not predictable either from his meager educational achievements or very low test score.

Case 3

Another case (Sarason, 1945) describes a girl who had been institution-alized when she was 15 years of age. On a battery of tests several years later her mental age ranged between 10 and 11 years, and on achievement tests her grade placement in reading was 3–9, in spelling 3–0, and in arithmetic 4–9. At the time of psychological testing this girl had been working for some time in the hospital laboratory. After one year of such work she was able to perform the following tasks:

1. Sterilization and chemical cleansing of glassware used in bacteriology and quantitative chemistry.
2. Preparation of bacterial media, physiological and chemical solutions used in bacteriology, hematology, and qualitative chemistry.
3. Cleansing of volumetric, graduated, and hematological pipettes and special chemical filters.
4. Complete urinalysis, except for microscopic including qualitative and quantitative sugars, albumin, acetone tests, and specific gravity.
5. Streaking and plating of bacterial cultures with aseptic technique.
6. Assistance in quantitative blood and tissue chemistry as in total proteins, lipids, sodiums, and potassiums.
7. Staining of hematology and bacterial slides.
8. Taking stool culture and finger blood tests alone.
9. Keeping daily record of work performed.
10. All blood typing (all work is, of course, checked by the head of the laboratory).

We presented the above not because it unequivocally demonstrates a surprising degree of problem-solving behavior (although this is likely) but because it illustrates (1) that much more attention should be given to nontest behavior, and (2) that the problems involved in describing the intellectual processes at work in nontest behavior are probably far more difficult than in the formal test situation where we have more control over the presentation of· the stimulus problem.

Case 4

The next example concerns an institutionalized woman of 30 who obtained an IQ of 49, her problem-solving behavior in any situation never seeming to be out of line with such a score. This case has been described by Schaefer-Simmern in great detail and the reader is urged to consult his full description. Selma was one of the "children" with whom Schaefer-Simmern worked in order to study the nature and development of artistic activity in the efforts of defective individuals. In choosing children for the study Schaefer-Simmern did not select on the basis of ability to draw but rather on the basis that the child's drawing did not reveal a tendency to copy or imitate nature or to represent objects schematically, e.g., stick figures. The initial drawing of the children would be considered most primitive by conventional artistic criteria.

Selma (as did the other participants) came to a workshop one day a week. When she was requested to show her first drawing:

   Her feelings of inferiority, her shyness, and even a certain anxiety gripped her. Turning her face away, she submitted her drawing with trembling hands. She obviously feared attention and criticism. Selma's first picture—according to her own statement, the only one she had ever done—indicates that even a mentally deficient person can create in a modest degree an ordered pictorial whole. It was astonishing that she was able to accomplish even so simple a pictorial result, and the writer praised her for her work. Her reserved attitude disappeared at once and a big smile spread over her face; apparently a word of encouragement was what she needed. Another fact was still more astonishing. While the writer was engaged in supervising the work of the other girls belonging to the same group, Selma took some drawing paper from the desk and started a new picture. She repeated almost the same subject. . . . Except for a little more careful execution of her drawing, there is no further development in the organization of form. But two essentials must be noted: the smaller trees show a different application of the stage of variability of direction of lines, a variation of form invented by herself; and furthermore, the fact that she drew this picture spontaneously indicated the possibility of an unfolding of energies that no one expected. (Schaefer-Simmern, 1948)

Language is an inadequate means for conveying to the reader what becomes evident from a study of Selma's artistic development—a development which can be labelled creative in that the content and structure of each of her drawings reflected her own decisions, her own way of solving the problems which such activity presents. Unfortunately, little interest in or research about the intellectual and problem-solving aspects of artistic activity is reflected in the psychological literature, although there can be no doubt that such activity is in large part of a problem-solving nature. The significance of Selma's case is not only that she was capable of a degree of sustained effort and achievement which was not predictable from her test or school behavior but also because it emphasizes how a particular kind of intellectual activity is not sampled by our tests. In addition, as a reading of Schaefer-Simmern's case description would clearly reveal, the problem of the content and structure of intellectual activity cannot be considered apart from that of motivation and the nature of the stimulus conditions (i.e., the pedagogical procedures and goals employed).[10] We have singled out the case of Selma only because of

---

[10] When Schaefer-Simmern's procedures are contrasted with those ordinarily employed in the occupational therapy units in institutions for defectives—for that matter, in art classes in our ordinary schools as well—one has a rather clear example of how the content, procedures, and goals of our schools restrict the range of problem-solving behavior which one can observe. This conclusion is identical to that which may be drawn from Wertheimer's (1945) observation of conventional procedures of teaching geometry. It is important to emphasize that both Schaefer-Simmern and Wertheimer discuss and describe intellectual processes (i.e., the creative, the productive) which are neither

our focus on mental retardation. Schaefer-Simmern's book contains many instances of individuals of differing test-score status where the development of a high degree of problem-solving behavior is indeed dramatic. It is difficult to avoid the conclusion that conceptions of the nature of intelligence underlying the development and use of our conventional tests give one a rather limited sample of intellectual activity.

We have been discussing the possibility that our intelligence tests measure a restricted range of problem-solving stimuli and intellectual activities, and we have focused on the suggestion that these tests may be excellent indices of educational achievement and poor indicators of nontest intellectual activity. Support for the conclusions drawn has been largely observational, a fact which reflects not only the absence of systematic research but, more important, the tendency to view intelligence from the perspective of our current tests. The often-heard statement that "intelligence is what intelligence tests measure" may have the virtue of being an operational definition but it may also have the vice of being scientifically nearsighted to a degree where one cannot see the forest for the trees.

Thus far we have discussed two problems confronting one in the diagnosis of mental retardation: the tests themselves, and the frequent discrepancies between level of functioning in and outside the testing situation. The third problem is of a much more practical nature, i.e., assessing the intellectual functioning of parents and sibs. In actual practice the appropriate kind of data are frequently not available, and even if one were disposed to obtain these data one would run into understandable resistance on the part of parents who, like so many of us, do not look kindly on having one's "brain" examined. In addition, assessing by formal means the intellectual functioning of parents and sibs is almost always impossible because of the time that would be required to do so. In practice, therefore, the kinds of data necessary for a diagnosis of familial mental retardation are rarely obtained. As a result, it becomes necessary to evaluate data which are frequently ambiguous and capable of being interpreted in varied ways. This problem has been well described by Blatt and Garfunkel in their discussion of the difficulties they encountered in a pilot study involving the selection of preschool mentally retarded children:

෨෮   Subject 1 and his family have resided at their present address for 11 years. The house is in an alley off a main street in Newtonville. All the homes on this street are in extremely poor condition and are adjacent to lumber yards and other business establishments. The house is in need of repairs, both inside and outside. The rooms are small, dark and dingy. Plaster is torn away from the wall, in many places leaving only beams showing. The furniture, which is sparse, is in poor condition—being torn and broken. The home is littered by debris, including

reinforced by pedagogical technique nor in any way reflected or measured in tests of intelligence, a point quite in keeping with Guilford's position presented earlier in this chapter.

empty beer bottles lying under the bed and garbage on the floor. There seems to be little attempt on the part of the mother to keep the house clean and in order. During visits to the home, the interviewers noted that the children were dressed with torn and dirty clothing and were in need of baths. It was also noted that all of the children were well behaved and friendly.

The father of Subject 1 is 36 years of age and went as far as the third grade in school. He then attended vocational school for "a few years." He is presently employed as a laborer, works hard all day and "has not the time to spend with the children that he would like." Mother is 35 years of age and stated that she went as far as the eighth grade in school. There are six children in the family—the two oldest from a previous marriage by the mother. The aforementioned two children are said to attend regular grades. An eight-year-old daughter is in a special class and a seven-year-old daughter is in the first grade, on the waiting list to attend special class. There are two preschool children, Subject 1—chronologically two and a half—is one of them. Mother reports that Subject 1 started to talk at about one year of age, although his speech is still somewhat limited and, in some instances, unintelligible. He started to walk at about eleven months and was toilet-trained prior to the age of two. He gets along very well both within the family circle and with neighborhood children. Although shy at first meeting, he warms up rather quickly and has an active interest in both adults and children.

With the evidence available, can this family be designated as cultural–familial mentally retarded? In one sense, it can. We have here instances of multiple school failures of parents and children. There appeared to be a low level of intellectual functioning of parents. In fact, the project social worker exhibited great skepticism as to whether the mother completed the eighth grade. The social worker felt the father was equally retarded. In addition to the aforementioned description of family life, we had evidence that this family was known to 16 social agencies in the Greater Boston Area, including: Public Welfare, Catholic Welfare, Family Service, Society of the Prevention of Cruelty to Children, and Aid to Dependent Children. There did not appear to be evidences of central nervous system pathology among either siblings or parents to account for the low level of school functioning or community dependency. Notwithstanding these data suggestive of a designation of cultural–familial retardation, we had difficulty in classifying this—our most "familial-like"—family in this category for the following reasons: the reported school successes of the two oldest siblings, the unverifiable school records of the parents, and our incomprehensibility in dealing with the meanings of such terms as "attended vocational school for a few years" and "completed eighth grade."

There were numerous other families in the Newton-Waltham group that presented themselves with more puzzling and ambiguous backgrounds. There were families having a child or two in a special class and other children doing adequate or superior work. There was another family with children in special classes and one parent who had attended special class; however, the other parent attended college for a period of time and one of the children was currently doing well in school. We were not sure what it meant to "attend a Southern Negro college for one year."

We were advised by colleagues well acquainted with the Greater Boston Area that attending (in fact, graduating from) vocational high school does not preclude the possibility of mental retardation. We were further advised that not all children who attend special classes are mentally retarded nor do all who are mentally retarded attend special classes. (Blatt and Garfunkel, 1965)

It is, unfortunately, rare that workers in the field face as squarely as have Blatt and Garfunkel the problems of meeting the criteria for the diagnosis of mental retardation. It is too frequently the case that those who append diagnostic labels to individuals are not acutely aware of the diagnostic criteria they employ (or should employ) and how these criteria determine what one has to do. The significance of this point is not only for the individual who is the object of our clinical concern but for a professional and scientific field of endeavor very much in need of clarity both on the theoretical and technical levels. Blatt and Garfunkel's monograph is a clear example of how serious examination of the diagnostic criteria of what they term familial mental retardation markedly influenced their research actions and strategies. It forced them to the conclusion that the practical difficulties of meeting the diagnostic criteria of mental retardation were such as to reduce their study population to a number which would make generalization of findings a hazardous, if not impossible, task. Rather than water down the criteria and run the risk of contributing to, rather than reducing, confusion and controversy, they changed the strategy of their research.

It will be recalled that in Chapter 3 we stressed the point that there was or should be an intimate relationship between diagnosis and action, a relation- ship which should never be taken lightly. This point must be raised again in the context of this discussion. The question may be put in a concrete way: Confronted with a child who is found to be intellectually and educationally retarded, and who comes from a social and familial context which is disorga- nized and culturally deprived, what difference in action would it make if one determined that one of the parents and/or one of the sibs were likewise retarded? But this question cannot be meaningfully answered without dis- cussing another question: Where, by whom, and for what purposes are such diagnoses made? It has been our experience that the bulk of these diagnoses has been made in the school setting and for the express purpose of providing a basis for administrative action within the setting, e.g., exclusion from school, special class placement. In actual practice there is no clear inten- tion of meeting the necessary diagnostic criteria and *in most of these instances the same action would be taken regardless of any other data available on family members.* We are here not concerned with the appropri- ateness of whatever actions are taken with regard to the child—this is not the issue. What is at issue is that labeling the child as mentally retarded very frequently affects the thinking of the diagnostician and others so that they selectively view the behavior of and knowledge about parents and sibs, and thereby make the explicit or implicit assumption that studies of them would result in fulfilling the criteria for cultural–familial mental retardation. One of Blatt and Garfunkel's major contributions has been to demonstrate that such easy assumptions frequently may not be justified. The important question, however, is whether challenging or testing these easy assumptions would result in differentiations, or an increase in the number of alternative actions to be considered, or point to new directions for program development. If a more intensive and comprehensive conception of diagnosis does not result in new information *and* different actions, it becomes an interesting but wasteful process.[11]

It is clear from our discussion in this chapter that an important concept in the statement of criteria of mental retardation is *cultural deprivation*, a concept which in recent years has gained wide currency but which, as we shall see in the next chapter, requires analysis and assessment.

---

[11] The specific point we are making here seems similar to the more general point made by Garfunkel (1964) and Brabner (1967), i.e., that existing diagnostic categories or definitions of mental retardation confuse rather than clarify issues. As Brabner well puts it in an abstract of his article: "The thesis is advanced that the concept of mental retardation, like the concept of mental illness, is a useless one for understanding and modifying non-adaptive behavior, primarily because the so-called 'condition' of mental retardation is not an identifiable behavioral entity. It is pointed out, further, that the relationship between subaverage general intellectual functioning and non-adaptive behavior is far from clear and that any 'explanation' of such behavior in terms of intellectual criterion is simplistic. Because of their grossness, present educational classification systems for *all* children tend to mask the extensive behavioral heterogeneity existing within categories and which should be of focal concern to the special educator. The need for more refined classification systems relating behavior to education is noted and a learning disability classification approach is proposed as a way of coping with instructional aspects of the heterogeneity alluded to above." The additional statement by Brabner is deserving of repetition: "Medical men, for convenience, will customarily toss various diseases of unknown etiology into one all-inclusive category, e.g., encephalitis, and gradually remove them from the category and reclassify them as they identify the etiological factors; gradually putting more of their professional house in order. When they identify phenylketonuria, for example, they haven't identified a form of mental retardation; they have identified an inborn metabolic error that produces many symptoms only one of which is subaverage general intellectual functioning. But for us as educators and psychologists to lump individuals in the petrifying categories we impose is presumptuous, unrevealing, unhelpful and confusing."

Cultural deprivation

Thus far in our discussion of mental retardation we have stressed several considerations. First, the official statement of diagnostic criteria is, in practice, extremely difficult to evaluate. Second, the most widely used psychological tests leave much to be desired as adequate and comprehensive measures of learning and intellectual functioning. Third, in everyday practice the implicit purpose of the diagnostic process is frequently not to understand the complexities of an individual but rather to obtain data which are required by administrative regulations.

This last point is certainly not peculiar to diagnostic practice in mental retardation. For example, admission to a state mental hospital requires a diagnostic conclusion that an individual is "psychotic." This conclusion is frequently arrived at with little understanding either of what in the past may have contributed to the individual's current status or of a variety of factors and situations in the present which are necessary for understanding his behavior. From the administrative (and action) point of view the aim of a diagnostic statement is not to understand the individual but rather to have a basis for deciding between courses of action, e.g., the individual is or is not eligible for admission. That a diagnostic process aimed at understanding may be wasteful, and a luxury which can only be occasionally indulged, is underlined by the fact that within the hospital the uses to which such understanding may be put are severely limited. If the pressures of numbers of cases result in the use of drugs as the primary and sometimes sole mode of intervention, the pursuit of understanding and individually tailored treatment programs remains a preoccupation of fantasy. We are not being critical of such diagnoses but merely emphasizing that they do not constitute an adequate individual diagnosis or contribution to our scientific knowledge and understanding of the particular conditions. It is this situation which, in our experiences, characterizes psychological diagnosis in mental retardation.

In the present chapter we shall not be concerned further with the purposes of diagnosis but with the following three questions: What have been the consequences to our scientific knowledge when there have been attempts to take the criteria seriously? What does the official statement of criteria leave unsaid and, therefore, unstudied? How might the criteria be recast so that they may be more useful in our quest for knowledge and more helpful in our diagnostic and helping practices?

The Concept of Cultural Deprivation

We have already noted that the 1959 statement of criteria of cultural-familial mental retardation differs from earlier statements in its explicit recognition of the partial etiological role of cultural deprivation. Although the term "cultural deprivation" is now a frequent one in our everyday speech, it is by no means clear what meanings it connotes or denotes. It is, in fact, somewhat surprising to find how, when challenged to define the term, most people have great difficulty explicating the concept in a way satisfying to them or to others. In the minds of many, cultural deprivation is synonymous with slum culture, i.e., it refers to undefined modes of existence in certain areas of our cities. It is not unusual to find even greater specificity, i.e., cultural deprivation refers to Negro slum or ghetto culture.[1] Such usages are both unrevealing and unduly restrictive. It is apparent, for example, that restricting the concept to a particular geographical unit in our cities, or to a particular group within that unit, does not allow one to understand the wide variation in intellectual development and functioning one inevitably finds. Equally important, how-

---

[1] In his recent book Gladwin (1967) makes it very clear that, however understandable it may be, the civil rights movement in this country obscured the pervasiveness of the poverty problem, i.e., that it involves many other groups in various parts of our country. As he says: "The historical fact that the poverty program was in a real sense born out of the civil rights ferment has resulted in such ambiguity and confusion that its consequences could in the long run prove disastrous. One set of problems and issues surround civil rights. Another set are operative with respect to the problems of the poor." The consequences of confusing the two sets of problems are in principle similar to what happens when one uses one term, e.g., mental retardation, to refer to a heterogeneous collection of people and problems.

ever, is that a narrow use of the concept of cultural deprivation diverts attention away from groups and areas where cultural differences may have effects similar to those presumed to be the consequences of cultural deprivation in urban areas. Appalachia, the American Indian, the Puerto Rican, the Mexican–American, the institutional setting—these are some of the places and groups characterized by a distinctiveness which seems to be related to intellectual and educational retardation. To restrict the concept of cultural deprivation to urban areas and groups has the unfortunate consequence of obscuring the cultural diversities existing in our society and, perhaps more important, restricting our understanding of how cultural and intellectual factors may be related to each other. These points have been illustrated and discussed by Sarason and Gladwin (1958).[2] The scope of the problem is revealed in the following excerpt from a report on Project Head Start:

In a remote West Virginia hollow, a Head Start art teacher from another area sat down at the round table, crayon in hand, eager faces around and said, "And now, we're going to learn to draw." "To draw?" asked a chorus of small voices. "To draw" to these children meant to receive a welfare check. Many, when asked what they wanted to do when grown answered, as though there were no alternative, "to draw."

Two rural counties in Arizona increased their census count by two percent. Children no one knew existed were discovered in remote Indian reservations and in the courtyards of adobe houses along the Mexican border. A social service staff determined to find the really needy, counted and transported these totally forgotten children to Head Start centers. School officials involved in the Head Start program wonder aloud how many older children have never gone to school at all—because nobody "fetched them before."

In a small Illinois town, a call was made on a mother living in extreme poverty. The woman's speech was unintelligible, due to a physical defect. The two physically normal children spoke exactly like her.

Through a series of visits by the Head Start center Director, accompanied by a social worker, the mother was persuaded to enroll her children in the center, and exposed herself to other social services, the existence of which she was totally unaware.

After a few weeks in the program, the children were able to communicate and to be understood. Without this experience, they would have been sent—as were their two elder siblings—to a school for the mentally retarded.

· · ·

. . . nationwide enthusiasm for Head Start was such that the program grew like a brushfire from Florida to Alaska, from Arizona to Maine. It reached the territories

---

[2] It is important to note that it was not until 1958 that a cultural anthropologist (Gladwin) made a systematic attempt to view and summarize the existing literature on the relation between cultural and intellectual factors. A major consequence of Gladwin's contribution was that it made clear that mental subnormality had to be understood in relation to a variety of cultural contexts and factors (e.g., ethnicity, bilingualism, social class), and that these relationships required the study and understanding of "mental normality and superiority." In other words, someone interested in cultural factors and their role in intellectual and educational development has to be concerned not only with inadequate but with adequate development as well.

of Guam, American Samoa, Hawaii, the Virgin Islands, and Puerto Rico. It called upon doctors, dentists, psychiatrists, teachers, businessmen, lawyers, civic leaders, welfare workers, and housewives, to contribute their time and talents to put together and administer an undertaking unique in our history. National voluntary and professional service organizations were solicited and made the backbone of the community response. (Richmond, 1966)

If there is anything common to the usages of the concept of cultural deprivation, it is that they refer to individuals or groups whose background or modes of existence are different from those found in what may be termed the prevailing or dominant groupings in our society and that these differences have the effect of reducing the likelihood that the norms of educational and intellectual development characteristic of the dominant groupings will be met. This is, however, a neutral statement in that it is not meant to pass judgment on the nature of the differences or their consequences. But ordinary usage of the concept of cultural deprivation clearly implies at least two types of value judgments which need to be made explicit:

1. Those whose backgrounds or modes of existence are different from those in the dominant groupings in our society are deprived of something "good," i.e., *our* way of thinking and living is better than *theirs*. By *our* standards *they* are deprived. *We* do not feel deprived. *They* should feel deprived.
2. The solution for those who are considered deprived is to change their condition so that in some distant future they will not be distinguishable—behaviorally, intellectually, educationally—from those in the dominant grouping. Those who think in this way tend never to describe aspects of the dominant group which should *not* be assimilated; and they rarely, if ever, focus on aspects of the deprived which should be reinforced rather than extinguished.

There is a world of difference between saying that two groups are different and saying that two groups are not only different but that the difference involves "goodness and badness," "inferiority and superiority" on a variety of dimensions. As we shall see later, the tendency for the concept of cultural deprivation to be associated uncritically with the above types of value judgments may be responsible for the failure of many remedial programs.

It is surprising that in recognizing the partial etiological role of cultural deprivation in cultural–familial mental retardation, the 1959 statement of criteria has little to say about the nature of cultural deprivation. It is safe to say that this silence did not reflect the assumption that the nature of the concept was sufficiently clear and recognizable so as to make definition unnecessary. One may hazard the guess that the silence reflected acute recognition of three things: the fuzziness of the concept; the likelihood that it was comprised of a number of different variables; and the fact that we are far from understanding the relationship among these variables, and between these variables and intellectual and educational development and functioning. The absence of guidelines, however, not only guarantees that different investigators will use the concept differently but that it will be next to impossible to compare the conclusions of these different investigators.

It will be recalled that in Chapter 4 we described the practical, methodological, and theoretical difficulties in assessing the intellectual functioning of the parents and sibs of children thought to be of the cultural–familial type of mental retardation. Our discussion in the present chapter forces us to the additional conclusion that the ambiguities of the concept of cultural deprivation, and particularly our lack of knowledge of the variables involved and their dynamics and effects, do not allow us to use this diagnostic category as if it had etiological significance. That is to say that at the present time we are not justified in drawing inferences about antecedent factors which have caused, or contributed to, the child's intellectual and educational status. Poverty, unstable family organization, restriction of experience, language deficits or differences, exposure to violence, the lack of appropriate models or materials for intellectual and educational stimulation and motivation—in some vague but nevertheless compelling way we assume that the interrelationships among some or all of these and other variables or experiences must have adverse effects on adequacy and level of performance when the child moves into the wider culture. We do not quarrel with this assumption but we must not allow this assumption to obscure the fact that we are far from knowing how these adverse effects are brought about. As we shall see in the next section, one of the most intriguing questions confronting us in this area is how to account for the obvious fact that many of those considered culturally deprived are *not* mentally retarded.

CULTURAL DEPRIVATION AND INDIVIDUAL DIFFERENCES

It has long been recognized that the incidence of juvenile delinquency, like that of mental retardation, was unusually high in certain parts of our urban areas. In fact, concepts like "poverty," "cultural deprivation," and "slum culture" have been used to explain the high incidence both of juvenile delinquency and mental retardation in these geographical areas. In this connection it is important to refer to the now classic study by the Gluecks, *Unraveling Juvenile Delinquency.* The focus of this study can be seen from the following:

As an illustration of the mass-culture approach to crime causation we may cite the studies of human ecology, the relation of neighborhood to human behavior, especially to delinquency. The numerous area-studies have revealed certain crude correlations between the gross physical make-up and composite culture of different zones of a city, on the one hand, and the incidence of delinquency and other aspects of social pathology, on the other. The most frequently quoted finding of these sociologic contributions is that there is a typical patterning of delinquency rates in different urban regions, the general trend of variation being from the highest rate in core-areas around central parts of cities and business districts to a lesser and lesser incidence in zones farther removed from the central section. The area of highest incidence of delinquency is also one of deterioration, in the sense that from a physical standpoint it is likely to be adjacent to industry and commerce and to be a neighborhood of dilapidated houses, dirty alleys, low rents, much poverty and dependency, and inadequate recreational facilities. From a cultural standpoint it is a place where the neighborhood has ceased to be an integrated and integrative agency of sentiments, values, behavior standards, and social control; has drawn in peoples of differing and more or less conflicting mores, morals, and standards of behavior; has to some extent developed a tradition of delinquency; and has largely failed to furnish unifying and edifying substitutes for the crumbling traditional patterns of behavior and authority.

This kind of approach to the problem of delinquency, although of much aid in studying the phenomenon in the mass, is of relatively little help in exploring the mechanisms of causation. These mechanisms are operative, not in the external area or culture, but in the mental life of the individual and in detail as well as en masse. The area-studies establish that a region of economic and cultural disorganization tends to have a criminogenic effect on people residing therein; but the studies fail to emphasize that this influence affects only a selected group comprising a relatively small proportion of all the residents. They do not reveal why the deleterious influences of even the most extreme delinquency area fail to turn the great majority of its boys into persistent delinquents. They do not disclose whether the children who do not succumb to the evil and disruptive neighborhood influence differ from those who become delinquents, and if so, in what respects. Until they take this factor into account, they cannot penetratingly describe even the culture of the delinquency area. For to say that certain bacteria have a fatal effect on some individuals but no such effect on the majority without describing the differently reacting persons or explaining the differential influences, is to describe that infective agent inadequately. (Glueck and Glueck, 1950)

The study by the Gluecks has obvious relevance for any discussion of the relationship between cultural deprivation and mental retardation, if only to remind us that many individuals who are characterized as culturally deprived are not intellectually retarded. This fact, long recognized and documented in research, clinical practice, and everyday experience, leads to the following inference and reveals several unanswered questions:

Among the so-called culturally deprived there is undoubtedly a good deal of variation on a number of individual and familial variables, i.e., however much the label "culturally deprived" tends to make us view the designated population as homogeneous, it is nevertheless true that there is a lot of variation within the population on those variables considered to be important in intellectual development. We are, however, far from understanding the sources of this variation, i.e., why in the same block and even within the same building families can differ dramatically in organization, stability, values, and child-rearing practices. But if our knowledge of the sources of variation *among* families is scant, it is even more scanty in regards to variation *within* families, i.e., why one and not another child in the family is intellectually retarded. (As is not infrequently the case, the study by the Gluecks provided an empirical foundation for "the obvious" which tends not to be taken seriously: First, psychologically speaking, at any one time the "same" family is not the same for the siblings within it; and, second, families change over time.)

It may very well be that one of the problems arising from the use of the concept of cultural deprivation is that it is not a psychological concept but rather a sociological one in the sense that it refers to characteristics of groups, e.g., education, income, housing, criminality, etc. As a sociological concept, cultural deprivation is not only important but has significance for the psychological understanding of the individual, i.e., it raises questions about the different ways in which group characteristics are reflected in or affect individuals and their relationships to each other. The point deserving emphasis is that as a sociological concept cultural deprivation does not in any clear way—as a sociological concept it is not intended to—tell us about or direct us to psychological or individual variation. Let us illustrate the point by presenting a case which sociologically speaking comes from an area or family possessing many of the characteristics of cultural deprivation. It is but one instance among many described by Sarason *et al.* in their description of their work in inner-city schools.

❧ Early in our experience in the schools a consultant came across a child who struck him as the most ragged and bedraggled child in the kindergarten classroom. The child was first seen crying in a corner of his classroom because he had not received milk that morning. Milk is provided for children only if the parents send money for it each week. This child had not had milk money before, finally had brought it, but still did not receive milk because it was Friday, and money brought in on Friday purchased milk for the following week. Subsequently, it was learned that the child was repeating kindergarten, that he was a pleasant child but hardly ever participated verbally in the classroom. Through the course of the year there were several incidents in which the child took things from the kindergarten classroom. These incidents were handled in an understanding but firm fashion by the classroom teacher.

Toward the end of the year the child was given a reading-readiness test on which he scored just about zero. An individual psychological examination revealed an IQ of about 85. At that point the consultant, the graduate student who tested the child, and the teacher had a conference with the boy's mother, in which the tests were interpreted to her. The conference seemed to be a pleasant one and the mother seemed to understand the findings indicating that the boy was probably of normal intelligence. She was told we were concerned about the possibility that his relative lack of communication would interfere with his performance in first grade. The graduate student agreed to make time available to see the boy through the summer, at no cost to the mother, to work with the child to help prepare him for first-grade work in the fall. On the surface the mother seemed to express her pleasure that the boy would have the opportunity, and she agreed to bring him to the Clinic, located within a ten-minute walk of her home.

She never kept the initial appointment and through the early part of the summer at least six letters and telephone calls setting up further appointments were made. At that time we had not yet adopted the policy of picking up and delivering such children to the Clinic, and after a number of broken appointments the mother was sent a letter indicating she could contact the Clinic if she wished to pursue the matter. She never did.

In first grade the child was placed in an experimental tutoring program. As part of the program the consultant and the boy's tutor visited the home to invite the parents to a meeting at the school to describe the program to them. On this visit the consultant and tutor observed enough in the home to leave a strong suspicion the woman was a prostitute and that the child's home was a brothel. Although the mother gave her approval for the child's participation in the program, she did not appear in school, which was across the street from her apartment.

The child worked effectively in the program but at one point was out for a period of a month or more because he had ringworm. After a period of time the school nurse went to investigate and discovered the ringworm was not being treated. It was not until she followed up and threatened to reveal the neglect to the ADC social worker that the mother made any effort to seek treatment for the child. On another occasion the child was found crying softly to himself in the classroom. Investigation revealed a chipped tooth that was paining him. Again treatment followed firm insistence by the school nurse that the mother correct the condition.

At the age of seven this child was involved with juvenile police from the youth bureau. He and another child were suspected of stealing money from the cash register of a local store. The juvenile authorities took him out of the classroom and questioned him in the school building for more than an hour. There is nothing to indicate the child's mother was ever notified of the incident. A casual interview on the street with the mother's "boyfriend" indicated he was aware of the trouble but neither he nor the mother had been informed that the police had questioned her child.

Not long after this incident the consultant received a call from the school indicating that the mother had been arrested on a charge of "lascivious carriage." (According to one attorney, it is a law applied almost exclusively to the Negro lower class, and characterized by him as one of the most unconstitutional laws on the books.) She was given five months in jail because she was already on probation, having previously been found guilty of breach of the peace. Five younger children had been placed with relatives. The two older children remained with a neighbor whose husband was a cousin of the children's mother. At this point the consultant called the ADC social worker and asked about the possibility of a permanent foster-home or institutional placement for these children. The ADC social worker's surprised response to the consultant's question provided a most revealing insight into the welfare program's problems. Her immediate and spontaneous reply to the request that the agency seek permanent foster-home placement for these children was, "Oh, we only do that in case of an emergency!"

As it happened the placement with the neighbor seemed to be beneficial for the child. The woman seemed to be a lively, warm individual with a good understanding of children, and willing to look out for the child in meaningful ways. Her husband, who had a police record of minor offenses, also seemed interested in the boy and told about how they were spending time with him. The family was receiving an allowance from ADC to care for the children, but the boy's response in school showed he was receiving more than minimal care. He was coming to school regularly and was working effectively in school. He seemed to be neatly dressed and clean most of the time. For the first two months of the placement the child apparently did not say anything at all about his mother, and repeatedly told the woman who was caring for him that he preferred to stay with her. None of the children knew what had happened to their mother. They had been told she had to go away "down south" to take care of a sick relative.

On the Monday following Mother's Day, both children were acting disturbed in school. The boy seemed somewhat bedraggled on the next two days. The consultant made several efforts to reach the boy's guardian by telephone. He visited the household and spoke to the man, who was very evasive about the boy. A telephone call in the evening finally reached the woman, who said that the boy had heard his mother was coming back for him and this was the reason he was upset. The consultant called the ADC social worker to ask what she knew of the situation and discovered she not only knew nothing about it but didn't even have a current telephone number for the family taking care of the children. Apparently no plans were being made for the mother's return.

After the consultant's telephone call, the ADC social worker called the probation department and discovered that the only probation officer who dealt with women prisoners was unaware of the date of her release. Further telephone calls revealed that there was no predischarge planning at the women's prison. The ADC social worker could not obtain authorization to visit the mother in prison. The probation worker would see her when she had time after she received notification of the woman's release. The ADC social worker also indicated they had no control over the woman's decisions about how she was to live until she reapplied for aid for children living in her home. When she left prison, without any planning that anyone was aware of, the mother would pick up the children, find her own place to live, and then come to the ADC office to apply for her welfare payments. At that point ADC would have some grounds to talk to her about her plans for her children and herself. The only alternative available to ADC, at least according to the way the social worker presented it to the consultant, was to institute a neglect charge against the mother and to make the children wards of the state. Because there were seven children involved, the worker felt she would have to institute a neglect petition for all the children and she was extremely pessimistic about receiving approval for such an action from her supervisory level, or about the possibility of finding a suitable home for the children. (Sarason, Levine, Goldenberg, Cherlin, and Bennett, 1966)

From the standpoint of everyday language the reader would probably agree that the child comes from a deprived background. But what if the psychologist had determined that the child was indisputably retarded intellectually? Would we not tend to conclude that the intellectual retardation was due to cultural deprivation? The fact is, of course, that the child was not considered intellectually retarded, which raises the question why is he not retarded? Given his background and life situation is it not important—and from a theoretical standpoint crucial—to try to understand why he functions intellectually as well as he does? It is clear that labeling his background as culturally deprived does not help us understand *that particular child*. It is all too easy to read such a case as a catalogue of horrors, which in a way it is. But is it not possible that our reaction is obscuring from recognition experiences and relationships which have been assets in this child's development? Is it not possible that our emotional, value-laden, middle-class response is preventing us from asking questions which would result in a somewhat different case description? We raise these questions not only to indicate that for psychological purposes (understanding the nature and sources of an individual's covert and overt patterns of behavior and performance) the concept of cultural deprivation is not adequate, but also to suggest the type of research which needs to be done if our understanding is to be enlarged to the point where the formulation of diagnostic criteria will serve (as they now do not do) the purposes of relevant and comprehensive description, psychological understanding, and a basis for remedial action and program planning. At the present time employing the concept of cultural deprivation in a statement of criteria for cultural–familial mental retardation may have the unfortunate effect of conveying the impression that we are dealing with a valid psychological concept the significances of which are clear and established. As a concept in sociological theory and research, cultural deprivation has been a fruitful one. As a rallying point for social action the concept has clearly served important purposes. To view cultural deprivation as a psychological concept overlooks the extent of our ignorance of the relationships between group characteristics and the behavior of individuals comprising the group.

Cultural Deprivation and Preschool Intellectual Functioning

It is important at this point to raise a question which will illustrate the complexity of the relationships between cultural deprivation and intellectual development. Before putting the question it is necessary to state that *in the elementary-school years* it is relatively easy to locate children who come from deprived backgrounds *and* who are intellectually and educationally retarded. It probably would not be difficult to locate a public school in certain urban areas in which the majority of children would be markedly retarded according to conventional intelligence tests. The question which has to be raised is: *Why has it been so difficult for researchers to locate preschool deprived children who are clearly intellectually retarded?* We are referring here to the difficulties encountered by Kirk (1952), Fouracre (1962a,b) and Blatt and Garfunkel (1965) in case finding. The following was Kirk's experience:

Locating mentally handicapped children already enrolled in a public school system, although presenting some problems, is relatively easy compared to locating children of preschool age. In a school system we rely primarily on the teachers recommendations or on group intelligence tests for referral of cases for individual examination. However, before children enter school the problem is a very different one. Then we must rely either on door-to-door surveys or on referral by parents, social workers, pediatricians, health departments, or other agencies. There is no procedure for identifying these children unless one were to examine all children below the age of six in a community.

During the planning stage of the experiment, names of preschool-age children were obtained from social workers, public health nurses, physicians, and school personnel who knew of younger siblings of children already attending special classes in the community. All physicians in the community were informed of the forthcoming project and asked to refer children of preschool age who they thought belonged in the category of educable mentally retarded. The initial list appeared large enough to warrant the selection of a sufficient number of children for both the Community Experimental and the Community Contrast Groups.

Examination of these children began in October, 1948. However, during the process of testing it was found that most of the children referred were of average intelligence. The judgment of social workers, public health workers, and other agency personnel was more closely correlated with unsanitary home conditions or domestic difficulties of the parents than with the test results. It was somewhat surprising to find that so few of the children referred as subnormal actually were mentally retarded according to psychometric and other evaluations.

The problem with physicians in the community was just the reverse. Nearly all the children who were referred by doctors were markedly mentally defective. In most cases referrals were made only where the defect was organically obvious, such as in mongolism. Very few of the children referred by physicians had IQ's within the experimental range of 45 to 80. It appeared that educable mentally retarded children of preschool age were not readily detected by members of the medical profession since few of them present evident organic disabilities. For example, three eligible children were eventually located in a speech clinic, where they all had been referred by the same pediatrician at the insistence of parents who felt that something was wrong. The children had not been referred directly for the preschool project, possibly because the pediatrician had not thought of mental retardation as a basic factor in their lack of speech development. The children most often referred by pediatricians had organic disabilities such as the effects of prenatal rubella in the mother, cerebral palsy, or other conditions associated with mental retardation.

The Community Preschool opened in Champaign in January, 1949, with only five children who met the criteria. It was not until the fall of 1949 that 14 children who fitted the standards of admission were found. It was impossible to find a sufficient number of educable mentally retarded children at the preschool level in a single community of approximately 70,000 to supply subjects for both an experimental and a contrast group.

Since the sources from which we had expected to find cases failed to provide a sufficient number, a systematic survey was made in the spring of 1951 by sending several psychologists to the lower socioeconomic areas of two cities where they tracked down cases by tapping on doors. The children in these areas were examined with both the Stanford-Binet and Kuhlmann tests. This type of approach was used for two purposes: (1) to locate children who could be used as contrast cases; and (2) to provide supplementary data to be followed by later retests in an effort to determine the development of children of low socioeconomic levels.

Apparently mental retardation (IQ's 45 to 80) is often not apparent at the preschool age, and social workers, doctors, or others dealing with children do not detect it. This, coupled with the small number of cases located, suggests that many children later placed in special classes or institutions are not recognized as mentally retarded at the ages of three, four, or five.

. . .

. . . many children later placed in special classes or institutions are not mentally retarded in terms of intelligence test scores at the ages of three, four, or five. Some children whose older brothers and sisters were in special classes, tested approximately normal at the preschool ages. This raises the question as to whether children from low cultural levels who are approximately normal at an early age may later become mentally retarded because of their cultural environment or other unknown variables. (Kirk, 1952)

We have already discussed the difficulties Blatt and Garfunkel encountered in locating children whose parents and at least one sib were intellectually retarded. When they changed their research strategy and chose preschool children because they lived in a Boston area that could be characterized as deprived on the basis of sociological indices, they ended up with a population of children who, at the age of 3.2 years, had an average Binet IQ of 91 and an average Vineland Social Maturity SQ (Social Quotient) of 106.

On the basis of our current knowledge we cannot answer the question which these researches raise in any secure kind of way—a point which should not be forgotten by those predisposed to need or give simple answers to very complex problems and issues. There is a difference between advancing an hypothesis which is capable of being studied and giving an answer which confuses hope with fact, or opinion with evidence. What we shall attempt to do here is to indicate the directions research will have to take if we hope to be able to arrive at a more satisfactory answer than can be given now.

One possibility which may in part answer our question is that the conventional tests used to assess preschool intellectual functioning simply do not measure what these tests measure at later ages. That is to say, the abilities or aptitudes or intellectual factors (in the psychological and statistical senses) which are sampled by tests in the preschool years may not be the same as those sampled by these same tests in older children. What must be noted here is that even within the infancy and preschool years there is apparently "unequal" sampling of intellectual factors (Stott and Ball, 1965). As a result of their factor analytic studies of infant and preschool tests Stott and Ball conclude: "The factor content of tests at different age levels for the same scale vary. Hence, one of the reasons for longitudinal changes in mental-test scores

is that the child is being tested for different abilities at the two age levels."
What is true within the preschool years may well be true between the preschool and school years. As was suggested in our discussion of intelligence
tests in Chapter 4, we are here not faced primarily with the problem of the
content of tests but with the necessity of developing a comprehensive theory
of intellectual structure and development which can serve as a guide to the
development of tests which are not, as is now the case, restrictive in terms of
abilities sampled and confuse the meaning of a test item with the name of the
item. Again as a result of their factor analytic studies Stott and Ball state:
"Observational guessing about related item meaning is shown to have little
validity in grouping together items in terms of the fundamental item relations,
as shown by factor analyses. For example, the Gesell items are quite differently classified by factor selectivity than they are by the labels in the
Developmental Schedules."[3] The following general conclusions by Stott and
Ball should emphasize for the reader how far we have yet to go and, consequently, how tentative we must be about interpreting the fact that it is much
easier to find intellectually retarded children in the school years as compared
to the preschool period.

. . . there is a real need for more adequate means of appraising the mentality of
young children. Recent research has provided a better understanding of the nature
of intelligence, its determinants, and the nature of its developmental change, thus
furnishing a sounder basis for new scale construction.
    The users of presently available tests generally feel the need for improved
testing devices and techniques. Our analyses of scale content have demonstrated a
great lack of consistency among and within the scales now in wide use, in terms of
factor content and meaning, thus pointing up the need for more consistent and
adequate test scales.
    Any attempt to develop a new intelligence scale, if it is to be an improvement
over what is now available, must first and foremost be guided by, and be consistent
with, the best conceived and most solidly based theory of the nature of mentality.
Research has made it quite clear that the human being, even at very early ages,
possesses not just one single general ability factor, but a number of abilities. It
should not be assumed without proof, however, that the same repertory of mental
abilities will be found at all levels of development. Guilford's structure of intellect
is presumed to be the structure to be found in young adults—the completed
structure. The structure of the infantile intellect is in its early stages of develop-

---

[3] Factor analysis is a statistical procedure by means of which one can determine the
degree of communality existing among a finite number of scores, the scores representing
individual items, or more global test scores, or any set of measurements. As a procedure,
factor analysis is rooted in statistical theory; and, as one might expect about any realm of
theory, there are differences of opinion about assumptions, applicability, and limitations.
These differences in opinion are not made any easier to resolve when factor analytic
theory and practices are confronted with the ambiguities of theories of intelligence (its
development and its measurement). The reader interested in this problem, particularly in
relation to mental subnormality, is referred to the illuminating papers by Meyers and
Dingman (1966) and Spitz (1966) and the stimulating open discussion of these papers
by a number of research investigators.

ment and, therefore, is presumably relatively simple, although its constituent abilities are indeed "intellectual" in nature. Since the young child's intellect is developing, it is changing constantly by the emergence of new abilities. However, as the repertory of abilities common to children at these different early age levels is determined through continued research, test items for their evaluation can be devised and appropriate scales constructed.

It must also be realized that it is always the child's level of acquired abilities that is available for testing, not the child's capacity or his mental potentiality. We can only observe or test what the child can do—indeed what he was "learned" to do. Children, of course, through use of their present abilities, acquire new abilities that are within the level of their developed capacity. A child who has been deprived of an environment that would stimulate and allow the exercise of his cognitive and perceptual abilities may perform at a relatively low level on a test, not because he has a low capacity, but simply because he has not learned to do the things required in the test performance although they may be well within his capacity to acquire. Perhaps one of the reasons for the lack of "predictive validity" of infant tests is that babies, as a result of wide variations in environmental stimulation, acquire varying degrees of ability within the limits of their developed capacity; tests measure the acquisition of the abilities rather than the capacity. (Stott and Ball, 1965)

The problem we are discussing goes beyond general theories of intellectual structure and development and the technical aspects of test content, development, and analysis. Sarason and Gladwin suggested in 1958 that social-class and ethnic-group membership may be related not only to level of intellectual performance but to the *patterning* of intellectual abilities. This suggestion has received substantial support in the recent work of Lesser, Fifer, and Clark. They studied four ethnic groups (Chinese, Jewish, Negro, and Puerto Rican), each of which was comprised of lower and middle social-class groups. This study is rich in findings and the following seems most relevant for the present discussion:

On each mental-ability scale, social-class position produced more of a difference in the mental abilities of the Negro children than in the other groups. That is, the middle-class Negro children were more different in level of mental abilities from the lower-class Negroes than, for example, the middle-class Chinese were from lower-class Chinese. On each mental-ability scale, the scores of the middle-class children from the various ethnic groups resembled each other to a greater extent than did the scores of the lower-class children from the various ethnic groups. That is, the middle-class Chinese, Jewish, Negro and Puerto Rican children were more alike in their mental-ability scores than were the lower-class Chinese, Jewish, Negro, and Puerto Rican children. . . . Ethnic group affiliation . . . affects strongly the pattern or organization of mental abilities, but once the pattern specific to the ethnic group emerges, social-class variations within the ethnic group do not alter this basic organization. Apparently, different mediators are associated with social-class and ethnic-group conditions. The mediating variables associated with ethnic-group conditions do affect strongly the organization of abilities, while social-class status does not appear to modify further the basic pattern associated with ethnicity. (Lesser, Fifer, and Clark, 1965)

A second explanation for the finding that it is easier to find intellecutally retarded children in the school years (in deprived areas) as compared to the preschool period involves the school culture itself. That is to say, it is possible that the introduction of these children to the school culture, the discrepancy between school and home in standards of behavior and expectations, the extinguishing or reduction in motivation to learn, failures in communication between child and teacher—these and other considerations may interact so as adversely to affect the child's intellectual and educational development. This possibility has been commented upon and discussed by countless people but we are still lacking investigations which could provide a solid basis for fruitful discussion and productive research.[4] Sarason and coworkers, for example, indicate *their* experiences in inner-city schools as follows:

There is not the faintest doubt in our minds that the effectiveness and scope of our work in inner-city schools were greater than in the suburban, middle-class schools. That there are more obvious problems in the inner-city schools goes without saying. Race, family disorganization, mobility, attitudes toward school, teacher morale, inadequate school facilities are only some of the major factors on which inner-city and suburban schools differ to a degree that has to be experienced in order to be appreciated. On the days we were in the suburban schools we could plan what classrooms we were going to visit, when we would have teacher conferences, or when we would be meeting with the principal or other supervisory personnel. In the inner-city schools such planning was sometimes wasteful because

---

[4] In recent years there has been increasing recognition of the significance of the relation between social class and language, on the one hand, and possible conflicts and interferences with learning produced by discrepancies between "school language" and "home language," on the other hand. We have had numerous opportunities to observe kindergarten and first grade classes in many inner-city schools and we have the very strong impression that the language of teachers—its content, style, syntax, and articulation—is different from that of many inner-city children and that this difference is unwittingly handled by child and teacher in a way which strongly suggests the importance of studying the problem in the classroom with a more direct focus on the language of children and teachers. (Bernstein, 1967; Jensen, 1967; John, 1963; John and Deutsch, 1960; and Semler and Iscoe, 1963) At the present time we know more about the language of children than we do about the language of teachers in relation to that of children. What we need to know is how differences in language, if they exist, create and obscure problems. Although not directly on this point—although his study grew out of the writings of Deutsch and Bernstein on language, social class, and time perspective—Gotkin's (1967) study illustrates what can be learned by focusing on teacher and child. He observed how teachers in inner-city schools taught calendar exercises. "In order to determine what children were actually learning from the usual classroom calendar exercises, we interviewed children from two classes in which these procedures were regularly being followed. It soon became obvious that the children were confused. Most of the children were confused about time units—concepts of day, week and month—even when a calendar was present for their reference. Those children who were able to read a few numbers were unable to deal with which number came next or unable to read two-digit numbers. The confusion of the children seems to be rooted in the fact that the teacher's procedures would be comprehensible only to those who could already read numbers and who possessed a left-to-right orientation, as well as a host of other skills. For the child who does not have these underlying skills, the usual calendar lesson is a meaningless ritual and one that may well orient the child to expect teachers to be incomprehensible."

crisis and catastrophe could be expected to involve us in all sorts of unplanned activities. A child hitting a teacher, fights among children, destruction of property, visits by police because of suspected out-of-school transgressions on the part of some children, violent temper tantrums, stormy visits by parents who were sometimes drunk and threatening to teachers were some of the unplanned events and their consequences with which we might be greeted. This is not to say that these events were daily occurrences (although there were periods when this seemed to be the case), but rather that they happened with a frequency sufficient to extinguish in us any surprise reaction. After a time we came to view ourselves as a kind of fireman who puts out psychological fires and then tries to determine their origins. (Sarason, Levine, Goldenberg, Cherlin, and Bennett, 1966)

These same authors present teacher-discussion groups which consisted primarily of teachers who were new to teaching and the bulk of whom were teaching in inner-city schools. The following excerpt from one of these teacher-discussion groups is given here to convey to the reader certain aspects of how teachers view their relationships with parents of inner-city children:[5]

TEACHER 5.   We just had this American Education Week, and the parents were supposed to come in. I had exactly three parents out. So they didn't come to see me. Monday I started going to see them. I sent little notes home, and I called. In some places, mama went across the street, or to the store at the hour I was scheduled to come. So it worked out beautifully. They don't want to see me.

CSM.   How many came, did you say?

TEACHER 5.   Three.

TEACHER 10.   I had four.

TEACHER 5.   I said, if they don't want to see me, I will go and see them. I think there is an awful lot that can be learned from a home visit, an awful lot. For example, I learned that one of my little boys is from a home where there is no father, and he is one of 13 children. The older children go to school here and there, and they come home and help out mommy. I had been screaming and shouting at this little boy for a long time, trying to force him into doing his work. I found yesterday that he just has a problem, and there is nothing that he can do about it himself.

It is a problem for which he is not responsible. This certainly helped me to understand him a bit better. I won't use the same methods that I have been using with him. The communication between the teacher and the home and the parents and school is important.

TEACHER 10.   There was something I always wondered about, a teacher going into the home. I could never quite make up my mind how I felt about that, whether or not it was correct.

TEACHER 5.   Well, correct or not, I did it. I went to the home. First I went home and put on my sneakers, my sweater, and old dress that didn't mind anyone

---

[5] Sarason et al. (1966) present four complete stenotyped transcripts of four different teacher-discussion groups with an aim, among others, to describe aspects of the school culture, particularly the inner-city school culture. In three of these transcripts the reader will find material which clearly suggests the importance of studying systematically the effects of the school culture on inner-city children.

spilling soda or anything on it, because I didn't know what to expect. Like a good salesman, I dealt with them on their level. I saw five Monday, and I saw four yesterday, and two were not home. Like a salesman, I went in.

I took their folders with me, and just talked with them. I certainly have a great deal more insight and understanding of the children. I told my principal beforehand that I was going to do this. So he said, "Well, if you are ambitious and want to—it's not required—but you may do so."

OBSERVER (OBS).   Did the parents respond to this?

TEACHER 5.   Well, some were very nice after they saw I wasn't coming in to see how many webs were in the corner, you know, this sort of thing. Some didn't like it at first. They kept their foot in the door, "Yes, Miss 5," and we just talked and talked. Eventually, with tactics here and there, they let me in. But some did object.

TEACHER 10.   How did they react, those that objected?

TEACHER 5.   Very nervously. "I'm fixin' to go to the store. Forgive me," that sort of thing. I said, "I will come back another day. Could we arrange it now?" They saw that I was determined, and they just let me talk. I found this in about two cases.

Also, I found that one of my little boys—I didn't realize it before—but his mother speaks Italian, and his father speaks fluent German. I didn't know this before. Sometimes he said, "Miss 5, what did you say? What did you say?" He has a language problem, and I didn't know this beforehand. This will help. No one, of course, told me that he was from this type of home, but now I found out.

TEACHER 6.   Do you have records where it says what language is spoken at home, about the family?

TEACHER 5.   It is in the pack. I have never read the packs, because I don't like to read the packs and build up this stereotyped idea about the children.

TEACHER 6.   But that would also give you a lot more insight.

TEACHER 5.   That is true. I haven't read them.

TEACHER 6.   Because many of them even have health problems.

TEACHER 5.   I did read those, yes.

TEACHER 6.   And family problems.

TEACHER 5.   I have just glanced through the yellow packs. But I did read the medical records. I have been a victim wherein the permanent record card has been read, and they build up these peculiar ideas. I have read about this. I don't know, sometimes you are influenced by what others say, and have a tendency to believe it. For this reason alone, I didn't, deliberately.

TEACHER 10.   I also didn't look at the reading records and marks that previous teachers gave, but I did look at the top of the yellow card, where it has a note if the parents are divorced, or if there is a foreign language spoken in a home, or when the child first entered school. I noted that, whether they were left back, things like that, so I would know the age of the child, and things like that.

TEACHER 5.   In the beginning of the year I submitted a little questionnaire. I didn't know, I didn't find out who was divorced. But I was concerned about, "Have you repeated a grade?" And I found out that much. But as far as scrutinizing those completely, I didn't.

csm. What feeling do you have about the home visitation? You indicated you weren't sure whether—you know.

teacher 10. That the parents can resent it. I don't know if it is the teacher's place to go and enter into the personal life. The teacher should make herself available, and should try to see a parent because, of course, you can learn a good deal. But I don't know, I really don't believe it is the teacher's place to take the step and walk into the home, go into the home.

teacher 5. Well, I certainly let them know beforehand.

teacher 3. What do you do in a case when your parents don't take the initiative, and it is imperative that you do see the parent? Because the parent has a very definite influence upon the child. You sort of can be counteracting each other as to what you are trying to achieve in the classroom situation, even in terms of a kid's attitude about school. This can come from a parent. In other words, some parents say, "Oh, well, he is getting by. Okay, that's it." Or they may say, "I was like this when I was a little boy. You have a behavior problem." And the parent is really taking pride in the kid acting up. What do you do then? You have to sort of help the parent see it.

teacher 10. Right. But if you have this type of a situation, you know, your first step would probably be to write to the parent, or try to contact the parent, or phone. If this doesn't work and the parent is going to resist this, then I think that would probably be the same type of parent that would resent your coming to the home to speak to them.

teacher 3. But how are you ever going to break that? How are you going to get the parent on the side of the school, or get them halfway, or partially interested in the school? Because school is something every child has to go through, and it takes up an awful lot of time. The sooner you start altering the attitudes toward this, and get cooperation from the home, and get sort of like a joint effort, you get a better reaction.

teacher 10. True, I agree with you. In the case where you are meeting resistance, I don't know if the teacher going into the home is the answer.

teacher 3. What I am speaking of right now is: all right, if this isn't the answer, what is? What is another method of handling it, or who handles it, or what? Because you just can't leave it there.

teacher 10. I know. That's the problem. Maybe somebody else has a suggestion.

csm. Isn't the question, under what conditions would one want to visit the home? What reasons would one have for wanting to visit the home? For example, why did you decide that you were going to visit the home?

teacher 5. To help me understand the children a bit better. And I like to see my parents. And they deliberately—well, not deliberately—but they didn't come. I had mimeographed a letter that one of the older teachers had, inviting them in September. And still the excuse is, "I work all the time. I have to hire a babysitter." So I made it convenient.

I sent notes home stating that I was coming. In some cases I called. But it was merely to have a better understanding of the child, to help me in some cases understand why the child behaves as he does.

csm. Why do you think so few parents came during American Education Week?

TEACHER 5.   I don't know. I am very sincere in it. I don't know.

TEACHER 3.   I would say, offhand, an average parent probably is not interested in American Education Week. You take the title "American Education Week," and what does it mean to a parent?

You work all day long. "My kid goes to school. All right, he's getting an education. That is what education is, my kid going to school, making sure he has something in his stomach, some clothes on his back, he is clean and neat."

This is all he can give. What are you going to do when you go there? You are going to sit and listen to a couple of recitals, or something like this, and some kind of an assembly program. This is a stereotype that I am sort of coming out with. But this would be my reaction if I were a parent. I would be more interested in just seeing the teacher, finding out how my kid was doing, and having a chance to sit down and talk about my child. This is what I am interested in.

TEACHER 10.   In my school, American Education Week, as such, wasn't played up. It was sent home, you know, "Come to school, and you can visit your child's classroom, see the class in action," although it wasn't the fact that it was American Education Week. And still I only had four parents come. I would say almost half the children in my room, probably both parents work. Or in the case where a number of parents are divorced, and the child is living with the mother, and the mother is working. A few of them have sick children. One boy, his mother has two children and a sick infant at home. There were problems like that also. But I know there were more that could have come that didn't. It is an apathetic feeling that I feel some of these parents have.

TEACHER 7.   I know every teacher in our school had at least half of the enrollment, the parents of the enrollment of their children. I know I had fourteen mothers out of my eighteen children. A lot of them stayed almost the whole day to watch the class. Now, I don't know if this is because I have a lower grade, first grade, where a lot of them are interested, "How do they begin reading? How do they begin arithmetic?" There was a tremendous—I don't know the word—interest, enthusiasm for what was going on. Maybe it is because of the neighborhood.

I don't know whether the people encourage school for these children.

CSM.   What school are you in?

TEACHER 7.   School W.

CSM.   Would that differ from the other ones?

TEACHER 7.   A little. I have a middle-class, a lower-middle Italian neighborhood. It is near the end of town.

CSM.   Is it likely that your school draws, in terms of social class, differently than the others?

TEACHER 7.   I think a little higher.

CSM.   I wonder what that means, though. You know these parents come and your parents don't come.

TEACHER 7.   Maybe as a community, school is more encouraged.

TEACHER 10.   I can look back to my own school days. If my mother or father would have gone to school and heard I wasn't behaving or wasn't doing, you know, what I should, if I was sitting during arithmetic and drawing or anything like that, I would have gone home and I would have gotten it. This wouldn't have stopped. My parents would have sat over me until I did what I was told, and until I got a better report.

Now, I have some children, and this one mother came to school in the beginning of the year, and there was a discipline problem. Her son could do no wrong. Her son William? No, absolutely not. And she has two children, one in each of the fourth-grade classes we have. She defends these children. They just can't do anything wrong. There are a number of other parents like that. There is just not the same feeling. If you speak to them as a teacher, and you want to cooperate with them and help their child do better, it doesn't work when you are up against such a wall.

CSM. You see, I am wondering whether, in fact, your parents are apathetic, whether they are really uninterested. I am wondering if there aren't—

TEACHER 3. Do you think they are embarrassed, in that they are not on the same social status or social level as the teacher, as the school? They don't have the pretty clothes to wear to school that they see the teacher in, and it shows them up. Also, there is the fact that you can't speak English properly.

CSM. It is very interesting that before Miss 5 went, she said she changed her dress and put on her sneakers; which is another way of saying, "I am going to try to put them at ease, and not to accentuate the obvious differences between me and them."

TEACHER 5. An "A" today.

CSM. I am just wondering if it is more than mere apathy. For the most part, you are drawing from a population where the parents are relatively uneducated, where their experiences in school were by no means happy ones, where it was a situation of relative failure and frustration for them. Why should it be easy for them to come to school? Let's ask that question.

Just imagine a situation where, you know, it is your child going to school. Would you feel any embarrassment, any hesitation about going to school to talk to the teacher, and the like? Why should they feel any differently? Why should they look upon the teacher and the school as a place to which they can comfortably come, and a place where they are unreservedly welcome?

TEACHER 3. Because their past has told them that school is not this kind of a place, in part. If their experiences have been unfavorable, they already don't like school, and they already have some notion of what teachers are like, having been a student, and having been picked on, or made to feel uncomfortable; and they realize that they have had the report card, and maybe their report cards weren't that good. So they realize there is a gap. That is one element.

And some teachers do have a way of pointing out the difference, not in a pleasant manner. They are sensitive already, and it only takes a little bit deeper. Maybe with one teacher a generalization can be made from that. Maybe they have made an effort and really didn't feel welcome. This is a possibility. Some teachers just don't really—it's a job, and that's it, and they don't want it. They want the kids to behave, and to learn, but they don't want to be bothered with anything else, if they can help it.

OBS.   What you are saying, in a way, is that if you are going to work with the parents, in some sense, as well as the kids, that you have to not only understand the kids, but understand the parents.

TEACHER 3.   I think in some cases that is true.

CSM.   What do the schools do to make these parents comfortable about school?

TEACHER 7.   Why is that important? I realize the importance, but they also have something to offer. I think there is more of a problem, the fact that the parents have been made uncomfortable for some reason, and therefore are uncomfortable for their children. I don't know how to word it, but you keep coming back to, "Why has it been made uncomfortable?" Whereas our problem is, "How do you get them into the school to overcome this, overcome their uncomfortable feelings, to get them in there and forget their feelings and take an interest in the children, and sublimate what happens to them?

CSM.   I agree. That is the question. You are assuming that they are uninterested. I am just saying, why do we assume that they are uninterested? It may be true. Certainly, for some it would be true. But why do we assume that they are not interested in what is happening to their kids?

TEACHER 3.   Well, like American Education Week, not very many of them showed up. In a sense, they haven't come to the school, or when they were invited they didn't come, or they have never come on their own to find out what is going on. Some of them might come after the report cards, I don't know. This would be the reason why you would say they are not interested, because you haven't seen them.

CSM.   What about P.T.A. attendance? Is it true that very, very few of the parents in your classes show up for P.T.A.?

TEACHER 5.   Well, we had a P.T.A. meeting last week sometime. I had exactly five parents out of a class of 29. I think that was a very poor attendance for 29 children.

TEACHER 7.   I had 17 out of 18.

OBS.   Miss 5 describes going to the home and seeing things that were going on, and she was able to understand some of the kids better, and in some sense felt that she had to change her approach with them, not to do what she had been doing, but sort of take into account some more things she learned about them, and try to deal with the kids and to do what she has to do in a slightly different way.

I wonder if perhaps the same may not be true of the parents. The ideal way would be to kind of just sit and wait for them to come and talk. In cases where this works, this is fine, and there is no reason to think about other ways. But when it doesn't work—just like when you know more about a child, you think of different ways to try to approach him. Perhaps the same could be true of the parents.

CSM.   I suppose I am raising the question whether it isn't a little too easy, whether it isn't an easy out to say, "The parents are uninterested," whether in fact we have done as much as we could to determine whether in fact they are that much uninterested.

When do parents hear from school? The one situation that a parent can count on hearing from the school is when something goes wrong. If things are going okay, the chances are you will not go out of your way to tell a parent that things are fine, and that you are gratified, and they should know this.

You may do it via a report card, but one doesn't go out of one's way to tell a parent something good in the same way that we do when we have something bad to communicate. Let's say you have Jimmy sitting in your class and Jimmy is doing fine. You take your sixth grader, the kid is reading on the sixth-grade level. So I would ask the question, "Have you gone out of your way when you became aware of how well this kid was doing, to make it your business to tell this to the parent?"

Or is it the situation that you thank God that you have got this kind of kid in your class, and you don't have to worry about him? (Laughter)

TEACHER 5.   Well, the moment the parent found out that he had had the Metropolitan Achievement Test, she came to find out, how well was he doing? So I didn't have the opportunity to do it. He was from the home on the right side of the tracks.

But this is very true. I think, as a whole, in our school—I will speak about our school because I don't know what is going on in the others—I think that is a very good generalization. When a child is doing well, we don't mention it. It is only when the bad things occur that we make it known, make sure the parent gets it. And this too could bring on attitudes on the part of the parents.

TEACHER 7.   I don't know if you have it, but isn't it usually the children who are doing well, it is their parents who show up for the P.T.A., who show up for American Education Week?

TEACHER 3.   That's right.

TEACHER 5.   Yes.

TEACHER 7.   The parents of the children who do well come, and the children who are doing poorly, or are having some trouble, they don't come.

TEACHER 6.   I have exactly that.

TEACHER 7.   I sort of remember from when we went to school, the same thing.

CSM.   You meant there aren't any kids that are doing well, who come from families that do not visit, do not attend P.T.A.?

TEACHER 3.   Occasionally, there are some; but the majority of parents that you do see at the P.T.A.—we used to have like classroom helpers and stuff like that— these are the parents where the children are functioning fine. They have a few problems, you know, general problems in learning how to do something new, but they catch on, not too many behavior problems. They are more or less the child that the teacher is glad to have.

CSM.   You know, a thought just occurred to me. Let's go back to some of our earlier sessions. I want to pick up the business of your seeing the transcripts of those earlier sessions, but we will take that up later. Earlier, essentially you were describing problems that you were running into with administration. Let's just group it that way. You were more or less saying, "Look, who the hell is interested? Who is really putting out for us? What about this? What about that?"

You know what it added up to, that you were alone, and there wasn't anybody who was really interested in what was happening to you and what you needed, and the like.

In a sense, I kept asking the question, "Well, why do you take it?" You remember, I was asking that question. The answer was kind of, "When you are up against a stone wall, there are so many concussions you are willing to subject yourself to."

I am wondering if this is not true for a lot of parents that we are discussing now. I mean, given their own lives in relation to these schools, their previous experiences with the schools, whether they don't start off with the assumption—for which in many cases there may be good grounds—"What is the sense in getting involved and getting mixed up in this?"

You know, it is a very uneven battle to begin with. Now, I am sure that if we had sessions like this for the administrators, they would be talking a great deal about what they really want the teachers to do and to feel and to think, and what have you. If we could read what you say and what they say, it is as if you are dealing with two different worlds, and yet there may be appropriate motivation on both sides.

Somehow or other, they cannot talk to each other. This was basically what was coming out in these early meetings. In terms of what you were experiencing, and whatever it was that they were experiencing, whatever frames of reference they had, somehow or other there wasn't a meeting of minds.

What I am asking is, may this not be the case as between yourselves and the parents that you are dealing with? I could ask the question, "Why should it not be comfortable for you to say outside of here what you said inside of here at this meeting earlier? Why can't you go to the superintendent, or why can't you go to whoever is the supervisor in your district, or why can't you go to your principal and say the things that you said here?"

What you were describing was a situation in which people could not talk to each other. We are dealing with a very similar situation here. Maybe we are dealing with this kind of a situation.

Now, I don't want to appear to have prejudged the issue, that is to say, that in fact parents are very interested, that they are not apathetic. I am, you know, merely raising the question, "Let's look at ourselves."

I can give you a personal example which I may have mentioned before, and which the obs, being in our department, can testify to. Several years ago the graduate students in our department made it clear finally to us that the only time that a student in this department ever heard from us was when we had something bad to say to him. And it was absolutely true. If they were doing all right, you know, they didn't need any special reward, and encouragement and motivation. But if he got a call from the director of graduate studies, he knew damn well that this was not going to be tea and cake.

So it is not that I am taking sides here. I just feel that it may be a more complicated issue. Or I am asking, is it possible that it can be a more complicated issue.

TEACHER 10.   This is making me do a little bit of thinking. I can look back and see where I have gotten notes from parents regarding why a child was absent, or some such thing, and the notes have been grammatically incorrect. You know, from the note, it was easy for me to tell that the parent had gone just so far in education. I can see why then, in this case—when we were younger, as students we looked up to the teacher, and the teacher was somebody up there whom we were afraid of. These parents probably in many cases still, you know, to a large extent put the teacher up on a pedestal, and feel very funny about coming and showing themselves to a school teacher, and not being able to hold a conversation, or something like that. They feel very inhibited, to a large extent.

csm. I often wonder about the schools in which you people are. Not only is it tough for a lot of them to write, but I sometimes wonder whether they can read some of the things that are coming home. It would be an interesting little study just to find out how many of them can really read a report card. I don't know about this city's report card. I have seen some report cards elsewhere that require a fair level of vocabulary in order to comprehend it. Some of these report cards look like railroad timetables.

teacher 5. As a rule, when there is a note to go home, I always explain it to them, because I have wondered this myself. I always tell them what it is about. I took a blank report card yesterday, before I issued the others, and explained it to them.

We know of no one who has maintained that schools in so-called deprived areas *in general* have a facilitating or positive effect on the intellectual and educational development of children. The question, of course, is whether the presumed effects are of such a nature and strength as to account, in part at least, for the finding that it is easier to discover intellectually retarded children in the school years than in the preschool period. At the present time we can only discuss the problem on the level of opinion or personal experience. One can only hope that a body of relevant research will develop that will provide a more solid basis for discussion and action.

Postschool Performance

In trying to understand why in the inner-city areas it is far easier to locate intellectually retarded children in the school years than in the preschool years, we are forced to consider a body of literature on the postschool performance of those who in school were intellectually retarded.[6] The

---

[6] There have been numerous follow-up studies of the mildly retarded: Abel (1940), Baller (1936), Bobroff (1956a,b), Charles (1953), Dinger (1961), Dunlop (1935), Fairbank (1933), Hegge (1944), Kellogg (1941), Kennedy (1948), Kingsley and Hyde (1945), McIntosh (1949), McKeon (1946), and Muench (1944). There are, in addition, the surveys of Onondaga County by the N.Y. State Department of Mental Hygiene (1955) and Baltimore by Lemkau, Tietze, and Cooper (1942). A close scrutiny of these studies leave little doubt that the bulk of the individuals who were followed were from so-called deprived areas. Although our primary focus here is not on the significance of these studies for the predictive validity of intelligence tests, it is important to note that Blatt and Garfunkel (1965) concluded that these studies "revealed that school tests of problem-solving behavior do not adequately predict non-school problem-solving behavior,

question now becomes: Does the educational, social, and vocational level of these children set them apart in any decisive way from others in their areas who were not considered intellectually retarded? After reviewing the literature Sarason and Gladwin conclude:

In other words, many children who through their final year of schooling are still labelled "retarded" immediately thereafter merge into the "normal" population with at least sufficient completeness no longer to be reported statistically. The compulsory school experience may therefore be viewed for many people as in effect the most difficult intellectual hurdle which will confront them throughout their entire lives, although later in other settings they may perform tasks of substantial complexity. (Sarason and Gladwin, 1958)

The recent study by Jastak, MacPhee, and Whiteman (1963) is relevant at this point. From a much larger population sample they chose 123 retarded individuals each of whom was considered retarded because for their particular age group they fell in the lowest 25 percent in average score of 15 psychometric tests, *and* in the altitude of the highest single score, *and* in an index of schooling completed, *and* in an index of occupational achievement. The retarded group was matched in age, sex, and race with 123 individuals from a nonretarded group. Although the cases were not selected in a way to permit the conclusion that this was a "cultural deprived group," it is likely that a fair proportion of the cases came from such backgrounds.[7] The two groups were compared on several indices: formal social participation, informal social activities, "aloneness," schooling satisfaction, and occupational satisfaction. It is not possible here to go into the wealth of data presented and analyzed by these workers. We present here what they consider a most important conclusion:

The most noteworthy result of the study is the striking similarity of the retarded and the nonretarded in many areas of personal-social behavior. The lower intelligence of the retarded group does not prevent a sizable number of them from working gainfully, effectively, with a good deal of stability, and with a great deal of subjective satisfaction. The retarded do not impose a disproportionate load upon community resources either in the form of legal infractions or excessive demands for social service. It seems that in many instances, mental subnormality need not connote an inability to fill an adequate community role. The general conclusion is quite similar to that of Kennedy who, after a follow-up study of noninstitution-

---

i.e., the group known as mentally retarded had demonstrated a greater degree of out-of-school success, both socially and vocationally, as compared with performance in school and predictions based upon psychological tests. This type of finding is but another basis for questioning the soundness of attempts to understand the etiology of cultural–familial mental retardation by depending solely on intelligence test data." This conclusion is identical to that we have drawn from the Ginzberg and Bray data (see page 56).

[7] The authors state (pp. 141–142) that "Those retarded at the 25 per cent and 9 per cent levels seem to differ from those retarded at the 2 per cent level in terms of social background factors. The former include more Negroes, represent the lowest income levels, and those in poor housing units."

alized morons, reported that most of them are ". . . in their humble way, worthy citizens who bear their share of the social burden and do nothing to threaten the welfare of society." (Jastak, MacPhee, and Whiteman, 1963)

It has to be emphasized that the above conclusion concerns "personal-social behavior." In relation to occupational level the nonretarded sample, as a group, performed at higher level, leading the authors to conclude that "It is probable that intellectual level sets limits to the adjustment potential of the retarded in terms of certain occupational, marital, educational, and social functions." This is a reasonable conclusion and we do not dispute it. However, one must point out that achieved level of occupation is a function of many things, among them being opportunity for exposure to certain occupations, favorable conditions of learning, and motivation. It could be argued that the occupational level of some of the retarded individuals in this study reflect not only intellectual limitations but some of the other factors we have just mentioned.[8] In this connection it is relevant to note that the study, although published in 1963, was initiated in 1950, long before the recent federal programs geared to upgrading occupational levels of inner-city populations. Future research findings from these programs will be of crucial significance in determining to what extent occupational level is a function of psychometric criteria of mental retardation. The experiences of the Yale Psycho-Educational Clinic with one of these programs strongly suggest that the opportunity to be exposed to and to learn certain occupational skills is extremely important in the vocational life of culturally deprived individuals. (Sarason et al., 1966)

As so many studies suggest, the postschool adjustment of retarded individuals from deprived areas requires explanation as does the finding that before the school years it is difficult to find retarded individuals. These kinds of findings force one to raise again the possibility that the school years in some ways have an interfering effect on the development of individuals in deprived areas. In attempting to arrive at some conceptual understanding of their findings, Jasak et al. directed their attention to the school setting as the following indicates.

Low intelligence and poor reading are instrumental in producing educational retardation, as manifested in the low index of schooling completed among the retarded. Educational retardation produces feelings of anxiety and frustration in the school situation. This latter postulated condition is assumed to have a number of different effects. First, it produces educational dissatisfaction, as manifested in the retarded group's low index of schooling satisfaction. This, in turn, probably

---

[8] The same statement would also be relevant for the nonretarded group, i.e., their level of occupational performance might have been, under other conditions, discernibly higher than that found by Jastak, MacPhee, and Whiteman. The question we are raising is *not* whether the retarded group potentially could do as well as the nonretarded group, but rather whether the retarded group could do better than they did. It is conceivable, and likely, that under some kind of ideal conditions, both groups could increase their occupational level discernibly and we would still find that the level of the nonretarded group was significantly above that of the retarded group.

induces educational retardation, which again contributes to negative feelings, thus producing a vicious cycle. At any rate, the feelings of anxiety in the structured group situation generalize to formal group situations, a postulate which makes comprehensible the findings that the retarded take a submissive role in planning group activities, score low in formal participation and, to the extent that self-selection is operative, do not receive formal instruction relevant to their current jobs. Negative feelings in the school situation may also be instrumental in producing a differentially greater ease of interaction with the family than with outside groups. This would account for several empirical findings: that the retarded marry younger than the nonretarded, that marriages and separations are no greater in number for the married retarded than for the married nonretarded, and that the retarded are more decisive with family members than with friends.

Related to the anxiety engendered by the school situation is a lowering of the occupational aspiration level after leaving school. It will be recalled that quite a few of the retarded reported having had high aspirations at the time they left school. This realistic lowering of aspiration level would then act as a contributing factor to the eventual occupational satisfaction of the retarded, to their job stability, and, of course, to their lower occupational status. Naturally, low intelligence and low educational attainment are also sizable contributors to low occupational status.

The postulated concepts and the network of relationships are admittedly ad hoc. However, these relationships have the merit of lending themselves to prediction and empirical test. This can be done either by converting the postulated concepts into empirical concepts through operational definition, and then testing in a new study whether the relationships specified . . . obtain, or by returning to the already gathered data and testing empirical concepts for the presence of new correlations. These latter could be predicted from the causal network through the operation of any postulated concept connecting two empirical concepts as a common cause or as a mediating factor, e.g., predicting that in the retarded group those with little formal participation would have had little special training for their current jobs because of the common factor "generalization of anxiety to formal group situations." Finally, it should be borne in mind that this postulation of causal factors does not imply that other causal factors are not at least as important. Thus, the lower economic status of the retarded is probably influential in determining a number of the observed reactions, independently or perhaps as a co-determinant of any specific anxieties. (Jastak, MacPhee, and Whiteman, 1963)

Without prejudging the etiological role of the school culture in affecting adversely the intellectual and educational development of many individuals from deprived areas, we think that systematic research on the problem is long overdue. Without such research we remain in the realm of opinion, uncertain theorizing, and heated but unilluminating controversy.

FAMILY DISORGANIZATION

If it is true that in the preschool years in deprived areas it is difficult to find intellectually retarded children—especially when such case finding is relatively easy during the school years—one might advance the hypothesis that it is not merely the process of schooling which has adverse effects but the *interaction* between family disorganization and the process of schooling. This hypothesis probably should be broken down into its component hypotheses.

1. What appears to an outsider to be an unhealthy family situation may not be as damaging to a preschool child as our theorizing and values suggest. It may be all too easy for many of us to observe how some of "these" families live and to conclude that it is inherently "bad" for the very young child. Our knowledge is not that great to permit one to dismiss the possibility that the young child in these families is receiving types of support and stimulation which at these ages enable intellectual development to take place. It may seem like an outlandish statement that the curiosity of these children about the world they live in may receive greater support than we think, perhaps greater support than children in other places of life. No one would deny that curiosity is an important, complex intellectual process in the intellectual development of children. The point we are trying to make is that *for the very young child* the "disorganized" family may not be as disorganizing as we imagine.

2. A second component hypothesis is that with the entrance in school, family disorganization begins to have adverse effects because what previously may have had supportive effects for the child no longer serve this function *as the child leaves the family*, i.e., as he spends most of the day in a setting which presents demands and stimulation which are novel and conflict producing. In short, family disorganization has adverse effects on children not because of disorganization per se but because at a certain point it begins to interact with the demands of a new nonfamily setting: the school.

These hypotheses receive some support in Blatt and Garfunkel's study of the effects of a preschool program on the school performance of children from a deprived area in Boston. In the next chapter we shall discuss their study in some detail. At this point we need only note that the measure most highly correlated with preschool intellectual development and academic performance in the first year of school was one concerned with degree of family stability and organization. In other words, children from the psychologically poorest homes tended to have intelligence test scores below those children from less poor homes, although it should be emphasized that the scores of the former group did not suggest mental retardation. The fact that children from the poorest homes also did less well in the first grade raises the possibility that over time the interaction of school failure and family disorganization or instability will have pervasive effects on their intellectual functioning. It is important to recognize (1) that children in the poorest families are by no means mentally retarded in the preschool period, and (2) that the term "culturally deprived" does not refer to a homogeneous group of people. As Blatt and Garfunkel (1965, p. 168) conclude:

There is a great heterogeneity both within and between families who meet criteria as culturally deprived. The degree to which we can positively intrude into the lives of these families depends upon numerous complex and interrelated factors which facilitate beneficial interaction with some families and cause difficulty with others. A blanket endorsement or condemnation of early and continued involvement with families who are culturally deprived demonstrates both an unwarranted prejudice and a grossly naive and doctrinaire approach to an extremely variable and relatively unstudied group of human beings.

As the studies by Lewis (1966) so well document, the "worst" families are fantastically complicated and the complications, from the standpoint of the preschool child, may not be all bad as long as the child is primarily in the family.

SUMMARY

In this chapter we have attempted to focus on certain factors, variables, or questions which need to be studied if we are to understand the finding that it is much easier to locate mentally retarded children during the school years than in the preschool period. In adapting such a focus it was not our intent to prove in any way the importance of these questions but rather to emphasize their potential relevance for future research which will alone determine whether the appropriate questions are being asked and appropiately studied. What is at stake are not only some important theoretical problems in child development but the rationale to be adopted in social action programs.

. . . some have the idea that the intellectual deficiencies of large numbers of culturally deprived children are due to a multiple genetic inheritance that causes these children to be born with inferior central nervous systems, resulting in school failure and mental retardation. On the other hand, there are those who contend that numerous children have normal intellectual development during the early years but that subsequent subnormality stems from requirements imposed by the schools and the alienation between the home and the school culture. Both of these assertions mitigate against an early involvement with families. If the behavior is due to an inherited subnormality it would appear to be of little value to intervene with the family for one would be intervening with comparably subnormal parents and, secondly, it hardly appears likely that one could prevent or reverse inherited subnormality. On the other hand, if school failures related to cultural deprivation are due to those conditions that obtain after the child enters school, an appealing strategy would provide for circumvention of the home, concentration on special programs to more adequately prepare children to ingest the school culture and to help schools become more tolerant of these children. We have provided some evidence to discourage the multiple genetic causation theory of school failure and to support the contention that impoverished early environments cause severe learning deficiencies. (Blatt and Garfunkel, 1965)

The primary purpose of this chapter was to discuss and illustrate the point that the concept of cultural deprivation is not a simple or clear one, or one which in its psychological or sociological meanings relieves its user of the necessity for carefully determining how, for what purposes, and on what empirical basis he is using the concept. Whether used in research, diagnosis, or social action the concept of cultural deprivation cannot be used without its meanings being stated as carefully as possible.

Educational intervention

Thus far in this book we have been primarily concerned, in one way or another, with problems of definition, diagnosis, and attitudes toward the mentally retarded. In discussing these problems it was not our purpose to labor the obvious facts that different people use the same terms differently, or that, in general, terms are used which are ambiguous or have a surface simplicity which does not hold up under close scrutiny, or that the tendency to give simple answers to complicated problems has mischievous effects. Our main purpose has been to stress a different kind of obvious fact, i.e., that the necessary and never-ending process of attaining clarity in conceptualization or theorizing must constantly be confronted with the possibility that it is not doing justice to the complexity of a problem as it occurs in reality.[1]

In this and the next three chapters our focus will be on the kinds and consequences of interventions which have had the aim of changing and

---

[1] Few, if any, would disagree with this point. It is an easy one to make in that it is for virtue and against sin. When in later chapters in this book we take up in detail the history of controversies centering around genetics and the heredity–environment issue, the reader may become more sensitive in his thinking, as well as in that of others, to the tendency to misperceive (or "underperceive") the complexity of a problem as it occurs in reality.

upgrading the functioning either of mentally retarded individuals of the cultural–familial or culturally disadvantaged type, or of nonretarded children from deprived areas where the prevalence of retardation is high. In a real sense we shall be concerned with interventions or actions which by their consequences allow evaluation of underlying conceptualizations and theories. It is one thing to attempt to evaluate prevailing conceptions and definitions by logical analysis and single case descriptions, and it is quite another thing to base such an evaluation on formal research interventions. At the very least, as we shall endeavor to indicate, intervening in the "real world"—in contrast to discussion of opinion or theoretically based deductions—often has the salutary effect of confronting one with the complexities of the problem as it occurs in the natural setting.[2] One of the main functions of research is to teach one that "the more you know the more you need to know."

Preschool Interventions

Kirk's (1958) pioneer study was designed to answer the following questions:

1. Does preschool training of mentally retarded children displace the rate of development of such children as compared to children who do not obtain the benefits of early training?
2. Does the rate of growth at the preschool age continue at an accelerated rate, or does it return to the original rate of development during the primary school years?
3. Are the results similar for children living in different environments, such as their own homes, foster homes, or institutions for the mentally deficient?
4. Are there differences in the changes in rate of growth as a result of training between children whose retardation is ascribed to cultural or environmental ones?

---

[2] It is not the sense of our statement to suggest that research involving real-world interventions is necessarily more difficult or necessarily more important. For example, the long-term research project by Zeaman and House (1963, 1966) has been concerned with the attempt to develop an "attention theory" to account for discrimination learning in a two-choice situation. They study retardates in laboratory-like situations which are not what we ordinarily mean by real-world situations. When one reads their publications in serial fashion one cannot but be impressed by the difficulties in theory, design, and interpretation encountered despite the apparent simplicity of the situations and the deliberate limiting of the scope of the problem, i.e., a two-choice discrimination problem. It is easy to overlook in their studies that the problem they study can have important practical and educational significances not only for mentally subnormal individuals but for others as well. Ultimately, when attempts are made to apply the theory and findings of this approach to real-world situations (e.g., the classroom) one can anticipate that a whole new set of difficult problems and issues will be encountered which will require changes in theory, further laboratory-like research, and further efforts at application. That is to say, they leave one set of difficulties to take on another set of difficulties. The major point we have tried to make is that when laboratory-like research findings and theory are applied to real-world situations theory, knowledge, and the mental health of the researcher are upset as new insights are gained.

Four groups of preschool children were studied:

1. Community Experimental Group. This experimental group consisted of 28 preschool mentally handicapped children from the community who were given an enriched nursery school environment from nine to three o'clock each day. At about six years of age these children were placed in a regular first grade or a special class. There were about 15 children at any one time in the nursery school.
2. Community Contrast Group. This group of children consisted of 26 young mentally handicapped children found in the same community or in neighboring communities. They were examined at the same intervals as those in the experimental group, but they did not attend a preschool. The term *contrast group* is used here instead of control group, since these children and the children in the Community Experimental Group were not randomized in the usual sense. It was impossible to find sufficient children at any one time to randomize them. The difficulties in selecting the children will be described later.
3. Institution Experimental Group. This experimental group consisted of 15 children who had been institutionalized as feebleminded in one of the state institutions. They were taken out of the wards and enrolled in a preschool in the institution from nine to three o'clock each day. The purpose of this setup was to replicate to some extent the organization of the preschool in the community and to determine the effects of this type of additional or specialized training on the development of institutionalized children.
4. Institution Contrast Group. Since sufficient children of the type needed for the experiment were not found in any one institution for both an experimental and control group, a contrast group was selected from another institution. Twelve such children, similar to the experimental children in essential characteristics, were identified in another institution, examined at the same intervals, but not given the opportunity for preschool education. In addition, a group of 10 institutionalized mental defectives, who had been tested and retested at the preschool level, was found in the files of the Lincoln State School. This group of cases was used as a subcontrast group from the same institution.

One of the major findings in Kirk's study was that those who benefitted the most in intellectual and social performance were the culturally deprived mentally retarded children; those who benefitted the least were those retarded children with organic impairments; and in between these two groups was a group of children considered to be culturally deprived *and* to possess organic impairments. These findings, it must be emphasized, are based on comparisons *among* the experimental groups, i.e., those groups receiving preschool educational experience. A finding that was not anticipated was that the Community Contrast Group showed no acceleration during the preschool period but did show acceleration in intellectual and social performance after school experience beginning at age 6 so that at the end of the study they were not significantly different from the experimental groups.

It had not been anticipated that the Community Contrast Group, showing no acceleration during the preschool period, would show acceleration in IQ's and SQ's after school experience beginning at the age of six. If these results are corroborated by later studies, it could mean that preschools for mentally handicapped children are not necessary, since the children will accelerate their rate of development after entering school at the usual age of six. It can be interpreted to mean that school experience is effective in accelerating the mental and social development of mentally retarded children even when school experience is initiated at the age of six.

At this point it would be well to clarify an apparent contradiction to this generalization. . . . It was shown that children from inadequate homes who did not attend preschool tended either to hold their rate of development or to drop in rate during and after the preschool years, whereas their siblings who attended preschool tended to increase in rate of development. Since the 14 siblings from inadequate homes did not accelerate their rate of growth before or during their school experience as did the Community Contrast Group as a whole, it is possible that children from adequate homes tend to accelerate their rate of growth during later school experience, whereas children from inadequate homes do not. In an effort to check this possibility, a further study of the Community Contrast Group was made. Eight of the 26 children in this group came from inadequate homes. An analysis of their changes in IQ's on the Binet and Kuhlmann tests indicated that their average change in IQ on both tests was less than the average change in IQ of the other 18 children whose homes were rated as adequate and semi-adequate, but that the difference was not statistically significant. (Kirk, 1958, p. 211)

From this and other statements it seems clear that Kirk was of the opinion that the effects of any kind of intervention—be those effects positive, negative, or neutral—must be understood, in part at least, by the adequacy of the home environment and that adequacy was not a matter of cleanliness and physical living conditions. Put in another way, among the so called culturally deprived population there are variations in family adequacy and these variations may be crucial for understanding the child's adjustment to and performance in school. Kirk seemed to be suggesting an hypothesis which, as we indicated in the previous chapter, Blatt and Garfunkel also put forward in their study done a number of years later. As we shall discuss later in this chapter, the nature and role of such a variable as "family adequacy" ("family organization") is not likely to be greatly clarified—or to have more than the status of a *post hoc* hypothesis—until it is used as a basis for selecting subjects *before* the research or intervention is initiated. By using this as one of the selection variables one is not only forced to make explicit what one means by the variable but, as important, it also facilitates obtaining sufficient cases enabling one to make statistically meaningful comparisons.

In the previous chapter we have already discussed in detail the possible significances of Kirk's difficulties in locating preschool mentally retarded children of the cultural–familial type, difficulties which may turn out to be of great theoretical and practical import. A second major contribution of his study is that it raises the question about the nature and role of "adequacy of home or family" in relation to school adjustment and performance, i.e., the problem of variation among those bearing a particular diagnostic label. A third major contribution made by Kirk consists in his clinical and statistical data indicating that planned interventions may have facilitative effects on the functioning of some retarded individuals.

A Critique of Method. Because Kirk's study paved the way for other studies, and because it concerns a problem of undoubted practical and theoretical import, it deserves close critical scrutiny.

Firstly, it is essential that the measures employed in research do not reflect the personal biases of the researcher, particularly when the hypotheses to be studied are of a kind which generate opposing positions and conceptions of human behavior. This is but another way of saying that the interpretation and scoring of the research data be carried out in such a way that they cannot be influenced by the researcher's personal value system or expectations.[3] Kirk's study is open to such criticism—this is not to say that the criticism is in fact true but that it may be true. For example, if an experimental child is being tested by someone who knows he is an experimental child and the tester hopes or expects the child to show improvement in score, it is possible that unwittingly the tester responds in ways, and scores in ways, that work in the direction of obtaining higher scores. Another example, when the criteria for determining "adequacy of home" involve an *interpretation* of case history material, there is not only room for personal bias to creep in but also the possibility that various people looking at the same data would not score the home in the same way. The intention to observe, score, and interpret in an objective manner is no guarantee that it is done in such a manner. We emphasize these points because we feel that the reader (like ourselves) needs to be made aware—particularly when the outcome of research fits in with his values and expectations—that he has an obligation to scrutinize the research to determine the degree to which the data and conclusions are truly independent of the researcher's personal hopes and expectations.

Secondly, in the case of the Community Experimental Group it is not possible—and indeed it was not Kirk's aim—to determine what aspects of the preschool experience may have played crucial roles in the lives of the children. There were undoubtedly differences among the preschool teachers in the types and depth of relationships they established with children, in the effectiveness with which they implemented the curriculum, and in their resourcefulness in dealing with difficult children and problem situations. If we had data on these points, it is conceivable that one might conclude that the results with this group could not be considered maximal. What we are here saying is that in addition to asking if findings are "real," one has also to ask if data are

---

[3] We are here touching on one of the most bedeviling problems in research on human behavior. An illuminating discussion of this problem is contained in Rosenthal's book *Experimenter Effects in Behavioral Research* (1966).

presented which would allow for a determination of the degree of change one might expect under different or more ideal conditions. (If four aspirin produce a certain effect one wants to know if the same effects could be obtained with three, or two, or one. If four aspirin produce a discernible but minimal effect it becomes important to know how much more would be necessary to obtain a desired effect.) The fact that Kirk obtained an effect does not mean, as Kirk recognized, that a greater effect would not or could not be obtained; but we do not have the data to evaluate such a possibility. Kirk's study does not contain a comprehensive description or searching evaluation of the contents and nature of the intervention.[4]

Thirdly, a variation of the preceding point concerns the finding that the Community Contrast Group (which did not have preschool experience) gained in score after their first year in school so that there was no longer any difference between the Experimental and Contrast groups. At the very least, this finding indicates that some culturally deprived children do benefit from the first year of school. However, as in the case of the preschool experience, we do not know the nature and atmosphere of the first year in public school. That is to say, we do not know how representative the particular schools were of schools in general, e.g., elementary schools in our larger urban areas. For example, it is in our experience unusual, now and particularly at the time Kirk's study was done, for special classes to be available to children who are entering public school for the first time. The fact is that in Kirk's study 7 of 18 Experimental children and 5 of 21 Contrast children spent their first year of public school in a special class, suggesting that these schools were unusual in facilities, diagnostic and other services, and perhaps quality. If this is true, and we must stress that we do not know if it is true, it would help us understand the accelerated performance of the Contrast children and it would limit the generality of the finding at the same time that it specified the conditions under which such a finding could be expected. It must also be pointed out that "The Community Experimental Group had many more inadequate homes than did the Community Contrast Group." This selective factor would

---

[4] At a symposium where Kirk's study was being discussed a member of the audience asked the following questions: "Was Kirk able to get the best teachers according to his standards? How frequent were children and situations not handled in the most appropriate way? Did Kirk have available the types of special personnel who could have helped teachers and children?" In the context of the discussion it seemed clear that this person was addressing herself to such variables as the degree and scope of the intervention. Both from a practical and theoretical standpoint these are crucial issues which confront one with an assessment of reality as it exists and reality as it potentially may be created—and with this statement we are back to one's conception of the potentialities of man. It may be an *argument ad hominem,* but we cannot bypass the opportunity, to state that the individual who raised these questions—unnamed and unknown to us—had an obvious degree of conviction which, if not recognized and controlled, can lead to research data, findings, and interpretations which are unwittingly contaminated by such conviction. We need only add that the literature is replete with examples of where the opposite type of conviction leads to research which is also of the self-fulfilling type.

probably have been statistically significant if the number of children in each group had been larger It does suggest, as Kirk emphasizes, that the effects of one year of schooling is in part a function of variation of home adequacy even within a culturally disadvantaged population.

We have commented upon and raised questions about Kirk's important study in order to draw attention to the point that terms like "education" and "intervention" and "curriculum" are global in nature and by themselves do not permit us to talk at all securely about what goes on. This point is as relevant to studies which do not have positive findings as it is to those which do. Future studies will have to address themselves to this problem if their results are to be compared to each other and unwarranted generalizations avoided. It is obvious that this will not be an easy problem to solve. It is equally obvious that bypassing the problem can stand in the way of realizing and studying what is indeed the complex reality subsumed under terms like "education" and "intervention."

Problems of Sampling and Interpretation.   A second major study, and one to which we have referred in previous chapters, is that by Blatt and Garfunkel (1965). As in the case of Kirk, these investigators had difficulty finding a sizable number of preschool children who met the criteria of the strategy of their research. They chose instead preschoolers who lived in an area previously determined by sociological indices indisputably to contain high incidence of problem children and families. Because the Blatt and Garfunkel study represents a serious attempt to do a methodologically sound investigation in a very difficult problem area, we shall focus on this attempt and its consequences if only to demonstrate to the reader that the life of the researcher can be frustrating indeed. With this focus, the first point to be made is that children were assigned to experimental (exposed to a preschool program) and control groups by random assignment, i.e., assignment to the two groups was done in a way so as not to be a function of any knowledge the investigators may have possessed about the children. This is a very important point because it avoids the criticism that groups were selected so as to unwittingly increase the likelihood that the investigators would get the differences they hoped to get. Despite randomization Blatt and Garfunkel painfully state:

. . . We [have] described our rationale for, and our activity in, selecting a sample of lower-class preschool children. Fundamentally, our interest resided in the study of the problematic relationship between cultural deprivation and mental retardation in the context of ongoing educational programs. . . .

While it is a fairly straightforward matter to set up an experimental design and to select measurements in order to evaluate the effects of certain specified treatment programs, it by no means follows that the application of that design in field research can be easily communicated to other investigators. For example, it is perfectly clear to social scientists what is meant by randomized groups, at least at that moment in time when subjects are actually assigned to one of several treatment or control groups. However, it is not at all clear what this random assignment means when there are experimental children who do not receive the full treatment and when there are control children who do not stay "controlled." It may very well be, and it is our contention, that a simple description of principles of experimental design as they apply to a particular study, without a careful discussion of how and if these principles worked, can do more to distort a description of what has taken place than to contribute towards its understanding.

In this light, our view of design is more that of interactions among statistical, logical and measurement principles, on one hand, and application, on the other, than a simple description of a plan that was designed before the intervention started. We will often refer, specifically, to what was planned before the formal phase of the investigation started but we will try to make it clear that the vagaries of field research often caused us to depart from our plans to such an extent that the departure was more significant than the original plan itself. In presenting the design in this way we have in mind to formalize the crucial problems of educational field research, particularly with reference to those studies that concern themselves with lower-class preschool children whose surroundings and opportunities can be loosely described as deprived.

The division of the principal sample into two experimental groups and a non-experimental group was done by stratified random assignment, utilizing the Stanford-Binet IQ, chronological age, and sex in the stratification. . . .

The designation of the group of children who were not involved in the intervention as "non-experimental" rather than "control" is the result of our insight into the design of field research of this type. The 21 children who remained home were certainly not a control group in the sense that they received nothing. On the contrary, during the first year of the intervention five of these children were involved in preschool programs in their immediate neighborhoods. Further, during the second year of the intervention 13 of them were involved in a kindergarten program at the local public school—one that consisted of classes which were relatively small (approximately eight to ten) because of the large exodus of children from the neighborhood into our experimental program. In addition to this obvious contamination of the control process there was similar contamination of the experimental process as not all of the experimental children were in daily attendance in the experimental program and there were a few who rarely attended the program in the two years of its existence. For these reasons, the apparent discrete dichotomy between experimental and non-experimental is, in reality, a continuous variable which includes children who had highly stimulating interventions for two years, either in or out of the project, and children who received practically no preschool or kindergarten program prior to their entrance in public school and, therefore, prior to the final evaluation.

We see this impurity of the independent variable as an ubiquitous problem in field research of this type, especially when investigators focus their attention on the intensive study of relatively small groups of children. (Blatt and Garfunkel, 1965)

What Blatt and Garfunkel essentially are suggesting is that they probably did not have contrasting groups and that it may very well be unwarranted on the basis of their study to talk about the effects of their preschool intervention. It should also be noted that later in their report they state not only that the nonexperimental children were in atypically small kindergarten classes in their inner-city schools but that these classes seemed to have unusually effective teachers.

We have emphasized the importance of collecting data in a way which avoids or minimizes the biases or expectations of the investigator. Blatt and Garfunkel were keenly aware of this problem and went to great efforts to have all psychological testing done by people not connected with the project, i.e., psychologists not aware of the grouping to which the child belonged. To accomplish this end is far more difficult than one might expect. For example, the psychologists may not be part of the project but they may be quite aware of the overall nature of the project and the hypotheses being tested. Blatt and Garfunkel became aware of this possibility and for their final testing they literally imported psychologists from a neighboring state. Few studies can compare with that by Blatt and Garfunkel in awareness of, and attempt to control for, investigator bias. Even so, as Blatt and Garfunkel point out, the use of "blind" psychologists achieved its purposes in the third and fourth testing but was only partially successful in the second testing when local psychologists were used. The problem did not arise in the first testing because the groups were organized after initial testing.

Another marked advance of this over previous studies is the detail provided on the nature of the preschool intervention. In fact, one gets a real feel for what these investigators tried to do and the atmosphere they tried to create. Perhaps the best indication of the efforts and dedication of these investigators is that over a four-year period *there was practically no loss in contact with all children and families, a most remarkable and atypical feat when working this population.* In fact, their knowledge of the children and their families—together with their findings about family adequacy—led Blatt and Garfunkel to state candidly that one of the major limitations of their intervention was their failure to deal with families.

Although we have been continually aware of the limitations of an intervention which restricts itself, for the most part, to dealing with children in a school situation, it was not within the plans of this study to treat families or to deal extensively with evaluations of siblings and other children in the community. Therefore, the curriculum was concerned with the Responsive Environment and the preschool program with peripheral attention to families during occasional meetings and home visits by teachers. It might very well be that the failure of this program, as described above, was due to the failure of the intervention to affect total family behavior. Since we found a relatively high correlation between a measure of family adequacy and the average school performance of all siblings, the inference follows that school failure is family linked and must, therefore, be family treated. (Blatt and Garfunkel, 1965)

Again in contrast to most educational intervention studies, Blatt and Garfunkel were able to secure a good deal of data relevant to family stability and organization. The quotation that follows well illustrates the depth and care with which family data were secured and, atypically, the critical stance which Blatt and Garfunkel adopted in relation to their data.

. . . we employed an experienced female social worker in the winter and spring of 1965. Eight scales were developed, all directly relevant to the home preparation of the child for school. These scales were developed by the social worker in conjunction with the project staff as a result of questions that were repeatedly asked about families in our continuing attempt to try to understand how and why they functioned as they did. For this reason, the scales do not represent a carefully structured and logical taxonomy. Rather, they represent the most pressing questions that were suggested by many hundreds of pages of process reports of interviews with each family. These reports were obtained through repeated interviews by the social worker and a male assistant who carried on interviews with all available fathers. Each family was visited a minimum of two times, and more often, three, four, or five times, in order to obtain extensive information about the parents' and children's functioning with reference to the questions raised by the eight scales.

The scales included the following:

1. Parents' Perception of Child's Functioning as a Student
2. Individual Behavior of Study Child as Displayed to the Social Worker on Repeated Visits
3. Marital Relationship
4. Individual Behavior of Mother and Father as Observed by Social Worker and Assistant on Repeated Visits
5. Mother-Child Relationship as Observed
6. Family Solidarity
7. Mother's Attitude Toward an Involvement in Study Child's Education
8. General Impression of Family Adequacy

Thus, it should be clear that our approach to measuring the environment of the home was not to ask or check off whether certain items were or were not present in the home or whether either or both parents held certain specific attitudes. We found that approach to be unworkable with the families we were studying. . . . Our intensive staffings of homes revealed, in a rather short period of time, that we had to take a global approach to the study of these homes and to ask a series of related global questions about mothers, fathers, and their children. In this way, we felt that we came much closer to measuring essential qualities of the homes than we would have had we utilized a more specific and formalized approach. On the other hand, a serious drawback to our methodology is that it is not easily and directly replicable because it was so dependent upon the caseworker and her assistant and the project staff, all of whom took part in the extensive staffings of individual families. However, two sets of independent ratings of the family protocols resulted in inter-rate correlations of .92 and .94. (Blatt and Garfunkel, 1965)

It is deserving of emphasis that in order to control for investigator bias an effort was made to obtain two sets of independent ratings of the family data, a methodological effort too frequently overlooked or avoided.

We have not presented the major findings of this study because we feel, along with Blatt and Garfunkel, that evaluation of educational interventions have not in the past, and must in the future, face the inordinate complexities of this type of research. At the present time findings are not hard to come by; the problem is one of their evaluation in terms of the realities from which they have emerged and to which, it is to be hoped, they are applicable. Particularly as a result of government support of preschool educational programs for the culturally disadvantaged, one may expect in the future many studies evaluating the effects of such programs. One may also expect that the findings will be far from uniform and will give rise to conflicting, and even contradictory, interpretations. It will be far from easy to keep one's head in the ensuing complex array of studies, findings, interpretations, and controversies. The following concluding statement by Blatt and Garfunkel not only indicates what the reader may expect over the next decade but also offers guidelines and attitudes which, if taken seriously, could prevent premature conclusions stemming from unrealistic conceptions of the complexity of the problem:

During the past few years, programs for the disadvantaged have mushroomed. Within recent months, we have been privileged to examine—in some instances, at first hand—the curricula and activities of approximately fifty preschool projects for disadvantaged children. In New York City, Chicago, Oakland, California, Norfolk, Baltimore, Ypsilanti, and in Boston—as well as in many other large metropolises and small hamlets—state colleges, large universities, and state education departments banded together with local communities and voluntary organizations to design and develop programs for these children. Although each program was to some extent unique, both in philosophical orientation and curriculum design, there was a common focus and expectation. That focus was on direct involvement with children in order to prevent an accumulation of learning and motivational disorders. Other common elements observed in most programs had to do with the conviction that early involvement with children was more desirable than delaying intervention until formal school entrance. Most programs did not seek deep and continuous activity with parents and other family members; more recently, one or two newer programs have sought such involvement. A few programs have—*a priori*—designed very specific curricula to prevent or remediate specific deficits; most programs developed more global curricula, this development taking place concurrently with involvement with children. However, all programs—more or less—appeared experimental and open-minded. That is, there are few hard and fast rules, either in the development of a theoretical position or in the execution of educational interventions with the deprived.

Insofar as formal experimental programs investigating the characteristics of deprived children, their genesis, and preventative and therapeutic programs designed to deal with mental retardation, learning disorders, and character defects are concerned, research activities are not nearly as extensive as those in service programs, nor have these efforts been as satisfactory. The major factors attendant to the quality of significant research in this field are two-fold. First, there are much more modest and restricted funds available for basic and applied research than for program implementation. Secondly, when research is funded, it appears as if each project is bedeviled with a massive array of strategic and tactical problems. In general, these have to do with researcher bias, the development of adequate research controls, notorious subject attrition, and the unavailability of suitable measurement instruments and tests. Therefore, until research workers can develop more tightly controlled studies and replications of studies—an extraordinarily difficult assignment for research with *any* group of human beings and, especially, with so complex and heterogeneous a group as the "culturally disadvantaged"—educational practitioners must, by necessity, continue to utilize interventional strategies that have "face validities" and must continue striving for a program climate dominated by open-mindedness and control over strong personal pre-judgments and pre-limitations of what might be accomplished under the best of conditions and what might reasonably be expected under modestly effective ones.

Insofar as our present study is concerned, at this time we have neither significant nor convincing data to substantiate our central hypothesis that intelligence is educable. However, this study revealed to us that we still have a great deal to discover concerning the nature-nurture interaction, about the most efficient and sufficient period to begin interventions, and about the varieties of possible intervention models that may have the greatest desired effects. What we do have encourages us to continue the quest for processes and methodologies to educate intelligence and, for certain children, to prevent mental retardation. (Blatt and Garfunkel, 1965)

Special Training Units: World War II

It may well be that the first attempt on the part of the federal government to deal with educational and mental retardation was in World War II when Special Training Units were set up with the following aims:[5]

1. To teach the men to read at least at a fourth-grade level so that they would be able to comprehend bulletins, written orders and directives, and basic Army publications.
2. To give the men sufficient language skill so that they would be able to use and understand the everyday oral and written language necessary for getting along with officers and men.
3. To teach the men to do number work at a fourth-grade level, so that they could understand their pay accounts and laundry bills, conduct their business in the PX, and perform in other situations requiring arithmetic skill.

---

[5] We have already discussed aspects of Ginzberg and Bray's study in earlier chapters. As these authors point out (1953, p. 79): "Without firm fact at their disposal those in authority were forced to base their judgment of the military performance of the un-educated on snatches of evidence that had come to their attention. The Army's impression of how the graduates of the Special Training Units performed could be summarized in a single word 'poorly.' The consensus was that the Army's investment in this group was not repaid." We would agree with Ginzberg and Bray's statement that their study, despite the limitations of which they were well aware, is the most searching done with the available data and supports the conclusion that "It was, in any case, not expected that the Special Training Unit graduates would include a great many outstanding soldiers. The question was rather whether any appreciable number would perform adequately and represent a clear gain to the Army. This question is answered unequivo-cally. Eighty-five percent of the graduates performed acceptably or better as compared to 90 percent of the control group. Clearly, at a time when the Armed Forces needed men badly, they were able with a small investment to turn many illiterates and poorly educated men into acceptable soldiers." When one realizes that those in the Special Training Units are strikingly similar to those who are currently the object of the "war on poverty" and "Great Society" programs, the study by and conclusions of Ginzberg and Bray have significance beyond the problems of the Armed Forces in World War II.

4. To facilitate the adjustment of the men to military training and Army life.
5. To enable the men to understand in a general way why it was necessary for this country to fight a war against Germany, Japan, and Italy.

To give the reader some feel for these Special Training Units we present the following excerpt from the History of the Special Training Unit, 1747 Service Command Unit, Fort Riley, Kansas which served the entire Midwest:

When a man first comes to the organization, he is temporarily assigned to Company C, the Receiving Company, where his "processing," already begun at the induction station, is continued. A series of tests are administered to determine the level of training to which the individual may be subjected. It has been found that men classified "illiterate" may be of several levels, and with that in mind, the several companies of the Unit are organized and equipped to take men falling into one particular level. The levels that have been established are classified as I, II, III, IV, progressing in that order from the lowest to the highest and comparable to the first grade through the fourth grade of school.

During the period of training, all men are given periodic tests to determine their academic advancement and careful progress record cards are maintained at all times on each man. The tests mentioned are standard War Department publications covering the academic subjects taught. These subjects are Reading, Language Expression, and Arithmetic. Language Expression includes reading and writing incorporated into the process of orientation and adaption to military life. War Department texts are also in use, among them the "Army Reader" and the "Army Arithmetic." The former is divided into four parts, each upon completion, followed by the appropriate test mentioned above. A fictional character, Private Pete, is followed through his military career and the entire course is designed along a functional level. It has been found that men will retain a great deal more if they are taught that "one man had four apples and another man gave him four more apples so that the first man then had eight apples," rather than four and four are eight.

The length of time spent in training in the Special Unit varies with the level of the man when he starts. Those having been determined as falling into Group I and II spent on an average of 4 to 6 weeks in the Unit, the lower levels requiring from 8 to 12 weeks of training.

Together with the basic academic training that the men receive while in the Unit, they are also given training in the basic military subjects, information they must know in order to fit themselves into military life and to help them adjust themselves to their new surroundings. Many of these courses will be repeated and more thoroughly covered at the Training Centers to which the men will go when they have completed their training here, but they will have the fundamentals so that they will be able to keep up with regular trainees. The emphasis in the STU, however, rests on the academic with approximately two hours of academic training to one of military.

A "cadre" or staff of enlisted personnel form the basis for all instruction in the Special Training Unit. Each man has been selected for the position on the basis of his academic background as well as being a capable military instructor. With but few exceptions, all of the instructors are college graduates, many of them possess Master's degrees and a few holding various Doctor's degrees. Formerly they were connected with civilian school systems, rainging from the elementary through the college level. The unit is staffed by 26 officers qualified both academically and militarily.

Experience has shown that men of the calibre that are received in the Special Training Unit learn more and faster if they are allowed to absorb the training given with the same group of men for the entire period they are here. For that reason, men are assigned to barracks and remain there until they leave. One classroom is set up on each of the two floors of the building and provided with tables, chairs, blackboards, and other instructional aids pertaining to the type of work being covered. For a short period of time after entrance into the barracks, some men are prone to exhibit shyness due to the fact that they have never associated closely with other men.

Gradually the spirit of teamwork and cooperation are developed and within a few days the men have made an adjustment sufficient to enhance learning. Since changing from one group to another would tend to prolong the period of adjustment, that method is not employed. The military instructor, a Corporal or Sergeant, lives in the barracks with the men, eats with them and works with them and it is rare that he fails to gain the complete confidence of his men almost immediately. The instructor's job lasts 24 hours per day. During the off duty hours much of his time is taken up writing letters for the trainees or giving them advice on their personal problems. Also he will devote considerable time to additional instruction for men who are learning slower than others.

After the war, Ginzberg and Bray, via a questionnaire sent through the mails, attempted to find out how their sample of subjects regarded their experience in the Special Training Units. From the data returned, and the samples of replies presented, the following conclusions seem warranted:

These replies tell us a considerable amount about the reactions of the poorly educated American to his experience with Army education during the war and the significance of this experience for his post-war adjustment. As indicated earlier, the men confirmed the findings of the earlier chapters which pointed to the success of the special training program as contributing to military victory. Although some of the men found shortcomings in the Army's program, the major complaint was directed against the short time that they were permitted to remain in it. From the military point of view, this was not a shortcoming since many of the men were able to perform at a generally satisfactory level after a period of instruction of no more than two months.

It is important that more than 50 percent of the men who received letters took the time and trouble to fill out the questionnaire. For the most part their replies were written in their own hand, although we have quoted one individual who indicated that he could not write the reply himself. There were probably others who did not specify that the questionnaire was filled in by a relative or friend. Thus, despite the limitations of penmanship, grammar, and punctuation the fact remains that men who entered the Army either totally or largely illiterate had acquired a sufficient basic knowledge of reading and writing during the eight or twelve weeks that they were given special instruction to be able to make use of these skills six years after demobilization. Admittedly, many of these men had added to their skills through education which they received after demobilization. However, the important point to note in this connection is the stimulation which they received, and which many of them commented on, from their exposure to the Army's training program.

One cannot review these materials without recognizing that the opportunity afforded these men to acquire in adulthood what most people acquire in childhood—the basic tools for communicating with their fellow men—gave new and heightened meaning to their lives. Several respondents commented on the fact that their whole adjustment to life had altered because they had acquired the ability to read and write. Clearly this episode in military history has significance far beyond the purely military domain. The national emergency of 1941–45 brought certain national problems into heightened focus. The measures that were taken to deal with these problems, in particular the problem of the poorly educated, must be evaluated, not solely by what they contributed to military victory, but by the lessons which they hold for civilian,welfare. (Ginzberg and Bray, 1953)

If one accepts, even in part, these conclusions, it becomes necessary—if only for the relevance of the study for contemporary "poverty programs"—to try to state those variables which seem to have been involved in the program.

1. The curriculum was obviously relevant to (and in a very concrete manner) the everyday problems which confronted the trainees. What they were expected to learn they needed to learn if they were to cope with the problems of living in the army.
2. The relationship between trainee and teacher was close and continuous, and apparently involved interactions not ordinarily occurring between teacher and student.
3. A point not emphasized by Ginzberg and Bray, but clearly one that comes out in the trainees' replies, is that *these adults were highly motivated to take advantage of the educational opportunity*. It was as if their prewar experiences had made them acutely aware of their educational and intellectual inadequacies and they seized upon the Special Training Unit as a means of making up for some of their inadequacies. It may have been true that motivation did not need to be engendered but rather reinforced and rewarded.

There are two major significances of the Ginzberg and Bray study. The first resides in the encouraging evidence it provides that adult slow learners, low test scorers, and culturally disadvantaged could benefit from an intensive, time-limited educational program. The second significance of the study resides in its implications for current and future war-on-poverty programs, i.e., it describes an atmosphere and conditions of learning which current programs with similar young adults do not always obtain. Where these conditions are approximated (Sarason, Levine, Goldenberg, Cherlin, and Bennett, 1966) the results are in line with those described by Ginzberg and Bray. The fact that these conditions are too often not developed may well account for the disillusionment which seems to surround contemporary community action programs for the inner-city or culturally disadvantaged populations. The results of any educational program—be these results positive or negative—cannot be judged solely on the basis of descriptions of curricula or services offered, or the amount of money spent. What one needs to know is wrapped up in such global terms as atmosphere, motivation, attitude, and conditions of learning. We can no longer be satisfied with these terms, particularly in research efforts where their use usually provides the reader with little but the opinion of the researcher. One of the major and formidable tasks of future research is to conceptualize these terms in ways which communicate clearly and objectively to the reader the attributes of the particular setting and their relationship to and interactions with the personalities involved. This is not a problem which will be solved by one or a team of investigators, but rather by a long succession of investigators over a long period of time. Just as it took scores of years for physics to understand and study appropriately the atomic and subatomic world of matter, one may expect that it will take a long time until we develop the conceptualizations and techniques adequate to mirror the complex realities of a classroom, a program, a setting. Until these issues begin to be clarified it will be difficult and hazardous to evaluate the significance of a single study, let alone to compare different studies. When one realizes that what is at stake is our understanding of the relations between conditions and human potentialities, it is not indulging the dramatic impulse to say that we can no longer be satisfied with educational results which do not recognize the shortcomings of conventional descriptions of the educational settings be they for the preschool child, the school-aged youngster, or the young adult.

The Effects of Special Classes

Special classes historically are the oldest means of educational intervention with the mentally retarded, and over the years the bulk of these classes have been located in urban areas. It is not surprising, therefore, that these classes have contained children largely drawn from inner-city, or lower-class areas, or racial and ethnic ghettos.[6] Despite the long history of special classes and their current proliferation there is no substantial evidence that this mode of intervention has positive effects. Stolurow, for example, states the following:

. . . Special classes for the mentally retarded were initiated in the public schools in 1896. Since that date almost all states have initiated special class programs in the public schools with state subsidies to local districts to encourage the organization of such classes. However, up to the present time no one has demonstrated that

---

[6] In the last decade there has been a dramatic increase in the number of special classes, in part as a result of the decision to provide educational programs for the trainable child whose degree of retardation was severe and associated with discernible central nervous system impairment. Until recently this type of child had been excluded from school. Special classes for these children, whose capacity to benefit from a formal educational program is extremely limited, represents less the desire on the part of educators to program for these children than it does parental pressures, mandatory state legislation, and increased state and federal appropriations. At the present time the bulk of all special classes are oriented to the educable, inner-city school child.

children in special classes develop mentally, academically, or socially at a more advanced rate than they might have, had they continued in the regular grades. In fact, three doctoral dissertations, one by Bennett, another by Pertsch and a third by Blatt showed the opposite. Bennett and Pertsch each found that the educable mentally handicapped child in regular classes generally was equal or superior in physical, personality, and academic performance.

These studies have three methodological deficiencies. The main one is selection. In studying the special versus regular class, in communities where special classes have already been established, it is impossible to control for selection factors which could bias such a study. Typically, the educable mentally handicapped children who exhibit behavior problems and marked learning disabilities in regular grades are the cause for the development of special classes or are the ones who are assigned to the special classes if they already exist. Thus, while the retarded child in special class might be comparable in IQ and MA to the retarded child in the regular class, for the special class child there have been reasons for his rejection from a regular class which could have important implications for his performance in school. Obviously, a variety of factors such as learning rate, ability, physical development, and personality characteristics could contribute to differences in the performance of those rejected from the regular class. A second factor is the specific experiences of the child prior to special class placement, especially as they relate to failure. These failure experiences could have important implications for the subsequent learning performance of the child. In the earlier studies, the special class children attended the regular grades from 2 to 5 years and then were placed in special classes for only a few years prior to the initiation of the study.

In addition to selection and experiential factors relating to failure, these studies did not identify special class programs in any of their important educational dimensions. This is the third potential contributor to the results reported; namely, the special class program itself. (Stolurow, 1961)

One could also cite studies by Cassidy and Stanton (1959), Johnson (1961), and Mullen and Itkin (1961) to substantiate further the conclusion that special classes have yet to demonstrate sufficient effectiveness to justify their existence as a way of intervening in the lives of children.

The study by Goldstein, Moss, and Jordan (1965) is not only the most recent and comprehensive but it is distinctive in that it attempted experimentally to evaluate the efficacy of special classes, i.e., at the beginning of first grade, children scoring below or at 85 IQ were randomly assigned into special classes or remained in their original first grade classes.

The purpose of this study was to determine the efficacy of special classes for educable mentally retarded children with respect to their intellectual development, academic achievement, and social and personal adjustment. The study was designed to take into account methodological inadequacies which had characterized previous investigations.

The major operational hypothesis was as follows: The placement of educable mentally retarded children in special classes at the beginning of their school careers, with specially trained teachers and an optimal special program, will have a more positive effect on their rate of intellectual development, academic achievement, and social and personal adjustment than will continuation in the regular public school classes.

The sub-hypotheses were as follows:

1. Educable mentally retarded children placed in special classes will develop intellectually at a more rapid rate than will similar children placed in regular classes.
2. Educable mentally retarded children in special classes will achieve academically at a higher level than will similar children placed in regular classes.
3. Educable mentally retarded children placed in special classes will show a more adequate social and personal adjustment than will similar children placed in regular classes. (Goldstein, Moss, and Jordan, 1965)

The following describes the selection of and placement of children:

1. The Primary Mental Abilities Test (PMA), Primary Battery, was administered during the first five weeks after the opening of school in September to every entering first-grade child (1,938) in the 20 cooperating school districts. The cooperating school districts were those within an 80-mile radius of Urbana, Illinois. These school districts did not already have primary level classes for the educable mentally retarded and the boards of education agreed to cooperate for the four-year period. All children who scored at or below 85 IQ on the PMA were scheduled for examination with the Stanford-Binet (1937, Form L).
2. The 290 children who scored at or below 85 IQ on the PMA were tested individually with the Stanford-Binet Scale (1937, Form L). Only 129 of the original 1,938 were found to score at or below 85 IQ on both the PMA and the Stanford-Binet tests (6.7 percent).
3. Four special classes were established in the three Illinois counties involved in the study. One class each was established in the two counties which were predominantly rural. Two classes were established in the one urban center of the third county.
4. Three of the original 129 children identified as appropriate for the study were lost prior to class assignment and the remaining 126 children were randomly assigned to one of the two conditions to be studied. Children to be placed in the special classes (experimental group) were transferred into newly established classes while the remaining children (control group) were left in their original regular first grades. The only restrictions placed on the random assignment of children to the special classes were that (a) a maximum of 15 children could be placed in a single special class, (b) placement had to be restricted to the child's originating county, and (c) permission for placement had to be obtained from the parents.

Of the 126 remaining children, 57 were placed in special classes while the remaining 69 became control subjects. The experimental children were divided 15 to a class with the exception that one rural class had only 12 children. Although there was a surplus of control children, they were all located in the other counties and could not be used to increase the enrollment in the rural county class. (Goldstein, Moss, and Jordan, 1965)

Data analysis clearly did not support the hypotheses about the efficacy of special classes, a finding consistant with previous research. In light of these negative findings Goldstein, Moss, and Jordan did further analyses in which each of the two groups was divided into those whose initial IQ was above and those whose initial IQ was below 80. The results of these *post hoc* analyses suggested that special classes may have some beneficial effects for those children whose initial IQ was below 80. The weight which these investigators give to this finding which was the result of analyses done after it was apparent that the major hypotheses received no support can be seen in the following:

Careful selection at age six, assignment of only children with IQ's of 75 or less to special classes, and careful observation and evaluation are requisites of early place-ment of educable mentally retarded children in special classes. Early placement opens to the child immediate involvement in a program and setting consistent with his abilities and needs. (Goldstein, Moss, and Jordan, 1965)

There are several reasons why one must regard with great caution the sugges-tion that special classes should be used in the manner described above. If Goldstein, Moss, and Jordan had said: "if the *only* selection criterion to be employed is an IQ score, then restrict placement to those with IQ's of 75 or less," we would raise no argument because it is a statement which reflects well the criterion employed in the study. But it seems clear from the word we italicized in the above quotation that Goldstein, Moss, and Jordan do not equate "careful selection" with an IQ score. This raises two important issues. First, since the data in this study are "group data" and whatever generaliza-tions may be drawn speak to the average child in the particular group, it is very likely that there are experimental children with IQ's below 75 for whom the generalization is not appropriate. This leads to the question: What are or should be the criteria for selection? This study provides no answer to this question. What now seems to be necessary, as a result of the leads provided by this important study, are further studies which place children in special classes on the basis of multiple criteria, i.e., criteria which take into account important social, intellectual, personality, motivational factors. The question is not whether special classes are effective but rather for what kinds of children they may be effective—and by kinds we obviously do not mean children who possess a particular IQ score. We have no doubt that Goldstein, Moss, and Jordan would agree with the statement that placing any child into a special class should never be done on the basis of conventional test scores and that they would regard it unfortunate in the extreme if their study was interpreted as supporting such a practice. Just as the failure to confirm their major hypotheses lead these investigators to subdivide their groups, future investi-gators will have to go beyond such an IQ subdivision if they are to contribute to our understanding of the problem: For whom is special class placement the intervention of choice?

In this chapter we have attempted to describe and discuss studies which were conducted in conventional types of educational settings and which had as their major aim the evaluation of the effects of programs on individuals who were considered mentally retarded or who came from those regions or parts of a community containing large numbers of mentally retarded children.

The results of these studies do not permit one to conclude in a general way that educational interventions have had their intended effects. It is also not permissible to conclude that more (and more sophisticated) studies are not necessary. It is our opinion that there is a basis for cautious optimism that future researchers, benefitting from the pioneering work of those whose work we have just described, can develop more complex theories and a more adequate technology which will bring forth new knowledge about the relations between conditions and human performance. The plight of the reader who desires or needs firm and substantial findings and conclusions is more than matched by the plight of the researcher who knows he is starting out on an obstacle course for which there are few maps to serve as a guide—and some of the maps to an undetermined extent are likely to be wrong or misleading.

$\mathcal{T}$he effects of institutionalization

$\mathbb{W}$hereas in the previous chapter we focused on planned interventions in conventional educational settings, we shall in this chapter turn our attention to planned and unplanned interventions occurring outside of the usual school setting. One such setting is the institutional one which up until recently (Sarason, 1964) was one of the major means society employed for dealing with all types of mental subnormality. Consistent with the aims of this part of the book we shall be discussing investigations where there is good reason to believe that the population under study would meet conventional criteria of familial–cultural mental retardation. However, as previous chapters have attempted to make clear, the reader needs to be forewarned that it is not always easy or possible to ascertain to what extent in any one study these criteria were seriously or systematically employed and, therefore, to what extent studies are comparable.

A Thirty-Year Study

It is fitting that we begin our discussion with one of the oldest and newest studies: "Adult Status of Children with Contrasting Early Life Experiences" by Harold M. Skeels (1966). This study covers a span of 30 years and the final report concerns the status as adults of two groups of children originally encountered in the Iowa institutions. The origin of the study (1939) deserves retelling:

Two children under a year and a half, in residence at the state orphanage, gave unmistakable evidence of marked mental retardation. Kuhlmann-Binet intelligence tests were given both children. C.D., thirteen months of age at time of examination, obtained an I.Q. of 46, and B.D., at sixteen months, scored an I.Q. of 35. Qualitative observations of the examiner substantiated a classification of imbecile level of mental retardation. In the case of B.D., the examiner felt that the child's actual level was perhaps slightly higher, but not to exceed ten points or an I.Q. level of 45. As check tests for further corroboration, the Iowa Tests for Young Children were used. Mental ages of approximately six and seven months respectively were obtained.

Obviously a classification of feeble-mindedness would not be justified if based on results of intelligence tests alone, particularly at these young ages. However, behavioral reactions in conjunction with the examinations of the pediatrician, and observations by the superintendent of nurses relative to activity or lack of activity of these children in the nursery in contrast with other children, gave ample substantiation for a classification of marked mental retardation. C.D., at thirteen months, was making no attempts to stand, even with assistance. She could not pull herself to an upright position with the aid of crib or chair, nor did she display much manipulative activity with blocks or play materials. Spontaneous vocalization also was lacking. B.D., at sixteen months, was not vocalizing, was unable to walk with help and made relatively no responses to play materials in the nursery. (Skeels and Dye, 1939)

Both children were illegitimate and their mothers had been adjudged feeble-minded. The two children were transferred to the school for the feeble-minded.

Six months after transfer, the psychologist visiting the wards of the institution was surprised to notice the apparently remarkable development of these children. Accordingly, they were re-examined on the Kuhlmann-Binet, C.D. obtained an I.Q. of 77 and B.D. an I.Q. of 87. Twelve months later they were tested again with I.Q.'s of 100 and 88, respectively. Tests were again given when the children were forty months and forty-three months of age, respectively, with I.Q.'s of 95 and 93.

In the meantime, inquiries were made as to reasons for this unusual development. Their "home" or ward environment was studied. It was observed that the attendants on the ward had taken a great fancy to the "babies." They were essentially the only pre-school children on the ward, other than a few hopeless bed patients with psysiological defects. The attendants would take these two children with them on their days off, giving them car rides and taking them down town to the stores. Toys, picture books and play materials were purchased by these admiring adults. The older, brighter girls on the ward were also very much attached to the children and would play with them during most of the waking hours. Thus it can be seen that this environment turned out to be stimulating to these pre-school children of low initial mental level. (Skeels and Dye, 1939)

As a result of these observations retarded children in the orphanage were transferred to the institution for the feebleminded. Thirteen children were transferred, the mean chronological age at transfer being 19.4 months, with a range from 7.1 to 35.9 months. The mean IQ was 64.3, with a range from 35 to 89. "That such retardation was real and observable was substantiated by the reports of the pediatrician and nurse in charge, indicating lack of development." The transferred cases were compared to a control group of 12 cases who had had intelligence tests before the age of two, were in continuous residence at the orphanage, and had not attended any kind of preschool. Social histories and psychometric data indicated that the parents of the children in both groups represented the lower educational and occupational levels. Of the five mothers in the experimental group on whom there were psychometric data, four had IQ's below 70 and one had an IQ of 100. Of the nine mothers in the control group on whom psychometric data were available, seven had IQ's below 70, one had an IQ of 79, and the other of 84.

When transferred to the school for mental defectives the experimental group was placed on wards with older and brighter girls. There were very few younger children on these wards aside from the experimental children.

The attendants and the older girls became very fond of the child placed on the ward and took great pride in its achievement. In fact, there was considerable competition between wards to see which one would have their "baby" walking or talking first. The girls would spend a great deal of time with the children, teaching them to walk, talk, play with toys and play materials, and in the training of habits.

Most of the clothing for these children was made by the older girls. The girls were so fond of the children that they would actually spend their small earnings and allowances to buy them special foods, toys, picture books, and materials for clothing. Similarly attendants gave of their time, money, and affection, and during their free hours frequently took the children on excursions, car rides, and trips. In addition, it was the policy of the matron in charge of the girls' school division to single out certain of these children whom she felt were in need of special individualization and permit these children to spend a portion of time each day visiting her office. This furnished new experiences including being singled out and given special attention and affection, new play materials, additional language stimulation, and contacts with other office callers.

An indication of the interest in these children was shown by the fact that a baby show was held for one of the Fourth of July celebrations. Each ward made a float upon which its "baby" rode, dressed in costume. Prizes were awarded for the winning baby, most attractive costume, and best float.

The spacious living rooms of the wards furnished ample room for indoor play and activity. Whenever weather permitted, the children spent some time each day on the playground, supervised by one or more of the older girls. In this situation, they had contacts with other children of similar ages. Outdoor play equipment included tricycles, swings, slides, sand box, etc. (Skeels and Dye, 1939)

In contrast to the experiences of the experimental group, the control group remained in an environment characterized by the relative absence of external stimulation and the lack of any enduring or consistent adult-child   relationships.

Up to the age of two years, the children were in the nursery of the hospital. This was limited to a rather small play room with additional dormitory rooms of two to five beds each. The children were cared for by two nurses with some additional assistance by one or two girls of ten to fifteen years of age. The children had good physical and medical care, but little can be said beyond this. Contacts with adults were largely limited to feeding, bathing, dressing, and toilet details. It can readily be seen that with the large number of children per adult, little time was available for anything aside from the routines of physical care. The girls who assisted the nurses accepted the work as a necessary evil and, in general, took little personal interest in the children as individuals. Few play materials were available and little attention was given to the teaching of play techniques. The children were seldom out of the nursery room except for short walks or short periods of time out of doors for fresh air. (Skeels and Dye, 1939)

In regard to the contrast group (those who remained in the orphanage):

When the children were examined, it was not known that they were or would become members of any study group. The re-examinations were merely routine retests that were given to all children.

At the ages when adoptive placement usually occurred, nine of the children in the contrast group had been considered normal in mental development. All 12 were not placed, however, because of different circumstances: 5 were withheld from placement simply because of poor family histories, 2 because of improper commitments, 2 because of luetic conditions, 2 because of other health problems, and one because of possible mental retardation.

The subsequent progress of the children in both the experimental and the contrast groups was influenced by individual circumstances. The groups were never identified as such in the resident institution; the members of each group were considered together only in a statistical sense. A child in the experimental group remained in the institution for the mentally retarded until it was felt that he had attained the maximum benefit from residence there. At that point, he was placed directly into an adoptive home or returned to the orphanage in transit to an adoptive home. If he did not attain a level of intelligence that warranted adoptive plans, he remained in the institution for the mentally retarded.

The contrast-group members remained in the orphanage until placement. One was returned to relatives, but in most instances the children were eventually transferred to an institution for the mentally retarded as long-term protected residents. A few of the contrast group had been briefly approved for adoptive placement, and two had been placed for short periods. None was successful, however, and the children's decline in mental level removed them from the list of those eligible for adoption. (Skeels, 1966, 11–12)

The actual follow-up study began twenty years after the postexperimental follow-up. Skeels describes briefly but well the "flexibility, ingenuity, and tenacity" required to locate and interview the subjects, particularly the experimental subjects. The following describes what he considered to be one of the more difficult instances of locating subjects.

〇～〇   On October 20, 1961, I stopped at Bradshaw, population 355, to try to find the Ted Mitchell family. Their daughter, Ruth, was one of the 13 experimental children, and the last contact with this home had been in 1941. I went to the Post Office but the postmistress said she did not know them at all. I asked her if there was some old-timer who might know them, and she suggested that I see Dr. Gifford, a dentist who had been the previous postmaster. I went to his office and waited until he had finished with the patient in the chair. I then stated my case and he indicated he had known the Mitchells, but did not know what had happened to them.

He suggested seeing John Richmond and Albert Johnson, farmers in the area where the Mitchells used to live. At the John Richmond farm no one was home. The man at the next farm did not know about the Mitchells, as he had lived there only 11 years. He pointed out the third house up the road as that of the Albert Johnsons, so I went there, but they were also away from home.

I then stopped at one or two farms on the way back, and an elderly gentleman told me that the Mitchells were members of one of the less common religious faiths, the only family of that denomination in the area, and that they had not had much truck with the people in the village, which probably accounted for the fact that it was so difficult to find out about them. He stated that Mr. and Mrs. Mitchell had separated, and Mrs. Mitchell had married again. He said that one person who had been in rather close contact with their daughter, Ruth, was a Mrs. Wilbur Marshall who lived out beyond the Albert Johnsons.

I went back out to see Mrs. Marshall, but no one was at home. I then stopped at a filling station on my way back to get the telephone numbers of some of these people, and the operator of the filling station told me that the Marshalls were building a house in town, and might be working over there. He showed me where it was and I went over, but apparently they had quit work and, I thought, perhaps gone home. I therefore went out again to the Marshall residence, but still no one was there. On the way back I stopped at the Albert Johnsons and was able to talk with him, but he did not know where the Mitchells had gone. Finding that John Richmond and his wife were now at home, I also stopped there, but they, too, did not know the present whereabouts of the Mitchells.

For the next three days I tried periodically to call the Wilbur Marshalls and had no success. Finally, the rural operator said that apparently they could not be reached because they had moved in to town and had no phone as yet in their new house. Therefore, I may have to go back to this town at a later time and see if I can possibly find Mrs. Mitchell.

. . .

October 25, 1961, I again drove out to Bradshaw, going directly to the Marshalls' new house. This time I found both Mr. and Mrs. Marshall there. Mrs. Marshall said that her daughter had been a friend of Elizabeth, a daughter by birth of the Mitchells; that Elizabeth was married to a Ralph Strand, and was living in Des Moines. She thought that Elizabeth could tell me where Ruth was, and where Mrs. Mitchell, the adoptive mother, could be located. She mentioned that Mrs. Mitchell had remarried. She couldn't remember the specific address, but thought Ralph Strand would be listed in the Des Moines telephone directory. (I had visions of there being several Strands listed.) On further question, she said they lived somewhere on Fourth Street Place.

I felt very fortunate to have secured this information. I drove back to Des Moines and immediately looked up the Ralph Strands in the telephone directory. As expected, there were two of them, but fortunately one lived on Fourth Street

Place. I went there that same afternoon, only to find no one at home. The next morning I went out there, and again no answer to my knock on the door. I then went to the house of a neighbor to ask if the Strands were on vacation.

From the neighbor I learned a great deal without divulging the purpose of my inquiry. She informed me that the Strands had separated, and that Ralph came home in the evenings. I indicated that in earlier years I had been acquainted with Mrs. Strand's mother, and that I was interested in locating either Elizabeth or her mother. She did not know where Elizabeth was, but the mother, formerly Mrs. Ted Mitchell, worked at the Green Lantern Restaurant; that she was now Mrs. Donald White, and lived at 4078 Grand Avenue.

The next morning I went to the indicated residence and had a very satisfactory interview with Mrs. White, the adoptive mother of Ruth, one of the 13 children in the experimental group. Early in the interview she asked, "How did you find me?" and I gave the obvious reply, "Well, it wasn't easy!" (Skeels, 1966, pp. 29–30)

Table 7.1 presents for the experimental and contrast groups the pretransfer test findings and ages at time of transfer; also shown are posttransfer test

T A B L E   7 . 1   EXPERIMENTAL AND CONTRAST GROUPS: MEAN, MEDIAN, AND STANDARD DEVIATION COMPARISONS OF MENTAL GROWTH FROM FIRST TO LAST TESTS (From Skeels, 1966, p. 19)

Measure	Chrono-logical Age Months	Mental Age Months	IQ	Chrono-logical Age Months	Chrono-logical Age Months	Mental Age Months	IQ	Length of Experimental Period Months	Change in IQ, First to Last Test
				Experimental Group (N = 13)					
	Before Transfer			Transfer	After Transfer				
Mean	18.3	11.4	64.3	19.4	38.4	33.9	91.8	18.9	+27.5
Standard deviation	6.6	4.2	16.4	7.4	17.6	13.0	11.5	11.6	15
Median	16.6	10.8	65.0	17.1	36.8	30.0	93.0	14.5	+28
				Contrast Group (N = 12)					
	First Test			Transfer	Last Test				
Mean	16.6	14.2	86.7		47.2	28.7	60.5	30.7	−26.2
Standard deviation	2.9	2.9	14.3		5.9	6.4	9.7	5.8	14.1
Median	16.3	13.6	90.0		49.3	29.3	60.0	28.8	−30.0

results, length of experimental period, and changes in IQ from first to last test. The differences between the groups in test score are obvious.

In regard to the experimental group at the end of the first period of study Skeels states:

As the evidence from the research studies accumulated, concern about the future of these children increased and led to the decision that some radical measure was justified. Coincidentally, a change had occurred in the administration of the state institution for the mentally handicapped which created a favorable climate for social experimentation. Those children who happened to be in the infant to 3-year-old age range, were not ineligible for placement for legal reasons, were not acutely ill, but who were mentally retarded, became members of the experimental group. The entire project covered a span of some three years and was terminated when a change in the administration of the state school reduced the tolerance for such untidy procedures as having "house guests" in an institution.[1] The onset of World War II and the departure of the principal investigator for military service effectively closed the project. (Skeels, 1966, pp. 8–9)

Tables 7.2 and 7.3 present some of the data which illustrate the striking differences in the adult status of the two groups of subjects. For a fuller picture the reader is urged to read Skeels' monograph. Skeels' concluding statement is worthy of quotation:

At the beginning of the study, the 11 children in the experimental group evidenced marked mental retardation. The developmental trend was reversed through planned intervention during the experimental period. The program of nurturance and cognitive stimulation was followed by placement in adoptive homes that provided love and affection and normal life experiences. The normal, average intellectual level attained by the subjects in early or middle childhood was maintained into adulthood.

It can be postulated that if the children in the contrast group had been placed in suitable adoptive homes or given some other appropriate equivalent in early infancy, most or all of them would have achieved within the normal range of development, as did the experimental subjects.

It seems obvious that under present-day conditions there are still countless

---

[1] Skeels is referring to the fact when the experimental children were transferred from the orphanage to the state school for retarded children, it was considered desirable that in order to avoid the stigma of commitment "children would be accepted as 'house guests' in such institutions but would remain on the official roster of the orphanage." Skeels' statement about reduced tolerance for untidy procedures on the part of the institution brings us back to the discussion at the end of the last chapter where we tried to emphasize that "one of the major and formidable tasks of future research is to conceptualize these terms (e.g., atmosphere, attitude, motivation, conditions of learning) in ways which communicate clearly and objectively to the reader the attributes of the particular setting and their relationship to and interactions with the personalities involved." If those who are responsible for any educational setting can legitimately be characterized as having "reduced tolerance for untidy procedures" is it not reasonable to ask if there is not something in the atmosphere of the setting which may adversely affect performance of the children in the setting, however clean and tidy the setting may be physically. Skeels' very brief comment may well speak volumes. At the very least, it points to a social psychological problem of which those who intervene in various settings need to be acutely aware.

TABLE 7.2   EXPERIMENTAL AND CONTRAST GROUPS:
OCCUPATIONS OF SUBJECTS AND SPOUSES
(From Skeels, 1966, p. 33)

Case No.	Subject's Occupation	Spouse's Occupation	Female Subject's Occupation Previous to Marriage
Experimental Group:			
1[a]	Staff sergeant	Dental technician	—
2	Housewife	Laborer	Nurses' aide
3	Housewife	Mechanic	Elementary school teacher
4	Nursing instructor	Unemployed	Registered nurse
5	Housewife	Semi-skilled laborer	No work history
6	Waitress	Mechanic, semi-skilled	Beauty operator
7	Housewife	Flight engineer	Dining room hostess
8	Housewife	Foreman, construction	No work history
9	Domestic service	Unmarried	—
10[a]	Real Estate sales	Housewife	—
11[a]	Vocational counselor	Advertising copy writer[b]	—
12	Gift shop sales[c]	Unmarried	—
13	Housewife	Pressman-printer	Office-clerical
Contrast Group:			
14	Institutional inmate	Unmarried	—
15	Dishwasher	Unmarried	—
16	Deceased	—	—
17[a]	Dishwasher	Unmarried	—
18[a]	Institutional inmate	Unmarried	—
19[a]	Compositor and typesetter	Housewife	—
20[a]	Institutional inmate	Unmarried	—
21[a]	Dishwasher	Unmarried	—
22[a]	Floater	Divorced	—
23	Cafeteria (part time)	Unmarried	—
24[a]	Institutional gardener's assistant	Unmarried	—
25[a]	Institutional inmate	Unmarried	—

[a] Male.
[b] B.A. degree.
[c] Previously had worked as a licensed practical nurse.

TABLE 7.3 EXPERIMENTAL AND CONTRAST GROUP: DISTRIBUTION OF
FAMILY HEADS BY SOCIO-ECONOMIC STATUS, COMPARISON
WITH SCORE FOR U.S. NORTH CENTRAL REGION, 1960,
IN PERCENTAGES (From Skeels, 1966, p. 38)

Socio-Economic Status Score	U.S. North Central Region[a]	Experimental Group	Contrast Group
0 to 9 (low)	2.0	0	54.5
10 to 19	6.7	15.4	36.4
20 to 29	8.1	7.7	0
30 to 39	11.7	15.4	0
40 to 49	14.8	0	0
50 to 59	16.4	15.4	0
60 to 69	14.9	15.4	0
70 to 79	12.2	15.4	0
80 to 89	8.1	15.4	0
90 to 99 (high)	5.1	0	0
	100.0	100.1	99.9

[a] U.S. Bureau of the Census, 1960 (1963a), p. 6.

infants born with sound biological constitutions and potentialities for development
well within the normal range who will become mentally retarded and non-
contributing members of society unless appropriate intervention occurs. It is
suggested by the findings of this study and others published in the past 20 years
that sufficient knowledge is available to design programs of intervention to
counteract the devastating effects of poverty, sociocultural deprivation, and maternal deprivation.

Since the study was a pioneering and descriptive one involving only a small
number of cases, it would be presumptuous to attempt to identify the specific
influences that produced the changes observed. However, the contrasting outcome
between children who experienced enriched, environmental opportunities and
close emotional relationships with affectionate adults, on the one hand, and those
children who were in deprived, indifferent, and unresponsive environments, on the
other, leaves little doubt that the area is a fruitful one for further study.

It has become increasingly evident that the prediction of later intelligence
cannot be based on the child's first observed developmental status. Account must
be taken of his experiences between test and retest. Hunt has succinctly stated
that,

. . . In fact, trying to predict what the IQ of an individual child will be at
age 18 from a D.Q. obtained during his first or second year is much like
trying to predict how fast a feather might fall in a hurricane. The law of
falling bodies holds only under the specified and controlled conditions of a
vacuum. Similarly, any laws concerning the rate of intellectual growth must
take into account the series of environmental encounters which constitute the
conditions of that growth.

The divergence in mental-growth patterns between children in the experimental and contrast groups is a striking illustration of this concept.

The right of every child to be well born, well nurtured, well brought up, and well educated was enunciated in the Children's Charter of the 1930 White House Conference on Child Health and Protection. Though society strives to insure this right, for many years to come there will be children to whom it has been denied and for whom society must provide both intervention and restitution. There is need for further research to determine the optimum modes of such intervention and the most appropriate ages and techniques for initiating them. The present study suggests, but by no means delimits, either the nature of the intervention or the degree of change that can be induced.

The planning of future studies should recognize that the child interacts with his environment and does not merely passively absorb its impact. More precise and significant information on the constitutional, emotional, and response-style characteristics of the child is needed so that those environmental experiences that are most pertinent to his needs can be identified and offered in optimum sequence.

The unanswered questions of this study could form the basis for many lifelong research projects. If the tragic fate of the 12 contrast-group children provokes even a single crucial study that will help prevent such a fate for others, their lives will not have been in vain. (Skeels, 1966, pp. 56–57)

Over the years the early reports of Skeels' study have been subject to various criticisms. A. D. B. Clarke succinctly and fairly listed these criticisms:

There are several criticisms which must nevertheless be made of this study. First, the testing of the infants in both groups was done at ages when these are anyway unreliable from a long-term point of view; thus their level at the commencement would normally give little clue about subsequent development, although admittedly gross developmental anomalies (particularly motor) seemed to have been present. Second, the groups were by no means matched even for I.Q. The experimental group had a lower mean initial I.Q. than the control; this raises the possibility of unknown selection factors. The experimental periods for both groups was markedly different; the experimental group had a shorter time on the average in better conditions, while the control group had a longer period under extremely poor conditions (30 months versus 18 months). A straightforward comparison of the effects of the two environments cannot therefore legitimately be made. Third, the inclusion of a control group was apparently an afterthought at the conclusion of the main experiment. Clearly, proper planning would have involved a control group from the outset. In a sense there was some sort of control, although it was not as efficient as it could have been; it is of interest that in both groups the initial I.Q.'s at these early ages gave little prediction of a relatively short-term outcome. The fourth point is that although members of both groups had apparently the same early experiences in the orphanage, they were not identically impaired at the commencement of the experiment. Thus, the initial differences between them were clearly due to factors other than environmental ones in infancy. Later, however, environmental factors apparently reversed the relationship. This must mean that unknown selection factors were operating, although, in fairness, it must be added that the initial superiority of the control group should have aided rather than penalized it. This, then, is an extremely interesting study, which, however, is not free from criticism. The results are strongly suggestive, and more recent work seems to have supported the findings. (Clarke, 1958)

With the final report by Skeels it is still not possible to answer criticisms having to do with the unknown selection factors or the different environmental conditions (and the variables of which they are comprised) to which the children in the two groups were subject. But the final report does buttress Clarke's opinion that the findings are important and in line with other research findings.[2]

We should not leave Skeels' study without emphasizing a point made in previous chapters, particularly in relation to the studies by Kirk (1958) and Blatt and Garfunkel (1965). We refer here to the complexities and realities of field research in which the investigator has far from the degree of control one can exercise in laboratory-type experimentation. All research is subject to the fallibilities of researchers, e.g., failure to anticipate difficulties or to exercise appropriate controls, or unwittingly to indulge one's pet theory or hopes, or to overgeneralize from limited data. When, to researcher fallibility are added the problems of studying individuals in fantastically complicated settings over which the researcher has far less control than he needs or would like to have, the consumer of such research reports must develop that kind of critical appreciation which reflects dispassionate, critical scrutiny and a sympa-

---

[2] Hunt has perhaps done the most scholarly and thoughtful review and analysis of the relations between intelligence and experience. The point of view which we have presented in this and previous chapters is similar to that of Hunt but his treatment of the problem goes far beyond problems of mental subnormality, and the reader with a special interest in the general problem of intelligence and environments is urged to consult his important book. The final paragraph in Hunt's book clearly indicates an opinion which seems supported by the existing research literature: "Further, in the light of these theoretical considerations and the evidence concerning the effects of early experience on adult problem-solving in animals, it is no longer unreasonable to consider that it might be feasible to discover ways to govern the encounters that children have with their environments, especially during the early years of their development, to achieve a substantially faster rate of intellectual development and a substantially higher adult level of intellectual capacity. Moreover, inasmuch as the optimum rate of intellectual development would mean also self-directing interest and curiosity and genuine pleasure in intellectual activity, promoting intellectual development properly need imply nothing like the grim urgency which has been associated with "pushing" children. Furthermore, these procedures, insofar as they tended to maximize each child's potential for intellectual development, would not decrease individual differences in intellectual capacity as assessed by tests but would not increase them. The discovery of the ways to govern the encounters children have with their environments for this purpose would require a great deal of expensive and difficult investigation of the effects of various kinds of early experience on later intellectual capacity. Even after the discovery of the ways, if they can be found, the task of effecting the necessary changes within the culture in child-rearing practices and in educational procedures would be Herculean. Nevertheless, ours is a technological culture of increasing complexity. Its development continually demands an ever larger proportion of the population with intellectual capacity at the higher levels. It calls also for intellectual giants to solve the problems that become increasingly complex. The fact that it is reasonable to hope to find ways of raising the level of intellectual capacity in a majority of the population makes it a challenge to do the necessary research. It is one of the major challenges of our times. It is a challenge, moreover, where the chances are fairly good that the behavioral sciences can make a contribution of great social, as well as theoretical, significance." (Hunt, 1961)

thetic understanding of what the field-research investigator inevitably encounters. This statement is not intended to be a plea to be "soft" on field
research but rather a plea that the reader's perspective take account of the
complexities of such research as well as the requirements of scientific procedures and logical thinking. It would indeed be unfortunate if the absence of
such a perspective intimidated researchers from doing field research because of
the expectation that the messiness of such research will subject them to the
critical brickbats of their colleagues.

Preinstitutional and Institutional Status

One of the questions that can be raised about the early status of Skeels'
institutional subjects (the experimental group) is to what extent their gain in
test score was a function of *removal from* the orphanage environment. In
other words, without denying the effects of the more stimulating environment
to which they went, one cannot overlook the possible effects of sheer removal
from a poor environment. Numerous investigators (McKay, 1942; Roberts,
1945; Spaulding, 1946; Burt, 1937; Guertin, 1949) have presented data on
increases in test scores with change in environment. Clarke and Clarke
(1954) noted similar test-score increases in institutionalized retardates, "in
some cases quite large increases in IQ, ranging from a decrease of five points
to an increase of 25 points on the Wechsler-Bellevue Test, Form 1, over a
time interval of about 18 months." By use of a control group the Clarkes were
able to indicate that these test-score increases could not be accounted for by
the effects of test practice, errors of measurement, or underestimation at the
time of the first test. A. D. B. Clarke then collected test-retest data over a 27
month interval on a representative sample of 59 institutionalized individuals.

Almost half of these patients showed gains of 8 points or more, and it was obvious
that for the majority of such persons the increments occurring over this relatively
short interval did not represent the total change which the individual had already
made or would make in the future. . . .
  Several hypotheses were examined to explain the results; control group data
disposed of the possibility of test practice or initial underestimation due to
nervousness affecting to any extent the data. There was a small but significant
tendency for those of lower I.Q. to make the larger changes ($r = -0.311$), but no
other relevant relationships emerged except for one. This final hypothesis was that
those whose history included early adverse environmental circumstances would be
those who made the larger increases. Twelve criteria such as "neglect,"
"N.S.P.C.C. intervention," "cruelty," etc. were formulated, and an independent
investigator, who knew neither the patients nor their test scores, applied them to
the 59 case histories, separating them into two groups, those from very bad homes
and the remainder (many of whom came from fairly bad homes). The former
showed a mean increment of 9.7, S.D. 6.3, and the latter a mean of 4.1, S.D. 4.9,
very similar to control group data.

The difference between the gains made by the two groups was significant at the 0.1 percent level, and confirmed the hypothesis that a record of early adverse experiences was related to I.Q. improvement, often many years later. This suggests that such experiences tend to retard mental development for many years, after which the effects begin to fade, I.Q. increments thus occurring. It was concluded that the increments seemed to be more the effect of being removed from a very adverse environment rather than of entry into a relatively better one, since there was no correlation with length of institutionalization, nor with particular type of treatment and training. These changes were related to I.Q. variability in normals, being different only in three respects: first, they tended to be unidirectional; second, they were relatively large in relation to the fairly short time-interval; and third; they took place at ages when mental growth is normally assumed to have ceased. It was suggested that further research might show how such relatively spontaneous changes could be both accelerated and improved. (Clarke, 1958)

In addition to these data Clarke (1958, pp. 109–115) discusses further studies of his and others which seemed to support the conclusion that "while early *negative* environmental influence had profoundly adverse effects, *positive* stimulation in adolescence or later excited little influence upon the IQ. It seemed that entry into any non-adverse environment would allow intellectual damage to fade to varying extents. Socially, however, these special conditions had resulted in profound changes in the subjects."

The interesting results by the Clarkes on the significance of the degree of preinstitutional deprivation were also the focus of a series of studies by Zigler and his colleagues. However, Zigler's main interest was on conceptualizing the relationship between motivation, social reinforcement, and social deprivation, the latter measured by a scale including such items as the economic circumstances of the home, the physical treatment accorded the child, the familial configuration, the adherence by the parents to social norms, and the attitude of the parents toward the child. In most of Zigler's studies social reinforcement was a function of the amount and type of supportive behavior shown by the experimenter to a child who was presented with a simple, monotonous, open-ended "put the marble in the hole game." The measure of motivation was usually the amount of time the child spent with the game under two conditions: supportive and nonsupportive.

In his first study Zigler (1961) found that institutionalized familial retardates experienced a great amount of preinstitutional social deprivation and that their performance on certain tasks varied as a function of the amount of social deprivation experienced. It was Zigler's hypothesis that social deprivation results in a heightened motivation to maintain interaction with a normal adult and to secure approval from him through compliance and persistence.[3]

---

[3] In Chapter 5 the point was made that concepts like culture deprivation and social deprivation tended to be sociological rather than psychological concepts, i.e., they are characterizations of groups of people and these concepts do not allow one to cope with behavioral variations within groups. One of Zigler's contributions has been his attempt to relate a measure of social deprivation to variations in individual motivation.

In a second study, using all available subjects from the first study three years earlier, Zigler and Williams investigated the proposition "that some systematic change in the effectiveness of social reinforcement occurs with longer institutionalization." The following are the major findings:

1. The results of the original testing clearly supported the view that the effectiveness of adult attention and approval is related to the degree of social deprivation experienced prior to institutionalization. Upon first examination of the children's performance on the same game 3 years later, this positive relationship between preinstitutional social deprivation and the effectiveness of social reinforcement appears to have vanished. All the significant effects found during retesting appear to be the result of the reinforcement conditions, while during original testing, performance was unrelated to the reinforcement conditions.

2. . . . children with the better preinstitutional histories show a much greater increase between the two testings than do children with the poorer histories. This finding points up the error of conceptualizing institutional living as if it affected all children in the same manner. The present study suggests that for children who have suffered the greater amount of social deprivation prior to being institutionalized, institutional living adds relatively little to the already high motivation for social reinforcers. Indeed, in light of the extreme social deprivation experienced by many institutionalized retardates, it would be surprising if institutional living were not less socially depriving for these subjects than their original homes, thus resulting in a lessened effectiveness of social reinforcers in the experimental situation. Children who have had comparatively good homes, on the other hand, have less motivation for social reinforcers early in their institutionalization. However, the institution is a relatively depriving environment for these children, and thus longer institutionalization produces a greater increase in the effectiveness of social reinforcers.

3. [An unexpected finding was the general decrease in IQ's between the two testings, contrary to the findings by Clarke and Clarke.] The failure to replicate the findings of Clarke and Clarke may be due to two factors: their subjects were older and had been institutionalized at a later age than the retardates used in this study; and the IQ changes reported by Clarke and Clarke took place during 2 years of institutionalization, while the IQ changes in the present study were based on 5 years of institutionalization.[4]

The early and later studies by Zigler and his colleagues (Zigler, 1963a, 1963b; Zigler, 1964; Butterfield and Zigler, 1965; Harter and Zigler, 1968) are of major significance because they draw our attention to the subtle as well as obvious effects of institutionalization and the variety of complex variables (preinstitutional status, the nature and amount of social reinforcements, birth order, attitudes toward peers and adults, and implied self-attitudes) which need to be better understood. There is, however, another significance to Zigler's studies which anyone concerned with the mentally retarded cannot afford to overlook: *What Zigler has demonstrated is that the testing and experimental situation—forms of interaction between an adult and a child—ex-*

---

[4] Zigler and Williams note in this connection that increases early and decreases later in institutionalization are consistent with similar findings on normal institutionalized children. (Zigler and Williams, 1963, pp. 203–204)

quisitely reflect and are affected by current and historical interpersonal experiences.[5] The psychologist or experimenter who views his numerical results apart from consideration of these experiences demonstrates a narrowness of view which current research has effectively discredited. Testing of the retarded child, institutionalized or not, is as demanding of knowledge and sensitivity as is the testing of other children—in light of the decisions which are often made on the basis of tests it could be argued that testing the retarded child demands the utmost in knowledge and sensitivity.[6]

INSTITUTIONALLY REARED INFANTS

Our primary purpose in returning to this problem is to indicate to the reader that research findings and social policy often are, unfortunately, in little relationship with each other. The study by Skeels is but one of the oldest dealing with the effects of institutional living on infants. Gesell and Armatruda have pointed out that the institutional infant may be

. . . propped up, possibly at regular intervals, and for predetermined periods; but not always at the psychological moments which are most favorable; nor with the endless variations and surprises which naturally enter into the flexible living of a domestic circle. The caretaker, having propped him for the sitting-up period, even places a toy at his disposal. But the propping is of necessity done in a somewhat hurried and impersonal manner, because the very same attention must be repeated for a sizeable number of babies. There can be no waiting for and adaptation to psychological moments. There is too much to be done. Nor is there much time for improvisation-play with the baby. . . . The institution tends to channelize the psychology of the baby by restricted and somewhat standardized impacts. It delimits the scope of the infant's behavior by paucity of impacts. This paucity has nothing less than an impoverishing effect. (Gesell and Armatruda, 1947, p. 321)

A systematic approach to the problem is represented by Goldfarb's (1943a,b; 1944; 1945a,b; 1947) studies of children who spent their early infancy in an institution. In one of these studies, 15 children who had been institutionalized at the average age of 4.5 months and transferred to foster homes

---

[5] It is not possible to describe in detail the many studies done by Zigler and his colleagues or to give a blow-by-blow account of how his conceptualizations determined and were in turn changed by each investigation. As we shall see in the next chapter, his studies on institutionalized and noninstitutionalized populations gave rise to new questions and studies of the climate of institutions. The reader interested in a more complete presentation of his theorizing and research should consult other of his publications.

[6] From another vantage point and with an intellectually normal population of children Sarason, Davidson, Lighthall, Waite, and Ruebush (1960), Sarason, Hill, and Zimbardo (1964), and Hill and Sarason (1966) have demonstrated that scores derived from testing and experimental situations have to be understood in terms of current and historical interpersonal experiences. In fact, the picture which emerges of the socially deprived, institutionalized, familial retardate in the testing and experimental situations—his fearfulness, compliance, need for approval, etc.—is far from dissimilar to the picture of the "high test anxious" child described by Sarason, *et al.*

at approximately 37 months were compared to 15 children who had experienced foster-home placement from early infancy. The occupational status of the mothers of the institutional children tended to be higher than that of the mothers of the foster-home group; both were equal in educational achievement. The foster homes to which the institutional children were subsequently sent seemed to have more favorable advantages for a child than the foster homes of the control group. When both groups were given psychological tests at 34 and 43 months of age, the institutional children received significantly lower test scores, showed immature speech development, and in general presented many more indications of maladjustive behavior. When similar studies were made with older age groups who also differed in regard to early institutional experience the incidence of feeblemindedness was markedly greater in the institutional group. Their behavior was characterized by aimlessness; impulsivity; inability to achieve or maintain personal relationships, respond to the needs of others, or express personal feeling.

Cold, isolated, depriving experience during the first months of life impedes the normal development of such mature qualities as personal security and independence, a deep, personal, reciprocating interest in others, appropriate inhibition, and a reflective, organizing mental approach to problems. The very absence of these qualities in deprived children has also made it very difficult to reach them on more than a casual basis or to affect significantly their adjustment subsequent to transfer from the institution. Treatment efforts, case work activity, and the best wishes of foster parents have been of limited consequence where the damage resulting from psychological privation first occurred at a very early age and was then exaggerated by a prolonged elaboration of the privation experience over several years. (Goldfarb, 1947)

The most recent study in this area was reported by Provence and Lipton in 1962. They studied clinically and longitudinally 75 infants in an orphanage and an equal number of family-reared infants. The following excerpts illustrate some of their most important findings with the institutional infants:

The first easily observable difference occurred in the second month and concerned a specific characteristic in the way the infants reacted to being held. There was a decrease in the extent to which they made appropriate postural adjustments to being held or carried. They did not adapt their bodies well to the arms of the adult, they were not cuddly, and one noted a lack in pliability. We do not refer to hypertonicity or muscle spasticity. All reflex behavior was normal. The best description is that they felt something like sawdust dolls; they moved, they bent easily at the proper joints, but they felt stiff or wooden as they were perceived through the holder's own sensory apparatus. These findings do not lend themselves to more precise description, because it is difficult to put into words the impression the infants conveyed. However, what the infant's body conveyed to the body of the holding person was distinct and real.

. . .

. . . observations in regard to the development of head control in the institutionalized babies compared to family-reared infants are of interest. In the average baby, the ability to control his head when he is pulled from his back into the sitting position occurs between four and five months of age. In the institutionalized babies this type of head control was delayed. Interestingly, however, most of the institutionalized babies of five months or over could be "taught" within a single testing session to control the head by the procedure of repeatedly being pulled to sit in a playful way by the examiner. They seemed, after a few trials, to be able to anticipate what was about to happen, to get set, and thereby to control the head. This appears to be a clear example of the interrelationship between readiness in maturational terms and the influence of experience. The capacity to control the head in the pull-to-sit play involves not only intactness of the neuromuscular apparatus but the capacity to anticipate and respond to the actions of the adult. Thus it reflects learning as well, and is based upon experience.

. . .

When one encountered the institutionalized infants at three to four months of age, one was immediately impressed with the lack of vocalizations and the intensity of their looking. The adult was looked at—even stared at—when near at hand or across the room, and the baby used all his available motor skills to keep the adult within his visual field. This visual attentiveness was such a prominent part of the infant's behavior that it was often difficult to get him to look at the test materials, and the examiner found it necessary to be as inconspicuous as possible when presenting them. The looking was accompanied by various facial expressions: sometimes the face was sober and immobile; often there was a smile; at times there was a wrinkling of the brow producing an expression that one was tempted to call puzzled. The looking, which was unusually intense and preoccupying, was the striking thing, however.

. . .

In the second six months one saw no evidence of increasing personal attachment to a particular person, nor did one encounter manifestations of aggression toward others. In those infants where a more positive response to the familiar attendant than to strange examiner existed, one was still startled by the tenuousness of the tie and the minimal emotional involvement of both parties. The evidence of understanding and participation in such traditional games as peek-a-boo, pat-a-cake, and others was markedly delayed. Indeed, all varieties of playful activity which are so much a part of the interchange between mothers and babies, and which the babies continue and elaborate on their own, were underdeveloped or scarcely ever seen in the institutionalized infants.

. . .

In the last months of the first year the language deficit was even more striking. An occasional mama or dada sound could be evoked after much effort from the adult, but these remained meaningless, nonspecific vocalizations. Altogether there was minimal vocalization of any kind. The repertoire of sounds through which the average baby by this time expresses pleasure, displeasure, anger, eagerness, anticipation, gleefulness, and excitement, or vocalizes something that sounds like a question or interjection was virtually nonexistent. None of the infants had even a single specific word by the end of the first year. Their understanding of the adult's language was also retarded, but less so than was language production.

. . .

The deviant nature and delayed development of the behavior with toys in the institutionalized infants was another aspect of their difficulty. The earliest visual and acoustic responses as well as the early approach and grasping activity were very similar to those of the normal infant. From about four to five months on through the first year there was a decrease of investment and in the approach, grasping, and exploitation of the toys. The looking, banging, biting, feeling, shaking, sucking, fingering, poking, dropping, and picking up again, which in the average baby become more elaborate day after day, were much less prominent in the institutionalized infants. They appeared to get some pleasure from the toys, but there was never any evidence of displeasure when they were removed. No evidence of preference of one toy over another was seen in the first year, and efforts to recover a lost toy were virtually nonexistent.

Additionally, a marked delay in the development of the mental concept of the existence of the inanimate object was characteristic of each of the institutionalized babies. When a toy with which he had been playing was covered or screened, it was as though it no longer existed. He might look briefly puzzled before he turned to something else; he did not look or search for it at the age one would expect him to be able to do so. It appeared that the hidden toy either was not remembered or was not important enough to be recovered. His failure to solve the problem presented by this situation continued throughout the first year. The capacity to evaluate the situation and to persist until the problem was solved (obtain toy) was greatly impaired. We suggest that this reflects a deficit in thinking in these babies. (Provence and Lipton, 1962)

Provence and Lipton (1962, Appendix A) present data which indicated that the developmental quotient of the institutionalized infants decreased over the year e.g., the *mean* quotient between 14–26 weeks was 101, between 27–29 weeks it was 87, and between 40–52 weeks was 85. It is also of interest that for the same periods the *range* of developmental quotients was 83–125, 72–107, and 72–92. Provence and Lipton were aware of Pinneau's (1955) criticisms of infant studies which did not take into account that it is characteristic of infant tests that they result in higher scores in the early months of life and lower scores in the later months of the first year. To cope with this criticism Provence and Lipton compared their orphanage infants with a group of 75 foster-home infants who had always lived in a family setting. They found that the decline in scores was significantly greater for the institutional infants.

That there is a discrepancy between what research and theory compellingly suggest, on the one hand, and social policy about institutionalization, on the other hand, needs no further documentation. Provence and Lipton voice the opinions of those who have been concerned with the problem:

Realistically, one must assume that institutions for infants will continue to serve a function not yet possible to fulfill in other ways. While they cannot duplicate the good home in the quality of maternal care, they need not be places in which an infant is damaged. They can be used in a constructive way as a temporary living situation, if they are adequately staffed and the staff includes people who understand some of the basic needs of infants—and these include, as our study convincingly shows, more than good physical care. We want to emphasize again that the infants in this study were meticulously cared for physically. But there must be more care and more personalized care for each baby. This can be effected (1) by an increase in the total number of persons available to care directly for the infants. It is both inhuman and unrealistic to expect that one person could provide anything like adequate maternal care for ten to twenty babies. Staff can be increased both by having more personnel and by the use of volunteers; (2) by an increase in the amount of time devoted to the care of every baby; (3) by a decrease in the number of different individuals caring for each baby. This requires that each of the staff members in the institutions take care of only a few babies, and that they care for the same babies day after day. They must have enough time to devote to them so that they can provide both the amount of care and the personal interest that are of such importance.

The implementation of a program designed to prevent the adverse effects of maternal deprivation requires support from the general public and from the various professional people involved—social workers, physicians, nurses, lawyers, legislators, and from the individuals and boards that set the policies of institutions, public health agencies and social agencies. It will involve changes in legal procedures; it will require greater numbers and better trained child-care workers, and a shift in cultural attitudes toward infants and children without families. Financial support while essential is not sufficient in itself to effect the changes that are considered necessary to provide better care for infants. (Provence and Lipton, 1962)

Since these and similar recommendations have been made in the past, one cannot avoid asking why so little has been done to implement them. We shall postpone an attempt to deal with this question until the next chapter in which we discuss the climate of institutions and the fate of recommendations for change and innovation.

The climate
of institutions and the problem
# of change

In the previous chapter we discussed some of the major studies concerned with the possible effects of institutionalization. One cannot study institutional *effects* without speculating about the nature of institutional environment and its probable variations within and among institutions. Until very recently, however, there has been little or no research on what may be termed the climate or culture of institutions. In 1958, Sarason and Gladwin posed the problem in the context of a discussion of the role of psychological and cultural factors in the etiology of cultural or familial mental retardation:

From the standpoint of our society one of the most neglected research areas concerns the psychological changes which are associated with institutionalization. When one realizes how many millions of dollars are spent in building and maintaining our institutions, it is surprising that very little research has been done to study the psychological changes which institutionalization brings about. Institutionalization involves a drastic change for the individual and there is every reason

131

for assuming that it is experienced as a stressful one involving (a) separation from loved or familiar figures, (b) pressures to adjust to a completely new physical and interpersonal (peer and adult) environment, (c) confusion and resentment about their helplessness, (d) anxiety in relation to the future. In the case of the mentally retarded individual, who usually comes from an unfavorable family situation, we are usually struck by the material differences between home and institution. But this is the way we view the change and one should not assume, therefore, that the child perceives it the way we do. What to us is a psychologically unfavorable family situation, and what may even be an unpleasant one to the child, may in the process of institutionalization be perceived by the child as his only source of security. As important as immediate effects are those of prolonged institutionalization. It is our clinical impression that the major effects of prolonged institutionalization are four-fold: (a) overt conformity to the institutional culture at the expense of personal spontaneity and expression, (b) excessive phantasying, especially about the "outside world," (c) avoidance and fear of new problem-solving situations, and (d) excessive dependence on the institutional culture, which becomes most apparent when the possibility of leaving the institution arises. The effects of institutionalization undoubtedly vary with age at commitment. In stressing the possible deleterious effects of institutionalization we are not unmindful that we are dealing with a very complex problem.

. . . We expressed the opinion that the bulk of the high grade cases in our institutions differed in no fundamental respect from those we have called mentally retarded but are not institutionalized. One could argue against such a conclusion on the grounds that the test scores of those institutionalized are probably significantly lower than the scores of those who are in the community and that such a difference may reflect a "basic" difference between the two groups. From all that we have said thus far in this report, it should be apparent that we do not think the grounds for such an argument are tenable. However, it should be noted that we do not have systematic studies on this problem. For example, we are not aware of any systematic study on factors associated with variations in intellectual performance within families of retarded children who have been institutionalized. The problems we are raising here seem very similar to that of why some children become delinquent while others in the same family or neighborhood do not. If studies of mental retardation similar to those of the Gluecks on juvenile delinquency were carried out, our understanding of the problem would not only be increased but, as in the case of delinquency, we would have a more rational basis for picking out much earlier than we now can those mentally retarded children who are likely to require institutionalization. (Sarason and Gladwin, 1958)

There are many reasons why research on institutions has been sparse; two require mention at this point. The first reason is that it is the rare institution that has the understanding and courage either to "look into itself" or to have "outsiders" come in to evaluate the ways in which the organizational structure and the quality of social and professional relationships affect those who are the primary concern of the institution. As we know well from research with industrial institutions, administrative staff do not look with enthusiasm on "being studied" and they, together with the rest of humanity, do not happily contemplate the possibility of real change in their thinking and actions. The second reason is that we are far from having the theoretical statements or relevant methodologies for studying so complicated a thing as an institution.[1] It is encouraging, however, that in recent years there has been an increasing interest in the practical and theoretical aspects of the problem and one may expect that as this interest gains momentum our understanding of the problem will deepen.[2]

Christmas in Purgatory

Around Christmas in 1965 Blatt and Kaplan (1966) visited five institutions for the retarded in four different states and were able to secure photographs of children, activities, and practices. In each institution they had secured the permission and cooperation of one important staff member who knew that a professional photographer, with a small camera attached to his belt, would be snapping pictures. This attempt to obtain a photographic essay of institutional living was motivated by Blatt's experiences in many institutions and the discrepancy between reality and the official statements and descriptions of institutional programs and practices. There was also the desire to bring to public attention a sorry state of affairs of which the public had little or no knowledge and, perhaps, no desire to know. Four of the institutions were large state facilities and these were compared to a "contrast" state institution which was relatively new and obviously possessing a different climate. The contrast between this latter and the other four institutions is a cause of both hope and despair—hope because of what can be and despair because of what so frequently is.

---

[1] It would, in our opinion, be a mistake if the reader were to view this discussion only in terms of the usual type of institution and fail to see that the problem is of far more general significance, i.e., that the problem goes beyond institutions for the retarded or defective child and holds also for a public school, a hospital of any kind, a community agency, a company, etc.

[2] In the first volume of the *International Review of Research in Mental Retardation* (Ellis, 1966)—a volume which organizes research around specific problems and theoretical points of view—five of the contributors (Bijou, Zigler, Haywood and Tapp, and Spradlin and Guardeau) specifically discuss the importance of institutional environments. It is our impression that there are at least three factors contributing to this increased interest. First, the renewed vigor and sophistication of "behavioristic theory," best illustrated by Bijou's (1966) chapter in which the importance of attending to the details of the environment and their reinforcing properties is succinctly and lucidly presented. Second, the attempts of the behavior theorists to apply their theories to clinical problems in natural settings, a willingness described by Spradlin and Guardeau (1966) in their review of the relevant research. Third, the demonstrable changes which those attempts have effected and the contrast between these changes and what ordinarily happens (as we shall see) in the natural setting, e.g., an institution. The total effect of this behavioristic approach has been to underline the importance of the setting in shaping behavior and how focusing on and controlling "stimulus settings" can produce desired changes. How far this behavioristic approach takes us—and how adequate it will be for conceptualizing complex interaction systems—remains to be seen. There can be little doubt that it has been productive and that it has helped direct our attention in a systematic way to the conditions of behavior modification.

It is always difficult, and in a basic sense impossible, to use words to convey pictures. The reader is urged to view the pictures in order to obtain for himself some feel for the atmosphere of certain institutions and the need for making institutions an object of scrutiny and study.[3] The title of the book, *Christmas in Purgatory*, well conveys the degrading circumstances in which many institutional children live. The following is from the introduction to the book:

There is a hell. It is on earth. And, in America, we have our own special inferno. We were visitors there during the Christmas Season, 1965.

During the early fall of that year, a United States Senator, Robert Kennedy, visited several of his state's institutions for the mentally retarded. His reaction to these visits were widely published in our various news media. These disclosures shocked millions of Americans as well as infuriated scores of public office holders and professional persons responsible for the care and treatment of the mentally retarded.

In the main, a segment of the general public was numbed because it is difficult for "uninvolved" people to believe that in our country in 1965, human beings are being treated less humanely, with less care, and under more deplorable conditions than are animals. A number of the "involved" citizenry—i.e., those who legislate and budget for institutions for the mentally retarded and those who administer them—were infuriated because the Senator reacted to only the worst of what he had seen, not to the worthwhile programs that he might have. Further, this latter group was severely critical of the Senator for taking "whirlwind" tours and, in the light of just a few hours of observation, damning entire institutions and philosophies.

During the time of these visits the senior author was a participant in a research project at The Seaside, A State of Connecticut Regional Center for the mentally retarded. The superintendent of The Seaside, Fred Finn, and he spent a considerable amount of time discussing the ongoing raging debate between Senator Kennedy and his Governor, Nelson Rockefeller. We concluded the following. It does not require a scientific background or a great deal of observation to determine that one has entered the "land of the living dead." It does not require too imaginative a mind or too sensitive a proboscis to realize that one has stumbled into a dung hill, regardless of how it is camouflaged. It is quite irrelevant how well the rest of an institution's program is being fulfilled if one is concerned about that part of it which is terrifying. No amount of rationalization can mitigate that which, to many of us, is cruel and inhuman treatment.

It is true that a short visit to the back wards of an institution for the mentally retarded will not provide, even for the most astute observer, any clear notion of the antecedents of the problems observed, the complexities of dealing with them, or ways to correct them. We can believe that the Senator did not fully comprehend the subtleties, the tenuous relationships, the grossness of budgetary inequities, the long history of political machinations, the extraordinary difficulty in providing care for severely mentally retarded patients, the unavailability of highly trained professional leaders, and the near-impossibility in recruiting dedicated attendants and

---

[3] The reader may wish to consult a series of newspaper articles beginning in the January 23, 1967, *Boston Traveler*. These articles describe the experiences of a reporter who obtained an attendant's job in a state institution for the mentally retarded. They suggest that Blatt and Kaplan's photographic essay may not be extreme in its import.

ward personnel. But, we know, as well as do thousands of others who have been associated with institutions for the mentally retarded, that what Senator Kennedy claimed to have seen he did see. In fact, we know personally of few institutions for the mentally retarded in the United States that are completely free of dirt and filth, odors, naked patients groveling in their own feces, children in locked cells, horribly crowded dormitories, and understaffed and wrongly staffed facilities. (Blatt and Kaplan, 1966)

We have not described this photographic essay with the intent to alarm, infuriate, or argue—nor was this the intent of Blatt and Kaplan. The significances of their work may be put as follows:

1. It forces into public awareness the question of how frequent these conditions are. The question is not do they exist but their prevalence.
2. It confronts the professional community with a problem area which they have neglected and which involves both scientific and professional issues, scientific because of the conceptual and methodological developments which will be needed if our understanding of institutions is to be deepened, and professional because action and change will be required.[4]

When the sensibilities of the public and professional community are aroused, it is understandable that actions will be recommended and carried out, and this is as it should be. However, it is precisely in these situations of public arousal that one falls prey to oversimplified explanations and solutions. This caveat was stated by one of the present authors (SBS) in his preface to the Blatt and Kaplan publication:

The contents, verbal and visual, of this book produced little surprise in me. Initially, it brought back a flood of memories surrounding a number of visits I made to various institutions twenty-five years ago when I first began to work in the field of mental retardation. As the years went on, it became increasingly clear to me that the conditions I saw—and which are documented in the present book—were not due to evil or incompetent or cruel people but rather to a conception of human potential and an attitude toward innovation which when applied to the mentally defective, result in a self-fulfilling prophecy. That is, if one thinks that defective children are almost beyond help, one acts toward them in ways which then confirm one's assumptions. This is similar to the situation several decades ago when, in many psychiatric hospitals, the diagnosis of schizophrenia contained the prognosis that the sick patients would never improve. That most of these patients did not improve did not reflect the validity of the diagnosis but the dishearteningly effective way in which state hospitals unwittingly went about confirming their diagnoses. In contrasting one institution (The Seaside), which views the defective child in one way, with other institutions which hold to another viewpoint, the

---

[4] The deplorable conditions visually described by Blatt and Kaplan apparently are not confined to institutions for the mentally retarded and it would be a mistake if the reader did not grasp the fact that the problem is more general and involves helping institutions of all kinds. For example, if the reader will consult New York City newspapers beginning June, 1966 he will find conditions described in city hospitals that are very similar to those described by Blatt and Kaplan.

authors have incisively made the point that the basic problem is in the realm of conceptions about human behavior and its amenability to change under specified conditions.

I would not deny that increased appropriations will make for better physical care. But spending more money is easy compared to the problem of how one gets people to change their conceptions and to view innovation and experimentation as necessities rather than as subversive suggestions or the terminal points of the meanderings of the academic mind.

At the end of this chapter we shall return to the nature of solutions and how they follow from the ways in which the problem can be formulated.

Aspects of the Institutional Culture

By using a "contrast" institution it was one of Blatt and Kaplan's aims to suggest that children in differing institutions look and act differently. Perhaps the first attempt formally to study the question is that by Butterfield and Zigler. Their introductory statement deserves quotation rather than paraphrase.

In research on mental retardation comparisons are frequently made between normal children living at home and institutionalized retardates. An implicit assumption in such a comparison is that all variables except intelligence which are capable of influencing the dependent measures are randomly distributed across the two populations. A number of investigators have now demonstrated that such an assumption is unwarranted (Stevenson & Fahel, 1961; Green & Zigler, 1962; Kaufman, 1963; Zigler, 1963). These studies have indicated that many behavioral differences found between these two populations are related to institutionalization rather than to intelligence.

A danger in these latter studies is that they may be interpreted as supporting the view that institutionalization represents a homogeneous psychological variable. That such a view is widespread is indicated by the generally accepted practice of equating institutionalization with social deprivation. The error here is the failure to recognize that institutionalization refers only to some vague social status whereas social deprivation must reflect specific social interactions. Anyone who treats institutionalization as a homogeneous entity must assume that certain critical social interactions are constant from institution to institution. It would be difficult to defend such a proposition in light of the empirical work of Spitz and the conclusion of Sarason and Gladwin that relatively little work has been done to investigate the exact nature of institutionalization.

In the course of their research the authors have been impressed by differences in the behavior of comparable groups of retarded children who resided in different institutions. The purpose of the present study was the experimental exploration of such institutional effects. Two residential schools for the mentally retarded in the same state having identical admission policies were employed. The social climates of the two schools impressed the authors as being strikingly different. In institution A, every effort is made to provide a noninstitutional, i.e., homelike, environment. School classes, residential units at the younger age levels, and frequent social events are all coeducational. Meals are prepared in the living units where the children eat in small groups. Emphasis is placed upon individual responsibility rather than upon external control by the staff. No buildings are locked; and all children who are ambulatory freely move about the grounds to school, work, and recreational activities. Isolation is rarely used as a punishment. Essentially no security force is employed. There are a large number of small residential units and a number of factors are considered before assigning a child to a unit, e.g., age, sex, intellectual level, the child's attitude toward the caretakers and other children residing in the unit, and their attitude toward him.

In institution B, little effort is made to provide a homelike environment for the children. School classes, all residential units, movies, and most other social events are segregated by sex. Meals are prepared and children eat in a large central dining room with virtually no individual supervision. Emphasis is upon external control of the children by the staff rather than upon inculcating individual responsibility. All buildings are locked, and no child moves about the grounds unattended by an employee. Isolation is frequently used as a punishment. A large staff of security officers patrols the grounds regularly. Residential units are all of the large, dormitory type, and no effort is made to group children except by the gross criteria of sex, age, and general intellectual level.

The climate at institution A strikes one as being much more conductive to constructive, supportive interactions between the children and their adult care-takers than the climate at institution B. In light of earlier work concerning the effects of social deprivation on children's desire for social reinforcement, one would hypothesize that children in institution B would be more motivated to receive social reinforcement than the children in institution A. To test this hypothesis children from both institutions were compared on a measure known to be sensitive to differences in need for social reinforcement. (Butterfield and Zigler, 1965a)

Butterfield and Zigler describe two experiments utilizing the marble-in-the-hole game. In the first experiment four groups of familial retardates (two groups from each of the two institutions) were run under support and nonsupport conditions. They found a clear difference in that children in Institution B (considered a less supportive climate than Institution A) played the game longer than children in Institution A, a result in keeping with the hypothesis that the more depriving the climate the greater the need to receive social reinforcement from the experimenter. Because in this first experiment the experimenters were aware of the differences in the climates of the two institutions and of the hypothesized effects, a second study was done with naive experimenters.

The findings of both studies clearly indicate that differing social climates result in different performance on a simple motivational type task. Results obtained with this task in other studies, as well as certain data in the present investigation, suggest that these differences in performance reflect differences in motivation for social reinforcement. Such a conclusion is consistent with the view that the more social deprivation experienced by the child, the greater will be his motivation for social interaction and support. A global assessment of the two institutions certainly suggested that one institution was more depriving than the other. However, it is far from clear what specific aspects of the social-psychological environments produced the differences found in this study. (Butterfield and Zigler, 1965a)

It should go without saying that the study of institutional climates is of major significance for increasing our understanding of the relationships between environments and behavior, relationships which have both theoretical and practical significances. From a theoretical standpoint these studies force us to face the inadequacies of present theories for handling individual–social-system relationships. Most, if not all, theories tend to be theories of individuals and say little of a systematic nature about the different social systems of which the individual is inevitably a part. As we saw in earlier chapters, this incompleteness in theory was a major obstacle in our understanding the significance of studies having to do with schools, classrooms, neighborhoods and other restricted geographical areas. Institutions are but one type of social system for which we have few guidelines in theory to help us understand how the behavior of the individual shapes and is shaped by the social system in which we find and study him.

The practical significances of studies in this problem area are well illustrated in Thormahlen's study:

Statement of the Problem

The problem of this study was to investigate the ward environment in a state institution for the mentally retarded relative to what is done by the ward staff (psychiatric technician) to formally train children in the skills and behaviors included in the *Cain-Levine Social Competency Scale*.

Procedures

An observation procedure was developed by the investigator as a means of obtaining detailed information relative to psychiatric technician-child interaction. Observations were conducted on the three wards in the institution studied that contained the largest number of trainable, mentally retarded children capable of being rated with the *Cain-Levine Social Competency Scale*. Ratings of the children with the Cain-Levine Scale were utilized to define appropriate training areas for trainable children and to determine the adequacy of the formal training the children received. The wards were studied for a total of 138 hours. The focus of the observations was on the ward personnel interaction with the children during the daily ward routine. A total of seventy-nine psychiatric technicians comprising the three work shifts on each of the three wards studied were observed for a minimum of one hour each. The written observations were coded utilizing nine descriptive categories developed during the research to represent formal training and other specific instances of the technician-child interaction process. The characteristic interaction of the ward personnel with the children was compared for all technicians, between wards, working shifts, and for activity on ward routines in terms of the three general categories of interaction that promotes: (1) independent behavior; (2) neither independent nor dependent behavior; and (3) dependent behavior. Formal training was analyzed with respect to area and adequacy. In addition, information was obtained regarding the age, sex, work experience, job performance rating, and education of the technicians.

An interview schedule was developed and thirty technicians of the seventy-nine included in the sample were interviewed in order to gain information relative to the kinds of factors the ward personnel see as affecting the training of children at the ward level, their understanding of the training process, their role as technicians, and their evaluation of their own work training.

Findings

1. The technicians interacted with the children in a manner that promoted independent behavior in the children on the wards for 12 percent of the total time observed. Formal training was included in this category.
2. The ward personnel formally trained children for 1.9 percent of the total time observed.
3. Interaction with the children in a manner that promoted neither independent or dependent behavior accounted for 51 per cent of all technician time.
4. Technicians interacted with the children in a manner that promoted dependent behavior 37 per cent of the total time observed.

Conclusions

1. The ward programs tend to emphasize physical care and there is little opportunity for exposure, training, and practice in the skills and behaviors defined by the *Cain-Levine Social Competency Scale.*
2. The marked emphasis of the ward personnel on promoting dependent behavior in trainable, mentally retarded children is in direct conflict with the stated goals and objectives of the institution and its formal school program.
3. If the orientation of the institution does, in fact, include the objective of developing socially contributory behaviors in trainable, mentally retarded children, the present inservice training program for psychiatric technicians appears to be inadequate for meeting the above objective. (Thormahlen, 1964)

The studies by Thormahlen, Butterfield and Zigler, and Blatt and Kaplan undoubtedly indicate a new line of investigation which may well have dramatic consequences for theories and practices beyond the field of mental retardation.[5] It has been all too easy in the past to view the behavior of the individual as if it were not crucially related to the complexities of the setting or social system in which it is embedded. It should not be as easy in the future.

The Problem of Solutions

How one thinks about the institutional problem, and the time perspective one adopts in relation to solutions, depends in large measure on what one considers to be the important issues. If one considers dilapidated buildings,

---

[5] The studies we have discussed were chosen because they addressed themselves to the relationship between the behavior of the individual child *and* characteristics of the total setting. The reader's attention is drawn to a series of papers and studies (Cleland and Peck, 1959; Cleland, 1962; Kimbrell and Blanchard, 1964; Cleland, 1964) on the selection and characteristics of ward personnel. These publications are important not only as indications of a growing awareness of how institutions are organized and who comprises them but, as important, in what they suggest about the self-defeating practices of institutions. One of the most salutary aspects of these publications is the recognition given to the fact that institutions for the retarded are but instances of institutions in general.

inadequate sanitation, shortages of attendants and professional personnel, and a generally unstimulating environment to be at the root of the problem, one is likely to view money as the vehicle for bringing about desired change. We agree that increased expenditures are likely to produce changes which will have some positive effect on institutionalized children. There is, however, one historical fact that should have a sobering effect on those who view expenditure as the vehicle for major change: In the past, whenever society has become aware of and upset about institutions (for the mentally retarded, the mentally ill, juvenile delinquents, criminals), the automatic reaction has been to spend money, with results which, although satisfying the public's understandable desire to do something, are temporary and quickly dissipated. When at some later date the problem erupts again into public awareness, questions about the adequacy of previous solutions are seldom raised.

It is certainly not our position in any way to derogate public awareness or to argue against increased expenditures and their intended purposes. The point we wish to make is that such efforts may be diluted in their effects precisely because they are not directed at the root questions. For example, if institutional programs reflect the assumption that not much can be done for retarded and defective children, it is not clear how increased expenditures would correct that attitude of hopelessness. The significance of Blatt and Kaplan's photographic essay lay in the suggestion that differences in how defective children looked and behaved reflected not differences in the amount of expenditure, but, rather, differences in expectations; i.e., they saw a relation between behavior and institutional climate. However clean and attractive an institution, however new it may be, however populated it may be by various professional personnel—none or all of these things can be given much weight if they are not reflections of a desire to experiment, innovate, and evaluate.

But what is meant by an attitude of hope and a desire to experiment, innovate, and evaluate? It is hard to be against these characteristics, yet it is by no means easy to describe them in a way so as to have a basis for determining the relation in any one instance between verbal intent and program implementation. The matter, however, is of such importance that we feel it necessary to describe a case which, in our opinion, beautifully illustrates what we mean by an attitude of hope and a desire to experiment, innovate, and evaluate. The case is one of the most detailed and illuminating reports dealing with an attempt to rehabilitate a defective child—Itard's study, *The Wild Boy of Aveyron*, published in 1801 (1932). The subject of this study was a boy, eleven or twelve years of age, who for a period of years had been living in the woods without contact with other people. On one occasion he had been seen completely naked seeking acorns and roots to eat. In 1799 he was seized by three sportsmen "as he was climbing into a tree to escape from their pursuit. Conducted to a neighboring hamlet and confined to the care of a widow, he broke loose at the end of a week and gained the mountains, where he wandered during the most rigorous winter weather, draped rather than covered with a tattered shirt. At night he retired to solitary places but during the day he approached the neighboring villages, where of his own accord he entered an inhabited house situated in the Canton of St. Sernin." When he was seen in Paris by the famous authorities of the day, he was pronounced an incurable idiot. Some even stated that his "wildness" was a fake and that it was inconceivable that such an idiot had fended for himself for years in the forests. Itard, however, believed that the boy's condition was curable and that his condition was due to the lack of intercourse with people. The boy was placed under Itard's care. His description of the boy follows:

ᛦᚢ   Proceeding first with an account of the sensory functions of the young savage, citizen Pinel showed that his senses were reduced to such a state of inertia that the unfortunate creature was, according to his report, quite inferior to some of our domestic animals. His eyes were unsteady, expressionless, wandering vaguely from one object to another without resting on anybody; they were so little experienced in other ways and so little trained by the sense of touch, that they never distinguished an object in relief from one in a picture. His organ of hearing was equally insensible to the loudest noises and to the most touching music. His voice was reduced to a state of complete muteness and only a uniform guttural sound escaped him. His sense of smell was so uncultivated that he was equally indifferent to the odor of perfumes and to the fetid exhalation of the dirt with which his bed was filled. Finally, the organ of touch was restricted to the mechanical function of the grasping objects. Proceeding then to the state of the intellectual functions of this child, the author of the report presented him to us as being quite incapable of attention (except for the objects of his needs) and consequently of all those operations of the mind which attention involves. He was destitute of memory, of judgment, of aptitude for imitation, and was so limited in his ideas, even those relative to his immediate needs, that he had never yet succeeded in opening a door or climbing upon a chair to get the food that had been raised out of reach of his hand. In short, he was destitute of all means of communication and attached neither expression nor intention to his gestures or to the movements of his body. He passed rapidly and without any apparent motive from apathetic melancholy to the most immoderate peals of laughter. He was insensible to every kind of moral influence. His perception was nothing but a computation prompted by gluttony, his pleasure an agreeable sensation of the organ of taste and his intelligence the ability to produce a few incoherent ideas relative to his wants. In a word, his whole life was a completely animal existence.[6]

In working with the young savage, Itard was aided by a woman who handled the boy "with all the patience of a mother and the intelligence of an enlightened teacher." The detail with which Itard describes the handling of the boy, the innumerable experiments he conducted with him, and the

---

[6] J. M. G. Itard, *The Wild Boy of Aveyron* (trans. by G. and M. Humphrey), Appleton-Century-Crofts, Inc., 1932. All quotations from this book are used by permission of the publishers.

various ingenious pedagogical procedures employed make condensation difficult. The following excerpts may give the reader some idea of Itard's attitude toward and handling of the boy as well as changes in the latter's behavior in light of the preceding description of him:

～ It is admitted by physiologists and political theorists that the inhabitants of the South owe their exquisite sensibility, so superior to that of the northerners, entirely to the action of heat upon the skin. I employed this stimulus in all possible ways. Not only was he clothed, put to bed, and housed warmly, but every day I gave him, and at a very high temperature, a bath lasting two or three hours during which frequent douches with the same water were administered to him on the head. I did not observe that the warmth and the frequency of the baths were followed by the debilitating effect attributed to them.

I should even have been glad if such had happened, convinced that in such a case the nervous sensibility would gain by the loss of muscular strength. But if the one effect did not follow, at least the other did not disappoint my expectations. After some time our young savage showed himself sensitive to the action of cold, made use of his hand to find out the temperature of the bath, and refused to enter when it was only lukewarm. For the same reason he soon began to appreciate the utility of clothes which until then he had only endured with much impatience. This utility once recognized, it was only a step to make him dress himself. This end was attained after some days by leaving him each morning exposed to the cold within reach of his clothes until he himself knew how to make use of them. A very similar expedient sufficed to give him at the same time habits of cleanliness and the certainty of passing the night in a cold wet bed accustomed him to get up in order to satisfy his needs. To the administration of the baths I added the use of dry frictions along the spine and even ticklings of the lumbar region. This last means was more exciting than most. I even found myself obliged to reject it, when its effects were no longer limited to producing movements of pleasure but appeared to extend further to the generative organs and to add the threat of perversion to the first stirrings of an already precocious puberty.

To these various stimulants I had to add emotional stimulants which were no less exciting. Those to which he was susceptible at this time were confined to two, joy and anger. The latter I only provoked at long intervals, for its attack was most violent and always apparently justified. I remarked sometimes that in the force of his passion his intelligence seemed to acquire a sort of extension which furnished him with some ingenious expedient in order to get himself out of trouble. Once when we wanted to make him take a bath which was as yet only lukewarm and our reiterated entreaties had made him violently angry, seeing that his governess was not convinced of the coolness of the water by the frequent tests that he made with the tips of his own fingers, he turned towards her quickly, seized her hand and plunged it into the bath.

Let me relate another act of the same nature. One day when he was in my study sitting upon a sofa I came to sit at his side and placed between us a Leyden jar lightly charged. A slight shock which he had received from it the day before had made him familiar with its effect. Seeing the uneasiness which the approach of the instrument caused him I thought he would move it further away by taking hold of the handle. He took a more prudent course which was to put his hands in the opening of his waistcoat, and to draw back some inches so that his leg would no longer touch the covering of the bottle. I drew near him a second time and again replaced it between us. Another movement on his part, another adjustment on mine. This little maneuvre continued until, driven into a corner at the end of the sofa, he found himself bounded by the wall behind, a table in front, and at my side by the troublesome machine. It was no longer possible for him to make any movement. It was then that, seizing the moment when I advanced my arm in order to guide his, he very adroitly lowered my wrist upon the knob of the bottle. I received the discharge.

But if sometimes in spite of the intense interest this young orphan inspired in me I took upon myself to excite his anger, I let no occasion pass of procuring happiness for him: and certainly this was neither difficult nor costly. A ray of sun reflected upon a mirror in his room and turning about on the ceiling, a glass of water let fall drop by drop from a certain height upon his finger tips while he was in the bath, and a wooden porringer containing a little milk placed at the end of his bath, which the oscillations of the water drifted, little by little, amid cries of delight, into his grasp, such simple means were nearly all that was necessary to divert and delight this child of nature almost to the point of ecstasy. (p. 16)

. . .

. . . I took him not long ago to the country house of citizen Lachabeaussiere in the valley of Montmorency. It was a most curious sight, and I venture to say one of the most touching, to see the joy that was pictured in his eyes at the sight of the little hills and woods of that laughing valley. It seemed as if the eagerness of his gaze could not be satisfied through the windows of the carriage. He leaned now towards the one, now towards the other, and showed the liveliest anxiety when the horses went more slowly or were about to stop. He spent two days in this country house and such was the effect of these outside influences, of these woods, these hills, with which he could never satisfy his eyes, that he appeared more impatient and wild than ever, and, in the midst of the most assiduous and kind attention and most affectionate care, seemed captivated by this dominant idea which absorbed all his faculties and even the consciousness of his needs, he scarcely found time to eat. He would get up from the table every minute and run to the window in order to escape into the park if it was open; or if it was shut, to contemplate, at least through the panes, all those objects towards which he was irresistibly attracted by still recent habits and perhaps even by the memory of an independent life, happy and regretted. I therefore resolved never again to submit him to similar tests. But in order not to sever him entirely from his country tastes, he was taken continually to walk in some neighboring gardens, of which the straight and regular arrangement had nothing in common with the great landscapes of which wild nature is composed, and which so strongly attach primitive man to the place of his childhood. Thus Madame Guérin took him sometimes to the Luxembourg and almost daily to the Observatory gardens where the kindness of citizen Lemeri has accustomed him to go every day for a lunch of milk. By means of these new habits, of certain recreations of his own choosing and finally, of all the kind treatment with which he knew existence was surrounded, he finished by liking it all. This was the beginning of the intense affection which he has acquired for his governess and which he sometimes expresses in a most touching manner. He never leaves her without reluctance nor does he rejoin her without signs of satisfaction.

Once when he had escaped from her in the streets, he shed many tears on seeing her again. Some hours after, he still had a high and broken respiration and a kind of feverish pulse. When Madame Guérin reproached him, he interpreted her tone so well that he began to weep. The friendship which he had for me was much less strong, and justifiably so. The care which Madame Guérin takes of him is of a kind which is immediately appreciated, and what I give him is of no obvious use to him. That this difference is unquestionably due to the cause indicated is shown by the fact that there are times when he welcomes me and they are the times which I have never used for his instruction. For example, when I go to the house in the evening just after he has gone to bed, his first movement is to sit up for me to embrace him, then to draw me to him by seizing my arm and making me sit upon his bed, after which he usually takes my hand, carries it to his eyes, his forehead, the back of his head, and holds it with his upon these parts for a very long time. At other times he gets up with bursts of laughter and comes beside me to caress my knees in his own way which consists of feeling them, rubbing them firmly in all directions for some minutes, and then sometimes in laying his lips to them two or three times. People may say what they like, but I will confess that I lend myself without ceremony to all this childish play.

I shall perhaps be understood if my readers will remember the paramount influence exerted upon a child's mind by the inexhaustible delights and the maternal triflings that nature has put into the heart of a mother and which make the first smiles flower and bring to birth life's earliest joys. (p. 23)

. . .

I ordered to be printed as a big character upon a piece of cardboard two inches square each of the twenty-four letters of the alphabet. I had an equal number of spaces cut in a plank a foot and a half square. Into these the pieces of cardboard could be inserted, without the use of paste, so that their places could be changed as required. I had an equal number of characters of the same dimensions made in metal. These were meant to be compared by the pupil with the printed letters, and were to be arranged in their corresponding places.

The first trial of this method was made, in my absence, by Madame Guérin. I was very much surprised on my return to learn from her that Victor distinguished all the characters and arranged them properly. He was immediately put to the test and performed his task without any mistake. Though delighted with such an immediate success I was still far from able to explain its cause, and it was only some days after that I discovered this by noting the way in which our pupil proceeded to make this arrangement. In order to make the work easier he devised of his own accord a little expedient which in this task allowed him to dispense with memory, comparison and judgment. As soon as the board was put between his hands, he did not wait until the metal letters were taken out of their places but he himself took them and piled them upon his hand, following the order of their arrangement so that the last letter, after all were taken from the board, was the first on the pile. He began with this and finished with the last of the pile, thus beginning the board at the end and proceeding always from right to left. Moreover, he was able to improve upon this procedure; for very often the pile collapsed, the characters fell out and he had to straighten everything up and put it in order by the unaided efforts of attention. So the twenty-four letters were arranged in four rows of six each, making it easier to lift them up by rows only, and even to replace them in the same way by taking letters from the second row only when the first was replaced.

I do not know whether he reasoned as I suppose, but at least it is certain that he executed the performance in the manner described. It was then a true routine, but a routine of his own invention, and one which was perhaps as much to the credit of his intelligence as was a method of arrangement hit upon shortly afterwards to the credit of his discernment. It was not difficult to set him off by giving him the characters pellmell whenever he was given the board. At last, in spite of the frequent transpositions to which I submitted the printed characters by changing their places, in spite of insidious arrangements, such as the O beside the C, the E beside the F, etc., his discrimination became infallible. In exercising it upon all these letters, the end I had in view was to prepare Victor for a primitive but correct use of the letters, namely the expression of needs which can only be made known by means of speech. Far from believing that I was already so near this great step in his education, I was led by the spirit of curiosity rather than the hope of success to try the experiment which follows:

One morning when he was waiting impatiently for the milk which he always had for breakfast, I carried to him his board which I had specially arranged the evening before with the four letters L.A.I.T. Madame Guerin, whom I had warned, approached, looked at the letters and immediately gave me a cup of milk which I pretended to drink myself. A moment after I approached Victor, gave him the four letters that I had lifted from the board, and pointed to it with one hand while in the other I held the jug full of milk. The letters were immediately replaced but in inverted order, so that they showed T.I.A.L. instead of L.A.I.T. I indicated the corrections to be made by designating with my finger the letters to transpose and the proper place of each. When these changes had reproduced the sign, he was allowed to have his milk.

It is difficult to believe that five or six similar attempts were sufficient, not only to make him arrange methodically the four letters of the word Lait but to give him the idea of the connection between the word and the thing. At least this is the justifiable inference from what happened a week later. One evening when he was ready to set out for the Observatory, he was seen to provide himself on his own initiative with the four letters in question, and to put them in his pocket; he had scarcely arrived at citizen Lemeri's house, where as I previously said he goes every day for some milk, when he produced them and placed them on a table in such a way as to form the word LAIT." (Itard, 1932, p. 45)

Itard's expectation that the wild boy could be trained into a normal civilized being was by no means confirmed. During the five-year period in which the boy was studied he never learned to utter more than a few words, his comprehension of abstract symbols was meager, his emotional expression was crude and diffuse, and his responsiveness to his environment was determined largely by biological needs. In light of Itard's original ambitious hopes it is understandable why he was disappointed with the results of his efforts. Itard's summary of his experiment, contained in his report to the French Minister of Interior, is distinguished by his attempt to evaluate his failures as scrupulously as his successes.

. . . I have made it my duty to present [the facts] without distinction, and to relate my reverses as scrupulously as my successes. Such an astonishing variety of results adds an element of uncertainty to any opinion which can be formed of this young man, while the conclusions that can be drawn from the facts related in this memoir consequently present a certain lack of harmony.

Thus, bringing together those facts which are scattered through [the report], one cannot help concluding: first, that by reason of the almost complete apathy of the organs of hearing and speech, the education of this young man is still incomplete and must always remain so; secondly, that by reason of their long inaction the intellectual faculties are developing slowly and painfully, and that this development, which in children growing up in civilized surrounds is the natural fruit of time and circumstances, is here the slow and laborious result of a very active education in which the most powerful methods are used to obtain most insignificant results; thirdly, that the emotional faculties, equally slow in emerging from their long torpor, are subordinated to an utter selfishness and that his puberty, which was very strongly marked and which usually sets up a great emotional expansion, seems only to prove that if there exists in human beings a relation between the needs of the senses and the affections of the heart, this sympathetic agreement is, like the majority of great and generous emotions, the happy fruit of education.

But if the happy changes occurring in the state of this young man are recapitulated . . ., one cannot fail to consider his education in a more favorable light. The following conclusions are then perfectly justifiable. First, that the improvement of his sight and touch and the new gratification of his sense of taste have, by multiplying the sensations and ideas of our savage, contributed powerfully to the development of his intellectual faculties; secondly, when one considers the full extent of this development, among other real improvements he will be found to have both a knowledge of the conventional value of the symbols of thought and the power of applying it by naming objects, their qualities, and their actions. This has led to an extension of the pupil's relations with the people around him, to the faculty of expressing his wants to them, of receiving orders from them, and of effecting a free and continual exchange of thoughts; thirdly, that in spite of his immoderate taste for the freedom of open country and his indifference to most of the pleasures of social life, Victor shows himself sensible to the care taken of him, susceptible to fondling and affection, alive to the pleasure of well-doing, ashamed of his mistakes, and repentant of his outbursts; fourthly and finally, my Lord, looking at this long experiment from any point of view, whether it be considered as the methodical education of a savage or as no more than the physical and moral treatment of one of those creatures ill-favored of nature, rejected by society and abandoned by medicine, the care that has been taken and ought still to be taken of him, the changes that have taken place and those which can be hoped for, the voice of humanity, the interest inspired by such a complete desertion and a destiny so strange—all these things recommend this extraordinary young man to the attention of scientists, to the solicitude of administrators, and to the protection of the Government. (Itard, 1932)

If this case is considered an example of what is meant by hopefulness or dedication as well as the desire to experiment, innovate, and evaluate, it becomes quite clear that very few institutional programs would possess these characteristics. Until more of our institutions contain personnel who possess (in greater degree than is now the case) these characteristics, we cannot expect that these settings will undergo any fundamental change, despite well-intentioned efforts to use money as the major vehicle for change. There are many things that money can easily buy but the characteristics we have attempted to describe are not among them.

A second major aspect of the "solution" problem stems from the fact that attendants (labels vary from one setting to another) are the ones in most frequent contact with children, have the least training for their jobs, and receive little or no supervision. Here too the approach has been to increase salaries of attendants in the hope of getting better people who will have more stable and prolonged job records, and, in addition, to provide more supervisory time. There is no evidence that either or both of these steps has a discernible effect on what happens to children. The crucial question, seldom raised, is *what constitutes supervision?* If one defines supervision as a sustained process in which one person informs, guides, *and observes* another person with the aim of determining to what extent psychological principles are being appropriately implemented—or to what extent a specific program for a specific child is consistently followed and evaluated—then one must conclude that supervision rarely takes place and that increasing salaries and employing more supervisors does not necessarily meet the problem.

It is indeed encouraging that in recent years researchers have begun to look at the climate, organization, and functioning of institutions with the purpose of describing and understanding how they affect those in their charge. In the next chapter Dr. Michael Klaber describes an on-going research project which may well be the most ambitious yet attempted in this problem area. His description and discussion of the study, and presentation of some of the early findings, emphasizes, concretizes, and brings together many of the points raised in the present and the previous chapter—but from the more secure vantage point of intensive experience with the problem and, more important, research data.

The retarded and institutions for the retarded— a preliminary research report

DR. M. MICHAEL KLABER[1]

During the past decade there has been an increased emphasis on the desirability of keeping mentally retarded children at home. Many studies and summaries have been published which suggest that the environment of the home is of greater benefit than that of the institution (Butterfield, 1967). While these results may prompt a strong effort to retain as many retardates as possible in the community, they are not helpful in illuminating the difficulties, advantages, and possible remedies of those persons who are and will have to be placed in residential centers. Currently, close to 200,000 retarded individuals are in residence in institutions, 82 percent of which are functioning below the educable or mildly retarded

---

[1] The research reported here was supported by Grant No. RD—1816—P of the Vocational Rehabilitation Administration. It was carried out under the auspices of the University of Hartford, David D. Komisar, Chairman of the Advisory Board. The author is indebted to Joseph Egan, Elaine Levering, Barbara Majer, Paul Mudry, and Michael Rondon who served as assistants during the data gathering process.

level of intelligence. There is a clear and pressing need to study and assess those variables which might enhance or retard the development of such a large group of seriously handicapped individuals.

Previous institutional studies have dealt almost exclusively with populations residing in a single facility from which generalizations pertaining to all institutionalized retardates are then drawn, the obvious assumption being that one institution for the retarded is representative of all such facilities. It appears, however, that while most residential facilities for the mentally retarded have some basic similarities, there are also many differences which affect the care, development, treatment, and growth of their residents. Institutions for the residential care of retardates are very complex systems which differ in their philosophy, goals, physical layout, size, and the professional expertise of their staff, as well as in their basic attitudes toward child care. In this respect, they are as dissimilar as other organizational systems, whether in the field of education, business or government. Thus, for example, state colleges within a state will differ from each other in their philosophy, academic emphasis, admission requirements, reputation, etc., while retaining some basic formal similarities, e.g., salary scales, campus maintenance, and other services. School systems, or even individual public schools, will acquire some very special characteristics depending on the areas they serve, the teachers they attract, and the key administrative personnel in decision-making positions.

Institutions for the retarded can thus be seen as individual systems, whose organic functional structure will produce differential effects on the growth, development, and self-sufficiency of the persons in residence. This chapter is based on the preliminary findings of a research project designed to investigate the differential properties of institutional systems for the retarded.

As a first attempt of this sort, it suffers necessarily from a series of limitations. The most obvious problem is reflected in capturing a living, functioning organism through static description—a process not much different from obtaining a still photograph of a moving object. The institutions described here are in a constant state of flux—their personnel changes, and their programs are modified. Our work therefore reflects merely a moment in the lives of the facilities studied. Our intention was not to evaluate a given institution but, rather, in broad strokes:

1. To demonstrate that institutions are different from each other.
2. To indicate that these differences are directly responsible for differential functioning among institutional residents.
3. To identify the reason for the differences.
4. To recommend changes in institutional management which will lead to maximal realization of the development and functional potential of institutional residents.

At the present time, there seems to be a general disagreement about the very essence and purpose of institutions for the retarded. Thus, for example, five of the six facilities investigated in this project had the official designation of "school" in their descriptive titles. Does this official designation mean that the facility is primarily educational in nature? If so, how congruent is this self-image with the fact that only 5 to 10 percent of the budgets of the institutions studied are designated for the purposes of "training and education"? Is perhaps the designation of "hospital" more appropriate to the institutional self-image (Bramwell, 1966)? If so, it is rather difficult to understand the extreme scarcity of nurses, licensed physicians, and board diplomates in medical specialties on the staffs of the facilities observed. If, on the other hand, recreation and vocational rehabilitation are the primary goals of the residential agency, then the scarcity of workshops, trained rehabilitation counselors, and fully educated recreation personnel are difficult to comprehend.

This lack of uniform purpose in institutional goals was clearly in evidence in our sample. Consider, for example, two of our facilities which were established within years of one another. One of these facilities was specifically designed to resemble home environment as much as possible and adopted a cottage layout for its architectural model, whereas the other was apparently designed for efficient custodial care with minimal interpersonal relationships in mind. Another pair of facilities constructed only five years apart from each other, reflects radically different attitudes toward segregation by sex: In one case, there are two completely independent "villages" with independent staffs, dining halls, recreation facilities, etc.; while in the other institution, males and females past puberty reside in separate dormitories, yet share recreational and dining facilities and have a common staff.

The more detailed our descriptions became, the more different the facilities appeared. The closer we observed the ward routine, the greater the individual quality of the ward experience became evident. The more involved we became in the institutional management, the more untenable became the assumed generality of the institutional experience. Prevailing throughout was the assumption by most members of administrative and professional staffs that things "have to be this way" because of circumstances.

THE INSTITUTIONAL SYSTEM

The institutional system emerged as an enormously complex, closed organization operating under certain political pressures. These outside pressures are primarily centered around parental demands (for admission or special consideration) and fiscal economies based on local tax conditions.

Unlike a private enterprise system, there is absolutely no measurement of success or failure of the institutional organization. No financial profit and loss sheet reflects the relative merits of a given administration, nor is there any built-in system of self-evaluation, such as that afforded public school systems by grade-specific achievement tests. The institutional administration is evaluated merely by its general reputation within the state, and by the fleeting impressions gained by visitors through observation or contact with staff members. This lack of any objective evaluatory method is fraught with obvious and severe limitations. Our own project staff had occasion to observe the frailty of evaluative impressions. One of our sample agencies enjoyed a reputation of severely neglecting its residents: The superintendent was uniformly disliked and distrusted, and struck us as barely competent on personal contact; the buildings were almost all old, poorly ventilated, and in urgent need of painting and repair. In spite of all these limitations the retarded children were assessed as looking more self-sufficient, happier, and enjoying a higher level of verbal functioning than those in another, better equipped, more congenially administered, and more expensively run institution.

It was our intent to investigate as objectively as possible the differential variables leading to better adjustment among institutionalized retardates. To this end our first task was to devise suitable measurement techniques which would tap crucial aspects of behavior of retardates, sample their interpersonal experiences on a day-to-day basis and assess relevant psychological and behavioral aspects in parents and aides.

Basic Methodological Considerations

Our basic approach involved the hypothetical case of admitting the same child to different institutions. Such an experiment is quite feasible in

TABLE 9.1 Matching Data on Subjects in Six Institutions for the Retarded

		Series I			Series II		
		Institution					
		A	*B*	*C*	*D*	*E*	*F*
MA	Mean	3.12	2.92	3.19	1.77	1.75	2.02
	SD	1.62	1.84	1.33	1.04	1.04	1.24
IQ	Mean	28.88	27.15	29.31	21.10	23.10	23.48
	SD	14.00	10.48	7.96	8.79	8.85	8.55
Age at admission	Mean	6.41	6.64	6.25	7.05	6.90	6.11
	SD	2.14	2.03	1.66	3.19	3.17	2.97
CA	Mean	10.96	10.52	10.52	15.48	15.40	15.48
	SD	1.88	1.99	2.22	3.91	3.84	3.83

physical science, but of course impossible under naturalistic behavioral science conditions. We therefore attempted to approximate this ideal condition by matching mentally retarded individuals as closely as possible on as many variables as practicable. Our assumption was that carefully matched groups would permit us to consider as comparable the experiences of retardates under separate institutional conditions.

For a number of administrative reasons, we divided our sample into two groups. Series I consisted of a matched sample of 17 children in each of three institutions, and Series II of 44 children in each of three other facilities. Series I was matched on the basis of current information, and Series II on the basis of five-year-old data. It was our hope to gain, thereby, a retrospective measure of behavior. Thus, for example, we would be able to discern whether differential growth in MA could be attributed to the institutional experience.

All matching was performed on a purely actuarial basis. Our workers perused institutional records and did not actually see the children selected for our study until much later. The data on which our sample was based thus emanated directly from the diagnostic work performed by the institutional staffs. Every precaution was taken so as to not bias and prejudice our workers.

Measuring Institutional Experience of Residents

In typical clinical situations it is customary to gather information through verbal responses of subjects. Individuals who are incapable or limited in their verbal abilities must, however, be subjected to other kinds of data gathering. Such data became available through observational methods. It was decided to observe our subjects systematically on a time-sample basis, a unit of two minutes constituting one time sample.

We were interested, however, not in mere behavioral description of the subjects but, also, in the impinging stimuli of the institutional environment. We wanted to observe the detailed interpersonal responses of each subject as related to events in his environment. To that end we constructed an observation schedule consisting of subject variables and of environmental variables. Included in our observations were: (1) the behavior of the child, and (2) the behavior of the individual interacting with the child. When observing the child's behavior we recorded self-directed behavior (crying, rocking, finger posturing, other stereotypies, inactivity, etc.), among outer-directed behavior we included such items as smiling, laughing, dancing, destructive and aggressive acts, playing with people and with objects, talking, listening, watching, and other items.

The "other person," the individual who interacted with our subject was described as being an attendant, a working patient (trainee), another retarded ward resident, or any nonretarded adult other than an aide. We recorded whether he responded to a demand on the child's part, or whether he initiated the interaction. We then went on to describe the interaction (taking care of the child's physical need, conversing with or punishing the child, playing with the child, showing physical affection, etc.).

Four research assistants, two men and two women, were employed in all the observations. This staff was composed of recent college graduates in psychology and education, but without background and experience in research or in the field of mental retardation. Their lack of preparation in scientific areas was more than compensated by their freedom from established attitudes to mental retardation and total naïveté with respect to our hypotheses.

The research assistants underwent an intensive training program (eight weeks) in the use of the observation scale. Training was terminated after an inter-rater reliability of .85 or better was achieved. The fact that this highly satisfactory level could be achieved after only two months of training suggests that observational assessment of the behavior of mentally retarded individuals is both feasible and practical.

While it is highly desirable to learn about the general behavior of institutional retardates, such information is insufficient in yielding the data necessary for the evaluation of adjustment. For this purpose, a number of experimental procedures have been developed and perfected under laboratory conditions. While these techniques have yielded reliable results in special situations, they have not been attempted in field conditions. Klaber and Butterfield (in press) have described rocking behavior among severely retarded as being dependent on external events. Such behavior can be measured with relative ease and can readily be used to assess the flow of external events (i.e., ward activities). We therefore decided to use this method to describe some of the interinstitutional differences.

Although social deprivation measures have rarely been used to measure interinstitutional differences, Butterfield and Zigler (1966) have demonstrated that two institutions for the retarded within the same state system may act in distinctly different ways upon mildly retarded children—one institution apparently satisfying the social needs of its residents much better than another. Through extending social-reinforcement techniques to tasks relevant to severely retarded children and adults, we were able to assess the social-reinforcement value of various institutions. Our findings are particularly interesting because they include a collection of behavioral measures of aide behavior, which is presumably one of the primary social-reinforcement agents.

Experimental evidence obtained under laboratory conditions are therefore also useful in this endeavor. We have adopted a special technique to this end and have demonstrated its usefulness in interinstitutional comparisons (Klaber, Butterfield, and Gould, 1968).

Child behavior was, of course, also assessed along the traditional lines of rating scales and psychometric tests. These measures are especially useful in serving as guideposts of functional levels along more conventional lines.

Our three approaches to the assessment of behavior of the institutional retardate can be summarized as follows:

1. Detailed behavior observations.
2. Laboratory techniques adapted to the life-space of the retardate, and to interinstitutional comparisons.
3. Psychometric tests and rating scales.

We believe that this three-pronged approach yields a substantial fund of data about the output of the institutional system or the product of the organization (were we to describe the agencies in question along business lines). As yet we have said little about the system itself, its workers (i.e., aides), managers (professional staff and administration), or consumers (the parents).

Assessment of Aide Behavior

While a substantial number of studies dealing with the expressed attitudes of institutional aides is available in the literature, (Butterfield, 1967) only one has been concerned with direct observation of aide behavior (Thormahlen, 1965). Thus, we have substantial data on how aides express themselves on paper-and-pencil inventories, but only scant information on their actual behavior. The evidence we *do* have suggests that the relationship between these two assessment methods is rather scant.

In order to overcome the inherent rigidity of a preformulated inventory, we supplement our evaluation of aide behavior with a sentence-completion test. Such a projective device requires the respondent to supply his own answer and thus overcomes the social-desirability effect which tends to be more powerful in conventional inventories. Rigorous scoring specifications permitted us to achieve 80 percent or better agreement between two raters. This instrument was used with parents and with aides. We also administered a revised version of the Parent Attitude Research Instrument to both aides and parents in the hope of using the projective and the objective instruments jointly.

The Institutions and the Matching Process

We studied six state-supported institutions for the retarded. Three of these facilities were in one state, two in another, and one in yet a third state. By matching every child with two other children, we were, in theory at least, studying the same child in three separate settings. The matching itself was performed on a purely actuarial basis, from records supplied by the institutions. We attempted to match the following variables as closely as possible:

age, age-at-admission, sex, race, IQ and MA. We eliminated from our study children diagnosed as mentally ill, and persons with disabling sensory handicaps. We also attempted to match gross diagnostic categories, and thus always matched mongoloids with other Down's Syndrome cases, seizure patients with other epileptics, etc. A close match of parental socioeconomic status proved to be too time consuming and of questionable reliability. A sample of 20 parent pairs, however, clearly demonstrated the comparability of the matched groups. We feel that our groups constitute a representative random sample of parental backgrounds.

The first series of matched triads consisted of 51 children, 17 in each of three institutions, A, B, and C.

Institution A is a medium-sized facility whose administrative organization represents three separate and distinct areas of service: a boys' village, a girls' village, and a compound for the severely retarded. The institution was originally designed to serve primarily the needs of the mildly retarded and efforts were made to simulate home environs through relatively small units and "house parents." As the institutional needs changed and younger and more severely retarded children were admitted, larger buildings were erected and greater emphasis on nursing-type care was provided. The official philosophy, however, still emphasizes the ideal of small units, educational approaches, and an atmosphere of homelike care.

Institution B is a large facility (population over 4000) which is divided into two strictly separated administrative units: male and female. These two segments are substantially autonomous with respect to child-care procedures and are geographically distinct. Apparently it was felt by the founders of the facility that their population would consist of ambulatory, reasonably self-sufficient individuals, whose major needs are shelter and food. Large dormitories and centrally located eating facilities suggest as much. The relatively new influx of more severely retarded, younger, and less self-sufficient residents prompted a building program stressing full-service edifices. These buildings are designed to meet all the needs of its residents, including food services and a variety of therapies. The philosophy is essentially medical and stresses physical habilitation.

Institution C is also a large facility whose apparent original design stressed efficiency and low-cost services for severely handicapped individuals. Buildings are very large, several of them have more than one story, and space was primarily designed for the placement of beds. Recreational facilities were minimized, as were all aspects of education and recreation. This institution was the only one in our survey which did not have at least minimal playgrounds for each building. The institution is not broken down into separate units and is administered centrally.

The second series consisted of 132 children in Institutions D, E and F, 44 children in each institution.

Institution D is a medium-sized facility whose original plant was composed almost entirely of multistoried buildings. It apparently also reflected the philosophy that ambulatory, self-sufficient individuals would reside there. Until recently, there was a total segregation of sexes but, more recently, there have been administrative changes permitting personnel and residents to move from one dormitory to another depending on need. Newer buildings are designed for full service and include day rooms and dining halls. Educational activities are carried out in a relatively new school building located at the outskirts of the grounds.

Institution E is one of a series of new retardation facilities of the state program. Located in older buildings, originally designed to serve chronically ill children and adults the physical plant, in spite of renovations, is not indicative of the philosophy of care of the facility. The number of residents is very small (less than 300) with a heavy emphasis on supplying the needs of the retardates through outside community resources. Schooling, medical care, etc., are provided by town or private resources. The per capita expenditure for residents in Institution E was more than double the average of the other institutions in our sample. Volunteers, a variety of specialists, and other personnel abound, thus creating a most favorable caretaker-to-retardate ratio.

Institution F is a medium-sized (close to 2000 residents) facility. It had the most neglected physical plant of all institutions studied, with old, multistoried buildings and unpaved roads. The original philosophy probably was essentially similar to that of Institution D, but a much older school building testifies to a much earlier interest in educational activities. Many of the old buildings had been modified to include school or education rooms. The institution is centrally administered without a sharp division between male and female services.

Residents of Institution A were matched with Institutions B and C, but a unique opportunity presented itself in Institution E. A number of its residents had been transferred five years earlier from Institution D for purely administrative reasons. It was possible to match these persons retroactively on measurements obtained at D with youngsters who had remained at D. This procedure of retroactive matching was also carried out at E. The second group of matched children represents, therefore, an attempt to obtain longitudinal measures, albeit, on a retrospective basis.

Results

The first task we had set ourselves was the investigation of the question, Does institutional experience differ among the matched triads? Are residents in one institution better off than in another, or does it really make little difference where a person is institutionalized? Do all residents function at similar levels of self-sufficiency, or does their ability to care for their needs differ from facility to facility? In short, we attempted to investigate whether the differences in the physical plants and apparent philosophies of the institutions had any effect on their charges.

Perhaps one of the most vital aims of institutional management is the development of greater self-sufficiency among its severely retarded residents. The published purpose of the so-called training programs in institutions stresses the fostering of greater independence among their charges. Fostering the ability to care for one's own needs; to dress, feed, and toilet oneself; to communicate; and to make ones needs known are surely among the most important aspects of caretaking.

In order to assess these vital aspects of behavior we constructed a special scale tapping the above mentioned areas of self-sufficiency. This instrument was more detailed at the more dependent end of the scale than the Vineland Social Maturity Scale and simpler than the Cain–Levine Social Competency Scale. It consisted simply of nine areas of self-sufficiency arranged in order of ascending independence (e.g., drinks from bottle; is spoon fed; feeds self with spoon, but is very messy; feeds self with spoon neatly; feeds self with fork; feeds self independently, but has meat cut; uses knife for cutting and spreading). We were not interested in what the child could do under ideal circumstances, but what he actually *did do* under the daily living conditions of institutional life.

Because such simple description requires mere observation we obtained extremely high inter-rater reliability. Our own workers achieved a correlation of .98, attendants achieved .94. Averaged scores of two attendants and two of our observers achieved a product-moment correlation of .92. This highly reliable instrument was used on the basis of the reports of two attendants in the institutions.

Since the children were matched according to measured intellectual ability, differences in self-sufficiency must, of necessity, reflect the effects of institutional programming. Figure 9.1 presents graphically the results of a comparison of self-sufficiency among the institutions.

It is clear that in both Series I and II one institution produces children who are much less self-sufficient than do the other two. In Institution C and Institution D, the residents do less for themselves in such areas as feeding themselves, toileting and dressing themselves, etc.

It may be argued that these residents do less by themselves because they are being properly cared for. The overriding question then remains whether children in various institutions experience similar degrees of happiness. We have attempted to assess the elusive quality of "happiness" or "adjustment" in behavioral terms. By sampling the behavior of mentally retarded individuals over substantial periods of time and throughout their waking day, it was possible to record their responses reliably. Certain behavior patterns are likely to reflect good adjustment (e.g., smiling, playing with toys, talking and inter-

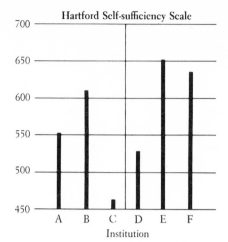

Figure 9.1

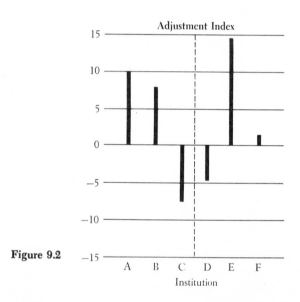

Figure 9.2

acting with others, etc.) while others are clearly symptoms of poor adjustment (e.g., autistic behavior, aggression, withdrawal, etc.). It was possible in this manner to construct an objective and reliable assessment of behavior indices of adjustment and apply them to our matched triads.

We developed an adjustment index based on our observations. By summing arithmetically the incidence of clearly adjustive behavior (talking, playing, laughing, etc.) and clearly maladaptive behavior (aggression, autism, stereotypy, total withdrawal, etc.). By assigning positive scores to the former, and negative scores for the latter, the predominance of adjustive over maladjustive behavior (or vice versa) can thus be readily ascertained. These data were obtained from almost 10,000 independent time samples, and are thus highly representative of behavioral observations the layman would term happiness.

Figure 9.2 clearly demonstrates that institutions differ in the state of adjustment (happiness) they confer upon their charges. In Series I Institution C is predominantly an unhappy one, while in Series II Institution D bears this distinction. The reader will recall that the very same facilities showed the lowest degree of self-sufficiency among their charges. It can be concluded that the ability of retarded children to care for their own needs is apparently related to the happiness manifested by them.

A third measure of institutional effectiveness is intellectual development. Since our sample was matched for IQ we could not demonstrate such differences on a cross-sectional basis for Series I, but Series II yielded data that could retrospectively be evaluated on a longitudinal basis. The matching data were based on tests administered by the institutional staffs to the cohorts six years or more in the past. It was possible to reexamine the children for the purposes of our research. These examinations were undertaken by the institutional staff at E, and by totally naïve psychologists at D and F. The results of this assessment is summarized in Table 9.2.

TABLE 9.2 Changes in IQ and MA over Six Years

	Institution D				Institution E				Institution F			
	IQ		MA		IQ		MA		IQ		MA	
	Mean	SD	Mean	SD	Mean	SD	Mean	SD	Mean	SD	Mean	SD
1960 or before	21.1	8.8	1.77	1.04	22.8	8.6	1.75	1.04	23.5	8.6	2.02	1.24
1966	10.8	8.7	1.75	1.22	16.6	11.3	2.33	1.58	16.2	10.3	2.35	1.54
Percent change	−49%		−1%		−27%		+33%		−31%		+16%	

It may be seen from Table 9.2 that Institution D manifests the greatest relative decline in IQ because of a failure to show any mental growth in the children; Institution E, however, shows a substantial increase in Mental Age (by as much as one third from the original baseline), whereas Institution F shows a moderate increment in MA, and consequently a moderate decline in IQ.

By relating the data on happiness, self-sufficiency, and intellectual growth to each other we can discern a high degree of similarity in these three variables.

Institutions in which retarded children are happy are also ones in which children grow intellectually and achieve greater independence.

Ancillary Experiments Demonstrating Institutional Differences

In order to support our argument concerning the differential effects of institutions we performed two ancillary experiments (Klaber and Butterfield, in press; Klaber, Butterfield, and Gould, 1968).

Rocking Index. The first of these experiments involved the observations of similar institutional wards rather than of individually matched children. The most convenient measure for our purpose was the number of retardates observed rocking rhythmically. By time sampling the number of ward residents who rock and by relating this figure to the total number of retardates in the ward, we have developed a "rocking index." Stereotyped rocking has been investigated repeatedly, typically under experimental conditions. It appears to be more prevalent among institution than noninstitution populations (Provence and Lipton, 1962), having been reported among as many as 69 percent of retardates under special environmental conditions (Kaufman and Levitt, 1965). If one feels that institution care for the severely retarded is generally inadequate, this finding would be expected. While stereotyped behavior is often associated with neurological impairment, it has been shown to be related to environmental events. Thus, it is most marked when the severely retarded person is placed in restricted, barren, and new environments (Berkson and Mason, 1963). Stereotypy is reduced by the availability of playthings and is most reduced by preferred toys (Davenport and Berkson, 1963). Stereotyped behavior is also influenced by social factors: It is increased by the presence of peers (Hollis, 1965). Furthermore, variations in ward activities influence the prevalence of stereotyped rocking, which is most prevalent immediately prior to meals and the coming and going of attendants during work-shift changes (Kaufman and Levitt, 1965). These findings suggest that the percentage of patients rocking in a ward for the severely retarded reflects inadequacies in the care provided in that ward. Guess (1966) has related this response pattern to restrictions in the sensorium and the ability to walk without help.

The mean percent of patients rocking in each of the wards compared are presented in Table 9.3.

comparisons among institutions. One between-institution comparison was made by combining the data from Wards 1, 2, 3, and 4 in Institution C and comparing their mean percent rocking scores to that of Ward 1 in Institution D. A t test revealed that there was a significantly ($t = 11.8, p < .001$) greater percentage of rocking in the four Institution C wards combined than

TABLE 9.3 MEAN NUMBER OF PATIENTS IN WARD, CA, IQ,
AND PERCENT OF PATIENTS ROCKING IN DIFFERENT WARDS
OF THE FOUR INSTITUTIONS STUDIED

Institution	Ward	Number in Ward	Mean CA	Mean IQ	Percent Rocking
C	1	67	10.6	27	12.7
C	2	57	9.4	23	7.2
C	3	56	10.2	22	12.0
C	4	61	9.9	26	10.1
B	1	126	12.2	14	7.7
D	1	36	9.0	22	5.3
D	2	39	14.6	13	10.2
D	3	27	10.8	15	15.7
F	1	108	24.5	21	8.9
F	2	146	37.7	18	5.7
F	3	147	37.2	18	8.8
F	4	97	23.8	29	8.9

in the Institution D ward. A second between-institution comparison was made by combining Wards 2 and 3 in Institution D and comparing their mean percent rocking score to that of Ward 1 in Institution B. A test revealed that there was significantly ($t = 2.29$, $p < .05$) more rocking in Wards 2 and 3 in Institution D than in Ward 1 of Institution B.

COMPARISONS WITHIN INSTITUTIONS. A one-way analysis of variance revealed that there were significant ($F = 3.38$, $p < .05$) differences between the four wards in the percent of patients rocking in Wards 1, 2, 3, and 4 of Institution C. Individual t-test comparisons indicated that this significant overall effect was due to the fact that Ward 2 had a lower percent rocking than any of the other three wards, which did not differ significantly from one another. Wards 1, 2, 3, and 4 of Institution F were compared by means of a one-way analysis of variance which revealed significant ($F = 6.39$, $p < .01$) difference between the four wards in percent of retardates engaging in stereotyped rocking. This overall effect was due to the fact that Ward 2 showed significantly less rocking than any of the other wards, which did not differ among themselves.

Institutionalization as Social Deprivation. The second ancillary experiment we employed was a laboratory method designed to tap experimentally the effects of social deprivation.

While there have been many investigations of the effects of institutionalizing children (reviewed in Butterfield, 1967; Casler, 1961; Yarrow, 1961), knowledge of the consequences of institutional rearing is still incomplete and equivocal. This is due largely to the methological problems of such investigations (see Butterfield, 1967; Casler, 1961). One of the key problems is that no matter how carefully one matches institutionalized and noninstitutionalized children, there is still much doubt about the comparability of their early life experiences and their constitutional endowments. This had led some investigators (e.g., Butterfield and Zigler, 1965a) to compare children who are placed in different institutions rather than children who are institutionalized with those who are not. The assumption underlying this type of comparison is that different groups of institutionalized children are more comparable on all variables except the character of their institutional experiences than are institutionalized and noninstitutionalized children. One advantage of interinstitutional comparisons is that they recognize that institutions differ and thereby reduce the chances of generalizing incorrectly from one institution to others. This approach also had the advantage of highlighting factors which might be changed in order to improve institutional care. It should come as no surprise to anyone that noninstitutional rearing is generally more beneficial for children than institutional rearing. But this knowledge offers little direction to improving institutional care because home rearing differs from institutional rearing in so many ways. However, isolating differentially beneficial institutions could lead directly to practical changes in less adequate institutions: It should be easier to discover the relevant differences between two institutions than between one institution and many homes, and there could be little question that the more beneficial procedure was feasible within an institutional setting.

Although it is reasonable to assume that children who are admitted to different institutions for the same ostensible reason, e.g., mental retardation, are quite comparable, it is still possible that different types of children find their way into different institutions. Therefore, in evaluating the effects of institutionalization, it would be most desirable to select closely matched children who were originally admitted for the same reason to a single institution and to then transfer some of them to another institution, later examining the differences between the transferred and retained groups. In the course of a broad-based experimental program to isolate dimensions of institutional care for the severely mentally retarded, we found that one of the seven institutions under study had, a few years previously, transferred a number of severely retarded children to an institution which was dramatically different in the type of care given to the children. The transfers had been made solely on the basis of the location of parents' homes, so that children would be closer to their parents. It was possible to find children who remained in the original institution and who matched the transferred children very closely on case-history and clinical data collected while all of the children were in the admitting institution. The present investigation reports the results of an experimental comparison of responsiveness to social reinforcement between the children who were transferred and the matched children who remained in the original institution.

A primary difference between these two institutions was the amount of contact between the children and their attendant caretakers. Attendants in the original institution provided the children with much less social interaction. It seemed reasonable to assume that the original institution was more socially depriving, and, accordingly, it was hypothesized that the children who remained in the original institution would show greater responsiveness to social reinforcement than those who were transferred.

Method

Subjects. The subjects of the experiment were 42 of the 88 children in Institutions D and E. They were ambulatory and capable of performing the tasks at hand. All the children at E, it will be recalled, had been transferred from D for administrative reasons.

Apparatus. The criterion measures were derived from a combination and modification of procedures employed by Kuethe (1962) and Weaver (1966). The apparatus consisted of a $3' \times 8'$ panel of green felt which was mounted on a wall, a group of 100 free-form felt cutouts, a tray to hold the cutouts and two chairs. The Ss chair was located eight feet in front of the midline of the felt panel and the Es chair was located at the end of the felt panel which was to Ss right. The E was a young woman who had had considerable experience as both a teacher and an experimenter with mentally retarded children.

Procedure. The Ss were brought to a spare room in either their cottage or school, asked to sit in the Ss chair, and were instructed to take one of the forms from the tray presented by E and to place it anywhere on the panel when E said to "Go." The E was then seated and told the child to "Go." After the child placed the cutout on the felt panel, E removed it and noted the distance it was placed from the end of the panel near which E had been seated. The E then offered the tray to the child so that he could select another figure. This procedure was repeated 12 times. After every odd-numbered choice, the E praised the child for his choice of forms. Otherwise, the E made no reinforcing comments.

Upon completion of the first twelve trials, an open-ended procedure was begun. The tray with the remaining forms was given to the child, who was instructed to take them one at a time and put them on the felt board, returning to his chair after each placement to get a different form. The child was told that he could stop playing the game anytime he chose. During this portion of the task, the child was praised after every third trial for his placement of the forms. The task was terminated when the child said he wished to stop, or when he remained at his chair or at the felt board for 30 seconds.

The two measures secured from the procedure were the average distance S placed the forms from E during the first 12 trials and the time he played during the open-ended procedure.

Results. On the 12 placing trials, the children who had remained in Institution D placed their figures an average of 41.1 inches from the Experimenter and children who were transferred to Institution E placed their figures an average of 52.2 inches from the Experimenter. This difference was statistically significant ($t = 2.35$, one-tailed $p < .01$), indicating that the children remaining in the institution which provided less social contact with adults approached significantly closer to the Experimenter.

On the open-ended portion of the task, the children who remained in the original institution played an average of 27.9 minutes and the children who were transferred played an average of 16.7 minutes. This difference was statistically significant ($t = 2.34$, one-tailed $p < .01$), indicating that the children in the more socially depriving institution played significantly longer.

Although the children in the two groups were comparable with respect to how far their parents lived from their respective institutions, a check was made on the frequency of visiting by the parents. Both institutions keep records of visits received by the children, and the number of visits received by each child during the calendar year preceding the experiment was determined from these records. It was found that the children remaining in Institution D received significantly ($t = 3.64$, $p < .01$) fewer ($M = 3.63$) visits than the children transferred to Institution E ($M = 15.48$). This finding raised the possibility that the differential responsiveness of the two groups was due to the amount of contact they had with their families rather than to the character of their institutional care. This possibility was evaluated by correlating the number of visits with both of the reinforcement measures separately for the two groups of Ss. None of these correlations approached statistical significance: the coefficients were .01 and $-.03$ for the time and distance measures respectively at Institution D and .07 and .14 for Institution E. Apparently, the differential responsiveness of the two groups to social reinforcement cannot be accounted for by the greater frequency of visits to the children transferred to Institution E.

Product-moment correlations were calculated between average distance from E for the first 12 trials and time played during the open-ended portion of the task. For Ss in the original institution, the correlation was .32 ($p > .10$) and for children who were transferred it was .37 ($.05 < p < .10$). Since the groups were small and the correlations were nearly identical, the groups were combined. For the combined group, the correlation was .40 ($p < .01$), indicating that those Ss who approached closer during the first 12 trials played longer on the open-ended portion of the game.

The findings that the transferred children approached less closely to E and played less long than children remaining in the more depriving institution indicate that one of the consequences of residing in a more depriving institution is a heightened responsivity to social reinforcement. Thus, the present study extends to severely retarded children the findings of Butterfield and Zigler (1965a) with mildly retarded adolescents. One of the important aspects of this heightened responsivity is that it may interfere with independent problem-solving behavior (Turnure and Zigler, 1964; Zigler, Sanders, and Butterfield, unpublished manuscript, Yale University, 1966) and that it results in a heightened reaction to socially defined failure experiences (Butterfield and Zigler, 1965b). As a consequence, it may interefere with intellectual development.

The Effective Institution

Assessing institutional effectiveness is made possible through use of the methods described above. An institution in which children are happy, self-sufficient, show intellectual growth, manifest minimal stereotypy (such as rocking), and manifest no excessive need for social reinforcement can be described as being an *effective institution*. A facility in which most of these factors are present only to a small degree is *ineffective* in terms of its therapeutic milieu.

In our sample of six state institutions, Institutions C and D are ineffective institutions. These two agencies stand out in the consistent low rank they obtained on all measures. These completely independently gathered assessments are so consistent as to allay any doubts about the validity of this conclusion. Institution E emerges as clearly effective, while F appears to be moderately effective.

Establishing the effectiveness of an institution is an important step in and of itself. It may have vital bearing on the question of institutionalizing a mentally retarded child (Klaber, in press). Yet such a designation merely enables us to label a facility—it does not explain the variables and causes which make for effectiveness.

It is reasonable to assume that effectiveness is dependent on many variables: per capita cost, physical plant, as well as the behavior of the professional and ward personnel. We were unable to investigate all these factors fully. We have, instead, concentrated on the human element, especially the ward personnel.

Aides and Their Charges

Since it is likely that the behavior of those persons who come in contact with the children will be most influential in modifying child behavior, we observed the behavior of attendants as they interacted with our matched triads of retardates.

Thus, for example, we recorded the percent of incidents in which we observed conversations between aide and child, we recorded the percentage of observed incidents when one of "our children" was ministered to physically, etc. Table 9.4 shows some of the results obtained from three institutions.

T A B L E 9 . 4 Incidence of Attendant-Child Interactions (Percent of Total Interactions)

	Institution		
	D	E	F
Shows physical affection	.44	.80	.37
Converses with individual child	2.20	4.36	1.96
Takes care of physical need	2.85	4.24	2.50
Responds to child	1.93	2.72	1.39

Clearly emerging from this table is the fact that our children received greater attention from aides in Institution E, than either Institution D or F. They had more conversations with aides, they received more physical care, and received responses to their demands more frequently. As we have already seen in Institution D, unhappy behavior predominates over happy behavior, intellectual growth is slower than in other facilities, and the residents do not act as independently as in the other two agencies. The strong relationship between the actions of the attendants and the capabilities of the children is thus self-evident. Moreover, the evidence of the social deprivation experiment is also fully consistent with the same variables.

The Retardate and His Interpersonal Environment

We do not mean to imply that the retardate in an institution receives all of his interpersonal stimulation from attendants. Quite to the contrary, by far most of his experiences are with other retardates and with older, less-handicapped persons called "working patients," "working boys," "trainees," etc. A surprisingly large number of interactions comes from other, nonretarded persons on the ward. These individuals are volunteers, professionals (e.g., physical therapists), and individuals employed specifically to interact with children.

Table 9.5 delineates the sources of interpersonal contacts of the children in our sample. In five out of six institutions peer contacts, i.e., other ward residents of similar degree of retardation, constitute the most prevalent source of interpersonal relations. Significantly, however, in Institution E, our most

TABLE 9.5 SOURCES OF INTERPERSONAL CONTACTS (PERCENT)

| Sources of Inter-personal Contact | Institution | | | | | |
| | Series I | | | | Series II | |
	A	B	C	D	E	F
Aides	21.987	11.348	23.687	25.854	30.768	23.420
Trainees	2.146	7.901	3.029	10.813	3.227	7.682
Peers	63.411	60.941	67.419	48.902	31.659	57.045
Nonretarded adults	12.456	19.809	5.865	14.430	34.345	11.852

effective facility, this is not the case: attendants and other nonretarded adults interact as frequently with the residents as the residents interact with each other. It will be recalled that Institution E is our most effective facility, in which the children were observed to be happiest. The often heard statement to the effect that "retarded children are happiest among their own kind" has therefore no basis in fact.

Another, to us rather surprising, finding derived from Table 9.5 was the significant contribution of nonattendant personnel. In the institutions which we observed, the contribution of these persons appeared to be much greater than we had anticipated. This observation led us to compute the expected rate of interpersonal interaction of this personnel and compare it with the observed rates. We may assume, for example, that if three attendants and one volunteer are present in a ward, the volunteer's contribution is 25 percent of the total observed interpersonal interactions. A quick glance at Table 9.6

TABLE 9.6 EXPECTED VS. ACTUAL INTERPERSONAL CONTACTS OF NONATTENDANT PERSONNEL

| | Institution | | | | | |
	A	B	C	D	E	F
Expected	.23	.51	.12	.36	.83	.37
Actual	.57	1.75	.25	.56	1.12	.51

will dispel this notion rapidly: most nonattendant personnel interact much more with the residents than expected on a purely statistical basis. We believe that this finding is highly significant and demonstrates the need for specialized personnel—free of housekeeping and administrative duties—whose job is the human relationship between child and adult. Our data also suggest that reliance on working patients or trainees is inadequate and, on the whole, not satisfactory. Our data would suggest, therefore, that programs using the services of such older and more capable retardates are probably of limited utility.

Most interactions involve other retardates both of positive (e.g., playing) or negative (aggressive) nature. There are, of course, further interactions with the working patients. The crucial determinant, however, is the amount of interpersonal stimulation received from aides and other nonretarded adults.

Perhaps one of the most potent indicators of satisfaction we have found was the amount of nonnutritive sucking the retardates engaged in. The incidents of oral self-stimulation (thumb-sucking; licking of objects, strings, rags, dolls, etc.) manifested a perfect negative rank order correlation with self-sufficiency and adjustment. It appears that this very simple behavior pattern which is so easily observed can serve as an excellent indicator of institutional effectiveness.

The Typical Institutional Routine

Although there are certain similarities in the observed institutional routines, there are some glaring differences. One example is given here to illustrate this point. Although all six institutions present the claim that schooling is available to all those who are eligible (i.e. educable and/or trainable) the percentage of matched children *actually* attending school varies greatly.

T A B L E   9 . 7   School Attendance

| | Series I | | | | Series II | |
	A	B	C	D	E	F
Number	13	12	3	6	15	12
Percent	76	71	18	14	35	27

As in all our previous measures, C and D have significantly fewer children attending school programs than the other two facilities in their respective series. It is concluded that a given child may have a two to three times better chance to attend formal school classes in one institution as opposed to another. Since it is reasonable to assume that teachers interact more with individual children than do aides, this fact contributes even further to the social deprivation of the residents.

On the ward the most typical "activity" was simple idleness, i.e., sitting down or doing absolutely nothing. In both series this factor appeared to be related to the amount of interactions available with aides and the other adults.

It is clear that the residents of E are much less inactive than the matched

INCIDENCE OF INACTIVITY (PERCENT OF OBSERVATIONS)

	Series I			Series II	
A	B	C	D	E	F
33.16	27.94	49.74	44.40	26.70	36.20

residents of D and F, and those in C receive less stimulation (external or internal) than their matches in A and B.

Roughly between one third and one half of the time of the severely retarded resident of a typical institution is spent in doing nothing (not even television watching). A substantial amount of time (between 15 and 20 percent) is spent in autistic behavior. It is necessary to mention here that we have found no effect of the institutional environment on this behavior pattern. Evidently none of the institutions we have studied have developed effective methods in treating such extreme withdrawal symptoms.

In order to understand the task of the aide better we observed attendants in Institutions C, D, and E while on the ward.

Here we did not observe matched residents, but attendants while they were in the immediate vicinity of the retarded children. We used a time-sample method of two-minute intervals (two minutes of observation followed by a two-minute rest period, in blocks of 30 minutes each). Child-care activities

TABLE 9.8 In-Room Activities of Aides in Three Institutions (Percent of Observations)

	Institution		
	C	D	E
Child care (active)	28.40	25.40	30.64
Talks to child	22.53	23.07	28.59
Plays	5.10	1.90	7.57
Punishment	2.82	5.12	4.38
Ward routine	11.77	15.00	11.65
Supervision(passive)	24.71	17.08	15.60
Self-directed	11.66	23.75	13.69

include feeding, bathing, etc., while passive supervision indicates that the attendant is merely standing by to see that no harm comes to the children. "Ward routine" refers to physical activities directed to the maintenance of the ward, while "self-directed" describes activities unrelated to the aides work assignment. It can be seen that Institution D's aides are more likely to be idle, watch TV, or engage in their own hobbies than are attendants at either C or

E. However, workers at C must spend much more time in supervising residents than the personnel at E.

The fact that aides in different institutions are maintaining significantly different work assignments is clear. That each institution has created its own typical work distribution is obvious. The reasons for this phenomenon are, however, not evident. Curiously, Institution D, which has emerged as the worst facility of all our measures, has maintained the most active in-service training program over the years, while E (our most effective facility) has only instituted such a service recently. The superintendents of all institutions claim to encourage interactions with children and seemingly attempt to do all in their power to implement their ideas. So far we have found little evidence that effective modification of aide behavior results from the administrative measures instituted by the directors of the facilities, or that in-service training changes attendants' interactions with children.

ATTITUDES OF ATTENDANTS

Attendant behavior is undoubtedly related to the attitudes which they hold with respect to the mentally retarded. Unfortunately we have been unable to find any studies which compare different institutions, nor are there any studies available which relate attendants' manifest verbalizations to observed behavior (Butterfield, 1967).

The attitudes aides express verbally (on tests or in interviews) in relation to their actual behavior have never been investigated. In evaluating training programs for attendants, such an approach seems crucial, for administrators are less interested in producing socially approved verbal responses than in proper, or desirable child-rearing activities. We attempted to measure verbal attitudes through the use of two instruments: (1) a modification of Schaefer and Bell's PARI (Schaefer and Bell, 1958) and (2) a sentence-completion test constructed by our own staff.

The modification of the PARI was a very simple one: we inserted the word "retarded" prior to any mention of child in the text, and substituted "retarded infant" for the word baby. We thus arrived at a new scale we called R-PARI ("R" standing for Retarded). We had hoped to be able to demonstrate the different attitudes of workers in different institutions and perhaps even to correlate these with attendant behavior. Our results, however, were quite disappointing. The relative agreement and disagreement of attendants in Institutions D, E, and F was almost complete. Only one sub-scale, of a total of 23, yielded a difference beyond the .01 level of probability. This sub-scale was entitled "Suppression of Sexuality." It contains such items as "Retarded children who take part in sex play become sex criminals when they grow up." Attendants at D agree much more frequently that suppression of sexual behavior is of importance in caring for retarded children. We wondered whether this attitude was related to the fact that complete segregation of the sexes was the rule at D until recently, whereas E and F were relatively more relaxed in this respect.

In spite of this one interesting difference we were much more impressed by the apparent general homogeneity of attitudes as expressed on the R-PARI. Although the attendants differ markedly in their behavior, they do not express verbally divergent opinions.

In order to maximize the possibility of self-expression on the part of the aides we constructed a Sentence Completion Task consisting of 25 sentence stems, all relating to mental retardation. The completed sentences were scored according to specific instructions for each sentence. We were able to achieve 87 percent agreement among raters, the remaining 13 percent were resolved by majority score (agreement of two out of three raters). Selected sentence stems relating to certain issues are discussed below.

Differences Among Institutions.   Although institutions differ in so many respects from each other, the attitudes of attendants show remarkable consistency. The differences which we found were, curiously, unrelated to job performance. We had expected, for example, the morale of the "bad" institution in a sample to be worse than in the other two facilities. Such was not the case. We attempted to measure this factor through responses to the sentence stem "as a rule state institutions for the retarded." By assigning positive or negative values to such responses it is possible to gauge the attitude of the respondents to state institutions. In this case about one half of all responses received a positive rating in Institutions D and E (48 and 57 percent respectively) but only 8 percent in Institution F felt kindly toward their place of employment and similar agencies. We were so surprised at this result (both the failure to differentiate between "good" Institution E and "bad" Institution D, as well as the extremely low rating of Institution F) that we investigated the relevant literature in industrial areas. We found that a review of studies affecting employee–management relationships concluded that "there is no simple relationship between job satisfaction and job performance" (Vroom, 1964). Our findings are evidently consistent with similar research in other areas.

The only other significant differences between institutions (at the .01 level or smaller) was in the general feeling of aides toward the retarded. The sentence stem "mentally retarded children are often" was completed in purely negative terms by 71 percent of the attendants in Institution D, by 48 percent of the aides in Institution F, and by a mere 33 percent of the personnel at E. Clearly, the attendants at E perceive retardates as less likely to possess a multiplicity of bad qualities (such as being hyperactive, difficult to manage, etc.), than do the personnel in other institutions. We might even say that they like them better.

Commonality of Aides' Attitudes.   Most attitudes we measured show typical response patterns among aides regardless of the institution which employs them, and regardless of the in-service training they received. Below are some of the highlights of our findings.

PARENTS. Aides have virtually nothing positive to say about parents of retarded children. They manifest negative attitudes towards "fathers of retarded children," "mothers of retarded children," and, not surprisingly towards "parents of retarded children."

	Positive (Percent)	Negative (Percent)
Parents	13	87
Mothers	12	88
Fathers	20	80

EDUCATION. Attendants are clearly in favor of "schooling for the retarded child" and 83 percent are for encouraging this activity. However, when the concept of schooling is made more concrete and their attitudes towards teachers is tapped, fully two-thirds (66 percent) respond negatively by criticizing the professional educators. Apparently, it is easier to be for "education" than to like the teachers personally.

INSTITUTIONAL PROBLEMS. In order to elicit a critique of institutional practices the sentence stem "the trouble with institutions for the retared" was used. Responses were scored in terms of administrative and physical difficulties, thus the response "are understaffed" would be an example of the former, while "have poor bathing facilities" would be an example of the latter. Attendants are overwhelmingly of the opinion that administrative practices are the root of the major problems (76 percent), with only 24 percent indicating physical shortcomings as being particularly vexing.

THE MENTALLY RETARDED AND THE ENVIRONMENT. Mental retardation is viewed on several items in relation to society at large, rather than as an isolated phenomenon (78 percent), the greatest danger to a retarded child is seen in psychological rather than physical injury (62 percent), and the greatest problem with a retarded child is seen in terms of external forces dealing with the child, rather than as an integral part of his being retarded (67 percent). The aides thus clearly view mental retardation as a social problem.

PROFESSIONAL PERSONNEL

Attendants and ward personnel are not the only people concerned with the welfare of the residents. The professional staff has certainly a major impact on the lives of the retardates residing in an institution. Observational methods are not suited for assessment of these persons, and we had to restrict ourselves to purely descriptive methods in dealing with this group. We surveyed the professional cadres of the institutions, somewhat informally, gathered some information about their qualifications, and interviewed the institutional directors.

Professional Qualifications.   It is impossible, of course, to judge the personality, efficiency, and competence of various professionals. We have to rely therefore on the standards, rules, and degrees bestowed on such workers by their professional peers. We were impressed by the relative dearth of fully qualified persons in positions which permit their coming in contact with residents.

MEDICINE. All six of the institutions in the sample offered medical services to the retardates. Five had a medical staff in residence. Only one institution, however, employed physicians holding a specialty diploma from a recognized specialty board in nonadministrative full-time positions. This institution employed four such well-qualified physicians all of which were pediatricians (it must be noted that less than 50 percent of the institution's residents were 16 years old or younger). Two facilities employed diplomates in psychiatry and neurology as superintendents, but neither of these people had time for individual treatment.

All institutions claimed to use medical consultants, but it was impossible to determine how frequently they would make use of them. None of the facilities used a Board Diplomate in Psychiatry in a strictly clinical capacity, i.e., working directly in the treatment of residents on a sustained basis.

CLINICAL PSYCHOLOGY. While all six facilities had full-time personnel in psychology, only two had a PhD on its psychology staff. Two additional facilities employed psychologists with doctorates in positions other than clinical (one in research and one in administration). A number of PhDs were used in part-time positions in five institutions for a variety of services, including clinical supervision, in-service training, and research. None of the psychologists were diplomates in clinical psychology or any other psychological specialty.

SOCIAL WORK. Only one of the six social service departments we visited was directed by a person holding a Master's Degree in the field of social work. All other persons serving in the capacity of social worker were either completely untrained college graduates, or people with some, though incomplete, social work education.

NURSING. Our survey of nursing personnel is very incomplete, especially in view of the fact that the administrators did not know the academic background of persons working as nurses on their staff. They were more concerned with meeting minimal state specifications rather than with outstanding or unusual professional excellence. As far as we could establish there were no nurses holding a Master's Degree employed in any of the institutions, and we guess that a high percentage of nursing positions designed to be staffed by Registered Nurses were in reality filled by Licensed Practical Nurses.

EDUCATION.   Comparatively speaking the professional training of educators was more adequate than in any other professional discipline. All institutions had individuals with Master's Degrees in charge of educational programs. Most of the teachers were licensed to teach in public schools in their respective states, though a relatively large number would not yet qualify for certification in the field of mental retardation in community programs.

Some Reasons for the Personnel Shortage.   Almost all administrators queried realized the shortages of their professional staffs, and attributed it to two specific factors: (1) low salaries (2) national shortages of personnel. They were united in claiming that properly trained professionals were not attracted to their facilities for these reasons.

An informal survey, however, revealed that the reasons most often given for professional shortages are open to question. It was possible to ascertain that a number of well-qualified persons had served in the six institutions but had left them. It appears that the problem of professional personnel is not in failure to attract them, but in a failure to retain them in service of the institution.

During the past five years two persons with doctorates in education had left the institutions, five psychologists with doctorates, two social workers with MSW degrees, and one RN with an MA were identified as having "passed through" the employ of the six facilities. We were unable to ascertain any Board Diplomates among physicians who left the agencies.

We were able to interview informally three of the psychologists, one social worker, the nurse, and one board-eligible physician. We also interviewed the superintendents. These interviews suggested strongly that the former employees viewed their reasons for leaving the institutions very differently from their employers. The tenor of complaints of the former employees was best described by one psychologist who said simply "I wasn't appreciated," whereas the typical response of the administrators was the answer "he simply didn't fit in."

All professionals complained that although their superior was not acquainted with their own specialty, he insisted that he was qualified to pass on the competence of their job performance. All felt harassed and required to conform to a general institutional pattern which was ill designed to meet the needs of professional personnel. They felt that their graduate education had prepared them for independent action, not for conformity.

Among the specific examples the workers gave as most upsetting were: opening of official mail addressed to them, lack of cooperation and interest in research activities (this area has been documented by Baumeister, 1967, and Wolfensberger, 1965), lack of professional associates, and most frequently of all, lack of respect for their professional recommendations. In a way, then, the superintendent who said that they "didn't fit in" was right. The question remains whether it is the institution or the professional worker who should accommodate the other.

The high degree of competence of all the people who had left the institutions is attested to by the fact that two of the psychologists and both educators are currently on the faculties of universities and the other professionals hold positions at least comparable to the ones they had left. They were unanimous in stating they did *not* earn substantially more money, but that their work assignments were much more pleasurable.

The Parents

The institutional system can easily be likened to any organization: its input is the newly admitted, retarded children; its output is the development of these youngsters. We have shown that the output varies from facility to facility. We have also shown that the process (i.e., behavior of personnel) is specific for each institution. One area is still unexplored—the consumers of the output.

In theory, all the citizens of the state are the consumers of state services. It is they or their elective representatives who decide upon the continuation, expansion, or contraction of the system. In fact, however, the average citizen knows little and cares less about the effectiveness of institutions for the retarded. The real consumers are the parents of the mentally retarded children.

Parents of children in institutions, and those whose youngsters might be admitted to such facilities, are the citizen-consumers of the institutional output. They are the only group of persons outside the system directly concerned with its operation.

It is surprising how little research has been done with groups of parents of institutionalized children. Two recent comprehensive research surveys in retardation fail to mention the word "parent" in their index. Most of the research has been conducted among those who have retained their children at home, not among those who have placed their offspring in an institution. We felt that our approach to the entire institutional system would be incomplete with the inclusion of the parent in our investigation.

We investigated both expressed attitudes and observable behavior among the aides and we intended to use a similar approach with parents. Verbal attitudes were tapped by using the same instruments we used with aides (the R-PARI and our Sentence Completion Task); the parental behavior we selected for our study was the number of visits they paid to their institutionalized children in the course of a year. We complemented our study by administering the verbal instruments to parents who had retained their children at home.

Parental Visits to Institutionalized Children.   When we first approached the area of parental visits to children in institutions we held the strong belief that distance from the parental domicile would be the determining factor of the relative frequency of such behavior. This assumption is widespread and by no means unusual (e.g., Cleland, 1963) and certainly logical.

Our method in investigating parental visitation was a very simple one: Through the institutional records of D, E, and F we obtained the number of visits each one of the children in our matched sample had during the course of one year (1965). We excluded children who had no relatives, and those both of whose parents had left the state. We recorded the parental home address, and measured the air mileage between home town and the institution on a road map. This method proved to be so easy as to arouse our suspicions that such research must have been undertaken earlier, especially in view of the crucial and expensive question of choosing sites for new institutions. In spite of a diligent search in the literature we found only one reference concerning distance and visitation rates. Schultz and Buckman (1965) claimed that a positive relationship between visits and distance exists, yet when their data were subjected to statistical analysis this impression proved to be illusory.

Our own data also caused us considerable surprise since they completely failed to substantiate our hypothesis. The overall product-moment correlation between number of visits in one year and distance to the parental home was insignificant ($r = -.12$). There seems to be no relationship between these variables.

In order to test this finding even further we computed the mean mileage of distance to parental homesteads of children who were never visited during 1965 and those who had visits. Table 9.9 demonstrates the absence of any

T A B L E 9 . 9 MEAN MILEAGE TO PARENTAL HOMES OF VISITED AND NONVISITED RESIDENTS IN THREE INSTITUTIONS

	Institution					
	D		E		F	
	Miles	SD	Miles	SD	Miles	SD
One or more visits	25.00	9.61	18.10	14.82	22.89	16.69
No visits	22.11	6.35	17.78	12.26	25.50	21.53

measurable differences in the mileage of visited and nonvisited subjects. Individual case studies revealed that several children whose parents resided within walking distance (less than 5 miles) from the institution were never visited, whereas some parents travelled over 80 miles to the facility almost every week.

Our data are, of course, limited to the distance and travel conditions prevailing in the northeastern states which we studied. It is quite possible that the greater distances which are common in other geographical areas will yield more substantial relationships. To date, however, there is no evidence that distance to an institution is a primary factor in parental visits.

Interinstitutional Visitation Differences.   While travel distance did not play a significant role in the frequency of parental visits, the institutions varied appreciably in the percent of parents visiting the matched children under observation. Table 9.10 and Figure 9.3 reveal that two thirds of our population were not visited at all during the course of one year at *D*, whereas only 30 percent of our subjects suffered this fate at *E* and *F*. More than eleven visits (about one a month) were recorded at *E* for almost half the group. If we

TABLE 9.10 PERCENT OF RESIDENTS VISITED IN ONE YEAR IN THREE INSTITUTIONS

Number of Visits	Institution		
	D	*E*	*F*
0	66	30	30
1–6	23	14	52
7–10	6	12	9
11+	5	44	9

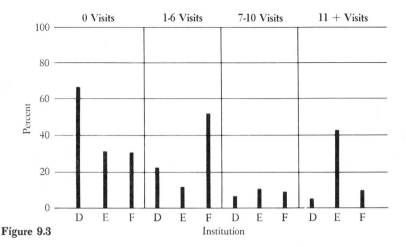

Figure 9.3

assume that parental visits are desirable (there is, alas, no experimental evidence to point up this fact), then Institution E would rank as the best facility, followed by F and D in that order. The reader will recall that the same rank order of these three institutions was obtained on the measures of institutional efficiency which we employed in that part of our study which dealt with adjustment, growth, and development.

The fact that institutional visitation patterns differ so markedly, while being unrelated to mileage travelled, suggests that the efficient institution reinforces the parents on their visits. It should be added here that all three institutions had similar administrative regulations governing visitations. The question must therefore be asked as to why some institutions manage to attract parental visits more than others. The answer appears to relate to the child's development. When parents see their children happy, developing, and responsive they will visit them; if they see that their children are failing to develop, they do not visit. The data at hand place the onus of abandonment by the family squarely on the shoulders of the institution and not on the parents.

Parental Attitudes.   Having established significant behavioral differences for parents in different institutions, we proceeded to search for possible variations of parents who have children in different facilities. To this end we administered the Sentence Completion Task to 14 parents with children at E and to 30 parents with children at D. These, admittedly very small, samples were obtained during parent meetings. The parents were visiting their children, and thus do not constitute a random sample. We have attempted to collect such data also from the parents of our sample who did not visit, but were able to obtain a response rate of only 30 percent. The fragmentary material, which was extremely expensive to collect, seemed to reflect the trends of the larger sample.

The most interesting finding of an analysis of the Sentence Completion Task was the lack of differences between the two groups. It seems that the verbal attitudes of parents with children in different institutions is homogeneous, while parental behavior is not.

The self-image of the parents was a poor one. Parents saw themselves overprotective or neglectful, feeling sorry for themselves, guilt-ridden, and ineffectual. It is evident from their responses that they are in need of psychological assistance which few of them had. Although several of the facilities studied claimed in brochures and interviews that therapeutic counseling was available to parents, we were unable to substantiate a single case of a sustained relationship between a qualified professional in the employ of an institution (i.e., psychologist, psychiatrist, psychiatric social worker) and a parent. The presence of the severe damage to the parental self-image points up the need for such a service.

The parents of children in both effective and ineffective institutions perceived the attendants in unrealistically favorable terms. The sentence stem, "Attendants in institutions for the retarded are" was frequently completed in quasi religious terms, e.g. "to receive a special reward in heaven," "angels of mercy." Frequently they were described as "better than the real father and mother," or as "wonderfully trained and well qualified for the job." Fully 91 percent of the parents had favorable comments about the aides. The distortion of reality testing in this area was highlighted by the total inability to distinguish between effective and ineffective institutional practices.

The same perceptual distortion with respect to the adequacy of institutional care was evident on answers to the sentence stems, "As a rule state institutions for the retarded" and "The trouble with institutions for the retarded." The latter phrase was, of course, deliberately slanted to elicit negative attitudes, yet it failed to do so in the majority of cases. Parents would admit problems in states or institutions other than their own, e.g., "I find no trouble at D," or "in X State I know of no trouble, I hear the other states are terrible." The institutions were seen as "making their lives more pleasant," "as a rule not as good as E," "are ideal and most essential for the children." A small minority stated there was some overcrowding and "lack of home atmosphere."

The sentence stem "I often wonder why the mentally retarded" yielded the greatest number of unanswered records. About one half (49.6 percent) of the parents left this item blank. Our puzzlement about this phenomenon was dispelled when we perused and analyzed those records which did have an answer: It became abundantly clear that the parents suppressed, or perhaps repressed, their wish that the retarded child did not exist. Typical sentence completions were: "are allowed to live often long lives by a loving God, especially severely retarded living on and on to a life of nothingness," "were put on this world by God," "are born," "are the way they are," etc.

These responses and lack of responses serve as an additional indicator of need for professional help for parents. Reliance on denial and repression in defending against the psychological trauma of retardation constitutes by definition a maladaptive response to environmental stress.

PARENTS WITH CHILDREN AT HOME. After we analyzed the responses of parents who had placed their children in residential state-supported facilities, the question as to whether their responses were the result of retardation in the family per se, or whether they are applicable to a special reference group arose. We attempted therefore to collect data from parents who had elected to retain their children at home, in the hope that such a comparison group would enable us to determine the psychological factors associated with institutionalization.

We obtained our sample from a local parent group and from a parochial school with a religious program for retarded children. The two groups of parents were comparable in education and income, but the home group was younger and their children were primarily moderately retarded; the institution group was older and their children were mostly severely and profoundly retarded. Such differences are in line with expectation, yet they impose certain limitations on the interpretation of the results.

There are some significant differences between the groups of parents who have elected to retain their retarded children at home and those who institutionalized their retarded offspring.

Mentally retarded children are seen in a more positive light by the home group, but mentally retarded adults are not. Almost half (40 percent) of the home group gave positive responses to the sentence stem "Mentally retarded children are often," but only 15 percent of the same group had a positive completion to the stem "Retarded adults tend to." The institution group remained consistent with 19 percent and 16 percent positive responses respectively.

INSTITUTIONS FOR THE RETARDED. There was a clear-cut difference in parental attitudes towards institutions and attendants. The institution group was convinced of the excellence of the facilities in which their children were placed, while the home group was convinced of the opposite. As mentioned earlier, the praise lavished on the institutions was so extravagant as to suggest severe distortions in reality in this area. Attendants were described as "angels," "much better than any parent could hope to be," "the most wonderful people I have ever met," etc. The item designed to elicit complaints about these facilities ("The trouble with institutions for the retarded") was frequently answered in terms of complete denial, and even more frequently in terms of "no trouble in X State, but bad in others." The home group was much less favorably impressed by the attendants, frequently referring to their lack of training.

Perhaps the most interesting difference found between the two groups was in relation to the realism of expectation expressed by them. The sentence stem "I often wish that retarded children" was scored in terms of specific desires (e.g., "had more school programs available") and magical fantasies (e.g., "could all be cured"). On this item, parents with children at home showed a high degree of realistic specificity, while almost half (46 percent) of the institution group expressed totally magical and frequently extremely rejecting attitudes (e.g., "I often wish that retarded children didn't exist").

The differences between parental groups suggest a partial breakdown in reality testing of parents who place their children in institutions. We do not know, of course, whether this difference occurred prior to or after the placement of the child. We suspect, however, that this impairment of judgment occurs *before* the decision to institutionalize a child is made and is symptomatic of it.

REGULATION OF INSTITUTIONS

As "consumers" the parents lack the objectivity and critical facility to serve as the regulatory agent which is inherent in a free-market economy. Supervisory agencies within the state system are too involved in the power politics of the larger state machinery. It appears therefore that an independently financed agency (perhaps one at a university, or a charitable foundation) will have to be given the authority and the necessary access to residential institutions. The most promising strategy involves interinstitutional comparison. No parent organization and no single state system has the necessary resources to undertake such studies. Regional and national authorities seem therefore to be a necessary part of a system of ongoing and permanent evaluation of institutional effectiveness.

SUMMARY

Organizational systems differ from each other in structure, operations, and aims. Residential institutions for the retarded are no exception. We set ourselves the goals of demonstrating some of these differences and investigating their causes. A sample of six residential state institutions in three northeastern states was chosen because of the very wide variation in style, philosophy, and size which they manifested.

We were primarily interested in the process and output of the system, by which we meant the operations leading to observed differences in the development of the children in residence. Our second effort was designed to investigate the psychological climate of the institutions and its relationship to the behavior of the persons most responsible for the welfare of the retarded residents.

In order to achieve our first objective we matched groups of severely retarded children in two series of three institutions each. By controlling for major diagnostic and demographic variables (including intelligence, age, age-at-admission) it was hypothesized that differences found between the matched triads would be the result of the actions of the respective institutional systems.

In the second of the two series of matched triads we were able to take advantage of a fortunate circumstance. One of the states in our sample had begun to decentralize its facilities for residential care five years prior to the advent of our investigation. We were thus able to match our triads in Series II on a retrospective basis with variables pertaining to intellectual measurements six years prior to our study. Our second series represents therefore a longitudinal investigation of matched triads of severely retarded children in three state facilities.

In order to obtain a comprehensive picture of our subjects' behavior, we devised a method of time-sampling their reactions to the environment and of the interpersonal stimulations they received from their surroundings. In this manner we collected over 10,000 individual observations, two minutes in duration and spanning the waking day of the children.

A compilation and analysis of these observations clearly showed one institution in each of the two triads to harbor less well-adjusted children than the other two. Autism, crying, inactivity, and other clearly maladaptive behaviors predominated over purposeful or enjoyable experiences. One institution in the second series was clearly superior in the adjustment of the residents to the comparable facilities.

The functional level of the residents was assessed through a Self-Sufficiency Scale which was administered by the aides. Significant differences were demonstrated among the different facilities on this variable. Since the children were matched initially with respect to intelligence, these differences were attributed to the effects of the institutional experience. The same two institutions which showed predominantly maladaptive behavior also manifested the lowest degree of self-sufficiency.

Records dating back over at least a decade permitted the retrospective matching of children with respect to intellectual functioning six years prior to the current study. Retesting of the triads in Series II yielded therefore a longitudinal record of intellectual development. In this area too, the institution which had already been shown to lag in self-sufficiency and adjustment manifests the least intellectual growth.

Our three independently obtained measures show a very close relationship to each other. We therefore designated as "effective" those institutions where self-sufficiency, adjustment, and intellectual growth were maximal, and as "ineffective" the institutions where these attributes were least well developed.

We proceeded to investigate some of the attributes of "effective" and "ineffective" institutions. Substantial differences in the ward behavior of attendants were established. These observations were also undertaken on a time-sample basis. They show that in some institutions attendants devote a much greater percentage of their time to the actual care of residents than in others. These behavior patterns did not seem directly related to such formal descriptive variables as employee—patient ratio, salary of attendants, or institution size.

"Effective" and "ineffective" institutions were not staffed by attendants holding substantially different attitudes on a Sentence Completion Task devised by us. In fact, attendant behavior seemed related to administrative practices, especially direct supervision, rather than to any measurable psychological variable. We were especially disappointed to note that institutional effectiveness and in-service training showed virtually no demonstrable relationship.

A sample of parents of children institutionalized in an "effective" or an "ineffective" institution also failed to yield a difference on the Sentence Completion Task. We interpreted this finding, as well as some of the specific response patterns as symptomatic of a breakdown in reality testing among the parents, at least with respect to their ability to evaluate their children's environs.

While the verbal and psychological attitudes of parents do not differentiate between "effective" and "ineffective" institutions, their behavior is indicative of an unconscious response to the more favorable environment. We found that parents whose children reside in an "effective" institution visit their offspring much more frequently than do parents whose children live in an ineffective institution. One by-product of our investigation was the finding that the frequency of parental visits is independent of the mileage required for travel. This surprising result suggests that the primary factor in the parent's interest in his child is his feeling that the child is happy, intellectually developing, and learning to become self-sufficient. In short, receives the benefits of an effective institution.

Implications

Perhaps the single most important implication of our study derives from the finding that institutions differ substantially from each other. Only too frequently have generalizations been drawn about "institutionalized retardates" on the basis of studying the population of a single institution. Any assertions, based on an institutional sample of one case, are highly questionable. It will be necessary to conduct studies on a regional, national, and in some cases even international basis to learn about the effects of institutionalization on retarded children.

We have shown that the matching method permits the objective assessment of the effects of different institutional environments. We believe that such methods as well as other objective indices should be employed to evaluate all publicly supported facilities, especially because parents of retarded children in institutions suffer from serious perceptual distortions in this area. An independent authority, working with but not of the responsible governmental agencies appears best suited for this task.

The recommendation as to whether or not to institutionalize a child will have to depend on the *specific* facility the child would be sent to, rather than be stated in global terms (Klaber, in press).

Some of the arguments for institutionalization in any form need to be reevaluated. Below are some specific assertions concerning the advantages of the institutional setting; they are frequently mentioned and therefore deserve special consideration.

1. The institution has better educational facilities than the public-school special class! Most states exempt their own, state-operated facilities from

the requirements of certification for teachers, remedial specialists, and other professional personnel. Thus the retarded child is less likely to be instructed by a fully qualified (i.e., certified) teacher in the state institution than in his own community (Cain and Levine, 1961). Moreover, the chances of a given child attending a school program fluctuate wildly from institution to institution.

2. Medical and behavioral specialists are readily available in the state institution! Our survey of six state institutions in three eastern states revealed a very small number of board diplomates among the physicians, not a single diplomate among the psychologists, and only one social worker with a Master's Degree. It is clear that fully qualified professional services may not be available in institutions. There is certainly no evidence whatsoever that institutional services are in any way superior to most community resources.

3. A retardate is happier among other retardates! The argument that certain individuals are happier among "their own kind" is indeed a specious one and has been used frequently for unsavory ends. In fact, our evidence strongly suggests the opposite, namely that retarded children are happiest when their contact with nonretarded adults is maximized. The greater the amount of contact the better adjusted they seem to be.

4. The therapeutic milieu of the institution, based on continuous training programs by aides, will effect an accelerated maturation among the retardates! Recent observations in a West Coast facility have clearly demonstrated that aides in one institution not only fail to train children in areas of self-sufficiency, but actually retard their progress by promoting dependent behavior (Thormahlen, 1965). Our observations show that such is indeed the case in certain facilities but not in others. The decision to institutionalize a child must therefore depend on the proposed placement as well as on the needs of the child and the family.

Among some other implications are the following:

Unit size is apparently more influential in institutional effectiveness than overall staff ratios. One attendant with ten children will be more involved with them than will ten attendants with one hundred children (though the ratio remained constant). Greater attention to smaller units is therefore of vital concern to administrators.

The contributions of nonattendant personnel is so great in relation to their relative number that the designation of better-educated and better-motivated persons for special purposes is necessary. Ideally, such people would be trained occupational or recreational therapists in charge of nonprofessional personnel. In line with this implication it seems logical that supervisory and promotional policies of institutions be reevaluated. It is our impression that promotion from the ranks is only minimally effective and perpetuates old and often undesirable policies. Career opportunities for trained therapists in the fields of occupational, physical, and recreational therapy appear most desirable. It appeared to us that institutions are reaching the limits of the use of untrained personnel. The in-service training programs in the facilities we visited were ineffective in modifying existing behavior patterns.

The parental image is in need of radical reconstruction. Staff will need greater help in dealing with parents, and parents are in need of skilled counseling and therapy (none of our six institutions had any program in these areas).

Highly skilled professional personnel must be permitted to work under conditions conducive to continued association with institutions. Without such leadership, it is unlikely that progress can be sustained. Should this prove impracticable, it will be necessary to draw on community resources on a part-time basis in preference to lowering of standards of employment.

CHAPTER

10

Siblings of the retarded

FRANCES KAPLAN

AUTHORS' NOTE:

THE INSTITUTION AND THE FAMILY

The institution, as described and studied by Dr. Klaber in the previous chapter, is an important setting for anyone concerned with the field of mental subnormality or with the more general question of the relation between behavior and environments. A far older "institution" is that of the family. In their 1958 monograph, Sarason and Gladwin emphasize the importance of studying how different cultural groups view and handle mental subnormality; and they discuss in some detail Eaton and Weil's (1955) study of Hutterite society. This study is well worth the reader's time not only because it describes a culture different from our own and therefore forces on one the awareness of how problems (their statement and resolution) vary from one culture to another, but also because it underlines the necessity of viewing variations within a society, particularly one such as ours which is pluralistic in so many ways. The family in our society is a highly complex and variable institution, a fact which should alert us to the possibility that its view and handling of a mentally subnormal member will vary considerably from one family to another. Just as the institutions described and studied by Dr. Klaber varied, we may expect significant variations from family to family.

In the following chapter Dr. Frances Kaplan presents the origins and history of a research project on the normal siblings of retarded or defective children. It would, in our opinion, be unduly constricting if the reader were to view Dr. Kaplan's experiences only in terms of the field of mental subnormality. As she so well states at the end of her chapter ". . . we see the problem of a family dealing with a retarded child and all it means to them, as one instance of a universal experience, i.e., how a family copes with unexpected disappointment and trauma. Few families can avoid such experiences, whether it be in the form of a retarded child, a chronically ill member, a serious accident, or some other stressful event. Despite the many specific differences in these experiences, the core issue seems to be how a family responds to severe stress, which often occurs without warning"—a point of view discussed and illustrated by Ross (1964).

Although Dr. Kaplan ends her presentation with a discussion of observations of siblings in a particular group situation, her research has not ended there. She is currently engaged in a more formal and comprehensive study of two college groups: those who have and those who do not have a defective sibling. Although it is too early to draw any specific conclusions, her preliminary findings encourage one in the belief that this type of study will illuminate the different ways in which family contexts seem to affect and be affected by a defective child.

INTRODUCTION

On the following pages is an account of the inception and development of a research investigation of siblings of retarded children. It is reported here neither as a completed project with specific conclusions about this population nor even for what tentative hypotheses we can offer about the experiences and difficulties of these brothers and sisters. Rather the report is intended as a case history of a research topic. In particular it illustrates how a certain point of view about a problem—in this case, retardation—causes one to focus on aspects of the situation often overlooked or disregarded. That point of view is the second reason for presenting the material. The premise is that retardation is not primarily a problem that resides in an individual but rather is an event that occurs in a family and in a community. To be maximally effective, clinicians addressing themselves to problems of retardation must consider them in this broader context. This research highlights the importance of this broader focus, as it illustrates the significance of having a retarded child in the family to a group that is commonly ignored, the siblings.

If this view of retardation as a family event is taken seriously, it has important implications for preventative interventions. Prevention in the area of retardation consists not only in finding ways of decreasing the incidence of retarded children. Families that do have retarded children must be helped to cope with the problems in a way that enhances, rather than constricts or distorts, the growth and development of all family members. In our work with siblings, we have found a surprising lack of awareness, both on the part of the families and professionals, of the siblings' roles in the families' total styles of coping with the retardation.

SIBLINGS

Cindy

Several years ago I began a psychotherapeutic relationship with an eleven-year-old girl, little suspecting that the questions raised by this experience would be the impetus for a full-scale research project on siblings of retarded children. Because many of the issues that emerged in the course of the treatment are still central to the research, my experience with Cindy will be described in some detail as the proper introduction to it.

The experience of treating this child is worthy of description in its own right, as well as in the context of siblings, as her case clearly illustrates the way that our prior conceptions of a child and of a category of dysfunction or "disease" so often enormously influence how we behave towards that child and ultimately become self-fulfilling prophecies as the child in turn responds in accordance with our expectations. Although at the present time Cindy's future is at best uncertain, her response to psychotherapy and to me suggests what might have been, had parents, teachers, and other people in her life treated her differently, or had any of these people seen her problems as potentially remediable and, consequently, brought her for treatment earlier. In this era of reawakened concern for all handicapped and troubled children, Cinday's story underlines the need for early intervention and for preventative approaches to mental health problems. This "might have been," tragic as it may be in this particular case, can still be possible for other similar children.

Finally, this case illustrates once again what we are slowly coming to know: the "case" is never just the disturbed child, the retarded infant, the delinquent adolescent. The "case" is the entire social system influencing and being influenced by the identified problem. It always includes the family and often the neighborhood, the schools, and the community (e.g., Farber and Ryckman, 1965; Sarason, Levine, Goldenberg, Cherlin, and Bennett, 1966). Cindy's pathology consisted not only of the difficulties she experienced in thinking and feeling; it was also part of an entire network of family interaction and patterns, which had in turn been deeply affected by Cindy's older brother—a severely retarded boy.

The initial contacts

⟡ Cindy's parents, Mr. and Mrs. B, first came to an agency that services retarded children because they were puzzled by what they described as her strangeness and were troubled by her increasingly inappropriate behavior in school. They decided to approach an agency for the mentally retarded because they considered Cindy retarded, as did the school, which had placed her in a class for the retarded. They expressed an interest in recreational activities for Cindy—with other retarded children—but did not seem to consider the possibility that whatever difficulty was causing her "retardation" and bizarreness might be, in part at least, remediable.

The social worker who visited the home reported that the mother suspected Cindy's difficulties to be due to an allergy to milk, since an older brother had such an allergic reaction. However, the social worker also expressed some puzzlement about his impressions of Cindy: She did not talk as he felt a retardate usually does. She had insisted on being present while he spoke with her parents, and she repeated such phrases as, "My life is over . . . I'm going to end it all. I'm very frustrated." He responded to her implicit pleas for help by referring her to me for a psychological and intellectual evaluation and possible treatment. Before I met with the B's, previous test material, doctors' reports, etc. were collected. They all gave a picture of a retarded, strangely behaving, brain-damaged child, and in fact she was diagnosed by several in just that way. The reports implied or stated the neurological, organic defect to be the basis for her retardation and strangenes. On the other hand, it was not clear to me how the diagnoses of brain damage explained this child's behavior. For example, the reports rated her reading as being at a high level, although she was given an IQ test score in the 60's. Why this discrepancy existed was not explainable in terms of an organic deficit. Consequently, it was with some feeling of puzzlement that I came to the first meeting with the B's. The B's are a middle-class Jewish family who showed signs of the strain they had been under. Mrs. B, a heavy, well-dressed woman, was quite overwhelming in her aggressive manner of talking, her demandingness, and her real sorrow. Mr. B. seemed to be a somewhat subdued man who let his wife do most of the talking.

Cindy herself appeared noticeably small for her age: At that time, she was prepubescent, and looked nearer eight or nine than her actual age of eleven. She had a somewhat strange appearance, probably due to the disarray in which she kept her clothes and hair. Nonetheless, she had a decided charm about her when she talked. In this first meeting, I was torn between an impression that she was an extremely "out of it," disorganized, and/or retarded child, and the occasional sharp realization from her comments of her acute and sophisticated awareness of what was going on.

Mrs. B actually provided the first major clue to Cindy's difficulties with her very first sentence to the therapist. Pointing to the one-way mirror in the treatment room, she said, "Oh, I know about those mirrors. They showed us how they work when we took Marvin to the institution." Thus, the identification in Mrs. B's mind between Cindy and her severely retarded, institutionalized brother was made clear from the beginning.

Although this tie between Cindy and Marvin was relatively clear from the beginning, many other aspects of that first interview with Mr. and Mrs. B and Cindy became comprehensible only over a period of 18 months and over 100 hours of treatment. Several aspects of this family's way of relating to each other were obvious even then. Mrs. B did most of the talking, describing their recent difficulties with Cindy with considerable affect and involvement, becoming tearful at points when she told of their fears that Cindy would become like her older brother. Cindy managed to look "crazy" and "stupid" during this discussion; she rolled her head around, played with her saliva, and maintained a silly grin.

However, when her mother likened Cindy to Marvin, she burst out, "You don't love me. You want to send me to an institution," indicating she was more in touch with the conversation than she looked or acted. However, she also "undid" this angry comment shortly afterwards by going up to her mother and nuzzling her as a small baby might, touching her face, leaning against her, etc. Mrs. B responded to this by touching Cindy, rubbing her and telling her she loved her. Thus, any real anger Cindy might have felt and expressed was withdrawn, as it were, and their "loving unity" reestablished.[1] Even then, the B's fear and conviction that Cindy, like her brother, was "incurable" and would end up in an institution was obvious.

Mr. B was generally quiet and let his wife do the talking, saying only that it bothered him when Cindy did all these strange things only because he knew it was not normal. He added that he knew she could not help it. I spent a brief time with Cindy alone at the end of this interview. Despite her peculiar, seemingly unrelated, and "unintelligent" behavior, when I suggested she might come back and talk with me, she said, "Yes, we should set up a schedule!" Thus she indicated from the beginning a strong desire to be helped and to establish a relationship.

The history of the difficulties—some of which they gave this hour, some of which emerged over the year-and-a-half of contact—began at least as far back as the birth of their second son. Their first-born, Richard, was a healthy boy, and two years later they had another son—Marvin. It shortly became evident that Marvin was retarded, and they began the troubled journey of so many parents of retarded children from doctor to doctor looking for advice and assistance. Much is unclear about this period of time, except that they kept Marvin at home for approximately ten years, and that during this time Mrs. B became very closely attached to and involved with this younger son. She maintained him as a complete infant, assuming he was totally unable to help himself and treating him accordingly. The decision to institutionalize him was extremely difficult for the B's to make and to carry out.

By their account, after Marvin was institutionalized, they took their first vacation since his birth and on that trip accidently conceived Cindy. (At another time, they reported she was born before their decision to institutionalize Marvin.) In either case, the intimate connection in their mind between the loss of Marvin and Cindy's birth was apparent.

From the time of Cindy's conception, they desperately feared she would be defective. Mrs. B was convinced she could not bear a healthy child. When Cindy was born, although no defects were apparent, they began taking her from one pediatrician to another, unable to believe she was not defective despite the physician's reassurances. By the time she was three, their prediction began to come true; she was beginning to seem somewhat slow in development. She was sufficiently "immature" at age five to be held back a year before starting kindergarten,

---

[1] One of the most clear characteristics of this mother-child relationship was its "double-bind" nature, i.e., the mother's behavior communicated two contradictory "messages" which can have the effect of keeping the child in a state of anxiety and uncertainty. This characteristic has been noted in the relationship between schizophrenic individuals and at least one of their parents, usually the mother (Bateson, Jackson, Haley, and Weakland, 1956).

then was kept in a combined first and second grade for three years, also because of "immaturity." Interestingly enough, Cindy did rather well those years. She had a sympathetic teacher who liked her, and she was able to learn some academic material despite some strange mannerisms, a reported short attention span, poor coordination, and other indications of difficulty.

When she finally left this class to begin third grade, with a different teacher and more emphasis in the curriculum on academic performance, she began to deteriorate. She cried, screamed, needed constant reassurance from the teacher, and could no longer maintain her previous level of academic work. At the school social worker's recommendation, she was transferred to a special class for educable retarded children, where, however, she continued to deteriorate. She frequently hit herself in the head saying, "I'm stupid, my brain doesn't work." She was frightened of being touched and screamed when another child accidentally brushed against her. She stopped doing any academic work. It was at this point that her parents appealed to the center for retardation for assistance.

I began to meet with Cindy twice weekly, while a social worker met regularly with Mrs. B and occasionally with Mr. B. In addition to the treatment sessions themselves, I immediately established contact with the school Cindy attended to find out what was happening and later to attempt to influence their handling of her.

The first three months of treatment

Cindy quickly established a relationship with me.[2] She made it clear she liked to come, and although she was silent much of the time, she was clearly involved in the process and thinking about it, in and out of sessions. The earliest focus of my comments, once she was comfortable with me, was the contrast between her rather sophisticated style of speech and her high-level ability to understand, on the one hand, and her seeming inability to learn at school, on the other hand. After being confronted with this a number of times, she began to reply with such comments as, "I can't do things any more, I think my mind is broken."

This theme of her inability to learn being associated with her own view of her "head being broken," of something being "wrong with my brain," ran through the first year of treatment, and she objected with increasing vehemence when this position was challenged. (At no time did she voluntarily mention her brother Marvin, who does indeed have "something wrong with his head.")

Seemingly related to Cindy's learning difficulty was her curiosity, which was obviously both strong and inhibited. She began acting out sexual questions using dolls—such as having them hug and kiss and then asking me what they were doing. When I offered to answer any questions she had about anything to the best of my ability, she became—for her—unusually direct and active in asking what people do when they are married, how babies are born, etc. Since she was at the time prepubescent, I also discussed menstruation with her in some detail. She was fascinated by these discussions and remembered in detail essentially all the facts

---

2 Since the focus of this account is Cindy as a sibling of a retarded child, no attempt is made to describe the psychotherapy in detail. Only those aspects relevant to the general issue are described here.

we discussed, giving further evidence of her ability to learn under certain conditions. However, when I commented on her intense curiosity she told me, "That's my sickness." It never became entirely clear why curiosity was so dangerous in the B's family. (Difficulty with curiosity has turned up in a large number of "normal" siblings of retarded children. This is discussed in detail below.)

The other major theme, which was already present in rudimentary form from the beginning, was her inability to express her enormous fury at her mother. A major concern of Cindy's was that if she showed her hatred, she would be sent away. In fantasy she imagined it would cause her total destruction. At this early point in treatment, I was aware that Cindy did not express an "expectable" amount of anger at her mother or at me, and talked with her about it. I was not aware for many months of the intensity of rage that would be released when it began to emerge.

The next nine months

Cindy was extremely upset when I left for a month's vacation, and became increasingly symptomatic. By the time I returned, she looked pitiful and bizarre, and I found it hard to be with her without feeling guilty and somewhat helpless. One symptom consisted of holding her breath and then tightening her entire body in a spasmodic manner; at its height, she repeated this many times a minute. She also began "wiping faces" which meant rubbing her hand down over her nose and gesturing as if she were wiping an invisible substance off her face and discarding it. At times she hit herself in the nose with her hand, occasionally hard enough to give herself a nosebleed.

The treatment of a child with a learning disorder can most effectively be carried out in close cooperation with the relevant persons in the school setting (Sarason, *et al.,* 1966). Although Cindy's special-class teacher wanted to help Cindy, her own point of view, as well as the orientation of the entire school system, resulted in treating children in special classes like "retarded children." That is, it was assumed that they could not understand things and that they would not be able to do very much work—academic or otherwise. In addition, Cindy's symptoms frightened the school personnel, causing them to treat her as if she were extremely fragile as well as retarded. Given this attitude and the series of expectations it set up, Cindy could only continue to behave as she had been and so confirm her own and others' views of her as incapable of learning or of behaving more normally.

After a relatively short attempt to influence the school and teacher, the need for a different setting became apparent. Several months after school began in the fall, Cindy was transferred to a private school that specializes in work with children who have learning difficulties.[3] I talked frequently with the principal and each teacher, emphasizing her ability to learn and to function normally.

Partly as a result of these efforts, partly by virtue of their own orientation and skills, they responded to Cindy as if she were a normal child. They behaved as if they expected her to act normally and to learn, thus making it possible for her to

---

[3] Great appreciation is due to the principal of the school and her staff, who were able to see Cindy as a child, rather than as a retardate, and consequently were able to teach her.

attempt to behave in these ways. This was undoubtedly the first time in her life outside of therapy that anyone ever acted towards Cindy as if she could be normal and intelligent. After an initial period of adjustment, when she first began to perceive this attitude, she became shocked and expressed violent disagreement with this view. We spent many hours talking about her alleged stupidity and I reiterated what I deeply believed, that nothing about the way she was born made it impossible for her to learn. Since she did not mention Marvin, I asked her about him. She did not want to talk about him at first, and when I asked she said she did not know what was wrong with him. Since she had been taken once or twice a month for many years whenever the family visited him in the institution, it seemed highly unlikely that she did not know and I commented on this to her. Finally, she suggested "Someone hit him on the head . . . I don't know who." This fantasy that he had been willfully damaged (by her mother) must have greatly aggravated her fears of displeasing her parents.

Once Marvin came up for discussion, the fight over whether she was defective began in earnest. She insisted she was, demonstrated it repeatedly by acting totally stupid (e.g., not being able to find a paint brush when it was lying in front of her on the table), said repeatedly she was just like Marvin and that she was born with something wrong with her brain. Finally, in utter desperation at her inability to convince me of her point of view, she said, "I'm sick like my brother. I don't have any originality, and my coordination isn't very good!" I told her I was aware that she thought that, and furthermore that her parents thought that as well. I discussed with her my idea that her parents had been so frightened that something might be wrong with her that they had come to believe there was. However, I pointed out numerous instances when she had been able to learn and again restated my disagreement with the family point of view about her.

After several months in the new school with the treatment focus on learning, she began one day in therapy to write a list of spelling words on the board, something she had never done before. Then she wrote a list of all her courses and a time schedule and a list of her teachers' names. I was delighted but afraid to talk directly to her about it for fear this new development would prove to be a mirage! However, my next visit to the school found the teachers jubilant. Cindy had started to learn. She seemed to have given up her previous view of herself as a nonlearner, which finally opened to her the possibility of learning. The spurt in academic work was impressive. In some fields—such as social studies—she rapidly began to catch up to the grade level of children her own age, while arithmetic remained difficult and tedious. But for the remaining time in treatment, even when her emotional life was utterly chaotic, she continued to progress in school, proving rather convincingly that her previous "retardation" was not a necessary result of neurological deficit, but also a response to her parents' and teachers' expectations that she could not learn.

Other events and issues were taking place concomitantly. Only a few major themes will be mentioned here. Her curiosity about sexual matters progressed to a more specific concern with what her parents were doing in bed together, what her newly married eldest brother did with his wife, and the forlorn questions to me: "What's an eleven-year-old girl to do?" Hints of some primitive sexual fantasies came up in her play, but at this time she did not share these thoughts.

Despite progress in several areas, however, I began to experience the hours as difficult, frustrating, and unproductive. Cindy was frequently silent the entire period, and often her behavior was stereotyped and rigid. Her behavior at home was more focused, having lost its previous diffuse and irrelevant quality; but she began having more temper tantrums. In particular, Mrs. B and Cindy had a major battle each morning before school. Although at this time I had no conscious awareness of the problem obstructing treatment, the information was available in the details of the morning battle, had I but paid attention to what I knew.

Cindy did not get up in the morning, despite her mother's scolding and finally screaming that she should. Then Mrs. B would come in and undress, wash, and dress Cindy in bed like an infant (or like a profoundly retarded child). Finally, Cindy would get up and go to the bathroom on her own. When the school bus arrived, Cindy would scream and cry, "Don't send me, don't make me go, and Mrs. B would feel she was killing her if she did insist. Sometimes she was able to get her on the bus; at other times she would give in. She described herself as being as upset as Cindy at forcing her to leave but also hating Cindy for putting her through such a difficult scene daily. When Cindy got to school, her behavior usually changed dramatically; she became pleasant and cheerful, with no signs of the early trauma.

The incredible infantilization and associated symbiotic intimacy, the rage and death wishes associated with separation, and the intimate relationship between Cindy's pathology and her interaction with her mother, were all present in these incidents. (Staver, 1953, has described a similar family pattern in a group of children with severe learning difficulties.) However, I did not yet see the problem clearly, but only knew I was getting increasingly discouraged about the treatment. Further, Mrs. B began cornering me in the hallway and talking in a very depressed and demanding way about the need to institutionalize Cindy. Cindy was getting more and more difficult, according to Mrs. B—and in particular, she could not tolerate more of these morning scenes. Mrs. B implied she herself was approaching a "nervous breakdown."

Since the social worker was leaving at this time, I decided to take over the contact with the parents, but in a different form. I continued to see Cindy twice a week individually, but met with Cindy and her parents together weekly for family treatment.

Two months of family meetings

Within an extremely short time, the central issue in the family pathology was unmistakable. These parents—and particularly the mother—were totally unable to accept *any* anger from Cindy. The family solution to this, with which they all conformed, was that she disguise her fury as "craziness" and that they view her expressions of anger as unmotivated, uncontrollable pathology. In the second family meeting, Cindy said to her parents with feeling, "I hate you!" They immediately responded by saying, "You don't really hate us, do you? You can't really feel that way." When I commented on their discomfort with Cindy's attack, they both said, "She doesn't really mean it." Cindy then ceased any direct expressions of anger, reverting instead to more "crazy" behavior, which involved running through a variety of symptomatic behaviors, all of which made her appear bizarre and also greatly irritated her parents.

In the next several meetings, Cindy expressed more and more openly her rage and fury. In one dramatic meeting, when they had been reminiscing about what a beautiful baby she had been she stood up and yelled at them, "I hate you, it's your fault, you didn't take care of me," and then covered her face and for the first time in my presence cried. Mrs. B also cried, and then both became increasingly guilty and depressed. They again began talking about the possibilities of institutionalization.

In individual sessions Cindy was openly angry and at the same time less symptomatic and indirect than she had ever been. She also began using individual sessions to share her fantasies and private thoughts. One fantasy that preoccupied her for many months was that she would stop up the toilet, then defecate in it, the toilet would run over, and her feces would entirely cover the house and her parents. Although the primitiveness of some of these fantasies was at times startling, I felt it represented significant therapeutic progress for her to be able to share and discuss her private world.

Although she was moving rapidly in treatment, the problem that eventually led to the destruction of the therapy had already begun to cause trouble. Cindy was unable to maintain the distinction between talking about her fury and acting out many of these fantasies and thoughts. She became increasingly destructive at home, tearing some curtains, breaking a window, and writing on the wall. She stopped up a toilet and did defecate in it, which was more openly expressed aggression and pathology than her parents were able to tolerate. The situation was rapidly reaching a boiling point.

The last two months

At this point in time, several events unfortunately coincided. I left for a month's summer vacation and during this time Cindy's maternal grandmother, who had been very close with both Cindy and Mrs. B, died while vacationing with the B's. Aside from the real deprivation and the fantasy concerns this caused Cindy, the major disruption was the loss to Mrs. B who had received considerable support from her mother. She felt herself to be even more deprived and resented Cindy's needfulness. Simultaneously she tried to turn more to Cindy for support. Cindy's expressed anger was, of course, increasing the distance between them rather than allowing them even their previous closeness and whatever support Mrs. B had derived from it.

Within a month of my return from vacation, it was apparent that Cindy could go no further while living in the home, since her parents could not tolerate her aggression. She had to begin to deal with her hatred before any further progress was possible. Further, she herself was at times overwhelmed by the intensity of anger released and the anxiety it aroused, and at least once became acutely disorganized in school at which time she uncontrollably screamed and ran up and down the halls. Mrs. B dramatically stated the conflict in a family meeting by saying she could not stand to have Cindy at home any more, she was driving her crazy, but she also could not and would not tolerate any separation from her! I finally insisted on the separation, saying I could not in good conscience continue working with Cindy or them unless they accepted this recommendation. We met daily for several days, during which time Mrs. B's stability was seriously in question. It became apparent that one factor making a breakdown seem attractive was the fantasy that if she could not be with Cindy at home, she could be her roommate in the hospital. I told her firmly that if she needed hospital support for a time, she would go to a different hospital. With this, the crisis subsided, and Cindy was hospitalized.

The end of the story cannot yet be written. Cindy profited greatly from two months of separation from her parents, and now needs a long-term residential setting. Even if a good residential treatment facility is available where she can receive continuing intensive therapy, her prognosis is at best doubtful.

The important issue is not whether Cindy can make her way to health at this point, but rather, if we could have gotten to her when she was younger, this child could have functioned far more adequately. If we had gotten to her parents to help them cope more effectively at the time when their son's retardation became apparent, or when they had to institutionalize him, or later when they began to express fears about the new baby, or even when Cindy was held back in the first grade, Cindy might have then had a chance.

Let me be explicit on one point. I do not mean to imply that Cindy is not brain damaged or not functionally retarded. She appears to be a child who came into the world less equipped to deal with it than some children (she does show a number of signs of "minimal brain damage"). She came into an environment that would have been difficult for a sturdier child. Similarly, her parents undoubtedly were not the most psychologically fit people before they had a retarded child, but they were then asked to handle a situation difficult for the healthiest of parents. If professionals in the field of retardation and mental health could have provided some assistance at any one of a number of points when the difficulties were first beginning, Cindy's story would be very different from what it is today.

Aside from its relevance to the treatment of this class of children, my contact with Cindy raised many questions in my mind. What happens to other siblings of retarded children? Do they have difficulties perhaps of similar kind but less in degree? How do young siblings of retarded children think about the retardate's difficulties? Do many suspect, as Cindy did, that someone has damaged them? Do many worry that they too may fall victim to the unknown (or possibly suspected) attacker?

Cindy seemed noticeably lacking in knowledge about her brother's condition, and made it clear she had some interest in remaining so. As she said, she felt her curiosity to be her sickness. Do other more normal siblings of retarded children know very much about the retardate? Is this the type of question they can ask about, or is it a family "secret" that the child must attempt to puzzle out on his own? What is the effect of lack of information on normal siblings? Finally, depending on the answers to these and related questions, what preventive measures might be helpful to normal siblings in dealing with the particular problems of having a retardate in the family?

NORMAL SIBLINGS

In other clinical contacts as a member of the staff at the New Haven Regional Center (NHRC) the weight of evidence has begun to accumulate to suggest that siblings of retarded children are often adversely affected. Parents frequently voiced concern to us about their normal children and the effect the retarded child had on their lives. Because of our emphasis on servicing the entire family in its natural setting, the home, the clinical staff was brought into increasing contact with the siblings. One staff member described a normal sibling who had unconsciously begun to imitate the petit mal attacks suffered by her older sister. There were no grounds for suspecting actual neurological pathology in this "normal" girl. Rather, all the available evidence suggested she was acting out her identification with her sister. This 10-year-old became quite depressed when her sister came into residence at the NHRC. When I talked with her, she denied having any troubling thoughts or feelings, with one exception. When she went to bed—her sister previously shared the room with her—she would suddenly become afraid the "boogey man will come and take me away," and then she was unable to stay alone in the room. Although she rationally knew why her sister was institutionalized, and that it would not happen to her, her fantasies reflected the underlying fears common to many siblings that perhaps it could happen to her. I suspect another fantasy in this girl was the idea that she might in some unknown way be defective herself. All of these experiences underlined the need for further study of the problem. A search of the literature revealed little work on siblings, although the need for professional aid has been noted from time to time (e.g., Carver, 1956; Caldwell and Guze, 1960; Graliker, Fishler and Koch, 1962; Farber, 1963; Farber and Jenne, 1963; O'Neil, 1965). Farber and Ryckman (1965) reviewed the literature on family interactions when a retarded child is present and concluded that the family relations of normal siblings are seriously affected. Our first article (Kaplan and Colombatto, 1966) described a project with younger siblings of retarded children in a Head-Start Program. Schreiber and Feeley (1965) described the only service program reported in the literature for the sibling population. They held biweekly discussions for a selected group of ten adolescents who had indicated an interest in participating in a meeting in which they could discuss the questions and problems they had in dealing with their retarded brothers and sisters. The project with young adolescent siblings (described below) and the one described by Schreiber and Feeley arose independently to fill a need experienced by staff members working with families having a retarded child.

Discussion Groups[4]

To pursue the questions about the sibling population, a project was undertaken to learn about young adolescent siblings of retarded children. Our interests were both to learn about siblings and also to learn when and in what ways preventive intervention might be effective. We had a chance to learn in at least two ways. First, we could find out if the kind of group we were establishing could alleviate and help resolve existing problems which, although not currently being treated, could lead to more serious disturbances in the future. Second, we could begin to explore, through retrospective analysis, what difficulties the siblings encountered when they first became aware of their brothers' or sisters' retardation, and how they might have been helped at that time. Unlike many functional disturbances, the problem of mental retardation as a family concern can often be traced to a particular point in time when the retardation was identified. Since a professional person is usually involved at that point (again unlike the situation in the development of most psychological disturbances), the chances for preventive work with other members of the family are maximized. Hence, if we could learn from these adolescents what pressing questions and fears they had related to having a retarded sibling, the opportunity to use such information for a preventive program would be great.

A third issue of major relevance which could be explored in a sibling program would be the extent to which such a program could have therapeutic effects on the retardate. We felt that any effective program for the patient—in this case, the retarded child—must involve family members. Participation in this group was seen as one method of helping the normal child modify his behavior towards his defective sibling. In this way, the group could help not only the siblings involved but could also help effect change within the network of family members' relationships and attitudes towards the retarded child.

Operating according to the general interests outlined in the introduction, we initiated a pilot project with siblings of retardates at the New Haven Regional Center for the Retarded (NHRC). The specific aims of this project were to understand more clearly the special problems of siblings of retarded children and to explore ways of meeting their needs.

This pilot project lasted approximately four months. At that point the program was reviewed, and on the basis of this evaluation, a second, and continuing, sibling program was established. Before describing the second group in more detail we will briefly discuss some of the many problems which arose in establishing the pilot project.

---

[4] This part of the research was carried out and written by the writer and Dr. Elizabeth Fox and is described in greater detail elsewhere (Kaplan and Fox, in press).

The Pilot Group

Technical Problems. The co-leaders originally tried to organize the group through the staff members of the NHRC. The idea of such a group had been raised at a number of staff meetings, and the leaders felt the staff had some basic understanding of the group's goals and possible therapeutic effects. The staff was asked to refer any siblings between the ages of 12 and 16 whom they felt would benefit from the group, and to contact their families to see if they would be interested in having these children come. Some contacts were made in this fashion and most of the families expressed an interest in the group. However, when a date for the first meeting was made, very few adolescents planned to come, and the inadequacy of this approach became apparent. Largely because of our own lack of clarity about how the group would function, the staff had little understanding of how the group was going to work and what it was going to accomplish. As a result, they could not easily feel that helping to organize the group was worth a substantial effort on their part. Yet, due to the deep concerns parents had about their children participating in such a meeting, it required a determined effort to maintain the parents' commitment to the program. This parental resistance represented a major obstacle, since the children were completely dependent upon their parents for transportation.

The project could have been abandoned when this "lack of motivation" became apparent. However, we were convinced that one cannot always wait for clients to come on their own to professionals—sometimes mental health workers must actively seek out those who may need help. In fact, our experiences in community mental health work suggests that it is those who do not come easily and willingly who most need the time and attention of professionals in the field (see Sarason, *et al.*, 1966). This group seemed to us to be important enough to these youngsters to warrant an intensive recruiting effort on the leaders' part.

We called all of the adolescents recommended, including those who had already been approached by other staff members. In most instances, the call was followed by a home visit, designed to explain the group further to the sibling and to deal with the many questions and concerns of the parents. The parents seemed primarily concerned that their children would reveal things about the family and the retardate which they wished to keep secret. One father, after talking with a coleader about the group and its purpose of providing a place for these young people to talk about their problems, agreed to his son's participation, then turned to the boy and said, "O.K., start talking. I'd like to hear what you have to say." Although he had agreed to having his son in the group, he was still very concerned about what the boy might say.

We discovered subsequently that retardation was not discussed openly in many of these families and that many parents were afraid of having their children even consider the subject. They seemed worried about the kinds of questions the siblings would ask, what they might say about how the parents treated the retarded child, and what the siblings' attitudes towards the retarded child might reveal. These home visits and the opportunity they provided for talking with the parents seemed to be sufficient to deal with their concerns. We felt fairly confident that they would prove reliable in providing the necessary transportation.

The adolescents contacted varied widely on a number of dimensions. In particular, no attempt was made to equate degree or type of retardation among their siblings, so their brothers or sisters ranged from a moderately retarded mongol and a severely physically involved cerebral-palsied girl to several mildly retarded children in educable classes in the public schools. Of that group, four were in residence in the NHRC and several others attended the NHRC day program. In addition, no attempt was made to screen the adolescents themselves, so their own intellectual level, degree of psychological health, and even social class varied fairly widely.

The Meetings.   The meetings of the pilot group were conducted by a staff psychologist (FK) and a third-year psychological intern (EF). The group met one evening a week for an hour and a quarter and refreshments were served. With the consent of the members, all meetings were tape recorded.

The leaders opened the first meeting by defining two major goals of the group. One was to help the psychologists learn what it was like to be a brother or sister of a retarded child, how it affected the siblings' lives, what difficulties if any it caused them, and what implications their experience had for people working in the field of retardation. The second was to provide the siblings with an opportunity to share their own thoughts and feelings with others in a similar situation in the hope that this sharing might be interesting and helpful to them. The leaders provided no specific format for the meetings but told the members that it was up to them to decide how they wanted to run the meetings and what they wanted to discuss. In general, the coleaders sought to encourage open discussion and expression of ideas and fantasies by the group members, and to avoid being perceived as experts who had the answers to all questions.

Although these ground rules may have been appropriate in the long run, they seemed to lead to tension and discomfort during the early meetings. These adolescents were not used to talking openly about retardation and their retarded siblings, especially with strangers. They had great difficulty finding a level of discourse which was neither banal nor anxiety-provoking. For the most part, they preferred to keep the conversation at a relatively superficial level and depended on the leaders to suggest topics and keep conversation going. The coleaders also had difficulty in deciding when and how to intervene in the discussions because of our inexperience with "normal" siblings and our uncertainty about what a group of "normal" adolescent siblings would be able to discuss. Occasionally, a member would bring up extremely anxiety-provoking ideas which aroused great discomfort and seemed to confirm the group's feelings about retardation. At the second meeting, for example, the conversation was dominated by the concerns and fantasies of a boy whose comments seemed quite disturbed and disorganized. He began by talking about seizures and said that his sister looked dead when she was having one. He later went on to say, when the discussion turned to the causes of retardation, that his sister's slowness was caused by a lump on the back of her head which secretes poison. He felt that if doctors could remove the lump, she would be all right. Both these topics fascinated every member of the group. However, raised in this way, and at this stage of group development, these subjects tended more to frighten group members and to discourage participation than to involve them in meaningful discussion. (In the second group, when the siblings had come to establish strong ties to each other and to the group, many of them were able to discuss these same topics with relative ease.) The siblings' anxiety interacting with the difficulties of the coleaders, led to long, painful silences which only the most courageous could break. At least three members stopped coming and all the others felt continued uneasiness.

Another factor contributing to difficulties in discussion was the constantly changing membership of the meetings. Contrary to our initial hopes, parents were not wholly reliable in providing transportation, so that even if the siblings wanted to come to the meetings, some of them were unable to. The uneven and disturbing quality of the meetings contributed to erratic attendance, for some group members would stay away for a week or two after a particularly upsetting meeting. As a result of all these problems, attendance varied from a low of five to a high of fourteen people, and each meeting had a slightly different membership from the one preceding or following it.

Despite these numerous difficulties, the coleaders felt that the group was fulfilling some of its aims. A number of fruitful and intriguing discussions had taken place. Siblings who attended fairly regularly began to show strong loyalty to the group and indicated its importance to them in many ways. For example, they were hurt and angry when, after several months, the leaders proposed adding new members to the group. One member who had never missed a meeting expressed his resentment by boycotting the meeting following this discussion, i.e., they felt they were "advanced" members who had learned a good deal and did not want to start back at the beginning with anyone new. In various ways, then, the leaders were encouraged to continue with the group if some of its major shortcomings could be overcome.

Issues Considered in Forming a Second Group

Issues such as transportation and parental resistance could be approached more effectively than had been done in the pilot project. However, the coleaders felt that some additional change was probably necessary to help adolescents verbalize their feelings in the group situation. One possibility was to limit group membership to highly motivated, relatively stable, and verbal siblings, as Schreiber and Feeley (1965) had done. In addition, we could have given the discussions an educational orientation and restricted the discussion to a relatively factual level. However, these possibilities seemed contrary to the original purpose. If the unmotivated, disturbed, or nonverbal youngsters were eliminated, the group would not be reaching those adolescents who most needed it. It was not consonant with our philosophy to restrict the group to those who came (without urging) and who could participate freely and appropriately. Similarly, limiting the discussions to an educational focus did not seem to be the solution. Only a relatively unstructured situation would permit and encourage the expression by the members of their underlying fantasies about their retarded brothers and sisters and about themselves, and we felt this to be essential to our understanding of the problems facing them, as well as to their own growth.

An alternative to placing limitations on group membership and discussion was suggested by an NHRC staff member. He proposed that the group spend part of its time doing volunteer work with some of the residents at the NHRC. Group members had asked from time to time if they could do volunteer work at the NHRC, and the idea of combining volunteer activity with the discussion group intrigued the leaders. This activity might allow the siblings to express themselves about retarded children without having to talk explicitly about their own brothers or sisters. Further, their contact with other retardates would help broaden their perspective on retardation and help them to think through their relationships with their own siblings. In addition this experience could provide a common basis for communication and help stimulate group discussion. When this combined activity–discussion group was proposed to the siblings, they responded with enthusiasm.

Various changes were incorporated into the establishment and functioning of the second group. The meeting, held only every other week, would last for two hours, the first forty-five minutes being spent with some of the retarded children in residence, the rest of the time devoted to a group discussion about what the siblings had done, what children they had watched or played with, and what ideas and questions they had as a result of this contact. We were able to offer transportation to about half of the members of the group.

Experience with the pilot group had underlined the importance of enlisting the parents' support and of allaying their anxieties as much as possible. To this end, after letters were sent out announcing the changes in the group and inviting several siblings who had not been members of the first group, we telephoned each family to give further information and encouragement. Both the parents and siblings were invited to the initial meeting, the parents meeting separately with one leader while the siblings held their meeting with the other.

A majority of the siblings had at least one parent present at this meeting, and these parents shared a number of feelings about having their normal children involved in such a program. Their attitude was highly favorable, but they also expressed some concern that their children might betray family secrets; they all indicated tremendous curiosity about what their children were saying. Their concerns and fears were clarified and discussed with them. Somewhat surprisingly to the leaders the parents indicated rather strongly their wish for a similar group, led by a coleader of the sibling group. Finally they arranged to meet occasionally with one of the coleaders to discuss how things were going.

THE SECOND GROUP

Phases of Development.   The new group started with fourteen members, several of whom had participated in the original group. The development of the new group seemed to fall into several phases. During the first several meetings the members were excited and fascinated by the experience of meeting the retarded children and of becoming acquainted with the NHRC. They also seemed to be buoyed up by the feeling that this group was going to "work," and that, frightening as the prospect might be, they were going to have a genuine opportunity to discuss their retarded brothers and sisters.

In contrast to the meetings of the pilot group, these first few meetings were characterized by active participation, with people frequently interrupting each other. During the time spent with the retardates, the coleaders worked actively to help the siblings interact with them. At this stage, the siblings wanted to do things for the retardates, organize activities, lead games, etc. As the novelty of the contacts wore off, the siblings realized that it was not so easy to keep a game going with a retardate. It was often difficult just to remain with one for any period of time.

This realization led into what seemed to be the second stage of the meetings. Although the prolonged and painful silences which typified the pilot meetings did not recur, the siblings began to turn away from the problem of retardation and their difficulties with their brothers and sisters towards thinking of the group as a club for organizing social activities for the children at the NHRC. For example, they wanted to pay dues which they could then use for parties for the retarded children. The little they said about their experiences with the children indicated that the siblings were having trouble thinking of activities for them and that they felt frustrated and help-less in trying to interact with them. In a group of nonsiblings this frustration might have been expressed and dealt with in an open way, but with these siblings it seemed to reactivate their feelings of helplessness towards their own retarded sibs, which was a difficult subject to discuss.

The group indicated by some of their comments their own awareness that they were avoiding important issues. The coleaders reraised the question of the purpose of the meetings. At the meeting where they had agreed to collect dues, we asked them if that was really what the meetings were for, and whether they wanted the meetings to turn into an organization to plan organized social events for the retarded children, or whether they wanted to talk about their own siblings and the problems of retardation. The siblings replied that they really did want to talk about their brothers and sisters. That was why they met, wasn't it? Several of them were able to influence the group to give up the idea of collecting dues and members began in greater earnest to approach problems concerning the NHRC children and their own siblings.

From that point, members of the group were able to keep more of the conversation directed towards topics related to their siblings or towards differ-ent problems associated with retardation. Before discussing these topics in detail, the interaction between the siblings and the children at the NHRC, as well as the effect of this contact on the meetings, will be described to provide the context for later discussions.

Relationships with the Retardates.   Just as the tenor of the meetings changed, so did the relationships between the members of the group and the children at the NHRC. The retardate group consisted of 30 high-functioning retarded children. They often spend their evenings in a large living room with couches and chairs, a TV, and various games and books, which is in their living unit.

Originally the siblings felt that they were there to think up things to do and games to play with a fairly unresponsive and possibly recalcitrant group. They expected to put effort into the interaction but didn't really feel that any would be expended by the retardates in return; and, indeed, this seemed to be the case for the first several weeks. However, as soon as the retarded children realized that the group would visit regularly, and as soon as they began to know something of the siblings, they started making definite demands on them. The siblings no longer had to seek out the retarded children—they sought out the siblings instead. It was no longer necessary to think up activi-ties since they emerged quite naturally within the matrix of friendship. Although this change did not occur with all the siblings, it occurred fre-quently enough to be considered a stable phenomenon.

In reviewing the ability of this group to deal verbally with issues of retardation and with their sibling relationships, it would appear that meeting with children at the NHRC facilitated their discussions in several respects. Perhaps its most important function was to serve as a "half-way house" in their approach to a very anxiety-arousing topic. Having this common experience with retarded children other than their own siblings allowed them to share thoughts and feelings which did not necessarily implicate themselves and their own siblings. Their experience with the children at the NHRC provided a safe context within which to discuss the problems. And the problems they had with these children mirror those they had encountered with their own siblings.

These meetings also seemed to provide the siblings with some perspective about the nature of retardation. For many, retardation had in the past been defined for them by their brother or sister. The contact with the NHRC children broadened their perspective and hopefully gave them a more objective view about their sibling.

Issues Raised in the Discussion

Given this framework of discussion, in which the group members can approach their problems either in terms of their experience with NHRC children or directly in terms of their own siblings, these adolescents were able to discuss a number of central concerns. For example, the issue of being similar to or different from the retarded sibling permeated many of the meetings and seemed to be a source of enormous concern to all of the group members. In fact, the experience with this group suggests that the main task of siblings of defective children is to avoid identifying with them. At times, group members frantically attempted to maximize the differences between themselves and their siblings. At one meeting, a boy described two normal siblings he knew from school. One was very fat and the other excessively thin. They all were impressed that two children so unlike could be from the same family. Implicit in their discussion was the question: If a very fat and a very thin child can come from the same family, can a very slow (retarded) and a bright child also come from the same family? In other words, is it possible for us to be normal, even though we have a retarded sibling?

A second issue that bothered members of this group is how their brothers and sisters understand their affliction, and, more generally, how the retarded children understand the world and what feelings they have about it. Group members agreed that retarded children have feelings, just like everyone else, but they were not sure how much their siblings could understand. This issue is complicated by the fact that siblings of group members represented a wide range of difficulties and levels of functioning so that, for example, several of the adolescents with severely handicapped siblings seemed to feel that they had little appreciation for their differentness from the normal population, and that it would mean nothing to explain this to them. Others saw this as a real problem. For example, one girl has a sister who is in an educable special class and who probably entertains expectations about getting married and pursuing goals similar to her normal sibling. As her normal sister put it, "What do you do, just sit her down and say 'Guess what, Susie? You're retarded!'?" Another problem in understanding was whether the retarded children can tell right from wrong, and whether their destructive behavior is intentional.

This last question is integrally connected with another common problem: How do you control and discipline your brother or sister? Most of these siblings have younger retarded brothers and sisters, and often act as parent substitutes in caring for their sibling. Do you hit your brother or sister when he or she does something bad, or do you just ignore it? Most of the group members seemed to agree that normal tactics do not suffice—their retarded siblings seem to persevere much more than normal children. Some felt that perhaps their retarded siblings did not understand enough to be punished; others felt that their brothers and sisters knew when they are doing something wrong, and should be dealt with accordingly. All seemed to agree that their parents are the final authorities and that they have little to say (and do not want to have more to say) as to how their brothers and sisters are handled. They were able to admit that they hit their brothers and sisters from time to time and received group acceptance of this behavior.

A problem about which all group members felt strongly was how they and their families relate to the community. They described, with mixed feelings of contempt and injury, the reactions of neighbors to the retarded sibling. Many had been harassed and had watched the sibling insulted and stared at by others. They did not know whether to defend the sibling or just to withdraw him from the situation. The question of what to tell their friends was also raised. Some had been teased at school; others seemed to have escaped this; but most felt that they could tell only their good friends, and then only if their friends would have to come into contact with the retarded child. They described varying degrees of involvement with their sibling outside the house. Some felt comfortable in taking their siblings on special trips, or having the sibling come along when they went shopping or to a movie. Others seemed to have as little to do with the sibling as possible. The sensitivity of these adolescents to the reactions of others was seen in miniature in the living unit at NHRC, since three members of the group had siblings in residence there. They had been remarkably reluctant to share this information with the group and the group equally adverse to perceiving it. One member's irregular attendance was probably due to his concerns about being identified with his sibling there. This issue is, of course, another part of their concern about being the same or different from their retarded siblings.

Another core topic, which was approached less directly by the group and which continued to evoke a great deal of anxiety, was how the issue of retardation is handled in the family. We had explicit statements from both siblings and their parents that talking about retardation is like talking about sex. One mother expressed this opinion in a parents' meeting, going on to say that she and her husband always answer any questions the children have. Clearly, many questions never get asked. Some questions that have been left unanswered, or at least not answered to the siblings' satisfaction include: What are seizures all about? Why should (or shouldn't) retarded siblings marry, and how is it that sometimes retarded people have children? What effects will having a retarded sibling have on the ability to have children that are normal?

It should be apparent by now that this group developed a real capacity to express their thoughts and feelings about their retarded siblings. Parallel to this was the development of a strong attachment to the group and to individual members of it.

Conclusion

This report of the sibling research consisted of clinical observation. The next step, which we have begun, includes the translation of our clinical impressions and hypotheses into a form that can be examined more systematically. For example, we have carried out extensive interviews with fifteen college men who have retarded siblings, and an equal number who do not; we are beginning to examine the similarities and differences between these two groups.

Of great importance are the broader implications of the research. Retardation is not simply a defect that occurs to, or resides in, an individual. Rather it is an event that involves and includes the total family unit and often parts of the larger community as well. This is most strikingly illustrated in those cases where the functional retardation itself is a result of the family dynamics (e.g., Staver, 1953). It is perhaps less obvious but equally true when the original retardation has an organic basis which then comes to have a variety of meanings for the family. These meanings and how the families deal with their significance effect how the retarded child and all other members of the family are encouraged and allowed to develop. Too often the eventual adjustment of the family limits and distorts one or more possibilities for growth. The fact that families thrive despite or because of the retarded child suggests that there are potentially adaptive ways of coping. An awareness of this fact opens the possibility of our providing some guidance to families to assist them in finding an adaptive and productive adjustment.

The most important point of this research is this: Preventative intervention can no longer be limited to developing ways of decreasing the incidence of defective children, although obviously this is vitally important. Prevention must also include helping families who do have a retarded child to cope in a way that enhances, or at least does not hinder, the family's and its members' opportunities for growth and development. The beginnings of the sibling research suggest the importance of several factors, e.g., the way the family talks about retardation and the problems of the retarded child, how they deal with their own aggression towards the retarded child, how they teach the normal children to do this, how they handle the community relationships with the retardate, and how they assist their normal children in understanding and explaining the issues involved. The time and effort required by professionals to talk with families about these issues when the fact of the retardation is first discovered is small. Trying to undo the damage done many years later is often impossible and at best prohibitive in terms of resources and personnel.

Even more broadly, we see the problem of a family dealing with a retarded child, and all it means to them, as one instance of a universal experience, i.e., how a family copes with unexpected disappointment and trauma. Few families can avoid such experiences, whether it be in the form of a retarded child, a chronically ill member, a serious accident, or some other stressful event. Despite the many specific differences in these experiences, the core issue seems to be how a family responds to severe stress, which often occurs without warning. One could argue that it is only when professionals and others can begin to see that retardation does not represent a unique set of problems unrelated to all other mental situations will the artificial separation between these areas disappear and fruitful interchange occur.

Biological science and social attitudes: the nineteenth-century view of mental subnormality

In previous chapters we have been considering mental subnormality mainly from the points of view afforded by the disciplines of psychology, education, and to a lesser extent by allied social sciences such as sociology and anthropology. We have in addition focused on the problem of mental subnormality as it presents itself to us today and in the recent past while orienting ourselves toward the research and program planning of the future. We hoped thus to take advantage of the fund of knowledge and the interests in current social problems which are already possessed by the student, the educator, or the psychologist who may for the first time be giving extended thought to the problem of mental subnormality. Although this approach may have gained us the didactic advantage we desired, it, of course, runs the risk of presenting a one-sided and somewhat ahistorical picture of the field. In the next several chapters we hope to rectify this by putting greater emphasis on both biological factors and historical developments.

The biological factors with which we shall be concerned relate specifically to heredity and pathology of the central nervous system. More extensive consideration shall be given to heredity factors because the issues involved therein have historically been of greater import to the field as a whole. In fact, the issues, as we shall see in our discussion of the eugenics movement, extend far beyond the field of mental subnormality, involving as they do our fundamental conceptions of the nature of man and society.

We are deeply impressed by how biological facts and theories—whether explicitly or implicitly expressed—have conditioned in the past and continue to condition the ways in which individuals and society as a whole have variously defined the problem of mental subnormality and how these facts and theories have both abetted and hindered our problem solving in this area.

We think it will be easy to document this in regard to various biological theories of heredity and their impact upon the field of mental subnormality, regardless of whether the theories were sound or were poorly constructed and badly supported by facts. In tragic truth, in the latter instance, it is not difficult to demonstrate how the so-called facts and theories of biological science have caused us to misperceive the problem and to act in ways obviously harmful and degrading to the retardate, less obviously but perhaps no less certainly, harmful and degrading to ourselves as individuals and as a people.

In the present chapter we shall consider some conceptions of heredity as they existed in the nineteenth century and endeavor to relate these conceptions to the way in which society viewed the retardate. We shall try in this presentation not to oversimplify, nor to mistake correlations for causal connections, but to give the reader some feeling for the complexity of the interactions among the attitudes with which society views the retardate, the theories concerning the nature of retardation, and the larger social context within which both theories and attitudes exist.

In subsequent chapters we shall trace out the ways in which continuing changes in biological theory and its interaction with various social forces were utilized in both defining the problem of mental subnormality and in attempting its solution.

Degeneration Theory and Its Antecedents

In the nineteenth century the role of hereditary factors in mental subnormality was often conceptualized either explicitly or implicitly within some form of the theory of degeneration. Erwin Ackerknecht (1959), following Georges Perrin, places the origin of this theory in France. Recognizing it as a development of ideas about heredity and mental illness that were already old at the time, he yet attributes the real creation of the degeneration theory to Benedict Augustin Morel (1860, 1857). For Morel "degenerations" were deviations from the normal human type, which were transmissible by heredity and which deteriorated toward extinction. Deviations from the normal human type included those afflicted with certain physical and psychiatric diseases, for example, the epileptic, the scrofulous, the psychotic, the mentally deficient, the moral deviate, and the alcoholic. The degeneration was subject to the "law of progressivity." The first generation of a degenerate line might be merely nervous, the second would tend to be neurotic, the third psychotic, while the fourth consisted of idiots[1] who would tend not to reproduce and so lead to the extinction of the line.

As Ackerknecht recognized, the roots of this theory may be traced a ways back. Certainly, some adumbrations of the theory may be seen in the work of Thomas Willis, 1621–1675, the English neuroanatomist and clinician. In one of the earliest systematic discussions of mental retardation Willis takes note of hereditary factors as follows:

For in the first place, *Stupidity* (as we but now observed) is sometimes original or born with one, and so it is either *hereditary,* as when Fools beget Fools, the reason of which is clear enough to wit, the same weak Particles flowing for the constituting the Animal Organs in the Son, which were in the Father: or *Stupidity* being born with one, is as it were accidental, to wit, it frequently happens, that wise men and highly ingenious, do beget Fools and Changelings, or heavy witted; which we suppose so to come to pass sometimes for this cause, for that the Parents being too much given to study, reading and meditation, the Animal Spirits that inhabit the Brain, are so much wasted, that for the supply of them, the most generous Particles of the Blood are still carried to the Head, and but few only, and small, are permitted to descend to the *Spermatick* Bodies. When the rational Soul becomes greatly solicitous in bringing forth its child (which are the works of the Intellect) then the Corporeal Soul (the Spirits being called away to wait on the other) becomes not at all, or very weakly prolifick.

Besides this reason, there is another frequently to be met with, wherefore the first implanted sagacity of men, as well as of *Brutes,* is not often propagated from the Parents to the Children. For when as we presume certainly, the Colt of a generous Horse, or of a delicate strain, or the Chickens of a Game-Cock, that they will *patrissare,* or be like their Sires, so that they are sold at a great rate, and the virtues of these, if not broken by inordinate and preternatural feeding or bringing up, descend by a long series to their young from age to age: This often happens otherwise to men, to wit, because the Parents do so enervate and weaken their bodies by intemperance, luxury, and evil manners, that they beget only languishing and unhealthy Children. Hence it is, that for the most part, those who are born of Parents broken with old age, or of such as are not yet ripe or too young, or of drunkards, soft, and effeminate men, want a great and liberal ingenuity or wit.

---

[1] Throughout this and following chapters when our interest is focused on historical developments we will not adhere to the terminology recommended by the World Health Organization. Instead, in our comments on mental subnormality and its subclassifications we will adopt the terminology of the author whose work is under consideration. This may cause some difficulty for the reader. But it is not always possible to translate a given author's terminology into ours. Even in those instances where it would be possible, we are not sure but that the result would be a barrier to communication rather than an aid.

Nor does there happen a less detriment to them of the Animal Faculty, whose fires are obnoxious to evil affections of the Brain, as the *Palsie, Epilepsie, Carus, Convulsions,* and the like; so that to be born of parents who *have a sound mind in a sound body,* is far beyond a large patrimony. (Willis, 1683, pp. 210–211)

That mental defect is sometimes directly transmissible—Fools beget Fools —is an observation antedating Willis by at least several centuries, for Zirkle (1951) points out a similar passage in Thomas Aquinas. Of greater interest is Willis' observation that mentally deficient children may be born of parents of sound mind, and his attribution of this, in part, to the enervated condition of the parents when they begat their children. We shall see this hypothesis appearing again in the degeneration theories of the nineteenth century.

Confusion of Mental Retardation with Insanity

The close association of idiocy and insanity in the degeneration theory of the nineteenth century follows readily enough from the knowledge of mental retardation obtaining at the time in which the theory had its roots. Philippe Pinel (1745–1826), the father of modern psychiatry, considered idiocy as one form of insanity. From the point of view of cultural history this is not surprising. However, we may find occasional definitions of idiocy antedating the nineteenth century which make a reasonably clear definition of idiocy and which even explicitly differentiate idiocy from insanity.

An oft-quoted passage from John Locke, 1623–1704, contemporary of Thomas Willis, will serve as an example:

In fine, the defect in naturals seems to proceed from want of quickness, activity, and motion in the intellectual faculties, whereby they are deprived of reason; whereas madmen, on the other side, seem to suffer by the other extreme, for they do not appear to me to have lost the faculty of reasoning, but having joined together some ideas very wrongly, they mistake them for truths, and they err as men do that argue right from wrong principles; for by the violence of their imaginations, having taken their fancies for realities, they make right deductions from them. Thus you shall find a distracted man fancying himself a king, with a right inference require suitable attendance, respect, and obedience; others who have thought themselves made of glass, have used the caution necessary to preserve such brittle bodies. Hence it comes to pass that a man who is very sober, and of a right understanding in all other things, may in one particular be as frantic as any in Bedlam; if either by any sudden very strong impression, or long fixing his fancy upon one sort of thoughts, incoherent ideas have been cemented together so powerfully, as to remain united. But there are degrees of madness, as of folly; the disorderly jumbling ideas together is in some more, some less. In short, herein seems to lie the difference between idiots and madmen, that madmen put wrong ideas together, and so make wrong propositions, but argue and reason right from them; but idiots make very few or no propositions, and reason scarce at all. (Locke, 1905, pp. 276–277)

Legal definitions such as that of Blackstone anticipated a developmental criterion not to be emphasized in medical science until the time of Esquirol.

An idiot, or natural fool, is one that hath had no understanding from his nativity; and therefore, is by law presumed never likely to attain any. (Blackstone, 1765, p. 292)

Nevertheless, in spite of such excellent definitions and discriminations the confusion between idiocy and insanity continued. The confusion was undoubtedly abetted by the fact that the best that society could offer these unfortunates and their families was custodial care for the patient. If diagnostic labeling does not lead to differential treatment or prognosis, it loses one of its main functions; and the society which must create and support the treatment facilities, and the practical physician interested in helping his individual patients, are not likely to pay attention to the problems of accurate diagnostic labels.

For Pinel, eminently practical physician that he was, there was perhaps an additional reason for confusion. This was his emphasis on symptomatology. He saw idiocy as a partial or total abolition of the intellectual powers and affections involving defective perception and "recognizance" of objects, with the greatest number of the afflicted either destitute of speech or confined to the utterance of inarticulate sounds. Torpor and apathy are prominent symptoms but some cases are characterized by transient and meaningless gusts of passion. This description, of course, would fit in general terms many severe forms of mental illness including some deteriorated and catatonic schizoprenias. Thus, within the same class Pinel places congenital forms of idiocy—which he notes are often accompanied by malformations of the cranium—and what would appear to be by today's standards of classification obvious forms of insanity, whether they be on an organic or functional basis. The following is an example of a case classified as idiocy by Pinel that would certainly not be classed as a form of mental retardation today, since the professional attainment of the individual concerned would preclude any great intellectual limitation existing at an early stage of development:

A young sculptor, eight and twenty years of age, in confinement at Bicetre, had been reduced to this state by excessive intemperance and venery. He remained almost always motionless and silent. At intervals his face would be distorted by a silly and stupid laugh. His features were devoid of expression. Every trace of his former condition was effaced from his memory. He shewed no symptoms of hunger; and even eating appeared to be a motion purely mechanical. He passed the whole of his time in a lying position. At length, he sunk under a fatal hectic. (Pinel, 1806, p. 165)

It is somewhat aside from our present argument but of interest to note that although Pinel confused idiocy with certain forms of insanity he yet advocated the separation of idiots from other classes of patients at lunatic asylums.

The natural indolence and stupidity of ideots, might in some degree be obviated, by engaging them in manual occupations, suitable to their respective capacities. With an able active man at their head, ideots are capable of being drilled into any sort of service where bodily strength alone is requisite. The new plantation at Bicetre was made almost altogether at their expence. (Pinel, 1806, p. 203)

Foreseeing a need for special treatment is to create a need for precise diagnostic discrimination.

Esquirol and the Developmental Criterion

Jean-Etienne-Dominique Esquirol, 1772–1840, a student of Pinel, greatly advanced the solution of the diagnostic problem by pointing out the importance of the developmental factor.

Idiocy is not a disease, but a condition in which the intellectual faculties are never manifested; or have never been developed sufficiently to enable the idiot to acquire such an amount of knowledge, as persons of his own age, and placed in similar circumstances with himself, are capable of receiving. Idiocy commences with life, or at that age which precedes the development of the intellectual and affective faculties; which are, from the first, what they are doomed to be, during the whole period of existence. Everything about the idiot betrays an organization imperfect, or arrested in progress of development. We can conceive of no possibility of changing this state. . . . Dementia and idiocy differ essentially; otherwise the principles of every classification are illusory. . . . A man in a state of dementia is deprived of advantages which he formerly enjoyed; he was a rich man, who has become poor. The idiot, on the contrary, has always been in a state of want or misery. The condition of a man in a state of dementia may change; that of the idiot is ever the same. (Esquirol, 1845, pp. 446–447)

Despite this diagnostic clarification, the association of idiocy and insanity was deeply rooted. And while Esquirol does not present us with any theory of degeneration, he does make note in discussing familial tendencies to idiocy that "sometimes also, in the same family, there is one idiot, and other children who are insane" (Esquirol 1845, p. 470). Esquirol was writing at a time when interest in hereditary factors had not yet commenced the rapid growth that it was shortly to experience.

Howe and the Massachusetts Report

The developmental criterion was utilized in the Report to the Governor of the Massachusetts Commission of 1848. This commission, headed by Samuel G. Howe, noted that,

One of the greatest difficulties in the consideration of this subject, is to distinguish between demented persons and idiots. In our lunatic asylums are found some, who are reduced to a state of complete idiocy, but who are not, strictly speaking, idiots;

their minds have once been in the normal condition; they have lost their understanding; they are *demented*. . . . We have considered, therefore, all persons whose understanding is undeveloped, or developed only in a partial and very feeble degree, or who have lost their understanding without becoming insane, to be proper subjects for examination. (Howe, 1848a, p. 22)

This Massachusetts report is of significance in that even before the publication of Morel's major formulation of the degeneration theory it subscribes to many of the major tenets of that theory.

It is said by physiologists, that among certain classes of miserably paid and poorly fed workmen, the physical system degenerates so rapidly, that the children are feeble and puny, and but few live to maturity; that the grandchildren are still more puny; until, in the third or fourth generation, the individuals are no longer able to perpetuate their species, and the ranks must be filled up by fresh subjects from other walks of life, to run the same round of deterioration. . . . It will be seen by the tables, that by far the greater part of the idiots are children of parents, one or both of whom were of scrofulous temperament, and poor, flabby organization. It is difficult to describe exactly the marks which characterize this low organization, but the eye of the physiologist detects it at once.

. . .

Suffice it to say now, that, out of 420 cases of congenital idiocy examined, some information was obtained respecting the condition of the progenitors of 359. Now, in all these 359 cases, *save only four,* it is found that one or the other, or both, of the immediate progenitors of the unfortunate sufferers had, in some way, widely departed from the normal condition of health, and violated the natural laws. That is to say, one or the other, or both of them, were very unhealthy or scrofulous; or they were hereditarily predisposed to affections of the brain, causing occasional insanity; or they had intermarried with blood relatives; or they had been intemperate—or had been guilty of sensual excesses which impaired their constitutions. (Howe, 1848a, pp. 78–80 and 57)

Another favorite hypothesis of the theories of degeneracy appears in the discussion of alcoholism in this report.

In seeking for the causes which lead to this sad deterioration of families, it will be found that the most prominent and prolific is *Intemperance*. By inspection of the tables, it will be seen that, out of 359 idiots, the condition of whose progenitors was ascertained, 99 were the children of drunkards. (Howe, 1848a, p. 82)

Nevertheless, Howe considers this a conservative estimate of the amount of alcoholism among the progenitors since many drinkers would not be publically known.

The effect of habitual use of alcohol seems to be to *lymphatize* the whole bodily organization; that is, to diminish the proportion of the *fibrous* part of the body—to make the *lymph* abound in all the tissues. The children of such persons are apt to be of the scrofulous character above described; and *their* children are very apt to be feeble in body and weak in mind. Idiots, fools, and simpletons, are common among the progeny of such persons. Thus, directly and indirectly, alcohol is productive of a great proportion of the idiocy which now burdens the Commonwealth. (Howe, 1848a, p. 83)

ISAAC RAY'S VIEW OF DEGENERATION

The theory of degeneration as espoused by Howe was only one variant of those prevailing in the last half of the nineteenth century and we may properly speak of a group of theories as "degeneration theories." Another variant is found in the writings of Isaac Ray, 1807–1881. Ray, a leading American psychiatrist, pointed out that the hereditary taint might fail to express itself in one generation only to reappear in the next, emphasizing that what is really transmitted is only a tendency to disease, the said tendency being more or less intense in different individuals within the hereditary line.

The multitudes who are understood to have a tendency to consumption may live long and comfortably under a judicious hygiene, and die at last of some other disease. This is precisely the case with mental disease. It is only the primordial germ—the taint—that is transmitted, in one degree or another of intensity. In answer to the question whether the insanity of any particular person is hereditary, it is not enough to show that the disease has occurred in none of his progenitors. The hereditary element is fairly established if it appears that some near progenitor suffered from any affection of the head. The change in the type of the disease, as it passes from one generation to another, which is so characteristic of insanity, is not less frequently from a higher to a lower grade of intensity than the reverse. Hence it is that we often see among the children of the insane one maniacal, another imbecile, another epileptic, another hysterical, another eccentric, another passionate, another alternating between exaltation and depression. To recognize the hereditary element in one of these cases and not in another indicates no very broad observation of the course of disease, nor a very nice perception of its affinities and relations.

. . .

Accordingly, we find that the transmission of any particular trait precisely as it existed in the parent, though not very uncommon, is, nevertheless, far from the invariable rule. It is a vulgar view of heredity which supposes that every or any trait must descend from parent to child in all its original vigor and proportions. But while temporary disappearance is compatible with the physiological law, it is equally true that traits may be transmitted in a latent form, and may reapear at some distant interval. Instances of this law, or a closely correlative one, will be better considered when we come to speak of the transmission of disease. At present we need only say that such instances furnish no support to the idea that a trait not derived from the immediate progenitor, though existing in uncles, aunts, or cousins, is not attributable to heredity. The simple fact is, that in some of the family it is fully developed, while in some it is latent but more or less ready to make its appearance in the next generation. This we are obliged to believe, unless we maintain that the recurrence of a trait, after it has once disappeared, is purely accidental, a recurrence which is too common to be explained in this manner. (Ray, 1869, pp. 13–14 and 9–10)

POLYMORPHOUS HEREDITY AND TRANSMISSION OF ACQUIRED TRAITS

In these quotations from Howe and Ray can be found two elements which appear to be held in common in sundry variants of the degeneration theory. The first is that the hereditary taint is polymorphous. That is, the degenerative tendency expresses itself in different ways and with different forms of disease. Thus different varieties of organic and functional disease may be expressions of one and the same hereditary tendency. It is necessary to understand the prevalence of this assumption in the latter half of the nineteenth century if we are to understand the "proofs" of hereditary factors in mental retardation advanced by leading authorities in the field such as Langdon Down, Martin Barr, and A. F. Tredgold. These "proofs" will be illustrated later on in this chapter.

The second factor which is common to various forms of the degeneration theory lies in the assumptions that acquired traits are transmitted to, and parental experiences have effects upon, the offspring.

The hypothesis of the transmission of acquired traits, which is frequently associated with the name of Lamarck—although he was not the originator— was widely accepted by prominent biologists and physicians in the nineteenth century. Since Charles Darwin was one of those accepting the transmission of acquired traits, his theory of heredity, which he called with characteristic caution "a provisional hypothesis of pangenesis," was designed so as to specifically provide a mechanism for such transmission. Thus Darwin envisaged that the various cells and units of the body cast off minute granules which he called gemmules. These gemmules were conceived as capable of self-multiplication and development into units like those from which they had been derived. Their development depended upon their union with other partially developed or nascent cells which preceded them in the regular course of growth. These gemmules were collected from all parts of the system to constitute the sexual elements and it was their development in the next generation that formed a new being. Traits that skipped a generation might be understood by assuming certain gemmules remained dormant in the skipped generation. Blending of parental traits might be understood by gemmules from both parents combining to form the cells and units. Dominance of a trait might be understood by gemmules from one parent being in greater number or possessing greater vigor. As for the transmission of acquired traits, any conditions of environment or use and disuse which would modify the cells and organ systems of the parent would result in modified gemmules being formed. The acquired trait would then be passed on via the modified gemmules.

It is equally or even more unintelligible on any ordinary view, how the effects of the long-continued use or disuse of a part, or of changed habits of body or mind, can be inherited. A more perplexing problem can hardly be proposed; but on our view we have only to suppose that certain cells become at last structurally modified; and that these throw off similarly modified gemmules. This may occur at any period of development, and the modification will be inherited at a corresponding period; for the modified gemmules will unite in all ordinary cases with the proper preceding cells, and will consequently be developed at the same period at which the modification first arose. With respect to mental habits or instincts, we are so profoundly ignorant of the relation between the brain and the power of thought that we do not know positively whether a fixed habit induces any change in the nervous system, though this seems highly probable; but when such habit or other mental attribute, or insanity, is inherited, we must believe that some actual modification is transmitted; and this implies, according to our hypothesis, that gemmules derived from modified nerve-cells are transmitted to the offspring. (Darwin, 1890, pp. 388–389)

DEGENERATION THEORY AT
THE TURN OF THE CENTURY

The theories of degeneration and the associated hypotheses on heredity gradually gave way before the new knowledge and theoretical constructions appearing about the turn of the century. But to demonstrate how deeply ingrained the theories of degeneration were in the field of mental retardation, and to demonstrate the usual time lag in the application of knowledge from the basic sciences to the clinical sciences, one can look at some of the classical texts appearing in the first decade of the twentieth century.

Martin Barr's *Mental Defectives: Their History, Treatment and Training* appeared in 1904. Barr was Chief Physician at the Pennsylvania School for Feebleminded Children at Elwyn, Pennsylvania. In discussing the etiology of mental retardation Barr emphasizes the condition of the mother during gestation. In this he follows Down and Howe among others and anticipates modern investigators such as Knobloch and Pasamanick (1960). Not only physical factors such as nutrition and disease but psychological stresses on the mother during pregnancy are assumed to affect the fetus. These factors are today still considered possible causes in some forms of mental retardation; but with a more sophisticated knowledge of hereditary mechanism, they are likely to be considered as prenatal environmental factors rather than true hereditary factors as they were so considered by Barr and some of his predecessors. In addition, it is extremely unlikely that any modern students of the field would assign to these factors the prominence or effectiveness which Barr assumed. Thus, today, some investigators speculate on the effects of chronic psychological stress upon the development of the fetus. But who, today, is likely to follow Barr when he concludes his summary of literature on the effects of psychological stress on the fetus by stating:

I have two cases somewhat similar among my patients. A boy born a veritable Esau, with a thick growth of reddish hair on back and chest; the mother during pregnancy was chased by a cow. A woman three months pregnant attending a circus was much frightened by a "freak" exhibited under the name of "What is it?" Her child—an idiot girl—born at full term, presented a most extraordinarily Calibanish appearance.

One might go on with such examples *ad infinitum,* but those cited are sufficient to show that the immediate effect of shock or physical strain, is such an abnormal condition in the mother as to result in direct transmission of idiocy or imbecility from her to the child. (Barr, 1904, p. 96)

In regard to the effects of phthisis—pulmonary tuberculosis—as a hereditary cause of mental retardation, Barr follows the lead of Langdon Down and others and presents tabulated data from his case histories to demonstrate that it is the casual factor in 7.57 percent of his 1978 cases. This percentage is considerably smaller than that reported by many of the authorities he quotes. The causal connection between phthisis and mental retardation is delineated as follows:

The immediate effect of phthisis upon the strongest constitution is a lowering of tone and a lessening of all the physical forces; but in enfeebled constitutions it cooperates readily with any neuroses patent or latent, in the work of disintegration and tearing down of tissue, nerve and fibre, inducing an enfeebled condition utterly unsuited to healthful procreation. It is this general poverty of the whole being which chiefly characterizes the victims of a phthisical heredity, and which is more to be dreaded than the inheritance of the actual disease, insomuch as such a condition is favorable to the development of idiocy either congenital or accidental. (Barr, 1904, p. 103)

A more obvious expression of the degeneration theory is also presented:

Insanity reproducing itself, is a fact as unquestioned as that of its frequency as a contributing cause to many forms of degeneration. As a sole agent Koch considers it less active than imbecility, finding in his studies 16 percent of the former as contrasted with 24 percent of the latter, and my researches confirm his opinion, showing insanity a predominating cause in 216 cases, or only 7.08 percent.

Associated with other neuroses, more especially idiocy, phthisis or epilepsy, it lends a psychologic force almost certain to develop mental defect. (Barr, 1904, p. 103)

The first edition of Tredgold's classic text appeared in 1908. Tredgold distinguished between intrinsic and extrinsic factors in the causation of retardation. Intrinsic factors were hereditary influences which modified the "germinal plasm" before conception took place and thus caused primary amentia. Extrinsic factors were those conditions of the environment which affected the development of the brain and body in utero or subsequent to birth and caused secondary amentia. Under intrinsic or hereditary factors Tredgold considered, among other factors, disease of the nervous system, alcoholism, and tuberculosis.

It is agreed by all who have studied this question, that the most frequent cause of amentia is some ancestral pathological condition—morbid heredity. It is also agreed that the commonest form of morbid heredity is disease of the nervous system. In a small proportion of cases the antecedent nervous disease consists of cerebral haemorrhages, paralysis, or various neuroses; but in the great majority it is insanity, dementia, or epilepsy. My own inquiries showed that over 80 percent of persons suffering from the severer grades of amentia were the descendants of a pronounced neuropathic stock. In 64 percent the heredity was in the form of insanity or epilepsy; whilst in 18 percent it consisted of a marked family tendency to paralysis, cerebral haemorrhages, or various neuroses and psychoses. (Tredgold, 1908, p. 16)

As regards alcoholism Tredgold states:

This is the hereditary factor next in importance, and in my own series of cases a pronounced history of family alcoholism occurred in no less than 46.5 percent. It is to be remarked, however, that in five-sixths of these definite neuropathic heredity was present in addition; whilst in most of the remainder there were other morbid influences. . . . There can be little doubt that long-continued, excessive indulgence in alcohol has a considerable effect upon the germ and sperm cells, and that it results in an impairment of the nervous system of the offspring. In fact, I believe that such psychoses as hysteria, migraine, epilepsy, etc., are often due to this cause. In my experience, however, alcoholism is rarely the immediate and sole cause of amentia, although where other factors exist—particularly neuropathic heredity—it is a most important contributory agent. (Tredgold, 1908, p. 18)

The indictment of tuberculosis as a causative factor is similar to Barr's.

I believe that this factor is but rarely the direct and sole cause of amentia; but my observations show that, like alcoholism, it has a very important indirect and contributory influence. Its indirect effect is seen in its undoubted potency to produce the milder forms of nervous instability in the offspring, such as migraine, hysteria, and mild epilepsy; whilst its importance as a contributory agent is shown by the large proportion of aments who come of a tuberculous stock. I found that in the families of 34 percent of aments there was a pronounced tendency to tubercular lesions. (Tredgold, 1908, p. 20)

In sum:

I regard these three morbid ancestral conditions—namely, disease of the nervous system, alcoholism, and consumption—as being far and away the most frequent causes of mental defect. The two latter appear to me to be rather remote than immediate in their action, their effect being to initiate the neuropathic diathesis, which (if unchecked) eventually culminates in amentia. It is comparatively rarely that they give rise to actual mental deficiency in the immediately succeeding generation, although they may do so in some cases. (Tredgold, 1908, p. 20)

THE CULTURAL SETTING OF DEGENERATION THEORY

Paul Cranefield (1966) has recently indicted the degeneration theory as a contributory cause to the catastrophic setback of the development of the understanding and treatment of the mentally retarded. Certainly, there does seem to be a setback if we compare the quality of the progress made during the first half of the nineteenth century with that occurring in the latter decades of that century and in the first decade of the twentieth. The custodial care of the mentally retarded had improved under the aegis of Pinel and Esquirol, even when the retarded were diagnostically confused and confined with the insane. But concurrent with increased diagnostic clarification toward mid-century, there developed methods of treatment and training by men such as Seguin and Howe that made demonstrable changes in the status of retardates and thus raised the highest hopes. But to attribute the pessimistic attitudes toward mental retardation around the turn of the century to the impact of the degeneration theories is to focus attention on only one of the relevant factors operative in the setback of the development of constructive programs for the retarded.

One might freely speculate that the pessimistic attitudes at the turn of the century were in part a reaction to the unrealistically optimistic attitudes prevailing at mid-century. The training methods introduced by Seguin and others had undoubted success but they did not live up to the expectations aroused by the advanced publicity. Society at large may have been experiencing what Itard experienced in his work with the Wild Boy, i.e., the disappointment of our most sanguine hopes leaves us blind to real advances, and an unrealistic optimism is replaced by an equally unrealistic dejection. Certainly, in this connection, it is intriguing to speculate why many of the leaders in the changing attitudes were directors of the training institutions which had so recently been established with great expectations.

However, more likely responsible for the change in attitude and programs in the field of mental retardation is the advent of the Darwinian theory of evolution. We might argue that the effect of Darwinism on the field of mental retardation was both widespread and deep. Generally speaking, Darwinism had its effect by its powerful influence on the zeitgeist. Science, medicine, philosophy, religion, ethics, politics, economics all felt the impact in one way or another. And, as thinking in these fields underwent change, there was undoubtedly a correlative change in the ways in which society began to view the problem of mental retardation.

For example, one might argue that we cannot understand the effect of degeneration theory upon the problem of mental retardation without understanding the effect of Darwinism upon degeneration theory and the way in which the figure of the degeneration theory altered with the changing background of the zeitgeist. The basic hypotheses and their interrelationships remained more or less the same, while the perception of the theory especially in its social action implications was radically altered.

Both Morel and Howe subscribed to a degeneration theory, but in neither case did the subscription lead to a pessimistic or alarmist attitude toward the problem of mental retardation. The hereditarian views of the day—which allowed for the transmission of environmental effects—could not in themselves lead to pessimism. One need only alter the environment and one could forestall or reverse the degeneration. Both men advocated social reform and especially the improvement of conditions for the working classes. In an impassioned article, "Causes and prevention of idiocy," published anonymously by Howe in the *Massachusetts Quarterly Review* of June 1848, Howe asserted that eight-tenths of the idiots were born of families that had degenerated to the lowest degree of bodily and mental condition. The immediate causes of degeneration included intemperance and unhygienic and immoral living; but the remote causes were ignorance and poverty.

This degradation is the result of ignorance, and this ignorance is the almost inevitable consequence of extreme poverty. Want is ever pressing so closely at the heels of the poor, that their whole energies must be expended in keeping ahead of it. In truth, the real and mighty evils of poverty are little known, or little thought about. Scanty food, thin raiment, comfortless houses—these immediate effects of poverty are but as the small dust of the balance, compared with the remoter ones which prevent the development and exercise of the truly human part of our nature. (Howe, 1848b, pp. 316–317)

The bugle call for the War on Poverty sounded at least that long ago.[2]

The pernicious implications of a theory of degeneration did not occur to a Howe or a Morel. They were the inheritors of a different spiritual and intellectual age. Seguin, who held no theory of degeneration, breathed the same air as these, his contemporaries, and on that atmosphere his voice rings the same note. Compare both tone and overtone in the following passages. The first, from Howe's 1848 Report to the Governor, is taken from a section dealing with a classificatory system for retardates consisting of three categories, simpletons, fools, and idiots. It is of interest in being one of the earliest applications of "the capacity for using language as signs of thought," as the classificatory principle. But of particular interest here is the attitude toward the retardate—and other deviate members of society—as revealed in Howe's warning against the misuse of classification.

This classification assumes that the subjects of it are *not* persons absolutely *devoid* of *mind*, but merely persons of feeble mind; that the idiot proper is the most feeble, the simpleton the least so. It is important that this principle should be kept in view, so that the great advantages of classification may be had, without the

---

[2] We, perhaps, need not labor to convince the reader that ideas that are fashionable today were held and discussed by people who lived long ago. What needs emphasis and reiteration is that the impact of ideas depends not only on whether they are right or wrong, appropriate or inappropriate, but on the social dynamics of, and the social forces within, a society at the time ideas are presented. The major purpose of this and subsequent chapters is to illustrate and discuss this point in the hope, expressed in Chapter 2, that the reader will gain a perspective which will prevent him from underselling the past, overselling the present, or overlooking the fact that the outlines of a "different" future are already in the process of development.

disadvantages that sometimes attend it. Nature produces individual men and not classes. Putting men into a class, is too apt to put them into a *caste;* sometimes even it puts them out of the pale of humanity. This is seen in the case of our artificial class of convicts or criminals;—they suffer by being considered as a class or caste, differing from other men not in degree of guiltiness only, (as is in truth the case) but differing absolutely and essentially,—being *criminals,* while other men are *not criminals.* Such classification may give undue pride to the one, and despair to the other. Similar effects may follow the classification of men into Christians and heathens; and the petty subdivisions into saints and world's people. Evil may arise from the misuse of the term *Idiot,* as the name of a class, if it causes them to be considered as a distinct order of persons, and different from other men in being utterly devoid of mind, for it will be considered useless to try to teach those who have no mind at all; but if they are considered as differing from others not in kind, but in degree only,—as merely having *feeble* minds, then their very feebleness, like that of little children, will commend them to our hearts. Whatever classification of men is made, the mantle of humanity should be thrown over the whole, that its ample folds may cover every one, and that none be lost to the human family.[3] (Howe, 1850, pp. 33–34)

The comparable quotation from Seguin is taken from his speech at Syracuse delivered on the occasion of the laying of the cornerstone of the first building in this country specifically designed for the training of idiots.

God has scattered among us, rare as the possessors of talent or genius, the idiot, the blind, the deaf mute, in order to bind the talented to the incapable, the rich to the needy, all men to each other, by a tie of indissoluble solidarity. The old bonds are dissolving; man is already unwilling to contribute money or palaces for the support of indolent classes; but he is every day more ready to build palaces and give annuities for the indigent or infirm, the chosen friends of Jesus Christ. To see that stone, token of a new alliance between humanity and a class hitherto neglected, is the greatest joy of my life; for I, too, have labored for the poor idiot. . . . (Seguin, 1866, p. 13)

That speech was delivered on September 8, 1854, five years before the publication of *The Origin of Species.* The view of the retardate and his relationship to the rest of society reflected in it, and in the quotation from Howe, highlights a common—and precious—bond of humanity. The impact of Darwinism was to contribute to the radical alteration of that perception.

SOCIAL DARWINISM

The Darwinian theory put the implications of the degeneration theory in a new light. If the evolution of a species is the result of *variation* in traits among members of the species, *hereditary transmission* of the variants, and *natural selection* of those variants most fit to survive in the struggle for existence, then the theory of degeneration is placed in a broader context. The "de-

---

[3] Howe's cautions about the uses of classificatory terms and labels—written over 100 years ago—are similar, if not in principle identical to, the cautions advanced by us, in relation to usage of current classificatory or labeling schemas (Chapter 3).

generates," the physically and mentally ill, are no longer seen as the unfortunate victims of environment and/or hereditary taint—of whom one might say "there but for the Grace of God go I"—but rather as those who are demonstrably members of an inferior race of mankind which in accordance with natural law ought to be allowed to die out as quickly as possible. This then would be an indirect but powerful effect of Darwinism on the perception of the mentally retarded. But it needed no special theory of degeneration to have that effect as witness the fact that many Social Darwinists—those who systematically and directly tried to apply the concepts of "struggle for existence" and "survival of the fittest" to an analysis of social life—made no mention of degeneration theory in their argument that the deviant members of society, the physically and mentally unfit, and the economically unsuccessful, had proven themselves unfit in the struggle for existence. To seek to alleviate the pain and burden of their lives was considered a misguided charity that would only perpetuate in future generations the evil it sought to rectify in this.

But Social Darwinism—a movement through which evolutionary theory was to have its impact on programs for the retardate—was in itself no simple product of evolutionary theory. Its roots can easily be traced further back.

In several passages appearing in his *Social Statics*, Herbert Spencer (1851) expresses views on the nature of life and society which one would readily attribute to Darwinian theory if they had not in fact been formulated nearly a decade before the appearance of *The Origin of Species*.

Spencer's argument is first presented in terms of nature at large.

Pervading all nature we may see at work a stern discipline, which is a little cruel that it may be very kind. That state of universal warfare maintained throughout the lower creation, to the great perplexity of many worthy people, is at bottom the most merciful provision which the circumstances admit of. It is much better that the ruminant animal, when deprived by age of the vigour which made its existence a pleasure, should be killed by some beast of prey, than that it should linger out a life made painful by infirmities, and eventually die of starvation. By the destruction of all such, not only is existence ended before it becomes burdensome, but room is made for a younger generation capable of the fullest enjoyment; and, moreover, out of the very act of substitution happiness is derived for a tribe of predatory creatures. Note further, that their carnivorous enemies not only remove from herbivorous herds individuals past their prime, but also weed out the sickly, the malformed, and the least fleet or powerful. By the aid of which purifying process, as well as by the fighting, so universal in the pairing season, all vitiation of the race through the multiplication of its inferior samples is prevented; and the maintenance of a constitution completely adapted to surrounding conditions, and therefore most productive of happiness, is ensured. (Spencer, 1851, p. 322)

In this best of all possible worlds, Calvinistically predestined, the argument is then extended to mankind:

. . . the well-being of existing humanity, and the unfolding of it into this ultimate perfection, are both secured by that same beneficent, though severe discipline, to which the animate creation at large is subject: a discipline which is pitiless in the working out of good: a felicity-pursuing law which never swerves for the avoidance of partial and temporary suffering. The poverty of the incapable, the distresses that come upon the imprudent, the starvation of the idle, and those shoulderings aside of the weak by the strong, which leave so many "in shallows and in miseries," are the decrees of a large, far-seeing benevolence. It seems hard that an unskillfulness which with all his efforts he cannot overcome, should entail hunger upon the artizan. It seems hard that a labourer incapacitated by sickness from competing with his stronger fellows, should have to bear the resulting privations. It seems hard that widows and orphans should be left to struggle for life or death. Nevertheless, when regarded not separately, but in connection with the interests of universal humanity, these harsh fatalities are seen to be full of the highest beneficence—the same beneficence which brings to early graves the children of diseased parents, and singles out the low-spirited, the intemperate, and the debilitated as the victims of an epidemic. (Spencer, 1851, pp. 322–323)

In a specific application of the thesis to a social problem, Spencer lashes at the defenders of the English poor laws:

Similarly, we must call those spurious philanthropists, who, to prevent present misery, would entail greater misery upon future generations. All defenders of a poor-law must, however, be classed amongst such. That rigorous necessity which, when allowed to act on them, becomes so sharp a spur to the lazy, and so stong a bridle to the random, these paupers' friends would repeal, because of the wailings it here and there produces. Blind to the fact, that under the natural order of things society is constantly excreting its unhealthy, imbecile, slow, vacillating, faithless members, these unthinking, though well-meaning, men advocate an interference which not only stops the purifying process, but even increases the vitiation— absolutely encourages the multiplication of the reckless and incompetent by offering them an unfailing provision, and *dis*courages the multiplication of the competent and provident by heightening the prospective difficulty of maintaining a family. And thus, in their eagerness to prevent the really salutary sufferings that surround us, these sigh-wise and groan-foolish people bequeath to posterity a continually increasing curse. (Spencer, 1851, pp. 323–324)

These passages anticipate the writings of the later Social Darwinists. Thus William Graham Sumner, in his *What Social Classes Owe to Each Other,* would argue:

We each owe it to the other to guarantee rights. Rights do not pertain to *results*, but only to *chances*. They pertain to the *conditions* of the struggle for existence, not to any of the results of it; to the *pursuit* of happiness, not to the possession of happiness. It cannot be said that each one has a right to have some property, because if one man had such a right some other man or men would be under a corresponding obligation to provide him with some property. Each has a right to acquire and possess property if he can. It is plain what fallacies are developed when we overlook this distinction. Those fallacies run through *all* socialistic schemes and theories. If we take rights to pertain to results, and then say that rights must be equal, we come to say that men have a right to be equally happy, and so on in all the details. Rights should be equal, because they pertain to chances, and all ought to have equal chances so far as chances are provided or limited by the action of society. This, however, will not produce equal results, but it is right just because it will produce unequal results—that is, results which shall be proportioned to the merits of individuals. (Sumner, 1883, pp. 163–164)

The application of this philosophy to the disadvantaged leads to the following argument:

. . . it may be said that those whom humanitarians and philanthropists call the weak are the ones, through whom the productive and conservative forces of society are wasted. They constantly neutralize and destroy the finest efforts of the wise and industrious, and are a dead-weight on the society in all its struggles to realize any better things. Whether the people who mean no harm, but are weak in the essential powers necessary to the performance of one's duties in life, or those who are malicious and vicious, do the more mischief, is a question not easy to answer. Under the names of the poor and the weak, the negligent, shiftless, inefficient, silly, and imprudent are fastened upon the industrious and prudent as a responsibility and a duty. (Sumner, 1883, pp. 20–21)

The Influence of Economic Theories and the Industrial Revolution

While the attitudes of the Social Darwinists were undoubtedly formed in large part by their reactions to evolutionary theory and the vivid analogies it suggested between life in nature and life in society, one must also recognize the fundamental influence of classical economic theory. Spencer's argument needed no Darwin. The classical economists had set the premises. They can be seen in Adam Smith's advocacy of free competition in the market place, in Ricardo's iron laws, and in Malthus' theory of population. As portrayed by these theorists, the laws of economic life were such that wage earners, employers, and landlords competed for the income of industry. There was a continuous pressure of population on subsistence, relieved only by war, famine, or disease, or sexual abstinence; and human nature being what it was not much could be expected from the last of these checks. Malthus' argument against the poor laws anticipates Spencer.

The poor-laws of England tend to depress the general condition of the poor in these two ways. Their first obvious tendency is to increase population without increasing the food for its support. A poor man may marry with little or no prospect of being able to support a family in independence. They may be said therefore in some measure to create the poor which they maintain; . . . Secondly, the quantity of provisions consumed in workhouses upon a part of the society, that cannot in general be considered as the most valuable part, diminishes the share that would otherwise belong to more industrious, and more worthy members; and thus in the same manner forces more to become dependent. (Malthus, 1798, pp. 83–84)

The effect of Malthusian theory upon Social Darwinism can be traced through another line of descent. For in Darwin's struggle with theoretical difficulties it was the reading of Malthus' essay on population that triggered the inspiration for his key concept of natural selection. That this seminal influence of the theory of population was not happenstance is suggested by the fact that the essay was also directive in the thinking of Alfred Russel Wallace, independent discoverer of the principle of natural selection and cofounder of modern evolutionary theory (Huxley, 1960).

If the classical economic theories are considered as causal antecedents of Social Darwinism, it is of course possible to take one further step backward in time and see the economic theories as intellectual by-products of the industrial revolution. The theories can then be viewed as an attempt on the part of their authors to systematize their observations and to provide explanatory concepts of the economic revolution occurring about them.

By pointing out these relationships, it is not meant to reduce the complex problem of changing attitudes toward the mental retardate to a simple economic determinism, or to substitute one set of biological or economic theories for the degeneration theory as the scapegoat. It is recognized that this schema of relationships, here presented, is a gross oversimplification. It focuses on a single causal chain where multiple causes acted, reacted, and interacted in a complex network. But gross as the schema is, it is used to suggest that at any point in time, society's attitudes toward its deviates are not shaped solely by the scientific theories or facts then available. The theories or facts will be seen to have different implications depending upon the general social matrix in which they occur.

This thesis should be kept in mind as we proceed to trace out in the following chapters a salient relationship in which Darwinian theory may be said to have had a direct effect upon the changing attitudes toward the retardate. This relationship was mediated through the eugenics movement.

The origin and early development of eugenics

In the preceding chapter we gave some consideration to the ways in which biological theories of heredity and evolution affected attitudes and programs in the area of mental subnormality. We noted that these theories in part reflected and in part helped to form the zeitgeist of the late nineteenth century. Within that zeitgeist attitudes toward the retarded and other dependents of sociey underwent a hardening and dehumanization if we compare them to the earlier feelings of brotherhood and identification that we find expressed by Howe and Seguin.

But the new biological theories and their continued development had their effect on the retardate not only through changes in the zeitgeist but also more directly through the formation of the eugenics movement. Eugenics served on the one hand to crystalize and organize the newer attitudes toward the retarded and other dependent classes of society at the same time it provided a vehicle for converting these attitudes into social action programs.

GALTON AND THE CONCEPT OF NATURAL ABILITY

Francis Galton, the founder of the eugenics movement, had been deeply impressed by the publication of *The Origin of Species*. The greater body of his work may be looked upon as an attempt to apply the key concepts of evolutionary theory—variation, hereditary transmission of variation, and natural selection—to mankind. His prodigious work on individual differences ranging from intellects to fingerprints reflects his interest in variation of traits in mankind. His pedigree studies, his twin studies, his correlational statistics are all techniques used in an attempt to demonstrate the hereditary transmission of traits. Eugenics itself can be seen as embodying the recognition that society alters the conditions of natural selection and that for the further evolution of mankind there must be a conscious control of differential reproduction rates among the members of society that will ensure that those possessed of the more desirable traits will reproduce at a faster rate than those possessing the least desirable traits.

Galton's first major publication on trait differences and their hereditary transmission was *Hereditary Genius* (1869). This book had a major effect on its times and was taken as proof that there was hereditary transmission of intellectual traits. The book had additional importance in that it presented a methodology—the pedigree study—which was in subsequent decades to be applied widely and uncritically in the study of mental retardation. It is also of more than historical interest in its attempts to conceptualize "natural ability." In this attempt we can see Galton grappling with the problem which Wechsler in our times would treat in his "global concept of intelligence."

Although Galton entitled his treatise *Hereditary Genius,* he was later—in the preface to the 1892 edition—to express regret for the choice of title and to indicate that *Hereditary Ability* might have been a less misleading title. He maintained that there was no interest on his part "to use the word genius in any technical sense, but merely as expressing an ability that was exceptionally high and at the same time inborn." The term genius throughout the text was used as the equivalent of "natural ability."

This concept of "natural ability" as used by Galton included more than just intellect.

By natural ability, I mean those qualities of intellect and disposition, which urge and qualify a man to perform acts that lead to reputation. I do not mean capacity without zeal, nor zeal without capacity, nor even a combination of both of them, without an adequate power of doing a great deal of very laborious work. But I mean a nature which, when left to itself, will, urged by an inherent stimulus, climb the path that leads to eminence, and has strength to reach the summit—one which, if hindered or thwarted, will fret and strive until the hindrance is overcome, and it is again free to follow its labour-loving instinct. (Galton, 1869, pp. 37–38)

It is not always easy to follow Galton's argument because of loose and shifting terminology. However, it does seem probable that in this passage when Galton uses the term "capacity" he was talking about intellect. In fact, on page 46, he states: "Again, we have seen that a union of three separate qualities—intellect, zeal and power of work—are necessary to raise men from the ranks."

Not only are there three components in natural ability, but Galton sees all three as being inherited:

The particular meaning in which I employ the word ability, does not restrict my argument from a wider application; for, if I succeed in showing—as I undoubtedly shall do—that the concrete triple event, of ability combined with zeal and with capacity for hard labour, is inherited, much more will there be justification for believing that any one of its three elements, whether it be ability, or zeal, or capacity for labour, is similarly a gift of inheritance. (Galton, 1869, p. 38)

Therefore, Galton's concept of natural ability includes not only intellective factors but also nonintellective factors such as motivation and energy levels. Although this may differ from the approach of succeeding generations of psychometricians who sought to measure intellectual ability divorced from other personality factors, it is interesting to note that Wechsler, among others, in recent years has sought to emphasize the importance of these nonintellective factors. It has been pointed out that it is impossible to obtain performance on an intelligence test independently of these other factors. Wechsler has even taken the position that it is desirable to include nonintellective factors in tests designed to evaluate intelligence. "General intelligence cannot be equated with intellectual ability however broadly defined, but must be regarded as a manifestation of the personality as a whole" (Wechsler, 1950, p. 78).

To elaborate the similarity between Wechsler's and Galton's points of view we can consider the former's conclusion to his discussion of some factor analytic studies of intelligence tests:

What are we to make of these two findings? First, that factors other than intellectual contribute to achievement in areas where, as in the case of learning, intellectual factors have until recently been considered uniquely determinate, and, second, that these other factors have to do with functions and abilities hitherto considered traits of personality. Among those partially identified so far are factors relating primarily to the conative functions like drive, persistence, will, and perseveration, or in some instances, to aspects of temperament that pertain to interests and achievement. (Wechsler, 1950, pp. 81–82)

As Wechsler recognizes, these factor analytic studies support what many clinicians were arguing all along, that personality components were an integral part of intelligent functioning. Or as Wechsler puts it, "Personality traits *enter into* the effectiveness of intelligent behavior, and, hence, into any global concept of intelligence itself" (Wechsler, 1950, p. 82).

Whether or not it is desirable to include nonintellective factors in an intelligence test as Wechsler urges—or to minimize them or to keep that at a relatively uniform value from subject to subject—is debatable. Much would depend upon the purpose for which the test is being used. If we would like to predict how the subject is likely to function in everyday life situations in which nonintellective factors are operating then it would seem reasonable to have nonintellective factors operative in the test situation. If we would like to know how a subject might function if nonintellective factors were not affecting his efficiency—if he were functioning in a less stressful environment or if he should undergo a successful course of psychotherapy—then we would probably wish to minimize nonintellective factors in the test situation. Be that as it may, it seems likely that failure to take nonintellective factors into account when testing mentally retarded individuals can cause serious errors in evaluation, as we have documented elsewhere in this volume. Therefore, it seems unfortunate that early workers in the field did not follow the lead given by Galton in his discussion of natural ability.

The Variability and Constancy of Traits

In developing his argument for the hereditary transmission of natural ability, Galton first argues for the variability of the trait under consideration. By analogy with physical measurements such as height and girth of chest, by a consideration of distribution of academic grades, and by a consideration of the different frequencies of various levels of ability, Galton argues that, "there must be a fairly constant average mental capacity in the inhabitants of the British Isles, and that the deviation from that average—upwards towards genius, and downwards towards stupidity—must follow the law that governs deviations from all true averages" (Galton, 1869, p. 32). This law is the normal probability curve. This distribution could conceivably result from innate causes, or environmental causes, or an interaction of these two groups of determinants. Galton unequivocally and eloquently argues for the first alternative.

I have no patience with the hypothesis occasionally expressed, and often implied, especially in tales written to teach children to be good, that babies are born pretty much alike, and that the sole agencies in creating differences between boy and boy, and man and man, are steady application and moral effort. It is in the most unqualified manner that I object to pretensions of natural equality. The experiences of the nursery, the school, the University, and of professional careers are a chain of proofs to the contrary. I acknowledge freely the great power of education and social influences in developing the active powers of the mind, just as I acknowledge the effect of use in developing the muscles of a blacksmith's arm, and no further. Let the blacksmith labour as he will, he will find there are certain feats beyond his power that are well within the strength of a man of herculean make, even although the latter may have led a sedentary life. . . . Everybody who has trained himself to physical exercises discovers the extent of his muscular powers to a nicety. When he begins to walk, to row, to use the dumb bells, or to run, he finds to his great delight that his thews strengthen, and his endurance of fatigue increases day after day. So long as he is a novice, he perhaps flatters himself there is hardly an assignable limit to the education of his muscles; but the daily gain is soon discovered to diminish, and at last it vanishes altogether. His maximum performance becomes a rigidly determinate quantity. . . . This is precisely analogous to the experience that every student has had of the working of his mental powers. The eager boy, when he first goes to school and confronts intellectual difficulties, is astonished at his progress. He glories in his newly-developed mental grip and growing capacity for application, and, it may be, fondly believes it to be within his reach to become one of the heroes who have left their mark upon the history of the world. The years go by; he competes in the examinations of school and college, over and over again with his fellows, and soon finds his place among them. He knows he can beat such and such of his competitors; that there are some with whom he runs on equal terms, and others whose intellectual feats he cannot even approach. Probably his vanity still continues to tempt him, by whispering in a new strain. It tells him that classics, mathematics, and other subjects taught in universities, are mere scholastic specialities, and no test of the more valuable intellectual powers. It reminds him of numerous instances of persons who had been unsuccessful in the competitions of youth, but who had shown powers in after-life that made them the foremost men of their age. Accordingly, with newly furnished hopes, and with all the ambition of twenty-two years of age, he leaves his University and enters a larger field of competition. The same kind of experience awaits him here that he has already gone through. Opportunities occur—they occur to every man—and he finds himself incapable of grasping them. He tries, and is tried in many things. In a few years more, unless he is incurably blinded by self-conceit, he learns precisely of what performances he is capable, and what other enterprises lie beyond his compass. When he reaches mature life, he is confident only within certain limits, and knows, or ought to know, himself just as he is probably judged of by the world, with all his unmistakable weakness and all his undeniable strength. He is no longer tormented into hopeless efforts by the fallacious promptings of overweening vanity, but he limits his undertakings to matters below the level of his reach, and finds true moral repose in an honest conviction that he is engaged in as much good work as his nature has rendered him capable of performing. (Galton, 1869, pp. 14–16)

The Argument for the Hereditary Transmission of Natural Ability

From our present-day vantage point, it is recognized that these assumptions of the innateness and constancy of differences in ability would not necessarily mean that the differences are hereditary. Prenatal environmental influences could account for innate differences as easily as hereditary factors. The effects of early training and/or environmental influences could be lasting and relatively irreversible. Nor was Galton so naive as to imagine that the relative ineffectiveness of training in modifying natural gifts was proof of their hereditary transmission. For Galton, the necessary proof was indicated by the very observations that suggested the hypothesis in the first place. It was in his study of the mental characteristics of different races that he first became aware that "characteristics cling to families." Then, reflecting upon his observations of acquaintances and their families he was struck how ability seemed to go by descent. The next step was an examination of the biographical data on illustrious men from all periods of history. This examination convinced him that genius was hereditary. Though others before him had espoused the theory of hereditary genius, Galton in his own estimate was the first "to treat the subject in a statistical manner, to arrive at numerical results, and to introduce the 'law of deviation from an average' into discussions on heredity" (1869, p. vi, Preface).

His accumulated researches on the subject as published in *Hereditary Genius* examined various groups of talented individuals such as authors, statesmen, scientists, poets, musicians, painters, athletes, judges, and divines. Galton argued—and convincingly—that the individual representatives of his various groups had not been selected to demonstrate his hypotheses but rather that they were unselected lists of eminent persons chosen from biographical dictionaries and such similar unbiased sources. Therefore, principles of heredity demonstrated within such groups were apt to be of general validity.

In using such sources as biographical dictionaries Galton was using "reputation" as a measure of natural ability, and he has been criticized both then and now for using such a suspect measure. But Galton argues tellingly for the use of his criterion.

By reputation, I mean the opinion of contemporaries, revised by posterity—the favourable result of a critical analysis of each man's character, by many biographers. I do not mean high social or official position, nor such as is implied by being the mere lion of a London season; but I speak of the reputation of a leader of opinion, of an originator, of a man to whom the world deliberately acknowledges itself largely indebted. (Galton, 1869, p. 37)

When one considers the level of ability with which Galton was attempting to deal—one that reflects itself in high, and socially acclaimed, achievement—his criterion does not appear to us to be especially suspect. We would be at some loss to suggest a better one. When we consider the objective tests of creativity that are currently being espoused by professionally trained members of the behavioral sciences, we rather think that one can still learn from Galton's approach. The difficulty lies, of course, not in the criterion but in its application, and even though Galton was generally careful there occur noteworthy lapses. His chapter on the judges of England contains one of the most suspect applications of this criterion.

The nearest collateral relation of the North family by the Montagu side is Charles Hatton, their first cousin. He is alluded to three times in Roger North's "Lives," and each time with the same epithet—"the incomparable Charles Hatton." Why he was so distinguished there is no information, but it is reasonable to accept Roger North's estimate of his merits, so far as to classify him among the gifted members of the Montagu family. (Galton, 1869, pp. 79–80)

This "achievement" of Hatton without further documentation, hardly meets Galton's stated criterion for eminence.

But even allowing that one might challenge a number of the entries on Galton's list of the eminent relatives of the eminent men constituting his various groups the remaining number would undoubtedly be considerable and more than one would expect on a purely chance basis. If we challenge none, then the argument is overwhelming. Thus in his list of 286 judges, he maintains 109 have one or more eminent relations. Among the groups of statesmen considered is the list of 25 English Premiers holding office since the accession of George III. Seventeen of this group are found with eminent relations. In nonpolitical spheres, of 83 scientists, 65 have eminent relations; of 56 poets, 20 have eminent relatives; of 120 musicians, 26 have eminent kinsmen, etc. A more detailed analysis of the relationships within his groups lends further weight to Galton's argument for it is convincingly demonstrated that the closer the degree of kinship the greater the likelihood of eminence. The sons of an eminent man are more likely to achieve eminence than are his grandsons. His nephews are more likely to achieve eminence than his cousins.

The argument that eminence clings to family lines is formidable but does it follow that the explanatory principle is to be found in nature rather than nurture? Galton recognizes this problem but dismisses the nurture argument on the basis of a number of observations which to him are convincingly in favor of nature. In all fields men of eminence have risen from humble origins and in spite of all adversity; and men with all social advantages are unable to achieve eminence, "unless they are endowed with high natural gifts." Adverse circumstances may hold back a man of mediocre gifts but not one whose gifts are exceptional.

If a man is gifted with vast intellectual ability, eagerness to work, and power of working, I cannot comprehend how such a man should be repressed. The world is always tormented with difficulties waiting to be solved—struggling with ideas and feelings, to which it can give no adequate expression. If, then, there exists a man capable of solving those difficulties, or of giving a voice to those pent-up feelings, he is sure to be welcomed with universal acclamation. We may almost say that he has only to put his pen to paper, and the thing is done. I am here speaking of the very first-class men—prodigies—one in a million, or one in ten millions, of whom numbers will be found described in this volume, as specimens of hereditary genius.

. . .

I have shown that social hindrances cannot impede men of high ability, from becoming eminent. I shall now maintain that social advantages are incompetent to give that status, to a man of moderate ability. It would be easy to point out several men of fair capacity, who have been pushed forward by all kinds of help, who are ambitious, and exert themselves to the utmost, but who completely fail in attaining eminence. If great peers, they may be lord-lieutenants of counties; if they belong to great county families, they may become influential members of parliament and local notabilities. When they die, they leave a blank for awhile in a large circle, but there is no Westminster Abbey and no public mourning for them—perhaps barely a biographical notice in the columns of the daily papers. (Galton, 1869, pp. 39–41)

A COUNTER ARGUMENT

The argument is fair and eloquently delivered. But in its detailed execution, as one peruses the list of eminent relatives of eminent men, one suspects that one is often dealing with individuals who could well be subsumed under the description of that last paragraph. And again, one has to raise the question, not of the adequacy, but of the application of the criterion of reputation. But grant that culled lists would still support the general contention of familial eminence, has Galton made too clean a dichotomy between environment and heredity? Let us assume that hereditary gifts in varying amounts are equally distributed in all families. Let us further assume that achievement in any field is some multiplicative function of hereditary endowment and environment. And assume that environment has its effect not only by the opportunity it affords for the development of natural gifts but by the motivational patterns it will induce for the use of those natural gifts—such inductions working by way of rewards and punishments for the exercise of those gifts and by the provision of appropriate models of behavior in the key individuals in one's environment. With these assumptions, take a number of upper-class families and a number of lower-class families each with the same total number of individuals and each with the same share of natural gifts. Now who in the eyes of society will achieve eminence? Certainly, those in the upper class who are highly gifted and those in the lower class who are so highly gifted that they will overcome all obstacles. But come down a few grades in ability and surely a point must be reached where a member of the upper class possesses enough ability that this combined with the opportunities and shaping forces of his environment permits the achievement of eminence while the member of the lower class with the same degree of ability does not possess sufficient opportunity to reach the same degree of eminence.

And within classes how easy it is to establish a familial subculture! One politician, one writer, one physician and a model is set, influential connections established, a family atmosphere created. The young are exposed to special kinds of experience, special kinds of behavior are signalled out for recognition and reward. A family line of politicians is established by a John Adams, or a Patrick Joseph Kennedy. A line of musicians by a Weit Bach.

In this case of familial transmission of special talents, consider the analogous argument that chance factors are the only or by far the predominant factors determining sex. Yet it is not impossible to find families that consist of six, eight, ten children all of the same sex. Nor is it difficult given sufficiently large samples to find families in which one or the other sex has predominated through several generations. Then given a sufficiently large number of upper-class families with a relatively small number of possible professions open to them, is it unlikely on the basis of chance alone that some families should exhibit their predominant eminence in science or politics or art? Add to that as we have indicated above that chance alone is not operative but that motivational patterns and social and economic opportunities are induced and handed down from one generation to the next and it may be no more necessary to infer a hereditary factor to explain the family of Bach or Adams than to explain the Jukes or the Kallikaks.

With such arguments, Galton's underlying assumptions can be cut away and his study is left as a demonstration that "eminence clings to family lines," but with no sound argument for the underlying cause. One can advance heredity, as did Galton, or with equal validity advance nurture or an inter-action of nature and nurture to explain the observed phenomenon.

THE EUGENICAL IMPLICATION AND IMPACT OF GALTON'S ARGUMENT

The question then is why did Galton's argument have the kind of im-pact and wide influence that it did? There are at least two obvious reasons.

It fit in naturally with the evolutionary zeitgeist. It was a convincing extension of the insights of evolutionary theory to mankind and particularly to those characteristics of man, intelligence and personality, to which they had not been previously applied even by Darwin himself. In the letter written to his cousin when he first began reading *Hereditary Genius,* Darwin states:

You have made a convert of an opponent in one sense, for I have always maintained that, excepting fools, men did not differ much in intellect, only in zeal and hard work. (Pearson, 1914, p. 6)

By contending that intellectual ability was a variable and inheritable trait in mankind Galton had applied to mankind the principle of natural selection and hence of evolutionary development of intelligence. He saw the various races of mankind as differing in intelligence in accordance with the degree of civilization that they were capable of developing and sustaining. These differences in races presumably occurred through the slow and chance-like operation of natural selection and led Galton to the converse argument of Darwin's *Origin of Species.* There Darwin opened his argument with obser-vations on the artificial development of races and species of animals and plants under domestication and then proceeded to develop his argument for natural selection. Galton, pointing to presumed intellectual differences naturally occurring between races, nations, and families, argued for artificial selection and breeding of man in order to produce a superior race. And in this proposal for an improvement of the human breed by artificial selection—with a con-comitant solution to existing social problems—lies the second and probably more important reason for the ready acceptance of Galton's argument.

Galton's approach to the conclusions of his own argument was cautious and thoughtful as befitted his essentially benign and scientific temperament. In *Hereditary Genius* he rejects as unthinkable the Spartan approach to im-provement of the breed by destruction of the weak and unfit and advocates in its stead the encouragement of the reproduction of the fit.

I shall argue that the wisest policy is that which results in retarding the average age of marriage among the weak, and in hastening it among the vigorous classes;

whereas, most unhappily for us, the influence of numerous social agencies has been strongly and banefully exerted in the precisely opposite direction. (Galton, 1869, pp. 352–353)

Galton then demonstrates with numerical examples how a familial line in which early marriage is the rule will outbreed one in which marriage is generally delayed, and concludes:

I trust the reader will realize the heavy doom which these figures pronounce against all subsections of prolific races in which it is the custom to put off the period of marriage until middle age. It is a maxim of Malthus that the period of marriage ought to be delayed in order that the earth may not be overcrowded by a population for whom there is no place at the great table of nature. If this doctrine influenced all classes alike, I should have nothing to say about it here, one way or another, for it would hardly affect the discussions in this book; but, as it is put forward as a rule of conduct for the prudent part of mankind to follow, whilst the imprudent are necessarily left free to disregard it, I have no hesitation in saying that it is a most pernicious rule of conduct in its bearing upon race. Its effect would be such as to cause the race of the prudent to fall, after a few centuries, into an almost incredible inferiority of numbers to that of the imprudent, and it is therefore calculated to bring utter ruin upon the breed of any country where the doctrine prevailed. I protest against the abler races being encouraged to withdraw in this way from the struggle for existence. It may seem monstrous that the weak should be crowded out by the strong, but it is still more monstrous that the races best fitted to play their part on the stage of life, should be crowded out by the incompetent, the ailing, and the desponding. (Galton, 1869, pp. 356–357)

Although the general principles of eugenics had been formulated in *Hereditary Genius* and in the studies that led up to it, the term *eugenics* was not introduced by Galton until the publication of *Inquiries into Human Faculty and Its Development* in 1883. In that work Galton advanced his argument for hereditable differences in individuals, families, and races of men, and presented as a moral duty encumbent on all the improvement of mankind by selective breeding—this selective breeding to be achieved in particular by the encouragement of early marriage upon the part of the most fit members of society.[1]

During these years before the turn of the century, Galton's preoccupation with eugenic theory received no direct translation into programs of social action. But his publications were not without effect; they were preparing the minds of many intellectuals for acceptance and participation in such programs when they finally did get underway. As an illustration of how Galton was

---

[1] In addition to advancing the cause of eugenics, the book was an important contribution to the development of psychological science. With its emphasis on laboratory measurement and statistical description of biological and psychological differences among men, it was a fundamental contribution to the founding of that branch of psychology which concerns itself with individual differences. Hence, it was one of the sources from which developed the psychological testing of intellectual and personality traits, a development which in turn was to have a profound importance for the field of mental retardation, as we shall later indicate.

influencing those who in turn shaped the thinking of others, we can take a passage from the second edition of *The Descent of Man* published in 1874. Darwin, after noting his indebtedness to Galton, among others, takes the following position:

> With savages, the weak in body or mind are soon eliminated; and those that survive commonly exhibit a vigorous state of health. We civilized men, on the other hand, do our utmost to check the process of elimination; we build asylums for the imbecile, the maimed, and the sick; we institute poor-laws; and our medical men exert their utmost skill to save the life of every one to the last moment. There is reason to believe that vaccination has preserved thousands who from a weak constitution would formerly have succumbed to small-pox. Thus the weak members of civilized societies propagate their kind. No one who has attended to the breeding of domestic animals will doubt that this must be highly injurious to the race of man. It is surprising how soon a want of care, or care wrongly directed, leads to the degeneration of a domestic race; but, excepting in the case of man himself, hardly any one is so ignorant as to allow his worst animals to breed. (Darwin, 1874, p. 149)

DEVELOPMENTS IN AMERICA PREPARING THE WAY FOR THE EUGENICS MOVEMENT

While Galton's efforts were having their main effect in causing intellectuals to consider problems of heredity in relationship to evolutionary progress of the race, there were concurrent developments in the social programs directed to the failures and misfits of society. These developments were to have much in common with the aims and methods of eugenics and would prepare the ground for rapid acceptance of eugenics after the turn of the century. In fact, it might be speculated that the role of the eugenics movement, coming along when it did, was to justify, organize, and intensify practices that were already underway. At any rate, these developments as they occurred in America have been summarized by Mark Haller in his book *Eugenics: Hereditarian Attitudes in American Thought* (1963). There it is pointed out that the period following the Civil War was characterized by rapid social change and mounting tensions: industrialization with labor strife; urbanization and the growth of slums; a huge influx of immigrants with attendant ethnic, religious, and economic problems.[2] Concomitant with the growth of these social problems was the growth of agencies, institutions, and professional specialties designed to cope with the problems. The almshouses which serviced alike the aged, the sick, the insane, the feebleminded, the alcoholic, the indigent, and the

---

[2] This brief description of some of the direct and indirect consequences of the Civil War is similar to the characterization of what happened in our society after World War II (Sarason, Levine, Goldenberg, Cherlin, and Bennett, 1966).

orphaned were gradually replaced in the more progressive states by specialized institutions. Social work became a profession. Within medicine, psychiatry underwent rapid development and increasing numbers of physicians became specialized in the care of the feebleminded. Members of the new professions and specialties formed organizations and founded journals which promoted the rapid dissemination of ideas within these fields and served as vehicles for affecting public opinion and legislation. From among these individuals and organizations specialized in the care of the outcasts and misfits of society came the developments that were to be the forerunners of the eugenics movement in America.

For example, many of the leaders in the efforts to restrict propagation of the feebleminded were superintendents of the recently created training institutions. These institutions, founded in optimistic faith that the mentally subnormal could be soon rehabilitated and returned to the community, proved disappointing. This, not so much because of their lack of achievement but because that achievement did not fulfill the unrealistic expectations of their founding. In addition, familial factors in mental subnormality and in its degenerative correlates were becoming more and more widely publicized. Earlier, the reports of the Massachusetts Commission in 1848 and the Connecticut Commission in 1856 (Davies, 1930) had emphasized familial factors in retardation. But as we indicated in our discussion of Howe, as long as one was optimistic about what could be done with the training of the retardate, one need not focus problem-solving efforts on the hereditary aspects. When training proved of small effect in removing the problem then other solutions had to be found and the familial factors came to the fore in the thinking of those concerned with the problem: If only this generation of defectives could be prevented from breeding, the number of defectives in the next generation would be greatly reduced.

Similar lines of thinking occurred to those working with other classes of defectives and dependents. Psychiatrists were greatly impressed with familial tendencies toward insanity and likewise concluded that a major solution of that problem was prevention of the reproduction of the insane. Those working with the pauper and criminal classes perceived a similar etiology and cause. That formidable lady Josephine Shaw Lowell, who had a life-long engagement in all manner of charitable activities and was the first woman member of the New York State Board of Charities, minced no words on the issue.

. . . while the acknowledgment is made that every person born into a civilized community has a right to live, yet the community has the right to say that incompetent and dangerous persons shall not, so far as can be helped, be born to acquire this right to live upon others. (Lowell, 1884, p. 68)

It is not surprising that in such an atmosphere and with such science and philosophy as they possessed—particularly the belief that these variously defective individuals were all expressions of the same hereditary taint—that individual members and groups within these professions would go on record advocating the asexualization of certain dependent classes such as the feeble-minded and the insane. Since the techniques then available—castration and ovariectomy—were repugnant to most members of society they were seldom used. There are, however, some instances of their use from the 1880s onward. Several of these experiments are summarized by Martin Barr in the section of his book *Mental Defectives* (1904) which advocates asexualization for the prevention of mental defect.[3]

While asexualization was advocated for some, less drastic remedies such as marriage restrictions and institutional segregation for the defective classes were advocated by others. Beginning with Connecticut in 1896, several states sought to regulate marriage of defectives for purposes of preventing their multiplication. In 1878, in part as a result of the efforts of Josephine Lowell, New York State undertook the founding of an asylum in Newark for the custodial care of feebleminded women of childbearing age. As Haller (1963, p. 28) points out, this precedent-establishing action was the first effort by a state to cut off the hereditary taint of feeblemindedness and so constitutes the first important recognition of eugenics principles by a state. In the succeeding decade the demand for custodial care of the feebleminded as a means of preventing the propagation of mentally defective children became widespread. It was repeatedly advocated by the standing committee on the feebleminded of the National Conference of Charities and Correction and was a recurrent theme in the annual presidential address of the medical officers of American Institutions for Idiotic and Feeble-Minded Persons (Haller, 1963).

---

[3] In most instances recorded there and elsewhere the ostensible reason was the control of behavior. The asexualization was presumed to reduce sexually acting out behavior— such as uncontrollable masturbation—and to cause the remission of other behavioral symptoms. One of the more notorious of these experiments was that of Dr. F. Hoyt Pilcher of the Institution for Feeble Minded Children at Winfield, Kansas. Dr. Pilcher, distressed at the debasing habits among the children in the institution and unable to affect changes by discipline, undertook the castration of 58 boys with claims of marked improvement both mental and physical in almost every case. There was considerable public reaction to this experiment, but Dr. Pilcher was sustained by his board of trustees who maintained, "All that would be necessary to convince those most horrified by this act of the wisdom of it, would be to have known the boys before and after the operation. Those who are now criticizing Dr. Pilcher will, in a few years, be talking of erecting a monument to his memory" (Barr, 1904, p. 196). Whether or not the monument was erected we have no record, but we must admit that an improvement in behavior on the part of the boys—from the point of view of the superintendent—may well have oc-curred. We might even expect that the increased tractableness would have generalized beyond the operated boys to those not yet castrated. At any rate, such improvements in behavior and well-being were cited by Barr in his argument for asexualization of the defectives, although he advocated asexualization primarily as a preventive measure to reduce the incidence of mental retardation.

INFLUENCES FROM THE SOCIAL
AND BIOLOGICAL SCIENCES

These developments were nineteenth-century forerunners of the eugenics movement, which did not really come into its own until the turn of the century. The blossoming of the eugenics movement after 1900 was abetted by immediately preceding and concurrent changes in social and biological science.

Social Darwinism and its advocacy of the "freely competitive society" had come under increasing attack around the turn of the century. Economists such as Henry George and Thorstein Veblen attacked the classical economic theories. Veblen particularly challenged Sumner's equation of the capacity to accumulate wealth with productivity and social usefulness. Lester Ward, becoming increasingly influential in American sociology, advocated social reform and state management, and emphasized the importance of education in determining intellectual differences. These are but a few of the influential leaders of thought on the American scene joining the attack.

As Hofstadter (1959) points out, it was in this period, when Social Darwinism was being put on the defensive, that it was resurging in a somewhat new guise in the literature of the eugenics movement, and in so doing achieved a new lease on life. When we come to examine that literature we shall quote some passages which can be read as echoing the social philosophy of Spencer and Sumner.

In the biological sciences, the great change preparing the way for eugenics was the overthrow of the doctrine of the hereditary transmission of acquired characteristics. Galton himself had some not inconsiderable role in this advance. He had challenged Darwin's theory of pangenesis and conducted a laboratory experiment testing that part of the theory that hypothesized that the gemmules cast off by the various body cells were carried by the blood to the germ cells and were thus permitted to have their effect on the offspring. In an experiment of classic simplicity he transfused the blood of the common lop-eared rabbit into a pure breed of silver greys. From three silver-grey bucks and four silver-grey does whose blood had been adulterated by approximately 50 percent, he bred 88 rabbits without any evidence of alteration of breed (Galton, 1871). However, as Connant (1947, p. 36) has documented, theories are not overthrown by facts but only by better theories. And Darwin, although admitting he would have expected the gemmules to be present in the blood, did not feel it was a necessary part of the theory of pangenesis (1890, p. 350). But better theory was on the way.

In the last decades of the nineteenth century numerous lines of investigation and theoretical development in biology converged to make Lamarckian theories of hereditary transmission of acquired traits more and more untenable. Not least among these theoretical developments was August Weismann's theory of the continuity of the germ-plasm.

What first struck me when I began seriously to consider the problem of heredity, some ten years ago, was the necessity for assuming the existence of a special organised and living *hereditary substance,* which in all multicellular organisms, unlike the substance composing the perishable body of the individual, is transmitted from generation to generation. This is the theory of *the continuity of the germ-plasm.* My conclusions led me to doubt the usually accepted view of the *transmission of variations acquired* by the body (soma); and further research, combined with experiments, tended more and more to strengthen my conviction that in point of fact no such transmission occurs.

. . .

There is now scarcely any doubt that the entire conception of the production of the "gemmules" by the body-cells, their separation from the latter, and their "circulation," is in reality wholly imaginary. In this regard I am still quite as much opposed to Darwin's views as formerly, for I believe that all parts of the body do not contribute to produce a germ from which the new individual arises, but that, on the contrary, the offspring owes its origin to a peculiar substance of extremely complicated structure, viz., the "germ-plasm." This substance can never be formed anew; it can only grow, multiply, and be transmitted from one generation to another. (Weismann, 1892, pp. xi, xiii)

Cytological research was also preparing the ground for new theoretical formulations. Among other advances Roux in 1883 described the behavior of the nucleus in mitosis and inferred from the activities of the chromatin that heredity was particulate and that the hereditary particles were in the chromatin. This conception was taken up by Weismann and incorporated into his formulation (Weismann, 1892, p. 26; Zirkle, 1951). By the end of the century, reduction division of the chromosomes in the formation of gametes had been described; and, in general, sufficient cytological knowledge was on hand to provide for the rapid integration of the rediscovered Mendelian principles of hereditary transmission of unit characters into a general theory of heredity that proved satisfactory not only in its explanation of known phenomena but in its ability to generate new and fruitful lines of research.

The initial consequences of this new knowledge in the science of heredity had anything but a happy effect upon developments in the field of mental retardation. So long as one accepted the hereditary transmission of acquired characteristics one was forced to take environmental conditions into account in any explanation of society's deviants. A family line might show a hereditary degeneration but one had to admit that timely social reform might have forestalled the degeneration or reversed its direction once it had begun.

Now, the advances in knowledge appeared to place eugenics on a firm scientific footing. Galton had demonstrated that intellectual and character traits were hereditary. The weight of accepted scientific theory and opinion now held that hereditable traits were not influenced by environment. No amount of social reform could reduce the numbers of the insane, the retarded, the social incompetent. We can readily imagine that the politically and socially conservative elements in society that had so readily embraced the Social Darwinism of Spencer and Sumner—and had found themselves on the defensive before the newer sociological and economic theories—would readily embrace the newer movement of eugenics which, like the Social Darwinism that preceded it, would advocate not a change in the organization of society but the elimination of those who could not or would not successfully adjust to that society.

These conservative elements were joined, as we have indicated, in the early stages of the movement by liberal reformers, superintendents of asylums for the feebleminded and insane, prison wardens, physicians, and social workers. It might be assumed that the individual members of these groups—most of whom were devoting constant efforts to betterment of the conditions under which the unfortunate classes of society lived—were not primarily motivated by any desire to maintain privilege. Rather, they were faced with problems which their best efforts had not resolved.

Indeed, there was much concern that the problems were growing larger. Estimates of feeblemindedness, insanity, criminality, and chronic pauperism were going up rather than down. To many of those who were concerned with the care and reform of these classes, eugenics was viewed as a scientific reform. A solution to problems that seemed insoluble by other means. It did not appear inconsistent to work for the betterment of the unfortunates of society and yet seek to prevent their multiplication.

The English Movement

Although the foundations of eugenics were firmly laid in America by the turn of the century, its subsequent organization and popularization was greatly influenced by Galton's efforts in England. Throughout the last decade of his life, despite growing infirmity, Galton was active, through lectures and publications, in furthering the advancement of eugenics. In 1901 he delivered his influential Huxley lecture on "The Possible Improvement of the Human Breed under Existing Conditions of Law and Sentiment." In this lecture Galton still emphasized positive eugenics, i.e., the improvement of the breed by increasing the productivity of the best stock. By 1908 when he published his biography, the emphasis had shifted toward negative eugenics, i.e., the improvement of the breed by decreasing the productivity of the less desirable stock.

The most common misrepresentations now are that its (*eugenic's*) methods must be altogether those of compulsory unions, as in breeding animals. It is not so. I think that stern compulsion ought to be exerted to prevent the free propagation of the stock of those who are seriously afflicted by lunacy, feeble-mindedness, habitual criminality, and pauperism, but that is quite different from compulsory marriage. How to restrain ill-omened marriages is a question by itself, whether it should be effected by seclusion, or in other ways yet to be devised that are consistent with a humane and well-informed public opinion. I cannot doubt that our democracy will ultimately refuse consent to that liberty of propagating children which is now allowed to the undesirable classes, but the populace has yet to be taught the true state of these things. A democracy cannot endure unless it be composed of able citizens; therefore it must in self-defence withstand the free introduction of degenerate stock. (Galton, 1909, p. 311)

He concludes these memoirs with the following observation:

This is precisely the aim of Eugenics. Its first object is to check the birth-rate of the Unfit, instead of allowing them to come into being, though doomed in large numbers to perish prematurely. The second object is the improvement of the race by furthering the productivity of the Fit by early marriages and healthful rearing of their children. Natural Selection rests upon excessive production and wholesale destruction; Eugenics on bringing no more individuals into the world than can be properly cared for, and those only of the best stock. (Galton, 1909, p. 323)

Blacker (1952, p. 111), in his study of eugenics, attributes this shift in emphasis from positive to negative eugenics to the then recently published Report of the Royal Commission on the Feebleminded. This report, appearing in 1908, was four years in preparation and placed a great and exaggerated emphasis on hereditary factors in mental retardation. Among other statements in the report are the conclusions of A. F. Tredgold.

Therefore, in 90 percent of patients suffering from mental defect, the condition is the result of a morbid state of the ancestors, which so impairs the vital powers of the embryo that full and perfect development cannot take place. In the milder cases the effects are seen in the nervous system only, since this is the most delicate and easily injured part of the organism; in the grosser cases other parts of the body are also affected as seen in the various imperfections and abnormalities of structure called "stigmata of degeneracy." . . . Amentia is thus not only hereditary, it is also the final expression of a progressive neuropathic degeneration. (Report of the Royal Commission, 1908, p. 398)

It is to be noted that although degeneration theory had been greatly discredited and although advances in basic biological science had made most of the theory's assumptions untenable, it still clung on with considerable vitality in the field of mental retardation at this late a date.

Important from the point of view of understanding Galton's shifting emphasis from positive to negative eugenics was the fact that the Commission's report not only exaggerated the extent of hereditary factors in mental retardation but also reflected the growing concern of the experts about the supposed fecundity of the feebleminded.

This fear of the fecundity of the feebleminded was to become one of the outstanding motivations contributing to the growth of eugenics. Tredgold was one of the leading authorities fostering this alarm.

As is well-known, the birth-rate of the country is steadily declining; but this decline is not general, it is selective, and unfortunately the selection is in the wrong direction. There is not the slightest doubt that the decline is chiefly incident in—indeed, one may say practically confined to—the best and most fit elements of the community, whilst the loafers, the incompetent, the insane and feeble-minded, continue to breed with unabated and unrestricted vigor. (Tredgold, 1910, p. 721)

In addition to the increasing popularity of his publications and lectures on eugenics, Galton improved the effectiveness of his campaign by securing institutionalized support for the study of eugenics. In collaboration with the University College of London he established a Research Fellowship in eugenics, a Research Scholarship, and a Eugenics Laboratory at the University College. These efforts were aimed at what for Galton was the essence of eugenics—the study of the laws of heredity and the agencies under social control that might improve or impair the physical and mental qualities of future generations.

Independent of these University-housed activities was the establishment of the Eugenics Education Society in 1907 by Montague Crackenthorpe. Galton was persuaded to serve as Honorary President. Among those active in the organization were such well-known figures as Havelock Ellis, George Bernard Shaw, H. G. Wells, and A. F. Tredgold. Ellis, better known to our generation for his studies on sex, was an active propagandist for race improvement. In the tract *The Problem of Race Regeneration* (1911), he recommended breeding the feebleminded out of the race by isolation in special colonies and institutions and by noncompulsory sterilization. He cited a study by the Council of the Eugenics Education Society.

It was found that paupers tend to belong to pauper families, even to the fourth generation, and that they tend to intermarry with pauper families; it was also found that they tend to manifest more or less obvious signs of mental weakness, and the conclusion was inevitable that their hereditary pauperism was based on an inheritance of mental defect. It is obvious that all our philanthropy directed to the present generation only will not remove this kind of pauperism but rather increase it; we need to extend our philanthropy to the generations to come. (Ellis, 1911, p. 68)

The simple solution to the problem as Ellis saw it in the case of these defective paupers was to withhold poor-law relief except to those who "voluntarily" consented, as a condition of such relief, to undergo sterilization.

Not all of those entering into the society's activities were assets. As in the case of all such movements which become faddish, it attracted assorted cranks and crackpots. Even the support of some of the more solid citizens was not without liability. Thus Shaw's point that it was "a national loss to limit the husband's progenitive capacity to the breeding capacity of one woman, or the wife's to an experiment with one father only" (Shaw, 1905, pp. 74–75), may have lost the society at least as many supporters as it gained in those post-Victorian years.

In addition to these minor difficulties a major problem developed in the rift between the biometricians—represented by Galton, Weldon, and Pearson—and the Mendelians—represented by the majority of the leaders of the eugenics movement in England and America. Before dealing with the theoretical issues here involved—issues which transcended the eugenics movement and were fundamental to the development of biological science—it might be added that the basic split was more than aggravated by the temperance issue. Throughout the nineteenth century the professions concerned about the care of the deviant and indigent had become increasingly concerned about the problem of alcoholism. As a social problem of major dimensions it needs hardly be documented since it is still with us. But what gave the concerns of the nineteenth and early twentieth centuries a different twist from those of our own day was the assumption of a close relationship between alcoholism and degenerative heredity. By some it was seen as the cause of degeneration in a breeding stock, to others it was in itself the evidence of hereditary taint. Small wonder then that many of the early eugenicists were also temperance leaders. Crackenthorpe, the founding father of the Eugenics Education Society, in particular, vehemently decried the "race poison" of alcohol. In 1910, Pearson published a statistical study purporting to demonstrate that the health of the children of alcoholics differed in no important respect from other children of similar age. He was immediately anathema to Crackenthorpe and other temperance leaders within and without the eugenics movement, so much so that it was necessary for Galton to publicly come to his defense (Pearson, 1930, pp. 405–409).

But the split between Pearson and other leaders of the eugenics movement involved a more basic issue concerning the nature of heredity. This issue did not originate within the eugenics movement; rather, it was a major dispute in biological science—especially in England—right after the turn of the century. But since many of the leaders of the eugenics movement—as we shall illustrate in the next chapter—were biologists, and since theories of heredity were germane to the eugenics program, the dispute naturally had repercussions in the eugenics movement. On one side of the dispute were Pearson and the biometricians defending Galton's theoretical views and on the other were Bateson and the Mendelists advancing the rediscovered theory of Gregor Mendel.

Unlike Galton's theory of heredity, which emphasized the blending of the parental traits in the offspring, Mendel's theory emphasized the particulate nature of heredity. Focusing on certain traits of the garden pea plant which occur in alternate forms—e.g., yellow seeds or green seeds, round seeds or angular seeds—Mendel had derived a number of generalizations about the inheritance of these characters. He showed that when one pure-bred line was crossed with a pure-bred line bearing the alternate character, the two traits would not blend. Rather, one—the *dominant* trait—would display itself in all the offspring of the cross. However, when this hybrid generation was self-fertilized the succeeding generation would display both the *dominant* and the alternate or *recessive* trait in the proportion of three to one. When this new generation, the offspring of the hybrids, bred by self-fertilization, the recessive trait bred true; but only part—one third to be exact—of these showing the *dominant* trait bred true; two thirds proved to be hybrid like the preceding generation by producing again a mixed progeny. With a series of elaborate and carefully executed experiments Mendel derived a number of generalizations about the inheritance of *dominant* and *recessive* traits which permitted precise statistical predictions about the results of various crosses among pure-bred lines of *dominant* and *recessive* characters and their hybrid offspring.

The rediscovery of these laws, and their independent confirmation by De Vries, Correns, and Tschermak at the turn of the century, was rapidly integrated with the advances in cytology occuring at about the same time to give us the essential outlines of our modern theory of heredity.

Many investigators like Bateson, in England, and Castle, in America, were quick to exploit and extend the explanatory power of the Mendelian model using various species of plants and animals as breeding material. But the model as it existed at the turn of the century was essentially limited in its explanatory power to qualitative traits that existed in an either-or state—green seeds or yellow seeds, tall forms or dwarf forms. Often the hybrid form was different from either parental stock, e.g., the cross of a white and a black chicken producing a spotted hybrid. The effect was only to increase the alternative forms of the trait to three and the offspring of the hybrids would display no more than the three alternative forms.

Even when Garrod (1902, 1908)—under the guidance of Bateson—first applied the Mendelian model to man, it was for certain inheritable forms of disease or errors in metabolism that existed in the either-or state. One had alkaptonuria or one did not, one was albino or one was not.

Pearson, preoccupied with the continuous variation in such traits as intelligence and personality, could not see how Mendelian heredity, granted it might play a role in some curious but relatively unimportant hereditable traits, could account for the continuous variation involved in the more important aspects of the nature of man.[4] At any rate, Pearson was out of step

---

[4] Eventually, around 1910, the work of the Swedish geneticist Nilsson-Ehle, and the American geneticist E. M. East, using as breeding material wheat and corn, extended the Mendelian model to fit the expression of continuously variable traits in which the quantitative trait under consideration results from the cumulative action of many independently transmitted genes, each gene producing only a fractional effect upon the expression of the trait. This is the *polygene* concept which maintains that several or many genes, located on the same or different chromosomes, will codetermine a particular

with other leaders in the eugenics movement who—especially in America—rapidly and uncritically applied the Mendelian model of unit trait inheritance to human behavior especially in the area of mental subnormality. These developments will be considered in the next chapter.

---

trait. It contrasts with single-factor inheritance in which a single gene locus, which may be occupied by variant forms or *alleles* of the same gene, determines the trait in question (Dunn, 1965; Stern, 1960). It is a tribute to the genius of Mendel that he foresaw, in his experiments on the quantitative variation in the flower color of the bean plant, need for the assumption that several independent determinants must be involved if the same basic law that applied to the inheritance of alternative characters in his pea plants were to be extended to quantitatively variable traits (Bateson, 1902).

The use and misuse
of Mendelism in eugenics

The rediscovery of Mendel's principles, their further development and wide dissemination, had a catalytic effect upon the progress of the eugenics movement in America. In our presentation of this effect, it will be noted that the growth of eugenics was closely tied to the new science of genetics. Often the leaders in genetic science were also the leaders in eugenics and several of the publications serving the new science of heredity also served for the advancement of eugenic programs. *In the perception of the lay public—and some of the scientists themselves—the boundaries between science and social action programs became badly blurred if not completely obliterated.*

THE LEADERSHIP OF THE EUGENICS MOVEMENT

W. E. Castle has pointed out that Mendelism received a hearty welcome from two groups of American biologists, those interested in the study of evolution and those who sought more efficient ways to produce improved varieties of plants and breeds of animals (Castle, 1951). Among the former was Charles B. Davenport who was to become, without serious challenge, the most influential leader of the eugenics movement in this country. Among the latter group were several outstanding plant breeders connected with either the United States Department of Agriculture or the state agricultural experiment stations. Most notable among these was E. M. East, who achieved his first eminence as a member of the staff of the Connecticut Agricultural Station and went on to a distinguished career in plant genetics at Harvard. His contributions to eugenic thought and the popularization of the eugenics creed received added weight from his well-deserved prestige as a scientist.

W. M. Hays, professor of plant breeding at the University of Minnesota, was instrumental in bringing these different groups of biologists together within the organization of the American Breeders Association which was formed in 1903. In the publications of that short lived association, spanning the years from 1903 to 1913, appear assorted papers devoted to theoretical expositions of Mendelian genetics, practical aspects of plant and animal breeding, and articles on human heredity and eugenics.

After the death of Hays, who was the moving force behind the Association, it was succeeded by the American Genetic Association and its publication the *Journal of Heredity*; both of which are still extant. W. E. Castle, a geneticist of major stature as well as an active eugenicist, played an important role in the founding of the new journal, which he maintained was designed to publish short articles suitable for the nontechnical reader (Castle, 1951). In its early years it was to prove an important organ for the dissemination of eugenical ideas and propaganda as well as a source of information about the growing science of genetics.

During its existence, the most important contribution of the American Breeders Association to the eugenics movement was the formation of its Committee on Eugenics. The first report of this committee, chaired by David Starr Jordan, a biologist and Chancellor of Stanford University, appeared in the fourth volume of the Association's Proceedings in 1908.[1] The objects of the committee, listed therein, were:

To investigate and report on heredity in the human race; to devise methods of recording the values of the blood of individuals, families, peoples and races; to emphasize the value of superior blood and the menace to society of inferior blood; and to suggest methods of improving the heredity of the family, the people, or the race. (Jordan, 1908, p. 201)

---

[1] Among the outstanding names on the committee at this time were Alexander Graham Bell, known to the general public as an inventor but an obvious choice for committee membership because of his studies on hereditary deafness. Luther Burbank, the plant breeder, was another prominent figure, but a somewhat less obvious choice since he still believed in the hereditary transmission of acquired characteristics. W. E. Castle, the previously mentioned Harvard biologist and "father of Mammalian genetics," was publicly less known, but like his colleague E. M. East served as an important link between scientific genetics and the eugenics movement.

The committee's activity moved into high gear when Charles B. Davenport took over as secretary. In his 1909 report he indicated the formation or proposed organization of a number of subcommittees including those on feeblemindedness and insanity. The subcommittee on feeblemindedness was chaired by A. C. Rogers, Superintendent of the Minnesota School for Feeble-minded and Colony for Epileptics; the secretary was H. H. Goddard of subsequent "Kallikak" fame. Adolph Meyer, the dominant figure in American psychiatry throughout most of the first half of the twentieth century, was chairman of the subcommittee on insanity. E. E. Southard, another promi-nent name in academic psychiatry of that period, was secretary (Davenport, 1911b).

In 1910, in recognition of its growing importance, the eugenics committee was raised to the level of a section coordinate with the plant and animal sections of the American Breeders Association. The old subcommittees were now raised to the rank of committees and by 1913 a total of ten of these research committees had been formed. Walter E. Fernald, superintendent of the Massachusetts State School at Waverly and one of the giants in the area of institutional care, had been added to the committee on feeblemindedness. The Committee on Heredity of Criminality included Charles R. Henderson, a University of Chicago sociologist known for his studies of crime and poverty—and William Healy, the great pioneer in the study of juvenile delinquency. The Committee on Inheritance of Mental Traits was studded with outstanding names from psychology. Robert M. Yerkes then at Harvard was chairman. E. L. Thorndike of Columbia and Madison Bentley of Cornell were also listed (Laughlin, 1913).

We detail some of the leadership of the eugenics movement at this time because we feel it is important to bear in mind that this movement was in large part a movement led by eminent scientists, intellectuals, and progressive reformers. The period of rapid growth of eugenics in America was in fact contemporaneous with the progressive era and those most anxious to work for the reform of society and the betterment of the conditions of life for the common man included those who were attracted to the eugenics movement.

These groups were readily joined by political and social conservatives who saw in the movement a rebuttal to the demands for social change. Snobs, cranks, and racists were quick to join the banner and, of course, there undoubtedly were the usual characters ready to espouse any cause that becomes fashionable whether or not they understand it. But among all these groups we feel it is most important to recognize the leadership of the "experts" especially in the formative years of the movement. For, as we shall elaborate later, there is always the danger when experts are involved in the advocacy of social action programs that the lay public fails to distinguish between the expertise and the value system. Expertise itself, a knowledge of facts and theories, never leads to a social action program. *It is only when the expertise interacts with a value system that social action programs arise.*

DAVENPORT AND THE EUGENICS RECORD OFFICE

Charles B. Davenport has been portrayed as a serious, insecure, driving individual who combined a capacity for organization with the ability to contact and enlist the aid of influential people in his causes. Rosenberg (1961) has viewed him as an example of "the statesman administrator. The ambassador to the laity from the world of science." Such he might be. With what distinction he fulfilled this role, judgments in his own lifetime were to be widely varied.

A product of Puritan ancestry, in which he took pride, he obtained his doctorate in zoology from Harvard and then taught at Harvard and at the University of Chicago for a number of years. Early in his career he became interested in the biometric work of Galton and Pearson. He published a text on biostatistics and was, at Pearson's request, the American editor of *Biometrika*. But following the rediscovery of Mendel's work—Davenport published one of the earliest American papers on the work of Correns and De Vries—he became a thoroughly convinced Mendelian. There was a subsequent falling out with Pearson, in part the result of temperaments, in part a reflection of the split in the eugenics movement between the biometricians and the Mendelians. The English group of biometricians within the eugenics movement were to become strong critics of Davenport's genetic interpretations of mental retardation—and justly so. Although the attacks were at times too personal and too intemperate to be in the best tradition of scientific debate, they correctly anticipated that poor research and extravagant claims in this area would redound to the discredit of the entire eugenics movement.

But before this dispute had erupted, Davenport had successfully campaigned to induce the Carnegie Foundation to establish the Station for Experimental Evolution at Cold Spring Harbor on Long Island. Davenport was appointed director at its founding in 1904 and remained in that position despite administrative reorganizations until his retirement in 1934.[2]

In 1910, with the financial support of Mrs. E. H. Harriman, Davenport founded the Eugenics Record Office at Cold Spring Harbor. This office had

---

[2] Although his research at Cold Spring Harbor involved breeding experiments with a variety of animals, he became more and more interested in hereditary factors in man. At first, his work was on skin, hair, and eye color. He published, with his wife, a paper that was important in that it was one of the first attempts to apply a polygenic model of inheritance to a human trait, the gradation of skin color. Eventually, he became more preoccupied with behavioral characteristics. Rosenberg has pointed out the irony of Davenport's interest in complex, quantitative characteristics. They were much more amenable to study by the correlational techniques of the Pearson School on which Davenport had turned his back than by the simple Mendelian analysis that he chose to use (Rosenberg, 1961).

close affiliation with the Eugenics Section of the American Breeders Association and the research committees of the latter cooperated with and advised the Eugenics Record Office on matters pertaining to their respective areas of interest. Subsequently the Eugenics Record Office was combined with the Station for Experimental Evolution by the Carnegie Institution to form a Department of Genetics under Davenport's direction. In this guise it continued its work until approximately 1940.

In his 1913 report on the operations of the Eugenics Record Office, Harry H. Laughlin, the superintendent, listed the varied purposes of the office. It functioned as a repository and clearing house for data on human heredity. All those who wished might deposit there on specially prepared forms the genealogies of their family traits and characteristics. In addition, field workers were trained for the gathering of eugenical data. Some of these workers were directly employed by the office, others were jointly employed by the office and various institutions interested in particular groups of defective or delinquent classes. A counseling service offered advice, to those seeking it, on the eugenical fitness of their proposed marriages. A major function was the publication of the results of eugenical research and dissemination of knowledge concerning eugenics. These and other functions of the office made it the center of the eugenics movement in this country (Laughlin, 1913).

The *Bulletins* and *Memoirs* published by the Eugenics Record Office consisted for the most part of studies on the heredity of such disorders as feeblemindedness, epilepsy, and insanity and discussions of various eugenic proposals for eliminating the undesirable members of society. The principal type of investigation was that of the pedigree study and the theoretical framework that of simple Mendelian genetics. The research data were gathered from institutions and in the field by a eugenics field worker who, in the course of a summer of training at Cold Spring Harbor, had mastered the basics of Mendelian genetics and the necessary interviewing and diagnostic skills to pursue her work.

THE MATING OF MENDELIAN THEORY WITH THE DEGENERATION THEORIES

The work of the psychiatrist Aaron J. Rosanoff published in the *Bulletins* is of particular interest to us in that it contained aspects of the old degeneration theories mated to the new Mendelian genetics. As the reader will recall, one of the consistent features of the degeneration theories was the assumption of a polymorphous hereditary taint that could express itself in various forms of illness. While he recognized that certain forms of mental disease like general paresis or "alcoholic polyneuritis" were probably on a purely exogenous basis, Rosanoff maintained:

One of the first facts that appeared in the study of the pedigrees was that any form of insanity or even all the forms of hereditary insanity do not constitute an independent hereditary character, but that they are closely related to imbecility, epilepsy, hysteria, and various mental eccentricities that are not usually included under the designation insanity. In other words, the distinction between these conditions as clinical entities cannot, in the light of their manner or origin, be regarded as deeply essential.

We find as manifestation of the neuropathic make-up in closely related persons cases of feeblemindedness, convulsion in childhood from trivial causes or chronic epilepsy, cases of grave hysteria, various eccentricities, cases of dementia praecox, manic-depressive insanity, paranoic conditions, involutional psychoses, and the like. (Cannon and Rosanoff, 1911, p. 4)

Committed to the applicability of the simple Mendelian ratios to mental illness and defect, given the flexibility provided by the concept of a polymorphous hereditary taint, and armed with diligent field workers who in Davenport's words were "trained in the rapid diagnosis of mental disease," it is not surprising that the data gave apparent support to the hypothesis that mental illness was the result of the recessive Mendelian transmission of a hereditary taint. Nevertheless, to shore up the argument at its weakest point—that all of these varied behavioral illnesses were on a simple genetic basis—it was necessary to add a few assumptions. Obviously, environment could affect the severity with which an illness expressed itself. Again, less severe forms of defect could be due to the hybrid condition rather than the pure recessive. Or, even more ingeniously, the polygenic model Davenport had introduced for skin color could be invoked so that the total number of recessive genes in the genetic group might determine the special type of defect to be observed clinically (Rosanoff and Orr, 1911).

At this point in his career, Davenport's own treatment of neurological and mental disorders also echoed degeneration theory in spite of the modern Mendelian dress. Since the two men, Rosanoff and Davenport, collaborated in committee work and research, it might be wondered whether Rosanoff had brought the degeneration theory from his psychiatric training and Davenport the Mendelian genetics from his biology to form this new theoretical marriage. At any rate, Davenport's treatment of inheritance in epilepsy has a model similar to Rosanoff's. First he notes from his pedigrees that imbecility and epilepsy are very closely akin, at least some feebleminded parents producing a large proportion of epileptic children. In addition, he notes that when both parents are epileptic, both are feebleminded, or one is feebleminded and the other epileptic, then all the offspring will be either epileptic or feebleminded. He concludes from his pedigrees that the conditions named migraine, chorea, paralysis, and extreme nervousness behave as though due to a "simplex condition," i.e., the hybrid or recessive carrier state. The symptoms of these conditions are due to the fact that the individual is hybrid or "tainted." The pedigrees further show that when such a tainted individual is married to a defective, about one-half the offspring are defective. When both parents are tainted, about one-quarter of the offspring are defective. The Mendelian ratios are thus nicely demonstrated—provided one accepts the classification of the parents as defective or tainted. Of course, occasionally a pedigree would show an epileptic arising from two seemingly normal parents. In such cases gross nervous defect could be found in close relatives and the assumption was that the normals were "simplex," i.e., carriers who in this instance did not show the taint usually characteristic of the simplex state. For a further echo of degeneration theory the data apparently show some evidence that alcoholism in the parent can poison the germ cell and result in defect (Davenport and Weeks, 1911). In his 1911 book, *Heredity in Relation to Eugenics,* the concept of polymorphous heredity is succinctly stated by Davenport.

But the mental defect that is "inherited" is not always of the same type. Thus in the same family may be found cases of manic depressive insanity, of senile dementia, of alcoholism and of feeble-mindedness. It would seem to be the neuropathic taint that is inherited. (Davenport, 1911a, p. 77)

In that book Davenport pays only limited attention to the inheritance of mental defect but, basing his argument partly on the work of Goddard, he does enunciate two laws which foreshadow, if they do not imply, a Mendelian interpretation of that inheritance. The first law is that two mentally defective parents will produce only mentally defective offspring. The second law is that, with the exception of mongolism, probably no imbecile is born except to parents who, if not mentally defective themselves, both carry mental defect in their germ plasm. These laws would obviously be corollaries of a Mendelian interpretation of recessive inheritance. The actual attempt to demonstrate the applicability of recessive Mendelian inheritance of mental defect was left to H. H. Goddard.

Goddard's Studies of Heredity

Henry H. Goddard, who had obtained his PhD under G. Stanley Hall at Clark University in 1899, became director of the Research Laboratory at the Vineland Training School in 1906. The training school at Vineland, New Jersey, was a privately operated institution for the education of the feeble-minded, which, at the time of Goddard's research, had approximately 400 inmates.

Goddard's work at Vineland was a major factor in the development of attitudes toward the retardate that prevailed from approximately 1910 to 1920—typified by the catch phrase "the menace of the feebleminded." In this view many of the major social evils of the times were seen as stemming in large part from mental deficiency. The contribution of the mental retardate to crime, prostitution, and pauperism was exaggerated to fantastic heights. This, combined with the assumed hereditary basis of mental retardation and the further assumption of the higher fecundity of the retardate, led to the frightful prospect of the degeneration of the race and the decay of civilization.[3]

Goddard's first published research on hereditary factors in mental retardation appeared in the *American Breeders Magazine* in 1910 and was considered of sufficient eugenical interest to be reprinted as *Bulletin No. 1 of the Eugenics Record Office.*

This 1910 publication, *Heredity of Feeblemindedness*, was in essence a preliminary report of on-going research and consisted of a selected sample of pedigree charts of inmates of the institution with accompanying commentary. The effect of the presentation was to indicate that, with the exception of a disorder such as mongolism, feeblemindedness tended to run in families. In this preliminary report there was little attempt to draw general conclusions concerning the mode of transmission of the defect.

The Kallikak Family

One of the pedigrees appearing in the 1910 report became, in extended form, the basis of one of the best known and widely influential of all studies of mental retardation, *The Kallikak Family*. In this work Goddard (1912) tentatively advanced the hypothesis of recessive Mendelian inheritance for feeblemindedness.

The name, Kallikak, was a pseudonym coined from the Greek by Goddard and meaning "good-bad." Although in this period before World War I there were to appear many family studies of mental defect, delinquency, and social incompetence, what led to the exceptional interest in the Kallikak family was precisely its good-bad quality. Two related family lines, one consisting of a feebleminded and socially incompetent strain, the other a strain of economically and professionally successful individuals for the most part exhibiting more than average social competence, could be traced back six generations to one and the same progenitor.

The unfolding of the family tree began with Deborah Kallikak, an inmate of the Vineland institution, who as a young woman obtained a mental age of approximately 9 years on the Binet Scale and was classified as a moron—a term Goddard had introduced to cover those functioning from a mental age of 8 to 12 years. Through her mother, Deborah's lineage was traced back to

---

[3] These concerns were not limited to the United States. The Royal Commission report of 1908 amply documented the case against the retardate in England and in subsequent years the British journals and popular press echoed and amplified the concerns of the expert testimony in that report. Some of this literature has been presented in Chapter 12. But for economy of presentation we will limit ourselves, now, to the United States and principally to the work of Goddard though we will touch upon the work of others where appropriate.

Martin Kallikak, Jr., the illegitimate son of a young soldier of the Revolutionary War, and a purportedly feebleminded woman he had met at a tavern. This branch of the family tree was the bad side and among the 480 descendants of Martin Kallikak, Jr. (the great-great-grandfather of Deborah), the indefatigable field worker, Miss Elizabeth Kite, was able to identify 143 feebleminded individuals. Some of the children who were descendants of Martin Kallikak, Jr., actually were tested by Miss Kite with the Binet Scale; but for the older generations Miss Kite was forced to rely chiefly on her observations of their behavior and the reports of neighbors and relatives in determining their intellectual status. For those who were deceased it was necessary to rely upon the verbal reports of elderly individuals who could remember them and upon such documents relating to their lives as might have relevance.

But feeblemindedness was not the only legacy of Martin, Junior. For among the 480 descendants, 36 were illegitimate; 33 sexually immoral, mostly prostitutes; 24 alcoholics; 3 epileptics; 3 criminals; 8 kept houses of ill fame; and 82 died in infancy.

In striking contrast is the good side of the family. After returning from the war, Martin Kallikak, Sr., married a respectable girl of good family and from that union there were tabulated 496 individuals in direct descent. All of Martin, Senior's legitimate children married into the best families in their state and among their descendants were nothing but good citizens—doctors, lawyers, judges, educators, traders, landholders, and men and women prominent in every phase of social life.

In this branch of the family tree there were no feebleminded, no illegitimate children, no immoral women, no epileptics, no criminals, no keepers of brothels. Only 15 children died in infancy. There was but one sexually loose male, and only two alcoholics. There was but one case of insanity.

For Goddard, the implications of this family pedigree were crystal clear. Two family branches diverging from the same father via different mothers and extending through six generations lived out their lives "in practically the same region and in the same environment, except in so far as they themselves, because of their different characters, changed that environment" (p. 50). Goddard refers to Winship's comparison of the Jukes and the Edwards, a family of paupers and criminals versus a colonial family of distinction, and notes that it is not a convincing demonstration of the power of heredity over environment. For though of different ancestral stock, the families were reared in different communities, different states, and "utterly different environments." The possibility exists that if the Jukes were of normal mentality and their places interchanged with the Edwards, the outcome would have been different.[4]

---

[4] There is apparently some ambiguity as to the extent to which Dugdale (1910) attributed the pauperism and criminality of the Jukes to heredity. It would appear that

Fortunately for the cause of science, the Kallikak family, in the persons of Martin Kallikak, Jr. and his descendants, are not open to this argument. They were feeble-minded, and no amount of education or good environment can change a feeble-minded individual into a normal one, any more than it can change a red-haired stock into a black-haired stock. The striking fact of the enormous proportion of feeble-minded individuals in the descendants of Martin Kallikak, Jr. and the total absence of such in the descendants of his half brothers and sisters is conclusive on this point. Clearly it was not environment that has made that good family. They made their environment; and their own good blood, with the good blood in the families into which they married, told. (Goddard, 1912, p. 53)

To Goddard, the Kallikak family was a natural experiment. On the good side is, "our demonstration of what the Kallikak blood is when kept pure, or mingled with blood as good as its own" (p. 68). On the bad side is the blood of the same ancestor "contaminated by that of the nameless feeble-minded girl" (p. 69).

The biologist could hardly plan and carry out a more rigid experiment or one from which the conclusions would follow more inevitably. (Goddard, 1912, p. 69)

Despite this sweeping claim, it is hard to imagine how any dispassionate consideration of the argument would not require a better control of the environment. Martin Kallikak, Sr., by Goddard's account, was an outstandingly successful farmer, with a passion for the accumulation of land, who "left large farms to most of his children." The exceptions are not detailed by Goddard, presumably they are the eldest legitimate daughter Miriam who married against her parents' wishes and Martin Kallikak, Jr. Not being raised in the home of a prosperous farmer and not receiving a bountiful patrimony, but rather being raised as the illegitimate child of a purportedly feebleminded woman could conceivably have made a difference for Martin, Junior. If one were in a carping mood one might even wonder if the failure of the descendants of Miriam to reach the social positions of the other branches of the legitimate heirs might not have been in part the result of their disinheritance. In contrast to Miriam, several of her legitimate siblings married into families prominent in Colonial and Revolutionary times. Goddard considered this an instance of good blood marrying with good blood, but it might

---

various commentators have interpreted his data and argument in terms of their own biases. Estabrook (1916), working out of the Eugenics Record Office, did a follow-up study of the Jukes in which he emphasized the role of hereditary feeblemindedness in this socially maladjusted group. Franklin Giddings in an introduction to the fourth edition of the Jukes emphasized Dugdale's belief in the effectiveness of environment, pointing out that Dugdale felt that environment could modify and even eradicate the vice and crime of such groups as the Jukes. (Dugdale, 1910.) When one recalls that the first edition of Dugdale's book appeared in 1877 it seems reasonable to us that, even though Dugdale never explicitly states his theoretical position, he was acting on a hereditary theory that allowed for the transmission of acquired traits and hence like Howe or Morel would believe that environmental reform could effectively reverse hereditary tendencies. This then would explain why subsequent commentators could quote Dugdale in support of either a hereditarian or environmental position.

also be viewed as an indication of the upwardly mobile family of Martin, Senior, consolidating its position in the social pyramid.

Because of the widespread popularity and the uncritical acclaim with which *The Kallikak Family* was first greeted, Goddard's view of the social burden of feeblemindedness therein presented was assured widespread influence that contributed much to the growth of the eugenics movement. That view was that feeblemindedness was largely responsible for the social problems represented by paupers, criminals, prostitutes, and drunkards. The Kallikaks were examples of that high grade of feeblemindedness—the moron type—that makes for a massive burden on society. In them,

. . . we have the type of family which the social worker meets continually and which makes most of our social problems. A study of it will help to account for the conviction we have that no amount of work in the slums or removing the slums from our cities will ever be successful until we take care of those who make the slums what they are. Unless the two lines of work go on together, either one is bound to be futile in itself. If all of the slum districts of our cities were removed tomorrow and model tenements built in their places, we would still have slums in a week's time because we have these mentally defective people who can never be taught to live otherwise than as they have been living. Not until we take care of this class and see to it that their lives are guided by intelligent people, shall we remove these sores from our social life.

There are Kallikak families all about us. They are multiplying at twice the rate of the general population, and not until we recognize this fact, and work on this basis, will we begin to solve these social problems. (Goddard, 1912, pp. 70–71)[5]

The solution to the problem, as Goddard saw it, could only be in the prevention of the transmission of hereditary feeblemindedness by the segregation of the feebleminded in institutions and colonies. In a single generation the number of feebleminded would be reduced, by Goddard's prediction, from 300,000—the estimated number in the United States at that time—to 100,000 or less. For he had found the hereditary factor in 65 percent of his cases and he pointed out that the estimates of other authors were as high as 80 percent.

Sterilization of the feebleminded as a solution to the problem was viewed by Goddard as an acceptable but less desirable solution.

In *The Kallikak Family* Goddard examined the marriages and progeny to show that the transmission of feeblemindedness in this family fulfills Mendelian expectations for a recessive trait but recognized that the data as there presented might be meager and inadequate. Nevertheless, he assures his readers that his larger study of pedigrees from the Vineland cases would be more convincing.

---

[5] This kind of thinking about the nature of the problem of slums and slum dwellers is, of course, still with us. Following the urban riots of 1967 a U.S. Senator was quoted as saying that, "Slums are made by slummy people."

Feeblemindedness:
Its Causes and Consequences

Goddard's larger work, published under the above title, appeared in 1914. In it Goddard considered the pedigrees of 327 unselected cases from Vineland. For 27 cases there was insufficient information to determine the etiology of the feeblemindedness but for those on which sufficient data could be obtained,

. . . one hundred sixty-four or 54% of the remaining 300 histories show other feeble-minded persons in such numbers or in such relation to the individual case studied as to leave no doubt of the hereditary character of the mental defect. In these cases it is evident from the charts themselves that we are, dealing with a condition of mind or brain which is transmitted as regularly and surely as color of hair or eyes. Thirty-four cases, 11.3%, have been grouped under the head of Probably Hereditary. The charts of these, while not showing so certainly as in the former group the hereditary nature of the trouble, yet have a high degree of probability and may be considered hereditary. (Goddard, 1914, p. 437)

For an additional 37 children, or 12 percent of the group, Goddard attributes the feeblemindedness to "neuropathic ancestry." In this group are the cases "in which there are not enough defectives to indicate hereditary feeble-mindedness, but there are more or less neuropathic conditions among the ancestry—such as paralysis, apoplexy, neurasthenia, epilepsy, etc." (p. 318). An additional 19 percent were considered "accidental," i.e., due to such varied causes as meningitis, mongolism, and pre- or paranatal stress (p. 448). In the remaining few cases no cause could be assigned.

The high familial incidence of feeblemindedness as revealed by his pedigree charts convinced Goddard that feeblemindedness was hereditary, and if one could make the assumption that feeblemindedness was a unit character an analysis of the pedigrees indicated that it followed the Mendelian modes of transmission for a recessive trait. Goddard came to this latter conclusion not without some concern and reservation. His faith in the Binet tests—which he had done so much to popularize—and their continuous distribution of intelligence scores must have made it a little difficult to perceive feeblemindedness and normality as unit characters—a qualitative either-or categorization. But the data were compelling: "Of 482 children of parents both of whom were feebleminded all were feebleminded with the exception of six. The exceptions are so few as to be hardly worth consideration" (p. 550). This is what might well be expected in the progeny of the homozygotic bearers of a recessive trait according to Mendelian principles.

That normal intelligence seems to be a unit character and transmitted in true Mendelian fashion is a conclusion that was forced upon us by the figures, and one that is difficult to make agree with previous conceptions. (Goddard, 1914, p. ix)

Eugenic action programs for mental retardation did not of course require the demonstration that it was a unit character recessively inherited. In fact, some eugenicists—such as Paul Popenoe, editor of the *Journal of Heredity*, and Roswell Johnson—raised serious question about Goddard's interpretation of his data. For Popenoe and Johnson, the mechanism of the transmission of defect was not crucial. What was crucial was that the defect be hereditary. In their widely popular treatise on eugenics they were to say:

For applied eugenics, it is sufficient to know that mental and physical differences are inherited; the exact manner of inheritance it would be important to know, but even without a knowledge of the details of the mechanism of heredity, a program of eugenics is yet wholly feasible. (Popenoe and Johnson, 1918, p. 99)

Though they questioned the adequacy of Goddard's study as a demonstration that feeblemindedness was a unit trait, recessively inherited, Popenoe and Johnson had no question about its adequacy as a demonstration that feeblemindedness was inherited. In fact, they use it as their authority for maintaining that "at least two-thirds of the feebleminded in the United States owe their condition directly to heredity." (p. 176).

Other eugenicists were more willing to accept the study not only as a demonstration of the hereditary character of feeblemindedness but also as a proof of its Mendelian inheritance. No less a figure than the outstanding Harvard geneticist, E. M. East, was willing to buy outright the contention of recessive Mendelian inheritance for epilepsy, insanity, and feeblemindedness—and that as late as 1927. In discussing the studies of Weeks, Rosanoff, and Goddard he was to assert:

. . . the result is that these disorders have been found to be inherited as simple recessives. Defectiveness in a single gene accounts for the divergence between a feeble-minded and a capable child, between an insane person and one who is sane, or between an epileptic and a normal.

The concordance of results is extraordinary, the apparent exceptions hardly worth noting. For example, matings of feeble-minded individuals with each other ought to give only feeble-minded children, according to this hypothesis. Among 482 children, resulting from 144 of such unions, Goddard found 6 apparently normal children. Statistically, such a limited number of exceptions is negligible; . . . Again, the results of unions between a feeble-minded parent (nn) and a normal heterozygote, a carrier (Nn), or between two carriers ($Nn \times Nn$), are remarkably in accord with theory. They are even more closely in accord with theory than Goddard makes out in his report, for he did not make the proper corrections when calculating the expected number of feeble-minded children . . . When the proper mathematical corrections are made in such cases, by a simple and correct algebraic method, the correspondence between theoretical expectation and actual result is so good as to be almost suspicious. (East, 1927, pp. 104–105)

As in the case of Davenport, there is some irony in East's ready acceptance of a single-gene factor in mental retardation. East's research in plant genetics had done much to introduce a polygenic model for the inheritance of complex, continuously variable traits. Today, those who would maintain that a large proportion of mental retardation is hereditary must invoke such a polygenic model for the inheritance of intellectual traits. As we shall indicate in a later chapter, the forms of retardation which can fit into a single-gene model constitute an extremely small percentage of the total cases of mental retardation.

METHODOLOGICAL PROBLEMS IN THE PEDIGREE STUDIES

As we have indicated, Goddard's study of the Kallikaks was only one—albeit the most influential—of the many studies of "degenerate" families appearing in the decade before America's entry into World War I. Several of these were direct products of the activities of the Eugenics Record Office. Thus there were: *The Nam Family,* a pedigree of alcoholics and indolent ne'er do wells reported by Arthur Estabrook and Charles B. Davenport in 1912; and *The Hill Folk,* a pedigree of mental defect characterized by crime and pauperism, reported by Florence Danielson and Charles B. Davenport in the same year.

In *The Hill Folk* the authors assume a relationship between mental defect and a variety of social problems:

From the biological standpoint, it is interesting to note that mental defect manifests itself in one branch of the pedigree by one trait and in another branch by quite a different one. Thus, in one line alcoholism is universal among the men; their male cousins in another line are fairly temperate, plodding workers, but the women are immoral. Another branch shows all the men to be criminal along sexual lines, while a cousin who married into a more industrious family has descendants who are a little more respectable. (Danielson and Davenport, 1912, p. 2)

The statement that "mental defect manifests itself" in the various forms of asocial behavior may well reflect the diagnostic bias existing in these pedigree studies. If the subject under consideration exhibits any of the undesirable social traits, there is presumptive evidence that he is feebleminded. Of course, Goddard and Davenport were sensitive to the questions that might be raised in regard to the diagnostic procedures which went into the construction of their pedigree charts. Their publications anticipated such criticism and they took pains to defend their procedures. The training of the field workers was emphasized.

These are women highly trained, of broad human experience, and interested in social problems. As a result of weeks of residence at the Training School, they become acquainted with the condition of the feeble-minded. They study all the grades, note their peculiarities, and acquaint themselves with the methods of testing and recognizing them.

. . .

In determining the mental condition of people in the earlier generations (that is, as to whether they were feebleminded or not), one proceeds in the same way as one does to determine the character of a Washington or a Lincoln or any other man of the past. Recourse is had to original documents whenever possible. In the case of defectives, of course, there are not many original documents. Oftentimes the absence of these, where they are to be expected, is of itself significant. For instance, the absence of a record of marriage is often quite as significant as its presence. Some record or memory is generally obtainable of how the person lived, how he conducted himself, whether he was able to make a living, how he brought up his children, what was his reputation in the community; these facts are frequently sufficient to enable one to determine, with a high degree of accuracy, whether the individual was normal or otherwise. . . . After some experience, the field worker becomes expert in inferring the condition of those persons who are not seen, from the similarity of the language used in describing them to that used in describing persons whom she has seen. (Goddard, 1912, pp. 13–15)

One can sympathize with the irony of Abraham Myerson who was to point out in 1925 that, "Really, it seems utterly unnecessary to have laboratories, blood tests, psychological tests, clinical examinations, and to take four years in a medical school plus hospital experience, etc., when a woman can as a result of a dozen or two of lectures make all kinds of medical, surgical and psychiatric diagnoses in an interview or by reading through a court record" (Myerson, 1925, p. 64).

To give a particularly striking, if perhaps extreme, example of the diagnostic liberties exercised in compiling the pedigree charts one might take the case of the illegitimate son of one Guss, a direct descendant of Millard the eldest son of Martin Kallikak, Jr. This illegitimate son of Guss had been born to a "feebleminded" girl. The child when young had a severe attack of scarlet fever which had resulted in the loss of his hearing. His mother subsequently married and bore four other children. The field worker, Miss Kite, gives a very vivid picture of her visit to this family for the purpose of determining the intellectual status of the deaf child, the illegitimate son of Guss.

◌◟ It was a bitter, cold day in February and about eleven in the morning when the field worker knocked at the door. Used as she was to sights of misery and degradation, she was hardly prepared for the spectacle within. The father, a strong, healthy, broad-shouldered man, was sitting helplessly in a corner. The mother, a pretty woman still, with remnants of ragged garments drawn about her, sat in a chair, the picture of despondency. Three children, scantily clad and with shoes that would barely hold together, stood about with drooping jaws and the unmistakable look of the feeble-minded. Another child, neither more intelligent nor better clad, was attempting to wash a few greasy dishes in cold water. The deaf boy was nowhere to be seen. On being urgently requested, the mother went out of the room to get him, for he was not yet out of bed. In a few moments she returned. The boy with her wore an old suit that evidently was made to do service by night as well as by day. A glance sufficed to establish his mentality, which was low. The whole family was a living demonstration of the futility of trying to make desirable citizens from defective stock through making and enforcing compulsory education laws. Here were children who seldom went to school because they seldom had shoes, but when they went, had neither will nor power to learn anything out of books. The father himself, though strong and vigorous, showed by his face that he had only a child's mentality. The mother in her filth and rags was also a child. In this house of abject poverty, only one sure prospect was ahead, that it would produce more feeble-minded children with which to clog the wheels of human progress. The laws of the country will not permit children ten years old to marry. Why should they permit it when the mentality is only ten? These and similar questions kept ringing through the field worker's mind as she made her way laboriously over the frozen road to the station. (Goddard, 1912, pp. 77–78)

If Miss Kite had any additional information for entering the boy as feeble-minded upon the pedigree chart, it is not mentioned. Yet the boy was deaf from early childhood and living in conditions of severe social and economic deprivation. This is a type of case which would require more than routine diagnostic evaluation by present-day standards.

It is an easy enough exercise to point out the methodological shortcomings with which the data were gathered in these pedigree studies. It scarcely requires more effort to attack the conclusions that were drawn from the data. Even assuming all diagnoses correct and the pedigree charts the most accurate and unbiased data, the hereditary nature of the disorders were not proven, let alone their transmission as Medelian recessives. Goddard's dismissal of environmental factors is glib if not naive. In reference to the "good" and "bad" Kallikaks:

Both lines live out their lives in practically the same region and in the same environment, except in so far as they themselves, because of their different characters, changed that environment.

. . .

Clearly it was not environment that has made that good family. They made their environment; and their own good blood, with the good blood in the families into which they married, told. (Goddard, 1912, pp. 50, 53)

The legitimate children were raised in the home of a prosperous farmer and with one exception the recipients of substantial patrimonies. The illegitimate child raised how? His mother is reported to have "lived in the woods"—and he without an inheritance. Impoverished and a drunkard, he raises a large family in a mountain hut. Are these grandchildren on the illegitimate side likely to have been within the same "environment" as the legitimate grandchildren?

The shortcomings of these studies are so obvious that pointing them out by themselves is without much interest. It only becomes of interest when we ask why these studies, so weak in method and so lacking in rigorous analysis, were so widely accepted and accepted not just by unsophisticated and gullible segments of the public but by professionally trained individuals of outstanding intellect?

In the next chapter we will address ourselves to the above question and consider some of the interactions that occur between science and the larger society of which it is part.

Sociopolitical factors in science

It would be a naive view of science to imagine that the acceptance or rejection of any given research finding or theoretical position was determined solely by its objective evaluation by the members of the scientific community. The history of scientific controversies is replete with instances where belief or disbelief were determined more by the personalities of the scientists involved or by social, political, and economic factors than by the available evidence and its logical treatment. This is true in the physical sciences but even more so in the biological, behavioral, and social sciences; for in proportion to which the state of science is characterized by rigor of methodology, generality of theory, and universality of its conventions, it is less vulnerable to the distortions and vagaries of personal or societal needs.

At the level of society such factors may be most easily observed in totalitarian cultures. Every school boy knows how badly the Copernicans fared under the Roman Church. Some are even aware that the Copernicans did not do particularly well under the Lutheran Church. The times, the issues, and the structure of the social institutions were similar enough for the outcomes to be essentially the same. But we needn't—and shouldn't—go so far into the past—the lesson is apt to appear less applicable for today.

The Lysenko Controversy

A closer example in time is the Lysenko controversy in Soviet Russia. It is particularly apt for our purposes since it deals with the science of heredity. In this controversy in Soviet biology, the Mendelian theory of heredity—and the genetic science that had grown up about it—was overthrown and replaced by a Lamarckian theory of heredity which provided for the inheritance of acquired characteristics. The controversy, which began in the 1930s, reached its climax in the late forties, when, with T. D. Lysenko leading the attack, the defenders of Mendelian genetics were overwhelmed and made public recantations of the error of their ways.

The causes of the destruction of genetic science in this period of Russian history are undoubtedly complex; but among the many speculations that have been advanced, those which are prominent and of most easy credence relate to the sociopolitical theories of the Soviet system.

A political system which assumes that there are no inborn class or race differences in man, and which emphasizes the importance of environmental manipulation in the production of desirable citizens and the perfection of the state, may perceive threat in a science of genetics which maintains that much of the variability in individual differences is hereditarily determined. To allow that individuals are hereditarily different not only makes it difficult to defend the position that there are no inherent class or race differences among men but admits to limitations on the effectiveness of education and environment in shaping the individual. Insofar as the Soviet political system requires—as does any political system—some theoretical position in regard to the nature of man, it requires a position which minimizes or denies the existence of inherited differences in man and maximizes the effects of environment.

The possibility of a clash between Soviet political ideology and the science of genetics obviously was inherent in the two systems. That the confrontation should have occurred in the thirties may have been in part a reaction of the Soviet political system to the aggressive, racist policy of Nazi Germany. The Nazi assertion of racial superiority based upon distortions and half-truths wrested from the biological, social, and behavioral sciences—and particularly genetics—was coupled with vicious eugenical practices aimed at the insane, the mentally defective, and the so-called inferior races. For an opposing political ideology, with its own authoritarian control over science, education, and all means of public communication the response must have seemed obvious. If the racism of Nazi ideology was based upon genetic science, then genetic science must be discredited, and a science of heredity more suited to one's own ideological position raised in its place. A suitable variant of Lamarckian theory—with the added advantage of having been fathered by a Bolshevik approved by Lenin, one I. V. Michurin—was at hand. An energetic, persuasive, and ambitious apostle, T. D. Lysenko was more than ready to proclaim the scientific dogma; and the science of heredity in Russia underwent revolutionary if regressive change.

The irony, of course, was that the Nazi racist position was not supported by genetic science—as many outstanding geneticists of the period were quick to point out. And for even greater irony, such geneticists as H. J. Muller would point out that the hereditary transmission of environmental effects would imply that colonial, minority, and primitive peoples, as well as the socially deprived classes who lived for generations under pernicious environmental circumstances, must be hereditarily inferior to their dominant exploiters. Was that not to yield the point to the racists? (Zirkle, 1949).

Nearly a hundred years earlier, those more humane proponents of a degeneration theory—Morel and Howe—could see the implication of a hereditary transmission of environmental effects and use it as a call for immediate social reform to roll back the process of degeneration within the oppressed classes.

One might object that the Lysenko controversy is no true example of sociopolitical factors influencing science qua science. It might be maintained that what Lysenko created was a pseudoscience with which he replaced a real science. Western geneticists have tended to view him as a charlatan, an opportunist, a limited intellect grappling with complexities beyond his power, motivated to destroy what he could not understand (Zirkle, 1949). All of these charges might be true. But Lysenko's personality and behavior suggest to us no characteristic we would consider qualitatively different from that displayed by other men from whom none are likely to withhold the name of scientist. Lysenko argued for a "false" theory and against a "true" theory, and did so with aggression, personal vehemence, and opportunism. But the history of controversy in science is full of such instances, with the aggression, vehemence, and opportunism being on the side of the angels as often as not. In a somewhat similar vein, although more subdued since the stakes were not so high—just one's academic career and not one's life being at stake—are numerous controversies in Western science.

THE MENDELIANS VS. THE BIOMETRICIANS

In fact, the very controversy that broke out shortly after the turn of the century between the Mendelians led by Bateson and the biometricians under Weldon and Pearson had many elements similar to the Lysenko struggle.

The recollections of R. C. Punnett (1950), a colleague of Bateson and himself a participant in the dispute, vividly portrays some aspects of the emotionally loaded atmosphere and the roughness of the infighting. The issue at stake was the continuity or discontinuity of variation—a basic issue in evolutionary theory at that time. The quarrel was begun by Bateson and

Weldon before the rediscovery of Mendel's work; but, as the contestants immediately recognized, the rediscovery of that work had major implications for the controversy. Weldon, supporting the orthodox view that natural selection worked by the accummulation of small continuous variations, belittled Mendel's work in the first volume of *Biometrika* and Bateson retaliated in 1902 with *Mendel's Principles of Heredity*. One small sample from a choice of many in that work conveys the emotional tone of the debate:

In the world of knowledge we are accustomed to look for some strenuous effort to understand a new truth even in those who are indisposed to believe. It was therefore with a regret approaching to indignation that I read Professor Weldon's criticism. Were such a piece from the hand of a junior it might safely be neglected; but coming from Professor Weldon there was the danger—almost the certainty—that the small band of younger men who are thinking of research in this field would take it they had learnt the gist of Mendel, would imagine his teaching exposed by Professor Weldon, and look elsewhere for lines of work. (Bateson, 1902, p. vi)

Weldon retaliated with a further article in *Biometrika*. Bateson submitted his rebuttal to *Nature—Biometrika* had previously refused his work and was closed to him as a publication outlet—but the editor refused to publish it. Fortunately other outlets were available.

The effective climax of the dispute was to occur at the British scientific meeting in 1904, when Bateson carried the day with scientific evidence and such oratory as: "the imposing Correlation Table into which the biometrical Procrustes fits his arrays of unanalysed data is still no substitute for the common sieve of trained judgment." (Punnett, 1950, p. 7).

The hostility continued and even such luminaries as Alfred Russell Wallace—codiscoverer of Darwinian evolution—backed Weldon; but Mendelism was now assured of a hearing.

Despite the obvious personality issues, the Machiavelian use of the professional journals to prevent one side from being heard, and the obvious reluctance of the scientists involved to consider the evidence without regard to or bias for a particular theory with which they had identified themselves, one may not be ready to grant the parallel to the Lysenko affair. But we would argue that the parallel is there and had Pearson and Weldon carried the day the situation might have been identical with the "false" theory winning out over the "true."

THE CONTINUING EFFECTS OF LYSENKOISM

The difference as we see it is that in England in the early 1900s, the orthodox scientists, despite their power and prestige, could not control all the means for public communication and were extremely limited in the type of penalty they could impose upon the unorthodox. In monolithic Russia, that was tragically not the case; and the "false" theory became part of the scientific framework within which investigators must work. That they must work within that framework is suggested by the cavalier dismissal of hereditary factors in mental retardation that one can find in the work of Russian investigators in the sixties. Thus, Luria recognizes that among the children who are unsuccessful in school there are those whose failures are due to such causes as pedagogical neglect, peripheral sensory defect, and enfeebled constitutions that keep them from maintaining the pace of the class. But all true cases of mental retardation are considered to be result of severe brain disease *in utero* or early childhood which has disturbed the normal development of the brain in these children.

In consequence all these peculiarities of their mental functioning and behavior which we have observed are not the result of a natural diversity of individual characteristics, but are the result of a severe disease which they have endured. (Luria, 1963, p. 11)

In the same volume with Luria's argument, Pevzner recognizes that some writers have attached significance to heredity but that others have correctly pointed out that oligophrenic feeblemindedness has the same symptoms of brain injury as aphasia, apraxia, and apoplexy. She further notes that scientists have talked less and less of the inherited nature of oligophrenia and more of them are accepting the view that it derives from external pathological factors that disturb the normal development of the brain. Metabolic errors like infection or intoxication can affect the development of the fetal brain. The error in phenylalanine metabolism is given as a case in point. There is not the whisper of a suggestion in her discussion that there exists a great mass of literature in the professional journals of the Western world devoted to genetic factors in such metabolic errors (Pevzner, 1963).

To be sure, in Pevzner's book *Oligophrenia: Mental Deficiency in Children* (1959), there is a greater recognition of the hereditary aspects of retardation as seen by Western investigators—she notes that Jervis believes that hereditary factors play a decisive role in the development of phenylketonuria. But the overall effect of her survey of the literature relevant to etiological factors is still to depreciate hereditarian interpretations and to emphasize exogenous factors. She ends on the hopeful note that, "An obvious tendency has been observed in recent years abroad to admit the significance of exogenous factors in the etiology of oligophrenia" (p. 8). Here, too, the cold war was thawing?

It would thus seem that regardless of how Mendelian genetic theory was overthrown in Russia—whether on the basis of adequate scientific evidence; honest errors in judgment upon the part of scientists; by quackery; or, as many Western observers maintain, by the requirements of sociopolitical issues—the fact remains that for succeeding generations of scientists a framework of orthodoxy exists within which their investigations will proceed. The young scientist is not likely to undertake a career of investigation on hereditary factors in mental retardation when his scientific elders and his textbooks tell him that such do not exist.

The ways in which sociopolitical factors can influence the development of science in an authoritarian culture is so apparent that there is the danger that a contrast effect will make them appear absent in a nonauthoritarian culture. Smaller and less effective they may be. In a cultural tradition like that of the West that has emphasized individualism rather than collectivism, in which there has been a relative looseness of the controls within and between groups, and a greater plurality of value systems, a diversity of viewpoints can more easily coexist; and the effects of sociopolitical factors in science as elsewhere are apt to display themselves in a more fragmentary and diffuse fashion. Certainly, one is less likely to find an instance where a Lysenko can rise before a scientific meeting and announce that his position on a scientific issue has the approval of the Central Committee of the Party, at which point all assembled stand in prolonged ovation and all opposition melts away.

SOCIOPOLITICAL FACTORS AND THE NATURE–NURTURE CONTROVERSY

That sociopolitical factors in a democracy are nevertheless active is suggested by a study such as that of Pastore (1949). Since Pastore's study concerned the heredity-versus-environment controversy, it has particular interest to anyone interested in the area of mental retardation. For, while its implications go far beyond the area, this heredity–environment controversy is a central issue for mental retardation.

Pastore's hypothesis was that a scientist's position in regard to the nature–nurture controversy would be related to his attitudes toward social, political, and economic questions. The hypothesis, as Pastore indicates, was not original with him. Others, including John Dewey and Lancelot Hogben, had advanced it before. What the hypothesis lacked and what Pastore sought to supply was documentary evidence.

For this attempt, Pastore selected twenty-four outstanding British and American scientists who had been active in the nature–nurture controversy and who had taken unambiguous stands as to the relative importance of heredity or environment in determining individual and group differences. These individuals were then classified according to their attitudes toward the potentialities of the "common man," toward democracy, toward social reconstruction, and toward the origin of social evils. The "conservative" classification included those who were pessimistic about the potentialities of the common man or critical of attempts to broaden the participation of the citizenry in the government. The conservative was for the status quo.[1] The

---

[1] In fairness, it should be pointed out that Pastore's characterization of the conservative is not necessarily identical with the way in which some might use the term to describe the sociopolitical attitudes of themselves or others. The same might be said for his definitions of liberal or radical sociopolitical attitudes. However, for the sake of his

"liberal" classification included those who believed in the necessity of social change. The "radicals" were those who believed in the necessity of a complete change in social, political, and economic institutions.

The result of Pastore's cross classification of his scientists on the nature vs. nurture and conservative vs. liberal-radical dimensions was to show a very marked correlation. Of the twelve emphasizing environmental factors, eleven tended toward liberalism or radicalism in their sociopolitical beliefs. Of the twelve emphasizing heredity, all but one tended toward conservatism. The specific list of scientists is of interest to us since it includes quite a few of the individuals we have discussed in tracing the history of the impact of biological factors on the field of mental retardation. The hereditarians were: Francis Galton, Karl Pearson, William Bateson, William McDougall, Charles B. Davenport, Frederick A. Woods, Edward L. Thorndike, Henry H. Goddard, Lewis M. Terman, Paul Popenoe, Leta S. Hollingworth, and Edward M. East. The environmentalists were: Lancelot Hogben, J. B. S. Haldane, Lester F. Ward, Charles H. Cooley, James McKeen Cattell, Franz Boas, William C. Bagley, Herbert S. Jennings, Hermann J. Muller, Frank N. Freeman, George D. Stoddard, and John B. Watson. Only Terman and Watson were exceptions to the hypothesis.

Although some of these men achieved fame in more than one field, Pastore's professional classification for them lists ten psychologists, nine geneticists and biologists, two sociologists, one anthropologist, one educator, and one statistician. One might expect the biologists and geneticist to emphasize heredity and the psychologists and sociologists environment. Actually four of the biologists and geneticists were environmentalists and five of the psychologists were hereditarians.

LIMITATIONS OF PASTORE'S STUDY

A study such as Pastore's is always open to criticism on the representativeness of the sample. The 24 names were drawn from a pool of 200 who expressed themselves on both nature–nurture issues and on controversial political and social issues. Those omitted from the final list either had not expressed themselves extensively enough to warrant inclusion or were quite similar to those who actually were selected for discussion. The basis for rejection in no case, according to Pastore, was determined by their sociopolitical outlook. If such indeed was the case, the correlation between sociopolitical outlook and position in the nature–nurture controversy seems definitely established; and, moreover, the correlation would appear to be exceptionally strong. There seems to be little likelihood that the strength of the correlation was due to any major errors in classification. Pastore quotes extensively from

---

argument it is not necessary that all agree to the same labels he applies to the sociopolitical attitudes he has under consideration. It is only necessary to admit that they are different sociopolitical attitudes and that they aptly describe the attitudes of the men he so classifies.

his scientists on both the nature–nurture issue and on sociopolitical issues and his classifications seem self-evident.

Of course, a correlation does not establish a causal relationship and one is as free to assume that the relationship goes from one's scientific position to one's sociopolitical attitudes as that it goes in the reverse direction. Nor is any light shed on the possibility of a third factor or group of factors determining the correlation between the two observed variables. Pastore considers the alternative explanations and arrives at his personal conclusion that:

In the opinion of the writer, the sociopolitical allegiances of the scientists were a significant determinant of their position on nature–nurture questions. It is his opinion that these allegiances had a marked effect upon the formulation of a hypothesis and the method of its verification, the conclusions drawn from an investigation, and the statement of implications of these conclusions for society. Different scientists were differently affected by their political allegiances. (For a given investigator, the effect of political allegiances upon his thinking depended much upon the nature of the problem under consideration.) The nature–nurture controversy, qua controversy, has been sustained by the conflicting social philosophies of the scientists. It seems that in a few cases the scientists concerned were able to hold their allegiances to one side and were able to discuss problems in terms of their intrinsic scientific merits. It is probable, however, that in most cases the scientists were not aware of the specific impact of their political loyalties upon their scientific thinking.[2]

In a footnote to this conclusion, Pastore allows that for some individuals the formulation of their social philosophy may have been strongly influenced by an earlier adherence or exposure to a particular scientific tradition; but, if such were the case, Pastore maintains the resulting social philosophy interacted, in its turn, with the initial scientific slant and sustained it.

One may or may not be willing to accept the generality of Pastore's conclusion. The results are in accordance with our own bias but the strength of relationship is suspiciously high and we suspect some selective factor may be at work to inflate it. Pastore himself suggests the possibility that many individuals with a definite point of view with regard to the nature–nurture question may not have expressed themselves in writing on sociopolitical issues because of the obvious contradiction between their sociopolitical and scientific outlooks. Nevertheless the hypothesis is a compelling one and the study appears to offer it some support. For our particular interests in the ready acceptance of Goddard's results it is of note that not only is Goddard, the originator of the research, listed among the conservatives as defined by Pastore but scientists most ready to accept his work as proof of the inheritance of mental defect—Davenport, Popenoe, and East—are also classed with the conservatives.[3]

---

[2] Nicholas Pastore, *The Nature-Nurture Controversy*. New York: Columbia University, 1949, pp. 181–182. By permission.

[3] Other instances of possible relationship between sociopolitical factors and one's position on "scientific" issues can be seen in our country. For example, many indi-

In this and the previous three chapters we have attempted to convey to the reader how the characteristics of a particular field (viz., mental subnormality)—the problems which dominate it, the favored theories, the preferred practices—must be viewed in the context of the wider society in which that field is embedded. Our attempt reflected the opinion that for too long the field of mental subnormality has been viewed and discussed as if it did not contain and reflect the most important aspects—social, moral, scientific, philosophical—of our society. It would indeed be a mistake, however, if the reader concluded that although our opinion had validity for the nineteenth and the early decades of the twentieth century, it was less relevant to the current scene. The fact is, as we have attempted to show that a particular field *always* reflects to a considerable extent major aspects of the larger society. It is easier to see in retrospect the relationships that existed in the more remote past than it is to see those existing during the time in which we live. This difficulty places a special obligation on us, *particularly those of us whose professional activities are intended to change the lives of other people:* We must strenuously resist assuming, implicitly or explicitly, that our practices are the result of cold logic and scientific facts unmediated by the knotty problems of values. As we pointed out earlier, social action and practices are not derivable directly from scientific facts; at some point there has been an explicit or implicit acceptance of certain values.

This thesis will receive further exemplification in the following chapters in which we shall attempt to trace the important and complex impact of the development of intelligence tests upon the field of mental subnormality.

---

viduals—in both lay and professional communities—take an extremely dim view of the concept of, and research on, instinctive behavior because these seem to conflict with their belief that everyone is born "equal" and that there are no inherent barriers to what man can be. It is as if instinctive behavior necessarily or directly has consequences for what man and society could be. Although somewhat less true today than in the first half of this century, research in instinctive behavior has never been a fashionable area, in contrast to what one finds in European countries; and this is not wholly due to the scientific status of the concept.

Intelligence tests and the social indictment of the retarded

We have tried in previous chapters to show how biological theories relating to heredity and evolution played a role in determining the way in which society came to view the problem of mental retardation after the turn of the century. Stanley P. Davies has pointed out that another determinant of this alarmist view was the development and application of the Binet intelligence scales (Davies, 1930).

Despite our frequent cautions about the misuse of tests, we feel the advantages of the tests for research and clinical practice are both real and important. But, whatever advantages the development of intelligence tests brought to the field of mental retardation, there is no doubt that one major initial impact they had was to contribute to the view of the mentally subnormal as a major menace to society. We think it should be noted that the intelligence scales had this particular effect upon society's view of the retardate because the theory of intelligence in which they were embedded by their major proponents on the American scene was a biological theory that assumed intelligence to be an hereditary, innate capacity little affected by environmental conditions.

THE DEVELOPMENT OF THE BINET-SIMON INTELLIGENCE SCALES

The Binet-Simon tests of intelligence were devised with a particular pedagogical problem in mind. In 1904 the Minister of Public Instruction in France named a commission and charged it with the study of measures to be taken for insuring the benefits of instruction to defective children. The commission determined such matters as the kind of school, the pedagogical methods, and the conditions of admission into the school. No child was to be barred from the ordinary school and admitted into a special class without a pedagogical and medical examination which would certify that because of his limited intelligence he was unable to profit sufficiently from the instruction given in the ordinary schools (Binet and Simon, 1916a).

Addressing themselves to the problem of a diagnostic examination for determining the intellectual level of retardates, Alfred Binet and Théodore Simon introduced in 1905 what they termed "a measuring scale of intelligence." This scale consisted of a series of thirty tests of increasing difficulty which started "from the lowest intellectual level that can be observed" and ended with normal intelligence. Thus the scale begins with the simplest of tests to determine if the subject has the ability to visually follow the movement of a lighted match, to grasp a presented object, to discriminate food from the inedible. It proceeds to test higher levels of ability such as imitation of gestures and knowledge of the names of body parts and of designated objects. The final test involves the definition of abstract terms, namely, the difference between *esteem* and *affection* and between *weariness* and *sadness*.

In this scale the authors attempted to evaluate the level of intelligence without regard to the subject's exposure to formal instruction.

We believe that we have succeeded in completely disregarding the acquired information of the subject. We give him nothing to read, nothing to write, and submit him to no test in which he might succeed by means of rote learning. In fact we do not even notice his inability to read if a case occurs. It is simply the level of his natural intelligence that is taken into account. (Binet and Simon, 1916a, p. 42)

And the nature of intelligence which they purportedly measure?

It seems to us that in intelligence there is a fundamental faculty, the alteration or the lack of which, is of the utmost importance for practical life. This faculty is judgment, otherwise called good sense, practical sense, initiative, the faculty of adapting one's self to circumstances. To judge well, to comprehend well, to reason well, these are the essential activities of intelligence. A person may be a moron or an imbecile if he is lacking in judgment; but with good judgment he can never be either. Indeed the rest of the intellectual faculties seem of little importance in comparison with judgment. (Binet and Simon, 1916a, pp. 42–43)

The test items of the scale were selected on the basis of a great deal of empirical work with both normal and subnormal children and were so arranged in increasing difficulty that it permitted an ordering of individuals in terms of the levels of their intellectual functioning. Idiot children did not succeed beyond test 6 which required the execution of simple orders and the imitation of gestures. Normal 3-year-old children typically succeeded through test 9 but not beyond. Five-year-olds did not succeed beyond test 14 which consisted of the definition of familiar objects. Imbeciles did not pass beyond item 15 which required the repetition from memory of various sentences spoken by the examiner. The highest grade of mentally retarded children, called *debilé* by Binet—and for whom Goddard coined the word *moron*—did not in general exceed the performance of a normal 12-year-old. (Binet and Simon, 1916a; Peterson, 1925).

Thus, as Peterson (1925) has pointed out, the authors had definitely grasped the conception of mental age levels, i.e., the levels of performance normal to children of different ages who are neither accelerated nor retarded in their mental development. With these mental age levels Binet and Simon had defined three degrees of mental retardation. But obviously these mental age limits for the various degrees of mental retardation were only usable when the chronological age level of the child was considerably in excess of his mental age. When such was not the case, one adopted a rough rule of thumb such that any child whose mental age was two years behind his chronological age was to be considered retarded. There was of course the difficulty that two years retardation at the chronological age of 5 did not appear to be quite the same thing as two years retardation at the chronological age of 13. This difficulty was not to be solved until the Terman revision of the Binet scales with its use of the intelligence quotient or ratio of mental age to chronological age.

In the development of the 1908 revision of the scale, emphasis shifted from the measurement of the intelligence of retardates to normal children.

We set for ourselves the following program: first, to determine the law of the intellectual development of children and to devise a method of measuring their intelligence; and, second, to study the diversity of their intellectual aptitudes. (Binet and Simon, 1916a, p. 182)

Binet did not live to carry out this ambitious program; but the 1908 revision presented, as he saw it, a usable method of measurement of intelligence established on correct lines. The tests were now grouped according to ages at which the majority of children succeeded in them. A subject was considered to have the intellectual development of the highest age at which he passed all but one of the tests. For every five tests that he passed above that base level he was allotted an additional year of intellectual development.

GODDARD'S ADAPTATION AND USE OF THE SCALES

It is a measure of Goddard's pivotal influence on the changing attitudes toward the retardate in this country that his contributions in the area of mental testing and the classification of retardates by use of the tests were as significant as his contribution to the hereditarian interpretation of mental retardation.

On a visit to Europe in the spring of 1908, Goddard learned of the 1905 scale through the work of Dr. Decroly and Mlle. Degand who had used this scale with defective children. These Belgian investigators had found the ranking of the children by the scale to be in rather close correspondence with ranking based on school success, clinical examination, and behavioral observations. Returning to Vineland, Goddard translated the scale and despite his feelings about its inadequacy began using it in the Training School. Upon the publication of the new 1908 scale, Goddard's initial reaction was negative. It appeared too easy and too simple to provide an adequate evaluation of intelligence. Nevertheless, he subsequently decided to give it a fair trial and with surprise and gratification found that it met his needs. The classification of children based upon this 1908 scale agreed with the experience of the Institution. In January, 1910, Goddard published a brief summary of the scale and from this time on the Vineland Laboratory became a major center for the dissemination of knowledge about the Binet method of intelligence testing. By 1916, the Vineland Laboratory had distributed 22,000 copies of the pamphlet describing the tests, and 88,000 record blanks. In that same year, 1916, under Goddard's editorship there appeared two volumes of translations of Binet's work on the intelligence scales and the mentally retarded (Binet and Simon, 1916a,b).

Goddard's translation of the 1908 scale was standardized on a sample of 2000 American children. Pintner points out that at this time the practical application of the scale was limited almost entirely for use with the feeble-minded. Normal children were tested principally for purposes of standardization. In this connection it is of note that both Huey and Kuhlmann, who published their own translations of the scale in 1910 and 1911, respectively, were both connected with institutions for the feebleminded (Pintner, 1923).

CLASSIFICATION OF MENTAL DEFECT BY MEANS OF TESTS

In 1909 Goddard proposed a classificatory system for mental defect based upon the Binet scale of 1905. In 1910, carrying out the ideas he had advanced in that proposal, he published the results of testing and classifying 400 feebleminded children by the Binet scale of 1908. Three major groups were proposed similar to those used by Binet: the *idiots*, whose mental age on the Binet scale did not exceed 2 years; the *imbeciles*, whose mental age ranged from 3 to 7 years; and the *morons*, whose mental age was greater than the imbecile group but did not exceed 12 years. Within each major group were three subdivisions of low-, medium-, and high-grade defectives. The objective classification of the retardates by the Binet tests matched very closely the subjective judgments of the staff of the Training School on the respective abilities of the various children (Goddard, 1910a).

This classificatory system was "tentatively" adopted by the American Association for the Study of the Feebleminded (Report of Committee on Classification, 1910). The important advantage of the classification and the reason for its popularity were that it emphasized psychological variables rather than pathological variables. Many of the classificatory systems of the nineteenth century had emphasized etiology and organic signs and symptoms. Martin Barr, among others, pointed out the limitations of such classifications for purposes of care, training, and education. In his book *Mental Defectives,* published in 1904, Barr had recommended an educational classification of the feebleminded which related to the degree of custodial care they required and to the skills they were capable of mastering. Goddard's work at Vineland suggested that the Binet scale provided an easy means of classifying the retarded in terms of an educational classification similar to Barr's. The mental ages obtained by the children on the Binet scale varied with the degree of self-care of which they were capable and with the complexity of the skilled tasks they were able to perform about the institution. Goddard pointed out that Barr's classification based on "trainability" was limited in its usefulness by the fact that the child had to be observed in the institution for a period of time before one could determine how trainable he was. During this period, in which the staff was getting acquainted with the child, valuable time was lost for training. Hence the desirability for a quick method of classification that would permit the immediate adaptation of the program to the child's ability. The Binet tests met this need.

Kuhlmann's experience at the Minnesota Institution for the Feebleminded gave strong support for Goddard's position. In 1912 he reported data on 50 children with mental ages ranging from 8 through 12 years. Teachers in the institution who knew these children well were asked to classify them into five groups of different grades of ability. No child was classified by less than three teachers. Over two months were used in the classifying. In this time, preliminary classifications were verified and special observations made on those children whose classifications were doubtful. A comparison of the teachers' classifications of any given child frequently indicated a wide range of disagreement. Nevertheless, the average grade assigned to each child was highly correlated with his mental age as obtained by the Binet.[1] Kuhlmann was struck by the wide range of variability in the classifications of a child by different teachers in contrast to the strong agreement of the average classification to the mental age. He then concluded that the Binet-Simon tests were more accurate than other available methods. They had the additional advantage of requiring only about an hour of examination time to obtain results similar to those obtained by weeks or months of general observation (Kuhlmann, 1912).

The striking success that these early workers had in applying the Binet to the problem of grading institutionalized retardates probably contributed to the subsequent overestimation of the value of an IQ score as a diagnostic sign of mental retardation. As Davies has pointed out:

For a time after the development of this measuring scale of intelligence, it was quite generally assumed that the presence or absence of feeblemindedness could be detected solely by the rating received in the intelligence test. (Davies, 1930, p. 2)

Another effect of these institutional surveys was that since the highest mental age level recorded for inmates was approximately 12 years, this was assumed as the upper level of feebleminded intelligence. And, with erroneous logic, the conclusion was drawn, not that *some* people with a mental age of 12 years are feebleminded, but that people with a mental age of 12 years *are* feebleminded.

Further Development
of the Tests and Their Theory

Binet's final revision of his scale appeared in 1911, the year of his death. Reports from investigators in a number of countries had indicated that the 1908 scale was too easy at the lower levels and too hard at the higher levels. This had resulted in too large a percentage of younger children being rated as of superior mentality, while in the older age groups a majority of the children were rated as having mental ages below normal. Taking account of some of these reports and of his own experience, Binet shifted a number of items to higher or lower age levels. Some old items were omitted and a few new ones added. An important change was the inclusion of a group of items for the adult level. It is of interest that three of the five items at this new adult level had formerly been set at the 13-year level (Binet and Simon 1916a). We will return to this point when we review the application of the 1908 scale to various delinquent and criminal groups.

---

[1] Kuhlmann presents his tabulated data without further analysis. We calculated a Pearson r of .62 for the mental ages of the children and the average grade assigned by the teachers. The correlation is all the more impressive when one remembers the limited range of the mental ages involved.

Despite the appearance of the 1911 scale, Goddard's adaptation of the 1908 scale remained the standard intelligence test in America until the advent of Terman's 1916 version which was known as the Stanford Revision of the Binet Scale. In the Stanford revision many new items were added to the original Binet scale and great care was devoted to placing the items at the proper age level. The method of calculating mental age was similar to that suggested by Binet. The basal mental age was the level at which all test items were passed, plus additional credit in terms of months of mental age allowed for every item passed at higher levels. A major innovation was the use of the Intelligence Quotient or IQ. This, following a suggestion by Stern, consisted of the ratio of the child's mental age to his chronological age multiplied by 100. This made it possible to compare the intellectual levels of children at different chronological ages.

In his book *The Measurement of Intelligence,* Terman (1916) advanced the argument that the similar nature of the distribution of IQ scores at the various ages—they all approximated the normal distribution curve—indicated that a child's IQ as measured by this scale remains relatively constant. He further maintained that retests of the same children at two- to five-year intervals supported this contention. This purported "constancy of the IQ" naturally seemed to minimize the effects of training and environment on intelligence. Thus the developing theory of the intelligence tests dovetailed nicely with the theory that intellectual ability was biologically based and hereditarily determined.

Application of the Tests
to the Delinquent Groups

Even before the introduction of the Binet intelligence test it was widely assumed that feeblemindedness was a major factor in the cause of delinquency, crime, prostitution, venereal disease, illegitimacy, alcoholism, and poverty. The eugenics literature previously cited gives many instances of this point of view. The use of the tests with their "objective," single-criterion diagnosis of feeblemindedness—a mental age below 13 years or an IQ below 70 as the case might be—permitted a "scientific" assessment of this assumption.

The early reports of the application of the Binet tests to delinquent youths gave such strong support for the hypothesis that it actually proved an embarrassment. Pintner (1923) reported that these early studies showed anywhere from 60 percent to 90 percent of the delinquents testing out as feebleminded. Some psychologists proposed a selective factor to explain the results: The tested delinquents were those not bright enough to escape the law. The brighter delinquents "got away" and hence the IQ of tested delinquents was lower than the IQ of the delinquent group as a whole. Other psychologists with less ingenuity but perhaps more accuracy held that the explanation lay in faulty construction of the scales. This was certainly so in the Goddard revision of the Binet scale in which the higher-level items were too difficult for their placement. As previously mentioned, Binet in his 1911 revision removed three items from the 13-year level to place them at the adult level. Yet other psychologists took the data at face value and assumed that the main difference between the delinquent and nondelinquent youth was the difference in general intelligence. Two of Goddard's studies reported in the *Training School Bulletin* will be representative of these early investigations.

Goddard's Early Studies with Delinquent Girls. Of 56 delinquent girls, 14 to 20 years of age, Goddard and Hill (1911) classified 93 percent as feebleminded on the basis of the Binet scale. In this instance the authors made use of a mental age below 13 years as the criterion for feeblemindedness. In interpreting the results, Goddard emphasized that test results were not influenced by school training:

Perhaps the reader may be inclined to say, "But these tests show that they are ignorant and that is because they have not been to school, or have not profited by their school experience." But such is not the case. These are not tests of school training; they are tests of mental development. Any person who has lived in any sort of average environment for the requisite number of years is able to do these tests, even though he has never been to school, even for a day, and by failing in these they manifest their mental defectiveness. (Goddard and Hill, 1911, p. 55)

The "average environment" is left undefined and no attempt is made to demonstrate that the girls grew up in such an environment.

In a later study, the criterion for feeblemindedness was changed with a resulting change in the percentage of those so classified. In this instance, Gifford and Goddard (1912) reported on the testing of 100 juvenile court cases chosen at random. Only one child obtained a mental age equivalent to his chronological age and was thus considered normal. Thirty-three children obtained mental ages from one to four years below their chronological ages. Some of these children, according to the authors, would eventually prove to be feebleminded but were not so classified. The remaining 66 percent of the children obtained mental ages more than four years behind their chronological ages. This group was classified as distinctly feebleminded by the authors.

Shifting Emphasis in Later Studies. The above two studies illustrate how readily the percentage of feebleminded varied with changes in the mental-age criterion. With such changes in criteria, improved test instruments, and more careful studies, and use of controls, estimates of the percentage of feebleminded in delinquent groups were to drop considerably. For example, Pintner (1923) arranged the studies he surveyed in chronological order from 1911 to 1922, presenting for each the percentage estimate of the number of retardates among the delinquents. The median percentage for the first 16 studies was 64 percent, for the last 16 studies the median percentage was 26 percent.

Pintner's survey of studies on adult criminals was similar. In fifteen investigations of inmates of state prisons and reformatories estimates of feeblemindedness ranged from 16 percent to 54 percent. Again, as with the adolescents and youths, the earlier studies gave markedly higher estimates.

The results of a later survey by Sutherland (1931) exhibits the same pattern of higher estimates of feeblemindedness in the earlier research. Examining 342 studies, comprising approximately 175,000 offenders, which were reported between 1910 and 1928, Sutherland notes a marked decline in the estimates of feeblemindedness. From 1910 to 1914, fifty studies gave estimates of the percentage of feebleminded offenders that ranged from 4 to 96 percent with a median estimate of 51 percent. In the period of 1925–1928 the estimates of 46 studies ranged from 2 to 58 percent with a median estimate of 20 percent. Sutherland discussed various factors affecting these estimates including changing criteria for feeblemindedness, differences in techniques of administration, and sampling differences.

These studies, of course, even when they used improved instruments and a more suitable test criterion for a diagnosis of feeblemindedness, still tended to give inflated estimates of the degree to which mental retardation was a factor in delinquent behavior. This resulted from the fact that allowance was not made for the degree to which cultural factors affected IQ scores. Thus it has been argued that a cultural factor such as a depressed socioeconomic level may act both to increase the frequency of delinquency and to depress the IQ scores of the group under consideration. Elsewhere in this book we have discussed the relationship of cultural factors to IQ scores. An introduction to the difficult problem of evaluating the interaction of cultural factors, retardation, and delinquency may be found in Shulman's (1951) review of research in this area. It is sufficient for our purposes to note that when attempts are made to take these cultural factors into account the delinquent groups do not look markedly different from control groups from the same cultural environment. That there may be a relatively small residual relationship between low IQ scores and greater frequency of delinquent behavior is, of course, possible.

Prostitution. The Binet tests were also used in a similarly unsophisticated way in studies of prostitutes. Typical investigations reported some 50 percent of the women feebleminded.

For example, in a study by Clinton McCord, published in 1915, fifty prostitutes were examined. The investigator with commendable concern for the conditions of testing and a becoming touch of gallantry records that:

Our tests were made in the houses, where the women, not being under arrest and not being accused of any misdemeanor, were free from excitement and antagonism, and, in all but two cases, free from nervousness. The examinations took place on Sunday afternoons when the girls were probably in a more rested and refreshed condition than at any other period of the week. The "madams" of the eleven houses in which cases were tested showed a spirit of friendly co-operation, and the tests were made under controlled conditions. (McCord, 1915, p. 387)

Of these women, 18 percent received a mental age of 9 or less representing for the author "definitely segregable types about whose mentality there would be little difference of opinion among trained observers." An additional 36 percent tested at a mental age of 10 and were considered high-grade morons.

The same author reports on a sample of 38 inmates of a home for "wayward" girls or sex offenders. Thirty-two of these girls and women tested at the mental age of 10 years or less and were accordingly classified as feebleminded (McCord, 1915).

The Conclusions.   Thus the relationship of feeblemindedness to crime and immorality which had been uncovered in the pedigrees of degenerate families received "objective" support from the investigations undertaken with the new testing instruments. The correlation was obvious, the causal connection was readily supplied by logic:

But why do the feeble-minded tend so strongly to become delinquent? The answer may be stated in simple terms. Morality depends upon two things: (a) the ability to foresee and to weigh the possible consequences for self and others of different kinds of behavior; and (b) upon the willingness and capacity to exercise self-restraint. That there are many intelligent criminals is due to the fact that (a) may exist without (b). On the other hand, (b) presupposes (a). In other words, not all criminals are feeble-minded, but all feeble-minded are at least potential criminals. That every feeble-minded woman is a potential prostitute would hardly be disputed by anyone. Moral judgment, like business judgment, social judgment, or any other kind of higher thought process, is a function of intelligence. Morality cannot flower and fruit if intelligence remains infantile. (Terman, 1916, p. 11)

SURVEYS AND THE OPINIONS OF EXPERTS

Further aspects of the indictment of the retardate as the source of all social evils were supplied by special surveys and reports, two of the most widely publicized being those of Anne Moore and Wilhelmine Key.

Dr. Moore's report consisted of a survey of cases selected from the ungraded classes of the City of New York and from the recipients of aid from public and private charity organizations. For the most part it was an urban population. By means of dramatically related case histories Dr. Moore illustrated the "causal" relationship of feeblemindedness to poverty, immorality, and crime. The report concludes with a plea for segregation of all defectives.

That the segregation of defectives costs money is remembered, that it saves money is often forgotten. The initial cost of segregation would be great but the saving effected by correcting our present lax methods would be greater. As tax bills are not itemized the ordinary citizen does not realize that he is at present paying for the unrestrained presence of the feeble-minded. An added tax for their segregation would be an apparent rather than a real increase, for through segregation of defectives, the number of criminals, the number of prisoners, the cost of trials, the demand upon public and private charity would be decreased; and as control of hereditary conditions resulted in decrease in the number of defectives, and training rendered many of them self-supporting, the expenditure necessary for their maintenance would from year to year grow less. The feeble-minded at large are as dangerous, if not more dangerous, than persons suffering from contagious disease. No consideration of cost, of parental affection and responsibility, or of personal liberty should be allowed to weigh against public safety. (Moore, 1911, p. 93)

Dr. Key's survey of a rural area of Pennsylvania was commissioned by the Public Charities Association of that state. The identification of the retarded in this study was without the aid of formal tests but accomplished rather in the fashion of the family pedigree studies that we have previously discussed. The statistical tabulations are accompanied by dramatic case histories illustrating the alcoholism, the immorality, and the criminal tendencies of the feeble-minded. A special argument is advanced to demonstrate the fecundity of defective women. For forty-five defective women in the sample who had reached the end of the child-bearing period, the average number of children produced was seven. Approximately 50 percent of these offspring by conservative estimate were considered defective. In contrast, a sample of forty-five normal women chosen at random averaged 2.9 children per mother.

To Dr. Key, the meaning of the data on fecundity was unmistakable:

It is to the unrestrained reproduction of the feeble-minded woman that we owe the disproportionate increase of the socially unfit, with their burden of pauperism, delinquency, and crime. Already this burden is almost intolerable. What will it be a few generations hence? (Key, 1915, p. 38)[2]

The experts for the most part concurred with the findings of the pedigree studies, the Binet research, and the surveys. Representative of these was Walter E. Fernald, superintendent of the Massachusetts State School. Fernald was then midway in a long and distinguished career in the area of mental retardation. In 1912, he addressed the Massachusetts Medical Society:

The social and economic burdens of uncomplicated feeble-mindedness are only too well known. The feeble-minded are a parasitic, predatory class, never capable of self-support or of managing their own affairs. The great majority ultimately become public charges in some form. They cause unutterable sorrow at home and are a menace and danger to the community. Feeble-minded women are almost invariably immoral, and if at large usually become carriers of venereal disease or give birth to children who are as defective as themselves. The feeble-minded woman who marries is twice as prolific as the normal woman.

We have only begun to understand the importance of feeble-mindedness as a factor in the causation of pauperism, crime and other social problems. Hereditary pauperism, or pauperism of two or more generations of the same family, generally means hereditary feeble-mindedness. In Massachusetts there are families who have

---

[2] Much has been written on the presumed fecundity of the mentally subnormal. Reported negative correlations between intelligence and family size have been viewed with alarm as indicative of a downward trend in the IQ of the population as a whole. For some recent thoughts on the problem which discount this danger the reader is referred to Penrose (1950; 1962, chap. VI); Higgins, Reed, and Reed (1962); and Reed and Reed (1965).

been paupers for many generations. Some of the members were born or even conceived in the poorhouse.

Every feeble-minded person, especially the high-grade imbecile, is a potential criminal, needing only the proper environment and opportunity for the development and expression of his criminal tendencies. The unrecognized imbecile is a most dangerous element in the community. (Fernald, 1912, pp. 90–91)

EUGENIC REMEDIES

In commenting upon the rapid change that occurred in society's attitude toward the retardate during this period, Davies (1930) has pointed out that in 1900 with the exception of the modest beginnings of the special classes in the public schools, mental deficiency appeared almost entirely as an institutional problem and interest in it was largely confined to those directly concerned with the care of the retardates in the institutions.[3] Judging by the facts that there were but 12,000 institutionalized cases of retardation and little discussion of mental retardation in the public press, it is reasonable to assume that at that time mental retardation was viewed as a very minor social problem.

But by 1915, Davies points out, mental deficiency was in the focus of public attention as perhaps the largest and most serious social problem of the time. Conservative estimates placed the number of defectives in the country at over 400,000. With mental defect seen as underlying all sorts of social maladjustment and antisocial behavior, the implications were grim.

Since mental retardation was viewed as basically a biological condition determined by a defective central nervous system, for the most part hereditarily transmitted from one generation to the next, the solution to the problem was naturally seen to be in the realm of biology. And as defective neural tissues could not be replaced or improved the major attack on the problem could only be preventive and not curative.

In 1911, the Eugenics Section of the American Breeders Association appointed a special committee "commissioned to study and report on the best practical means for cutting off the defective germ-plasm in the American population." The reports of this committee appeared in the *Eugenics Record Office Bulletin* in 1914.

Although the committee recognized many groups presenting problems for eugenical study such as paupers, alcoholics, criminals, epileptics, the insane, and the deformed, it was forcefully maintained that, "The greatest of all eugenical problems in reference to cutting off the lower levels of human society consists in devising a practical means for eliminating hereditary feeble-mindedness". (Laughlin, 1914, p. 18)

---

[3] As we indicated in Chapters 7 and 8, it is only in recent years that some thought has been given to the deleterious effects of institutionalization. The issues and implications of Dr. Klaber's study (Chapter 9) could not have been formulated—indeed, the study could not have been done—in the earlier decades of this century. Undoubtedly there were a few individuals who saw the issues; however, the theories and practices of those times did not allow these issues to be raised.

Various alternative solutions were considered from laissez-faire to euthanasia. The committee concluded that the two most socially acceptable and effective remedies were life segregation—or at least segregation during the reproductive period—and sterilization. Other remedies, such as restrictive marriage laws, were seen as ineffective. As for euthanasia, the committee, while deprecating Sparta's custom of exposing undesirable offspring to the elements, could not but "admire her courage in so rigorously applying so practical a system of selection."[4] But for modern eugenics, the committee felt that the aim must be, "preventing the procreation of defectives rather than destroying them before birth, or in infancy, or in later periods of life."[5]

Sterilization Laws. The report of this committee further considered the legal, legislative and administrative aspects of sterilization (Laughlin, 1914). Existing state laws—twelve in number, headed by the pioneer Indiana law of 1907—were criticized by the committee on such grounds as failing to provide for due process of law, inadequate provisions for administration, and the unsuitable procedures for the selection of candidates for sterilization. A model sterilization law was proposed circumventing these difficulties.

A number of these early state laws were declared unconstitutional for causes such as those pointed out by the committee. This led to the revision and construction of laws more in line with then current constitutional interpretations and in 1927 the United States Supreme Court handed down a decision upholding the Virginia sterilization statute. The object of this law passed in 1924 was frankly eugenic and based upon the premise that heredity is a major component in the etiology of insanity, mental deficiency, epilepsy and crime. The law applied to inmates of the state hospitals for the insane and the State Colony for Epileptics and Feebleminded. Provision was made for safeguarding the rights of the inmates by providing for a hearing before a special board of directors of the hospital or colony. At this hearing the inmate and his legal guardian were entitled to representation by counsel and provided with a right of appeal to the state courts for any decision of the special board.

A campaign for the enactment of sterilization laws was undertaken with considerable success by various members of the eugenics movement. But as Haller (1963) points out, many within the movement objected to the sterilization laws either in principle or as a matter of policy. Some had reservations about the state of scientific knowledge which was presumed to obtain in the area and felt that until we knew better the precise modes of hereditary transmission, legislation was ill advised. Others such as Fernald saw this solution creating other social and moral problems.

The presence of these sterile people in the community, with unimpaired sexual desire and capacity would be direct encouragement of vice and a prolific source of

---

[4] *Op. cit.,* p. 55.
[5] *Loc. cit.*

venereal disease. Sterilization would not be a safe and effective substitute for permanent segregation and control. (Fernald, 1912, pp. 95–96)

Nevertheless, despite the lack of a unified front and because of the dedicated efforts of men like Harry Laughlin of the Eugenics Record Office many states were won over to the enactment of sterilization laws. Yet the victories were more apparent than real. Davies (1959) notes that by 1926, 23 states had enacted sterilization laws. But the early spurt soon slacked off and by 1955, nearly 30 years later, the total number of states having such laws on their statute books was only 28. Even more telling was a consideration of the actual number of sterilizations performed under these laws. By 1925, 1374 operations had been performed on the mentally retarded within the United States. By 1958 the total had swelled to 31,038. Regardless of what benefits one assumes may have been achieved from the point of view of the management of individual cases, it is obvious that the eugenic impact of this limited number of sterilizations, over a fifty-year span, must have been minimal.

Segregation Programs.   Conditions were much more favorable for the segregation program. All eugenicists were in accord. A national committee on provision for the feebleminded was formed with financial support from Mrs. Harriman and with membership from state boards of charity and the National Committee for Mental Hygiene. It included such familiar names as Davenport, Goddard, and David Starr Jordan. This committee worked with local civic and charitable groups to further the end of increased institutional facilities for the care and segregation of the feebleminded (Haller, 1963).

Although the campaign had the worthwhile results of abetting the establishment of several new institutions—a gain of especial value in the southern states where there had been almost no provision for institutional care—its success from the eugenical point of view was minimal.

Davies (1959) points out that in 1910, the number of patients in institutions for the retarded was 14,347 or 17.5 per 100,000 population. In 1923, after over a decade of active propaganda for extensive segregation of the retarded, the number of patients in institutions was 42,954 or 39.3 per 100,000. At first glance, a gratifying increase—which to be sure had begun before the propaganda campaign and continued long afterward—but from the eugenical point of view, which was only secondarily concerned with patient care and primarily concerned with cutting off defective germ-plasm, only 2 percent of the population's retarded individuals could be segregated in 1923.

Thus it would appear that the eugenics movement—despite the great assist mental tests provided in furthering the social indictment of the retarded—met with no real success in its efforts to provide remedies for the problem in the form of sterilization and segregation programs.

Intelligence testing, eugenics, and racism

While the campaign for the sterilization and segregation of the retarded had small success, the eugenics movement in the United States attained a much more solid achievement in its efforts for restrictive immigration. This success was predicated upon an alliance with racism. The alliance of racism with eugenics in the pre- and post-World War I era has been documented by Haller, and we do not propose to go into great detail on this aspect of the eugenics movement. Nevertheless, since we have been following the growth of the eugenics movement for the light it sheds upon the development of our attitudes toward the retardate, some passing notice of racism is necessary for, as Haller maintains, "The extreme racism associated with eugenics did more to bring eugenics to public notice and to cause eventual scientific repudiation of the early eugenics movement than any other single factor" (Haller, 1963, p. 144).

But not to wander too far from our main theme—mental subnormality—we will pick those aspects of racist attitudes that are connected with considerations of the intelligence of racial and ethnic groups and the incidence of mental retardation among them.

THE ORIGINS OF RACIST ATTITUDES AND
THEIR DEVELOPMENT IN THE EUGENICS MOVEMENT

In discussing the relationship of racism and imperialism in America about the turn of the century, Hofstadter (1959) makes the point that the Anglo-Saxon form of racism then prevalent was basically a product of modern nationalism and the romantic movement. To be sure, it derived strong support from Darwinism which with its leitmotif of struggle and survival of the fittest provided vivid analogies and "scientific" support for the proponents of racial superiority and aggressive international politics.[1]

This "scientific" support for racism began with Galton, the founder of the eugenics movement. Although he was apparently not guilty of racial animosity as such, he nevertheless felt that the theory of evolution and the available evidence led inevitably to the conclusion that various human races differed not only in physical characteristics but in intellectual and behavioral traits. In his book *Hereditary Genius* (1869) he attempted to demonstrate the existence of these differences. His principal argument was based upon estimations of the frequency with which men of genius had been produced by different races. Thus with complete obliviousness of cultural, historical, and environmental factors he estimated that the Anglo-Saxon race was superior to the Negro and the Negro to the Australian aborigine. Unlike many racists who would accept that much, Galton was broad-minded enough, and objec-

---

[1] While Anglo-Saxonism saw the international scene as a struggle for survival between nations and races and hence generally supported American imperialism in the decades before World War I, there were nevertheless those among the Anglo-Saxon enthusiasts who strongly deplored warfare for its dysgenic effect. Such was Henry Fairfield Osborn, distinguished paleontologist and active eugenicist, who saw in the Great War the destruction of the best of American stock. Emotionally moved by his observations of the mobilization of troops, he commented: "Whatever may be its intellectual, its literary, its artistic or its musical aptitudes, as compared with other races, the Anglo-Saxon branch of the Nordic race is again showing itself to be that upon which the nation must chiefly depend for leadership, for courage, for loyalty, for unity and harmony of action, for self-sacrifice and devotion to an ideal. Not that members of other races are not doing their part, many of them are, but in no other human stock which has come to this country is there displayed the unanimity of heart, mind and action which is now being displayed by the descendants of the blue-eyed, fair-haired peoples of the north of Europe. In a recent journey in northern California and Oregon I noted that, in the faces of the regiments which were first to leave for the city of New York and later that, in the wonderful array of young men at Plattsburg, the Anglo-Saxon type was clearly dominant over every other and the purest members of this type largely outnumbered the others. . . . With a race having these predispositions, extending back to the very beginnings of European history, there is no hesitation or even waiting for conscription and the sad thought was continually in my mind in California, in Oregon and in Plattsburg that again this race was passing, that this war will take a very heavy toll of this strain of Anglo-Saxon life which has played so large a part in American history" (Osborn, 1919, xi–xiii).

tive enough, within the limits of his science, to allow that another race might be superior to his own. Thus basing himself on the frequency of eminent men in the golden age of Athens he argued that:

. . . the average ability of the Athenian race is, on the lowest possible estimate, very nearly two grades higher than our own—that is, about as much as our race is above that of the African negro. This estimate, which may seem prodigious to some, is confirmed by the quick intelligence and high culture of the Athenian commonalty, before whom literary works were recited, and works of art exhibited, of a far more severe character than could possibly be appreciated by the average of our race, the calibre of whose intellect is easily gauged by a glance at the contents of a railway book-stall. (Galton, 1869, p. 342)

While it would appear that Galton's argument for racial differences in intellect and personality was derived in part or at least conditioned by evolutionary theory, the hypothesis—and the racist attitudes that so often accompany it—is of course at least as old as recorded history, and it may be presumed that whatever objective evidence exists for the hypothesis, the accompanying racist attitudes derive from and are supported by primitive and widely prevalent psychic needs of both individuals and social groups. Thus, we interpret Hofstadter's indictment of modern nationalism and the romantic movement as causes of racism to refer to the particular form that racism took during this period of modern history. At any rate, there would appear to be no question, as Hofstadter and others have documented, that the aggressive and expansionist international politics of the United States around the turn of the century received strong support from Anglo-Saxonism.

If on the international scene Anglo-Saxonism was concerned with bearing the white-man's burden and spreading the benefits of Anglo-Saxon civilization, on the domestic scene it joined with other variants of racism then prevalent in a concern for preserving the purity of the breed. The growing racist attitudes in America in the latter part of the nineteenth century were expressed in the increasing demands for immigration restrictions which would preserve the blood of the old immigrant stock from northern Europe—the blood that had founded this country and made it great (Haller, 1963). The increasing flood of immigration from southern and eastern Europe with its alien Catholic and Jewish religions, its foreign folkways and strange tongues, alarmed a native population already stressed by the rapid social and economic changes that followed the Civil War. Spokesmen readily appeared for the racist attitudes that emerged in this period of strain, and in 1894 a group of young Harvard graduates formed the Immigration Restriction League.

The development of the eugenics movement in this country provided these advocates of racial exclusiveness another outlet for their propaganda and one that had the advantage of "scientific" respectability. In 1911, Prescott Hall, a leader of the Immigration Restriction League, in conjunction with his old Harvard classmate Charles Davenport, arranged to have a committee on immigration attached to the Eugenics Section of the American Breeders Association. The first report of the committee appeared in the *American Breeders Magazine* in the following year. The report advocated more rigorous enforcement of existing restrictions on the admission of the alien insane and feebleminded and a further tightening up and extension of these regulations. The feebleminded were viewed as perhaps an even greater menace to public health than the insane, for the latter were more likely to be segregated in institutions. But great as the danger was from classifiable defectives it was seen as "less than the danger from the much larger class of aliens who are below the mental and physical average of their own countries and cannot fail to lower the average here" (Cance *et al.*, 1912, p. 252).[2]

INTELLIGENCE TESTING AND THE ARGUMENT FOR RACIAL AND ETHNIC DIFFERENCES IN INTELLECTUAL ABILITY

While Galton's argument for racial differences in intellectal ability was circuitous, the development of intelligence tests appeared to give a means for a direct comparison of racial and ethnic groups.

Goddard's Testing of Immigrants.   Goddard was one of the first to apply Binet tests to immigrant groups, with the intent of determining whether methods for keeping out defective aliens could be improved. His report on his experiences at Ellis Island included the following in which he demonstrated the "uncanny" ability of one of his field workers for identifying the feebleminded:

We picked out one young man whom we suspected was defective, and, through the interpreter, proceeded to give him the test. The boy tested eight by the Binet scale. The interpreter said, "I could not have done that when I came to this country," and seemed to think the test unfair. We convinced him that the boy was defective. That was so impressive that the Commissioner urged us to come back on the following Monday. We did, spending the day there and trying some experiments. We placed one young lady at the end of the line, and as the immigrants passed, she pointed out the ones she thought defective. They were taken to the quiet room, and we proceeded to test them. She picked out nine, whom she thought were defective. The result was that every one of the nine were below normal, according to the Binet test. (Goddard, 1913, p. 105)

This work was continued and reported in full in a 1917 issue of the *Journal of Delinquency*. In this report six groups of steerage passengers were selected from the immigrants at Ellis Island. They were chosen only after the

---

[2] Franz Boas dissented from the conclusions and recommendations of the committee and subsequently resigned. This dean of American anthropologists and long-time critic of racism surely must have found himself among strange bedfellows. He was replaced by Irving Fisher, a Yale economist and a leading eugenicist. With the transformation of the American Breeders Association into the American Genetic Association, the reports of this committee on immigration subsequently appeared in that association's official organ, the *Journal of Heredity,* and they continued to advocate restrictive immigration policies.

physicians of the immigration service had culled out all the mental defectives that they recognized as such. Two of the groups, one Italian and the other Russian, had been selected by one of Goddard's field workers as appearing defective. Out of a combined total of 37 in these two "defective" groups only one achieved as high a classification as borderline on the Binet, the remainders were either morons or imbeciles. The remaining four groups consisting of Jews, Hungarians, Italians, and Russians, respectively, were selected as representative of steerage passengers in general but to compensate for the fact that the immigration authorities had already removed the obviously mental defective from among the passengers, Goddard excluded from his groups a small but unspecified number of obviously intelligent immigrants. In the resulting select but "representative" samples the Binet tests revealed an average of 80 percent feebleminded immigrants.

With such a rich mine of feeblemindedness, the success of the field worker's "look see" diagnoses for the two "defective" groups previously discussed becomes more understandable.

Apparently embarrassed by riches, Goddard removed some of the test items that had proved most difficult for the immigrant groups and rescored the tests. But even with this liberal treatment approximately 40 percent of each group proved feebleminded, failing to make a mental age score of 10 years or better. Not only were these results true for the immigrant groups where it had been necessary to use a translator in the administration of the tests but they held as well for the Jewish group where it was possible to use an examiner who spoke the language of the group.

Presenting these results, Goddard then addressed himself to the skeptical reader:

Doubtless the thought in every reader's mind is the same as in ours, that it is impossible that half of such a group of immigrants could be feeble-minded, but we know that it is never wise to discard a scientific result because of apparent absurdity. Many a scientific discovery has seemed at first glance absurd. We can only arrive at the truth by fairly and conscientiously analyzing the data. (Goddard, 1917, p. 266)

First, Goddard points out that the immigration of recent years is inferior in quality to the past. "It is admitted on all sides that we are getting now the poorest of each race." Second, Goddard points out the great majority of these feebleminded immigrants belong to the moron class, a class that is capable of earning a living under favorable circumstances. These favorable circumstances according to Goddard usually existed for the immigrant.

He is watched and protected because he does not know the customs of the country. He is excused because he does not understand the language. His every act and movement is more or less closely supervised because he is a foreigner. In a large percentage of the cases he goes at once, when he lands, to his own group. They protect and care for him, partly through racial pride, partly through common humanity, extending to him the care and oversight and patience which we have just mentioned. (Goddard, 1917, p. 268)

Thus the moron immigrant is capable of succeeding after a fashion in the New World and our average citizen who is likely to have contact only with the more successful and prosperous of the immigrant stock would on the basis of his limited experience easily underestimate the surprisingly large percentage of immigrants who are of relatively low mentality.

Goddard concludes his report with a consideration of hereditary factors that is startling coming as it did from the author of *The Kallikak Family* and *Feeblemindedness*. He asks whether the immigrants of low mentality are such because of hereditary defect or cases of apparent mental defect by deprivation. While admitting that there is no data on this point, he points out that it might be indirectly argued that it is more probable that their condition is due to environment than that it is due to heredity. First, the environment of these immigrants had been poor and seemed able to account for the result. Second, Goddard recognized that this immigration had been going on for a number of years, and if the condition were due to hereditary feeblemindedness we would expect a noticeable increase in the proportion of the feebleminded of foreign ancestry. This was not the case. Goddard's own survey of a few years back had shown that only 4.5 percent of inmates of institutions for feebleminded were of foreign ancestry. However, the other alternative that these are cases of hereditary defect is not lightly to be dismissed and Goddard's position in the end remains somewhat equivocal. But perhaps this allowance of an argument for an environmental effect was one of the early signs of the shifting winds of opinion on the part of the experts in the area of eugenics. At any rate, the article was considered of sufficient importance to eugenics that it was given an extensive review with many quotes in the December 1917 issue of the *Journal of Heredity*.

Pintner's Studies of Racial Groups. During this period around World War I there were numerous other applications of the Binet and other newly developed tests of intellegence to the study of ethnic and racial groups. Rather than deal with further individual examples of this kind of research we think we might achieve some desirable brevity, and at the same time get an appreciation of the way in which this research appeared to an expert in the field and the way it was presented to students, if we look instead at one of the early and outstanding college textbooks in the area of intelligence testing. Rudolph Pintner, a professor of education at Columbia University, published his text in 1923. He was then in full stride in a distinguished career that included many contributions to the testing movement including the development of special tests such as the Pintner-Patterson Performance Test and Pintner Non-Language Test with which he pioneered in the application of intelligence tests to deaf children.

In his review of the use of intelligence tests with various "racial groups" in America Pintner reports on six studies of Italian children in which median Binet IQs range from 77.5 to 85. For three comparison groups of children of native American stock the median IQs range from 95 to 106. He discussed briefly the variables of social status and language in these studies but concluded that although the median IQ of the Italian in the United States might not be as low as indicated by the results it was probably still below 100. In discussing Binet test results on other ethnic groups he urges caution since the data are not as extensive as that available on the Italian groups but concludes that it might be that the groups coming from southern Europe are inferior in intelligence to those of northern Europe. This, of course, although Pintner does not mention it, would be in support of the then prevalent racist belief in the superiority of Nordic blood.

Pintner then refers to the results of the Army testing program in World War I—we shall shortly consider this work in detail—and indicates that it also gives support for the assumption of a superiority of the northern European over the European from the south or east.

In his concluding remarks on these "racial" or ethnic groups Pintner carefully points out that the results are indicative of differences in these "racial" groups as they are represented in this country and points out a need for comparisons between races in their home countries.

As regards the American Negro, Pintner presents three Binet studies comparing Negro and white school children. The median IQs for the Negro groups ranged from 7 to 24 points below the white groups. There is no discussion of possible educational, cultural, or socioeconomic factors that might concomitantly vary with the racial groupings. Another study discussed by Pintner compared a group of Negro and white children in terms of the mental age obtained on the Goddard revision. Approximately 30 percent of the Negro children were more than one year retarded in comparison to their chronological age whereas only 10 percent of the white children were similarly retarded. It was maintained that the Negro children were more retarded even when compared with the "poor whites" as represented by the children of mill workers. A final Binet study compares Negro college students with white college students. The 55 Negro students obtained a median IQ of 103 and the 75 white students a median IQ of 112. Pintner further discusses the results of the testing of Negro and white soldiers in World War I and concludes that all results show the Negro decidedly inferior to the white on standard intelligence tests.

Thus the results of approximately a decade of research on the question of racial and ethnic differences in intelligence appeared to a competent expert and were so presented to his students in one of the outstanding schools of education in this country.

The Army Testing Program in World War I

In Chapter 2, when we discussed the effect of World War II on the field of mental subnormality we noted that one of the effects of war is to force a society to evaluate its human resources. This was certainly as true of World

War I as it was of World War II. One of the results of this pressure for evaluation of human resources in both wars was a tremendous development in that area of psychology specifically concerned with individual differences. In World War I the focus was on the measurement of individual differences in intelligence, for this appeared to be what was needed and what psychological science of that time was in the best position to do. In World War II, although psychology's contribution in the area of the measurement of intelligence and ability continued, it expanded into the area of the evaluation and treatment of emotional disturbances. In both wars, as a result of military needs and the readiness of the military to support appropriate research and action programs to meet those needs, psychology made rapid strides in the development of its techniques, the advance of its knowledge, the training of its professional members, and the advancement of its public image. But advances made under such pressures are not an altogether unmixed blessing. Too much ground covered too quickly often must be retraced, and imperfect knowledge and rough instruments are pressed into action programs with resultant loss as well as gain.[3]

With no intent to detract either from the undoubted gains to the field itself or to the services it rendered, we would like to touch upon some aspects of this forced development during World War I which we think did much to foster racism during this period and so constituted one of the definite ill effects of the crash program.

In this connection we shall refer to the work of distinguished psychologists who both before and after their war service did much to advance the science of behavior and to whom society is therefore in debt. When we indicate how their work on the army tests led to the fostering of social attitudes and programs that many if not most of us would repudiate today, we have no intentions of indicting or maligning these men. No more than we had intentions of indicting or maligning Galton—whom we truly admire—for his naive racism. We reiterate that *the opinions and beliefs of scientific men reflect not only the state of their science but the state of the society in which they function. Man is a social being embedded in the social matrix of his times. He reflects the past and present ideals of that society and in his actions he anticipates their future development. In a complex society the ideals and values will be pluralistic and no man will reflect them all. In such a society the ideal citizen is the one that identifies with the best of his traditions and in his actions preserves and develops them. The ideal citizen is found among psychologists and scientists no more than he is in other walks of life, and each man will achieve in his public and private life some mixture of acts reflecting both the worst and best of his times.* To say that the judgment of a man and

---

[3] To the reader acquainted with another kind of war, i.e., the War on Poverty begun in the mid-sixties, the mixed consequences of programs started under strong societal pressures are familiar phenomena.

his times calls for an exceedingly fine balance is not to imply such judgments should not be made. It indicates that in the instances with which we deal we do not feel competent on our partial knowledge to make them. Nevertheless, we feel we may use these instances of men and their times to pursue our main purpose which is that of obtaining some understanding of the inter-action of science and value systems as they affected attitudes and programs directed toward the problems of mental subnormality.

Upon the entry of the United States into World War I, the leadership of the American Psychological Association undertook prompt action to determine the ways and means by which professional psychology could offer national service in this time of emergency. These efforts were facilitated by the formation of a psychological committee within the organization of the Na-tional Research Council. Robert Yerkes, president of the American Psycho-logical Association, served as chairman. A number of subcommittees were formed, the chief one of note for us being a committee concerned with the psychological examination of recruits. The importance of that subcommittee is attested to by the fact that it also was chaired by Robert Yerkes. A proposal originating in that subcommittee and calling for the psychological examina-tion of recruits for the determination of intellectual deficiency and psycho-pathic tendencies was submitted to the Surgeon General of the Army. While this proposal was going through channels, Yerkes sought and obtained financial aid from the Philadelphia committee on provision for the feeble-minded for the initial planning of such a program of testing. With this support, the Committee on the Psychological Examination of Recruits met at the Vineland Training School in May of 1917. Included on the committee were such outstanding names as Robert Yerkes, W. V. Bingham, H. H. Goddard, L. M. Terman, and G. M. Whipple. Considering the possible contribution of psychology to military efficiency, the committee decided that intelligence testing offered the best possibilities of practical service.

Taking into account the number of men who would eventually have to be tested and the available time, the committee determined that its first task was to devise a suitable group test of intelligence. Arthur Otis who had de-vised group tests capable of objective scoring made his tests available to the committee through Terman and with these as take-off point the committee undertook the planning and development of a suitable intelligence scale. The National Committee for Mental Hygiene supplied further financial aid to test the reliability and serviceableness of the tests in various army and navy organizations. By August a report on these trials was available and included such encouraging results as a correlation of .5 between the psychological examinations and officers' ratings for the 4000 men examined.

Yerkes was appointed a major in the Sanitary Corps of the Army and the official military trial of psychological examining got under way. The psycho-logical testing of recruits was only one of the activities of the Division of

Psychology as headed by Yerkes but in scope and impact it far outweighed the Division's contributions in other areas. The test program as it finally evolved employed both group and individual tests of intelligence.

Group Testing.

ARMY ALPHA. The Army Alpha was a group paper-and-pencil test consisting of eight subtests including among others an arithmetic test, a test of general information, a test of practical judgment, and a number series test. It was the test of choice for the majority of English-speaking, literate recruits.

ARMY BETA. The Army Beta was a group test for illiterates or foreign born who had difficulty in either reading English or in understanding spoken English. It was administered by a combination of pantomime instructions and demonstrations and consisted of seven tests including one on maze tracing, a picture completion test and a digit-symbol test, these tests being similar to those now used in the well-known Wechsler Intelligence Scales.

Individual Testing.
For individual examinations several tests were available. Frequent use was made of a shortened form of the Stanford-Binet. Occasionally the abridged Yerkes-Bridges point scale was substituted for the Binet. For illiterates and non-English-speaking people the individual examination was accomplished with a composite performance scale consisting of items from the Knox tests—developed by the immigration service at Ellis Island—and the Pintner-Patterson nonverbal tests.

Procedure.
In the typical procedure for examining a detachment reporting for psychological examination, the first step was the separation of the English-speaking, literate troops from the non-English-speaking and the illiterate. The first group was given the Alpha and the rest the Beta. Those who obtained low scores on Alpha were reassigned to Beta. An attempt was then made to give individual examinations to all those who obtained low scores on Beta. With the limitations of time and personnel this last goal was not always achieved. During the war, scores on the different scales were converted to one general scale of letter grades corresponding to differences in ability as measured by the tests.

The Official Report.
The results of the Army testing program were not made available to the public until 1921 when the Official Report of the Division of Psychology of the Office of the Surgeon General was published as Volume XV of the *Memoirs of the National Academy of Science*. It is this account that we have been following in our presentation. Chief among those active in the preparation of the report were Robert M. Yerkes, E. G. Boring, L. M. Terman, and H. C. Bingham.

According to the report, from September 1917 through January 1919 a grand total of 1,726,966 men were given psychological examinations. Of this number about 42,000 were officers. More than 83,500 enlisted men included in the total had been given individual examinations.

Between April 28, 1917, and January 31, 1918, 7,800 men (0.5 percent) were recommended for discharge because of mental inferiority by the psychological examiners. An additional 10,014 (0.6 percent) were recommended for assignment to labor battalions because of their low-grade intelligence. Another 9,487 (0.6 percent) were recommended for assignment to development battalions for observation and training to determine how they could be used in the Army. Thus a total of 1.75 percent of the men examined were considered unfit for regular military service. During this same period a total of 46,347 men obtained scores on the tests equivalent to less than ten years of mental age and the report concluded that "It is extremely improbable that many of these individuals were worth what it cost the Government to maintain, equip, and train them for military service" (Yerkes, 1921, p. 100).

Analysis of the Army Test Results

In addition to the aid it provided in the identification of the mentally subnormal, the testing program provided intelligence ratings which were useful in the selection of men for various kinds of specialized training and assignment. From our point of view, however, the military achievements of the Army testing program are of less interest than is the very great effect the results of the program had on attitudes toward mental subnormality and upon the eugenics movement.

Perception of Mental Subnormality.   The third section of the official report consisted of a statistical summation of the results of the testing program. Since nearly two million soldiers had been examined it was decided to select only a sample, albeit a large one, for analytic treatment. Securing a representative sample was difficult—because of the ways in which tests had been reported and filed—but the authors succeeded in making a reasonable compromise between the ideal and the possible. As finally selected, the sample consisted of several groups, the ones of primary interest to us being 96,354 white enlisted soldiers, 25,392 Negro soldiers, and 15,528 white officers.

Since individuals were tested on different examinations it was necessary to derive a score for each soldier that would be comparable to all other scores regardless of the examinations used. By means of various assumptions and statistical treatments which made use of correlations between the scales it was possible to derive a score for each soldier—called the "combined score"—which could be used for pooling the data from all soldiers. The report also made use of mental-age scores by transmuting via statistical procedures the combined score into mental-age scores. Yerkes offered the following reason for presenting parts of the summary data in mental ages.

The transmutation into mental age is given because those terms have now acquired some absolute meaning and are therefore familiar. Rejections from the Army as well as special treatment of the feeble-minded in civil life can be thought of best in relation to units of mental age. (Yerkes, 1921, p. 789)

When reported as mental ages the results of the testing were quite startling in their implications. Thus, for the "white draft" the median mental age was approximately 13 years. If the classification standards recommended by God-dard were then used, nearly 50 percent of the white draft would be classified as feebleminded.[4] Even if selective factors were allowed for—such as the higher intelligence of the army officers not included in the sample, or those exempted from the draft because of their vital contributions to industry—it would be hard to conclude other than that the average mental age of the draft-age men of this country was not very far above that of the average 13-year-old child.

News of the Army test results had begun to filter out even before the publication of the official report and immediately eugenical alarms arose. Fears began to be expressed for the future of democracy if such was the intellectual level of the mass of its electorate. Writing in *Scribner's Magazine* in 1921, Edwin Grant Conklin commented on the Army tests as follows:

Assuming that these drafted men are a fair sample of the entire population of approximately one hundred millions, this means that forty-five millions, or nearly one-half of the whole population, will never develop mentally beyond the stage represented by a normal twelve-year-old child, and that only thirteen and a half millions will ever show superior intelligence [i.e., attain a mental age of 16 years or more].

When it is remembered that mental capacity is inherited, that parents of low intelligence generally produce children of low intelligence and that on the average they have more children than persons of high intelligence, and, furthermore, when we consider that the intellectual capacity or "mental age" can be changed very little by education, we are in a position to appreciate the very serious conditions which confront us as a nation. (Conklin, 1921, p. 354)

However, despite the alarms, a saner view set in and both psychologists and the public at large soon realized that any definition of feeblemindedness that classified 50 percent of the population as feebleminded must be suspect to say the least. And long-time critics of the abuse of test scores in the diagnoses of feeblemindedness were quick to point out the implications of the Army results for the assumed high frequency of feeblemindedness among the dependent and delinquent classes.

---

[4] It is important to recall from our discussion (Chapter 2) of Ginzberg and Bray's (1953) study of the World War II draft that the number of individuals rejected for service because of "mental deficiency" was also very high. When one contrasts their handling and discussion of the problem with the reports we are discussing from World War I, one can see how much the thinking in this area had changed—a change in thinking which reflected tremendous changes in the nature of our society *and* our science.

So the Army testing program in a sense marked a high-water mark in the indictment of the feebleminded. At any rate, the use of tests as a sole criterion for feeblemindedness was to come under increasing attack and by 1928 even Goddard was gracious enough to allow, "It was for a time rather carelessly assumed that everybody who tested twelve years or less was feebleminded" (Goddard, 1928, p. 221).

Racism, Eugenics, and the Social Climate.   While the Army results thus had a mixed effect on the development of those attitudes toward mental subnormality that have been epitomized in the phrase "the menace of the feebleminded," on the one hand heightening the alarm and on the other hand causing a reaction to set in because it made patent the absurdity of a definition of feeblemindedness that would encompass half the population, its effect on the alliance of racism and eugenics was more uniform. This resulted from the fact that the analysis of the test results in terms of racial and ethnic groups gave "very evident" support for the arguments of the racists for the superiority of the white Nordic breed.

The Relationship of Intelligence Ratings to Nativity.   Of the approximately 94,000 men in the white draft sample, 13,200 reported that they were born in a foreign country. There was wide variation in the number of men born in different countries, with Italy and Russia leading with 4000 and 2300 men, respectively. However, in the analysis no country was included unless it was represented by at least 100 men. This reduced the overall sample size to some 12,400. The analysis yielded mean scores for the various foreign-born draft as presented in Table 16.1.

T A B L E 1 6 . 1 Army Test Results for the Foreign-Born Draft

	Mean Combined Score	Mean MA
Canada	13.74	13.29
England, Ireland, and Scotland	13.37	13.00
Denmark, Norway, and Sweden	13.30	12.95
Germany and Austria	13.17	12.85
Greece	11.90	11.86
Russia	11.16	11.28
Italy	11.04	11.19

It will be noted that the differences are considerable (an extreme range of practically two years mental age) and that the countries tend to fall into two groups: Canada, Great Britain, the Scandinavian and Teutonic countries all fall in the class interval between 13 and 14 points, whereas the Latin and Slavic countries fall in the class interval between 11 and 12 points. Most of the successive differences, when the difference is compared with its probable error, are significant. (Yerkes, 1921, p. 699)

In the official report of the Army examinations the results of the examinations were stated "factually." There was relatively little attempt to explain ethnic or social differences or to speculate upon the implications of the data. However, as soon as the data became available to the public, psychologists and laymen alike freely interpreted the data and spelled out what to them were obvious implications.

The most authoritative of these interpretations was that of Carl C. Brigham in his *A Study of American Intelligence* which appeared in 1923. Brigham had served as an Army psychologist during the war. His extensive presentation and further analysis of the data was aided by Carl R. Brown, E. G. Boring, and Mark A. May, all of whom had worked on the original Army report. The book was further supplied with an introduction by Robert Yerkes.

Before we consider Brigham's book in detail we think it is important to get some feel, however slight, of the climate of the times in which it appeared. As we have indicated previously, this was a period of American history when racist attitudes were at high, e.g., one need only recall that it was the period of the revival of the Ku Klux Klan and of extended and intense agitation for restrictive immigration—the restrictions to be based not on numbers but on ethnic and racial origin. Madison Grant's paean on the Nordic, *The Passing of the Great Race,* which had first appeared in 1916, reappeared in a revised edition in 1919. This widely popular survey of European history saw most if not all of the greatness of that past as the product of Nordic blood. Thus we read:

The chief men of the Cinque Cento and the preceding century were of Nordic blood, largely Gothic and Lombard, which is recognized easily by a close inspection of busts or portraits in northern Italy. Dante, Raphael, Titian, Michael Angelo, Leonardo da Vinci were all of Nordic type, just as in classic times many of the chief men and of the upper classes were Nordic.

. . .

In depicting the crucifixion no artist hesitates to make the two thieves brunet in contrast to the blond Saviour. This is something more than a convention, as such quasi-authentic traditions as we have of our Lord strongly suggest his Nordic, possibly Greek, physical and moral attributes. (Grant, 1919, pp. 215, 230)

In this work, racism and eugenics were closely allied:

Those who read these pages will feel that there is little hope for humanity, but the remedy has been found, and can be quickly and mercifully applied. A rigid system of selection through the elimination of those who are weak or unfit—in other words, social failures—would solve the whole question in a century, as well as enable us to get rid of the undesirables who crowd our jails, hospitals and insane asylums. The individual himself can be nourished, educated and protected by the community during his lifetime, but the state through sterilization must see to it that his line stops with him or else future generations will be cursed with an ever increasing load of victims of misguided sentimentalism. This is a practical, merciful and inevitable solution of the whole problem and can be applied to an ever widening circle of social discards, beginning always with the criminal, the diseased and the insane and extending gradually to types which may be called weaklings rather than defectives and perhaps ultimately to worthless race types. (Grant, 1919, pp. 50–51)

Thus wrote Madison Grant—chairman, New York Zoological Society; trustee, American Museum of Natural History; Councilor, American Geographical Society—in a book prefaced by Henry Fairfield Osborn, Research Professor of Zoology at Columbia University.

Lest one think that this kind of thinking was limited to expression in a few books or a specialized professional journal or two, it might be worthwhile to belabor the reader with a further quote from this period that appeared in *Scribner's Magazine*, a journal with wide public appeal to the intellectuals of that day comparable perhaps to our present-day *Harper's* or *Atlantic Monthly*. For the reader to appreciate the change in zeitgeist he might try imagining his reaction if he ran across this in his favorite monthly.

The result of our lax system of admitting immigrants is shown not only in the great number of mental defectives but also in the large number of criminals among the foreign born. Of late we have heard much of the "crime wave" in this country, but this wave is only a ripple on the flood of crime which we have with us continually. For example, Chicago, with a total population about one-third that of London, had in 1916 nearly twelve times as many murders. . . . New York in 1916, 1917, and 1918 had in each year six times as many homicides as London. . . . That a disproportionate amount of this crime is traceable to recent immigrants, or to unassimilated races, is shown by the fact that more than three-fourths of the total population of these cities are immigrants or the children of immigrants. . . . How much of this lawlessness and crime is due to inherited traits is not indicated, but in view of the fact that certain classes of crime are associated particularly with certain races it seems probable that there is in these races an inherited tendency to peculiar forms of lawlessness and crime. For example, in New York, in the number of hospital cases treated for drunkenness, the Irish lead all other foreign-born stock.[5] Very probably the excessive amount of insanity among the Irish as well as this disproportionate amount of alcoholism are indicative of an unstable nervous organization which is inherited. In crimes of violence, kidnapping, and blackmailing the Italians lead all foreign-born stock with more than two times their proper proportion. In this case, also, it seems probable that there is inherited as a racial characteristic a highly excitable and emotional disposition with deficient powers of inhibition and control.

In gainful crimes such as robbery, larceny, and receiving stolen goods the Russians and Poles lead all foreign-born stock; in white slavery and prostitution the Hebrews lead, and in crimes against chastity the English are pre-eminent; however, it is impossible to say to what extent this larger incidence of these

---

[5] One can't help fondly remembering Shelley's dutiful and gentle wife Harriet who accompanying her husband on his quixotic mission to settle the "Irish Question" wrote home, "Poor creatures, they live more on whiskey than anything, for meat is so dear they cannot afford to purchase any."

particular crimes in the races named can be regarded as due to bad heredity, and to what extent it is the result of bad education and environment. Of course no race has a monopoly of good or bad qualities, and we breed our own criminals as well as import them, but this merely emphasizes the importance of shutting out more effectively those who may be expected to add to this group not only in their own persons but also in those of their children. (Conklin, 1921, pp. 355–356)

Brigham's Analysis.   This then was the climate in which Brigham undertook his evaluation of the Army data. To indicate how closely that climate enwrapped Brigham we might note that in Yerkes' foreword to *A Study of American Intelligence* as well as in Brigham's own introduction, special mention is made of Charles W. Gould. Gould, in 1922, had published a racial interpretation of history that equated the rise of a civilization with the purity of its racial stock, and its decline with its mongrelization. He concluded that work with an impassioned plea for the exclusion of alien races from our shores.

We know that our institutions depend on the intelligence of each citizen. We know that a republic is possible only to men of homogeneous race, determined and united in intelligent control of their own affairs. We know that the greater the common impulse, the greater the common intelligence, the more community of action and individual capacity are fostered, the better, the more splendid, the happier will be the result. . . .

No naturalization certificates can carry with them any part of this, our heritage, impalpable, intangible, and yet more worth on the great altar of our country than the suffrage of untold millions of the ignorant and debased. . . .

Americans, the Philistines are upon us. Burst the fetters of our unseemly thraldom. Bar out all intruders. Repeal our naturalization laws. Deafen your ears to the clamor of demagogues. Make strong your hearts against the appeals of emotional humanitarianism. . . .

Arise—stand alert—trifle no more with Opportunity. She knocks but once. Repeal our naturalization laws; bar out the feeble-minded, the vicious, and the debased; secure our children and our children's children in their legitimate birthright. (Gould, 1922, pp. 163–165)

Yerkes' foreword to Brigham's book has this to say of Gould:

It appears that Mr. Charles W. Gould, a clear, vigorous, fearless thinker on problems of race characteristics, amalgamation of peoples and immigration, raised perplexing questions which drove Mr. Brigham to his careful and critical re-examination, analysis, and discussion of army data concerning the relations of intelligence to nativity and length of residence in the United States. In a recently published book, *America, a Family Matter*, to which this little book is a companion volume, Mr. Gould has pointed the lessons of history for our nation and has argued strongly for pure-bred races. (Brigham, 1923, p. vi)

In his Acknowledgment section Brigham points out his indebtedness to Charles Gould who suggested and sponsored the work.

In my treatment of the race hypothesis I have relied on his [Gould's] judgment and on two books, Mr. Madison Grant's *Passing of the Great Race,* and Professor William E. Ripley's *Races of Europe.* (Brigham, 1923, pp. xvii–xviii)

Brigham's estimate of Grant is conveyed in a footnote to a section of the book in which he compares his findings of race differences to those proposed by Grant in the *Passing of the Great Race:*

The quotations I have chosen from Mr. Madison Grant's chapter on *Racial Aptitudes* most certainly do not do justice to that author, but they seemed to me to summarize his general position briefly. The entire book should be read to appreciate the soundness of Mr. Grant's position and the compelling force of his arguments. (Brigham, 1922, p. 184)

The reader may refer back to our own quotations from Grant's work to savor "the compelling force of his arguments."

Brigham's statistical handling of the Army data left the findings essentially unchanged and we shall refer to them only in relationship to the interpretations that were placed upon them.

The Foreign Born. Although both the official Army report and Brigham's reanalysis showed the foreign-born draft as a group obtaining significantly lower scores than the native born, it was difficult to interpret this simply, i.e., as demonstrating that the foreign born were innately the intellectual inferiors of the native born. For, when the immigrants were categorized in terms of the number of years they were resident in the United States, it became evident that the longer the immigrant was resident in the United States the higher his scores on the test (Brigham, 1923, p. 89):

	Years in the U.S.				
	0–5	6–10	11–15	16–20	>20
Combined-scale average	11.41	11.74	12.47	13.55	13.82

In comparison, the average combined-scale score for the native-born white draft was 13.77. Thus there was no significant difference between the native born and those foreign-born residents in the U.S. for over twenty years. In view of the gradual decrease over time in the difference between the foreign-born groups and the native-born, one might be tempted to hypothesize that the acculturation of the foreign born during his increasing years of residence in the U.S. was responsible for decreasing the difference in test scores. This would, however, be a temptation only if one did not believe that intelligence tests measure ability uninfluenced by experience or if one did not believe that there were such a thing as intellectually superior and inferior races. Many of the psychologists of this period were not free of these beliefs and hence the matter could not be dropped with such a simple explanation. It is true that in the official Army report an acculturation hypothesis was recognized, but scientific caution required the consideration of other alternatives.

Apparently then the group that has been longer resident in this country does somewhat better in intelligence examination. It is not possible to state whether the difference is caused by the better adaptation of the more thoroughly Americanized group to the situation of the examination or whether some other factor is operative. It might be, for instance, that the more intelligent immigrants succeed and therefore remain in this country, but this suggestion is weakened by the fact that so many successful immigrants do return to Europe. At best we can but leave for future decision the question as to whether the differences represent a real difference of intelligence or an artifact of the method of examination. (Yerkes, 1921, p. 704)

Brigham allowed that the hypothesis offered in the Army report might be possible but pointed out that one of its weaknesses was that it would require a marked difference between the intelligence of the returning immigrants and those who stayed to account for the size of the effect. The alternative explanations as he saw them must be either an error in the method of measuring intelligence or the inferior intelligence of recent immigrant groups as compared to those who had immigrated more than twenty years previously. A number of statistical analyses and arguments are then advanced for rejecting the assumption that there is an error of methodology. Thus, for example, he compares different periods-of-residence groups in terms of whether they took the Alpha test or the Beta nonlanguage test, and demonstrates that on the basis of either test there is an increase of score with increasing period of residence. The assumption is of course implicit that Beta is influenced neither by language nor acculturation.

This indicates, then, that the five years of residence groups are groups with real differences in native intelligence, and not groups laboring under more or less of a linguistic and educational handicap.

. . .

We must therefore accept the conclusion that under the conditions of this experiment the differences shown in the average scores of the five years of residence groups indicate real differences in intelligence and not a defect in the measuring scale. Instead of considering that our curve indicates a growth of intelligence with increasing length of residence, we are forced to take the reverse of the picture and accept the hypothesis that the curve indicates a gradual deterioration in the class of immigrants examined in the army, who came to this country in each succeeding five year period since 1902. (Brigham, 1923, pp. 102, 110–111)

The question then is, What change in the character of the immigration has occurred in the period under question? Brigham presents data on immigration obtained from issues of the *Statistical Abstract of the United States* to demonstrate that in the period under question the proportion of immigrants from northern Europe, England, Germany, and the Scandinavian countries has been on the decline while the proportion from eastern and southern Europe, Russia, Italy, etc., has been on the increase. He then argues: If the decline in intelligence of the immigrant is due to a change in the source of supply then we would expect the Army data to show that immigrants from northern Europe would show higher test scores than those from the East and South. The Army data are utilized to show this is a fact. The difference holds even if one considers only the non-English-speaking immigrants from the North. The possibility of socioeconomic differences existing between northern Europe and the East and South is not considered. We suspect that they are not considered, not because of an oversight, but because to anyone holding that Nordic blood is superior it would be obvious that northern Europe had a higher socioeconomic standing because it was inhabited by the superior race. Superior blood produced both superior intelligence and superior socioeconomic conditions. Then how could one argue that superior socioeconomic conditions produced superior intelligence?

These results on nativity groups then suggested to Brigham that the race factor might underlie the large differences found in intelligence scores among the various foreign-born groups. To test this hypothesis it was necessary to compare, not the proportion of immigration from northern Europe with that from the South and East, but rather the proportion of Nordic, Alpine, and Mediterranean blood in each European country sending immigrants to this country. Racial classification at this time was determined by such anthropometric data as skull proportions, physiognomy, height, skin and eye pigmentation, and hair characteristics. And on these bases anthropologists had distinguished the three major European races. Race distribution was not completely coextensive with national borders—e.g., the Norman type of northwestern France was Nordic; the shorter, darker inhabitants of southern France were Mediterranean. It was, therefore, necessary to reanalyze the immigration data, which had been obtained in terms of country, in the more important terms of race. Thus, while Brigham estimated the English immigrant stock to represent 80 percent Nordic blood and 20 percent Mediterranean; French immigrants represented 30 percent Nordic, 55 percent Alpine, and 15 percent Mediterranean. When the immigration data was analyzed in this fashion, it was evident that in the period from about 1890 to World War I there had been a drop in the proportion of Nordic blood in comparison to Alpine and Mediterranean blood. Despite the subtleness of the analysis, a problem remained in that most of the drop in the proportion of Nordic blood occurred prior to 1900 while the drop in intelligence in the immigrants occurred after 1900. Therefore, Brigham allowed that the race hypothesis could not entirely account for the observed drop in intelligence. Nevertheless, he continues:

In a very definite way, the results which we obtain by interpreting the army data by means of the race hypothesis support Mr. Madison Grant's thesis of the superiority of the Nordic type. (Brigham, 1923, p. 182)

The poor showing of the Mediterranean race was also interpreted by Brigham as supporting Charles Gould's contention that these people had degenerated since historical times when the Mediterranean was the center of civilization. We have previously mentioned Gould's thesis that the root of this degeneration was the mongrelization of the race by interbreeding with other races.

Negro Intelligence and the Army Data. Brigham's comparison of the Negro-draft and the white-draft groups—like that of the Army official report—indicates the clear superiority of the white-draft test scores. On the combined scale the mean score for the white draft was 13.54, for the Negro draft it was 10.41. Approximately 86 percent of the white draft obtained scores above the mean score of the Negro draft, while only 13 percent of the Negro draft scored above the mean of the white draft. The difference between the groups was of course highly significant. In commenting on these results Brigham notes:

Our results showing the marked intellectual inferiority of the Negro are corroborated by practically all of the investigators who have used psychological tests on white and Negro groups. This inferiority holds even when a low intellectual sampling of whites is made by selecting only those who live in the same environment, and who have had the same educational opportunities. . . .

The discrepancies between data from various investigators as to the *amount* of difference between Negroes and whites probably result from different methods of selecting whites. If we compare Negroes only to those whites who live in the same neighborhood, and who have had the same educational opportunities, our differences are smaller than those obtained by comparing samples of the entire white and Negro populations.

Some writers would account for the differences found between white and Negro by differences of educational opportunity alone. The army tests showed the northern Negro superior to the southern Negro, and this superiority is attributed to the superior educational opportunities in the North. The educational record of the Negro sample we are studying shows that more than half of the Negroes from the southern states did not go beyond the third grade, and only 7 percent finished the eighth grade, while about half of the northern Negroes finished the fifth grade, and a quarter finished the eighth grade. That the difference between the northern and southern Negro is not entirely due to schooling, but partly to intelligence, is shown by the fact that groups of southern and northern Negroes of *equal schooling* show striking differences in intelligence. (Brigham, 1923, pp. 190–192)

Brigham attributes this superior intelligence of the northern Negro to three factors, greater educational opportunity, a greater admixture of white blood, and "the operation of economic and social forces." Interestingly enough, only one of the three groups of factors is genetic. Yet a few sentences later Brigham warns,

Particularly misleading and unsound is the theory that disregards all differences found between racial groups unless the groups have had the same educational and environmental opportunities. . . .

If intelligence counts for anything in the competition among human beings, it is natural to expect that individuals of superior intelligence will adjust themselves more easily to their physical and social environment, and that they will endow

their children not only with material goods, but with the ability to adjust themselves to the same or a more complex environment. To select individuals who have
fallen behind in the struggle to adjust themselves to the civilization their race has
built as typical of that race is an error, for their position itself shows that they are,
for the most part, individuals with an inferior hereditary endowment.

In the same way, our educational institutions are themselves a part of our own
race heritage. The average Negro child can not advance through an educational
curriculum adapted to the Anglo-Saxon child in step with that child. To select
children of equal education, age for age, in the two groups, is to sample either
superior Negroes or inferior whites. (Brigham, 1923, pp. 193–194)

While following this argument of Brigham, the reader may be interested in
referring back to our earlier discussion (Chapters 2 and 6) of the Ginzberg
and Bray study on the uneducated. For Brigham, equal education in a comparison of northern and southern Negroes apparently refers to an equal
number of grades of schooling, while Ginzberg and Bray concern themselves
with the quality of the schools in the North and the South by taking into
account the monies spent for educational purposes.

Brigham's Afterthoughts.   While our main interest here is the impact of the
Army test results on racism and eugenics, it would be unfair to Brigham to
close this section without noting that he was subsequently to drastically revise
his opinions about the implications of the Army tests. This revision took the
form of an article in the *Psychological Review* of 1930 which questioned the
statistical validity of the analysis of the Army data. Basically, the question was
"Could the subtests of the Army Alpha be added together to obtain a total
score?" Brigham concluded that several statistical considerations involving the
varying amounts that subtests contributed to the total score, and the presence
of disparate group factors within the test indicated that the eight subtests of
the Army Alpha should not have been added to obtain a score, or, if
added, similar total scores should not have been considered to represent similar
performances in the tests.

If the Army Alpha test has thus been shown to be internally inconsistent to such a
degree, then it is absurd to go beyond this point and combine Alpha, Beta, the
Stanford-Binet and the individual performance tests in the so-called "combined
scale," or to regard a combined scale score derived from one test or complex of tests
as equivalent to that derived from another test or another complex of tests. As this
method was used by the writer in his earlier analysis of the army tests as applied to
samples of foreign born in the draft, that study with its entire hypothetical
superstructure of racial differences collapses completely. (Brigham, 1930, p. 164)

Again Brigham takes an entirely different view of the language factor in its
effect upon test scores than he had in the earlier study.

For purposes of comparing individuals or groups, it is apparent that tests in the
vernacular must be used only with individuals having equal opportunities to
acquire the vernacular of the test. This requirement precludes the use of such tests
in making comparative studies of individuals brought up in homes in which the

vernacular of the test is not used, or in which two vernaculars are used. The last condition is frequently violated here in studies of children born in this country whose parents speak another tongue. It is important, as the effects of bilingualism are not entirely known.

This review has summarized some of the more recent test findings which show that comparative studies of various national and racial groups may not be made with existing tests, and which show, in particular, that one of the most pretentious of these comparative racial studies—the writer's own—was without foundation. (Brigham, 1930, p. 165)

We know little of Brigham as a person. We suspect that he may have been a man of considerable size. But what interests us more is Brigham the "expert." Was he more of an expert in 1923 or in 1930? We hope the latter, but nevertheless we fear the expert of 1923 was more influential than the expert of 1930. And that is one of the problems in the relationship of the expert to social programs. No matter how much their expertise may be needed, there is no guarantee that for any given expert the degree of expertise is directly related to the degree of influence. Society needs its experts but must choose and use them with care.

THE SUCCESS OF RACISM AND EUGENICS IN THE AREA OF RESTRICTIVE IMMIGRATION

Thus the testing movement in its studies of immigrant groups and in particular through the results of the Army testing program—by charging various racial and ethnic groups with inferior intelligence and proportionately higher rates of feeblemindedness—contributed to both racist and eugenical thought and helped to cement the growing alliance between racism and eugenics. This alliance was to insure for eugenics one of its greatest successes in social action programs. This success consisted in furthering the enactment of increasingly restrictive immigration laws throughout the twenties. These laws not only strictly limited the number of immigrants but, with repeated revisions, also insured that future immigrant stock would have proportionately more Nordic blood than that coming into this country since the turn of the century. The quotas for immigrants were so set that immigrants from northern Europe were given preferential treatment over those from the South and East. The measure of this success is that it was not until the mid-sixties that revision in the law changed these quota systems to conform slightly more to rational considerations and slightly less to racial and ethnic bias.

Much of the agitation for restrictive immigration was spearheaded by the eugenicists and the racists but it is not to be imagined that their success in this instance as contrasted to the relative lack of success that the eugenicists achieved in their goals for the segregation and sterilization of the feeble-minded was simply the result of more cogent arguments or a more intensive campaign. It would seem more probable that success in the restrictive immigration campaign was due to the fact that other powerful social forces, seeking the same ends, were operative at the same time. Thus, organized American labor, which in the past had vacillated in its position on immigration, during this period of the twenties reacted primarily to the threat of competition from cheap immigrant labor. This attitude on the part of labor occurred at a time when industry, which in the past had often opposed restrictive immigration, no longer had a great need for large supplies of unskilled labor. Therefore, in this period of our history, economic forces were favorable for the enactment of restrictive immigration at the same time that heightened racist attitudes on the part of large segments of the citizenry were receptive to a campaign for such legislation. But as we shall see in the next chapter, the eugenics movement paid a high price for its alliance with racism whatever the temporary triumphs it insured.

The decline of the social indictment of the feebleminded

As we indicated earlier, one of the beneficial effects of the Army test results was that they led to the eventual recognition that there must be something wrong with the then current definition of feeblemindedness when such a definition led to the categorization of nearly 50 percent of the population as feebleminded.

It is true that, despite the 1910 endorsement of the American Association for the Study of the Feeble-Minded, not all psychologists had been willing to accept Goddard's definition of feeblemindedness, based as it was wholly on mental age. In fact, J. E. Wallin, drawing on his own wide experience in testing normal and subnormal children, had been protesting the use of such a rigid and misleading criterion since before the war.[1] Other psychologists gradually added to the protest. Nevertheless, up until the twenties it was still common practice to consider a mental age below 13 years sufficient for a diagnosis of feeblemindedness. This is brought out in Wallin's comments on the Army test results:

Fortunately the work of the division of psychology in the army which has conducted the most extensive intelligence survey ever attempted, involving the

---

[1] See our statements on page 7 concerning the pioneering role of Wallin in the fields of clinical psychology and mental subnormality.

examination of a million and three-quarters of soldiers of the selective draft, has, finally, yielded results which probably will settle definitely the controversy regarding the morons or the upper level of feeble-mindedness. This survey shows that the intelligence age of the white American soldiers, as so far reported, was 13.1 years. It has been alleged that this intelligence level may be even higher than for our adult population at large because masses of soldiers who had been rejected as mentally and physically unfit were not included in the army survey. If this is true, the prediction we made many years ago that "many millions of our citizens" would be found feeble-minded by the XII-year standard was entirely too conservative instead of too radical. The army results now justify the presumption that 50,000,000 of our white citizens only reach, or will eventually only reach, approximately the intelligence level of the "high grade morons." Forty-seven percent of the white recruits, and 89% of the colored, in the army had an intelligence level of less than XIII years. Must we believe that in California, where a feeble-minded person has been legally defined as one who "will not develop beyond the level of the average child of twelve years" (fortunately the only state in the union which has enacted such a definition), almost half the white citizens have about the intelligence level of the high grade feeble-minded?

It should be obvious that we will render the conception inane if we place the upper intelligence level of feeble-mindedness only about a fifth of a year below the average intelligence age of our white adult citizens; or, in fact, equal to or above the average intelligence age, because the XII-year standard when adopted was based on the 1908 scale and all authorities are agreed that the higher age-standards in this scale were considerably too difficult. And yet, such a conception of mental deficiency is still followed in the practical diagnosis of dependents and delinquents. (Wallin, 1920, pp. 47–48)

As Wallin had expected, the mental-age criterion as the sole criterion for a diagnosis of feeblemindedness proved untenable; and, with its gradual abandonment, it was recognized that those studies that had purported to demonstrate that feeblemindedness was the basis of crime, alcoholism, prostitution, and pauperism were clearly undercut.

The Waverly Survey

At the same time that rejection of the mental-age criterion was taking place other research was also making for a reappraisal of the mentally subnormal. One of the better known and more influential of these studies was conducted by Walter Fernald, a former ardent advocate of segregation for the feebleminded (Fernald, 1919; Davies, 1930). As a result of his survey of the community adjustments of patients discharged from the Waverly institution in Massachusetts, Fernald drastically revised his opinions on the purported dangers to society and to retardates themselves if they were not segregated.

The survey, following the account of Davies (1930), involved patients who had been discharged—the majority against the advice of the institutional authorities—between the years 1890 and 1914. Of 470 discharged males, the survey found that 28 were earning a living without supervision, 86 were working for wages while supervised by their families, 77 cases were not working for wages but were able to do some work at home, and a more severely retarded group of 59 cases were living at home with the families able to assume the burden of support and protection. Fifty-four individuals had died since discharge.

On the negative side, 68 had been readmitted to Waverly, 43 committed to other institutions, 32 had been sentenced to penal institutions, and 23 had been arrested but not sentenced.

Thirteen of the 470 males had married and there were but 12 children to these marriages. Eleven of these men were making good wages without supervision. Two of the men who had been making wages capable of supporting their homes had been sent to the reformatory for larceny.

Of the 176 discharged females, 27 were married. With one exception these women were classified as morons. Nearly all had married above the social level of their own parents. Eleven of the married women "were living useful and blameless lives," had neat and attractive homes, bore good reputations in the community, went to church, and apparently were making good in every way." These 11 women had 34 children, all apparently normal. Eight of these women had been discharged against the advice of the institution, and only upon court order.

The remaining 16 married women had records of problem behavior after discharge and their marriages turned out poorly. Four developed syphilis, the only recorded instances of venereal disease among all 176 women. To these 16 women, 24 children were born.

In the total group of 176, there were 11 unmarried mothers who had given birth to 13 illegitimate children. Twenty-one additional women were recommitted to Waverly or other institutions because of sexual behavior problems.

From the economic point of view, one could count the 11 successful wives, 8 additional unmarried women who were self-supporting and self-supervised, and 32 women working capably at home under supervision. Thus 30 percent of the whole group could be considered economic assets at least to the extent of earning their own keep.

While there were a considerable number of social failures in these discharged patients, the startling thing from the point of view of Dr. Fernald and his contemporaries were the number of successes. In fact, Dr. Fernald confessed that the results were at such variance with the then currently accepted theories of dealing with mental deficiency that he hesitated to publish the results for some two years.

How much this research had changed the view of mental deficiency for Dr. Fernald and his contemporaries may be seen by contrasting our earlier quotations from Fernald on the "menace of the feebleminded" with his comments on the Waverly study as they appeared in *Mental Hygiene* in 1919:

At Waverly, a careful study of the discharges for twenty-five years showed that a very small proportion of the discharged male morons had committed crimes, or had married, or had become parents, or had failed to support themselves, or had been bad citizens.

It has been fairly well demonstrated that the average male moron, without naturally vicious tendencies, who has been properly trained in habits of obedience and industry, and who is protected from temptation and evil associations during his childhood, can be safely returned to the community when he has passed early adolescence, if his family are able to look after him and give him proper supervision. A very much larger proportion of these trained male defectives would be suitable for community life if the above-described extra-institutional control and supervision could be provided. . . .

The after-care studies of the female morons who have received training in the institutions were not so favorable, but many of these, too, led moral and harmless and useful lives after their return to the community. The study of discharged female cases at Waverly showed a surprisingly small number who became mothers or who married. While it is true that defectives with undesirable habits and tendencies are not easily controlled, it is equally true that defectives who are obedient and moral and industrious are apt to continue these traits permanently. (Fernald, 1919, pp. 571–572)

Thus during the twenties the eugenics movement began to lose some of the steam of its campaign against the feebleminded. Other factors also helped to discredit this campaign. For example, as the science of genetics grew in scope and precision the absurdities of the early applications of Mendelian genetics to the problem of feeblemindedness became more and more apparent. Scientists such as H. S. Jennings (1925) attacked those assumptions relating to heredity that underlay the more extreme eugenical thought. The interaction of heredity and environment was emphasized. And the reckless application of the unit character interpretations to complex behaviors was challenged.

Chesterton's Attack on Eugenics

Popular writers reaching wide audiences also challenged not only the scientific but the moral basis of the eugenics movement. Thus G. K. Chesterton published in 1922 a volume entitled *Eugenics and Other Evils*. E. M. East the geneticist—in one of his eugenic tracts—summarily dismissed Chesterton as a "medieval mind." What little we know of the medieval mind leads us to conclude that it was a complex one and we suppose that there may have been more than one way in which East's epithet may have been justified. But certainly Chesterton shows a similarity to the medieval mind in that he was a man whose value system was consciously and explicitly possessed and who felt that good and evil were real things that could be determined by absolute standards. Passages in his work blaze with the indignation of a man certain of his principles and convinced of their importance. In our age, when even churchmen take a relativistic view of morals and preach situational ethics, the mind and the style of Chesterton is not without a certain charm and refreshment. Thus in commenting on eugenical interpretations of the incest taboos:

It is only right to say here, though the matter should only be touched on, that many Eugenists would . . . claim that there was a consciously Eugenic reason for the horror of those unions which begin with the celebrated denial to man of the privilege of marrying his grandmother. Dr. S. R. Steinmetz, with that creepy simplicity of mind with which Eugenists chill the blood, remarks that "we do not yet know quite certainly" what were "the motives for the horror of" that horrible thing which is the agony of Œdipus. With entirely amiable intention, I ask Dr. S. R. Steinmetz to speak for himself. I know the motives for regarding a mother or sister as separate from other women; nor have I reached them by any curious researches. I found them where I found an analogous aversion to eating a baby for breakfast. I found them in a rooted detestation in the human soul to liking a thing in one way, when you already like it in another quite incompatible way. Now it is perfectly true that this aversion may have acted eugenically; and so had a certain ultimate confirmation and basis in the laws of procreation. But there really cannot be any Eugenist quite so dull as not to see that this is not a defence of Eugenics but a direct denial of Eugenics. If something which has been discovered at last by the lamp of learning is something which has been acted on from the first by the light of nature, this (so far as it goes) is plainly not an argument for pestering people, but an argument for letting them alone. If men did not marry their grandmothers when it was, for all they knew, a most hygienic habit; if we know now that they instinctly avoided scientific peril; that, so far as it goes, is a point in favour of letting people marry anyone they like. It is simply the statement that sexual selection, or what Christians call falling in love, is a part of man which in the rough and in the long run can be trusted. And that is the destruction of the whole of this science at a blow. (Chesterton, 1922, pp. 8–9)

Though Chesterton's *Eugenics and Other Evils* is written with a bit too much feeling and indignation for sustained cogency of argument, he nevertheless repeatedly touches the heart of the matter. In a eugenics program, what shall be the criteria for those classes of men whose procreation shall be restricted or encouraged, and who among us shall set the criteria?

In discussing legislative provision for the segregation of the feebleminded, he commented:

The Eugenic State has begun. The first of the Eugenic Laws has already been adopted by the Government of this country; and passed with the applause of both parties through the dominant House of Parliament. This first Eugenic Law clears the ground and may be said to proclaim negative Eugenics; but it cannot be defended, and nobody has attempted to defend it, except on the Eugenic theory. I will call it the Feeble-Minded Bill, both for brevity and because the description is strictly accurate. It is, quite simply and literally, a Bill for incarcerating as madmen those whom no doctor will consent to call mad. It is enough if some doctor or other may happen to call them weak-minded. Since there is scarcely any human being to whom this term has not been conversationally applied by his own friends and relatives on some occasion or other (unless his friends and relatives have been lamentably lacking in spirit), it can be clearly seen that this law, like the early Christian Church (to which, however, it presents points of dissimilarity), is a net drawing in of all kinds. It must not be supposed that we have a stricter definition incorporated in the Bill. Indeed, the first definition of "feeble-minded" in the Bill was much looser and vaguer than the phrase "feeble-minded" itself. It is a piece of yawning idiocy about "persons who though capable of earning their living under favourable circumstances" (as if anyone could earn his living if circumstances were directly unfavourable to his doing so), are nevertheless "incapable of managing their affairs with proper prudence"; which is exactly what all the world and his wife are saying about their neighbours all over this planet. But as an incapacity for any kind of thought is now regarded as statesmanship, there is nothing so very novel about such slovenly drafting. What is novel and what is vital is this: that the *defence* of this crazy Coercion Act is a Eugenic defence. It is not only openly said, it is eagerly urged, that the aim of the measure is to prevent any person whom these propagandists do not happen to think intelligent from having any wife or children. Every tramp who is sulky, every labourer who is shy, every rustic who is eccentric, can quite easily be brought under such conditions as were designed for homicidal maniacs. (Chesterton, 1922, pp. 19–21)

In commenting on the work of an "expert" on heredity:

It is his business to study human health and sickness as a whole, in a spirit of more or less enlightened guess work; and it is perfectly natural that he should allow for heredity here, there, and everywhere, as a man climbing a mountain or sailing a boat will allow for weather without even explaining it to himself. An utterly different attitude is incumbent on any conscientious man writing about what laws should be enforced or about how commonwealths should be governed. And when we consider how plain a fact is murder, and yet how hesitant and even hazy we all grow about the guilt of a murderer, when we consider how simple an act is stealing, and yet how hard it is to convict and punish those rich commercial pirates who steal the most, when we consider how cruel and clumsy the law can be even about things as old and plain as the Ten Commandments—I simply cannot conceive any responsible person proposing to legislate on our broken knowledge and bottomless ignorance of heredity. (Chesterton, 1922, pp. 68–69)

Chesterton was suspicious of the expert's claim that he could determine who was fit to reproduce and who was not:

There is no reason to suppose that Dr. Karl Pearson is any better judge of a bridegroom than the bridegroom is of a bride. (Chesterton, 1922, p. 40)

And he clearly saw the abuse to which legislated procreation was liable in the hands of ordinary men—expert or not.

. . . while we can always get men intelligent enough to know more than the rest of us about this or that accident or pain or pest, we cannot count on the appearance of great cosmic philosophers; and only such men can be even supposed to know more than we do about normal conduct and common sanity. Every sort of man, in short, would shirk such a responsibility, except the worst sort of man, who would accept it. . . . It should be noted here, of course, that an individual biologist may quite honestly believe that he has found a fixed principle with the help of Weissmann or Mendel. But we are not discussing whether he knows enough to be justified in thinking (as is somewhat the habit of the anthropoid *Homo*) that he is right. We are discussing whether *we* know enough, as responsible citizens, to put such powers into the hands of men who may be deceived or who may be deceivers. I conclude that we do not. (Chesterton, 1922, pp.84–85)

ECONOMIC AND POLITICAL FACTORS

In addition to these direct attacks on eugenic thought, the 1930s saw the development of economic and political factors that resulted in social attitudes directly unfavorable to the eugenics movement.

We have already called attention to the wide-ranging effects of the great depression of the 1930s upon American life. We would add here its effect upon those social attitudes related to Social Darwinism which we indicated had been absorbed into the eugenics movement. The emphasis on individualism, the assumption that social and economic failure was the result of possessing inferior traits of intellect and personality, the laissez-faire attitude toward the problems of the depressed and dependent classes. To an America whose faith in its economic and social system had been shaken to the roots it was no longer possible to complacently assume that those at the bottom of the economic heap were there because they merited no better. Those who had not suddenly seen their life savings, business, or job wiped out, had certainly seen such among friends and relatives. Poverty touched oneself, and those one esteemed and loved. When poverty was remote, its victims could well be assumed to merit no better. But when oneself and one's loved ones were impoverished it was obviously more rational to recognize that it was the system that was at fault and not the individual. Thus the great depression led to an emphasis on environmental and social factors as the root of social ills, and a de-emphasis on hereditarily inferior strains of the human race.

On the international scene, the rise of the Nazi party to power in Germany; the promulgation of the so-called eugenic laws of 1933; and the undertaking of the campaign of extermination against the insane, the mental and physically defective, and the so-called inferior races, demonstrated that Chesterton's worse fears were anything but overdrawn and caused a general revulsion against the kind of eugenics that had been promulgated in America since the turn of the century.

THE NEW LOOK IN EUGENICS

At the same time that the eugenics movement was being set back by external events, efforts were being made for internal reform. The old leadership passed with age, retirement, and death; and Frederick Osborn, who had retired from a highly successful business career at the age of 40, began to assume leadership of the American eugenics movement. Under the guidance of the anthropologists Clark Wissler and Harry L. Shapiro of the staff of the American Museum of Natural History he undertook a program of studies in genetics, psychology, and sociology. Soon he and those associated with him were publishing criticisms of the research on intellectual differences between races, emphasizing socioeconomic and cultural factors that would affect test performance of different groups (Haller, 1963).

As Osborn moved toward leadership in the American Eugenics Society he became instrumental in dissociating the American eugenics movement from the racism that had characterized it in its earlier period. He entered government service in 1940 and the American Eugenics Society became inactive for a number of years. In 1950, Osborn reactivated the Society, which then undertook the publication of the *Eugenics Quarterly*, a scholarly journal "devoted to furthering the discussion, advancement, and dissemination of knowledge concerning the biological and sociocultural forces which affect the structure and composition of human populations." In striking contrast to the publications associated with the eugenics organizations of an earlier day, this journal not infrequently carries articles critically attacking research purported to demonstrate the intellectual inferiority of minority groups.

When issues of the *Eugenics Quarterly* are compared with the older publications of the Eugenics Record Office it readily becomes apparent that the philosophy of the American eugenics movement has a new look. Comparison of Osborn's *Preface to Eugenics* (1951) with the eugenic writings of E. M. East or Madison Grant will emphasize the point. In contrast to the antidemocratic prejudices and racism of those earlier eugenicists, Osborn deplores racism and argues that a safe and effective eugenics program could only develop within a democratic framework. His social action programs would emphasize social and economic reforms designed to lift the burden of poverty from the deprived classes by providing public programs of welfare, education, and recreation in order to relieve parents from many of the direct economic burdens of child rearing.

Eugenics and democracy are significantly interrelated. The eugenics ideal calls for a society so organized that eugenic selection will take place as a natural and largely unconscious process; one in which those persons who make the most effective response to their environment will, in the normal course, have more children than will those who respond less effectively. That kind of eugenics would be the only kind possible in a democracy where, except in the case of extreme defect, no one would be given or would assume any right to decide who should or who should not have children. The right to have or not to have children would be safeguarded in a democracy along with the right to free speech and to freedom of worship. This is a necessary protection to eugenics, for man himself is not fitted to judge right and wrong so clearly that broad power over survival would be safe in any hands except those of the parents who are directly concerned. Only in a dictatorship would such power be taken from the mass of the parents and put under arbitrary control. A system of arbitrary control would not be eugenics, but would be simply the application of genetic science to the breeding of specific kinds of men and women. This is something which could easily be done. It would be as dangerous as putting any other tools of modern science in the hands of arbitrary power.

Democracy is therefore the necessary safeguard of eugenics. But on the other hand, it is doubtful whether democracy can long continue in any society except one so set up that the more competent people in every social and occupational group are favored for survival. (Osborn, 1951, pp. 324–325)

In comparison to some of the eugenical proposals of the past, Osborn's would certainly seem to be much less obviously objectionable. In fact it is not without a certain appeal in its utopian idealism, and we imagine a Chesterton might be mollified by such admissions as that "man himself is not fitted to judge right and wrong so clearly that broad power over survival would be safe in any hands except those of the parents who are directly concerned." But what would he make of that ideal juxtaposed in the same passage with, "except in the case of extreme defect, no one would be given or would assume any right to decide who should or who should not have children?" Is this perhaps an inconsistency of thought processes? We will consider the case of "extreme defect" in the next chapter but note here that in spite of all its appeal Osborn's new society might be objected to by a Chesterton for its quality of "Prussian scientism" and "creeping socialism."

We, perhaps unwisely, lack Chesterton's concern for "creeping socialism"; for we would be willing to buy some of Osborn's social reforms outright. But we do share Chesterton's concern for "Prussian scientism," at least insofar as we understand his use of that term to encompass the conduct of state affairs and the development of social action programs on the partial and shifting insights of "scientific knowledge." We must move by the best light we have but as Matthew Arnold reminded us we must take care that our best light be not darkness. A handful of studies, or a pocketful of correlations, are neither light nor science when we deal with the complexities of a human culture.

Osborn's argument for a eugenical program with concomitant social reforms is based on the assumption that "all available evidence indicates that the most intelligent parents bear fewer than the average number of children." Because these parents, under conditions of modern civilization, have no great comparative advantage in bringing their children to maturity, there is little chance for natural selection to work. "But if natural selection ceases to work or goes into reverse, our civilization is not likely to make much further advance" (Osborn, 1951, p. xi).

Yet there are experts on evolution, such as Huxley (1951, 1960) who would question whether man's future evolution in a strictly biological sense is not likely to be negligible in comparison to the potential of his cultural evolution. There are even those scientists favorably disposed to eugenics such as Reed and Reed (1965) or Penrose (1950, 1962) whose analysis of the differential birth rate for families of high and low intelligence lead them to conclude that the brighter half of the human race is not reproducing at a slower rate than the duller half and possibly may even be reproducing at a faster rate. If these latter scientists are right, should we give up the advocacy of Osborn's social reforms, since their desirability would no longer be derived from our scientific analysis of natural selection operating in modern civilization?

We would not belittle the motivation of men like Osborn that makes them seek in science the knowledge that will enable us to solve our social problems. In that motivation and in that search is the hope of the future. But the zeal for the application of scientific knowledge to social problems is often in need of curbing if for no other reason than that the "scientific knowledge" of one expert is apt to be wild speculation in the eyes of another, and in the complex areas of the nature of man and society the "scientific knowledge" of today is apt to be myth of tomorrow.

The problem, of course, and the reason we use quotation marks, is the definition of "scientific knowledge" as distinct from scientific methodology. In retrospect the "scientific knowledge" on which the early eugenicists based themselves was just so much hogwash. What is the assurance that Osborn is basing himself on a better brand of "scientific knowledge?" The problem—a knotty one—is again one of criterion. Our limited capacity for abstraction makes us hesitate to define "scientific knowledge," but we suspect that before the term is meaningfully used in any area some "critical mass" of integrated fact and theory must be reached. It would appear far from likely that such a "critical mass" exists in our knowledge of race, class, ethnic, or social group differences in hereditary intellectual and personality traits. That such differences may exist, the future may demonstrate. Whether such differences— when and if demonstrated—should result in the designation of more or less valuable kinds of men is quite another order of question. That is a question of values to which we shall return.

A Modern Family Study of Mental Subnormality

In our consideration of eugenics we tend to drift to wider social issues than those that are encompassed solely by considerations relating to mental subnormality. This is not surprising in view of the interrelatedness of all social problems. But to bring our consideration of eugenics back more in focus on mental retardation we would like to treat in some detail one of the more ambitious studies on hereditary factors in mental retardation to appear in recent years. It is a longitudinal study whose historical roots are in the eugenical past and it leads its authors to eugenical recommendations for the future.

Initial Phase: 1911–1918. This family study of mental retardation reported by Reed and Reed (1965) began in 1911 as a cooperative project of the Eugenics Record Office and the State School and Colony at Faribault, Minnesota. The study in its initial phase was under the direction of A. C. Rogers, superintendent of the state institution. During that period, Rogers also functioned as editor of the *Journal of Psycho-asthenics* and was a member of the committee on the feebleminded of the American Breeders Association.

With the financial support of the Eugenics Record Office and the Minnesota legislature two field workers undertook collection of data on the inmates of the state institution. In all, during the period from 1911 to 1918, 549 families of inmates at the institution were investigated. All material available in the institutional records of the patients was collected. In addition, the field workers visited the patients' homes and interviewed as many relatives as possible in order to assess the mental, social, and economic status of the family. Interviews of teachers, physicians, employers, and neighbors were also included in the data collection. Test data were also available, since by 1911 intelligence tests were administered routinely to applicants to the institution and at times to their parents and siblings as well.

In the opinion of the Reeds, the evaluations of the field workers were accurately and carefully done. A few mistakes were made in the case of untested young persons whom they classified as retardates but who actually were "underachieving juvenile delinquent types who later became successful in life." The most extreme case, according to the Reeds, was that of a youngster who later became a U.S. Congressman—certainly a measure of success, but a cynical citizen might wonder if he really had been misclassified.

This initial phase of the study came to an end because of the death of Mr. Rogers, a lack of funds, and loss of personnel.

The Reeds' Study: 1949–1961. In 1949, the study was reopened and criteria set up to determine which of the original families would be followed. The first of these criteria was that all the original patients studied—i.e., the probands or index cases—were to have IQ scores of 69 or below. Secondly, they must have been resident in the institution between 1911 and 1918, and thirdly, the probands selected must have had no history of epilepsy prior to institutionalization. With these criteria, there remained 289 families to consider. By mail contact of relatives of the probands up-to-date information was gathered on the families. In addition, the cooperation of state and county agencies and the schools provided additional information on the families as well as an independent check of information obtained from the relatives. IQ scores were usually made available by the schools, and the records of the state psychological testing bureau were also accessible.

All relatives with IQs equal to or less than 69 were considered retarded. For persons with no available IQ scores, the criteria for retardation included many grade failures in school, leaving school at the sixth or seventh grade at ages 15 or 16 years, or the expressed opinion of the teacher that the individual was retarded. The authors grant that an occasional underachiever might be erroneously classified by these latter criteria.

Pedigree charts were drawn up for each proband and are presented in the published report. The pedigree charts represent 82,217 individuals and comprised all the known descendants of the grandparents of the 289 probands. Three and a half percent of these individuals—including miscarriages and abortions—did not survive beyond 2 years of age. The remaining 79,376 individuals included 2,156 retardates. This 2.7 percent of retardation is not very different from what one would expect in any large random sample of the population and the Reeds point out that the biased selection of 289 retardates (the probands) is not sufficient to raise the proportion of retarded very much. As of 1961, 202 of the original 289 probands were deceased, of the remainder, 36 were still institutionalized.

CLASSIFICATION OF THE PROBANDS.   The probands were divided into four groups. The *first group* consisted of 84 cases where in the opinion of the authors genetic factors were of primary importance. It included well-defined anomalies and syndromes such as Down's syndrome (mongolism) and phenylketonuria. Although the former disorder is rarely hereditary it is based on a genetic imbalance and, hence, here classified. Presence of consanguinity in the parents was also taken as evidence of a genetically based disorder. A third alternative criterion for this group was the presence of one or more siblings or half-siblings with apparently identical types of low-grade mental retardation.

The *second group,* of 55 probands, consisted of those in which genetic factors were probably of primary importance. Three or more generations of mental retardation without a break was considered sufficient evidence for the assumption of the primary importance of genetic factors. In such families, the authors assume that the primary factor is assortative mating at the lower end of the curve of normal intelligence, i.e., marriages are not random with respect to intelligence but the less intelligent tend to marry among the less intelligent. They point out that in such families even though both parents are retarded there can be normal or intellectually superior children. Genetic segregation, in the view of the Reeds, would explain the extreme intelligence variation found in some of these sibships much better than assumed trivial differences in the environment.

This is an important group from the point of view of the development of the Reeds' argument. Therefore it is probably worthwhile pointing out that not all authorities in the field would accept the Reeds' assumptions. For example, we could imagine that Knobloch and Pasamanick would argue that in lower socioeconomic families reproductive risks leading to various degrees of minor brain damage are high. In the lower socioeconomic levels, this higher risk would exist across generations and would account for the sporadic appearance in each generation of some retarded individuals who are neurologically impaired even though the impairment is not gross enough to be picked up by neurological examinations. We shall consider this argument of Knobloch and Pasamanick in a later chapter but refer to it here to indicate alternative arguments to the Reeds'. Another alternative might consist in the argument that a family line classified in this "probably genetic" category might not be genetically different from a family of average, normal intelligence which may—as is often the case—show marked variability in intelligence even though no member is mentally retarded. We could imagine such a genetic line of average intelligence being placed not in an average environment but in a substandard environment capable of shifting the mean IQ some 10 or 15 points below 100. With the genetic variation occurring around a mean of 90 or 85 we could expect some of the members of this family line to fall in the mentally retarded group. Then consider a large number of families with average genetic endowment living within this substandard environment, would we not expect—purely on the basis of chance—to find a number of the families who show several consecutive generations in which one or more individuals meet the Reeds' criterion for retardation of an IQ below 69? This argument is similar to the one we used in dealing with Galton's families of hereditary ability. Hereditary ability may be evenly distributed in all family lines but if only some family lines are in exceptionally favorable circumstances for the development and display of that ability then men of ability will occur more frequently in those family lines than they do in the population at large. We do not say that this argument disproves hereditary mental retardation or hereditary ability within family lines; we do say it indicates a factor that must be taken into account in any discussion of familial intellectual traits.

The *third group* in the Reeds' study consists of 27 probands where environmental factors are assumed to be of primary importance. This group included patients whose retardation was the assumed sequelae of infectious disease of the child or the mother during pregnancy, birth injury, or postnatal traumatic injury.

The *fourth group* of 129 probands consisted of those who did not meet the criteria for classification in one of the other groups and for whom it was therefore unknown whether genetic or environmental factors were of primary importance.

Retardation Among the Relatives of the Probands. As we indicated earlier, of the total 79,376 individuals related to the probands there were 2,156 or 2.7 percent retarded individuals. However, the important consideration is not the overall rate of retardation but the way in which the retardation rate varies with the degree of kinship to the probands and whether or not the rate varies for different kinds of probands. These variations are most succinctly revealed in Table 17.1.

In the table, the first degree of kinship includes parents, siblings, and children of the probands. The second degree includes grandparents, uncles and aunts, half-siblings, nephews and nieces, and grandchildren. The third degree includes half-uncles and -aunts, half-nephews and -nieces, great nephews and nieces, and first cousins.

It is obvious from the table, which deals only with relatives within the third degree of relationship, and from the retardation rate of 2.7 percent for the total sample of all the relatives of the probands, that the percentage of retardation increases with nearness in kinship to the probands. The percentage of

TABLE 17.1 THE PERCENTAGES OF RETARDATION IN THE RELATIVES OF THE PROBANDS ACCORDING TO DEGREE OF RELATIONSHIP AND CATEGORY OF CLASSIFICATION[2]

Category	First Degree	Second Degree	Third Degree	Average Percentage Retarded
Primarily genetic	33.6	9.2	3.7	8.8 (452 of 5,149)
Probably genetic	50.7	16.8	5.3	13.2 (496 of 3,759)
Environmental	21.4	2.0	1.1	3.3 (60 of 1,831)
Unknown	15.6	2.6	2.1	3.7 (275 of 7,327)
All categories Percentages	28.0	7.1	3.1	7.1
Totals	(532 of 1,897)	(434 of 6,070)	(317 of 10,099)	(1,283 of 18,066)

retardation in the third degree of kinship (3.1 percent) is not particularly different from that of 2.7 percent for the overall sample. But there is a sharp jump to 7.1 percent at the second degree of kinship and an even sharper jump to 28 percent retardation at the first degree of kinship. The authors take note of the fact that there is some bias in sampling in that the probands were institutionalized and presumably the percentage of retardation in the first degree of kinship is somewhat inflated. A retarded child with parents or grandparents who are retarded might more readily end up in an institution due to a lack of competent adults to meet the child's needs outside of the institution. A special point is made of this bias in considering the 21.4 percent of the environmentally retarded group with a first degree relationship. For this group, whose retardation is due to infection, injury, etc., we would not ordinarily expect as high incidence of retardation among close relatives as we would for genetically determined forms of retardation. That there is some biasing factor in this group is further suggested by the fact that when we get to the second degree of relationship there is a sudden sharp drop off in the retardation rate, whereas in the case of genetically determined retardation we would not expect and do not obtain such a sharp decrease.

In contrast to the environmental group, the primarily genetic group still shows an elevated retardation percentage in both the second and third degree

[2] Reprinted by permission from E. W. Reed and S. C. Reed, *Mental Retardation*. Philadelphia: Saunders, 1965, p. 31.

of kinship. This would be expected for both dominant and recessively inherited traits and for that form of mongolism which is hereditarily transmitted; presumably these types of retardation constitute part of the primarily genetic group. That the primarily genetic group does not have higher frequencies of retardation among relatives is probably due to the fact that the authors included in it a number of mongol children whose disorder was not of the hereditarily transmissable type.

As regards the frequencies for the probably genetic category, we will let the authors speak for themselves:

The probably genetic category shows the highest frequencies of mental retardation in all degrees of relationship. This is due in part to the definition of the group: that of three consecutive generations of mental retardation. These values of 50.7 percent retardation for all first degree relatives, and 16.8 percent and 5.3 percent for the second and third degree relatives indicate large genetic and environmental influences on the people involved. Attempts to identify specific variables of any kind were unsuccessful. However, these "loaded" families have two characteristics of interest: they show assortative mating to a very high degree and the retarded are predominantly of the 50 to 69 IQ level. It is clear from the structure of the normal curve of intelligence that the majority of the higher grade retardates must result from the interaction of the many genetic and environmental factors which operate at the left end of the normal curve of intelligence. The result of each gene and each environmental factor is assumed to be so small that individual identification is impossible. This situation is the same as that for the polygenic traits of height or size in man and the laboratory animals. (Reed and Reed[3])

The Eugenic Implications of the Reeds' Study

The authors draw a number of implications from their study but we shall concern ourselves here with only those that are directly related to eugenic considerations and their advocacy of voluntary sterilization as a solution to the problem of mental retardation. The Reeds are apparently convinced that their study provides strong argument for the assumption that, with the exception of certain environmental events of a traumatic or infectious nature directly affecting the neurological substratum of intellectual functioning, mental retardation is basically genetically determined. This is obviously so in the case of those identifiable genetic defects such as phenylketonuria. Where one may disagree with the Reeds is in the area of that large group of familial defectives or the also large group of sporadic defectives where single gene or chromosomal defects or traumatic events are not identified. When we discussed the Reeds' criteria for the probably genetic group we tried to indicate some of the reasoning that might lead to a conclusion on etiology different from that offered by the Reeds. It may be objected that we haven't done full justice to the Reeds' argument, and that may be so, but we are only interested in

---

[3] *Op. cit.*, p. 36.

indicating that alternative arguments are possible. It is even possible that the Reeds are not fully convinced by their own argument of genetic determination, for in their advocacy of sterilization they take a rather interesting position which we would like to document with their own words:

There has been a myth in circulation during the last few decades that sterilization would not be immediately efficient in reducing the frequency of a trait because if the trait depended upon a recessive there would be so many more carriers of the trait than affected persons, that progress would be imperceptible. This might be true for very rare recessives but we are not concerned with such usually sterile anomalies. We are concerned with a polygenic trait in which assortative mating is high and the trait is transmissible and frequent. With such a trait, even if it has no genetic basis, sterilization will have an important effect which will be greatest in the first generation.

Few people have emphasized that where the transmission of a trait is frequently from parent to offspring, sterilization will be effective and it is irrelevant whether the basis for the trait is genetic or environmental. (Reed and Reed[4])

We feel certain that there are those, including ourselves, who would take the position that the means used in the solution of a problem are not irrelevant to the nature of the problem. We might feel that a biological solution is appropriate to a biological problem but not necessarily to an environmental problem. Some of us might even react as Chesterton and regard the Reeds' line of argument as an example of "that creepy simplicity of mind with which the Eugenists chill the blood." For if such reasoning is acceptable in regard to the problem of mental retardation is it not applicable in the area of other social problems? For example, since Dugdale's study of the New York State prisons, and even earlier, familial tendencies in crime have been noted. One might feel that socioeconomic factors and personality factors not genetically based are involved, but if we follow the Reed model this would be irrelevant. The familial "transmission" of a behavioral trait whether it is genetic or environmental would be solved equally well with sterilization. At the risk of adopting that favorite technique of the sophomoric mind—the reductio ad absurdum—we might point out that this solution could even handle the "social problem" of the political opposition for we as others have been forcibly struck by the familial "transmission" of adherence to the Republican and Democratic parties.

To be sure, the Reeds propose that their sterilization program would be one of voluntary sterilization. But we tend to cynicism and we mistrust the label "voluntary" as we mistrust other labels. We remember that in 1911 Havelock Ellis also spoke of a solution to the problem of hereditary pauperism by sterilization. The reader may recall that "voluntary" in that instance was spelled out to mean the withholding of poor relief until the pauper volunteered to be sterilized. Havelock Ellis in his published works, we must admit, appears reasonable and humane—and of the height of his intellect we have no

---

[4] *Op. cit.*, p. 77.

doubt—but we fear we disagree with him on the definition of "voluntary." The Reeds, for their part, have not spelled out what they mean by voluntary. Obviously it could not be anything as simpleminded as saying to an individual, "Now see here, you have tested out with an IQ of 69 on the Stanford-Binet. We feel that in your best interest and in the best interest of society you ought to submit to sterilization." Such an approach is very likely to receive a flat rejection. The Reeds, however, do appear to hold up Kemp's report on the Danish experiments in this area as a model.

Sterilization in Denmark is on a voluntary basis and the best interests of the retarded persons are scrupulously looked after. There is no program in the formal sense, but the whole population is educated regarding the usefulness of the operation for the retarded, so no major difficulties develop. The climate of opinion in the United States should change gradually toward a greater realization of the advantages of voluntary sterilization for the retarded who remain in the community . . . if the number of retarded in the United States could be reduced by 50 percent each generation by any humane means, the advantages of such methods are clear. This could be achieved with the aid of voluntary sterilization.

When voluntary sterilization for the retarded becomes a part of the culture of the United States, we should expect a decrease of about 50% per generation in the number of retarded persons, as a result of all methods combined to reduce retardation. (Reed and Reed[5])

This is certainly a beguiling argument. The prospect of a 50 percent reduction in the number of retarded persons is very impressive. But we do think if "voluntary sterilization" is to be added to other methods for reducing mental retardation in order to achieve that 50 percent rate, we ought to be told how much of this contribution will result from "voluntary sterilization." As we understand the Reeds' position, they would expect no gain from the sterilization of the mentally retarded who are homozygotic for rare recessive genes since these individuals are usually too severely afflicted for reproduction. Those retarded on the basis of traumatic injury, infection, etc. will not pass on their retardation in any hereditary fashion and hence there is little to be gained from their sterilization. And, with rare exceptions, chromosomal errors such as mongolism will not be hereditarily transmitted. There remains then that group, undoubtedly very large, where we—if not the Reeds—cannot be sure whether we are dealing with polygenic inheritance, or environment, or an interaction of the two.

Let us assume that the Reeds are right and that the cause of retardation in this latter group is polygenic inheritance resulting from assortative mating at the lower end of the normal distribution of intelligence. Is "voluntary sterilization" so simple a solution, in this case? What shall be the selection procedure? Do we recommend that a person with an IQ of 69 volunteer for sterilization but not a person with an IQ of 70 or 75? Having tested hundreds of retardates, the present authors would be at a complete loss to say what is

---

[5] *Op. cit.,* pp. 77–78.

the psychological difference between a 69, a 70, or a 75 IQ score for any given individual. With only that kind of information as a guide we would be even at a loss as to whether to recommend a special class placement or not. In fact, on occasion we have obtained lower IQs and recommended with successful outcome placement in a regular class. To decide whether or not a 75 IQ represents a better set of genes than a 69 IQ or even a better capacity for parenthood is far beyond our technical skill. We would tend to agree with Chesterton that the decision calls for a "cosmic philosopher."

The problem of selection of "volunteers" is not in our opinion a simple one. It is possible, of course, to disregard errors of commission and care only that there are no errors of omission. In that case the selection criterion—whether it be IQ or social competence—can be set as arbitrarily and as high as one dares or as high as the "educated public opinion" will allow. Which, obviously, will be the temptation because it is grossly inefficient when dealing with a "polygenic trait with assortative mating" to cull out only the least desirable—i.e., the most retarded—for sterilization. To sterilize the 69 IQ child and to permit his two 75 IQ parents to go on breeding would be an obvious absurdity. Would we not be tempted into educating them into "volunteering" for sterilization?

Now if the Reeds are wrong, and the retardation of this group is not primarily on a genetic basis, is it ethically defensible to educate the public into accepting the expediency of sterilization on the assumption it would solve the problem anyway? We would be deeply concerned about a citizenry which would allow itself to be so educated and we are concerned that a scientist should so advise. If the problem of retardation in this group is in part or in whole socioeconomically and culturally based, is it not the best part of science and citizenship to point that out? For if the basic problem is cultural, in whole or in part, then it is a symptom of illness within our society and it is likely to be far more important to diagnose that illness correctly and to seek proper remedy than to seek the temporary alleviation of secondary symptoms by measures of expediency.

To sum up, if the Reeds' interpretation of the polygenetic basis for the familial forms of retardation is correct, we can see the logic of a program of sterilization, although we have considerable concern that such a solution may carry with it temptations for abuse which should cause all thoughtful men to pause. If they are wrong, and polygenic factors are not the major or sole cause of familial retardation, then their advocacy of sterilization as a solution to the problem is to prostitute both science and citizenship to expediency.

The concern of the Reeds for posterity is commendable but Chesterton's question demands thoughtful response:

What can we do for posterity, except deal fairly with our contemporaries? (Chesterton, 1922, p. 82)

Phenylketonuria (PKU): biological, psychological, and social aspects

THE BEGINNINGS OF HUMAN GENETICS

While the Davenports and the Goddards were glibly misapplying Mendelian genetics to the area of mental retardation and advocating drastic social programs—with a supposed scientific basis—sounder applications of the new genetic knowledge were being undramatically advanced. By 1902, Garrod following up a suggestion of Bateson was able to demonstrate that alkaptonuria —a congenital metabolic disorder characterized by darkening of the patient's urine on exposure to air[1]—fulfilled a major criterion for the establishment of hereditary transmission by a rare recessive gene. This criterion is that the proportion of first-cousin marriages among the parents of the afflicted individuals should be in significant excess over the proportion of cousin marriages in the population at large. This increased likelihood of the homozygotic appearance of a rare recessive gene in the offspring of a marriage of cousins

---

[1] The darkening of the urine is due to the presence of homogentisic acid, a metabolite of tyrosine, which in its normal metabolic pathway would have undergone further change rather than excretion in the urine. The disorder involves no health problem in early life but results in a form of arthritis in later years (Knox, 1958).

follows from the fact that cousins have a greater likelihood of having identical genes at a given locus than do two unrelated individuals.

Out of the 18 families of alkaptonurics reported by Garrod, in which neither parent showed the anomaly, 12 of the marriages were between first cousins, thus giving a cousin-marriage rate of 60 percent. This was contrasted with data on cousin marriages for the English population as a whole which indicated that such marriages were not in excess of 3 percent of all marriages (Garrod, 1902).

In his Croonian lectures of 1908, delivered before the Royal Academy of Medicine, Garrod further considered the hereditary aspects of alkaptonuria and three additional disorders, pentosuria, cystinuria, and albinism. The latter two disorders had been considered briefly in the earlier report and all four were now referred to as "inborn errors of metabolism." In these lectures, the germinal idea of the "one gene, one enzyme" hypothesis was sown in that Garrod assumed that a normal enzyme responsible for the conversion of homogentisic acid was not present in alkaptonuria and that the presence or absence of this enzyme was genetically controlled.

In the first of these lectures, Garrod pointed out the striking similarity in the modes of incidence of alkaptonuria and albinism and made an argument for their hereditary transmission on a recessive Mendelian basis.

Both are apt to occur in several brothers and sisters of a family whose parents do not exhibit the anomaly and direct transmission of either from parent to child is very rare. It has been repeatedly stated that a considerable proportion of human albinos are the offspring of consanguineous marriages. Thus Ascoleo found that of 24 families which included 60 albino members five were the offspring of the mating of first cousins. In only two instances was albinism directly transmitted from parent to child. Of the cases of alkaptonuria, concerning which the necessary information is forthcoming, a very large proportion have been in children of first cousin marriages. (Garrod, 1908, p. 4)

Garrod recognized that the ratio of affected to normal sibs in his data was inconsistent with Mendelian expectations, being closer to 1 : 2 rather than the expected 1 : 3. However, he felt the data were an unfair test of the Mendelian ratio in that several of the families consisted of a single child who was affected. He noted that if one limited oneself only to those families in which there were five or more children the approximation to the expected Mendelian ratio was quite close. We shall return to this problem of deviations from the expected Mendelian ratios when dealing with data obtained from human families, but note here that Garrod was correct in his judgment that his raw data was an unfair test of the Mendelian ratio. At the time, Garrod felt that the strongest argument that could be made for the view that alkaptonuria was a Mendelian recessive character was afforded by the fact that albinism, which so closely resembled alkaptonuria in its incidence in man, behaved as a recessive character in the experimental breeding of animals.

Despite this auspicious and early start, the scientifically sound application of Mendelian genetics to human traits was slow to develop. L. C. Dunn, in his discussion of this slow growth, rejects the assumption that it was due to the lack of appropriate methods and concepts in those early years. He has pointed out that the basic principle of population genetics, Landsteiner's blood groupings and the demonstration of their genetic basis, and Garrod's insightful observations on biochemical genetics in man were all available by the end of the first decade of the twentieth century (Dunn, 1962, 1965). But the fruitful exploitation of these early advances was not to be effected for several decades.

It will, I think, be clear to anyone who examines the records of the period from 1900 to about the middle thirties that the manner in which the eugenics movement developed cast a long shadow over the growth of sound knowledge of human genetics. The ideals of eugenics as originally proposed by Galton in 1883 and restated in more concrete form in 1901 can hardly be held responsible for this, for they will appeal to most people as embodying a noble conception. But there grew up within the eugenics movement ambivalent attitudes through which it tended to become all things to all people, here a science, there a social movement, and in Germany an instrument, through the so-called eugenics laws of 1933, of the ferocious application of prejudice which seemed to many people to be the logical extension, the reductio ad absurdum, of ideas to be found in eugenics programs elsewhere. One effect of all this was to deflect attention from the essential scientific problems and to discourage persons interested in these from pursuing them with human material. It seems as though some perverse kind of Gresham's law might have been operating here, bad coin driving out the better.

A second cause of failure and delay in human genetics was the all too frequent relaxation of critical criteria and a lowering of standards which would not be tolerated in other branches of genetics. In course of time this, like the handicap imposed by eugenics, became less important in relation to the rising tide of good scientific work, both practical and theoretical, in human genetics. . . . As these changes went on, the name eugenics disappeared from several institutions and publications dealing with human genetics. On the other side some of the eugenical organizations (like the American Eugenics Society) tended to assume a more responsible attitude toward the scientific facts underlying social applications and toward research in human genetics. (Dunn, 1962, p. 3)

Whether or not Dunn's analysis provides a sufficient explanation,[2] the fact is that the development of human genetics did proceed rather slowly for several decades following Garrod's discoveries. Limiting ourselves to the area of mental retardation and monofactorial inheritance, it was not until the mid-thirties that there occurred a major breakthrough in the form of Følling's discovery of phenylketonuria and its genetic basis.

SOME GENERAL CONSIDERATIONS OF SINGLE-GENE FACTORS IN MENTAL RETARDATION

Before we discuss phenylketonuria in detail we would like to point out some general facts and principles regarding single-gene effects in the area of mental retardation. The first point to underscore is that single-gene-deter-

---

[2] See Schultz (1967) for an alternative view.

mined forms of mental retardation are rare not only in terms of incidence in the total population but even in terms of the retarded population itself. For example, phenylketonuria, one of the most common and best studied of these disorders, has an incidence of less than 1 person in 20,000 and contributes less than 1 percent of the inmate population in institutions in the northeast United States (Jervis, 1939).

Dominant Defects. In the case of dominant genes causing mental defect, there is obviously a strong selective factor operating against such genes. Severely defective individuals are unlikely to reproduce. Even moderate degrees of retardation impose a reproductive handicap, and over the course of generations causative genes are likely to become a smaller and smaller fraction of the total genetic pool available within the population. Therefore, dominant defective genes, if they are to persist in the population, must have characteristics which mitigate the reproductive handicap.

Thus Huntington's chorea, a degenerative neurological disease caused by a dominant gene, is maintained in the population in part because its mean age of onset—calculated at approximately 35 years in a Michigan survey—assures that many of the afflicted individuals will have reproduced before the disease takes its toll (Reed *et al.*, 1958). To be sure, Huntington's chorea, like other disorders with variable age of onset, can be considered a cause of mental retardation—by current definitions—only when the neurological deterioration develops in childhood.

Other dominant defective genes are maintained in part by the fact that they vary a great deal in the severity with which they express themselves—the degree of intellectual defect may vary from severe to none—or as revealed in some family pedigrees some individuals may be presumed to have carried the gene and yet never to have shown its phenotypical effects. In such cases the presence of modifying genes in a particular individual may account for the reduced severity or absence of the phenotypical traits. Epiloia—a condition characterized by numerous small tumors of the skin and brain—exemplifies this variation, showing all possible levels of intellectual functioning from normality to the severest retardation.

In addition to these factors, and most powerful in keeping the defective dominant gene present in the population, is the continuous spontaneous mutation of normal genes into the defective allele. When such mutation occurs in the germ cell that enters into the formation of a new individual, obviously the disease will appear without any previous family history. The rate of spontaneous mutation varies from gene to gene. By the appropriate combination of theory, observation, and statistical analysis it is possible to make estimates of the frequency of such mutations for both recessive and dominant genes. When selective factors working against a gene's maintenance in a population are balanced by the rate of spontaneous mutation the incidence of defect in the population will be stable.

Recessive Defects. In contrast to the dominantly determined defects the recessive defects are often more severe in their manifestations and show less variability of expression from one patient to the other. In addition, Penrose points out that family histories are highly characteristic. Sharp differentiation in phenotype from affected to unaffected sibs is the rule and parental consanguinity is an important sign. In diseases where mortality in early life is the rule, evidence of inbreeding may be more diagnostic of a recessive trait than the estimation of the Mendelian ratios (Penrose, 1962).

Penrose, in his 1962 edition of *The Biology of Mental Defect,* discusses approximately a score of rare autosomal gene defects associated with varying degrees and frequency of mental defect. A glance at recent journals in the area of pediatrics and human genetics shows the list to be still growing. To compile a complete list and to discuss the various disorders of this nature is beyond the scope or intent of this book. Nevertheless we feel that a somewhat detailed presentation of the growth of knowledge about a representative of this group will have value for the nonmedical and genetically untrained reader. We feel on the basis of our own experience in acquainting ourselves with the literature in this area that problems and solutions applicable to one form of genetically determined mental retardation have a considerable degree of generality. Thus the extent to which the deleterious effects of a defective gene may be modified by successful biochemical and clinical research can be illustrated in the consideration of one disorder and suggest how it may be similarly achieved in the case of another. Again the psychological and social problems presented by a single disorder will be similar for others in the group.

In choosing such an example of a genetically determined form of mental retardation, the choice logically appears to be that of phenylketonuria since this is probably the best understood and most thoroughly investigated of such disorders.

Phenylketonuria: Symptomatology

In 1934, according to the account of Centerwall and Centerwall (1961), a Norwegian mother concerned about her two children, both severely retarded, was referred to Dr. Asbjorn Følling, a biochemist and physician by training. Both children had seemed normal at birth and in the early months of infancy. The older, a girl, was observed to be slow in her development at 1 year of age and did not learn to walk until 2. She never learned to speak more than a few words. The younger child, a boy, had appeared alert at first, then his development slowed, and he never learned to walk or talk. The children were approximately 7 and 4 years of age when seen by Dr. Følling. The parents were particularly concerned about a musty odor which seemed associated with the urine of the children. This odor was especially distressing to the asthmatic father of the children. It was felt that in view of Dr. Følling's biochemical training he might be in a position to help. Having first ruled out chronic infection as a possible source of the odor in the urine, Dr. Følling tested it for diacetic acid by adding ferric chloride, but instead of a red brown color indicative of that acid, the urine turned green. Ruling out other alternatives that might account for the unexpected reaction, Dr. Følling undertook the series of chemical separations and extractions necessary to obtain the chemical substance in the urine responsible for the green coloration. The pure crystaline extract obtained, its chemical structure was analyzed and identified as phenylpyruvic acid, a metabolite of phenylalanine, not usually found in the urine of normal individuals. Følling therefore hypothesized that the children were afflicted with a disturbance in the metabolism of the amino acid phenylalanine. A survey of several hundred institutionalized retardates led to the discovery of additional cases, including two more sibling pairs. Within the same year that the first two children were brought to him, Følling published a report on ten cases with the new metabolic disease (Følling, 1963). This was the first specific inherited metabolic disease to be recognized in the field of mental retardation, and with the publication of Følling's findings the interest of various workers in the field led to quick confirmation, notably by Penrose in England and Jervis in America. Penrose and Quastel (1937) suggested the name "phenylketonuria" for this disease and it has supplanted Følling's designation of "imbecilitas phenylpyruvica" and the American alternative of "phenylpyruvic oligophrenia." Less cumbersome and less offensive to the relatives of the patient, and more accurate—since later investigation showed that retardation was not an inevitable accompaniment of the disorder—phenylketonuria has become the more widely accepted term.

In Penrose's confirmatory study (1935) consisting of a survey of 500 institutionalized patients, the urine of one 19-year-old male idiot gave the characteristic reaction. The urine of the parents and three sibs was tested, with positive results only in the case of a 5-year-old brother also severely retarded. The remaining living members of the family appeared to be unaffected. The description of the institutionalized boy and his younger brother may be used to present some of the characteristics of the disorder.

Male, aged 19, idiot, urine contains phenylpyruvic acid. Blood Wassermann reaction negative. The birth was normal at full term and the child was, at an early age, recognized to be mentally defective. He had no convulsions. He has never walked or talked; he cannot feed himself and he is wet and dirty in habits; he sits or lies with his limbs contracted while he occupies himself with mannerisms of the fingers and with rocking movements of the trunk. He appears to notice a bright moving object. His head is small and brachycephalic (head measurements: length 17.1 cm.; breadth 14.3 cm.; cephalic index 0.84). There is a pigmented patch of skin on the right side of the forehead. The shoulders are broad but there is a marked kyphosis with depressed sternum; the teeth are widely spaced and the molars are decayed. He has long tapering fingers, thin legs, flat feet with partial syndactyly of the second and third toes. The testes are undescended bilaterally and the penis is small. Deep reflexes in the limbs are all very brisk; there is bilateral extensor plantar response. The abdominal reflexes are present. The forearms and legs show pronounced muscular wasting. The pupils react irregularly to light, there are signs of old iritis with adhesions especially in the right eye, bilateral cataract, and small corneal opacities. He once had an epileptic fit, when aged 14.

Male, aged 5, idiot, urine contains phenylpyruvic acid; unable to walk, talk, or stand, he can now crawl a little but hardly uses his legs at all and sits tailorwise; wet and dirty in habits; brachycephalic (head measurements at the age of 2 years 1 month: length 6.2 cm.; breadth 5.4 cm.; cephalic index 0.87). He suffers from constipation. The deep reflexes in the legs are very brisk; plantar responses extensor. Fits started when he was a few months old; they consisted of twitchings associated with apparent loss of consciousness. They have continued ever since and often occur several times in one day. (Penrose, 1935, p. 24)

The two cases just described were more severely affected mentally than those described by Følling. But several of their symptoms can be considered characteristic of the disorder. The degree of mental defect is usually severe. Penrose (1962) maintains that 60 percent of the cases are of the idiot grade and 30 percent imbecile. The remaining 10 percent range from mild subnormality to average. The Colchester Survey of 1938 gives a mean IQ of 19.9 with a standard deviation of 12.6 for 47 institutionalized cases. Since the upper intellectual ranges attained by phenylketonuria would not be represented in an institutionalized sample, this is of course a slight underestimate of the true mean for all cases.

In addition to mental subnormality these brothers displayed other symptoms which according to Penrose (1962) are characteristic of severe cases of phenylketonuria. These include the kyphosis or humpbacked curvature of the lumbar region of the spine, the hyperkinesis which often takes the form of digital mannerisms, the epileptiform seizures in infancy and childhood, the accentuation of reflexes both superficial and deep, widely spaced incisors, and variable pigmentation of the skin. Not observed or reported in these cases but also frequently present according to Penrose are light hair pigmentation in comparison with normal sibs, blue eyes, susceptibility to dermatitis and abnormal electroencephalograms.

Paine's (1957) survey of 106 phenylketonurics—mostly institutionalized—corroborates and fills out the above picture. Approximately 60 percent of the cases were adults and all but five were over 5 years of age. The patients were classified into two groups, low grade (IQ below 25) with an N of 78, and a combined group of high and middle grade (IQ above 50 and IQ between 25 and 50) with an N of 28. The developmental histories indicated a mean age for walking alone of 2.5 years for the entire group. All of the high—middle group were walking, but only 54 percent of the low group were walking independently. If six cases under 6 years of age are excluded, the remaining high–middle group talked. In the low-grade group only six, constituting 8 percent of the group, talked and their speech was confined to single words.

Nineteen percent of Paine's patients had a history of eczema and 26 percent a history of seizures. In both instances the incidence was greater in the low-grade cases. Seventy-nine percent of the limited number of patients on whom electroencephalograms were obtained showed abnormal tracings. Interestingly enough, the incidence of abnormality in the electroencephalograms did not differentiate the groups. The hand posturing described by Penrose was found in 63 percent of the low-grade but only 7 percent of the high–middle group. Paine, unlike Penrose, does not report any unusual incidence of skin pigmentation or kyphosis.

Despite the fact that many investigators agree on the high incidence for certain of the physical signs, diagnosis by physical signs alone would appear to be difficult. Penrose (1962, p. 150) suggests that the skilled observer may occasionally diagnose a case correctly before the urine has been tested. Paine emphasizes the variability of the symptom picture and indicates that some of the neurological signs such as hand posturing and rocking are common to other forms of severe retardation. Without the biochemical analysis he would view diagnosis of phenylketonuria by physical symptoms as more of a guessing game than a medical exercise. Certainly the most prevalent symptom—retardation—is only a symptom suggestive of a most complex differential diagnosis, and even it is not an invariable accompaniment of phenylketonuria.[3]

Phenylketonuria: Genetics and Incidence

In his survey of families of institutionalized phenylketonurics Jervis (1939) documents the argument for considering phenylketonuria a genetically determined disorder, recessively transmitted. On the assumption of a single, autosomal, recessive gene, without influence on viability, the Mendelian expectation would be 75 percent of the sibs normal and 25 percent afflicted when both parents are heterozygotic. Different expectations would obtain if one or both parents were afflicted. But for an extremely rare disorder which drastically lowers fertility—only a few cases are known in which a phenylketonuric-parent produced offspring and there are no known cases in which

[3] Recently, Koch (1967) and other investigators have emphasized the importance of vomiting, eczema, and urine odor as diagnostic signs in early infancy. In connection with the problems of differential diagnosis, this report of Koch is especially interesting in that in his sample of 109 phenylketonuric patients, six were considered autistic until urine tests of phenylpyruvic acid revealed the true basis of their behavior. To quote these authors, "The PKU child is usually hyperactive and exhibits unpredictable, erratic behavior. Excessive rocking movements, grinding of teeth, arm waving, and overall aimless behavior occasionally are misdiagnosed as early childhood schizophrenia."

both parents were afflicted—we can neglect the other alternatives as contributing a negligible amount to the incidence of the disease and assume that all or nearly all offspring are the product of a mating between two heterozygotes. Therefore, if the offspring of all pairs of heterozygotic parents were sampled, we would expect the Mendelian ratio of 3 : 1 to be fulfilled. Now let us see how Jervis' data fits this expectation.

The Families of Phenylketonurics.   Jervis' data which was collected by a survey of 20,300 institutionalized patients, turned up 161 phenylketonurics. The families of these phenylketonurics were then investigated to determine the existence of additional cases of phenylketonuria among the siblings of the institutionalized cases. In 13 instances it was impossible to obtain sufficiently adequate information on the families; thus, these cases were dropped from the study. There then remained in the study 125 families—in some instances a family had more than one institutionalized child—with a total of 467 children of whom 197 or 42% of the children, both institutionalized and noninstitutionalized, were afflicted with phenylketonuria. This percentage of afflicted children at first seems to contradict an interpretation of a Mendelian recessive gene. However, as Jervis indicates, it is typical when dealing with human recessive traits for the observed percentage to be high. The explanation is simple and depends in large part upon the method of ascertainment. In such studies we typically identify the heterozygotic parental pairs by the observed defect or trait appearing in our survey of such children. This so-called index case, which may be picked up in an institution or clinic, gives us a biased selection of our heterozygotic parental pairs. This is true because a certain number of the heterozygotic pairs—especially in view of the small size of human families—will have, by chance, no affected children. If we consider only those sets of parents who have only one child, obviously three of these families will have a normal child to every one that has an affected child, and three children who should be in our sample will be missed for every one that we pick up. As the number of children per family increases, the chances of missing a heterozygotic pair of parents decreases but it remains considerable within the usual range of family size. For example, we may consider the chance that a pair of heterozygotic parents will give birth to four consecutive children none of whom display the recessive trait. The chance of the first child being either a homozygotic dominant or a heterozygote who is phenotypically normal is ¾. The chance that each succeeding child would be the same is again ¾ and the combined chances for all four being normal is ¾ × ¾ × ¾ × ¾ or 81/256. The latter figure tells us that in samples of 256 families, each with 4 children, on the average 81 of the families would have all normal children and hence not be counted in a survey ascertainment method such as that used by Jervis. Fortunately, there are a number of statistical techniques for correcting this bias in sampling. The simplest to describe—not necessarily the preferred—is a method devised by Weinberg. The essence of this method is that the index case is not counted. He serves only to identify a pair of heterozygotic parents. The count of afflicted and nonafflicted offspring is then made for the remaining sibs in that family. The count of afflicted and nonafflicted among these children is not affected by the existence of the index case—"chance has no memory"—and we should expect to find that on the average a group of such families so counted will give us the expected Mendelian ratio. The method is only a trifle more complicated when, as often occurs, the original survey turns up two or more sibs in the same institution or clinic and hence the identification of the same hetero-zygotic parents occurs with several index cases. In this instance we in essence consider each index case and his family—including his institutionalized sibs—separately. An institutionalized sib serves as an index case in one instance and is not counted among the afflicted children of that family although his institutionalized siblings are counted. But when his brother or sister in the institution serves as an index case, he now becomes part of the count of afflicted sibs and a second entry for the family is made in the tabulations. Thus we may consider two institutionalized cases, brother and sister, who have two normal sibs and one afflicted noninstitutionalized sibling. A first entry—when the institutionalized brother is considered the index case—includes two normal sibs and two afflicted, the institutionalized sister and the noninstitutionalized afflicted sib. A second entry is made in the tabulations for this family in which the institutionalized sister serves as the index case, and the entry consists of two normal sibs and two afflicted, the noninstitutionalized sib and the institutionalized brother.

Using such a statistical method, Jervis' data yield an observed percentage of afflicted sibs of 24.8 percent which is not significantly different from the expected Mendelian percentage of 25 percent.

Another test of a rare recessive Mendelian trait is a measure of the frequency of consanguineous marriages in the parents of the afflicted children. If a defective gene occurs but rarely in a population, it is much more likely that two related individuals will both possess it than that two unrelated individuals will. In Jervis' data the parents were cousins in 7 of the 125 families. They had 10 affected offspring. In the American population at large we would not expect cousin marriages to exceed 0.5–1 percent of the total marriages. Therefore, Jervis' obtained percentage of approximately 5 percent cousin marriages exceeds expectation and is of the same order as the value usually obtained for cousin marriages in the case of rare recessive traits when the general incidence of cousin marriages in the population under consideration does not exceed 1 percent.

Incidence of Phenylketonuria in the General Population. Estimates of the frequency of phenylketonuria have varied from country to country and between samples taken from the same country. Part of this variation is un-doubtedly due to sampling error and part of it to the types of assumption made in extrapolating from the incidence observed in a particular sample to an esti-mated incidence for the population at large. For example, Jervis' actual data gave an incidence of 0.793 percent (161 in 20,300) of phenylketonuria among institutionalized defectives. By assuming that 1 percent of the general population was mentally deficient and that one-half of these were in the in-stitutions, he deduces that the frequency of phenylketonuria in the general population is of the order of .004 percent or 1 in 25,000. Obviously, somewhat different estimates would result from assuming a different incidence of mental retardation in the general population or a different incidence of institutional-ization for mentally deficient individuals. Nevertheless, Jervis' estimate is of the same order as that made by other authorities on the basis of other surveys of institutionalized defectives and serves nicely to indicate the rarity of the disease. Even if we were to use the more recent data resulting from surveys of newborn infants by biochemical tests, the incidence rate would not be higher than 1 in 10,000 (Koch, 1967). It is of interest for understanding the genetics of phenylketonuria and the problems of genetic counseling to deter-mine the frequency of the heterozygotic carriers of the phenylketonuria gene. This can be done if we know the frequency of those afflicted with the dis-order in the general population and can make the assumption that breeding within that population is essentially random, i.e., that there are no inbreeding isolates in the population that would affect the distribution of genes in such a way as to alter the probabilities for the occurrence of the various genotypes. This involves an application of the Hardy-Weinberg principle which essentially states that for a randomly breeding population in which two alleles (variant forms of the same gene) A and A' occur in frequencies p and q the equilibrium proportions for the three genotypes AA, AA', and $A'A'$ are in the proportion $p^2 : 2pq : q^2$. As applied to our case of phenylketonuria, q^2 equals the proportion of afflicted individuals in the population, $2pq$ equals the pro-portion of phenotypically normal carriers of the defective gene, and p^2 equals the proportion of individuals homozygotic for the normal gene. Since the formula is based on the assumption of a randomly breeding population, we will follow Penrose's treatment of Jervis' data by omitting those cases in his sample which were the product of cousin marriages. Then the estimate of the incidence is reduced to approximately $1 : 30,000$, or expressed as a fraction $1/30,000$. If q^2 is $1/30,000$ then q, the frequency of the defective gene, is $1/173$. Since $p + q = 1$, i.e., the sum of the proportion of normal genes and the proportion of defective genes equals one, $p = 1 - q$ or $172/173$. Then the proportion of heterozygotic carriers is $2pq$ or $2 \times 172/173 \times 1/173$ which is equal to approximately $1/86$ for the carrier frequency. Thus it is seen that despite the extreme rarity of the disorder, the number of heterozygotic carriers of the disorder is by no means extremely rare. The rarity of the disorder results from the facts that on a random mating basis, the chances of two heterozygotes marrying is $1/86 \times 1/86$ or one chance in 7,396 and the chance that any given child from that marriage is phenylketonuric is, according to the Mendelian analysis, ¼. Hence the combined probability for a child of unrelated parents being born a phenylketonuric is $1/86 \times 1/86 \times$ ¼ = 29,584 or approximately 1 in 30,000. Of course once a set of parents give birth to an affected child, the probability of the next child being phenylketonuric is radically altered since we now know both parents are heterozygotic and the odds are 1 in 4 that the next child will be afflicted.

These frequency estimates are of course subject to more or less error, depending on the accuracy of our population sampling and the validity of our assumptions on such factors as random breeding for the population under consideration. Again, reasonably accurate estimates for one population do not necessarily hold for another population. For example, it is known that the incidence of the disease varies with ethnic groups. Thus the disease is exceedingly rare in American Negroes and in Ashkenazi Jewish populations throughout the world (Penrose, 1962).

Since the introduction of routine testing of newborns for phenylketonuria—in some states such testing is required by law—it has been possible to obtain estimates of incidence that are less subject to the uncertain assumptions necessary in estimating incidence on the basis of the number of identified phenylketonurics in institutions. The screening of newborns is preferably done by any one of several tests for estimating phenylalanine blood levels, since phenylpyruvic acid may be absent from the urine of newborns for several weeks after birth. The Guthrie screening test depends upon the effect of phenylalanine on the growth of a specific bacteria, *Bacillus subtilis*. In suitable preparations, a single drop of the infant's blood will demonstrate this effect and so provide a rough index of the level of phenylalanine in the blood.

On the basis of newborn screening programs conducted in various hospitals in the United States, the estimate of the incidence of PKU has risen to 1 in 10,000 births. But questions have been raised as to whether all such detected cases are truly classic PKU cases (Koch, 1967).

Variations in Intellectual Functioning in Phenylketonurics

The number of reported individuals with untreated phenylketonuria who reach borderline or above levels of intellectual development are not many. Some surveys suggest that such individuals approximate 1 percent of the actual cases of phenylketonuria (Paine, 1957; Knox, 1960).

The Range of Intellectual Development.   The following cases illustrate some examples of individual exceptions to the general rule of severe retardation.

〜   In 1959, Leonard and McGuire reported on a child diagnosed as phenylketonuric at 6 years of age. At 7 years of age she obtained IQs of 70 and 80 on the WISC and Stanford-Binet, respectively. A year after initial contact with the clinic she was making adequate adjustment in the special education classes of the local school system.

A case reported by Allen and Gibson (1961) is of particular interest because it raises the question of the effect of the method of ascertainment on our estimates of the frequency of phenylketonuria accompanied by higher levels of intellectual functioning. Except for infants, the usual untreated phenylketonuric is picked up either by a survey of an institution for the mentally retarded or by examination of the relatives of a known phenylketonuric. The present effective screening techniques for identification of phenylketonuria in newborns, of course, insures that such cases when identified will be given treatment and hence will not contribute to our knowledge of the range of intellectual functioning possible in untreated phenylketonurics. Therefore our ascertainment of untreated cases remains a biased one. In the case of Allen and Gibson, the identification was unusual in that the primary referral reason was not retardation but hyperactivity for which psychiatric evaluation was requested.

〜   Psychological testing of the child in his tenth year gave a Stanford Binet IQ of 109. On the WISC in the same year he obtained a Verbal IQ of 111, a Performance IQ of 100, and a Full Scale IQ of 107. Both tests indicated considerable variability in functioning. Word definition and verbal abstract reasoning were consistently higher than other abilities. There was some suggestion of deficit in visual motor functioning. At the time of initial psychiatric contact, the history noted that the patient had just completed the third grade and his academic work was satisfactory. However, he was a hyperactive, anxious youngster whose behavior had become increasingly disruptive in the classroom. The diagnostic impression was of chronic brain syndrome of unknown cause. Referred for pediatric-neurological evaluation, an electroencephalograph recording proved abnormal with paroxysmal features, urine was positive to ferric chloride, and phenylalanine blood levels were elevated.

The authors indicate that this case suggests the need for continued search for phenylketonuria, not only among mental defectives but also in any individual in whom an abnormality of cerebral function exists.

One other case of interest in this regard is reported by Caudle (1960).

〜   The patient, a 3½-year-old boy, was first identified as a phenylketonuric after the diagnosis had been made on a younger, severely retarded sibling. Despite positive urine and blood tests this child obtained a Performance IQ of 121 on the

Merrill-Palmer at 2½ years of age, and an IQ of 134 on the same test three months later. On a follow-up of this case, Koch *et al.* (1967) report that at age 10, still without therapy, he obtained an IQ of 115. He is healthy and his EEG is normal despite elevated serum phenylalanine values and urine findings on chromatography that are classic for PKU.

We have placed considerable emphasis on the proper caution essential to the interpretation of IQ scores in the diagnosis of mental retardation; therefore it is well to end this discussion of the range of intellectual development in untreated phenylketonurics with the account of the first two reported cases of phenylketonuria in a Jewish population (Cohen and Kozinn, 1949).

⌒ A 6-year-old Jewish boy showed typical features of phenylketonuria. He walked at 19 months; didn't say a word until he was 3; had an IQ of 34; and his urine was persistently positive for phenylpyruvic acid. The mother and a younger sibling had normal mentality and negative urines. The father, however, showed phenylpyruvic acid in the two specimens of urine tested. He obtained an IQ of 69 on the Wechsler-Bellevue. He was employed as a presser of gloves, worked steadily, and provided an adequate income for his family. The authors state, "despite his borderline intelligence, he made a satisfactory and independent economic and social adjustment in a strongly competitive community such as New York City."

Explaining the Variation. The wide range of IQ and social functioning associated with phenylketonuria poses a problem in our understanding of the disease. The literature presents a considerable number of instances in which the variation among sibs, all with elevated phenylalanine levels, is from profound idiocy to normality. It would be stretching an environmentalist explanation beyond the breaking point to seek the major source of this variance in environmental differences, especially in view of the fact that not only is the difference in psychological functioning but it occurs also in the absence or presence of very obvious physical findings such as seizures, microcephaly, and eczema. From the genetic point of view, a theoretical explanation is readily at hand, for no gene is assumed to operate in a vacuum. Rather it acts in an extremely complex biochemical environment, the exact specification of which depends upon the nature of each and every other gene present in the organism; the quantity and quality of nutrients available, past and present; and many environmental conditions external to the organism, past and present, that can modify the internal biochemical environment. That biochemical environment will determine within wide latitudes the net effect of the gene; it can enhance, suppress, or mitigate the gene's effects. Theoretically, explanation of the variable effects of a gene presents no problem. In actuality, the specification of the cause of the variation may so exceed our ability that we content ourselves with some sort of actuarial statement such as that 60 percent of the cases are of idiot grade, 30 percent imbecile, and 10 percent from mild subnormality to average. If we are lucky, and the relevant variables gradually become identified and understood, our explanatory power increases; and the area in which we must resort to simple actuarial description becomes narrowed. As for the present, in the case of phenylketonuria we appear to be in a stage where actuarial description is all we can offer, though speculations and possible leads can be found sprinkled here and there in the literature.

Penrose offered one of the earliest of such sepculations in his 1946 discussion of the problems of eugenics in relationship to PKU. While recognizing that the degree of mental defect varies within families where more than one case occurs, he yet on the basis of limited data estimated that the correlation of the mental grade of affected sibs was of the order of + 0.3. This suggested that the differences in mental grade between families could be due to genetic modifiers present or absent in the different family lines. Penrose's argument can of course be objected to on the grounds that we have no way of knowing but that environmental factors varying between families might be the cause of the correlation. Even if the patients studied were all institutionalized, we would assume some part of their early lives was spent at home. However, Penrose advances his argument with the following case:

A sibship consisted of five living affected children and six normal children. Two of the phenylketonurics were idiots, two were imbeciles, and one a moron with severe juvenile diabetes. The two imbecilic children had glycosuria—excretion of an abnormal amount of sugar in the urine—and Penrose suggests that they may have been mild diabetics. The two idiots never showed glycosuria. The question is raised whether the diabetes, which was presumed to be of genetic origin in this sibship, actually modified and alleviated the manifestation of the phenylketonuria.

With data limited to one sibship one can only speculate, but it suggests the desirability of a closer medical and genetic evaluation of these rare phenylketonuric cases with relatively high levels of intellectual functioning. In view of their rarity, one might call attention to the case reported by Coates, Norman, and Woolf (1957).

A 6-year-old boy was referred with a history of walking at 20 months and muscular weakness and clumsiness from at least his third year. At the time of referral there was in addition to the weakness, definite wasting of muscular tissue, and an electromyogram and biopsy indicative of myopathy. A diagnosis of muscular dystrophy of Gowers' type was made. The investigators, looking for aminoaciduria in muscular dystrophy, tested the boy's urine by paper chromatography. The pattern was characteristic for phenylketonuria, as were later tests of blood and cerebrospinal fluid.

In relationship to techniques of ascertainment biasing against the pick-up of high-IQ phenylketonurics, it is interesting that this case like others reported also was an "accidental" find.

ᖆᖆ Tested with the Stanford-Binet at 6 years and 4 months, the boy obtained an IQ of 103. In two retests done within a four-month period, he obtained IQs of 101 and 105. Since the average IQ of the parents and three siblings of this child was considerably higher than his, the authors allow that some mental deterioration might have occurred but assert that it is minimal and quite negligible compared with most phenylketonurics. Unfortunately, in a two-year follow-up the child's IQ had fallen to 89 on the Stanford-Binet, suggestive of some degree of deterioration.

The authors are struck by the fact that like some other phenylketonurics with relatively high intelligence their case showed relatively less excretion of phenyllactic acid and phenylpyruvic acid in the urine. They also noted the resemblance between their case and that of another phenylketonuric with an average IQ of 94. In both cases, the hair was dark. The light hair found in many phenylketonurics is attributed by some investigators to an inhibition of formation of the pigment melanin by high concentrations of phenylalanine. Coates and his colleagues feel that the presence of normal hair color with normal intelligence in these two cases can hardly be coincidence and suggest that it is indicative of a change in the chemical reactions of these phenylketonurics as compared to others. They do not suggest the possibility that the altered physiology accompanying the muscular dystrophy may have, just as hypothesized in the case of Penrose's diabetic, somehow served to mitigate the effects of the phenylketonuria.

Whether such exceptional cases in which identifiable genetically determined traits or disease would occur simultaneously with modified expression of the phenylketonuric genes with sufficient frequency to throw light upon the mechanisms involved remains to be seen.

Biochemical Factors in Phenylketonuria

Følling's hypothesis of an error in the metabolism of phenylalanine was followed by efforts to specify the error, its effects, and their prevention. In its oxidative metabolism, phenylalanine is normally converted to tyrosine—another essential amino acid—which in turn is oxidized to other metabolites. When a deficiency in phenylalanine hydroxylase blocks the conversion of phenylalaline to tyrosine, alternative pathways are used in the metabolism of phenylalanine. Specifically, phenylalanine is transaminated to phenylpyruvic acid which in turn may be metabolized to phenyllactic acid or phenylacetic acid. However, much of the phenylpyruvic acid is excreted in the urine where it may readily be identified with the ferric chloride test.

Jervis in 1947 demonstrated that the normal rise in the blood concentration of tyrosine following the administration of phenylalanine did not occur in phenylketonurics. The enzyme—phenylalanine hydroxylase—which converts phenylalanine to tyrosine was subsequently obtained by Jervis from normal liver tissue but he could not obtain it from the liver of a phenylketonuric (Nyhan, 1963; Hsia, 1966).

In a confirming study Hsia (1966) demonstrated that when liver tissue biopsied from a normal individual was incubated with phenylalanine, tyrosine not originally present would subsequently appear, indicating the conversion of phenylalanine to tyrosine. When the same study was repeated with a phenylketonuric patient the tyrosine did not appear.

The clinical importance of this conversion is that it permits the discrimination of phenylketonuria proper from disorders which may cause an elevation of phenylalanine levels in the blood but not as a result of the metabolic error peculiar to phenylketonuria. In cases in which phenylalanine levels are elevated but tyrosine levels normal, we are dealing with a hyperphenylalaninemia which may be due to a variety of causes but not to phenylketonuria. In phenylketonuria the elevated phenylalanine levels are accompanied by tyrosine levels that are below normal. Not only is this relationship important for diagnosis but recent findings suggest that it is crucial for the proper dietary treatment of the disease.

In a recent review, Carpenter, Auerbach and DiGeorge (1968) discuss various forms of phenylalaninemia, their possible causes and biochemical features. These men distinguish several groups of disorders characterized by elevated blood phenylalanine levels. In "classical PKU" according to these authors, the patients if untreated will develop the typical form of Følling's disease with retardation. In contrast, patients with "atypical PKU" exhibit only moderate increases in blood phenylalanine levels with or without phenylpyruvic aciduria and with or without mental retardation. In still another group with "mild phenylalaninemia" blood levels of phenylalanine are slightly elevated but there is no phenylpyruvic acid or its metabolites in the urine. This latter group would not appear to require treatment in the opinion of these authors. Still other cases of elevated phenylalanine levels in infancy may be due to a delay in the maturation of the associated enzyme systems or other biochemical defects unrelated to classical PKU.

These various biochemical complexities pose formidable—and in large part as yet unsolved—problems of diagnosis, treatment and genetic counseling.

DIETARY TREATMENT AND ITS EFFECTS ON INTELLECTUAL FUNCTIONING

The first suggestion that phenylketonuria might be treated by a dietary restriction of phenylalanine appears to be that of Woolf and Vulliamy (1951) in their report of an unsuccessful attempt to lower blood phenylalanine concentrations in patients by the feeding of glutamic acid.

In 1953, Bickel, Gerard, and Hickmans reported the results of treating a phenylketonuric child with a low phenylalanine diet. Following the suggestion of Woolf for removing phenylalanine from casein acid hydrolysate by treatment with activated, acid-washed charcoal, a diet preparation was made which provided the other essential amino acids.

⟨~⟩ The patient, a 2-year-old girl, was severely retarded, unable to stand, walk, or talk. She showed no interest in her surroundings, was uninterested in food, and spent her time groaning, crying, and head banging. On four weeks of a phenylalanine-free diet, phenylalanine blood levels fell to normal, urine test turned negative, and the characteristic musty smell disappeared. However, there was a loss of weight and eventually abnormal amounts of amino acids were excreted in the urine. This was evidence that in the phenylketonuric as in the normal individual complete deprivation of phenylalanine was incompatible with normal metabolism and even life itself. Therefore, phenylalanine was added to the diet in small amounts in the form of whole milk. Normal weight gain and a return toward normal biochemical findings occurred. This diet, supplemented by some protein-free foods was continued and in ensuing months the child learned to crawl and stand, she no longer banged her head or cried continuously. Two trials were made of increased phenylalanine intake. On each occasion there was rapid deterioration in the child's condition. She lost her ability to stand and crawl. She resumed head banging and crying. In addition, on the second trial, she developed facial eczema, became ataxic, and vomited repeatedly. With resumption of the low phenylalanine intake, the child's condition improved. For this child the beneficial effects of a low phenylalanine diet seemed unequivocal.

Following this demonstration, numerous studies were undertaken to determine the effects of a low phenylalanine diet on growth, neurological status, and intellectual development. Commercial dietary preparations were soon made available such as Lofenalac in this country and Minafen in England. The diet might take several forms. A typical example would consist of the commercially available low-phenylalanine synthetic foods, supplemented by a proportion of natural foods of low phenylalanine content, the patient's family being provided with a list of such foods and special recipes. Sufficient milk is given to prevent blood levels of phenylalanine from falling too low. Repeated experience has shown that if phenylalanine levels are *too* low the child fails to grow and thrive.

Almost from the beginning, investigators using the low phenylalanine diets were concerned with accurate measurements of the intellectual changes of the treated children. But such research faced two formidable problems. The very rareness of the disorder insured that the sample size of any one research team would be strictly limited. Secondly, it quickly became apparent that striking effects on the intellectual functioning of older phenylketonurics were not to be expected, although, occasionally, improvements such as a reduced frequency of seizures or a decreased irritability would be reported. This meant that in the age group where most improvement might be expected, i.e., within the first few years of life, the measuring instruments were most unreliable and poor prognosticators of future performance.

In spite of the difficulties, by 1960 sufficient numbers of treated cases had been reported in detail for Knox to attempt a summary presentation and analysis.

The Importance of Early Treatment.   Knox (1960) found 44 reported cases in which dietary treatment had been instituted at an age greater than 3 years. These included one group of 19 patients treated for one year on a low phenylalanine diet and compared with a matched group on a similar diet containing phenylalanine (Hsia *et al.*, 1958). None of these 44 cases had demonstrated impressive change in neurological or mental status.

There were 43 cases in the literature in which treatment was instituted at a mean age of 16.2 months and a range from 10 days to 36 months. The duration of treatment for these cases ranged from 3 to 61 months with a mean duration of 16.8 months.

To evaluate the intellectual development of this treated group, Knox used as a control the IQ distribution of 466 untreated cases of phenylketonuria of all ages as culled from the literature. In comparing this distribution with that of the phenylketonurics who had been treated at less than 3 years of age, the following striking differences may be noted: 44.5 percent of the treated cases had IQs or developmental quotients in excess of 60, whereas only 2.5 percent of the untreated cases had IQs that high. In contrast, only 16 percent of the treated cases had IQs or DQs below 21, whereas 64.4 percent of the controls had scores that low.

Since the argument could be made that many of the treated cases were being tested within an age range where the test scores are notoriously unreliable, Knox again compared the treated and untreated cases, this time eliminating from the treated group those who were tested before 2 years of age. This reduced the treated group to 31 cases who ranged from 2 to 6 years of age. Again the treated group was clearly superior, having 36 percent of the cases with test scores above 60 and only 16 percent below 21.

To further evaluate the importance of early treatment, Knox subdivided his treatment group into those who had begun treatment before 16 months of age ($N = 23$) and those who began treatment between 16 and 36 months of age ($N = 20$). The difference in intellectual functioning is strikingly in favor of the early treatment group. In the early treatment group 69 percent tested higher than an IQ or DQ of 60 and only 9 percent tested below 21. In contrast, the later treated group had only 5 percent scoring above 60 and 25 percent scoring below 21.

Knox emphasizes the importance of early treatment by a correlational analysis which for the entire treated group gives an r of $-.67$ between the final IQ obtained after treatment and the age at which treatment was begun. Knox estimated an average loss of nearly 5 IQ points for each 10 weeks' delay in treatment.

Comparisons of the EEG findings and the incidence of seizures in the groups showed the same significant differences with more abnormal tracings and higher incidence of seizures in the untreated group than in the treated and in the later treated group than in the early treated group.

There are certain reservations that one might have about the generalizations that Knox draws from his survey. The difference in method of ascertainment for the two groups of treated and untreated cases undoubtedly accounts for some of the variation. The untreated cases, for the most part, are cases identified in institutional surveys. Not only are those in the treated group noninstitutionalized but many showed no sign of developmental retardation at the time of identification. We cannot be sure that the disease course in this latter group would follow the same course that it did in the institutionalized group or that, if untreated, their mean IQs would be identical to the institutionalized group at the same age. The age differential between the treated and the controls presents additional problems. For example, the clinical literature on untreated cases gives more than a few instances of a decline in IQ at ages in excess of the oldest child in Knox's treated group (Koch *et al.*, 1967). If to that is added the fact that the institutionalization of. Knox's untreated group may have further depressed IQs, it is difficult to assess accurately the effect of the diet on the younger children using the older phenylketonurics as our control.

Nevertheless, one can make quite liberal allowances for these and other possible sources of error and still find the results of the study quite compelling. And, fortunately, further studies with tighter controls seem to bear out the general implications of Knox's review. In light of these studies the question would appear to shift from one of whether or not the diet can reduce the incidence or degree of mental defect to whether or not it can completely prevent the usual intellectual deterioration.

Biochemical Control and the Effectiveness of Treatment. In 1961, Berman *et al.* reported a study of 22 children from 6 families. Eight of the children were prenylketonurics under dietary treatment, the remaining children were their siblings, 11 were unaffected and 3 were untreated phenylketonurics. Five of the treated children had been placed on the diet at less than 3 months of age, one began treatment at 12 months, and the remaining 2 at approximately 24 months. The following table derived from Berman's data gives the mean and range of IQ scores, and other relevant information for the various sibling groups.

TABLE 18.1 IQ Scores for Phenylketonuric Sibling Groups

	N	Age at Start of Treatment	Average Age at Testing	Mean IQ	Range of IQ
Treated	5	3 months	14 months	83	72–93
PKU	1	12 months	32 months	84	—
sibs	2	26 months	46 months	46	45–48
Untreated PKU sibs	3	—	54 months	24	18–29
Unaffected sibs	11	—	65 months	117	95–155

All of the children were retested within six months to a year of the original testing and the resulting IQs were substantially unchanged from those reported. In all but one instance the test used was either the Stanford-Binet (Form L, 1937) or the Cattell Infant Intelligence Scale.

The results are clear-cut, with the treated group scoring significantly higher than the untreated group, but significantly lower than their unaffected sibs. The authors maintain that the "loss" in intelligence should not be attributed to poor chemical control as "treated children maintained phenylalanine levels within the normal range throughout treatment, with occasional brief exceptions." Like the Knox data, despite the small sample, there is the suggestion that the treatment in early infancy is more effective than treatment in later infancy.

On neurological examination two of the untreated PKU's and two of the treated PKU's showed positive findings, two additional treated children showed suggestive findings. None of the unaffected sibs showed either positive or suggestive neurological findings.

This study therefore suggests—if we make the assumption that the averaged IQ scores of the untreated sibs represents the premorbid potential of the phenyketonurics—that although a preventive diet in early infancy may reduce the amount of deterioration, either it does not completely prevent deterioration or some degree of damage may exist at birth or shortly thereafter.

The contention of Berman *et al.* that the loss in intelligence could not be attributed to poor chemical control is based on the assumption that adequate control involves keeping phenylalanine blood levels within normal limits. More recent findings suggest that adequate dietary control for the phenylketonuric child may require serum phenylalanine levels somewhat above normal levels.

The early experience of Sutherland and her co-workers (1966) demonstrated to their satisfaction that serum phenylalanine levels under 2 mg/100 cc resulted in failure to support weight gain and well-being of the patients. They determined that for their patients serum phenylalanine levels ranging from 3 to 8 mg/100 cc were better suited for maintaining growth and development. Since there are individual differences in the utilization of phenylalanine in the patient population, and since the utilization varies with periods of growth and with the presence of other factors such as febrile illness, these investigators felt it necessary to maintain a strict monitoring of the biochemical control with appropriate dietary adjustments.

The results of their investigation are consistent with that of others in demonstrating that the earlier treatment is undertaken, the higher the IQ. Thus, for 7 children where treatment was begun prior to 3 months of age, the average IQ was 110. For 5 children where treatment was begun between 9 and 12 months of age the average IQ was 78. Fifteen children who began treatment at more than 1 year of age had an average IQ of approximately 51. Where the results show an interesting difference to those of Berman *et al.* is in the fact that 10 unaffected siblings of the group that started treatment prior to 3 months of age had an average IQ of 106. Here there is no evidence for a "loss" of IQ in comparison to the potential suggested by the unaffected siblings.

In a subsequent report of their work, (Berry *et al.*, 1967) Sutherland's group report some additional data, now giving results on a total of 8 early treated cases with a mean IQ of 108 with 10 unaffected siblings averaging 106. Data available for 8 of the parents gave a mean IQ of 109, again offering no support for the assumption that the treated phenylketonurics were not reaching their full potential for intellectual growth.

Other investigators have also moved in the direction of less stringent restriction in phenylalanine intake, maintaining serum levels somewhat in excess of normal although still well below the levels usually found in the untreated phenylketonurics (Koch *et al.*, 1967; Kennedy *et al.*, 1967).

Berry *et al.* (1967, p. 5) suggest that "over-restriction of phenylalanine resulting in a dietary deficiency of an essential amino acid during the critical period of brain development in early infancy may also be responsible for the moderate mental retardation which has been reported in some phenylketonuric patients who were diagnosed and treated very early in life."

The results of Kennedy *et al.* (1967), whose treatment of phenylketonurics also involved mean blood phenylalanine levels above those formerly recommended for treatment, would seem to bear out the contention of Berry *et al.* For thirteen patients who appeared severely affected with phenylketonuria in the newborn period (as judged by such criteria as the rate of blood phenylalanine rise and the presence or absence of urinary metabolites of phenylalanine), an average IQ of 102 at a mean age of 30 months was obtained. Six cases considered to be mildly affected in the newborn period obtained an average IQ of 109 at a mean age of 26 months. The children were tested with either the Cattell Infant Intelligence scale or the Stanford-Binet.

Kennedy *et al.* rightly caution on the predictability value for later intellectual functioning of test scores obtained between 2 and 4 years of age. This same caution is applicable to the work of the Sutherland group who were tested at an average age considerably below that of their sibling controls. But the results to date are encouraging and suggest that with improved dietary control and management of the disease, mental impairment may be reduced to a negligible degree if not completely eliminated.[4]

Duration of Diet and Psychological Effects.   Although accumulated experience is far from extensive, there have been several reports suggesting that continued or life-long dietary restriction of phenylalanine intake is not a requirement for successful treatment (Farquhar, Richmond, and Haldane, 1963; Solomons, Keleske, and Opitz, 1966). Horner *et al.* (1962) report three cases whose diet was ended for one or another reason at an early age. Two of these children who began treatment at under 2 months of age had IQs in the nineties at 4 years of age. They were then taken off the diet. Follow-ups two years later on one of the children and several months later on the other revealed no intellectual deterioration. A third case treated from 6 weeks of age till 4 years had an IQ of 70 at termination of the diet. Again, there was no deterioration after termination of the diet.

It would appear from such cases that the intellectual damage must occur

---

[4] Although the general consensus of opinion in the field holds that dietary treatment, when started early in life is effective in reducing, if not preventing retardation, there have been occasional voices of caution and dissent. For example, Birch and Tizzard (1967) have recently challenged the evidence for effectiveness of dietary treatment. They—as we have also indicated—point out the biases inherent in the method of ascertainment of cases: The untreated or late-treated cases are often ascertained through the presenting symptom of mental retardation; the early-treated cases are usually obtained through screening programs. Thus in a research program the follow-up IQ may be simply the reflection of the original IQ rather than the age when treatment was undertaken. O'Flynn and Hsia (1968) have, however, presented data on 37 treated PKU cases which they interpret as a rebuttal of the assumption of Birch and Tizzard. This data of O'Flynn and Hsia confirms the usual finding that the later-treated groups have lower IQs subsequent to treatment than those in which treatment began prior to two months of age, but an examination of the IQ changes over time does not suggest that the final IQ is solely a product of the initial IQ. Of special importance, in the view of the present authors, is the fact that some of the later-treated cases reported by Flynn and Hsia show marked improvement in IQ even though the group's average is below that obtained by the earliest treated group. Thus, in a group of 8 patients in which treatment began between 25 and 60 months of age, the average IQ rose from 44 to 66 when tested at least one year subsequent to the start of treatment. This data suggests a somewhat more optimistic outcome for delayed treatment than much of the earlier work. But at best, the conflicting findings that are still appearing in the literature—almost invariably with small samples, and often without sufficient specification of the degree of biochemical lesion and its control—suggest the need for further research and the need for caution in our interpretations.

within the first years of life and that, subsequently, the older child is able to tolerate the elevated phenylalanine levels without deterioration. Assuming that such is the case, it is not quite clear when dietary treatment can be discontinued. Various estimates from 6 years to adolescence have been offered (Farquhar, et al., 1963; Solomons et al., 1966; Bickel, Gerard, and Hickman, 1953).

Solomons' group have emphasized the negative psychological aspects of dietary management, i.e., the tensions and conflicts induced in parent–child interactions. In his investigation parents were concerned about the necessary controls inherent in the diet, the length of therapy and the slow apparent improvement. Some parents were overly concerned about any breakdown in dietary control, other parents were skeptical of the value of the diet. These concerns and conflicts in the parents resulted, by their own estimation, in less effective handling of their child.

In a study of seven children who had started dietary treatment at a mean age of 4 years, with a mean duration in excess of 3 years, Solomons reports that after dietary cessation there was an improvement in behavior, school performance, and the emotional climate in the family. IQs for this group of subjects ranged from 26 to 106 while on diet, with an average of 58. Off diet the range was 24 to 104, with a mean of 58. Follow-up periods ranged from six to eleven months and were admittedly short, yet, Solomons maintains that the results were encouraging and suggests that termination of diet after the age of 6 years is safe.

One of the problems in using Solomons' data for a guide is that with the exception of one child beginning dietary treatment at 9 months of age, all the other children were over 2 years of age when the diet was instituted. Therefore the group as a whole began treatment at an age at which one would have expected little benefit from treatment. The data as presented do not give any indication that the institution of the diet had improved intellectual status or adjustment, although the average IQ is above that found in an unselected and untreated sample of phenylketonurics. Therefore, the question arises, if this is a group that did not achieve any benefits from the diet would we have expected any losses on going off the diet? If there were no losses to be expected as a result of biochemical and physiological factors, then why wouldn't the removal of a rather burdensome dietary restriction cause general relaxation in child–parent interactions with resultant improvement in the child's adjustment? The important question as we see it would be in those cases when early institution of diet has led to preservation of normal psychological and neurological functioning—Will the removal of dietary restrictions at a later age occur without risk of deterioration?

Nevertheless, Solomons' findings are important in that they suggest that a family probably does not maintain a child on dietary restriction as strict as that required for the treatment of phenylketonuria without paying a psychological price in the form of family tensions and conflicts. When the preservation of the child's intellectual and neurological functioning is at stake, that price is well worth paying. When such preservation is questionable or of trivial degree then one may well question the price. The problem is to judge when the preservation is questionable or trivial. The accumulation of data is as yet so limited that a clinician is apt to put greatest reliance on his own personal experience, and so Koch, at the other extreme from Solomons, wonders if life-long therapy may be needed. This position is apparently taken primarily on the basis of one striking case in which a youngster treated from 16 months to 4 years of age showed a rise from a developmental quotient of 39 to a Stanford-Binet IQ of 89. After dietary therapy was discontinued there was no obvious intellectual deterioration but increased restlessness, irritability, and sleeplessness. Some two years after cessation of treatment this child began to experience psychomotor seizures and the EEG revealed a diffuse abnormality with spike foci (Koch *et al.*, 1967).

Regardless of what experience will ultimately dictate as the optimal duration for treatment, Solomons' point that we are not treating a phenylalanine blood level but a "total child" living in a family environment is well taken. The physician concentrating on biochemical aspects of the disease and ignoring the child's and family's psychological reactions and adjustments to the disease and its treatment, at best runs the risk of needlessly crippling the child's personality development and fostering the growth of tensions within the parents; at worse, he runs the additional risk of losing biochemical control through loss of cooperation from parents and child.

Eugenics and Genetic Counseling

At the close of the previous chapter we discussed some aspects of eugenics as they applied to the area of mental retardation. The difficulties as we saw them involved two groups of factors. The first of these constitutes the scientific basis on which eugenic proposals are based. Crucial in this area is the degree to which polygenic inheritance plays a role in that large undifferentiated category of retardates in which no obvious anatomical or physiological defect is ascertainable. In regard to that category we expressed our conviction that the frustratingly difficult problem of separating the factors of heredity and environment makes for an extreme degree of unreliability in any estimation of the importance of polygenic inheritance. The second group of factors are those subsumed under the heading of ethical and social considerations, and the difficulties in this area were compounded by the shaky scientific base upon which they proposed to rest.

In comparison, it might seem that when we come to deal with the eugenical aspects of single-gene determined mental defect, the problem is greatly simplified. We are no longer dealing with a conglomerate group whose retardation is due in some cases to a genetic cause, in others to biological trauma or social environment, and in still others to all sorts of combinations of the three preceding factors. In the single-gene defects that have been identified to date, not only are we reasonably certain that the affected individual's retardation has a hereditary basis, but in the instance of several major afflictions we are even able to ascertain the carrier state with a considerable degree of reliability. In addition, the laws of hereditary transmission of these defects are accurately known. So it would seem that on the side of the scientific basis for our proposed eugenic plans we are in a much better position than is the case for polygenic defect. It would therefore seem reasonable that since our scientific basis for action is more solid, our ethical and social problems may yield more easily to a solution. Certainly, there seems to be a difference between sterilizing or pressuring an individual into "voluntary" restriction of procreation when we definitely know he is a carrier of defective genes, and the adoption of the same tactics toward an individual who may *possibly* be a carrier of defective genes.

To see the extent to which this is really so, we shall take a look at the problems of eugenics and the related problems of genetic counseling as they apply to phenylketonuria. As a starting point we will contrast the recommendations of Jervis and Penrose as they appeared in the literature of a few decades ago. Knowledge of the disease has since altered, particularly in regard to treatment and identification of the carrier state. We do not know whether, or to what extent, this altered state of knowledge would cause either author to change his position. For our purposes, this does not matter. *What we wish to illustrate is that at a given point in time with presumably similar knowledge available to them, two experts viewing the same single-gene form of mental defect can take positions that are radically different in their implications for genetic counseling or public policy in the area of eugenics.*

In the conclusion of his article on the genetics of phenylketonuria which appeared in 1939, Jervis took the following position:

A final practical consideration may be added. Parents of affected children would be discouraged from having other children since one-fourth of these will be affected and one-half will be carriers. Whenever possible, parenthood should not be encouraged in brothers and sisters of affected individuals, since half of them are carriers.[5] Consanguinous marriages among members of families of patients should particularly be prevented. Obviously, the patients should be segregated to prevent child bearing. (Jervis, 1939, p. 24)

The direct forcefulness of these recommendations reminds us of James Joyce's delightful description of Mrs. Mooney, the boarding house mistress: "She dealt with moral problems as a cleaver deals with meat" (Joyce, 1947).

---

[5] As Penrose notes below, if the sib does not show signs of the disease his chance of being a carrier is 2 in 3.

In contrast, the position of Penrose was presented in an inaugural lecture delivered as Galton Professor of Eugenics in the University of London.

The situation at present is, then, that we are for practical purposes still unable to identify carriers. Persons who are related to phenylketonurics, nevertheless, inquire whether they are likely to have affected children, and they must and can be given information.

Let us take the case of the normal brother or sister of a phenylketonuric imbecile. His chance of being a carrier is 2 in 3. Unless he chooses a wife who is a cousin of his or an inhabitant of the Norwegian Hvaler islands, she will have the ordinary chance of being a carrier, and this has been shown to be of the order of 1 in 100. The chance that a child of this union will be affected is, therefore, a quarter of two-thirds of a hundred—i.e., 1 in 600. In my opinion, this risk is no adequate ground for discouraging the union.

There is, however, a wider eugenic aspect. Are we justified in allowing the further spread of a noxious gene in the population? Here I think we must accept the inevitable, which is not, after all, very bad. It is obviously unfair to discriminate between one carrier and another regarding which shall be allowed to have offspring and which not, and we cannot reasonably sterilise 1% of the population. The practical medical aim is to reduce the incidence of phenylketonuria. This can be accomplished by preventing consanguineous matings in affected families, and ultimately by preventing all matings of two carriers. These procedures are, paradoxically, slightly dysgenic. Haldane (1939) has calculated that the general tendency in recent years for the degree of inbreeding to diminish in human populations will actually tend to produce a slight increase in the abundance of carriers of most rare recessive diseases. The point is that in the past there has probably been a balance between extinction of genes (through infertility of affected homozygotes) and new mutation.[6] The proposed eugenic practice of discouraging the mating of partners who are both carriers denies, as it were, natural selection its legitimate prey. The argument, however, is contingent on the normal fertility of carriers. Mutation of the gene for phenylketonuria, moreover, is probably not sufficiently frequent to cause any alarming increase in carriers for a long time to come. (Penrose, 1946, pp. 952–953)

Let us look more closely at these positions and consider some of the questions that might be raised. Both authors are aware that normal sibs of afflicted individuals run a greater risk of having phenylketonuric children than an individual without affected relatives. To one, Jervis, the implication is straightforward and obvious. Their parenthood should not be encouraged. Given our cultural values, to deny the right of parenthood to a man or woman entails a considerable deprivation. To base the deprivation on the argument of their "unfitness" as parental stock is to further deliver a blow of considerable magnitude to their self-image. Then why should we impose such restrictions based upon such arguments on some members of society and not on others? Shall the restriction be imposed because these individuals might inflict a burden upon society and/or themselves by producing defective children? We

---

[6] The assumption is that the defective gene is a mutant form of the normal gene and that spontaneous mutations from the normal to the abnormal form occur at a given rate.

leave aside for the moment how such restrictions shall be imposed—by force, by social pressures, by persuasion. Some are undoubtedly more humane than others, and, certainly, Jervis appears to advocate nothing more strenuous than persuasion.

Yet it would appear that none of us is without some risk of producing genetically defective offspring. Considering such factors as the elevated death rates in childhood for the offspring of first-cousin marriages, geneticists have made estimates as to the likelihood of any individual possessing genes which if present in homozygotic form would cause death in early childhood. Combining these figures with estimates on the number of recessive genes that are likely to be responsible for abortions, premature deaths of adults, and various abnormalities, Curt Stern (1960, p. 396) arrives at the conclusion that the total number of genes per person which are detrimental in homozygotes is likely to be much larger than ten.

Such being the case, it is obvious that if anyone having a high likelihood of possessing defective genes were refused the right to procreate, we would run an immediate danger of extinguishing the race. The question then arises, if the state of our science is such that we can identify the presence of some defective genes in some individuals but cannot identify the defective genes present in the rest of us, why should the identified group be singled out for restrictions? It might be argued that for those who have been identified as carrying a particular defective gene, the overall likelihood that they would produce a defective child from any gene is greater than for the average individual. Such may well be the case. But then it becomes a matter of probabilities and a question arises as to what probability level should be the cut-off point between those who will and those who will not be allowed to procreate.

Penrose calculates that the risk for the normal sib of a phenylketonuric to produce an affected child under the conditions stated is 1/600. Presumably his risk for producing a child with another type of defect is on the same order as that for the average individual in the population at large. For Penrose, this increased risk of 1/600 is not great enough to warrant restriction on procreation. For Jervis, it apparently is. Where would the cut-off point be for another expert? Would he agree with Penrose when the increased risk was 1/600 but balk when the increased risk was 1/100, or with a gambling instinct would he even go to 1/10 before he reached his cut-off point?

Another aspect of the complexity of the problem arises when we think not only in terms of the particular defective gene an individual is carrying but in terms of the overall quality of his genetic makeup. Let us assume a married couple, possessed of admirable physical, mental, and personality traits, some not inconsiderable component of these traits being assumed to possess a genetic base. They desire children. They are capable of providing an excellent family environment for the rearing of children. But both possess in heterozygotic form a defective recessive gene. Now assume another couple possessing the same gene in heterozygotic form but lacking all the admirable qualities and also the ability to provide as good an environment. Would one be inclined to let the decision on procreation rest solely on the probabilities of producing an offspring with the particular genetic defect under consideration?

Conceivably, society could decide to deny the right for procreation solely on the basis of the probability of producing defective offspring. It could seek to enforce this restriction by various educational, legal, and medical techniques. We have seen such recommendations in the public press within the past year coming from experts in medicine as well as other disciplines. Yet we would suggest that if society so acted it would be a society whose value system had changed considerably from that which we have known. We do not think that the alteration in values would express itself only in attitudes toward defective genes. We would expect that it would be a society in which the needs of the individual would—for better or worse—count much less heavily in relationship to the needs of the state than is now the case.

Since Penrose and Jervis took their positions, the knowledge of phenylketonuria has undergone change. This change simplifies some aspects of the counseling and societal problems but complicates others. It is no longer true as it was when Penrose wrote that we are unable to identify carriers of the phenylketonuric gene. Hsia and his colleagues in 1956 demonstrated that the oral feeding of phenylalanine to carriers resulted in elevation of blood plasma phenylalanine levels that were on the average twice as great as those of noncarriers. While the test is not infallible, it does permit a separation of the normal sibs from the carier sibs of the phenylketonuric patient with a good deal of accuracy. Presumably, Jervis would have no objections to a "demonstrably" normal sib marrying and procreating. His strictures against the carrier sib presumably would in no way be changed.

Penrose's position might be a bit more difficult to transpose into the changed conditions. Not only could the carrier sib be identified but it would be possible to test the prospective spouse. If the test of the prospective spouse was negative, Penrose would probably have no great concern about marriage and procreation. If the test were positive, the implications of his 1946 position might be a bit ambiguous. On the one hand he points out the practical medical aim of reducing the incidence of phenylketonuria and indicates that this could be achieved by preventing all mating of two carriers. On the other hand he points out that such procedures are slightly dysgenic in that they deprive natural selection of its legitimate prey and tend to increase the proportion of defective genes in succeeding generations. This assumes, of course, that the carriers forbidden to marry each other will marry noncarriers and pass down the defective gene to the children of these acceptable marriages. In a sense, Jervis' position of discouraging any procreation on the part of carriers—limited to the problem of phenylketonuria—is more logically sound, if less sympathetic.

If now we take into account the fact that dietary treatment of phenyl-ketonuria is available, the problem takes on new dimensions. From the point of view of the individuals concerned, the availability of treatment may make the subjective risk of producing a phenylketonuric child relatively negligible, for such a child if treated would pose little more burden on the parent than would a normal child. From society's point of view, the problem may be more acute.

To illustrate this, let us take further liberties with the positions taken by our two experts. Jervis had recommended segregation of all phenyletonurics in order to prevent reproduction. In view of the extreme rarity of untreated phenylketonurics reproducing—Penrose in 1946 noted only 3 such incidents in 500 cases of phenylketonurics—his recommendation sounded heroic to say the least. But with treatment preserving normal IQ and a normal degree of social functioning in phenylketonurics, the likelihood of such individuals reproducing may not be very different from other individuals in the population at large. Now what would Jervis' position be toward these individuals? Segregation for phenylketonurics who are functioning at normal intellectual levels and with normal social efficiency? Sterilization without segregation? At the very least, strong social pressure against allowing such homozygotic individuals to reproduce? But what means will be both effective and acceptable within the framework of societal values now prevailing?

As for an extrapolation of Penrose's position, the argument would no longer hold that the denial to two carriers of the right to mate might be dysgenic. Such a position was based on the assumption that homozygotic individuals would not reproduce and so the defective gene would not be passed on by the homozygotic offspring of carriers. Treated homozygotes without mental or physical defect in all likelihood would reproduce.

At the beginning of this section we maintained that the scientific basis of our understanding of a single-gene determined form of mental retardation—such as phenylketonuria—was much more sound than our understanding of possible polygene-determined forms of mental retardation. We therefore suggested that the ethical and social problems of a eugenics program aimed at single-gene defects might be more easily solved. We considered the position of two eminent scientists who have done much to advance our knowledge of this disease. For sake of argument, we took a certain amount of liberty in speculating how their positions might have altered in view of changing knowledge in the area. Our purpose in contrasting these positions and raising a host of speculative questions in relationship to them—which we have left unanswered—has been twofold.

On the one hand, we wish to point out that although the social and ethical problems in a eugenics program for single-gene defects may conceivably be less difficult than is the case with polygene defects, the order of difficulty may still be well in excess of our problem solving skill if we are to achieve this solution within the present framework of societal values.

On the other hand, we wish to make some general observations on the relationship of science and scientists to public and private action programs. In our consideration of the divergent views of Jervis and Penrose we hope the reader may have been led, as we were, to the conclusion that the divergence of these experts does not derive from difference in their understanding of scientific theory or fact as it relates to phenylketonuria but rather to their respective value systems, values which are never explicitly referred to in their advocacy of one program of action or another. Yet we can think of no other hypothesis but that the implicit value systems must be the cause of their divergent conclusions when they are both looking at the same facts and operating within the same theory. We further suspect that the value system has led one—Penrose—to select additional facts and theories which in conjunction with those originally under consideration may make his divergent conclusion more logically tenable.

The point that we would advance is that the inexpert individual and the public must be able to recognize that the value system of the expert is always operative and that it may be different from one's own. The problem, and no easy one since the expert's value system is more often implicit than explicit, is to determine when one's own value system is different from that of the expert, and when it is different to determine if the facts and theories are now perceived in a different light, i.e., one that makes the implications of fact and theory assume different form.

The experts supply us with facts and theories and recommendations but in the end it is the inexpert public that will have to decide what use shall be made of these facts, theories, and recommendations. And justly so, the value system of any individual or community extends beyond the reach of any expertise.

We think one further point might be made on the relationship of value systems to action programs in the areas of eugenics and/or genetic counseling. In the praiseworthy concern for the biological heritage of succeeding generations we must not be unmindful of their cultural heritage. Not the least component of that cultural heritage—our personal bias would even lead us to say the basic core of that heritage—is the value system. If we were allowed only one alternative we would much prefer to impart to the next generation not the best of our genes but the best of our values. In an atomic world society capable of destroying itself and all of life with it, we think the next generation and the generations that follow can afford a considerable increase in the genetic load of undesirable genes much more readily than they can afford even a slight decrease in the quality of their value systems.

The risk as we see it—the history of the eugenics movement illustrates that risk as do the more recent overly simplified discussions of the relationship of hereditary factors and social problems appearing in the public press—is that in either the genetic counseling area or in public policies with eugenic implications biological considerations become primary and individual and societal values secondary. We have a bias that transcends the smattering of facts and theories we have been able to master and it is that the dignity and worth of a group is predicated upon the dignity and worth with which that group views its individual members. We shall not defend that thesis. Such a thesis in all probability derives from sources beyond the narrow span of the categories of logic. But we do ask, when others propose programs for action, that they make explicit not only the scientific theories and facts upon which the program is based but that they make equally explicit the value system in which those facts and theories are embedded and by which they are connected to the proposed program for action.

In this age in which the experts, scientific and otherwise, are called upon more and more frequently to formulate and implement programs of social action it becomes ever more crucial for the individual and the public to be able to discriminate between what is expertise and what are value judgments. The argument is relevant to our programs for the retarded. It obviously extends beyond, for the problem of retardation is only one aspect of the totality that is the human question. In defining the retardate and our attitudes toward him we define ourselves.

Mongolism and other chromosomal anomalies

In the last chapter we considered hereditary mental defects that resulted from qualitative variations in the genetic material. In the present chapter we shall consider mental defects resulting not from qualitative differences but from quantitative differences in the genetic material due to an excess or deficiency in the normal chromosomal complement.

As the reader undoubtedly knows, the genes are assembled in larger units called chromosomes, and the somatic cells of a species such as man are characterized by a specific number of chromosomes.

This number of chromosomes is called the diploid number. In the development of the sexual cells this number of chromosomes is reduced by half during the process of reduction division and the chromosomal count of the sex cells is then haploid. In fertilization, the male and female sex cells unite to reconstitute the diploid number. It is possible in the maturation of the sex cells for errors to occur in the reduction division process resulting in sperm or egg cells with either a deficient or excessive number of chromosomes. If such a sex cell participates in fertilization, the resulting zygote—or a new individual—will of course have an abnormal number of chromosomes. In the case of man, these abnormal chromosomal counts—or aneuploids—if they are not inconsistent with life itself will result in an individual more or less defective due to a genetic imbalance presumably resulting in the overproduction or underproduction of particular metabolites necessary for normal development.

Sometimes the error resulting from reduction division does not involve an excess or deficiency of chromosomes but rather a structural change of a chromosome in which there is the deletion or addition of chromosomal material. Here again the resulting genetic imbalance can cause a more or less serious defect in development.

Since the discovery of the first chromosomal defect in man—that which results in mongolism or Down's syndrome—in 1959, the number of definite clinical entities demonstrated to be accompanied by chromosomal aberrations has grown at an astounding rate. Thus Lejeune (1962) has noted that in the thirty months following the demonstration of the abnormal chromosal count in mongolism, there appeared in the literature accounts of approximately forty different abnormalities of chromosomal number or structure. A glance at recent journals of medicine and genetics does not suggest any notable slackening in the rate of discoveries in this area. Fortunately, with a few exceptions the incidence of these abnormalities is extremely low, and in this chapter we shall concern ourselves principally with those few that are prevalent enough to constitute a problem of more than theoretical interest.

Mongolism: History and Clinical Picture

The first of the chromosomal abnormalities we shall consider is mongolism, or Down's syndrome, as it is referred to with increasing frequency in recent literature.[1] This disorder was first described by Langdon Down as a separate entity in 1866 and independently in the same year by Seguin. Seguin referred to the disorder as "furfuraceous cretinism," emphasizing an assumed relationship to cretinism, while Down, struck by some aspects of the physiognomy of the patients superficially similar to certain Mongol peoples, called it Mongolian idiocy.

Down's designation of this Mongolian type of idiocy was part of his attempt to develop a general ethnic classification of idiots with the view that the various kinds of idiocy were the result of degeneration or alteration of racial type.

෨෨   A very large number of congenital idiots are typical Mongols. So marked is this that when placed side by side, it is difficult to believe that the specimens compared are not children of the same parents. The number of idiots who arrange themselves around the Mongolian type is so great, and they present such a close

---

[1] In this chapter we shall be using the terms mongolism and Down's syndrome interchangeably. A patient with this disorder is referred to in the literature as either a mongol or a mongoloid. Again, the terms are used interchangeably in this chapter.

resemblance to one another in mental power, that I shall describe an idiot member of this racial division, selected from the large number that have fallen under my observation.

The hair is not black, as in the real Mongol, but of a brownish colour, straight and scanty. The face is flat and broad, and destitute of prominence. The cheeks are roundish and extended laterally. The eyes are obliquely placed, and the internal canthi more than normally distant from one another. The palpebral fissure is very narrow. The forehead is wrinkled transversely from the constant assistance which the levatores palpebrarum derive from the occipito-frontalis muscle in the opening of the eyes. The lips are large and thick with transverse fissures. The tongue is long, thick, and much roughened. The nose is small. The skin has a slight dirty yellowish tinge and is deficient in elasticity, giving the appearance of being too large for the body.

The boy's aspect is such that it is difficult to realize that he is the child of Europeans, but so frequently are these characters presented, that there can be no doubt that these ethnic features are the result of degeneration.

The Mongolian type of idiocy occurs in more than ten per cent of the cases which are presented to me. They are always congenital idiots, and never result from accidents after uterine life. They are, for the most part, instances of degeneracy arising from tuberculosis in the parents. . . . They have considerable power of imitation, even bordering on being mimics. They are humorous, and a lively sense of the ridiculous often colours their mimicry. This faculty of imitation may be cultivated to a very great extent, and a practical direction given to the results obtained. They are usually able to speak; the speech is thick and indistinct, but may be improved very greatly by a well-directed scheme of tongue gymnastics. . . .

The improvement which training effects in them is greatly in excess of what would be predicated if one did not know the characteristics of the type. The life expectancy, however, is far below the average, and the tendency is to the tuberculosis, which I believe to be the hereditary origin of the degeneracy. (Down, 1866)

The racist implications in Down's ethnic classification of "mongolism" have been one of the objections to the term and in recent years the eponymic "Down's syndrome" has been gaining in favor. It is of course possible that Down was reflecting some of the racial attitudes prevalent in his time just as was the case with Galton whose *Hereditary Genius* appeared in the same decade. In Down's defense it might be noted that he saw in his ethnic classification evidence for the unity of mankind.

Apart from the practical bearing of this attempt at an ethnic classification, considerable philosophical interest attaches to it. The tendency in the present day is to reject the opinion that the various races are merely varieties of the human family having a common origin, and to insist that climactic, or other influences, are insufficient to account for the different types of man. Here, however, we have examples of retrogression, or at all events, of departure from one type and the assumption of the characteristics of another. If these great racial divisions are fixed and definite, how comes it that disease is able to break down the barrier, and to simulate so closely the features of the members of another division. I cannot but think that the observations which I have recorded are indications that the differences in the races are not specific but variable.

These examples of the result of degeneracy among mankind, appear to me to furnish some arguments in favour of the unity of the human species. (Down, 1866).

Down's attribution of the etiology of mongolism to degeneration of tuberculous stock is an example of the prevalence of degeneration theory in medical thought at the time he made his observations, and it of course has not stood the test of time. Nevertheless, his clinical observations were quite astute. The generality of some of his clinical signs might be challenged as we shall see; others would hold up quite well.

Although mongolism or Down's syndrome is characterized by a large number of clinical signs and practically every organ system of the body is more or less involved, no patient will show all the signs while many will be present in other types of patients and indeed in otherwise normal individuals. In addition, the signs are not constant for different age groups. Therefore, diagnosis without chromosomal analysis will depend on the presence of multiple signs, the pattern differing somewhat from one patient to the next.

Among the readily recognized external signs of Down's syndrome are peculiarities of the skull, eyes, tongue, and hands. The skull is small, rounded, and brachycephalic with noticeable flattening in the occipital region. In infancy the anterior fontanelle is unusually large and late in closing. The palpebral fissures of the eyes slant upward toward the outer corners or canthi. In very young mongols there is frequently a small semicircular fold of skin at the inner corner of the eyes which goes from the upper to the lower lid and which is called an epicanthic fold. These characteristics of the eyes contribute to a somewhat Mongolian facial appearance. Actually, the epicanthic fold is quite different in anatomic origin from the Mongolian fold found in people indigenous to the Far East—the latter consists of a skin fold originating in the upper lid and coming down at the inner corner of the eye. In contrast, the epicanthic fold is an embryonic feature not uncommonly found in many normal newborns. The chief distinction between normals and mongols in regard to the epicanthic fold is that the latter group has a greater incidence in infancy and for that group it disappears at a slower rate[2] (Benda, 1960; Solomons et al., 1965).

Blepharitis, or inflammation of the eyelids, is also a fairly common disorder in Down's syndrome. Other disorders of visual functioning encountered more

---

[2] Generally speaking, the physical signs, or stigmata, of mongolism including the epicanthic fold and the oblique palpebral fissures are as diagnostic in a Chinese population as in a Caucasoid population. (Emanuel, Huang, and Yeh, 1968)

frequently in this group than among normals include nystagmus, strabismus, myopia, and cataract. Of no known functional significance, but of diagnostic use, are anomalies of iris pigmentation, such as "speckling," that occur more frequently than they do in normal control groups (Benda, 1960; Solomons *et al.*, 1965).

The oral cavity is small and this contributes to the tongue protrusion noted with fair frequency in this group. The tongue is sometimes enlarged and frequently furrowed.

The adult mongol tends to be dwarfed in size. In 368 cases Benda (1960) noted only 15 with a height in excess of 5 feet. The fingers are short and the little finger curves toward the third finger in over 60 percent of the cases. The second phalanx of the little finger is often rudimentary or missing and the usual two flexion creases may be replaced by one only. A single transverse crease may run across the palm of the hand, the so-called simian or four-finger line (Benda, 1960; Penrose, 1962). The epidermal ridges on fingers, palms, and soles of the feet show pattern types that differ in frequency from those of the general population. Thus the finger prints of mongols have a frequency of whorls and arches which is about half that in the general population. There has been increasing interest in recent years in the study of these patterns in the epidermal ridges since chromosomal anomalies other than mongolism also show differences from the general population. Since such configurations are constant through life they provide an additional aid to diagnosis in the neonatal and newborn period (Holt, 1963).

RANGE AND SEVERITY OF INTELLECTUAL DEFECT

Down's syndrome is typically characterized by a moderate to severe degree of intellectual defect, though estimates by different authorities will show variation. Tredgold and Soddy (1963) emphasize the variability of defect, indicating that the majority belong to the imbecile grade of defect, while a few are pronounced idiots and another few merely feebleminded. Penrose (1962) estimates the mean IQ for institutionalized cases to be between 20 and 25, but recognizes that a sample of institutionalized cases is biased and that those cases living at home may be on the average of higher intelligence. Nevertheless, he believes that the highest mental age is hardly ever above 7 years, which would make for an IQ of less than 50 in an adult mongol. Benda (1965) gives an estimate of "±50 IQ points," and notes (1960) that the number of mongoloid children who maintain an IQ of 60 to 70 is not as small as some studies would suggest.

In discussing the development and intellectual growth of the mongol, Benda (1965) is critical of the unduly pessimistic prognosis that some physicians offer the parents of a mongol infant. This prognosis is sometimes accompanied by a recommendation for immediate institutionalization on the grounds that the child is "an idiot who will never learn to walk or talk."[3] Benda emphasizes that the average mongoloid child learns to walk at 2 years and sometimes as early as 18 months. Speech, however, tends to greater retardation. The 3-year-old mongol may use words and phrases but rarely speaks in sentences before 4 to 6 years of age.

Benda maintains that the Stanford-Binet test does not do full justice to the mental ability of the mongol. Despite the lower IQ scores, he maintains that many mongols are actually in the educable range and are capable of development through the first three school grades. Benda apparently takes the position that placement of mongoloid children in "trainable" classes on the basis of IQ scores is to fail to utilize the full learning capacity of many of these children.

Social and Personality Development

Benda and other investigators maintain that the mongol's social maturity is apt to be greater than his intellectual maturity. Clinical descriptions of the mongol's personality have typically emphasized his good-natured disposition and his warm, affectionate response to others. This "prince charming" characterization of the mongol has, however, received occasional challenge in the literature.

One of the more recent studies, by Menolascino (1965), reported on 86 mongols under 8 years of age who were evaluated by a multidisciplinary team. Eleven of the children (13 percent) were described as having prominent psychiatric disturbance. Classified according to the American Psychiatric Association Nomenclature, the breakdown was: six children diagnosed chronic brain syndrome with behavioral reaction; four children, chronic brain syndrome with adjustment reaction; and one child, chronic brain syndrome with psychotic reaction.

Of interest was the high incidence of abnormal EEG tracings among the disturbed mongols. This group gave 50 percent abnormal EEG tracings as compared with 13.4 percent abnormal tracings for the remaining 75 mongols. This finding raises the question as to whether the cerebral dysrhythmia was of etiological significance in the emotional disturbance.

Despite evidence of a significant incidence of emotional disturbance in the mongol group, Menolascino notes that this incidence of 13 percent is similar to the 15 percent incidence of emotional disturbance reported by other

---

[3] One such instance is described in detail in Chapter 3, but there the emphasis is on the adverse affects on the family of such a precipitous move—a good example of Dr. Kaplan's point (Chapter 10) that failure to view the family as a social psychological unit can produce serious problems. The material contained in Chapters 8 and 9 (Dr. Klaber) should make one wary of routinely advocating institutionalization. Further discussion of this issue, particularly in relation to mongolism, can be found in Sarason et al. (1966, ch. 22). The position there is similar to that taken later in the present chapter.

authors for the general population under 8 years of age. Apparently the mongoloid child runs no greater risk of developing an emotional disturbance than do other children. On the other hand, Menolascino reports an incidence of 30 percent psychiatric disturbance for a total group of 616 retarded children evaluated by his multidisciplinary team. Therefore, the mongols who were part of this total group were showing a considerably smaller incidence of emotional disturbance than the retarded group as a whole.

These figures, of course, are only suggestive of the incidence of emotional disturbance among either the mongols or the retarded group as a whole since there are likely to be some biasing factors in sample selection, e.g., children with an emotional disturbance may be referred to a diagnostic evaluation and treatment unit, such as the one where this data was collected, with greater frequency than retarded children without emotional disturbance.

EXCEPTIONAL CASES

In spite of the generally marked limitation on the intellectual development of the mongol, occasional cases are reported where the intellectual attainments, while below the average for the general population, are nevertheless markedly above the average for the mongol group.

Buck (1955) reported on an exceptional mongol who first entered an institution for the retarded in his early forties. Mr. Bolt had been raised by devoted parents who refused to accept the opinion that their child was uneducable. His mother had spent many years in the intensive tutorial instruction of her child. Mr. Bolt's commitment to an institution followed on the death of his parents.

Physically, Mr. Bolt presented many of the typical signs of mongolism including flattened occiput; fissured, thick, pointed tongue; thick, guttural speech and eye defects of myopia, internal strabismus and nystagmus. Medical examination including skull x-rays, confirmed the diagnosis of mongolism suggested by Mr. Bolt's appearance.

On intake examination the psychologist was surprised at Mr. Bolt's extensive vocabulary and courtly manner of address. On the *Time Appreciation Test* the patient obtained an Age-corrected I.Q. of 111. He was able to tell what words the initials B.C. and A.D. stood for and he knew the meaning of the term "autumnal equinox." On the Wechsler-Bellevue he obtained a Verbal Scale I.Q. of 80, a Performance Scale I.Q. of 73 for a Full Scale I.Q. of 75. The scatter on the subtests was extreme. Verbal weighted scores ranged from 12 on Information to 1 on Arithmetic. His highest success on Information was in answer to "Who wrote Faust?" to which he unhesitatingly replied, "Goethe." On the Performance Scale weighted cores ranged from 0 on Picture Competition to 5 on Block Designs and Object Assembly. On the Performance Scale the severity of his visual handicap undoubtedly penalized him. Despite powerful correction lens, it was necessary for him to work with his nose pressed against whatever it was he was trying to see.

On the Wide Range Achievement Test administered shortly after admission to the institution, he obtained a Reading grade of 8.7, a Spelling grade of 6.7 and an Arithmetic grade of 4.1. At the same time he obtained an I.Q. of 70 on the Stanford-Binet Form M, with the basal mental age established at six years and final success on Sentence Building II at the Superior Adult I level.

Two years after admission, Mr. Bolt was again tested with the Wechsler-Bellevue. This time he obtained a Verbal I.Q. of 88, a Performance I.Q. of 81 and Full Scale I.Q. of 83. On the Vocabulary subtest his highest full credit definition was earned on *recede;* his highest half-credit definition was on *espionage.*

The reader is referred to Buck's original report for a detailed and interesting account of Mr. Bolt's psychological adjustment documented by much projective test material.

As a further testament to the level of intellectual development that some few mongols can reach, there has recently been published a 12,000 word diary of a mongoloid youth, *The World of Nigel Hunt* (Hunt, 1967). The authenticity of the document is attested by Professor L. S. Penrose who has personally known the boy and observed his development. In his foreword to the diary Professor Penrose calls attention to several personality and intellectual qualities of Nigel, which while they are uniquely Nigel, yet reflect characteristics often found in less able mongols. Thus the diary reveals Nigel's preoccupation with music, his friendliness and sense of humor. Intellectually, his knowledge of words is astonishing for a mongol and his powers of observation and memory for discrete events are good. But as Penrose notes, the manner of thinking is entirely concrete. Nigel never generalizes, nor compares similar events with one another. Again, the concept of number is rudimentary with some apprehension of one, two, three, and four, but no apparent appreciation of the use of number in addition and subtraction.

Nigel typed his own manuscript and a reproduction of one of the original typewritten pages indicates that his errors are few. Nigel began his book at the age of 17. A few passages will be used here to give an idea of the quality of the work.

Nigel who could read reasonably well by the time he was 6 recalls his mother's teaching.

My mother has been so kind to me all my life. My mother taught me to read. When I was very tiny we used to play together with plastic letters and a book with huge letters in it. I learnt the sounds of the letters from my mother as we played.

After I had learned the sound of every letter mother held things up and sound-spelt them like "This is a C-U-P" and soon I could do it all by myself; all our friends were amazed and pleased with me when I began to read properly from books.[4] (Hunt, 1967, pp. 97–98)

---

[4] Nigel Hunt, *The World of Nigel Hunt.* New York: Garrett Publications, 1967. By permission.

In one of his adventures Nigel slipped away by himself to see a "Trooping of the Colour" at Buckingham Palace. Positioning himself he waits for the band.

So I stood and waited for at least one and a half minutes. I heard a terrific throb and my ears were lifted and with a Biff bang the band came along, and when they turned the corner up came their oompahs and the miserable trombones and blowed me in the middle of nowhere.[5] (pp. 54–55)

Nigel's father, in a preface to the book, details some of Mrs. Hunt's teaching of her child. Almost as soon as Nigel could talk she began to spell short words to him phonetically. While doing her house chores she would spell out the names of objects she was using, or had in hand. For example, "Ker, A, Per—Cap." In this way she exploited the echolalia which is so typical of mongolism. When he was little more than 5 years of age his mother would play with him by throwing a number of plastic letters upon the floor telling him to pick out a certain one. When the child succeeded in picking out the correct one the mother would say "That's right, Nigel. That is an M. What does he say?" And Nigel would answer with the phonetic equivalent "Mer." The Hunts found this method of spelling words phonetically far more successful than the "look and read" method, by which a child is shown a picture.

However, the precise techniques the Hunts used in teaching their child are not of prime interest to us here. What is of interest to us is the attitude they had toward their child's learning capacity and the loving endless patience and inventive skill with which they went about the task of helping him to utilize that capacity to the full. We think that Nigel like Mr. Bolt must have been unusually well endowed for a mongol. Perhaps the extrachromosomal material that has such baneful effects on the intellectual capacities of the mongol, in these instances, acted against genetic backgrounds unusually well equipped to counteract its harmful effects. However that might be, we do think that Nigel and Mr. Bolt were probably very lucky in having the kinds of parents they did.

Nigel's father notes that a fortnight after the birth of their son, they were told that no matter how much love and care they lavished on their son he would be an idiot and nothing would alter that fact. He then comments, "If we had accepted this, it would have become true." Again, at the end of Nigel's diary, his father recalls that when Nigel was 5 a senior officer concerned with mental affairs summoned them to help plan for Nigel's future. Observing the child was a mongol, she expressed the opinion that he was quite uneducable and asked if they wanted him "put away." Mr. Hunt notes that if they had been more easily impressed by "experts" they might have said "Yes."

Many who read Nigel's diary—and know the usual severity of intellectual

---

[5] *Ibid.*

handicap in mongolism—will marvel at the intellectual achievement it represents. To some parents—and this is obviously the intent of Nigel's father in publishing the book—it will prove of comfort and inspiration. We think there is much of comfort and inspiration in Nigel's diary for all of us. But with our bias we would hope that the comfort and inspiration would not derive solely or basically from the fact that Nigel, a mongol, learned to read and write. For Nigel that could only be of importance insofar as it enriched his life. For us its importance is that it allows us to perceive that life as Nigel experienced it. It is in the perception of that life that we find the marvel of the book. In reading Nigel's descriptions of marching bands and of the mountains and of the towns he visited with his parents, one feels that in Nigel's life there has been fun and joy. The kind of fun that pains no other; the kind of joy that spills out and over his companions. And when met with the raw shock of pain—for Nigel, the death of his mother—he can yet cover over the hurt and move about the daily chores of home and the training center and writing his book. It is this achievement, a capacity for joy and courage, that makes this mongol's life a comfort and inspiration and it is this that makes Nigel unique not among mongols but among men.

INCIDENCE AND LIFE EXPECTANCY

Estimates of the incidence of mongolism among newborns varies according to the authority from 0.5 to 4 per thousand (Tredgold and Soddy, 1963; Penrose, 1962). Benda (1960) points out the difficulty in making such estimates. If the child dies at birth the diagnosis is more apt to be registered as prematurity, asphyxiation, or congenital heart disease even though mongolism be the underlying cause. Making allowances for this sort of error, Benda estimates that it is safe to assume a frequency of 2 to 3 instances of mongolism per 1000 births.

It is even more difficult to make reliable estimates of the incidence in the general population. However, since mongols have a relatively short life expectancy compared to the general population, the incidence must be lower than among the newborns.

Kirman (1964) has reviewed some of the literature on life expectancy in mongoloids. Referring to Carter's life table on 700 mongoloid children attending an English hospital between 1944 and 1955, he notes that of live-born mongols 30 percent are dead by the age of 1 month, 53 percent by 1 year, and 60 percent by the age of 10 years. Nevertheless, within the span of years covered by the survey there was a sharp drop in the mortality rate from the first half of the period to the second half. Major causes of death in the series were bronchopneumonia and congenital heart disease.

Kirman also refers to a 1963 survey in Australia which found that 25 percent of mongol infants died within six months of birth and 50 percent within five years of birth. These figures, while not as high as those from England, are nevertheless of the same order and also indicate the excessively high death rate in early infancy.

Benda (1960) estimates that with the decrease in mortality rate among mongols in recent years a life expectancy of 30 years would be a conservative estimate. At the time of that publication, 1960, Benda reported that the oldest known mongoloid patient living in an institution was over 74 years of age.

The drop in mortality for mongols in recent years is undoubtedly due in part to the fact that in the area of illness where mongols tend to be most susceptible—severe respiratory infections—medicine, via the introduction of the sulfa drugs and the antibiotics, has made some of its most impressive gains. The mongol's life expectancy will also be lengthened by the current improvement in surgical and management techniques for congenital heart disease. Benda reported in 1960 (p. 148) that abnormalities of the heart were found in 75 percent of the mongols who died in the first two years of life.

Benda (1960) indicates that estimates of the frequency of mongolism in comparison to other forms of mental subnormality are also difficult to obtain with precision. These estimates will vary from study to study depending upon whether the survey involves institutional or outpatient material. They will also vary with the age group under consideration. The most reliable figures available concern the institutionalized cases. Benda indicates that in an eight-year period in which there were 12,066 admissions to the New York State schools, 9.8 percent of the cases were mongoloid. This agrees with Penrose's estimate of 10 percent mongols for all hospitalized cases of mental subnormality. This percentage is undoubtedly higher than the percentage of mongols in outpatient populations. This inference would appear reasonable since as a group, among the mentally subnormal, the mongols are likely to have lower IQs than many other groups and hence more likely to be hospitalized. This is shown in Penrose's table on intelligence quotients for hospitalized patients where the mongols rank near the bottom of the list (Penrose, 1962, p. 346). In addition, because mongols are very frequently diagnosed at birth or shortly thereafter, they are often institutionalized without there being an opportunity to see if adjustment of the child and family will be adequate enough to forestall the need for institutionalization.

RELATIONSHIP TO MATERNAL AGE

Numerous studies have indicated that there is an increasing risk of the birth of a mongol child with the increasing age of the mother. Penrose (1962, p. 208) gives the mean age of the mother at the birth of a mongol child as 36 years as compared with a mean age of 29 years for all births. Benda (1960, pp. 4–5) notes that the incidence of mongol births is 1.25 to 1.68 per 1000 births in the maternal age group 18 to 29 years. After 30 years there is an accelerating rise in the incidence—maternal-age curve, so that in the age group 35 to 39 years the incidence is 8.5 per 1000, and in the over-40 years age group it reaches 39 mongols per 1000 births.

Although maternal age is highly correlated with paternal age, Penrose (1962) has demonstrated that the partial correlation between paternal age and mongolism for a constant maternal age is negligible and concludes that the paternal age has no detectable effect on the incidence of mongolism.

Cytogenetics of Down's Syndrome

By Penrose's account the suspicion had existed some time before its proof that a chromosomal aberration might be implicated in the pathology of mongolism. As early as 1932 Waardenburg had suggested that an excess or a deficiency of chromosomes might be the cause of the disorder. Chromosomal aberrations were known to exist in other species, where they were observed to be accompanied by profound and pervasive effects on the organism. Mongolism was a congenital disorder involving multiple organ systems yet its incidence was not compatible with any model of Mendelian genetics or theory of prenatal trauma; thus the hypothesis of chromosomal error had a certain plausibility. Unfortunately, at the time, cytological techniques were not up to an adequate testing of this hypothesis. Mittwoch in 1952 attempted a chromosomal count on the cells of a mongol patient but the results were consistent with the then accepted assumption that the normal chromosomal count in man was 48 chomosomes in the somatic cells and 24 chromosomes in the mature sex cells. Therefore there seemed to be no reason to assume that the mongol's chromosomal count was any different than that of normal individuals (Penrose, 1962).

However, during the 1950s cytological techniques for preparing satisfactory material for chromosomal analysis improved. In 1956 Tjio and Levan, using some modification of these newer techniques, found that chromosomal counts for cells prepared from four human embryos indicated that 46 and not 48 was the normal chromosomal complement for somatic cells.

In their technique, tissue cultures from the embryos were treated with colchicine which stopped cell division at a point where the chromosomes—ordinarily invisible in the resting cell—can be made visible. Other technical treatment of the preparation was necessary in order to insure that the chromosomes for any one cell would be spread out sufficiently well to permit accurate counting. The chromosomes so spread out are seen to differ in size and configuration in such fashion that classificatory systems can be devised. Twenty-two of the chromosomes can be paired off with an identical looking mate. These are known as autosomes. The remaining pair of chromosomes are known as the sex chromosomes since they determine the sex of the individual. In the human female the sex chromosomes, like the autosome pairs, are of the same size and shape. In the male, the sex chromosomes are of unequal size. One, the larger, is identical to the sex chromosomes of the female and it is known as the X chromosome. The other smaller sex chromosome in the male is the Y chromosome.

In the Denver classificatory system, the chromosomes are arranged in seven groups according to their size and to the position of the centromeres. The centromere is a specialized region of the chromosome with staining properties different from the rest of the chromosome. Within some of these groups the individual chromosomes are also easily distinguished. In others the size and configuration of the group members does not permit discrimination by visual examination. Thus Group 1–3 is a group of large chromosomes with approximately median centromeres in which the three pairs of homologous chromosomes in the group are distinguishable from each other by size and configuration. Group 4–5 includes two chromosome pairs difficult to distinguish from one another. Group 6–12 also includes the X chromosome. This group presents greatest difficulty in discriminating the individual members. Group 13–15 are medium sized chromosomes with nearly terminal centromeres. The remaining groups decreasing in size are 16–18, 19–20, and 21–22. The Y chromosome is similar in appearance to the very short chromosomes of Group 21–22 (Report of a Study Group, 1960).

Following Tjio and Levan's determination of 46 as the diploid chromosome number in man, confirmation occurred in several other laboratories. The question of a chromosomal aberration in mongolism was now reopened.

In 1959, Lejeune and his coworkers (Lejeune, Gautier, and Turpin, 1959) reported chromosomal analyses on tissue cultures obtained from nine mongoloid children which indicated the presence of 47 chromosomes. The extra chromosome was a small one with the centromere located near the end. Lejeune and his coworkers advanced the hypothesis that this extra chromosome was a product of nondisjunction during the reduction division that occurs in the maturation of the sex cells. They further noted that in the fruit fly, *Drosophila*, nondisjunction is greatly influenced by maternal aging. Such a mechanism would then account for the increase in frequency of mongolism as a function of the advanced age of the mother.

Other investigators quickly confirmed Lejeune's findings and it was determined that the small extra chromosome would correspond to number 21 in the Denver classification system (Polani, 1963).

The etiology of Down's syndrome was then postulated to result from an error in the reduction division that occurs in the maturation of the ovum or egg cell. In the maturation of an egg cell a specialized cell called an oöcyte undergoes two successive cell divisions to produce the mature egg cell and three polar bodies. The result of this complicated process is to reduce the chromosomal number of 46 existing in the oöcyte to the 23 existing in the mature egg cell. Thus the oöcyte, like the somatic cells, contains 23 pairs of chromosomes for a total of 46. The germ cell, in this case the egg, has only one representative of each pair for a total of 23. In the maturation of the sperm a similar process of two successive divisions occurs starting with a spermatocyte and ending in four sperms. Again, during the process the chromosomal count is halved, but unlike the process in the maturation of the egg when only one of the final cells, the ovum, can participate in fertilization, all four sperm cells are capable of participating in fertilization.

In the case of Down's syndrome it is assumed that an error in reduction division occurs so that the ovum instead of possessing the normal complement of 23 chromosomes, contains 24 the number 21 being in duplicate. If such an ovum is fertilized by a normal sperm with 23 chromosomes, the resulting zygote and the individual developing from it will be characterized by 47 chromosomes.

It is of course possible that the extra chromosome will be contributed by the sperm cell rather than the egg, but the strong correlation between maternal age and the occurrence of Down's syndrome makes it likely that in the usual case the egg bears the extra chromosome.

TRANSLOCATIONS

Soon after the demonstration that mongols had a chromosomal number of 47 rather than 46, exceptions to the rule began to be reported. These consisted of rare individuals with Down's syndrome who had a normal chromosomal count of 46. However, examination of their chromosomes revealed differences in structure in one of the 46 chromosomes. In some of these instances it appeared that a normal member of the 13–15 group of chromosomes was missing and in its place was a larger chromosome whose structure would be consistent with the interpretation that the missing member of the 13–15 group had combined end to end with a number 21 chromosome. This is an example of a translocation in which one chromosome becomes attached to another chromosome. Thus, although such an individual appeared to have the usual chromosomal count of 46, there actually was an extra number 21 chromosome present, attached in this case to a member of the 13–15 group. Therefore the two normal number 21 chromosomes and the translocated number 21 resulted in trisomy for number 21—or Down's syndrome.

In other instances in which a case of Down's syndrome exhibited a chromosomal count of 46, it was demonstrated that there was a different type of translocation, this time a number 21 combining with a member of its own 21–22 group.

The demonstration of the existence of these translocations made possible the understanding of some aspects of Down's syndrome that cannot be explained by the usual trisomy for number 21.

FAMILIAL TRANSMISSION OF DOWN'S SYNDROME

As was indicated earlier, the great majority of cases of Down's syndrome cannot be explained on the basis of any Mendelian pattern of inheritance. Nevertheless, familial mongolism, though rare, has been reported in the literature, including cases of affected sibs, first-cousin pairs, and affected uncles and aunts of the mongol child.[6]

The existence of chromosomal translocations makes this familial incidence of mongolism understandable. Chromosomal studies undertaken on the parents of a mongol with the translocation type of Down's syndrome sometimes reveal that either the father or mother has an abnormal chromosomal count of 45. However, one of the 45 chromosomes will be abnormal and on closer examination prove to be a translocation. Such a parent will then have approximately a "normal" amount of chromosomal material although the chromosomal count is 45. We say approximately the normal amount because a translocation usually involves a small loss of chromosomal material on the part of the two chromosomes joining together.

This parental "carrier" of the translocation will produce various kinds of gametes, or sex cells, depending upon the nature of the compound chromosome resulting from the translocation. If the translocation involves the fusing of a number 21 to a member of the 13–15 group, three gametic types will occur which in fertilization will result in a viable zygote.[7] These various zygotes will develop into normal children, children who are phenotypically normal but carriers, and children who will have Down's syndrome of the translocation type (Polani, 1963). If the translocation involves a number 21 attached to a number 22, again three types of children will result, normals, carriers, and affected individuals. If however the compound chromosome consists of two joined number 21, then we would expect only individuals with Down's syndrome among the survivors.

In addition to the usual trisomy number 21 and the translocation type of Down's syndrome, there exists a mosaic form in which the individual shows an admixture of normal and abnormal trisomic 21 cells in varying proportions. Such mosaic forms may result from an error in mitotic division of a somatic

---

[6] As is usual in cases of severe defect, individuals with Down's syndrome would appear to be relatively infertile. According to Penrose's account, as of 1962, no example of a mongoloid father was known. However, there were 13 instances of female mongoloids giving birth. Two of the instances involved still births. Of the live born, 5 were mongols, 2 were mentally retarded, and 4 were normal.

[7] Some gametes which would be formed in these various reduction divisions are apparently incompatible with life. Thus, a gamete which is minus chromosome no. 21 would, if fertilized, result in a zygote with 45 chromosomes, only one of which would be a no. 21 chromosome. The absence of one member of a pair of autosomes would appear to be generally incompatible with life.

cell after the formation of the zygote. The proportion of trisomic cells in the bodily tissues might then depend upon how early in embryonic development the error occurred. In such individuals the number of features of Down's syndrome observed and even the intelligence of the individual may vary with the proportion of normal and abnormal cells (Penrose, 1962; Polani, 1963).

RECURRENCE RISKS

The existence of the translocation type of Down's syndrome has implications for the counseling of the parents of a mongol child if they are concerned about the likelihood of a future child being afflicted with mongolism. Ordinarily, a woman who has given birth to the typical trisomy number-21 form of Down's syndrome runs a risk of having a second child born with Down's syndrome that is only slightly higher than that for the general population of her maternal age at the time of the next pregnancy (Wright, Day, Muller, and Weinhouse, 1967).

Wright and his colleagues (Wright et al., 1967) compiled data from the literature and from their own studies to give the frequency of trisomy and translocation among 1382 patients. The data indicated that translocations are more frequent in the children of the younger mothers. About 9 percent of the cases of Down's syndrome born to mothers less than 30 years of age have a translocation, whereas only 2 percent of the patients born to mothers over 30 years of age show a translocation. However, the presence of a translocation in the child did not mean that one of the parents would also prove to have the translocation. In fact, in approximately 75 percent of the cases the parents did not exhibit a translocation; and the authors assume that the presence of the translocation in the offspring represents a new mutational event. They distinguish these "sporadic" translocations from the inherited translocations in which the translocation can be demonstrated to be present in one of the parents. The percentage of sporadic translocations varies with the nature of the translocation, being much more common for the translocations that involve the joining of a number 21 chromosome to another member of the 21–22 group (92 percent) and considerably rarer for the translocation involving number 21 joining with a member of the 13–15 group (60 percent).

If the patient has a sporadic type of translocation—in which neither parent shows the translocation—the risk of recurrence in a future child is probably low (Wright et al., 1967). If one of the parents is identified as a carrier of the translocation, the empiric recurrence risk will vary from several percent to 100 percent, depending upon such factors as the type of translocation and the sex of the parent carrying the translocation.

Fortunately, the number of instances in which the risk of recurrence is high are rather rare. Wright et al. estimate that at maternal ages less than 30 years at parturition there is a chance of approximately 1 in 50 that chromosomal analysis will detect an inherited rearrangement in the affected offspring. The likelihood of detecting an inherited rearrangement of the chromosomes in those cases where the maternal age was 30 years or older at the time of parturition is about 1 in 333. These estimates, of course, would apply when there is no known instance of mongolism in previous generations or collateral lines of the family. When such instances are known, the likelihood that the patient has an inheritable rearrangement of the chromosomes will be higher.

INSTITUTIONALIZATION

We have discussed institutionalization of the mentally subnormal at length in two earlier chapters but think it desirable to briefly consider institutionalization again in connection with the child with Down's syndrome. As a group, mongoloid children are among the earliest of all the mentally subnormal to be institutionalized. Two factors would seem to contribute to this state of affairs. First, unlike many other forms of mental subnormality, Down's syndrome is apparent in early infancy and, in fact, the diagnosis is often made at birth. Second, there is an attitude prevalent among a large number of the medical profession and the laity alike that little can be done for the mongoloid child and it is really best for the family as a whole if he is removed from it as soon as possible.

In an editorial in the *American Journal of Diseases of Children* in 1965 Dr. Donald K. Grant refers to the phenomenon of "Instant Institutionalization," which occurs when a doctor having diagnosed severe retardation "incontinently advises incarceration."

This attitude on the part of some physicians and its effect on children with Down's syndrome and upon their families is nicely documented in a study by Robert Kugel and his colleagues (Kugel *et al.*, 1964) which analyzed the reasons behind the institutionalization of 77 children with Down's syndrome. These children, between 2 and 18 years of age, were resident in a "hospital-school" for the mentally retarded. The authors note that "In Iowa, as elsewhere, there had been a long tradition among professional people of recommending early institutional placement for most mentally retarded children, especially for the readily identifiable mongoloid children" (p. 69).

The study had three aims: to determine if there were medical reasons for the institutionalization such as would require day to day hospital care, to determine if educational programs comparable to what the institution was offering the child would also be available in the child's own community, and finally, to obtain by parental interview some understanding of why the parents had institutionalized the child. Of the 77 sets of parents only 62 were available for interviewing but institutional records were also available to shed some light on the questions of interest.

Medical evaluation indicated that with the exception of two children with congenital heart disease, the group did not have any organic illness which might warrant hospital management in either an acute or chronic sense.

Consultation with the State Director of Special Education indicated that appropriate school facilities were available in the communities of residence of 50 of the children.

The actual reasons advanced for institutionalization by the families are considered under six headings. A given family might be placed in more than one category if its response indicated more than one reason for seeking institutionalization.

In 43 instances the advice of a physician was cited as a substantial influence for seeking admission. In eleven of these 43 cases the child was admitted under 1 year of age, and in 29 of the 43 cases the child was placed in the institution exclusively on the advice of the physician.

In the second category, 35 families felt that their inability to cope with the problem contributed to the placement. Within this category, 15 families stated that their physician had helped them to accept the fact that they and their other children would be better off if the mongoloid child was institutionalized. In all of these 35 families the child had been institutionalized at less than 3 years of age.

In a third group the family in the judgment of the authors had shown little or no desire to try to cope with the problem. No consideration had ever been given to the possibility of home care. Ten families fell into this category.

In a fourth group the reason given was a lack of suitable educational and training facilities in the community. Twelve of the 14 cases in this group were admitted after the child was of school age and in the area of their family residence, school provisions for the mentally retarded were inadequate. But interestingly enough two families giving the lack of educational facilities as the reason for institutionalization placed the child in the institution at less than 1 month of age. The authors speculate that in these cases concerns about educational facilities could hardly be the primary consideration and believe it more likely that the parents were reacting to fears about the problems involved in raising the child at home.

In the sixth and final category there were six families who maintained that their child was so ill that they could not care for him at home. This in spite of the fact that only two of the children could be so classified on the basis of medical evaluation.

In summation, the authors indicate that of the 77 children, two could be considered as having sufficient medical reasons for their institutionalization and 12 came from communities with inadequate facilities for their education. The remaining 63 children had been institutionalized for neither medical nor educational reasons but for reasons that were largely social in nature.

To indicate that there are not valid medical or educational reasons for the institutionalization of a child does not mean that there are not other circumstances which would make institutionalization the best solution for both child and family. But Kugel's study of the kinds of reasons families advance for the institutionalization of their children suggest that often too little thought and planning go into the decision to institutionalize, on the part of both the physicians and parents. One feels that there would be less "Instant Institutionalization" if both parents and physicians had a better understanding of the probable course of development of the handicapped child, a realistic picture of the burden of the child upon the family, and some knowledge and understanding of the ways and means by which that burden can be made more bearable.

We do not wish to present any pollyanna view of the difficulties of raising at home a child as severely handicapped as the average mongol. There are burdens upon the parents and siblings that should not be discounted. These burdens involve psychological stress as well as the strain of physical care, as Dr. Kaplan's presentation (Chapter 10) demonstrates.

The birth of any handicapped child is likely to invoke in the parents feelings of shame, inadequacy, and hurt; and it does little good to be offered the reassurance that such feelings are irrational. The day-to-day care of such a child is likely to involve much energy and time, with dependency in feeding, dressing, and toileting lasting far beyond the normal period. The physical and emotional strains involved in caring for the child may raise the tension level of all family members to the detriment of harmony within the home. There are concerns for the future welfare of the child that are more intense and more constant than those that afflict the parent of a normal child. There is the especially poignant pain that results from the awareness that other loved members of the family circle, spouse and children, must also bear the burden. Yet many families manage to carry the burden with dignity and with benefit not only to the handicapped child but in some instances to the family unit as a whole.

It would seem to us that the role of the professional, be he physician, psychologist, or social worker, in dealing with a family so burdened, should not be that of one who imposes upon the family his own "expert bias," be it for instant institutionalization or home rearing at all costs. Rather it should be one which endeavors to help the parents to see the problem realistically with neither exaggeration nor denial, to see the needs of the child and of the family unit as a whole, and to evaluate their own resources and the resources of the community and thus to help them formulate the best plan for this individual child and this unique family. Nor would we conceive such a plan as being static and unchanging with time but rather in need of constant reevaluation as the child and family develop and old problems dissolve and new ones take their place.

In addition, we think it should be pointed out that too often the community as a whole offers the family with such a burden only two alternatives: institutionalization in which the community takes over the complete responsibility for the child or home rearing with the community offering at most special education classes during the school-age years. We would think it much wiser from the point of view of the development of such children and in the interest of the community itself if appropriate services were offered their families throughout the lifetime of these children. Preschool programs, day-care centers, organized voluntary baby-sitter services, homemaker services during a mother's temporary illness, sheltered workshops, etc., would lighten considerably the burden of rearing severely mentally handicapped children at home. The net result would be improved development for the children and reduced costs to the community, for such services would probably cost less per child maintained at home than would equivalent provision for the child in an institution.

Sex-Chromosome Anomalies

In the same year that the abnormal chromosome count in mongolism was reported in the literature there also appeared reports of abnormal chromosome counts in patients with certain forms of gonadal dysgenesis.

Jacobs and Strong (1959) reported the case of an apparent male with small testes, enlarged breasts, poor facial-hair growth, and a high-pitched voice. Tissue obtained by a sternal marrow puncture was cultured and examined for its chromosomal complement, with the result that the individual was discovered to have 47 chromosomes. The extra chromosome was assumed, on the basis of size and shape, to be an X chromosome and the patient was considered to be of an XXY chromosome constitution rather than the XY constitution of the normal male.

The patient of Jacobs and Strong is representative of a group exhibiting Klinefelter's syndrome. Patients with this syndrome develop fairly normally until puberty at which time the abnormalities of the primary and secondary sexual characteristics become apparent. Testes are atrophied and there is some degree of feminization such as scant facial hair, high-pitched voice, and breast development. In the many chromosomal studies that have been done on Klinefelter's syndrome since the Jacobs and Strong report more than one type of anomaly involving the sex chromosomes have been found. Thus some patients show a constitution of XXXY, XXXXY, or XXYY. But in all chromosomal anomalies accompanying Klinefelter's syndrome there is more than one X and at least one Y.

The intellectual range of this group of patients is wide, varying from severe defect to above average. There is the usual problem of sampling because the more severely affected—either physically or intellectually—are more likely to come to the attention of the clinician. However, in the main, these individuals do not show severe degrees of mental defect and are likely to be in the educable class if they are retarded. Penrose (1962) estimates that the majority of individuals with Klinefelter's syndrome are probably intellectually normal.

Sex-chromosome anomalies also exist in females with gonadal dysgenesis, the first reported case involving the chromosomal analysis of a patient with Turner's syndrome (Ford *et al.*, 1959). Turner's syndrome is characterized by retardation in growth and in sexual development, accompanied by assorted congenital anomalies which may or may not be present in any given case. These include digital anomalies, imperfect extension of the elbows, cardiac malformations, and the presence of a band of tissue alongside the neck (described as a webbed neck). Ford's patient at the age of 14 was short (51″) and without secondary sex characteristics. In addition she was retarded at school. On chromosomal analysis she was found to have only 45 chromosomes with the missing chromosome assumed to be an X. The chromosome constitution was designated as XO, the O being used to denote the absence of the second sex chromosome.

The majority of Turner's-syndrome patients are intellectually normal; when retardation is present it is not severe. Polani (1960) feels that subnormality is more likely to be present in those patients that display the webbing of the neck, but even in this group it would not appear to exceed 25 percent of the cases.

Other sex-chromosome anomalies in the female may involve an excess number of X chromosomes. Penrose (1962) describes the triple-X female as similar to the normal female though in some instances menstruation may be delayed or absent. Intellectually, however, they tend to be subnormal, usually in the educable range. Cases of females with four X chromosomes have also been reported, again with no notable physical defect but with intellectual retardation.

OTHER CHROMOSOMAL ANOMALIES

Among other chromosomal errors a trisomy of a member of the 13–15 group and of the 17–18 group have been reported. Both of these chromosomal errors result in clearly defined clinical pictures.

The trisomy in the 13–15 group is also referred to as the D_1 trisomy after Patau's scheme (1960) of classification which assigns letters to the different chromosomal groups. The D_1 trisomy syndrome was actually familiar to clinicians long before its chromosomal basis was demonstrated under the designation of *arrhinencephaly*.

The infant displays many anomalies of development at birth. Those readily apparent include cleft palate, cleft lip, microphthalmos, polydactyly and posterior prominence of the heel. There is an incomplete differentiation of the brain with an absence of the external olfactory tracts. Anomalies of the heart and other internal organs are also found. (Smith, 1963)

Trisomy in the 17–18 group is also referred to in the literature as E_1 trismony or No. 18 trisomy. Like the D_1 trisomy, it involves multiple anomalies. An underdeveloped lower jaw, low-set ears, prominent occiput, and narrow pelvis are among the external features. Internally, cardiac and renal defects are common. (Smith, 1963; Rhode, et al., 1964; deGrouchy, 1965)

Both the D_1 and E_1 trisomies are accompanied by severe mental defect and the children tend to die early in infancy.

Estimation of the incidence of these disorders is difficult because of death in early infancy and failure of correct diagnosis. Smith (1963), however, gives some suggestive figures. Of 4412 babies examined, 2 had D_1 trisomy (0.45 per 1000), one had E_1 trisomy (0.23 per 1000). In the same sample, 7 infants had Down's syndrome (1.6 per 1000), for a total incidence for known autosomal trisomy syndromes of 2.28 per 1000.

In addition to the anomolies, involving an abnormal number of chromosomes, the literature in recent years presents numerous cases of abnormal development accompanied by structural changes in the chromosomes—i.e., either a deletion or addition of chromosomal material. These structural errors may also result in mental defect and a number of definite clinical syndromes have been described (deGrouchy, 1965; Nitowsky et al., 1966; Falek et al., 1966; and Reisman et al., 1967). In some instances of structural change in the chromosomes there has been evidence of familial transmission via a normal carrier similar to the transmission that occurs in the translocation type of Down's syndrome (Falek, Schmidt, and Jervis, 1966; Shaw, Cohen, and Hildebrant, 1965).

There is other evidence, consisting of the accumulation of several of the rare chromosomal patterns within one family line or within one individual, which suggests that there may be genetic factors involved which favor non-disjunction of chromosomes in cell division (Hauschka, et al., 1962; Therman et al., 1961; deGrouchy, 1965). Genetic control of the meiotic process has been demonstrated in other organisms and supports the hypothesis that the same may be true of man.

Increased knowledge in the area of familial transmission and possible genetic factors controlling the disjunction of chromosomes will obviously have relevance to practical clinical problems of genetic counseling. Further study of the chromosomal abnormalities also has importance for the genetic mapping of chromosomes in man.

Brain damage

If a definitive history of the development of the field of mental subnormality during these past several decades is ever written, one of the larger sections will undoubtedly be devoted to the development of the concept of brain damage, its associated theories, diagnostic and therapeutic techniques, and its associated programs for remedial education. It will be a difficult area for the historian to organize since brain damage is a concept that has lent itself to shifting, ambiguous, and often contradictory meanings which have reflected themselves in both theory and clinical practice.

We begin our own account of this area with the awareness that our presentation will be—of necessity, within the confines of a chapter—overly brief and arbitrary in its approach. Much of importance in the way of theory, research, and clinical practice in this area will not be touched upon; moreover, the arbitrary organization of our material will be readily apparent. Thus, the reader may have already challenged the introduction of a chapter specifically titled, "Brain Damage" with the query, "Is not the mongol child or the phenylketonuric child with mental subnormality, previously discussed, also brain damaged?" And, of course, the anatomical and neurological evidence would say, yes. We treated those disorders where we did following our interest in the development of biological theories of the inheritance of mental subnormality which led us to a consideration of genetic and chromosomal factors. Others may have chosen, with justification, to organize the material in a different fashion.

But now, arbitrarily, we would like to consider those forms of brain damage in which the etiological agents are presumed to be mainly environmental—though the environment may be intra-uterine as well as extra-uterine. This is not to say that genetic factors are irrelevent to such forms of environmentally determined brain damage. In some instances such as kernicterus resulting from genetically determined blood incompatibilities between mother and fetus the genetic determination of these incompatibilities are all important, though from the point of view of the child the effect of the incompatibility occurs through the intra-uterine environment. Or again the resistance of the child to infectious agents that may cause meningitis may well be in large part genetically determined, but the immediate etiological agent—the infectious organism—is an environmental one.

This delimitation which we place on the material of this chapter is, of course, not only arbitrary, it is ideal, and we are not certain to what extent we shall be violating the ideal when we discuss the work of various theoreticians, researchers, and clinicians in that these authorities may not feel they are limiting their use of the term brain damage to environmentally determined forms. However, in bulk and in rough measure, the material selected appears to be concerned with environmentally determined forms of brain damage.

Within this general category of environmentally determined brain damage we shall deal with mental subnormality attributed to lesions of the central nervous system. In some instances the lesions are demonstrable, and we shall speak of gross brain damage. In other instances the lesions are only presumed and we, following the literature, shall speak of "minimal brain damage," or "diffuse brain damage."

The Relationship of Demonstrable Brain Lesions to Mental Subnormality

In Chapter 3 (The Use and Misuse of Labels) we indicated that the coexistence of brain injury and certain types of behavior or levels of performance is no reason for assuming a *direct, unmediated* relationship between the two.[1] We would like to open our consideration of the relationship of demonstrable brain lesions to mental subnormality by reemphasizing this point with a consideration of case material that has been reported in the literature over

---

[1] This, in fact, is one of the major points discussed and illustrated in the previous two chapters, i.e., among individuals with the same condition or etiology there is tremendous variation both in behavior and level of performance. The concept of brain damage, like that of cultural deprivation (Chapter 5) is not adequate to "explain" observed variations in behavior and performance.

the past thirty years. We shall present this material, insofar as possible, in the context of theories of brain functions to which it is relevant. As we shall see, the problem of relationships is not peculiar to the field of mental subnormality.

Goldstein and Lashley. Beginning in the late thirties Donald Hebb undertook a critical attack upon the then existing theories on the relationship of brain injury to behavior. In particular, his psychological analysis and evaluation of a series of cases that had undergone surgical removal of diseased cortical tissue led him to challenge the formulations of theorists such as Goldstein and Lashley (Hebb, 1939, 1945, 1959).

Goldstein, a neurologist, on the basis of his experience—particularly with brain-injured veterans of World War I—had advanced the theory that cortical injury, especially when it involved the frontal lobes, was apt to lead to marked behavioral changes in both personality and intellectual functioning. The basic deficit underlying the various behavioral symptoms was characterized by Goldstein (1939) as a loss of the "abstract attitude." This loss of the abstract attitude, Goldstein maintained, could account for many of the varied behavioral symptoms exhibited by his patients, such as their concretisic thinking or their extreme anxiety attacks which Goldstein characterized as "catastrophic reactions." The concretistic thinking involved an inability to abstract or to generalize from experience, an inability to plan ahead, and an inadequate ability to handle symbolic thought as in mathematics or, even in more extreme cases, language itself. Thus one of his aphasic patients presented with a ball and asked what it was could not respond but only squeezed it and then tried to eat it. Finally, in disgust he threw it away and as it bounced the patient's face lighted up and he exclaimed, "ball." This for Goldstein represented the concretistic language of this patient. He could not recall the name for the object until he inadvertently put the object to use by throwing it. Language for him was not abstract but tied to concrete activities. Similarly, a severely affected patient could not be induced to drink or to pretend to drink a glass of water unless he were actually thirsty. The possibility of assuming the "as-if" attitude was beyond his concretistic level of functioning.

The acute emotional upsets—or catastrophic reactions—which his patients showed in reaction to apparently trivial stresses, e.g., a change in the physical surroundings on their ward or in the plans for the day's activities, were seen as a result of the patients' need to have a well-structured, highly predictable environment. Without this kind of environment, they could not function. A complex and constantly changing environment would demand a degree of flexible planning and anticipation, the invocation of higher and more abstract thought processes, and of all this they were not capable (Goldstein, 1939).

While Goldstein's theoretical position in general was that of Gestalt psychology and his emphasis was on the functioning of the organism as a whole, his emphasis on the importance of the frontal lobes for abstract levels of functioning was reminiscent of the localization principle of brain function. Lashley (1929), on the other hand, had advanced the theoretical principle of cortical mass action which maintained that large areas or masses of the brain function as a whole in learning and intelligent behavior, but within these areas the loss of function from surgical ablation is dependent not upon the specific locality of the lesion but upon the quantity of tissue destroyed.

Hebb's Clinical Material and Theoretical Formulation.   Hebb undertook his research program with the expectation that except for the speech function —for which the evidence indicated localization in specific areas of the temporal and parietal lobes—he would not find topological representation of the higher functions in the cortex. But he did assume that, in general, the principle of mass action would be upheld (Hebb, 1959). Thus he expected that while removal of cortical tissue outside of the speech, sensory projection, and motor areas would not result in specific intellectual defects, he did expect that the reduction in intellectual performance postoperatively would show a relationship to the extent of tissue removed. The results as he interpreted them supported the first hypothesis but not the second. One of the more striking cases, reported in 1939, involved a 20-year-old male who had been having epileptic convulsions over a period of nine years. The patient was operated on to remove an intracerebral cyst in the left frontal lobe. In addition to the destruction of tissue due to the cyst itself a minimum of 55 grams of neural tissue were removed in the course of the operation. Preoperatively, there had been only a slight increase in intracranial pressure and the encephalogram gave no evidence that the cyst was producing pressure on neighboring tissue. The subjective condition of the patient seemed good and the preoperative IQ was taken as a reliable index not of the patient's original level of functioning but his level as of that time. This preoperative IQ as measured by the Stanford-Binet (Form L) was 124. Postoperatively, the subject was tested at 3, 3½, and 5 weeks with Stanford-Binet forms M, L, and M, respectively. The obtained IQs were 122, 117, 129, for an average of 123.

In the same article Hebb reported the case of a 25-year-old man who, following the drainage of left frontal intracerebral abscesses several years previously, underwent surgery for the removal of scar tissue thought to be the cause of his epileptic seizures. Four years after the surgery the patient made no errors on the Stanford-Binet Superior Adult tests (Levels I, II, and III) to obtain a perfect score and an IQ of 152.

Two other cases of left frontal lobectomy reported in this series obtained postoperative Stanford-Binet IQs of 87 and 110. The total mass of tissue removed in each of these four cases, while difficult to determine precisely, was estimated as between 4.5 and 10 percent of the total mass of the cerebrum.

The conclusion that Hebb drew from these results was that any effect of frontal lobectomy on intelligence test performance must be relatively small. He also noted the lack of classical "frontal lobe signs" that other authors had described in pathological conditions of the frontal lobes, such as Goldstein's "loss of abstract behavior." Hebb then argued that the presence of such signs or symptoms in the presence of a pathological lesion such as a tumor had best be considered the result of the interference by the pathological tissue with the normal physiological activity of the brain rather than to the destruction of the tissue itself. Therefore, the existence of certain frontal lobe signs in the presence of a pathological lesion in the frontal lobes could not be used for inferring the localization of certain functions in the frontal lobe.

In subsequent articles Hebb (1942, 1945) brought forth and reviewed additional clinical material that led him to a number of important conclusions about the effects of brain injury, which in turn led to the development of his general neuropsychological theory of behavior (1949).

In his review (1942) of 38 cases of adult brain operation he estimated an average Stanford-Binet IQ of 108 for the group. For 19 of the cases for which there were both pre- and postoperative scores the average drop in IQ was but one point. The individual changes in IQ score ranged from a loss of 14 points to a gain of 11 points. Hebb considered the possibility that the apparent lack of effect might be due to "the compensating removal of dysfunction, with the effect of surgical destruction balanced by recovery from the pre-operative disturbance." But he maintained that this effect if it was present was small, since the preoperative status of the patients was generally good.

In one of the cases in this sample the patient had surgical removal of the entire right hemisphere above the basal ganglia. This patient's Stanford-Binet examination had not been completed because of her fatigue but there was no question that in at least some of the areas tested her functioning was above normal. Thus at year XVI of the 1916 Stanford-Binet she passed "differences between abstract words" very readily. At year XVIII, she obtained a score of 46 on the vocabulary list was able to pass the "memory for digits" item by repeating a series of 8 digits forward and 7 backwards.

Considering test data on nonaphasic cases Hebb concluded that:

Ability to do certain tasks which form an important part of Binet-type tests may not be greatly affected even by large injuries to the mature brain: these tasks include word definition, comprehension of and memory for complex verbal material, and the solution of unspeeded verbal problems which are hard to classify apart from the fact that they appear to be of a familiar kind, dealing with matters of general significance (though even this may not be true in all instances). The evidence shows also that there is likely to be deterioration in other abilities, although the extent and kind of loss in any individual case is unpredictable. The particular tests which have been found to show the effect of late brain injury, in the various cases cited, include: maze tracing, sentence completion, differentiation of abstract words, giving of opposites, analogies, speeded block-manipulation tasks, and picture absurdities. (Hebb, 1942, p. 281)

In the case of aphasic patients Hebb had less clinical material to work with and the psychometric evaluations were not as thorough. Nevertheless, he felt that the facts seemed to be "(a) that in aphasia there is frequently a wide disparity of abilities, but also (b) that in most cases both verbal and non-verbal indices show evidence of loss" (Hebb, 1942, p. 282).

Having reviewed the effects of adult injury on intelligence Hebb attempted a comparison of these results with the effects of brain injury in infancy upon performance in later childhood. His sample of children were, with the addition of a few cases of his own, obtained from the data of Strauss and Werner and consisted of Stanford-Binet scores, vocabulary scores derived from the Binet, and Arthur Performance Test scores. The children ranged from 10 to 19 years of age with Binet IQs ranging from 43 to 99.

A comparison of vocabulary-age scores with chronological-age scores indicated that vocabulary was generally depressed by birth injury. In addition, unlike the psychometric pattern for the adults, the vocabulary score did not tend to be one of the high Stanford-Binet subtest scores. A comparison of the Binet and Performance IQs indicated that the nonverbal IQ of the birth-injured patient tends to be higher than his verbal IQ. A more detailed analysis of the results indicated that these psychometric patterns revealed no similarity to either the pattern for the nonaphasic adults or the aphasic adults.

Hebb then concludes:

The weight of evidence points to a more widespread and less selective effect of the large infant injury than of the large adult injury. Unless known cases of exogenous mental defect involve lesions in the speech areas (the possibility already discussed), to account for the uniformly low vocabulary and verbal test scores, it must be that *low verbal test scores are produced by early lesions outside the speech areas*. With vocabulary at least it appears that a cerebral lesion may be deleterious at infancy and not at maturity, for such lesions at maturity do not affect vocabulary to a detectable degree. If this is so, the development and the retention of an ability may depend on the brain in different ways. An intact cerebrum is necessary for the normal development of certain test abilities, but not for their retention at a nearly normal level. In other words, *more cerebral efficiency or more intellectual power is needed for intellectual development than for later functioning at the same level*. (Hebb, 1942, p. 286)

Though the results of the adult brain ablations suggested that Lashley's equipotentiality theory had limitations, the generalized effect of infant lesions, in Hebb's view, argued for some degree of equipotentiality of the cortex in early development. He maintained that even the verbal abilities so sharply localized in the speech areas of the adult were dependent upon the integrity of the whole cerebrum for their development in childhood.

This assumed difference in the functioning of the immature and mature cortex, derived from a consideration of the effects of early and late brain injury, led Hebb to the construction of his neuropsychological theory of behavior. This theory has been of great heuristic value as attested by the large amount of research it has generated in such areas as the effects of early experience on behavior of the adult organism, the effects of perceptual isolation, and the relationship of various neurophysiological phenomena to behavior. As an aside we might indicate that it is another instance of where coping with clinical material has led to theoretical formulations of the most general relevance to the science of behavior.

Regardless of the heuristic value or the viability of Hebb's theory, it seems necessary to consider whether Hebb was really justified in assuming his data indicated that brain injury in the adult was essentially different from brain injury in infancy. This necessity would seem forced upon us by clinical material such as that offered by Kennedy and Ramirez (1964).

Kennedy and Ramirez. In the first case we shall consider from the Kennedy and Ramirez series, an 8-year-old was evaluated for uncontrolled petit mal seizures and a severe behavior problem.

∽   The seizures and behavior problem dated from infancy and were subsequent to a severe illness requiring hospitalization. At the time of evaluation at 8 years, "he was a third grade pupil in a private school and said to be bright." But the parents complained of demanding, aggressive, and destructive behavior. At meals, he would smash dishes and scream without provocation. Pneumoencephalography demonstrated left cerebral atrophy and a hemispherectomy—removal of the cortex on one side—was performed. Subsequent to recovery from surgery the child's behavior problem disappeared and he remained seizure free without anticonvulsant medication.

Another even more striking case reported by Kennedy and Ramirez concerned an infant with Sturge-Weber syndrome, a disorder often accompanied by hemiplegia, epilepsy, and mental retardation—although the latter is usually of a mild degree.

∽   The infant was born with a hemangioma covering her entire right cerebral hemisphere. At the age of of 11 months, after the development of hemiparesis and seizures, the right cerebral hemisphere was removed leaving "only the basal ganglia, thalamus and middle portion of the visceral brain on the involved side." Evaluated at 8 years she proved an attractive and responsive child. She was able to walk although there was motor impairment in the left arm and leg. She had the expected visual-field defect corresponding to the absence of the right visual cortex. Despite these expected sensory and motor impairments, the child was progressing normally in school and her IQ was estimated at 132.

A third dramatic case in this series was a 7-year-old boy with marked hydrocephalous.

∽   After a stressful period at birth the development was normal except that walking was delayed until 2½ years due to spasticity of the lower limbs. At the time of evaluation, he was capable of normal physical activity in spite of some pyramidal tract signs and tremulousness. His head measured 60 cm, markedly in excess of the norms for a 7-year-old child. Pneumoencephalography revealed marked dilatation of all ventricles and basal cisterns. There was but a centimeter of brain tissue at the periphery of the lateral ventricles. Despite these very obvious organic findings the child was considered very intelligent and well behaved with an excellent school record and an IQ of 137.

These cases—and there are others in the literature with similar import—are obviously very unusual. In the discussion accompanying the Kennedy and Ramirez paper it is pointed out that in other cases removal of the hemisphere had not resulted in a functionally effective child. Every clinician has seen numerous instances where less marked hydrocephaly has apparently resulted in severe retardation. But the point is that when we are dealing with surgical ablations of cortical tissue and with specific pathological lesions in childhood, it is possible to find the same kind of exceptional cases that Hebb reported in adults. This raises the question whether or not injury to the brain in infancy is essentially different from injury to the brain in the adult. Hebb, himself, pointed out the difference between the loss of cortical tissue by disease or surgery and the interfering effects that the presence of diseased or scar tissue may have upon the physiological functioning of the rest of the brain. Kennedy and Ramirez also emphasize that the absence of tissue and the presence of malfunctioning tissue may be quite different in their physiological effects. It would seem reasonable to us to question whether the difference between Hebb's adults and the "exogenous" brain-damaged children may not be due to the type of lesions present in the two groups rather than the age at injury. We are in no way maintaining that the age at injury is not relevant to the effects on behavior; we are maintaining that all the evidence to date suggests that the relationship between behavior and brain injury is fantastically complex, subject to few generalizations that will hold up across all cases.

Even in the relatively simple area of the effects of penetrating wounds involving the visual projection area of the occipital lobe, Teuber and his colleagues (1960) have shown that the relationship between visual field defects and the anatomical damage cannot always be reconciled. For example, a patient wounded in the occipital lobe presents with a visual scotoma (an area of blindness in the visual field) that is in the form of a ring. Teuber maintains that he cannot conceive, on the basis of knowledge of the visual tracts and projection areas—knowledge that is some of the best we have regarding the function of the central nervous system—how anatomical damage resulting from the wound can account for a scotoma in the form of a ring.[2]

---

[2] From the same laboratory (Semmes et al., 1960) data on somatosensory changes after penetrating brain wounds indicates further complexity in simple sensory function. It had been generally conceded that the left and right parietal lobes were not functionally equivalent but the differences were assumed to lie solely in the areas of complex disorders

SOME GENERAL CONCLUSIONS ON GROSS BRAIN DAMAGE

The foregoing considerations of exceptional cases involving gross brain damage or removal of cortical tissue, and of the complexities of the relationship between brain injury and behavioral impairment, are in no way meant to imply that brain damage does not often or even always result in some impairment in function. What we would iterate and emphasize is that in any individual case one cannot automatically attribute behavioral impairments or disturbances to the presence of brain injury. This then means that the diagnostician, the therapist, and the educator cannot approach the task of aiding any individual child and his family with the preconception that the behavioral problem, be it intellectual or emotional, is the result of a known brain lesion. The lesion and the behavior may be related causally, in part, even principally, or not at all. It is the task of the clinician and the educator, partially with professional skills and techniques, partly by trial and error, to determine the extent to which the behavior is modifiable by environmental manipulations and by learning experience. For even if the behavior is determined to the extent of 99 percent by the organic lesion, exploitation of the remaining 1 percent susceptible to environmental manipulation and learning may make the difference between an adjustment to the handicap by the child and his family that constitutes a liveable solution to the problem and one that is a total catastrophe for the family unit. With these thoughts in mind we will now consider the problem of cerebral palsy—a most typical form of gross brain damage—and its relationship to mental subnormality. For while we feel that often the capacity of the handicapped child to progress is not fully exploited by educators and parents alike, we are aware that unrealistic expectations for a child can result in demands for performance that are frustrating to child, parent, and teacher alike. There is a difference between the attitude that assumes there is always room for progress and expresses itself in warm, supportive encouragement of the child, and the attitude that assumes that realistic limitations do not exist. The line dividing the two attitudes is un-

---

such as the aphasias, agnosias, apraxias, and anomalies of spatial orientation. Thus, in right-handed people speech is specifically vulnerable to injury in a rather restricted region of the left hemisphere. But for left-handed people the speech function is likely to be more diffusely represented in the cortex and cases of speech disturbance have been reported with injury to either the left or right hemispheres. But to this recognized complexity of the higher functions, Semmes' results add complexity to even such primary sensory functions as sensitivity to pressure or the localization of a point touching the skin. Her data would indicate that "the localization and nature of sensory decrement, as well as the distribution of decrement between the hands, are not the same with respect to lesions of the left and right hemispheres." It appears that the sensation of the left hand is more diffusely represented in the contralateral hemisphere than is the case for the right hand, and that sensation of the left hand unlike the right is frequently affected by lesions of the ipsilateral sensorimotor areas.

doubtedly a fine one, but it should be possible for teacher and parent—with the aid of the clinician if necessary—to keep from developing unrealistic expectations without swinging to the other extreme of assuming that progress is impossible.

THE CEREBRAL PALSIES

As Crothers and Paine (1959) have pointed out, the term cerebral palsy does not designate a disease in the usual medical sense. However, they consider it a useful "administrative term" covering individuals who since early life have been handicapped by motor disorders which are due to nonprogressive abnormalities of the brain.

The cerebral palsies may be subdivided depending upon the site of the motor impairment. Thus, monoplegia refers to paralysis of a single limb, hemiplegia to paralysis of one side of the body; in paraplegia the involvement is basically limited to the lower limbs; cerebellar ataxia involves impairment of the muscles controlling maintainence of posture. Or the classification may emphasize the nature of the impairment and categorize the cases as those involving flaccid paralysis, spasticity, rigidity, tremor, athetosis, or ataxia.

Crothers and Paine have preferred a simpler classification into two large groups: spastic cases and "extrapyramidal" cerebral palsies. The site of brain injury in the cerebral palsies may involve the pyramidal or extrapyramidal systems or the cerebellum. Where spasticity is an outstanding feature, pyramidal involvement is most likely. Lesions in the extrapyramidal tract or basal ganglia sometimes result in athetosis—a condition characterized by slow, wormlike, purposeless movements which are exaggerated by voluntary action. However, in many cases both pyramidal and extrapyramidal tracts are involved and there are relatively few cases showing pure spasticity or pure athetosis.

Etiology of Cerebral Palsy. In some instances of cerebral palsy specific etiological agents can be identified. But in most instances it is difficult to pinpoint the causative agent. Since Little's classic paper on the disorder in 1861, birth injury has been indicted as an etiological agent. Cerebral anoxia either before or during birth has also been suspect. Bilateral anomalies of the brain in some cases of cerebral palsy suggest developmental malformation occurring in utero. All of these factors and more would apear to add to the total incidence of cerebral palsy. But as yet it is not clear which etiological agents are the more important (Crothers and Paine, 1959).

An example of an etiological agent that is fairly well understood occurs in cerebral palsy associated with kernicterus. Kernicterus is an acute encephalopathy of the newborn period occurring subsequent to hemolytic disease. The hemolytic disease itself may result from blood incompatibilities between mother and fetus involving the Rh or other blood-group factors. In hemolytic disease of the newborn there is a breakdown of the red blood corpuscles which starts before birth but may not reach its maximum until after delivery. The infant is jaundiced and there is an elevation of the blood level bilirubin, a pigment released during the breakdown of the hemoglobin of the red blood corpuscles. The physiological state of the newborn is such that this elevated bilirubin level may lead to a deposition of this pigment in the brain, particularly in the basal ganglia, the hippocampal cortex, and the subthalamic nuclei. The deposition of this pigment in the brain constitutes kernicterus which in its acute phase displays itself clinically in a neurological syndrome characterized by lethargy and muscular rigidity. If the infant survives the acute phase of the disease he may subsequently show a variety of residual neurological effects ranging from comparatively minor motor disturbances to severe cerebral palsy. Deafness and mental retardation may also be part of the clinical picture (Zueler, 1960). Fortunately, since the introduction of exchange transfusions for neonates with hemolytic disease the incidence of kernicterus has been reduced.

Intelligence in Cerebral Palsy.   Estimates as to the incidence of mental subnormality among the cerebral palsied have varied considerably. It may be assumed that part of this variability is due to the difficulty of testing patients with pronounced motor handicaps often accompanied by speech and sensory deficits. Clinicians have generally felt that there must be some adaptation of the testing procedures to allow for the handicaps of the child. Such adaptations, with their often unspecified variations from standard test procedures, will, of course, introduce some degree of unreliability into the test scores.

One of the earliest writers to point out the problems involved in testing brain-damaged children was G. B. Smith (1926). Most clinicians would still concur with his practical suggestions for the administration and interpretation of tests.

We wish to emphasize, however, the need for careful re-examinations in which the actual intelligence quotient determination plays the least part. We should be extremely careful to note the character of the scattering, the deviations in mental reactions, and the manual performance in the performance tests. If the tests are graded in the manner usually done for other defectives, we are not fair to the child, for they consistently are undergraded rather than being given too high a score. A great deal of difference is noted in individual examinations and much depends upon the interest and perseverance of the examiner. I have found, especially in the group with the associated speech defects, that it is wise to have the teacher or the mother present to interpret the child's answers. Each test must be analyzed in the light of existing defects in the special senses, for defective eyesight, hearing, lack of coordination as well as diminution in sensibility and discrimination, all play a very important part. (Smith, 1926)

Other experienced clinicians in the field, e.g., Lord (1937) and Taylor (1959), have also emphasized the difficulties in estimating the intellectual abilities of these children. Edith Meyer Taylor, who continued Lord's pioneering work at the Children's Hospital in Boston, summarized the reservations she and Lord had about the use of IQ scores for such children.

Both of us have recognized the limited merits of intelligence quotients in children with cerebral palsy. In our psychological studies we have tried to evaluate the child's ability to adjust to his present life-situation, and to adjust to the demands of his environment. Dr. Lord was interested especially in the child's educational potentialities and his prospects to learn how to read and write and do arithmetic. Coming from a slightly different psychological background, I have myself become more and more interested to see the educational problems as symptoms of broader difficulties. We have concentrated especially on the study of reasoning ability, perceptual organization, learning ability, etc., as they pertain to general adjustment of the individual. While the methods have varied and evolved in the past 23 years, the basic philosophy has remained the same: we have tried to judge and to predict how far the child could be expected to adjust to the ordinary demands of his life-situation. (Meyer and Crothers, 1953, p. 153)

However, despite the reservations most clinicians would have about a straightforward administration of a standard IQ test to a severely handicapped child, Schonell has presented evidence that, at least for the Stanford-Binet, modification of the test procedures to adapt to the child's handicap may not make as much of a difference as might be expected if one is concerned about a mean IQ or a distribution of IQs for a *group* of cerebral-palsied children as a whole. The following description of Schonell's work is from Doris (1963).

In a survey of cerebral palsy in Birmingham, England, 354 children were seen by the psychologist, and for 340 of these between the ages of three and fifteen years it was possible using the Stanford-Binet (Form L) to obtain estimates of intelligence. For each child three scores were obtained. The first of these was the *tested* I.Q. obtained when the instructions for administration were adhered to irrespective of the child's handicap. The second was the *modified* I.Q., obtained by scoring as successes those items which the psychologist judged the child would pass except for some special disability which prevented him from carrying out instructions. Schonell includes in her report some details of the ways in which testing was modified to adapt to the child's handicap. The third score was the *estimated* I.Q., and in each instance in which this *estimated* I.Q. differed from the *tested* and *modified* I.Q.s a short report was written explaining the *estimated* I.Q.

In 253 cases (74%) the three I.Q. scores, *tested, modified,* and *estimated* were identical. With these children the test was administered and scored with strict adherence to the usual procedures. In 87 cases (26%) some modification of test administration was undertaken. It is of interest to note that modification of testing procedure was deemed necessary with more of the athetoid and mixed athetoid-spastic cases than with the pure spastic cases. It is in these groups of athetoid and mixed types that the greatest discrepancies between *estimated* and *tested* I.Q.s occurred. On the whole, differences between the *estimated* I.Q.s and the *tested* and/or *modified* I.Q.s were slight. In the 87 cases where the *estimated* I.Q. was different from the *tested* and/or *modified* I.Q., only 44 involved a difference of more than three I.Q. points; 43 involved a difference of only one or two points, which would certainly be considered negligible for all practical considerations. The average difference between *estimated* and *tested* I.Q.s for all 87 cases was only 2.7

points. The six largest differences reported range from 9 to 14 points. All of these latter cases were severely handicapped. Thus, these findings suggest that in the majority of cerebral-palsied cases there is no need for modification of standard test procedures in the use of the Stanford-Binet. They further suggest that when modification of testing procedures are judiciously undertaken by the psychologist or when he makes an estimation of intelligence based upon a modified administration, the results on the average are not greatly different from those obtained by standard administration. However, in some individual cases the differences between the scores were substantial. (Doris, 1963, p. 177–178).[3]

Schonell's data are not, of course, to be interpreted to mean that the results obtained on the Stanford-Binet are the same as might be obtained if the motor handicaps, speech, and sensory defects were not interfering with the performance of the children. Her work does, however, give us some reason to assume that test scores obtained on the Stanford-Binet, and possibly other tests, when a group of cerebral-palsied children are considered as a whole, are likely to be fairly stable despite the fact that different test examiners may deviate somewhat in their administration of the test to accommodate to a child's handicap.

Schonell (1956) presents other important data on the reliability of Stanford-Binet IQ scores for the cerebral-palsied group. In her Birmingham study, a correlation coefficient of .89 was obtained for test–retest scores on 29 children at a twelve-month interval. Another sample of 50 children tested at a cerebral-palsy clinic in Brisbane gave a correlation of .96 after twelve months. For both samples, the average IQ in both the test and retest were within a range of 78 to 82.

Schonell's data then suggests that in the hands of a competent psychologist the Stanford-Binet is a reliable instrument for use with cerebral-palsied children even when the psychologist uses his clinical judgment to make allowances for the child's handicaps in the administration and scoring of the test.

It is also of interest that Schonell (1958), basing herself on a review of relevant clinical and research literature as well as on her own extensive research and clinical experience with the testing of the cerebral-palsied child, concludes that the Stanford-Binet is the best single instrument for testing of the cerebral-palsied youngster. This, of course, is not to say it is an ideal instrument; and the clinician testing a severely handicapped child will and should interpret the obtained IQ score with considerable caution.

Having set some rough limits for the confidence with which we may view tests scores in the case of cerebral palsy we would like now to look at two studies which will give us some limited idea of the relationship of cerebral palsy to mental subnormality. In addition, these studies, presenting as they do

---

[3] From the clinical point of view, it is of interest that Schonell gives data on eleven of the children who had *estimated* IQs higher than their *tested* IQs. These children were accepted into the day-care program of a cerebral-palsy center. They were retested at twelve-month intervals, one to three retests per child. Schonell maintains that the retests showed that the increase of the *estimated* IQ over the *tested* IQ was fully or partially justified in all but one case.

longitudinal data, will give us some idea, in the case of cerebral palsy, of the predictability of test scores obtained in childhood for test performance at a later stage in development.

TAYLOR'S LONGITUDINAL STUDY. From a large sample of over 1800 cerebral-palsied patients who had been seen at the Children's Hospital over a period of years, Dr. Edith Meyer Taylor (1959) was able to obtain follow-up psychometric data on a subsample of 214 cases.[4] These cases had for the most part been initially tested before the age of 6 years. Reevaluation was from three to twelve years later, at which time chronological ages ranged from 3 to 20 years. The Wechsler-Bellevue Intelligence Scale or the Wechsler Intelligence Scale for Children was used with older patients. The revised Stanford-Binet Scale was used for children under 7 years of age. In cases where administration of the whole scale was not possible the results were prorated.

As a result of the psychological examination at reevaluation all cases were classified in the following categories: superior (IQ score greater than 110), average (IQ 90–110), borderline (IQ 70–90), defective (IQ 50–75), low-grade defective (IQ below 50). Unfortunately, since this follow-up study was not set up at the time of the original testings, the data from the original test reports were not in a directly comparable form and the psychological findings were not expressed in definite quantitative terms. Therefore, the results of the earlier psychological evaluations were classified into categories assumed to be roughly equivalent to the reevaluation categories set up on the basis of the actual IQ scores.

An examination of Taylor's data indicates that on the initial evaluation the distribution of patients in the categories of intellectual competence were as follows: superior, 9; average, 48; borderline, 50; defective, 107. Thus, while approximately 25 percent of this sample of cerebral-palsied individuals achieved average or better intelligence ratings, 50 percent were in the defective range. The sample is, of course, selective, and we cannot say how representative the distribution would be for cerebral palsy cases in general. Obviously, very mild cases of cerebral palsy are less likely to appear in a clinic population and it is not unreasonable to assume that the very mild cases, if included, would raise the proportion of bright children in the group. Taylor's interest, however, focussed on the changes in intellectual level with the passage of years. A comparison of the classifications of subjects at initial evaluation and at reevaluation indicates that of the 214 cases, 157 (73 percent) were in the same category in both examinations, 33 cases (15 percent) were

---

[4] In such a study, one can well appreciate the difficulty of getting in contact with patients, often after years have elapsed since their last contact with the clinic, and inducing them to return to the clinic for a reevaluation. Therefore, our indication of the size of the total sample and the much smaller size of the subsample for whom it was possible to obtain retest data is in no way intended as a criticism; it is merely to make the reader aware that many selective factors work to limit the generality of the findings.

in a lower category on reevaluation, and 24 (11 percent) were in a higher category. Only four cases differed by more than one step in category placement. For Taylor this indicated that:

. . . in 57 cases (those in categories "average" and "superior") the psychologist could assure parents and doctors before the child was of school age that it was of normal intelligence (in 9 cases of superior intelligence). Forty of these children developed as well and two even better than anticipated (a total of 42 children or 72% of the 57 cases). In 107 cases the psychologist believed the child to be mentally defective at an early age. In 91 (85%) of these cases, this evaluation was proved correct by subsequent events. Of 50 children who were originally considered borderline cases (between defective and normal) 6 were better developed when reexamined than they had seemed before; 18 were more noticeably defective than they had appeared when younger; 26 remained in the borderline category. (Taylor, 1959, p. 28–29)

These findings offer evidence for the reliability of this kind of classification over considerable time intervals. In the examination of the causes of disagreement between initial and follow-up categorizations the study supplied additional dividends of information.

It is not easy to determine for each case the extent to which the differences between original and later examinations result from the child's condition or from incorrect original appraisal. In a number of cases physical deterioration went with decline in mental alertness. In some others it seemed that improved physical condition and increased opportunity for experience had bettered the mental situation also. However, study of the psychological records reveals some other significant causes of possible errors. It appears that most of the disagreements are found in cases where the first examiner tended to place more emphasis on the child's ability to use or respond to language than on other signs of comprehension. For instance, the most flagrant disagreements between original and later estimates are found in the group with pure extrapyramidal involvement—often among the earliest patients. Of the eleven cases in this group who were originally thought to be defective but turned out to be of borderline (6) or average (5) intelligence when examined more than ten years later, five had by then proved to be deaf or hard of hearing. (Medically they belonged to the kernicterus group.) The others all had more or less serious speech delays due to dysarthria. In some other instances where the original estimates were lower than the reevaluations, children classified in other medical groups had difficulty in speaking and learned to talk late. However, errors of prediction probably due to overemphasis on the importance of speech development also occurred with children who talked early. They had earned high ratings as young children because of their verbal fluency; later this facility was not as useful to them, since at higher age levels good performance is determined more by reasoning power than by fluency of speech alone. (Taylor, 1959, pp. 29–30)

THE LONGITUDINAL STUDY OF KLAPPER AND BIRCH. A recently reported study by Klapper and Birch (1967) sheds some further light on the intellectual capacities and development of cerebral palsied children. In 1948, 141 children of a total patient population of 155 at a cerebral-palsy clinic were administered the Stanford-Binet, Form M. In the distribution of scores, 11 percent of the cases were below an IQ of 50; 57 percent were between an IQ of 50 and 89; 32 percent obtained an IQ score of 90 or above. These results are roughly equivalent to those obtained by Taylor, showing a preponderance of low IQ scores, but with a considerable proportion of the group obtaining average or better IQs.

In a follow-up of these children 14 years later, Klapper and Birch were able to obtain psychological tests on 54 of their patients. Forty-five of these were administered the Wechsler Adult Intelligence Scale, the remaining nine were too defective for the Wechsler and were administered the Peabody Picture Vocabulary Test. In the authors' detailed analysis only the WAIS data were used since the Peabody and Wechsler were not considered sufficiently comparable. For the group of 45 patients tested with the Wechsler, the correlation between initial IQ rankings on the Stanford-Binet scores and the ranking on the Wechsler at the time of follow-up was .64 (Spearman rho; p. < .01) indicating that the two tests at a 14-year interval discriminated the group with respect to intelligence with a considerable degree of agreement. Like the Taylor study, it suggests that psychological estimates of intellectual functioning of the cerebral palsied obtained in childhood can have considerable predictive value for psychological test scores obtained at a much later date.

Twenty-eight of the total group of 45 shifted less than plus or minus 14 IQ points from the first to the second testing. Seventeen showed a shift of 15 or more IQ points. However, 14 of these latter cases showed an increase and only 3 showed a decrease in IQ scores.

Therefore, although there was noteworthy stability for the IQ scores of the group as a whole, a considerable number of individual children apparently made quite large shifts in intellectual functioning. Fortunately, most of the large shifts were in the direction of an increase of IQ score. The authors further note that the predictive worth of the earlier estimates of intelligence varied with the earlier test score. Initial IQ scores of less than 50 were excellent predictors of retest scores. Initial test scores ranging between 75 and 89 were the poorest predictors of retest rank and IQ score. This finding of greater unreliability for the initial estimates of intelligence when dealing with IQs from 75 to 89 is similar to Taylor's data which indicate that her borderline group (IQ estimate from 70–90) gave the greatest unreliability, a point which the clinician might find of some value.

Klapper and Birch indicate that their data show a mean increase in IQ score for the group as a whole of 6.5 IQ points ($t < 3.1$; $p < .01$). They consider the possibility that the intellectual functions of the cerebral-palsied patient are transiently depressed in childhood because of the early restriction in sensory and motor experiences attendant upon the disorder, and the degree to which the environment may tend to reinforce the child's invalidism.[5]

---

[5] The early effects of cerebral palsy on sensory-motor experiences have hardly been studied systematically. In a large number of cases we know that visual defects have

Alternatively, they suggest that there may be a compensatory reaction to motor and sensory handicap leading to an acceleration in the development of verbal skills. We also wonder to what extent it is simply a reflection of differences in the test instruments since, relative to one another, different IQ tests may give somewhat higher scores at one or the other end of the scale, or scores may be higher or lower on two scales depending on the nature of the group being tested. But the difference, if further study should support it, is of great practical and theoretical importance.

Social and Emotional Adjustment of the Cerebral Palsied. The psychometric evaluations of the cerebral-palsied patients reported by Taylor were only part of the follow-up study conducted under the direction of the neurologist Bronson Crothers and his staff at the Children's Hospital in Boston. The experience and observations of this group of clinicians in evaluating and handling the emotional and social adjustment of these patients appears to us to have too much significance, not only for the problem of cerebral palsy, but for the entire area of mental subnormality, to be passed by without consideration.

Introducing case material on the emotional adjustment of their patients Crothers and Paine (1959) note:

It is difficult but possible to arrive at tentative conclusions about the course of physical growth and development and its effect upon the motor patterns and to come to grips with the complicated problem of appraisal of physical therapy. It is far more perilous to generalize about educational procedures, although we can appraise psychological levels and check on school progress. The most difficult and perhaps the most important matter of all is related to the way in which these handicapped children deal with the pressures which are imposed upon them and the degree of emotional stability they acquire. It is particularly important to find out what we can about the way in which independence, however incomplete, is fostered or impeded by the adults whose power is so greatly increased by the disability of the child. (Crothers and Paine, 1959, p. 218)

Crothers and Paine felt that many of the more marked failures in emotional adjustment concerned a small group of children of defective or borderline intelligence who were subjected to incessant pressure to achieve beyond their capacities. For example, a spastic, tetraplegic boy evaluated at 6 years of age could neither walk nor sit alone though he had fair use of his arms. He could say a few words but was considered "grossly defective." The parents would

---

existed from birth and that these visual defects alter the way the infant and young child experience the world. For example, the experience of being picked up—indeed the "visual intake" even when at rest—is not the same for the cerebral-palsied child with a visual defect as it is for the normal child. In light of this, one may raise the question of how, knowing that the child has some kind of visual defect, one might take this into account in the many different kinds of situations in which someone changes his position, and therefore, his visual field. This is not an easy question to study but it does allow us to make the point that research may tell us how the environment can be changed so as better to help the very young child compensate for the visual defect.

not accept a realistic appraisal of the boy's limitations but undertook their own program of goals and training for the child. The patient returned for reevaluation in his mid-thirties, bringing with him a series of notebooks in which the same simple words and short sentences were written over and over. He spoke a few words and short sentences. Given paper and pencil by the examiner he wrote with incredible and agonizing slowness a series of words. If any letter showed the slightest irregularity he erased it and rewrote it. If he were told to ignore the irregularity and go on with his writing he became irritated and insisted on the correction. He absolutely refused to attempt to write a new word that might be dictated to him. Crothers and Paine compare this performance to that exhibited by Goldstein's brain-injured patients, and they comment: "The whole product of his effort was a stereotyped duplication of simple patterns. The incessant training had no obvious relation to education" (p. 221).

The reader may compare these parents and their child to the case of the mongoloid child, Nigel Hunt, which we considered in an earlier chapter. In both cases a determined set of parents refused to accept the advice and the prediction of the experts. What accounts for the difference in outcome? *We emphasize most strongly that the difference in outcome is not simply in the intellectual achievements of the children.* The records, as brief as they are, indicate a radical difference in the overall adjustment of the children. Nor is the difference solely the result of the nature of the organic impairment. Crothers and Paine give several cases of success and failure in social adjustment and achievement when the degree of physical handicap and the level of intellectual functioning in childhood are not noticeably different.

The factors that make for successful adjustment to and circumvention of a handicap or an intellectual impairment by a child and his family are undoubtedly fantastically complex and subject, at this time, to few generalizations that can be stated with any degree of precision. It is easy enough to make some vague statement to the effect that the child must be encouraged and motivated to overcome his handicap insofar as possible but he must not be pressured beyond his capacity. *But in concrete behavioral terms how do we distinguish encouragement from pressure?* Every clinician and most parents will recognize the extremes of pressure, but instances less extreme gradually fade into that desirable category of encouragement. Precisely the same kind of parental behavior is for one child pressure and for another encouragement. At times the advising clinician may be no less bewildered than the perplexed parent. As for the child's motivation, one finds apathy at one extreme and at the other a degree of motivation that, out of touch with realities, is foredoomed to frustration. Extremes are easily recognized but how does one go about developing and recognizing in a given child the optimal level of motivation?

The problem is obviously a pressing one for the clinician. It ought to be equally pressing for the research worker. For this problem—in both its practical and theoretical implications—is not limited to the handicapped and the mentally subnormal. In every family unit there are interactions between child and parents that foster or impede a child's successful exploitation of his own individual pattern of abilities for the purpose of his overall social and emotional adjustment. *The problem exists for the average and the gifted child just as surely as it does for the mentally subnormal.* If it did not, we would not as parents, clinicians, and educators be faced with the common problem of the average or gifted child underachieving, and unhappy in his underachievement. Nor would we face the allied problem of the gifted child who develops his intellectual gifts at the expense of other important psychological needs, to the overall detriment of his social and emotional adjustment.

At this stage of behavioral science, perhaps the best that can be done is to carefully assess the available clinical material for some suggestions that might be of value to the clinician working with the problem of a given child and his family at the same time that they provide challenging hypotheses for the research worker. For this purpose we think some of the case material of the Boston group is worth closer attention than we can give it here, but we would like to touch further upon some of the generalizations that they draw from that experience.

In commenting on the more obvious failures in adjustment Crothers and Paine noted:

It is always absurd to pay too much attention to the classification of short series of cases in which the patients are seen only a few times, but it is very striking that a considerable number of children went into one or another critical emotional reaction. The usual story was that the cerebral palsy as a motor disorder was well managed and frequently not the major cause of disability. The outstanding difficulty seemed to be related to two factors, first, an increasing loss of warm confidence by one or both parents, and second, the fact that over a long period medical emphasis was focussed on the care of physical disability rather than on the supervision of growth and development. (Crothers and Paine, 1959, p. 240)

In regard to the more successful cases they comment:

One point that impressed us throughout this study was that most of the successful individuals had rebelled against their advisers from time to time and made their own experiments and often their own decisions. Since we believe that the aim of successful treatment is the achievement of maximal independence, it has been disturbing to consider how little respect for initiative and independence there is among some of the people who control treatment. Docility and persistence are respected and rebellion is regarded with distaste. (Crothers and Paine, 1959, p. 269)

We suspect that these factors, which may make for success or failure in the development of the cerebral-palsied child, are not irrelevant to the development of any handicapped child—be the handicap physical or intellectual.

In an earlier report from the Boston group Edith Meyer Taylor had commented upon the social and emotional adjustment of their patients and suggested goals that might be set for work with the cerebral palsied.

Dr. Crothers, as you know, for many years has stressed the importance of the family setting and the family's attitude toward the cerebral palsied child and his handicap. It is interesting to find this thesis substantiated in the details of the psychological studies. I am thinking of two children with comparable situations—acquired right hemiplegias—a boy, 19, and a girl, 22. The boy belongs to an ambitious, intellectual family with an energetic, driving mother. His nurse's remarks at age 15 months state, "If she only would let him be a baby." The girl belongs to very solicitous, relatively unambitious parents who were overwhelmed by the child's illness and all through her childhood were startled by the child's ability to do anything. Both children are amongst our ablest patients and have been ever since we have known them. The boy has always been and still is an insecure, hesitant, rather unhappy youngster, who said at age 7, "I do not know anything about anything." In spite of quite marked specialized difficulties, he has kept up reasonably well in school, though not at the rate his family was accustomed to. However, he is now shy, slow moving, and very careful. While the boy never was able to live quite up to his family's expectations, the girl always went beyond those of hers and spent her life proving to people that she could do more than they thought. She is now a pleasant, driving, rather insistent girl, who has finished a college course, in spite of many rather striking difficulties in perceptual organization. Her approach to all intellectual problems is intuitive and quick, not at all always careful. Everything she does is marked by a rebellious, but successful quality.

The pattern described in these two patients appears in one form or another modified in most of our cases, and confirms in the psychological study the thesis that *attitudes that surround the child* mold more than in normal cases the personality of the cerebral palsied child. The prolonged dependence on parents and the many contacts with authoritative figures, such as doctors, physiotherapists, speech therapists, etc., prolong the stages of unilateral relationships which in the normal child's development are soon offset and counter-balanced by his growing independence and outside contacts with contemporaries on equal terms.

Second important result: It is futile to say that cerebral palsied children are "just like normal people," and should be treated as such; the majority are not and should not be requested to be. They have a great many difficulties of all sorts; there is an appallingly small number of people with even high average abilities, and even these almost without exception have demonstrable distortions in mental functioning. One may say—what does it mean? How important is it to have normal perceptions or well regulated thinking processes? Still it becomes evident that these distortions are not isolated quirks but represent distorted modes of adjustment, and are reflected in social adjustment just as well. Except for the two college people who are still in training, only a very few of our patients have a job of responsibility, and few are fully self-supporting. One of the ablest and most sociable of the women is desk secretary at Harvard, but subordinate to a head person. Very few of our patients read for pleasure; most of them are surprised when asked how many books they read a year, and can at best think of one or two.

Their *social life* is even in the best cases different from normal. Most of them are lonesome; they either admit that they have only a very few or no friends, or they talk quite frantically about the fact that "everybody is nice with them and is their friend." In most cases one finds that these are hardly ever friendships on equal terms. One of our star patients, the before-mentioned girl, felt that she was popular in a college course in which she was the only girl, but she stated that she had 26 "brothers" carrying her brief-case, but no boy-friends. Most satisfying social relationships are in club activities, etc., where they can meet in "a cause" rather than for their own sakes. The social-sexual relations obviously are a great problem in this group. None of our adult patients who were observed here is married, although others have been; none of these seems to have very satisfactory sexual relationships. Most of them appear either much inhibited or strangely immature when questioned in this direction. Some of them—a minority it seems—are openly rebellious and unconventional in a rather adolescent way; the majority must find refuge in fantasy and day-dreams. This was evidenced in direct conversations rather than through psychological tools that apparently are not adapted too well to our particular patients.

Last, I would like to mention briefly their own *attitude toward their own handicap*. It is striking to see that most of the patients either seem to be somehow self-conscious and apologetic, or show apathy and resignation. They seem to reflect the attitudes of their surroundings. They either have been made to believe that they could do just as well as everybody else if they tried, and found this was not so, or they knew from the beginning that they were hopelessly out of step, but tried just the same. Only very few seemed realistic and adjusted, and able to appraise objectively their assets and liabilities.

What have we learned from our patients, and what new goals should we set for ourselves in the work with the cerebral palsied?

1. Give early attention to the parents' attitudes; try to shorten and minimize periods of exclusive dependence on authoritative people; try possibly in the nursery school to start some group activities that may help to avoid prolonged egocentricity.

2. Appraise difficulties early and realistically; do not try the impossible, but set the goal so that social, motor, and intellectual difficulties are taken into account and reckoned with. Aim toward a life situation in which patient can function with relative ease and minimum emotional strain.

3. Stress most of all the development of acceptable social situations. Further also, at later age levels, groups of patients where competition and exchange are possible, and avoid competition in normal groups where the patient is always hopelessly outnumbered. This would seem the best solution for the personal-social-sexual, and also for ultimate economic, problems.

4. Develop more realistic attitudes toward the handicap in the patient as well as in the community: While nobody expects the deaf to try to hear or the blind to try to see, many athetoids are still being encouraged to make speeches, or hemiplegics to handle abstract arithmetic. If the cerebral palsied patient would be allowed to develop his assets and to circumvent his liabilities, one would avoid much frustration and embarrassment all around, that is, in the patient as well as in those who live with him.

5. Whether home adjustment or institutional living should be the ultimate goal is a wide-open question. Long periods away from home early in life have seemed undesirable to us except in hopelessly unresponsive cases. For older, and especially for adult patients, one might be inclined to strive for some group living, but both aspects are obviously still open to discussion, require much

thought, and, on the whole, will depend on the individual case. (Meyer and Crothers, 1953, pp. 154–156.

A Case Study. We present below a psychologist's report of a cerebral-palsied woman for whom institutionalization was recommended.[6] We present this case because it underlines the significance of Meyer and Crothers' discussion, i.e., it illustrates the consequences of well-intentioned but problem-creating family behavior at the same time that it demonstrates what can be done when the environment can be adapted to the needs and defects of the individual.

Background Material

ᘒ   Helen was brought to the Outpatient Clinic of the Training School to be tested in order to determine eligibility for commitment. Since birth the left side of her body has been paralyzed. Up until 1943 Helen had been living with her parents and when both of them died during that year she went to live with her brother. The brother indicated that Helen had been overprotected all her life and had not been given an opportunity to learn tasks which were within her reach and from which she could derive satisfaction. The brother, who is single, stated that Helen is alone most of the day and has become increasingly unstable. He would like to commit her until she is trained to do things which will give her a feeling of independence. Helen's family, who appear affluent, are very attached to her and look upon commitment as a means of her obtaining feelings and habits of independence which will make her happier when she returns to live with them permanently. A report of a previous electroencephalographic examination was supplied by the brother; the record "indicates a mild degree of diffuse cerebral damage more on the right than on the left and with a definite focal attenuation in the right parietal region. There is no indication of an expanding lesion." Aside from the fact that she had attended school only for several years and that private tutoring had not been successful, no other data were available at the time of the examination.

Psychological Report (1/23/45) (C.A. 35–8)

General observations

Helen, who was very neatly dressed, is a dark-haired and dark-complexioned woman with dark circles under her eyes. Her left hand appeared stiff, with some of the fingers clenched and the others extended rigidly. She seemed unable to engage in any activity which involved the coordination of both hands, and usually prearranged the fingers of her left hand in a position to enable them to be of some aid. She was able to move her left arm quite well, although not as freely as her right one. Helen held a pencil clumsily and could not write easily. Hand tremors were observed. She was able to print letters with long bold strokes. Her left foot was stiff and dragged a bit.

---

[6] We are indebted to Dr. Esther Sarason for use of this report, and to Mrs. Helen Kreitler for her painstaking and successful efforts to teach this girl how to read and write.

Helen was very fearful during testing and frequently rubbed her eyes and exclaimed excitedly, "I'm too nervous to talk. Look how I'm shaking." Although she became more relaxed as testing progressed, she was prone to anticipate and become upset by failure. It seemed that she was fearful of having her inadequacies exposed and tried to cover for them by giving vague, general answers which could be applicable to most any question. Helen had great difficulty in comprehending directions; how much of this difficulty was due to a mental defect and how much to the anxiety aroused by her feelings of inadequacy is difficult to estimate. In conversational speech, as well as in response to the vocabulary list, this girl's enunciation and use of words were excellent and in marked contrast to her overall test inadequacy. When responding to questions about her activities and family relationships, the coherence, fluency, and "insightfulness" of her replies were atypical for mental defectives. Helen's verbalized feelings of inadequacy usually were followed by statements about her strong desire to learn to do something useful so that she would not be dependent upon her brothers and sisters. It seemed clear, however, that her need for achievement was not as strong as the fear of failure or the tendency to avoid any situation because of the anticipation of inadequacy. Her tendency to self-derogation is so strong that any achievement on her part would be viewed by her as insignificant and consequently be no source of encouragement.

Tests		*Results*
Terman-Merrill (L)	MA 8.8	IQ 58
Wechsler-Bellevue (Verbal Scale)		IQ 71

Discussion

Terman-Merrill (L):   Basal was established at 5 years with final successes at the average adult level. Within this range all items requiring the definition of words were successfully passed. At the average adult level her sole success was in giving differences between abstract words. In contrast to these successes it should be noted that all items involving the presentation of a visual stimulus (picture absurdities, drawing a diamond, memory for designs, etc.) were failed. Although she seemed to recognize the inadequacy of her diamonds, she could not improve her performance. That her failure on the diamonds is possibly due to a defect in visual perception rather than in the motor sphere is indicated by the following: When she was asked to read a word she was usually unable to do so, but if she spelled aloud the letters of the word she was then usually able to read the word correctly. It was as if she was able to respond to auditory cues more adequately than to visual ones. Also, when she had finished a word, she was likely to go to a word on the line above or below from where she had started. She was not aware of her inability to focus on successive words in a line. In this connection it should be noted that on the fourth picture absurdity at year 7 Helen stated that "a girl is smoking a pipe"—a most unusual faulty perception. Helen was completely unable to adopt a critical attitude toward any kind of absurdity problem. Although fearfulness and anticipation of failure may have affected her efficiency, the discrepancy between her unusual verbal facility and her severe inadequacy with problems involving a sustained conceptual process or a response to a visual stimulus suggests that nonemotional factors are playing a decisive role. Her performance is similar to that found in some mental defectives with a known brain injury. It may well be that her emotional behavior is a learned response to inadequacies due to a brain injury.

Conclusions

To interpret the intelligence quotients earned on the tests according to usual psychometric classifications would be to neglect important aspects of Helen's behavior. Though technically the intelligence quotients suggest mental deficiency, her vocabulary, verbal expression, and social reasoning as revealed in conversation hardly resemble that commonly associated with a mentally deficient person. It might be said that her facility with and correct use of language would not be expected to be acquired by the ordinary defective. That her mental functioning is uneven is evident. This irregularity is probably due in large part to brain pathology on the one hand, and, on the other, to emotional instability. How much of her social incompetence is due to the brain defect and how much to overprotection is difficult to estimate. The present problem is to decide whether commitment to the Training School is warranted. The brother indicated that he desired commitment so that his sister might learn to do certain things which would eventually give her a feeling of independence and an opportunity to improve in reading. He indicated that he was not interested in custodial care but would take Helen out when she could more or less get along on her own. Until about two years ago Helen lived with her parents and was apparently not trained to engage in activities for self-occupation. Now that her parents are dead and Helen lives with her brother, she is left alone a large part of the time, and as a result has become more unstable. To expect institutionalization to reduce anxiety and instill independence in a girl who has been overprotected all her life seems a hardly possible task. It would even be difficult with someone who does not possess Helen's handicap. To compensate for the privations that the girl has experienced all her life by being so handicapped would take a very large amount of individual attention to effect even a small change. To expect a woman whose only security has been the affection of her family to become more stable in surroundings where this feature does not exist is to remove the very thing which can aid her. In terms of the brother's purposes, institutionalization is not feasible.

It was felt that learning some tasks was essential for Helen's well-being and a plan which could utilize community resources was recommended. It was suggested that she be enrolled in the training program of the Workshop of the Society for Crippled Children in her city. When it was suggested that this possibility for training should be tried before commitment, the brother said that this still would not solve the problem of Helen's being left alone most of the time. The possibility of a companion was discussed and the brother indicated that the family had tried to get one but those who applied for the job were unsatisfactory. This examiner favors the training at the Workshop if Helen can be placed in a foster home or if a similar living arrangement can be made. Commitment is recommended only as a last resort.

Subsequent History

Helen was enrolled in the Workshop. It was the opinion of the staff that she could be taught to go to and from home, increase her use of her left hand, and learn to do tasks which would occupy her when she was alone. Although she gained considerably in self-confidence as a result of the Workshop program, she was unable to go from her home to the Workshop without completely losing her direction. Since it was not possible to get a companion for her and she was still alone a good part of the time, the Workshop recommended that she be admitted to the Training School. This recommendation was carried out. Because of this girl's experience of overprotection and the traumatic shock of her separation from her family, it was arranged that she be seen each day by the psychologist on a psychotherapeutic basis. An initial problem was Helen's inability to go from her cottage to the psychologist's office, a distance somewhat less than a quarter of a mile, without getting lost. At first she refused to go, saying that she would get lost. On the first few trips she was accompanied by the psychologist, who attempted to point out cues that Helen might use as a bearing. Being accompanied by the psychologist reduced Helen's apprehension, increased her desire to come to the office, and made it easier for her to attempt the trip herself. The first couple of times she came alone she was told that the psychologist would be watching from her office in order to see where Helen might make a mistake and to make sure that she did not get lost. After a few trials Helen was able to come to the office without any difficulty. She was also able to go to other parts of the institution without any difficulty in orientation. For the first few weeks the interviews were largely taken up with Helen's attitudes toward the other girls in her cottage. She was surprised at how rough they were and the coarse language they used, and she was afraid that they might not like her and would pick on her. Her adjustment to the other girls was complicated by their jealousy of the fine clothes she had and the attention and affection which her family demonstrated. She constantly reiterated that the girls "are not my type." The chief functions of the interviews seemed to be to give Helen an opportunity to unburden her feelings, to feel that despite her separation from her family there was someone who was interested *in her,* and to anticipate and reduce the apprehension which would arise with each new situation. The fact that her family visited her frequently also prevented any strong feelings of rejection.

Helen was enrolled in the occupational therapy and continuation-school programs. Because of her intense desire to read and in light of her severe visual defect, special reading techniques were employed. A gadget was devised which Helen could manipulate and which allowed only one line at a time to be exposed, thus preventing her tendency to wander all over the page. She was also instructed to spell each word to herself, then to spell it aloud, and then to attempt to pronounce it. She was aided at all times by the continuation-school teacher, who began with words which Helen already knew. Within a period of two years Helen was able to read and comprehend on about the fifth-grade level, although for optimal results it was necessary for the teacher to observe her directly because even with the mechanical aid there was a noticeable tendency for her visual gaze to shift unexpectedly to other parts of the page. Helen, who had never been able to write before, was also taught to write a legible and coherent letter.

In educational circles one frequently hears that one teaches children and not subject matter—a goal infrequently attained by teachers be they in an elementary, high school, or college. Similarly, as Crothers and Taylor emphasize, one treats a child and not an abstraction called cerebral palsy. It would be more correct to say, as Dr. Kaplan stresses (Chapter 10), that the focus of attention should be not the child but the family. What we need is not *an* individual diagnosis but a family one. This is not only a shift in diagnostic focus but in tactics and program planning. As we emphasized in Chapter 3, diagnosis is a form of decision making which has important consequences for what one does for those who call on us for help. To the extent that our diagnostic focus is *the* individual we reduce the chances that we shall understand and influence the social context in which he lives—the social context which he has influenced and which has influenced him. This increase in scope of diagnosis is not justified as a matter of theory or clinical esthetics but simply on the ground that the problems are social and not individual in nature.

Minimal Brain Damage

The diagnostic category of "minimal brain damage" presents many difficulties both in its rationale and in its practical application. Nevertheless, its durability and its persistent use, despite various cogent criticisms, suggest that it fulfills some of the needs of clinical theory and/or practice. In the following pages we shall endeavor to sketch some aspects of the development of the concept of minimal brain damage. This we hope will give the reader an understanding of the rationale that may be advanced in justification of the use of this term as a diagnostic entity. We shall then indicate some of the limitations and pitfalls that may attend that use.

Development of the Concept. One of the earliest references that would appear to be conceptualizing an entity of minimal brain damage (although the term was not used) much as it is done today is that of G. B. Smith in 1926. Dealing with cerebral accidents of childhood and their relationships to mental retardation, Smith wrote:

At the time of birth, too often the minor injuries are overlooked, or later if noted they have spontaneously improved, so that later in life we often see a picture of mental deficiency in which there is no outward expression of brain injury or apparent cause. I cannot help but feel that many of the cases of mental deficiency which present atypical pictures, especially those which do not readily conform to average personality patterns and which show a scattering in intellectual ability, can be explained on such a basis, especially when we realize that the association pathways all develop after such an injury. (Smith, 1926)

There are two points of note in this passage. First, Smith postulates that although the brain has been injured there is "no outward expression of brain injury." Secondly, Smith feels that when the mental deficiency is accompanied by certain patterns of personality or intellectual functioning brain damage can be assumed. This in essence, as we understand it, is the way in which minimal brain damage is conceptualized today. However, there have been modifications. While Smith apparently referred to cases where neurological signs were absent, today, the term is often used for cases where certain "soft" neurological signs may be present, such as motor awkwardness or difficulty in making rapidly alternating movements. Again, the term has been extended by various clinicians to refer to those children who are in no way intellectually retarded but who display certain behavioral characteristics or patterns of intellectual and perceptual–motor functioning that are considered indicative of minimal brain damage. These behavioral characteristics and patterns may include: hyperactivity, impulsivity, emotional lability, short attention span, uneven functioning in different areas on intelligence tests, difficulty in discerning the figure from the ground in complex perceptual tasks, concretistic modes of thinking, etc. These behavioral characteristics and patterns are also found in some individuals with gross brain damage. Similar behavior in both groups of children—those with gross brain damage and those with minimal brain damage—constitutes, as we shall see, one of the arguments for assuming the underlying cause to be the same: damage to the central nervous system.

It is also of interest that when Smith referred to "scattering in intellectual ability" the context makes it clear that he was referring to "scatter" *as variation in level of performance on different kinds of intelligence test items.* The use of scatter on intelligence-test items has continued to be one of the main diagnostic criteria for minimal brain damage.

The fact that knowledge of the sequelae to neurological disease and injury increased rapidly during and after World War I must have been another factor strengthening the hypothesis that a minimal or diffuse injury to the brain might result in intellectual or behavioral effects in the absence of gross sensorimotor impairment. In his discussion of epidemic encephalitis, Kanner (1957, p. 285) quotes Jelliffe, writing in 1927, to the effect that of all the great advances made in neuropsychiatry in the preceding decade no single advance approached in importance that made through the study of epidemic encephalitis. Epidemic encephalitis first came into medical prominence following the wide-spread flu epidemic during the latter part of World War I. There was a wide variety of clinical manifestations but in one of its more typical forms the encephalitis was accompanied by lethargy, prolonged sleep, and various disturbances in the neuromuscular control of the eyes such as nystagmus and strabismus. Of interest to us in the development of the concept of minimal brain damage are the many studies of the sequelae to encephalitis that appeared in the literature during the twenties and thirties.

An example of this literature and its relevance to minimal or diffuse brain damage concepts would be that of Patterson and Spence (1921). In a study of the aftereffects of epidemic encephalitis in twenty-five children they indicated that various degrees of permanent physical and/or mental disability follow an acute episode of epidemic encephalitis. In their sample of twenty-five, one child died and six of the group made a complete recovery. Among those children with sequelae, mental changes varied from complete idiocy to slight mental deficiency. Changes in the character and habits of the children were also noted. In one instance a severe behavior disorder occurred without intellectual or physical impairment. Physical changes following the encephalitis included spastic diplegia, hemiplegia, muscular rigidity, and tremor. The severity of the initial attack of encephalitis appeared to be in direct proportion to the severity of the aftereffects.

Thus, in the case of encephalitis, the various sequelae—physical, intellectual, and behavioral defects occurring in all degrees and either simultaneously or independently—following upon a known infection of brain tissue provided a model by which it was possible to postulate varying degrees and kinds of brain injury—with or without gross neurological signs—accompanied by certain patterns of behavior and/or intellectual defect.

Among the various behavioral and intellectual disorders occurring among these postencephalitic children certain typical patterns stood out and were emphasized by various writers. These patterns came to be accepted as diagnostic for minimal or diffuse brain damage. Thus in Bender's (1942) report on the experience of her group with the evaluation and treatment of postencephalitic children, there is emphasis on hyperkinesis and other impulse disturbances, and on the presence of typical psychometric patterns.

Studies on the relationship of prenatal and paranatal factors affecting subsequent development of the child also served to strengthen the hypothesis of a relationship between undetectable neurological lesions and behavioral and intellectual impairment.

In a statistical study demonstrating a correlation between certain disorders of pregnancy and parturition with the development of cerebral palsy, Lilienfeld and Parkhurst (1951) introduced the hypothesis of a "continuum of reproductive wastage."

There appears to exist a relationship between stillbirths, neonatal deaths and cerebral palsy. The pattern of factors, such as complications of pregnancy, prematurity, etc., which influence infant loss seems to behave in a similar manner with regard to cerebral palsy. On the basis of these related patterns, it is possible to broaden the concept of "reproductive wastage" to include cerebral palsy and possibly other related disorders. One might postulate the existence of a "continuum of reproductive wastage" which can be subdivided into lethal and sublethal manifestations. The lethal component includes abortions, stillbirths and neonatal deaths. The sublethal component includes cerebral palsy and, possibly, other disabilities. Although this concept has never been stated as such, insofar as the present authors are aware, it has been implied previously by those investigators who have emphasized the role of cerebral hemorrhage in the etiology of cerebral palsy. These workers felt that the cerebral palsy group represents those infants who have survived the lethal effect of the hemorrhage. It has also been implied by Ingalls and Gordon in their epidemiological investigations of such conditions as mongolism and is probably equivalent to their concept of disease described as the "biological gradient of disease." It would appear that other congenital stigmata, such as malformations, mental deficiency, etc., should be similarly investigated in an attempt to delineate possible antecedent factors. (Lilienfeld and Parkhust, 1951, p. 278)

It is of interest that Lilienfeld and Parkhurst in advancing this hypothesis recognize that, even as etiological agents, biological factors do not operate in vacuo:

At this point it would be well to emphasize that the various factors that are apparently involved in producing this "continuum of reproductive wastage" are, in turn, probably the result of a complex of biosocial factors. There is, no doubt, an interplay of both genetic and environmental (both socioeconomic and intra-uterine) factors. The various factors of pregnancy and parturition probably represent specific manifestations of this biosocial complex. (Lilienfeld and Park-hurst, 1951, p. 278)

This hypothesis was subsequently elaborated by the work of Lilienfeld and Pasamanick and various coworkers and may be found in its more fully elaborated form in the work of Knobloch and Pasamanick, where it is known as a "continuum of reproductive casualty."

Some time ago we constructed the hypothesis of a "continuum of reproductive casualty" which has been investigated in a series of retrospective and anterospective epidemiologic studies. According to this hypothesis, there is a lethal component of cerebral damage which results in fetal and neonatal deaths and a sublethal component which gives rise to a series of clinical neuropsychiatric syndromes depending on the degree and location of the damage. We have found that these abnormalities range from the more obvious disabilities, such as cerebral palsy, epilepsy, and mental deficiency, through the learning and behavioral difficulties, such as reading disabilities, tics, and the behavior disorders of childhood, probably as a result of cerebral disorganization after minimal cerebral damage. The retrospective investigations have indicated that three prenatal and paranatal factors appear to be most highly associated with the components of this continuum; namely, prematurity, toxemia, and bleeding during pregnancy. In the retrospective study of children with behavior disorders, this association was found to be particularly high in the hyperactive, confused and disorganized group. (Knobloch and Pasamanick, 1959, p. 1384)

In this same article Knobloch and Pasamanick present data on the developmental examination of premature and full-term infants to demonstrate that the neurological status of the infant at 40 weeks of age is related to prematurity as defined by birth weight, with increasing degrees of prematurity attended by increased frequency of neurological impairment. The definition of minimal brain damage as adopted there is as follows:

The syndrome of minimal cerebral damage as we define it is manifested by minor but clearly defined deviations from the normal neurological and behavioral developmental patterns, usually with more or less complete compensation by 15 to

18 months of age, as determined by the standard neurological examination. These developmental abnormal neurological signs persist well into the preschool period but require special techniques and a knowledge of maturity to elicit and interpret them. The syndrome is important in the early identification of expanding lesions of the brain, in following the progress of a child with a neurological abnormality, and in identifying those infants who, because of their cerebral disorganization, might be more apt to develop neuropsychiatric disorders later in childhood. (Knobloch and Pasamanick, 1959, p. 1384)

Gesell and Amatruda as early as 1941 had expressed related views:

An entirely negative birth history and an uneventful neonatal period may nevertheless demand a diagnosis of minimal injury because of persisting or gradually diminishing behavior signs. In obscure or doubtful cases the following is a safe rule: Do not assume that there has certainly been a cerebral injury, but assume that every child who is born alive has run the universal risk of such injury. (Gesell and Amatruda, 1941, p. 231)

Thus the variability of sensorimotor defects, behavioral and intellectual impairments after traumatic injury, or infectious disease affecting the brain whether prenatal, paranatal or postnatal, have led to the assumption that brain damage can be of such nature that it may not reveal itself in unequivocal neurological signs but yet may affect personality and intellectual functioning. This has led many clinicians to the converse proposition that if children displayed the kinds of personality, intellectual, and perceptual-motor patterns found as sequelae to known insult to the central nervous system, then one could assume—especially if they had histories which might be suggestive of pre- or paranatal stress or had subsequent infection or trauma that might have involved the central nervous system—that these children were brain damaged.

Strauss and the Concept of the Brain-Injured or "Exogenous" Child

Alfred A. Strauss was one of the foremost and influential proponents of the view that the diagnosis of brain injury could rest primarily, or exclusively, upon behavioral indications. In 1947, Strauss published with Laura Lehtinen an influential book on the psychopathology and education of brain-injured children which was based in part upon nearly twenty years of clinical observation, research investigations, and educational experience with brain-injured children.

Within the general group of the mentally subnormal, Strauss distinguished the brain-injured or "exogenous" child (where the mental subnormality was assumed to be the result of damage to the central nervous system) from the "endogenous" child with familial and other types of mental subnormality not based upon brain injury. Strauss opened his consideration of the brain-injured child with the following definition.

A brain-injured child is a child who before, during, or after birth has received an injury to or suffered an infection of the brain. As a result of such organic impairment, defects of the neuromotor system may be present or absent; however, such a child may show disturbances in perception, thinking, and emotional behavior, either separately or in combination. These disturbances can be demonstrated by specific tests. These disturbances prevent or impede a normal learning process. (Strauss and Lehtinen, 1947, p. 4)

The definition obviously includes both gross brain damage and minimal brain damage. A consideration of minor brain injury, by itself, led to the following criteria:

A complete diagnosis of minor brain injury includes the following four criteria:

1. A history shows evidence of injury to the brain by trauma or inflammatory processes before, during, or shortly after birth.
2. Slight neurological signs are present which indicate a brain lesion.
3. When the psychological disturbance is of such severity that a measurable retardation of intellectual growth can be observed, the immediate family history indicates that the child comes from a normal family stock and that he is, in general, the only one of the sibship so afflicted.
4. When no mental retardation exists, the presence of psychological disturbances can be discovered by the use of some of our qualitative tests for perceptual and conceptual disturbances.

Although the first three criteria may be negative, whereas the behavior of the child in question resembles that characteristic for brain injury, and even though the performances of the child on our tests are not strongly indicative of brain injury, it may still be reasonable to consider a diagnosis of brain injury. (Strauss and Lehtinen, 1947, p. 112)

As we read this, it would appear that the diagnosis would hinge on criterion 4: the patient's performance on qualitative tests of conceptual and perceptual performance.[7] Criterion 4 would also indicate the existence of a group of minimally brain-damaged individuals with normal IQ. This is made more explicit later in the text: "Behavior and learning, it is now beginning to be recognized, may be affected by minimal brain injuries without apparent lowering of the intelligence level" (p. 128). This is elaborated in a subsequent publication by Strauss and Kephart (1955), where the "clinical syndrome of exogeneity in brain-injured, mentally defective children" is enlarged "to include the clinical syndrome of the brain-injured child who is not mentally defective, but who in spite of 'normalcy in I.Q.' as tested is still 'defective.'" As near as we can tell from the case material in this second book,

---

[7] There has been much research on the perceptual and conceptual differences between brain-damaged and nonbrain-damaged individuals and at times the findings have been conflicting or have lent themselves to alternative interpretations. For some introduction to this extensive literature the reader should consult several of the following references: Birch and Lefford (1964); Bortner and Birch (1960); Cruickshank, Bice, and Wallen (1957); Gallagher (1957); Goldstein (1939); Keller (1962); Weatherwax and Benoit (1957).

Strauss and Kephart are using the term "defective" to mean that the child has a school learning problem related to an uneven development of intellectual skills and/or behavioral difficulties which are presumed to be due to brain injury.

Thus for Strauss—and for many other clinicians—the brain-injured child is a broad and elastic category including on the one end children with gross brain damage easily demonstrated by neurological examination and at the other end children with "minimal brain injury" not at all detectable by neurological examination or special neurological techniques but assumed to be present because of perceptual and conceptual difficulties which could be revealed by special tests and which were assumed to be the result of a hypothetical brain injury. The logically minded may of course object to a reasoning which appears to go like this: Some individuals with known brain damage have certain behavioral characteristics, therefore individuals with these same behavioral characteristics must be presumed to be brain damaged.

EISENBERG'S POSITION ON THE CONCEPT OF BRAIN DAMAGE

Eisenberg (1964), with considerable sophistication, presents a defense of such reasoning. He recognizes that the frequency of the diagnosis of brain damage would decline precipitously if its use were restricted to patients with unequivocal sensory or motor defect. He recognizes further that there would thus be a reduction in the number of false-positive diagnoses; he feels that this would be offset by too many false negatives, i.e., cases in which brain damage was ruled out as the etiological agent for the observed behavior when in fact such brain damage does exist. These false negatives would occur, in Eisenberg's opinion, because the epidemiological evidence indicates, "that children with behavior disorders but without neurological manifestations have a disproportionate loading of fetal and neonatal complications known to be associated with central nervous system pathology" (p. 62). Therefore, Eisenberg concludes that we cannot restrict the diagnosis of brain damage to patients with the classic neurological findings. Nevertheless, his advocacy of the use of the diagnosis of brain injury includes cautions:

Let me at once add that, in making this diagnosis, we should specify the criteria upon which we base our diagnosis, the level of confidence we assign to it, and the type of syndrome the patient exhibits; the greatest fallacy of all is the common assumption that there is *a* brain-damage syndrome. (Eisenberg, 1964, p. 62)

Eisenberg feels that some of the objections to the use of the term "organic" brain injury arise because to many physicians, teachers, and parents the term conveys a sense of irreversibility and hopelessness which is not present in the assumption of a psychological behavior problem. Eisenberg, however, rejects this assumption of irreversibility and hopelessness and indicates that:

When we have assigned the patient to this general category the diagnostic task has just begun; we must go on to specify (*a*) the type of disorder, (*b*) the areas of function secondary to damage, (c) the loci, and (d) the causative disease. (Eisenberg, 1964, p. 63)

In Eisenberg's recognition that brain-damaged patients may exhibit more than one type of syndrome, in his insistence that the criteria for the diagnosis should be specified along with the level of confidence assigned to it, and in his recognition that diagnosis does not end with the attachment of a label, in all of this there is sophisticated conceptualization of the problem. Nor can one lightly dismiss the argument, based on epidemiological evidence and the varying sequelae to infectious disease and traumatic injury of the central nervous system, that there are probably individuals who have lesions of the central nervous system that are undetectable by present neurological techniques and that these lesions yet determine—along with intrapsychic and environmental factors—behavioral attributes of personality and intellect. It would even appear that, insofar as such a hypothesis leads to productive research on the relationship between brain injury and behavior and to the development of increased diagnostic skills and techniques for determining the presence of brain injury, the hypothesis may be highly useful.

Difficulties in the Clinical Application of the Concept of Minimal Brain Damage

But one may grant the value of such a hypothesis for research and yet object to the use of the term "brain injured" or "minimally brain damaged" for a given child presenting with a problem in behavior or intellectual functioning when the existence of an organic lesion has not been demonstrated. For this is to assume that the behavioral characteristics noted in some brain-damaged children—hyperkinesis, inattention, uneven development of intellectual abilities, etc.—can *only* occur in the presence of a brain lesion. Such an assumption instead of being—as Eisenberg would have it—the beginning of the diagnostic task may, in fact, be a deterrent to an adequate diagnostic formulation of the child's problem. *Too often in our experience have we observed that not only is the diagnosis terminated with the label of brain damage, but the prognosis and the treatment, or more likely the lack of treatment, are automatically predetermined by the attachment of that label.*

Some of the dangers involved in labeling are brought out by Doris and Solnit (1963) in their article on the treatment of brain-damaged children in a child-guidance center.

Although our assessment of these children touched on all areas of their lives, the nature of their deficits often emphasized their need for assistance with formal educational tasks. We undertook our work with such children aware of the fact that the psychiatric approach to these problems was often limited because of a prevailing bias that psychotherapy is not well used by children with central nervous system defects and that a child guidance clinic has little help to offer such children and their parents. These assumptions often exclude such children from psychiatric treatment or limit work with them to brief psychiatric evaluations and counseling of the parents. The school learning problem is usually attributed to deficient mentation attested by the low scores many of these children obtain on standard I.Q. tests. The specific learning handicaps of the brighter child are assumed to be an expression of his organic deficit. In any case, the learning problem is assumed to be a problem for the educator rather than the psychiatrist. Special schools for the brain damaged may be recommended if such exist in the clinic's locality. Behavioral problems of such children in the school and home are often attributed to the "organic syndrome" and some attempt may be made to alleviate this with drugs. Psychotherapy is rarely considered, and counseling of parents and teachers is undertaken, if at all, on a short-term basis.

We would readily grant that these attitudes are not characteristic of all clinics or of all workers in this field. But our experience within a medical center has repeatedly brought to our attention cases that have been handled in just the manner we depicted within our own and neighboring states. In addition, we have sometimes completed a diagnostic workup on a child such as we have described and then referred the patient to a child guidance clinic in his own geographical area. Subsequently the child's distressed parents have returned to us with a story of brief treatment followed by discharge from the clinic. Our experience indicated that a child guidance clinic working within its own limitations and with only the usual community resources could devise diagnostic and therapeutic approaches that would provide more effective aid to these children, their parents, and their teachers. (Doris and Solnit, 1963, pp. 619–620)

The diagnostic and therapeutic approach advocated by Doris and Solnit emphasizes the complexity of the interaction between biological, psychological, and social variables and the necessity for the clinician to constantly keep these complexities in mind when dealing with the behavior of a child who may be considered brain damaged.

The diagnostic aspect of the work with these children involves a neurological and psychological evaluation of the nature and extent of their defect, an assessment of the child's psychological adjustment to his defect, and an awareness of the environment's reaction to the child's defect and to his personality as a whole. Usually, the interaction of the child and the environment is so intimate and of such long duration by the time the child reaches the clinic that it is often impossible to make an accurate assessment of what each has contributed to the presenting problem. Therefore, we content ourselves with tentative working hypotheses which will undergo continuous change as our work with the child progresses, and we are prepared to change our diagnostic formulations as our knowledge of the child increases. In addition to these diagnostic considerations, it is also clear that the child's problem is not a static one. With growth and development and with concurrent changes in the family's environment, the child's problems assume new aspects. Although the clumsy four-year-old may not be rejected by his play group because of his awkwardness, the same child at ten may be rejected by his playmates because his awkwardness does not make him a desirable member of the ball team. Therefore, the diagnosis of the child's problem in adjustment is a continuing one for as long as the clinic continues to work with the child.

From the therapeutic point of view, the clinician having formulated his diagnostic impression must design and implement a therapeutic program that is directed at the defect, the child's adjustment to the defect, and the environment's reaction to the child. Again this therapeutic program must be a flexible one, capable of continuous change and shift in emphasis to keep abreast of our developing diagnostic formulations. (Doris and Solnit, 1963, pp. 620–621)

With this degree of complexity in the diagnostic and therapeutic process for patients with *detectable* neurological damage, one may ask are we doing justice to the child with *presumed* minimal brain damage by attaching a label to him without sufficient evidence? It is all very well for Eisenberg to caution that we should specify the criteria on which we base our diagnosis of brain damage and give the level of confidence with which we assign the diagnosis. But we suspect, as information is conveyed from clinic to clinic, from clinic to school, and from the clinic to parent, that the criteria and the degree of confidence with which we assigned the label will recede into the background and what will be in the foreground and hence likely to induce stereotyped attitudes and behaviors toward the child on the part of parents, teachers, and physicians, will be the "fact" that this child is brain damaged.

We cannot see what would be lost in the clinical management of such children if judgment were suspended on the possible existence of a central nervous system defect, and a diagnostic formulation of the child's adjustment drawn up which takes into account the child's various patterns of abilities and behavioral reactions and the nature of his interactions with the environment. We would think that for clinical work one might approach the problem as Doris and Solnit approached the problem for their sample of brain-damaged children—omitting the designation of "minimal brain damage" for those children in which neurological signs are absent or equivocal.

We feel that from the clinical point of view the approach of Doris and Solnit with slight modification is applicable to all children. Every child with a problem of behavioral adjustment and/or intellectual functioning has a constitutional pattern consisting of relative strengths and handicaps. The handicaps may range from gross motor impairment, or cortical blindness, through relatively minor handicaps such as obesity, myopia, acne, susceptibility to respiratory infection, poor physical stamina, or a less attractive physical appearance than his peers. In the diagnosis of the behavioral or learning problem and the therapeutic approach to it, account of the child's constitutional equipment and the psychological and social reaction of child and environment to that equipment cannot be ignored. The clinician must diagnose the areas of relative strength and handicap and then capitalize on the strengths and circumvent or remove the handicap so that the child's behavioral and intellectual functioning may reach an optimal level. In some cases the handicaps may have reality aspects to them that make the problem of adjustment for child and family more difficult in the sense that the handicap cannot be greatly modified and what must be modified is the perception of that handicap by the child and family. And this modification in perception must be accompanied by the creative exploration—by clinician, child, and family—of ways in which the effects of the handicap can be circumvented or minimized. In other cases the problem may be somewhat easier. The prescription of glasses, the introduction of a therapeutic diet, or the use of anticonvulsive medications, may make a direct attack upon the handicap possible. Regardless of the nature and extent of the handicap, and regardless of the degree to which it can be directly overcome, the clinical problem always has biological, psychological, and social components; and diagnosis and therapy must be pushed in all areas. In some clinical problems biological components may be more to the fore, in others psychological or social components. But in no clinical problem can any one of these components and its interactions be ignored.

Although a diagnostic label such as "minimal brain damage," when it neither specifies the nature of the clinical problem, nor implies a prognosis, nor dictates the appropriate therapeutic intervention, might conceivably, as we have granted, have some heuristic value for research and theory, its utility for clinical work is questionable. It suggests no approach to a child's learning or behavioral problem that would not be undertaken by a dynamic diagnostic formulation of that problem. On the other hand, it may cause one to assign undue weight to the presumed biological aspect of that problem and thus invoke stereotyped attitudes in the parents and educators dealing with the child. It may even evoke such stereotypes in the clinician himself, to the detriment of diagnostic formulation and therapeutic approach.

Case Reports

In concluding this chapter on brain damage we will present two cases which we think will emphasize the complexity of the interaction between biological, psychological, and social variables and the necessity for the clinician constantly to keep these complexities in mind when dealing with the behavior of a child who may be considered brain damaged.

The first of these cases, taken from Doris and Solnit (1963), concerns a child who—although not mentally subnormal—presents in association with epilepsy a rather clear example of the interaction of biological, psychological, and social factors in the etiology and development of a learning problem. The relevance of this case to problems of mental subnormality should be readily apparent.

     Allen came to us at six years of age. The parents complained of a school phobia, temper tantrums, and depressive moods. Subsequent to the initial clinic contact, Allen had one major and several minor akinetic seizures. The etiology of these seizures is still open to question although the child's difficulties in motor coordination and the positive EEG findings leave no doubt as to the presence of a neurological problem. Allen also is handicapped by strabismus for which he had undergone two surgical procedures prior to clinic contact.

The presenting problems of school phobia and difficult behavior at home rapidly resolved themselves during the first months of clinic contact. However, the problem of a severe learning handicap in the area of reading came to the fore.

When first tested at our clinic Allen obtained a Full Scale I.Q. of 120 on the WISC. His Verbal I.Q. was 105, and his Performance I.Q. was 132. It was assumed by the tester that part of Allen's relatively low performance on the Verbal Scale was due to his anxiety which seemed to inhibit his verbal productions. At any rate, the Verbal I.Q. would not in itself suggest the severity of the reading problem which Allen later developed. By the time Allen reached the third grade he had fallen far behind his classmates in reading.

At the 3.2 grade level Allen was at the 1.8 grade level in reading vocabulary and at the 2.1 level in reading comprehension. Near the end of the third grade Allen was retested at our clinic with the WISC. He obtained at this time a Full Scale I.Q. of 123, a Verbal I.Q. of 120, and a Performance I.Q. of 121. The drop in Performance I.Q. in the year and a half since his first I.Q. test was assumed to be in part a result of temporary inefficiencies during the second test. But in addition, there was a notable drop in his Coding score. At the time of the first test he was under eight years and so given the A form of this test; at the second test he was given the B form. He apparently had a great deal more difficulty with this second form. We are not quite certain why this was so, but an examination of the two forms indicates that the A form with its widely spaced symbols may be an easier perceptual task than the B form with its closely crowded stimuli. Therefore, the explanation for the decrease may lie in Allen's visual handicap. The contrasting increase in Verbal I.Q. on the second test might be interpreted as support for the psychologist's belief at the time of the first test that the Verbal I.Q. had been depressed due to his anxiety.

One of our major problems during the second year of Allen's contact with the clinic was the diagnosis and the treatment of his reading handicap. We knew that many psychodynamic factors might be playing a role. At the time when Allen was just learning to read in the first grade, the ophthalmology clinic had prescribed eye exercises which involved reading. These exercises were administered at the ophthalmology clinic, and it is not unreasonable to suspect that these early experiences with reading became involved with Allen's traumatic feelings about his strabismus and the frightening surgical procedures that he underwent. In addition, Allen's parents are professional people with high standards of academic achievement for their children. Allen was not meeting these standards, and the parents had come to view him as a dull child. Allen's third grade teacher was at a loss as to how to help Allen and she was puzzled by the child's uneven functioning; yet she objected to the suggestion of a tutor for Allen because she felt this was a slur on her ability as a teacher. Moreover, she was somewhat frightened by what she had heard of this boy's seizures. Over and against these psychodynamic considerations we had to consider the effect of a certain degree of residual diplopia which, according to the child, was most noticeable when he attempted to look at moving objects at short range. We also had to consider the possibility of an additional perceptual defect such as is often found in brain-damaged children. The questions which we then asked ourselves were: What kinds of psychological attitudes and conflicts does this child bring to the reading situation as a result of the close association between the reading task and his concerns about his vision? What effect does the derogatory attitude of the parents toward this child's intelligence have upon the self-confidence with which he approaches the reading task? What effect does the teacher's confusion about the nature of Allen's difficulty and her fears of his epilepsy have upon the way she poses and seeks to help him with the reading task? What directly interfering effect, if any, do the organic factors have upon the reading skills?

In Allen's case we assumed an active role in contacting various people involved with him. In addition to his parents, this group included his pediatrician, ophthalmologist, and neurologist, his classroom teachers, remedial reading teachers, and school principal. Each had something to say which clarified certain aspects of the problem. But single contacts were not sufficient; not only his parents, but also his teachers and physicians saw Allen's problem differently as time went on. Sometimes the change in view was due to a change within Allen himself; at other times it was simply that physician, educator, or parent had increased their knowledge of Allen and so saw his problem in a different light. It often was the psychotherapist's role to act as an interpreter among the individuals concerned. Information gathered from the ophthalmologist was of use to the remedial reading teacher; similarly, observations of the remedial reading teacher could help the ophthalmologist improve his comprehension of Allen's visual difficulty. Misunderstandings between parent and physician or between parent and teacher often came to the psychotherapist's attention, and clarification of these misunderstandings had an important therapeutic effect on the boy's environment. In our school visits we were able to dispel the teacher's fears about Allen's seizures and to help her understand the benefits of special tutoring as a supplement to her own work with Allen. Similar cooperation with the remedial reading teacher was also fruitful, leading to a discussion of their pragmatic methods for aiding the child with his disability. These discussions appeared to encourage the application of the remedial teacher's knowledge and inventiveness in devising more successful techniques for this child's particular difficulty. Thus, it was discovered that the use of a blank card placed under each line of type enabled Allen to read more effectively, possibly because it helped his eyes to track more easily.

It was found that Allen's anxiety was most handicapping when he was expected to read aloud. If the teacher patiently helped him through these first anxious moments, he began to relax and to function more effectively. Allen, as was the case with many of our brain-damaged patients, was found to work more effectively when he was given individual attention. This attention could be effective even if it was limited to the teacher's close physical presence as the child worked. It seems as if the physical proximity of the important adult often has an organizing and energizing effect upon the functioning of the child with brain damage. The continuing discussions and cooperation with Allen's teachers, tutors, and the principal helped the therapist and educators to be more effective in dealing with the child's inattentiveness and low motivation in the learning situation, and his distorted self-esteem. The role of sports and physical activities in the school program also were considered since Allen's inadequacy in these areas was a cause of frustration and lowered self-esteem.

Our work with the parents involved a clarification of their perceptions of their son and his handicaps. We helped them to see through the obscurations of their own hopes and fears to the realities not only of the child's handicaps but of his assets. This enabled them better to absorb the narcissistic injury that had been part of their reaction to Allen's defects. They could then make good use of assistance in organizing specific supervised activities to help the child not only with his learning handicap but with his problems of body mastery. These activities varied from formalized programs such as swimming lessons at the local Y to increased father-child engagement in outdoor activities including gardening chores and ball playing. In his psychotherapeutic work the boy was able to increase his insight into the relationships between his physical defects and his self-attitudes. This enabled him to reflect upon and talk about the traumatic experiences of his surgery, his seizures, and his physical defects. He was also helped to explore his feelings about his reading handicap and the associated feelings of intellectual inferiority. Proceeding in this way it was possible to help him to see himself a bit more realistically, with what we believe was a concomitant improvement in self-esteem and a reduced sense of vulnerability. This permitted him to apply himself more effectively to his academic work. Although regular therapeutic sessions with Allen were stopped some six months before completion of the third grade, we remained in frequent contact with family and school. At present, the social problems related to school adjustment have decreased. The child and parents live more harmoniously with one another and with greater appreciation of each other's worth. Academically, the reading problem is being overcome at a satisfactory rate. At the end of the third grade Allen's reading vocabulary had increased to the 2.9 level, which is slightly more than a full school year's gain in this grade, and his reading comprehension had increased to 3.8, which is equivalent to more than a year and a half gain.

In Allen's treatment the therapist provided explanations to the child about his eye defect and the eye surgery he had experienced as well as the nature of his seizures and their medical management. Explanations of this kind to a child require a certain degree of technical knowledge that is not always available to the parents, and an understanding of the child's fears and psychodynamics not readily available to the surgeon or neurologist. In this aspect of his work the therapist assumes an educational role in which the interpretation of knowledge to the child is so timed and so regulated that the child can most effectively use it. All brain-damaged children will have fears and concerns about their bodily intactness and even of impending death, especially if they are subject to such frightening experiences as seizures. Although the realistic aspects of these fears should not be dismissed, the therapist can help the child to cope with them. The irrational aspects can be helped not only by a resolution of the underlying and associated conflicts but by imparting to the child the necessary information for a reality-oriented understanding of his defects. (Doris and Solnit, 1963, p. 621–625)

In the following case, taken from Doris (1963), we are dealing with a child who under the definitions considered in this chapter could well be considered minimally brain damaged. Many of the supposed behavioral signs are present including hyperactivity, short attention span, susceptibility to anxiety, and the appropriate psychometric pattern. The developmental history—with its prematurity and delay in language function—plus the neurologist's opinion might, however, give greater credence to the existence of brain damage than is sometimes the case of children assigned to the minimally brain damaged group.

∽ *Robert* . . . was brought to our clinic at the age of six with a school learning problem. His parents were also concerned about his hyperactivity, his short attention span, his nervousness, and his overexcitability. They described him as a sociable child who related well to adults but had difficulty in relating to children his own age. His low frustration tolerance, his sensitivity, and his inability to assert himself put him at a disadvantage in the give-and-take, rough-and-tumble atmosphere of six-year-old children at play. In addition, other children were likely to view him as "odd." His father explained this in part as Robert's overreadiness to please and to make friends.

Birth and developmental history were as follows. There had been a moderate amount of vaginal bleeding in the fifth month of pregnancy requiring the mother to remain in bed for several days. Birth weight was 4 lbs., 14 oz. and Robert was placed in a premature unit. He was in an incubator and given oxygen during the first few days after birth. He was discharged in two weeks. Colic was present until about eight months. He walked at fourteen months. Simple sentences were used before the second birthday, but the parents considered him a slow speaker and maintained that he did not talk clearly until after his fourth birthday. He was bladder trained at three years, but even at six years he had to be reminded to go to the bathroom. Bowel training was difficult. He would not sit on the potty chair, and training was done by having him stand on newspapers spread upon the floor. Neurological examination at the time he came to our clinic was essentially within normal limits, with the following exceptions: Robert exhibited some difficulty with gross and fine motor coordination. He was unsure of his orientation in space, clumsily bumping into objects. He could skip only on one foot. There was definite difficulty in performing alternating repetitive movements. Even with eyes open he could not sustain his weight on one foot. He grasped a pencil with marked awkwardness and had trouble copying a triangle. The neurologist's impression was that there was no active neurological disease but probably some organic brain deficit, prenatally determined. On psychological examination, Robert obtained a Full Scale I.Q. of 68 on the WISC, a Verbal Scale I.Q. of 79 and a Performance Scale I.Q. of 62. With the notable exception of the vocabulary subtest, scores on all other subtests both Verbal and Performance were markedly below age-level expectation. On the vocabulary subtest Robert achieved a test age of 7-6 which was above his chronological age level of 6-7. On the arithmetic subtest he achieved a test age of 5-2. All other subtests fell below this level. On block designs he was not able to obtain a single raw-score credit. On object assembly he obtained just a single credit but was nevertheless able correctly to recognize and name the puzzles, although he could not put them together. On the Bender Gestalt most of his reproductions were unrecognizable, only the dotted patterns maintaining a semblance of the original Gestalt.

At the time of Robert's initial contact with our clinic, the school was prepared to leave Robert back and was seriously considering his candidacy for a special class. The psychologist who examined Robert and the therapist who was treating him for the emotional aspects of his problem were of the opinion that it was not meaningful to plan for Robert's education in terms of the I.Q. score or his present level of functioning in the class. They were impressed by the fact that the boy had shown some progress in learning to read; that the history indicated no serious retardation in development; that although he could not solve the puzzles in the object assembly test, he had sufficient perceptual skills to recognize what they were; that he showed evidence of considerable social skills in his interactions with adults; and that his vocabulary was fully age adequate not only in the test situation but in his everyday speech. The therapist further felt that Robert's anxiety and short attention span must be a major handicap in the learning situation and was of the opinion that if Robert could be helped with his emotional problems by psychotherapy, or if the teaching situation could be slightly modified to take into account his particular problems, he might perform more efficiently in school. In consultation with the principal and his teacher it was decided that Robert should repeat the first grade instead of being placed in a special class. It was further decided that a teacher would be employed for part-time individual tutoring. Individual tutoring was thought desirable, for it had been observed that Robert worked best in the classroom when the teacher stood beside him. It was not so much a matter of the teacher's offering direct help to him, but rather it seemed that her presence was necessary to keep him oriented toward his work. Why this was so we are not quite certain, but we do know that Robert had a high investment in his interpersonal relationships. For Robert it was important, even more than for the average child, that everybody like him, and since he painfully experienced the rejection that his odd behavior patterns sometimes evoked from other children, he was especially pleased when someone showed an interest in him. The teacher's presence near him when he worked and her expression of approval when he succeeded may have been sufficient for him to overcome the problems in attention span and distractibility that usually interfered with his work. With this program, Robert repeated the first grade successfully. In the second grade he got along so well that the tutoring was not thought necessary, although at times the teacher would keep him after school to give him a little extra help or to permit him to finish an assignment that his slower work patterns had not permitted him to finish with the other children. At the end of the second grade his reading ability was above class average; his arithmetic skills placed him in the lowest quarter of the class but still sufficiently high for promotion. On the last follow-up contact we learned that he had been promoted to the fourth grade, after an adequate performance in the third grade. (Doris, 1963, p. 187–190)

Some comments on this case, not available in the original report, might be relevant in the context of this chapter.

๑๛ On the decision of the neurologist, no electroencephalography was undertaken. There was no indication in the history or in the physical examination of seizure activity. Therefore, the neurologist felt that an EEG was not warranted for the determination of either the presence or the locus of a focal lesion. In addition, he felt that should the EEG show a non-focal "abnormality" it would be without significance from his point of view since such "abnormalities" are quite common in clinically normal children. Finally, he maintained, he knew the therapist well enough to know that the presence or absence of such an abnormal EEG tracing was not likely to affect in any significant way the psychotherapeutic planning for the child. In this he was right. Under these conditions, the neurologist then felt that the likelihood of a significant gain in information that would affect the treatment of the child was too negligible to warrant subjecting the child and his family to the stress and expense of an EEG.

The second comment on this case concerns the use of labels.

In interpreting the child's learning and behavioral problems to the parents the therapist felt that it was appropriate to point out that the child's learning and behavioral difficulties were not likely to be exclusively the product of emotional disturbance or parental handling. Rather it was emphasized that it was the therapist's impression that there was a constitutional predisposition in the child for the kinds of learning and behavioral difficulties he was experiencing. This position was taken after an extended professional contact with the family which had convinced the therapist that this problem was not basically psychogenic and that these parents were coping with a difficult problem with much greater than average skill. A correct perception by the parents of the nature of the problem seemed to require an emphasis on the "biological component." To speak with greater precision on the nature of the "biological component" seemed speculative and unnecessary. The parents could apparently accept and "understand" the import of the therapist's communication. They were dealing with a problem where the child's emotional conflicts and their behavior toward the child were certainly important, but it was a problem where the biological equipment of the child seemed to be a major determining factor.

Subsequent to the conference with the therapist, the mother spoke to the neurologist who described the child as "brain damaged." The mother returned to the therapist after this "new" piece of information quite depressed, concerned that she had not taken sufficient care of herself during the pregnancy, pessimistic about the boy's future. When the therapist contacted the neurologist it became apparent that both viewed the child's problem in essentially the same way. The neurologist did not wish to maintain that there were definite anatomical lesions of the central nervous system. He felt that there was reason to believe that in some way, whether anatomically, physiologically, or biochemically, there was a dysfunction of the central nervous system. He did not know whether the dysfunction might be hereditarily based or acquired. This was consistent with the therapist's view that there was a constitutional basis for the child's learning and behavioral difficulty. Both professionals felt that emotional and environmental factors had been and would continue to be important modifiers—for good and for ill—of the way in which the underlying biological handicap was translated into behavior.

Fortunately, it was possible to convey this essential agreement between the therapist and the neurologist to the mother, and at the same time in subsequent conferences the neurologist and therapist both supported the parents in the development of a more optimistic view of the child's problem. An optimistic view that proved realistic in view of the outcome.

It might be argued that the only difference between the neurologist and the therapist in their communications to the mother was a difference in the choice of words. The meaning was essentially the same. But the mother's differential reaction to the two communications indicates that there were connotations and implications in the two communications that, for her, were radically different. We would not argue that one label, "constitutional predisposition," is inherently preferable to another, "brain damage." Two professionals, agreed on what they are talking about, can communicate just as well with one term as with the other. *But what is important in the clinical situation is that the clinician and the patient or his family are agreed upon the meaning of the terms they use.* We suspect that in the above case both the neurologist and the therapist may have been tactically in error in assuming that their labels of "brain damage" or "constitutional predisposition" conveyed to the mother of the child the complicated and extended set of meanings that they conveyed to themselves. Therefore, in clinical work we would think that a diagnostic formulation conveying the nature of the patient's difficulty in adjustment without the use of jargon—especially when the jargon lacks precise definition —is by far the best way of communicating one's findings to the parents, the educators, and the other professionals concerned with the child. We suspect it may also be the clinician's best defense against that tendency—present in all of us—for slipping into fuzzy and stereotyped thinking that aids in neither the definition nor the solution of the problem at hand.

In this chapter we have attempted to convey that in cases of actual and presumed brain damage our diagnostic, prognostic, and remedial capabilities are far from securely based—a fact which apparently has not intimidated some individuals from presenting themselves to the public as possessing "the truth" in this complex area. Like all other fields, mental subnormality has had, and will continue to have, its share of faddish practices and solutions. Strong belief in the validity of what one is doing is necessary in any form of sustained endeavor. One cannot long persist in the helping professions if one feels that one's endeavors have little or no justification. The problem is that strong belief is too often a double-edged sword in that passionate commitment to a way of thinking and practicing makes it easy to confuse assumption with fact, to screen out alternative possibilities, to fail to recognize contradicting instances, and to oversimplify what is in fact fantastically complex. It may not be a source of comfort, but it is nevertheless true, that the relationships encompassed in the phrase "the brain-behavior problem" are staggering to the mind not only because the brain is so complex but also because its external environment is equally complex, and these two complexities are always in a dynamic relationship to each other.

The next chapter, concerned with infantile autism, is but a varient of what we have been discussing. As we hope to demonstrate, the controversy surrounding infantile autism concerns every important issue we are aware of in the area of the brain and behavior. It would be more correct to say, perhaps, that it involves practically every major issue taken up in this book—hopefully, a helpful way of concluding our efforts.

Infantile autism: the continuing controversy

We have endeavored to convey to the reader how the field of mental subnormality and many, if not all, of the problems contained in it, change over time as a function of a variety of factors, e.g., events in the contemporary society, the status of the field in relation to other fields of investigation, the acquisition of new knowledge, the development of new theories. An important example including many of these factors is the problem of infantile autism, not because of the number of afflicted children, which is very small, but because the unravelling of the nature of the problem may well have fateful consequences for the entire field of psychology—a point made in 1958 by Sarason and Gladwin and given support by Bettelheim's recent book (1967).

As we shall see in the following pages, infantile autism raises most of the important issues in mental subnormality: the role of organic brain defect, genetic factors, parent-child relationships, the development of the complexity we call the self, and amenability to remedial or therapeutic efforts. As Bettelheim (1967) has stated, and demonstrated, one can devote a large volume to autism without doing full justice to all aspects of its history or problems. In the present chapter we shall restrict ourselves to a partial account of its modern history in a way so as to highlight the issues involved, alternative explanations, and the more general significances of the problem.

KANNER'S CLINICAL PICTURE

In 1943 Kanner described eleven children whose condition he ascribed to an inborn autistic disturbance of affective contact. "The combination of extreme autism, obsessiveness, stereotypy, and echolalia brings the total picture [of this condition] into relationship with some of the basic schizophrenic phenomena. . . . But in spite of the remarkable similarities, the condition differs in many respects from all other known instances of childhood schizophrenia." Kanner pointed out that whereas in childhood schizophrenia there were usually at least two years of essentially average life, "the children of our group have all shown their extreme aloneness from the very beginning of life, not responding to anything that comes to them from the outside world. This is most characteristically expressed in the recurrent report of failure of the child to assume an anticipatory posture upon being picked up, and of failure to adjust the body to that of the person holding him." In contrast to the young schizophrenic, Kanner's cases were able to establish and maintain a purposeful and "intelligent" relation to objects "but are from the start anxiously and tensely impervious to people, with whom for a long time they do not have any kind of direct affective contact." The course of development of these children also seems to be different from that found in early schizophrenia.

The basic desire for aloneness and sameness has remained essentially unchanged, but there has been a varying degree of emergence from solitude, an acceptance of at least some people as being within the child's sphere of consideration, and a sufficient increase in the number of experienced patterns to refute the earlier impression of extreme limitation of the child's ideational content. One might perhaps put it this way: While the schizophrenic tries to solve his problem by stepping out of a world of which he has been a part and with which he has been in touch, our children gradually *compromise* by extending cautious feelers into a world in which they have been total strangers from the beginning. Between the ages of 5 and 6 years, they gradually abandon the echolalia and learn spontaneously to use personal pronouns with adequate reference. Language becomes more communicative, at first in the sense of a question-and-answer exercise, and then in the sense of greater spontaneity of sentence formation. Food is accepted without difficulty. Noises and motions are tolerated more than previously. The panic tantrums subside. The repetitiousness assumes the form of obsessive preoccupations. Contact with a limited number of people is established in a twofold way: people are included in the child's world to the extent to which they satisfy his needs, answer his obsessive questions, teach him how to read and to do things. Second, though people are still regarded as nuisances, their questions are answered and their commands are obeyed reluctantly, with the implication that it would be best to get these interferences over with, the sooner to be able to return to the still much desired aloneness. Between the ages of 6 and 8 years, the children begin to play in a group, still never *with* the other members of the play group, but at least on the periphery *alongside* the group. Reading skill is acquired quickly, but the children read monotonously, and a story or a moving picture is experienced in unrelated portions rather than in its coherent totality. All of this makes the family feel that, in spite of recognized "difference" from other children, there is progress and improvement. (Kanner, 1943, pp. 249–250)

The only case in Kanner's series who did not follow this course of development was a girl who at the age of 5 had been "dumped" into a training school for the feebleminded. Her behavior was markedly different from that of the other children in the school: over a period of years there was no change in it, the institutional setting presumably making for a continuation of her behavioral pattern rather than a change in it. Several of the other cases described by Kanner had also been considered at one time as mentally defective but their development was as described above.

Kanner also noted that the parents of these children were in some ways unusual.

One other fact stands out prominently. In the whole group, there are very few really warmhearted fathers and mothers. For the most part, the parents, grandparents, and collaterals are persons strongly preoccupied with abstractions of a scientific, literary, or artistic nature, and limited in genuine interest in people. Even some of the happiest marriages are rather cold and formal affairs. Three of the marriages were dismal failures. The question arises whether or to what extent this fact has contributed to the condition of the children. The children's aloneness from the beginning of life makes it difficult to attribute the whole picture exclusively to the type of the early parental relations with our patients. (Kanner, 1943, p. 250)

There were three interrelated reasons for the subsequent impact of Kanner's descriptions (1944, 1946, 1948). The first was that they were a model of descriptive clarity, and thus enabled others to perceive their clinical cases from a new perspective. The second was that he advanced two hypotheses that were certain to arouse controversy: There was an inborn component; parent-child relationships were somehow involved. The third reason was a pessimism that anything could be done for most of these children—a position certain to arouse opposition in those who for theoretical or other reasons look optimistically at the capacity of any human organism to change or be changed.

Not long after Kanner's initial publications, Rank (1949) described four children who showed many of the characteristics described by Kanner. However, perhaps because her description grew out of an intensive therapeutic involvement with the children and their parents, Rank gave much more weight to the role of the mothers who tended to be highly intellectual, prominent people in whom immaturity and narcissism were marked. Rank's description of the psychological structure of these mothers and its effect on the child follows.

The need to be a mother, the hope and expectation that through this experience she may become a real person capable of true emotions, is so desperate that of itself it may create anxiety, ambivalence, fear of failure. Because she is so barren of spontaneous manifestation of maternal feelings, she studies vigilantly all the new methods of upbringing and reads treatises about physical and mental hygiene. Her greatest fear is of "spoiling" her child. Frequently she insists on an aseptic environment, and the child grows in an orderly, scientific atmosphere where routine and dietary prescriptions prevail. The sunshine which is radiated by the spontaneous, tenderly devoted mother is missing. The result may be passive inertia of the infant or at the other extreme, restlessness and sleeplessness. The passive child is less of a threat because he does not make exaggerated demands on the mother, who feels constantly in danger of revealing that emotionally she has little or nothing to offer, that she is a fraud. Parallel with this or independently, we may find in her personality structure the "messianic idea," not in the psychotic sense, but as a symbol of hope that through identification with the child, her own flesh and blood, she may experience vicariously the joys of real living, of genuine feeling.

If then, as frequently occurs, she becomes aware that this is not the case, she is compelled to face the fact that she is really without magic. She fights desperately for control, no longer of herself perhaps but of the child. The struggles over weaning and toilet training are generally battles in which she tries to redeem herself. The child becomes the real victim—victim of the mother's helplessness which in turn creates an aggression in her that mounts to destruction. The only way for the child to survive is to retreat, to withdraw not only from the dangerous mother but from the whole world as well. A world of his own is created, a world of fantasy, but of fantasy so primary, so repetitious, so remote from our own feelings and experiences that he appears to us odd, bizarre, and dull intellectually and emotionally. He may then remain arrested in this stage, showing a scattered development, or regress even further to a complete breakdown of all social patterns. He becomes a restless wanderer in search of no one and no place, weaving about the room, swaying back and forth, circling the walls as if they were bars he would escape through; and he frequently does escape into the neighboring yard or the street, unconcerned with danger, absorbed in his own world. Unaware of the people he encounters, he stumbles over their feet or their most precious possessions. But all at once he may get panicky and in his fury and anguish throw himself to the ground when suddenly aware that his mother or mother-substitute is not at his side. It is as if he had been running away from her only to be able to return to her over and over. This special quality of pulling away and yet leaning on one, is one of his many enigmatic characteristics. Because he tries so desperately to be invulnerable in his own world, he is pathetically helpless at the same time. (Rank, 1949, pp. 131–132)

As we shall see later, Rank's formulation in 1949 is very similar to that of Bettelheim in 1967. In the writings of Kanner and Rank the basic controversy—not about the clinical picture of infantile autism but about its origins, development, and therapy—was already in the literature.[1]

---

[1] This statement holds for the recent or modern history of the problem. In the last part of this chapter where we take up the work of Witmer in the early decades of this century—a contribution apparently unknown to modern writers (Sarason and Gladwin, 1958)—we shall see that in certain respects he anticipated the formulations of Kanner, Rank, and Bettelheim.

The Idiot-Savant and Infantile Autism

Although the idiot-savant has been described and discussed many times over the years, it was not until 1945 that a really penetrating and comprehensive review and discussion of the problem appeared. In that year Scheerer, Rothmann, and Goldstein (1945) published their monograph, a work which has not received the attention it merits. The reader is urged to read this monograph from which we give below the authors' summary statement:

৩৴ L, an 11-year-old boy, with behavioral peculiarities has been studied over a period of 5 years and a reliable record of his previous development obtained. L showed distinct musical aptitude—he played melodies on the piano by ear—and was remarkable in verbal retentiveness. His skill in rapidly manipulating simple numbers was also unusual, and he performed so-called calendar calculations amazingly well. Numbers he remembered with the same ease as occurrences which to his mind had once become connected with them, so that he volunteered dates, names, places, and times of events at the slightest provocation.

In spite of all this, L's general information was surprisingly subnormal, and, with the exception of the just mentioned aspects of his surrounding, nothing aroused his interest. He never absorbed or learned in a normal fashion, nor could he attend a regular school. He was retarded in the mastery of many skills, commensurate to his age, and he was lacking in social awareness with a limited repertoire of social responses. L had an IQ of 50 which classifies him technically an "idiot-savant."

An investigation of L's personality structure was carried out with specially devised experiments, with standard tests and with careful exploration of his spontaneous behavior in everyday life. An analysis of all data and of the findings in multiform performance fields failed to disclose an individual segmental defect or several specific defects. Instead, his various deficiency symptoms pointed to a functionally common disturbance, a general impairment of abstract capacity (e.g., in the semantic use and ideational understanding of language, of social contents and relations; in reasoning, in the grasp of causation, of logical meaning, of symbols, of conceptual number relations; in the cognitive structuring of visual performances and visuo-motor tasks). This picture of general abstract impairment was corroborated by the experimental evidence that L succeeded in his own performance-specialties without having a genuine understanding of their meaning as to content and implication. Further exploration of his thinking, learning, and social behavior revealed an abnormal concretization. He could only grasp and learn what made situational or tangibly patterned sense to him. Otherwise, if he retained at all, it was in an automatic, associative manner by habituation.

A positive evaluation of his successful performances, abilities and skills was attempted. After having experimentally ruled out other alternatives, it was found that L possesses an initial endowment in the acoustic and audiomotor sphere, probably supported by kindred imagery. This endowment expressed itself particularly in his sensory motor receptiveness for melodies, i.e., for acoustic "Gestalten" and for verbal patterns. On this basis his musical performances, his verbal and tonal memory (absolute pitch), and his aptitude for serial grouping became explicable (e.g., his rapid oral counting and spelling, forward and backward, his large digit span and his calendar performance).

Further analysis of his procedure in the utilization of this endowment revealed however, that it did not operate in a normal manner. It was bound to an abnormally rigid concreteness and functioned in a sterile, bizarre and undiscerning form. Symptomatically, in music he could not develop his talent through study or practice. His performances were desultory, depending on specific circumstances and his interest ranged from obsession with a special phonograph record to appreciative enjoyment of opera arias or Handel's "Largo" on records and indifference to *any* radio music. Correspondingly anomalous function of his talent was manifest in his excessive tendency to count indiscriminately, and to resort to enumerative verbalization and inane speech clichés whenever he was confronted with a task that overtaxed his power.

We find then that an individual who is handicapped in abstraction and endowed in a particular field of performance shows a *sub*normal intelligence and an *ab*normal canalization of his endowment. In interpreting this personality picture we concluded: owing to his impaired abstract attitude, L cannot realize his remaining potentialities in a normally integrated manner. He is therefore driven in an abnormal degree and direction to exercise those functions which nature permits him to develop, because these are the only performances through which he can actualize himself and come to terms with his surroundings. The least impaired function thus becomes a coping mechanism of adjustment, but, since it can only operate on the level of concrete reactions, it becomes canalized into atypical forms of expression. This result seems to point to an organizational interdependence of basic psychological functions. Certain pertinent implications with regard to normal personality structure and with regard to the problem of idiot-savant are discussed and the following generalizations considered:

1. How an endowment operates and develops, depends upon the organization of the person as-a-whole.
2. There exists a functional interrelation between abstract capacity, intelligence and special endowment.
   a. The abstract capacity is essential for the normal functioning of intelligence. The bearing of this on the association theory of intelligence is followed up.
   b. The abstract capacity is conditional for the normal functioning and development of an endowment, although the latter may be anchored in concrete processes, e.g., of Gestalt type.
3. The term idiot-savant is a misnomer. Idiot-savants are talented aments who possess an amented talent.

In order to test these conclusions a comparative study of other reported cases of idiot-savant was undertaken and various explanatory hypotheses of other authors were critically examined. The evaluation of this case material seems to confirm our interpretation, since no cases were found in which a talent functioned normally in an individual with abstract impairment. These led to the establishment of certain criteria for the psychological identification of a talented ament.

In studying the reported superior abilities in aments two phenomena invited particular attention because they posed an intriguing psychological problem. These were (1) the relative frequency of number manipulation and retention, and (2) unusual features of memory.

(1) The analysis of the psychological processes involved in these number performances laid bare their origin in concrete perceptual counting procedures with specific limitations. A comparison between this stage of primitive, concrete grouping and the initial procedures in arithmetical prodigies showed basically common characteristics. It became clear, however, that the arithmetical prodigy who developed further towards a cognitive understanding of mathematics outgrew this original stage of concrete dependency in his number operations, because he could increasingly adopt an abstract approach. In contrast the abstract impairment prevented the talented ament from passing beyond the initial stage of concrete grouping procedures.

(2) The striking retention of numbers or of outlandish and irrelevant data, as, e.g., railroad tables or an entire newspaper column, is all the more surprising as in most every instance the retained material is not understood by the ament in a normal way. A psychological appraisal of the changes in figure-ground organization as experienced during pathological concreteness led us to set forth a new explanation of these peculiar memory processes. The observations on the cases studied indicate that a defective organism will cling tenaciously to those aspects of a situation and those features of material which make concrete palpable sense to him, i.e., with which he can deal successfully. These aspects are thrust into the foreground of the phenomenal organization as the "figure." Such a difference in perceptive centering in the abnormal's coming to terms with the world of the "normal" leads to a different centering of performance. Therefore, these aments retain easily what may appear senseless or peripheral or irrelevant to the normal observer. To the aments in question, however, this is the only "sense" possible and pivotal in the experienced contents. This explanatory attempt is tested on diversified case material. Finally, comparing abnormal concreteness in aments with stages of concrete reaction in normal children the following question is raised: Does the atypical memory organization in a subnormal child represent a lawful modification of a normal development phase which has become pathologically "eccentric" and conditioned as a coping mechanism? (Scheerer, Rothmann, and Goldstein, 1945, pp. 59–61)

It has indeed been a rare event in psychology or psychiatry when clinical problems that have been considered rather different are brought in relation to each other. For this reason we quote the following passages from Scheerer, Rothmann, and Goldstein:

Recently Kanner has discussed 11 cases of personality deviation in children in terms of "autistic disturbances of affective contact" which he considers a special syndrome. Pointing to the misplaced eagerness of parents to promote precociousness in their children he states: "Their excellent rote memory, coupled with the inability to use language in any other way, often led the parents to stuff them with more and more verses, zoologic and botanic names, titles and composers of Victrola record pieces and the like. Thus, from the start, language, which the children did not use for the purpose of communication—was deflected in a considerable measure to a self-sufficient, semantically and conversationally valueless or grossly distorted memory exercise. To a child 2 or 3 years old, all these words, numbers, and poems (questions and answers of the Presbyterian Catechism; Mendelssohn's violin concerto; the twenty-third Psalm, a French lullaby; an encyclopedia index page) could hardly have more meaning than sets of nonsense syllables to adults. It is difficult to know for certain whether the stuffing as such has contributed essentially to the course of the psychopathological condition. But it is also difficult to imagine that it did not cut deeply into the development of language as a tool for receiving and imparting meaningful messages."

Kanner's behavioral observations on these children represent new valuable material for mental pathology. Since his case histories show many parallels to those here presented it may be in order to make some comparisons between his interpretation and our hypothesis on the role of concreteness in defective children and their retentivity.

According to Kanner "the outstanding, 'pathognomic,' fundamental disorder is the children's *inability to relate themselves* in the ordinary way to people and situations from the beginning of life." He explains all behavioral abnormalities found in these children from their *affective* disturbance, from their "desire for aloneness and sameness." To Kanner the inconsistent picture of intellectual ability, the obsessive repetitiousness, the shock reactions to loud noises and moving objects, and the "truly phenomenal memory" in these children is accounted for by their emotional resistance against change in the outer situation—the insistence upon "identical spatial or chronological order." In following Kanner's impressive observations in support of his view, it appears nevertheless as if Kanner has neglected the qualitative nature of the intellectual abnormalities in this picture. The case histories abound with instances of compulsive concreteness in thought and action. In our opinion this is only explicable on the basis of an impairment of abstract attitude which is intimately bound up with the affective disturbance. To mention only a few problems, it is hard to see how an affective disturbance alone can account for what Kanner calls the "literalness" in these children, their inability to use "yes" as a *general* symbol of affirmation, detached from the specific situation in which it had been acquired; their inability to understand prepositions in the abstract sense. (Asked to put something down, the child puts it on the floor—understanding the word only in the originally acquired situational sense.) It is hard to follow Kanner when he makes the affect-anomally responsible for: "the absence of spontaneous sentence formation and the echolalia type of reproduction, which in every one of the 8 speaking children has given rise to a peculiar grammatical phenomenon. *Personal pronouns are repeated just as heard.* The child once told by his mother 'now I will give you your milk' expresses the desire for milk in exactly the same words. Consequently he comes to speak of himself always as you and of the person addressed as I." We have encountered this reversal of pronouns in three cases here presented all of which showed pronounced impairment of abstraction.

This peculiar "grammatical" phenomenon appears to be more than a mere grammatical one or a purely mechanical echolalia. The child hears himself addressed as "you" and the other person speaking of himself as "I." Only on a concrete level of thinking is the literal application of the word "you" to the child himself and "I" to the other person explicable, because the child cannot detach the words from their experienced "belongingness" in the actual situation and reverse this belonging in terms of a relational symbol. (The corresponding phenomenon in normal children is their frequent use of their first name or the third person in referring to themselves.)

Is the child's inability to shift the word "you" from himself to the other person, and the word "I" from the other person, is this inability to grasp the relational meaning of "you" and "I" in the abstract, merely the result of the affective disturbance or (is it) not a symptom of impaired abstraction and limitation to the concrete as well?

In discussing their peculiar memory Kanner speaks of parrot-like repetitions of heard word combinations, of "delayed echolalia."

As in the case of L, "the children had learned at an early age to repeat an inordinate number of nursery rhymes, prayers, lists of animals, the roster of presidents, the alphabet forward and backward, foreign (French) language lullabies . . . even long and unusual words were retained with remarkable facility." Yet in contrast to these recitals, their spontaneous language-development and understanding was retarded. In Kanner's concepts it is the need for "sameness and autistic aloneness" that sufficiently accounts for both, this semantic retardation and for the abnormal retention of verbal material, which latter he characterizes as completely senseless for the children. This makes it quite difficult to understand *why* they so eagerly and readily absorbed and reproduced such material, and even liked to spell out words. Is perhaps the fact that the children did not grasp the meaning of language in the normal way the motive for their heightened responsiveness to and their tenaciously obsessive reproduction of phonetic sound patterns? In the light of our own case-material it seems highly probable that these children excelled precociously in verbal memory for the same reasons as we outlined in our hypothesis. And the question may arise, whether the disturbance in affective human contact they suffered is not secondary to the defect in abstraction or parallel to it. Perhaps this hindered a normal grasp of the semantic aspect of language and impelled these children to cling to that aspect of speech which was concretely sensible and apprehensible for them in terms of auditory motor patterns. (Scheerer, Rothmann, and Goldstein, 1945, pp. 57–58)

In their discussion of the hypotheses put forward by Scheerer, Rothmann, and Goldstein, Sarason and Gladwin (1958) state the following:

How is such an explanation to explain (or to be integrated with) the impression, reported by Tredgold (1922) and supported by our own review of the literature, that the large majority of idiot savants are males? There also seems to be a preponderance of males among the reported cases of infantile autism.

There appear to be no grounds for doubting that there is an impairment of abstraction in both the idiot savant and the autistic child. When Scheerer, Rothmann, and Goldstein cautiously suggest that in these cases we may be dealing with a lawful modification of a normal development phase which has become pathologically "eccentric and conditioned as a coping mechanism," at least two questions arise. Is the coping mechanism always a response to the impairment of abstraction—that is, is the impairment of abstraction always the *etiological* factor "forcing" the child to develop atypically? Is development normal up until that phase when the organism should be able to respond abstractly? To answer either question in the positive would certainly conflict with the experience of those clinicians who report having discerned the characteristics of autism well before the period when abstraction as an intellectual characteristic normally becomes manifest. In other words, factors other than intellectual seem, in some cases at least, to be primary.

To explain the idiot savant and the autistic child primarily in terms of an impairment in abstraction would be more plausible if these were cases with demonstrable central nervous system pathology. In the published literature many, if not the large majority, of these cases have no such discernible pathology. Because these conditions can and do appear in the presence of positive neurological evidence of brain injury does not allow one to assume that where such evidence is lacking it is because of the crudity of neurological procedures. This may be the case but the burden of proof would seem to be on those who make the assumption. Because schizophrenia can follow alterations in the central nervous system does not mean that all schizophrenia can be explained in this way.

Perhaps our most serious reservation to Scheerer, Rothmann, and Goldstein's discussion of the idiot savant and the autistic child concerns their failure to consider the possible ways in which familial personalities and organization either interact with or cause or exacerbate the impairment of abstraction. For example, Kanner, who has reported the largest series of cases of infantile autism, comes to the conclusion that the personality of the parents and their techniques of child rearing are not irrelevant factors in attempting to understand the autistic child. It may be that Kanner's sample is in some ways a biased one but until this is demonstrated one cannot dismiss the possibility that factors external to the autistic child are important in the development of the condition. In this connection it might be pointed out that in the case of the idiot savant which Scheerer, Rothmann, and Goldstein describe there is practically no discussion of the possible role of parental personality on the child. We point this out because of our impression that what little is contained in the monograph on parental personality and behavior suggests similarities to Kanner's descriptions of the parents of his cases. Unfortunately (but not unexpectedly) in the entire literature of the idiot savant there is not a single acceptable personality description of the parents. We are here not contending that parental personality and behavior is the etiological factor—for reasons to be discussed later we feel such a statement to be unjustified on theoretical grounds. However, for similar reasons, we are contending that any explanation of behavior which is based exclusively on factors "inside" the individual is likely to be a very incomplete one.

If one were to assume that the kinds of cases we have been discussing were in some way primarily a function of non-environmental factors (e.g., brain-injury, genetic, constitutional, etc.) then one would expect that they would occur in any culture, e.g., the so-called primitive ones. There is no evidence that this is the case. However, since anthropologists have not been interested in these types of problems, and are not trained to pick them out, the absence of evidence in this instance means little or nothing. We would suggest that cross-cultural studies of infantile autism and idiot savants might be fruitful regardless of the direction of the evidence which would emerge.

In summary, Scheerer, Rothmann, and Goldstein have made an important contribution in pointing out and discussing the similarities between the autistic child and the idiot savant. There is little doubt that in both these conditions there is an impairment of abstraction. In raising questions about the adequacy of such an impairment for explaining these conditions, we have tried to suggest that such an explanation does not seem to cover what apparently are certain facts—particularly the sex difference in the incidence of the two conditions. In addition, we expressed the opinion that discovery of those factors which antedate and are related to the impairment of abstraction may be of vast importance for our understanding of the early development of intellectual functions—their nature, course, and relation to the external environment. The importance of these cases to the development of a science of psychology would seem to be vastly beyond what their relatively rare occurrence in the general population would suggest.

We hope it is clear from the previous discussion that we are dealing with conditions the etiology of which is very ambiguous. These cases are certainly not homogeneous in terms of presence and degree of organic pathology. It is also impossible to do other than grossly speculate about the possible role of environmental factors. It seems fair to say, then, that neither in the case of infantile autism nor in the idiot savant can one justifiably ascribe the condition to either, environmental or organic pathological factors. It would indeed be surprising if the ultimate explanation required knowledge of but one of these factors—the conditions seem far too complex to hold out hope for such simple explanations. (Sarason and Gladwin, 1958, pp. 211–214)

The Etiology of Infantile Autism: Psychogenic or Biological

In their 1958 monograph, in connection with their discussion of the relationships among autism, idiot-savant, and Bourne's (1955) "protophrenia," Sarason and Gladwin raise the following question: "Why is it that some children who have been subjected to the kinds of experiences and relationships which Bourne describes do *not* develop the picture of severe subnormality he calls protophrenia?" It is important to emphasize that although Sarason and Gladwin did not deny that organic and environmental factors had to be viewed in relation to each other, they considered that the type of variable they had in mind was perhaps independent of both, at least in the earliest months of life. They referred specifically to the "unusual sensitivities in very young children" described by Bergman and Escalona (1949):

It was several years ago that the authors were first struck by the observations to be reported here. Some very young children possessed unusual sensitivities manifesting themselves in several, if not in all, sensory modalities (visual, auditory, tactile, etc.). Colors, bright lights, noises, unusual sounds, qualities of material, experiences of equilibrium, of taste, of smell, of temperature, seemed to have an extraordinarily intensive impact upon these children at a very early age. They were "sensitive" in both meanings of the word: easily hurt, and easily stimulated to enjoyment. Variations in sensory impression that made no difference to the average child made a great deal of difference to these children. They were also characterized by a certain precocity, though this was very unevenly distributed among the diverse functions of their personality. The first impression which some of their reactions and abilities gave was that of unusual giftedness such as might be observed in the budding of a genius. Further observation, however, suggested comparison with individuals suffering from a traumatic neurosis, or a psychosis, and even with feebleminded children. Closer study and follow-up then made it appear that childhood psychosis was the fate of these children, though we are not sure yet that all children of the type to be described eventually develop a clear psychotic picture. . . .

If we examine more closely those facts that impressed us as bespeaking unusual sensitivity in the described children, we become aware that they differ from each other in several respects, and can be grouped accordingly. We find that we have observed facts pertaining to many parts of the sensorium, i.e., to visual, to auditive, to tactile, to olfactory, to gustatory, to equilibrium, and to temperature experiences. Some of the children reported on reacted very sensitively to light or colors, to noises and music, to materials that came in contact with their skin, to smells and perfumes, to foods, to rocking and swinging, to cold air or cool objects.

Thus, one obvious principle of grouping our observations is furnished by the sensory modality.

Then we find that what impressed us in some observations was the reaction to the intensity or quantity of stimulation, while in other cases the observation is more easily understood as a reaction to quality. Thus if any kind of slight sound seems to awaken a sleeping infant, or arouses a reaction from the waking one, we will consider that he reacts to the intensity of the stimulation, in fact here to a very low intensity. But if certain sounds or combinations of sounds attract a child, while other sounds or combinations of sounds of equal loudness repel him, it seems plausible to consider this a reaction to quality. Other reactions to quantity that we find in our material are, e.g., reactions to light of a certain brightness, reactions to normally imperceptible (or at least not usually reacted to) amounts of odor, reactions to slight disturbances of the equilibrium, to slight impressions on the feeling of temperature. On the other hand, observations pertaining to certain colors, certain materials, specific odors, foods, we can group with reactions to quality. Whether a special fondness of rocking should be grouped with reactions to quality or to quantity may be debatable. With some sensory modalities this distinction does not seem to make much sense. We would not be able to say, e.g., what a reaction to quality would be like in the modality of the sense of temperature. (Bergman and Escalona, 1949, pp. 333, 340)

Bergman and Escalona advanced the hypothesis that unusual sensitivities in young children may result in premature defensive reactions which are inadequate in the face of later trauma:

The hypothesis will be offered that the infant who is not sufficiently protected from stimuli either because of a "thin protective barrier," or because of the failure of maternal protection, may have to resort for such protection to premature formation of an ego. When this premature ego breaks down, possibly as a consequence of a trauma, the psychotic manifestations are thought to set in. (Bergman and Escalona, 1949, p. 347)

Sarason and Gladwin then raise the following questions

. . . (a) To what extent do autistic children have a history of unusual sensitivities?—a question which Bergman and Escalona raise but which existing studies cannot answer; (b) To what extent would the histories of idiot-savants indicate unusual sensitivities preceding the appearance of unusual intellectual behavior?; (c) To what extent do the children described by Bourne have unusual sensitivities? *Perhaps of more significance than these questions is the assumption that the crucial factor in these types of atypical development is the interaction between unusual sensitivities, on the one hand, and environmental factors, on the other hand.* Whether the infant with unusual sensitivities develops atypically may be a function either of parental handling of these sensitivities or fortuitious organic conditions or some combination of both.[2] In other words, not all children with

---

[2] The occurrence in the same child of an unusual sensitivity and an organic pathology does not, of course, mean that the two are causally related, although this may be the case in certain instances. The presence of an unrelated organic pathology may make it more difficult for the child (and parent) to cope with the sensitivity. For example, Frankl (1942–1943) described a case of severe autism in a child with tuberous sclerosis. Although most cases of tuberous sclerosis are severely defective, there are some whose intellectual functioning is less, or not at all, affected by the condition (Tredgold and Soddy, 1956). In any event, extreme autism is not a marked behavioral characteristic of

unusual sensitivities would be expected to develop atypically. Similarly, objectively similar environments or organic pathologies would have differing effects on individuals who differed in terms of the unusual sensitivities described by Bergman and Escalona. For example, the "protophrenics" described by Bourne may be those who had unusual sensitivities, while other children with similar or worse experiences and relationships but who did not show such extreme subnormality may not have had such sensitivities.

It is reasonable to assume that sensory hyperreactivity is but one of several ways in which the young child may be unusual. Put in another way: the very young child can be viewed in terms of various behavioral continua, and extreme placement on any of these continua, as in the case of unusual sensitivities, may be the predisposing factor which when interacting with environmental or organic factors has untoward effects. The work of Fries on "congenital activity types," [as well as the recent intriguing investigations of Richmond and Lustman (1955)] supports the contention that the study of temperamental and physiological variations in the very young child may provide at the least a partial answer to the question why different children are differentially affected by similar external events or similar organic conditions. This is clearly not a problem of peculiar significance to the area of atypical development but one which is truly basic to our understanding of normal development, the nature and range of the earliest individual differences in relation to rearing and educational techniques. (Sarason and Gladwin, 1958, pp. 216–217)

In their review of the literature up until the time of their monograph in 1958, Sarason and Gladwin were quite aware of the tendency of writers to view the problem of etiology in an either-or kind of way, i.e., it was inborn or it was environmental, it was organic or it was not organic, it was potentially remediable or it was not, etc. What Sarason and Gladwin tried to indicate was that, however committed they or others might be to a particular hypothesis, the available evidence simply did not permit one to regard the problem of etiology as simple or resolved. But such a view did not long hold sway, if indeed it ever held sway. Not only did the theoretical battle lines continue to be drawn but it seemed as if clinicians, educators, and researchers began to apply the label "autistic" in a way so as to overwhelm one with the heterogeneity of children to which the label was applied. As Kanner ruefully states in his foreword to Rimland's book in 1964: "The concept of 'early infantile autism' (I could not think of a better name) was diluted by some to deprive it of its specificity, so that the term was used as a pseudodiagnostic wastebasket for a variety of unrelated conditions, and a nothing-but psychodynamic etiology was decreed by some as the only valid explanation, so that further curiosity was stifled or even scorned."

Rimland's Review and His Hypotheses for Biological Causation. Twenty years after Kanner's initial publication, Rimland published his book *Infantile*

---

these cases. The extreme picture of autism which Frankl describes need not be related, in its initial phases at least, to the central nervous system pathology. It is conceivable that their origins are independent but that the central nervous system pathology exacerbates the autistic tendencies. (Sarason and Gladwin, 1958, p. 216)

Autism. The Syndrome and Its Implications for a Neural Theory of Behavior
—the subtitle accurately reflecting Rimland's hypothesis about the etiology of
the condition. How one reacts to this book will probably be a function of one's
tendency to polarize or "either-or" problems. This will not be helped any by
Rimland's somewhat polemical style. For example:

> Perhaps it should be made explicit at this point that the writer does not presume to
> have shown that autism is biologically determined and that the psycho-social
> environment plays no part in its etiology. What the writer *does* assert is that a
> careful review of the evidence has revealed no support for the psychogenic point
> of view. The evidence is instead highly consistent with expectation based on
> organic pathology. . . .
>   It is probably too early to suggest that psychogenesis as a *hypothesis* no longer
> be considered. ("Hypothesis" is used advisedly, because there appears to be too
> little evidence to support use of the term "theory.") No avenue for learning all
> that we can about the etiology of mental disorder should be unexplored. The
> detailed explication in this chapter of the arguments concerning the etiology of
> autism was in part intended to facilitate, and perhaps even to provoke, some long-
> overdue, rational and articulate consideration of the problem, even at the expense
> of jointly provoking a measure of articulate and inarticulate wrath.
>   It is not questioned that distinction should be maintained between a disproven
> and an unproven hypothesis, but neither should there be a failure to distinguish
> between an unproven and an uninvestigated hypothesis. The psychogenic hy-
> pothesis is by no means uninvestigated.
>   Whatever may be the merit in being patient with psychogenesis as a hypothesis,
> there is much less in being patient with it as an assumed force-in-fact. The all too
> common practice of blatantly assuming that psychogenic etiology *can* exist or *does*
> exist in any individual case or in any given class of disorders is not only unwar-
> ranted but actively pernicious.[3]

Despite their polemical *style*—which was intentional—it should be emphasized that Rimland's statements are hard to quarrel with: To assume that the
case for psychogenesis is proved is unreasonable; attempts to gather data
relevant to the hypothesis should be encouraged; and extreme commitment to
an hyopthesis can be blinding. The fact that Rimland has a strong commitment to a contrary hypothesis should not blind the reader to the merits of
his critique of the hypothesis of psychogenesis.

In Table 21.1 we have brought together the arguments and assumptions for
the hypothesis of psychogenesis, and those for the hypothesis of biological
causation as Rimland tabulates them. Rimland reviews comprehensively the
literature relevant to both hypotheses, and, as the above quotation indicated,
he quite clearly recognizes that neither hypothesis has been satisfactorily
proved although he equally clearly believes that available evidence favors the
hypothesis of biological causation. But Rimland does not rest with a review of
the existing literature. He goes on to develop and present an avowedly specu-

---

[3] *Infantile Autism, The Syndrome and Its Implications for a Neural Theory of
Behavior* by Bernard Rimland. New York: Appleton-Century-Crofts. Copyright © 1964
by Meredith Publishing Company, pp. 61–62. Reprinted by permission.

TABLE 21.1 THE ETIOLOGY OF INFANTILE AUTISM[a]

A. The Arguments for Psychogenesis of Infantile Autism	B. The Case for Biological Causation
1. No consistent physical or neurological abnormalities have been found in autistic children which could account for their condition.	1. Some clearly autistic children are born of parents who do not fit the autistic parent personality pattern.
2. Many autistic children have been raised by parents apparently deficient in emotional responsiveness, which could have pathogenic effects on the child.	2. Parents who do fit the description of the supposedly pathogenic parent almost invariably have normal, nonautistic children.
3. Certain children raised in hospitals or orphanages where maternal contact was sparse have been reported to show an undue frequency of emotional difficulties.	3. With very few exceptions, the siblings of autistic children are normal.
4. The behaviors of the child—his indifference or aggressiveness, his refusal to speak (or "elective mutism"), his apparent withdrawal from the outside world—are interpreted as signs of "punishment" or "retaliation" against the parents.	4. Autistic children are behaviorally unusual "from the moment of birth." 5. There is a consistent ratio of three or four boys to one girl. 6. Virtually all cases of twins reported in the literature have been identical, with both twins afflicted.
5. Certain incidents in the life of the autistic child appear to be pathogenic and permit the disorder to be traced to them.	7. Autism can occur or be closely simulated in children with known organic brain damage.
6. Psychotherapy or otherwise placing the child in a kind and understanding environment has beneficial effects.	8. The symptomatology is highly unique and specific.
7. The high incidence of first-born and only children suggests that parental attitudes may be causative.	9. There is an absence of gradations of infantile autism which would create "blends" from normal to severely afflicted.

[a] From pp. 42, 51, and 52 of Rimland's text, 1964, by permission. Material has been juxtaposed to contrast the opposing arguments that Bernard Rimland has assembled.

lative set of hypotheses in an attempt to explain and integrate a number of factors crucial to a biological hypothesis:

. . . we have presented evidence indicating that early infantile autism is caused by an inability to associate stimuli in the foreground of consciousness with all but a limited fragment of the content of memory instilled by previous experience. We have suggested that the symptoms could be the consequence of an impairment in the function of the reticular formation of the brain stem, and have presented data from the neurophysiology laboratory and elsewhere in support of the hypothesis of reticular impairment. The prevailing feeling that autism is a form of psychosis rather than of mental retardation has been explained as an expected consequence of effective sensory deprivation (or more exactly, of perceptual disability). A number of case studies were reported which led to the hypothesis that, at least in some instances, early infantile autism could be caused or very accurately stimulated by an excess of oxygen given in early infancy. In view of known vast differences in infant reactivity to oxygen, it was suggested that even atmospheric oxygen tension might exceed the tolerance threshold for a small fraction of genetically predisposed infants, as it appears to in some cases of retrolental fibroplasia.

Still unanswered by the theory as thus far presented are some of the most puzzling and paradoxical aspects of the problem of early infantile autism. Why are only certain children afflicted with early infantile autism? Why predominantly first-born males? Why mainly children of highly educated and intellectual parents?

. . . we will propose and cite evidence to support the final postulate of the theory: Children stricken with early infantile autism as a primary disorder were genetically vulnerable to autism as a consequence of an inborn capacity for high intelligence. This postulate brings what is known about infantile autism into a consistent relationship with a considerable body of pre-existing theory and knowledge. Our major task . . . is to make explicit the relationship between this aspect of the present theory of autism and related theories in the neighboring fields of psychology and biology.[4]

The reader is urged to consult Rimland's book not only because it contains a comprehensive review of the literature, or because it takes a strong stand on a number of issues, or because of his attempt to formulate a coherent theory of biological causation, but also because this book must be viewed together with that of Bettelheim's (1967) recent volume which is sure to raise the battle of theory, etiology, and treatment to a more intense level.

Bettelheim's Argument for Psychogenesis. The subtitle of Bettelheim's (1967) book *The Empty Fortress: Infantile Autism and the Birth of the Self,* accurately suggests the author's commitment and position. Any reader interested in infantile autism will have to familiarize himself with Bettelheim's book. Here we can only outline the major aspects of what Bettelheim attempted to do:

1. Initially Bettelheim presents a picture of the early years of development from the standpoint of modern psychoanalytic theory and experience—an unusually lucid and concise presentation independent of the problem of infantile autism.

2. The first "critical period" occurs during the first year of life and is one in which an emerging framework of selfhood develops primarily through the child's relations with "real objects," particularly the mother. Through a variety of circumstances and parent-child interactions the child can react as if "one's own efforts have no power to influence the world, because of the earlier conviction that the world is insensitive to one's reactions."

---

[4] *Ibid.* (pp. 119–120)

Bettelheim emphasizes that it is the failure of the child to become active in the face of frustrating experiences that can result in the beginning of the picture of infantile autism. Bettelheim (1967, p. 45) recognizes that this process may depend on individual differences in temperament, i.e., the infant predisposed to passive responsivity is far more vulnerable to conditions of threat and catastrophe.

3. The second critical period, beginning at about 18 months of age, is one in which "the child can much more definitely shape his relations to his environment if permitted to do so." Here too autistic withdrawal can appear, or become stronger depending on events in the first critical period, in the face of conditions which produce overwhelming anxiety consequent to persistent frustration of needs. Bettelheim is aware that these periods are gross approximations and that the number of critical periods may be more than two. The point he stresses is that infantile autism is indeed a "fortress" erected to shut out the world the price being one of internal emptiness.

4. Bettelheim then presents in great clinical detail several cases with whom intensive therapeutic work in a therapeutic milieu was carried out over a period of years. He draws a number of conclusions from work with these children but two require special noting: (a) the children *did* relate in their own way to the external world and (b) their condition is a defense against unbearable anxiety and "that the source of this anxiety is not an organic impairment but the child's evaluation of the conditions of his life as being utterly destructive."

5. Bettelheim concludes that parental behavior is a necessary but not sufficient factor in the etiology of infantile autism and the clinical picture of the mothers he presents is very similar to that of Rank which we gave earlier in this chapter.

6. Therapeutic outcome is, according to Bettelheim, more favorable than Kanner or Rimland suggested although the best outcome appears to be with those autistic children who possessed some degree of speech.

7. "I find it equally hard to accept as proven that autistic children are different 'from the beginning of their extra-uterine existence.' Despite the most careful scanning of the literature, and study of the many cases that have come to our attention at the Orthogenic School, we found no tangible evidence that autism was recognized at birth or right afterward. While some parents do make such claims, none that we examined stood up under scrutiny. On closer examination it always appeared that what was later recalled as being present at birth, was behavior not actually observed for the first time until weeks or months later." (Bettelheim, 1967, p. 392)

There is little doubt that Rimland and Bettelheim differ passionately about how the final story of infantile autism will read. There is even less doubt about their differences in regard to what should be done now in cases of infantile autism, i.e., their differences of opinion lead them to view clinical intervention and disposition in radically different ways. However, if one gets past the obvious fact that they take a dim view of each other's expectations, the areas of agreement are larger than one might think. This is most clearly seen in Bettelheim's (1967, pp. 403–404) summary statement in which he says "far too little is known about infantile autism to settle this question of organicity versus a psychogenic origin." Bettelheim emphasizes that his quarrel with Rimland does not concern matters of approach but rather Rimland's "insistence that the psychogenic approach should be discarded."

Lightner Witmer and Early Therapeutic Intervention

Psychologists, psychiatrists, and educators of today may know of Witmer's name in connection with the fact that he organized the first psychological clinic in this country in 1896 at the University of Pennsylvania. What has been forgotten, unfortunately, is that in the early years of this century he was concerned with and wrote most illuminatingly about the differential diagnosis between mental deficiency and childhood psychosis. Years before the autistic and schizophrenic young child was described and recognized by American psychiatrists, Witmer published his "orthogenic" case reports in which the major characteristics of this type of child were delineated. To be sure, Witmer's descriptions are not as sophisticated or complete as those of today, but the serious reader who studies Witmer's writing will probably agree that he must be considered one of the real pioneers of American child psychiatry.[5]

Aside from his awareness of the importance of differentiating between mental defect and childhood psychosis, the significance of Witmer's work lies in his therapeutic approach to and success with these instances of differential diagnosis. We give below excerpts from one of his reports:

At the age of two years and seven months this boy responded to every test like a feebleminded child and he was diagnosed by competent experts as feebleminded. Today he is a normal boy, not quite seven years old, reading, writing and doing the number work of the second school year. Either he was not feebleminded and the diagnosis was a mistaken one, or feeblemindedness can be cured. What is feeblemindedness—a performance level or an irremediable mental defect? Don's response to treatment shows that he had grave but not irremediable defects. His arrest of development was nearly complete, the results of disease and the psychosis which accompanied the disease.

---

[5] In 1907 Witmer started the journal called *Psychological Clinic*. It is no longer in existence. Some of his case reports (1907–1908, 1908–1909, 1916–1917, 1919–1922, 1928, 1928–1929) are more concerned with subnormality than others. Throughout the journal will be found similar cases by his students. As would be expected, there is much in the journal which is now outmoded, but the serious student of the problem will gain much by scrutiny of all the volumes.

When a normal adult becomes insane we observe a marked change in character. "He is no longer himself," we say, and a prominent symptom is a reduction of mental level called technically "dementia." Auto-intoxication, disease and shock may cause insanity. Let us suppose that one or all of these causes affect a child in his first or second year. We shall not be able to observe much change in the child's mentality except that his mental development will be arrested. I maintain that one type of feeblemindedness, better called arrested development, is due to the same causes which produce insanity in an adult, and that in some cases the psychosis or mental disorder can be cured and the child restored to completely normal condition, provided the case be taken in hand early enough.

Except to the very observant eye of an experienced expert, these cases look more like feeblemindedness than insanity. Nevertheless, they are a species of feeblemindedness or insanity, whichever name we choose to apply, very different from the congenital imbecile, one of the mongolian type, for example. The mental disorders of children which cause arrest of development and apparent feeblemindedness are as diverse as the mental disorders observed and classified by the alienists. A child may be either feebleminded or insane, or he may be both feebleminded and insane. Some of the Orthogenic Cases reported in the earlier numbers of the *Psychological Clinic,* notably Orthogenic Cases Nos. 4, 6, 12, and 13, are not primarily cases of congenital defect, but cases of mental disorder in which there is a greater presumption of possible cure than in the cases of the child who is both qualitatively and quantitatively feebleminded.

. . .

He was five years old last July, and so I entered him the following autumn in a near-by school, where he is the youngest of a group of first-grade children. His teacher says that he reads better than any of them and, except that he is poor in handwork, she considers him as competent as the other children.

"Terence," said he to his pal, the gardener, who was taking him to school the first day, "don't call me Donnie when we get near the school; don't call me Donnie or Don; call me Donald, which is right."

I saw Donald for the first time when he was two years and seven months old. His father carried him into my office, and deposited him, a soulless lump, upon the couch. He sat there with the stolidity of a Buddhist image, absorbed in the inspection of a card which he held in his pudgy hands, as regardless of his father and mother as of the new objects about him. While his gaze moved over the card, he scratched the back of it gently and incessantly with his fingernails. At times he gritted his teeth; and then again he made a crooning, humming sound with which it is his habit to lull himself to sleep.

He paid no attention to a rattle, to a bright-colored ball or to a picture book which I held before him, but every effort to remove the card from his hands he resisted. His face, already crimson, became empurpled. His physiognomy took on an expression of angry hostility; and I retreated before the approaching storm, leaving him again to his absorption in the card.

"He is fond of music," his mother said; but the liveliest strains of the talking machine were powerless to distract him from his chosen preoccupation. In the months to come I was to discover that by preference he would sit or lie in bed for hours, looking attentively at the object which he happened to be holding in his hands. It appeared to be persistent, concentrated attention, that most difficult and valuable of mental powers to cultivate.

From two to six years the child has the flitting attention of a monkey. "How do you select your monkeys for training?" a trainer of animals was once asked.

"I hold a lighted match before them," he replied, "and pick out as the easiest to train those that look longest at the burning match."

Donald would look at nothing but his card. One could not guess what lay behind those dull blue eyes. Was it interest, or only emptiness of mind—the dreamy listlessness with which the corner loafer looks at the passing world?

"What are those abrasions about the mouth and ears?" I asked.

"When he gets angry," his mother said, "he will scratch and tear at them."

"What else can he do?" I asked, not venturing to break in upon this obstinate immobility by trying to get him to perform the simple task which might, perchance, reveal some hidden mental ability.

"Can he walk?"

"A little, but he only began about two months ago," she replied. "Until he was over two years old he hadn't even crawled; and he only learned to crawl by his nurse taking hold of his knees and advancing them one after the other."

As the flower blooms, the fish swims or the bird flies, so the child crawls, walks and talks. It is the unfolding of his own instinctive impulses. But this child had to be taught to crawl and to walk, and even yet he could only toddle about uncertainly. If he fell upon his face he would lie helplessly crying with his nose to the floor. Either he did not have the strength to change his position, or he did not know how, or he was unwilling to make the effort.

He never uttered a word spontaneously and he could repeat at command only a few words like "Kitty," "Mama"—eight words in all. His understanding of language seemed to be limited to pointing to his head, eyes, ears and nose when these words were spoken. Even a chimpanzee of the same age as this boy, if brought up in human surroundings, will give evidence of understanding more of spoken language than this boy did. He could not feed himself. A much younger child can hold a cup or a spoon, but this boy could not even close his lips upon a cup when it was offered to him. He was still in diapers, and weeks were to pass before he could be safely clothed like the normal boy of two years and a half.

At two years and seven months, Donald was doing no more than many a child does at twelve months, no more than every child should do at fifteen months. No one who saw him needed to consult an expert before deciding that he was subnormal. You had only to look at the large head—"top-heavy Bill" one of his teachers called him—the fat red face, the expressionless eyes and the helpless body to arrive instantly at the conviction that "this child is feeble-minded."

And feeble-minded I thought him—of such low grade that I refused at first to accept him for educational treatment in my school. With reluctance I finally yielded to the parents' pleas. He was the youngest child I had ever accepted for psychological treatment, and apparently the most hopeless.

The expert, like the parent, bases his opnion on the child's appearance, behavior and history. But even more important than these is the *"attempt to teach."* In doubtful cases I do not like to express an opinion until after I have observed the results of attempting to teach the child something new. This can often be done at the first examination, but I could not even begin to teach Donald.

"I should like to see him walk," I said. But when he was lifted from the couch, put upon his feet and made to walk, he burst into a paroxysm of rage. His eyes became bloodshot; even his gums bled. When he was put back upon the couch he returned to his contemplative absorption in the card. Offered a block, he made no effort to take it. He even closed his eyes, as though the very sight of it and me were more than he could endure.

When I took the card away, so as to secure his undivided attention, he had another paroxysm of rage. From this, however, I derived a little hope, for passion and rage may be an expression of strength. The child at least had energy at his disposal. His violent resistance evidenced resolute determination. Obstinate children are better material for training than the overpliant sort. I looked at him, sitting impassive, but always bolt upright, and this, too, I thought an encouraging sign.

"He is a very easy child to neglect," one of my teachers entered in her report soon after he came to the school. "If you let him alone he will sit or lie in bed for hours and give no trouble. It is only when you try to do something with him, to dress him, or bathe him, even at times to feed him, that the trouble begins."

It takes some time and care to adjust a child to new surroundings, so I considered it no great misfortune that Donnie promptly got the measles. For a couple of weeks it was necessary to isolate him in the care of a trained nurse. This probably helped to make him less resistant to strangers. Perhaps there also awoke within his soul some responsive feeling of gratification when the soothing hand of the nurse or the doctor brought him relief from his distress of body. One month after Donnie's arrival I began his education.

"What to do" and "How to do it" are two puzzling questions confronting teacher and parent at every turn. To answer the first question is to present the aims of education. In the early years of education, the three R's are the chief objective. The answer to the second question, "How to do it," will determine our method of procedure.

Educational aims and practice are commonly the outcome of theory. For example, an interesting and important theory of recent origin is the Montessori method. It aims to develop a child's natural abilities. It also has a theory of educational practice. It emphasizes and, in the opinion of many, relies exclusively upon appealing to the child's natural inclinations and desires. Deprecating the use of constraint and force it throws the reins over the neck of the horse. Several children have been brought to me for examination and educational treatment who were nearly ruined by too close adherence to this supposed Montessori method.

I hold that constraint and liberty have equal value. At one time constraint, at another liberty, will bring the best results. The wise employment of constraint and force calls for greater intelligence and judgment on the part of teacher and parent than the leaving of the child free to work out his own salvation and development.

I try to approach the problem of educating a child like Donald without any preferred theory. More than twenty years of experience has led me to see that there is some good in most theories. A few are fit only for the scrap heap. One guiding principle, however, has stood the test of time and use: "The first task of teacher and parent is to gain and hold the child's attention by giving him something he *can* do, and after that something he *can't* do"—this in general is my method.

My educational aim is to develop attention by choosing tasks which develop it. Whether a child be one year of age, or two years, or six, whether he be in high school or college, the guiding principle of the educator should be to gain and hold attention first, and then to cultivate concentration, alertness, persistence, and endurance, all of these being attributes of attention.

For the rest, I feel my way. I watch the child to discover what he does with interest and with ease, and from here I get him to take a step forward in the direction best calculated to bring him to what I am aiming at, "the next higher level of attention." Montessori provides the child with stimulating objects—her didactic material—and leaves it with the child to make the next step forward. This is doubtless an acceptable procedure; but suppose the child refuses to take a step in any direction. He must be shoved.

To shove a child in the direction you want him to go is easy if the child is pliant and submissive. If he is a fighter like Donnie, and if, like him, he has no desires except to be let alone, the development of attention and the enforcement of obedience must go hand in hand.

When you have a trout on a hook at the end of a thin line, the only way to land him is to play him. He is lively and vigorous. He has desires which conflict with yours. If you use too much force you will break the line. If you use skill, yielding and yet constraining, you will in time get him into your basket. In this way the skillful teacher "plays" the child. The hook of attention is attached to the line of obedience, and then she watches the child's every move to insure his advance in the required direction. Shall she coax or force him? On the lee shore of this question many a gallant educational craft lies shipwrecked.

You can coax most children, some of the time at least, by appealing to their interests and desires, even as the hunter entices the deer to come within gunshot by appealing to its curiosity. But some children can't be coaxed, any more than you can wheedle a trout into your basket.

For example, take Donald. He did not have a keen desire even for food. He would not eat prunes, apparently because he disliked their appearance, and so they had to be mixed with his cereal in order to get him to eat them. He would not drink milk or water from a transparent glass. It must be offered to him in a cup. In the early days, indeed, he declined to drink water at all, and got his only liquid in the shape of milk or soup.

He declined to accept a sugarplum offered as a reward of merit; and if you took away the object he so fondly clasped in his hands, and then yielded to his ragings and returned it to him, he would very likely throw it violently across the room. He disliked to be dressed. He disliked to be taken out of bed and put on the floor. He disliked to be taken for a walk.

All these things aroused angry resistance; and in his passion he went so far as to do himself bodily injury; but as long as Donald held something in his hand there was peace and quiet.

"What to do with him?" He could not be bathed and dressed in this happy state of calm contemplation. Take away what he held and his hands went up to his ears and mouth, tearing at them till they bled. Tell him to keep his hands down, they went up just the same; perhaps he only scratched himself a little more strenuously. Put mittens on him, as his former nurse did, and he still went through the motions.

Smack his hands, anger and passion intensified the violence of his resistance. The only thing to do was to hold his hands. Could he be compelled to keep them down after they were released? The historic battle lasted for an hour and a half. His hands were held while his teacher spoke to him from time to time: "If I let your hands go, will you keep them down?"

He raged, he stormed, he grew apoplectic, but the hands were firmly held. At every lull in the storm they were released, and up they went again. In the end he gave in. Ninety minutes showed remarkable endurance, determination and consistency of purpose, qualities which might be successfully employed in his educational development later.

Never again did Donnie hold out for so long on this or any other issue. My records show that though he raged at intervals during the ensuing twelve months, the longest period of resistance lasted for ten minutes only. He had learned his lesson. There was an inevitable persistence that would outlast his own. He might as well give in first as last. (Witmer, 1919–1922, pp. 97–103)

The subsequent development of this boy under Witmer's supervision was both dramatic and heartening. That Witmer was an astute observer who did not allow dramatic change in the patient to cause him to overlook problems and weaknesses may be gleaned from Witmer's concluding remarks:

ᐫᐤ If I began my work without a theory and without understanding Donnie's mental status, I am far from that position now. I have unraveled much of the mystery, and I find the understanding of this one child of important value in interpreting the behavior and progress of other normal children. I believe that Donnie was at the start dominated by fear, which plays still an important role in his behavior. His concentration on the card was in the nature of a defensive reaction. He disliked to get out of bed because he was afraid to get out of bed. He disliked to walk and talk because he was afraid—perhaps of failure.

It was noted on one occasion that when taken outdoors he would not stop screaming even after he had been put on the back of a pony. I know now that this was the worst thing that could have been done to him. Donnie is afraid of all animals. He takes kindly, however, to little creatures and has often alarmed his teachers by bringing them caterpillars and worms.

One day Donnie, while seated at a table playing with a train of cars, had his attention called to the fact that a little gray kitten was in the room. He was mortally afraid of it, so he would not turn his head to look, but kept moving the train back and forth, saying "Puff! Puff!" in the same absorbed concentration which was characteristic of him at the beginning. He was ignoring the kitten just as he used to ignore people he disliked by closing his eyes when they came into the room.

He was afraid to look down a well, he was afraid of a doll, of a soft rubber ball, of a balloon, a loaf of bread, a spinning top. He was afraid to go on a sailboat the first time, but the second time he went with joy. He took a fearful pleasure in trains, for he loved them as moving things, and yet they terrified him. He would say: "Let us go to town in the three trolleys;" but when you asked him why he would rather go in the trolleys than in a train he would never tell you.

He has never verbally admitted that he is afraid of anything. "Won't hurt you," he very early exclaimed whenever he was frightened by anything; and this was one of his first spontaneous reflections. "Don't have to pat the pony," he would reiterate during the many weeks required to get him to overcome his fear of the school pet. The effort to take him out driving in a little pony cart, which it was thought would entertain him, only succeeded after a period of two months. But then, as was usual with him, he couldn't get enough of driving behind the pony.

Even yet he is afraid. "I like dogs," he declared lately, as he started on his way to school. "Nice kind dogs which don't bite," he added thoughtfully. Nevertheless, he managed unobtrusively to place his companion between himself and every dog. "I like to pat dogs," he boasted; but when one appeared unexpectedly he excused himself tactfully: "I don't like them that color."

So, while Donnie is fearful, he is not a coward. He is doing his best to overcome his fears, and he has worked out his own method of doing this. He had no fear of dark or of the supernatural.

Fears and desires are the two greatest motive forces of mankind. No problem is more perplexing and none so absolutely fundamental as the proper treatment of fears and desires so that these motive forces may excite the actions desired. As I understand Donnie now, he had no desires, but many fears. We compelled him to do those things which he feared. As soon as he had done the fearful thing, the fear, in many instances, disappeared and desire took its place. Donnie is now afraid chiefly of what surprises him.

Donnie's obstinacy measured the intensity of his fear, but in part it measured also the intensity of his desires. Always, from the very beginning, Donnie has known just what he wanted. Never was there any wobbly uncertainly of choice. He either desired it or he didn't desire it. This, to my mind, is a strong and valuable trait of character if you can turn it to the right use.

The desire for possession gives rise perhaps to his keenest pleasure. He held on to his card, not only because it enabled him to ignore the fearful things of the world about him, but he held on to it because here was something "all his own." Not until recently has he been willing to share any of his possessions with others. For a long time he not only clung passionately to his own possessions, but appropriated the playthings of all the other children as well, so much so that his room was known as the "Robber's Den." He is now so far advanced on the road to generosity that he will give away his second-best toy.

He has always shown the same concentration of attention which he showed at the beginning. One day recently he wore to school a necktie which he had borrowed from the gardener, Terence. The teacher could do nothing with him that day because he persistently explored the attributes of his new possession. He met Terence, who came to take him home, with the matured fruit of his morning's work: "Terry, can you see the top of *your* necktie?"

His first craze was for automobiles, and then for sailboats, bicycles, trains and cars—anything that moved. As he learned to talk, he went through the magazines. "It's an automobile, see the automobile," he kept reiterating. When he grew fond of excursions abroad, "Are we going out, Agnes?" he would say, "Agnes, are we going out?" a thousand times until he threatened to drive his nurse to distraction.

No child can have a better endowment for future accomplishment later than this power of persistent concentration.

Donnie's traits of character are therefore positive traits. He has a definite array of abilities, keen desires, self-dependence. Even from the first he preferred to walk alone, though in constant fear of falling, rather than hold someone's hand. He only sought the hand if a terrifying object came in view. With strong desires and fears, strong likes and dislikes, Donnie has an equal capacity for happiness and great unhappiness, for success and failure. He can be sweet-tempered or angry and resentful. His emotional balance is easily disturbed, and he still requires very careful handling.

Of the cause of Donnie's mental condition when he came to us, and which led several experts to diagnose him as feeble-minded, I cannot be sure. He had an illness after birth, which I now believe left his brain so devitalized that it permitted fear to gain the upper hand over desire. Of one thing I am certain: If Donnie had not been given the painstaking and expert training to which we subjected him he would by now have fallen into a state of irremediable feeble-mindedness. (Witmer, 1919–1922, pp. 108–111)

The single case is no secure basis for deciding issues. Its significance resides primarily in underlining the need for intensive therapeutic intervention early in the lives of children for whom the diagnostic picture is ambiguous (and Witmer's case can be considered ambiguous diagnostically, particularly because he presents little or nothing about parental background and behavior).

The Continuing Controversy

When one considers that the controversy we have outlined dates from 1943, it is understandable that the puzzling nature of infantile autism has been only somewhat clarified. That we are not even secure about what constitutes the "facts"—let alone the interpretation of them—is, perhaps, less due to a short history than to the strongly contrasting views of human nature which are held. It is precisely because the condition represents such a clear challenge to these contrasting views or theories, each of which have clear and direct practical consequences for clinical practice and child development, that led Sarason and Gladwin (1958) to state that infantile autism was a significant problem for the science of psychology.

Controversy, like gossip, seems to have an irresistible attraction which satisfies a number of human needs. In this connection we can do no better in concluding this chapter than to quote from Boring's presidential address, "The Psychology of Controversy," to the American Psychological Association, in 1928.

Discussion is relevant to scientific work, but controversy is more than discussion. It involves emotion; and passion, while of itself irrelevant to scientific procedure, enters to prejudice reason and to fix the debaters more firmly in their opinions. If it were possible, scientific discussion should be dispassionate, not only in form but in spirit, for otherwise progress toward the truth is hindered.

Since the controversy of a movement is apt to be less personally pointed, especially when there is only one active party to the quarrel, participation in a movement may have the advantage of blinding the scientist less than participation in a personal controversy. On the other hand, movements, in so far as they are blind, have the further disadvantage of lending to blindness the social support of the group within the school.

As psychologists, we cannot, however, afford to condemn controversy, be it ever so emotional. If we could read out of the body scientific every investigator who lost his temper with an opponent and kept it lost, we should read out those very men who, because of their drives or prejudices or whatever we like to call that conative component of their personalities, had made the positive contributions to the science. Research is something more than a habit and it requires something more than patience. It requires, among other things, an irresistible urge, bolstered up, I think, not so much by curiosity, as by egotism. This urge may carry one to the truth, beyond it, or even directly away from it. Vision and blindness are here alike, for both are attention, and attention to one thing is inattention to another. The same urge helps and hinders progress.

Must the truth then forever transcend the individual? Is the stage of science like the court of law, where attorneys contend and only the judge speaks the truth? This is the view of research that I find so personally abhorrent and yet seem forced to accept.

There is, however, an incomplete solution for the dilemma. A scientist should, I think, cultivate dissociation. Too much has been said in favor of the integration of the personality, and too little in favor of dissociation. The scientist needs to be a dual personality. He needs to be able to become the prosecutor or the judge at will. He can then stand off and evaluate himself at times, and perhaps even arrange things so that the prosecuting personality will fare more happily when it returns to dominate his person. But I would not have him be the judge too often, for then the assured, prejudiced, productive personality might get "squeezed out," and science would be the loser.

I recommend this dissociation, not because it will make us happier, not merely because it is fun to be the judge as well as the prosecutor, but because I have no expectation that it could be so complete that there would be no interaction between the two personalities. I should hope for a tempering of the prosecutor by the judge so that there would really be more vision and less blindness, and so that psychology would benefit thereby. Then we should have less futile controversy, fewer people devoting their lives to lost causes, even more candid and thus more fruitful discussion, less talk and more research. (Boring, 1929, pp. 111–121)

A CONCLUDING COMMENT

Professor Boring's comments are applicable to much, if not all, of what is contained in this book because, as we hope we have made clear, the field of mental subnormality contains so much controversy. This characterization probably does not differentiate this field from any other field concerned with human behavior. This kinship, however, in no way makes the task of the reader easier. It may, in fact, make the task harder because as one becomes increasingly aware of similarity among the fields of human behavior—a similarity which extends to substantive problems as well as issues of social action and planning—it will demand the acquisition of more and new knowledge, and require an ever increasing degree of scope and capacity to generalize. There is an illusory comfort in viewing the field of mental subnormality as distinct from anthropology, sociology, psychology, education, government, political science, etc. At certain times and for certain problems it is possible, and even necessary, to study them apart from larger contexts. Controversy, however, tends to be generated when the individual investigator draws conclusions which go beyond the confines of his particular problem or study, i.e., when he develops a formulation which covers both his data and that of others. This is a difficult and hazardous endeavor when one is dealing with circumscribed problems, but for so many of the problems we have taken up in this book the problems are far from circumscribed and involve what we ordinarily consider to be different fields of endeavor. This complication would be enough to insure "reasonable" controversy sufficient to satisfy the most contentious of individuals. But what generates explosive controversy are formulations or generalizations which explicitly or implicitly reflect a value system, i.e., what is good and bad, what actions or programs should be instituted or dropped, how lives should be lived, etc. The answer, clearly, is not to avoid facing the issue, unless one wants to guarantee continuing fruitless controversy. The answer, as Professor Boring suggests, is how to be both a "prosecutor and judge." This answer is not in the nature of a "final solution" but rather in the nature of an attitude which helps one recognize and tolerate ambiguities, incomplete solutions, and imperfections in one's own thinking as well as in the thinking of others. "Must the truth then forever transcend the individual?" When Professor Boring answers in the affirmative, and candidly admits to personal difficulty in so answering, he reflects and underlines what a rare commodity humbleness is.

Bibliography

ABEL, T. M.   A study of a group of subnormal girls successfully adjusted in industry and the community. *American Journal of Mental Deficiency*, 1940, *45*, 66--72.

ACKERKNECT, ERWIN.   *A Short History of Psychiatry.* New York: Hafner, 1959.

ALLEN, R. J., and R. M. GIBSON.   Phenylketonuria with normal intelligence. *American Journal of Diseases of Children*, 1961, *102*, 115–122.

AMERICAN ASSOCIATION ON MENTAL DEFICIENCY.   Etiological classification manual. *American Journal on Mental Deficiency*, 1957.

BALLER, W. B.   A study of the present social status of a group of adults, who when they were in elementary schools were classified as mentally deficient. *Genetic Psychology Monographs*, 1936, *18*, 165–244.

BARR, M. W.   *Mental Defectives: Their History, Treatment and Training.* Philadelphia: Blakiston, 1904.

BATESON, G., D. D. JACKSON, J. HALEY, and J. H. WEAKLAND.   Toward a theory of schizophrenia. *Behavioral Science*, 1956, *1*, 251–264.

BATESON, W.   *Mendel's Principles of Heredity.* Cambridge University Press, 1902.

BAUMEISTER, I. A. (Ed.)   *Mental Retardation: Selected Problems in Appraisal and Treatment.* Chicago: Aldine, 1967.

BENDA, CLEMENS E.   *The Child with Mongolism.* New York: Grune & Stratton, 1960.

BENDA, CLEMENS E.   Mongolism. In Charles H. Carter, *Medical Aspects of Mental Retardation.* Springfield, Illinois: Charles C Thomas, 1965.

BENDER, L.   Post-encephaletic behavior disorders in childhood. In J. B. Neal (Ed.), *Encephalitis.* New York: Grune & Stratton, 1942.

BERGMAN, P., and S. K. ESCALONA.   Unusual sensitivities in very young children. *The Psychoanalytic Study of the Child.* New York: International Universities Press, 1949. Vols. 3–4.

BERKSON, G., and W. A. MASON.   Stereotyped movements of mental defectives: III. Situation effects. *American Journal of Mental Deficiency*, 1963, *68*, 409–412.

BERMAN, P., F. GRAHAM, P. EICHMAN, and H. WAISMAN.   Psychologic and neurologic status of diet-treated phenylketonuric children and their siblings. *Journal of Pediatrics*, 1961, *28*, 924–934.

455

BERNSTEIN, B. *Social structure, language, and learning.* In J. P. DeCecco (Ed.), *The Psychology of Language, Thought, and Instruction.* New York: Holt, Rhinehart & Winston, 1967.

BERRY, HELEN K., BETTY S. SUTHERLAND, BARBARA UMBARGER, and D. O'GRADY. Treatment of phenylketonuria. *American Journal of Diseases of Children,* 1967, *113,* 2–5.

BETTELHEIM, B. *The Empty Fortress.* New York: Free Press, 1967.

BICE, H. V. *Mental deficiency, moron level.* In A. Burton and R. E. Harris (Eds.), *Case Histories in Clinical and Abnormal Psychology.* New York: Harper & Row, 1947.

BICKEL, H., J. GERRARD, and E. HICKMANS. Influence of phenylalanine intake on phenylketonuria. *Lancet,* 1953, *2,* 812–813.

BIJOU, SIDNEY W. *A functional analysis of retarded development.* In N. R. Ellis (Ed.), *International Review of Research in Mental Retardation.* New York: Academic Press, 1966.

BINET, A., and T. SIMON. *The Development of Intelligence in Children.* Trans. Elizabeth S. Kite. Baltimore: Williams & Wilkins, 1916a.

BINET, A., and T. SIMON. *The Intelligence of the Feeble-minded.* Trans. Elizabeth S. Kite. Baltimore: Williams & Wilkins, 1916b.

BIRCH, H. G. The problem of "brain damage" in children. In H. G. Birch, *Brain Damage in Children: The Biological and Social Aspects.* Baltimore: Williams & Wilkins, 1964.

BIRCH, H. G., and A. LEFFORD. Two strategies for studying perception in "brain-damaged" children. In H. G. Birch, *Brain Damage in Children: The Biological and Social Aspects.* Baltimore: Williams & Wilkins, 1964.

BIRCH, H. G., and J. TIZARD. The dietary treatment of phenylketonuria. *Developmental Medicine and Child Neurology,* 1967, *9,* 9.

BLACKER, C. P. *Eugenics: Galton and After.* London: Gerald Duckworth, 1952.

BLACKSTONE, W. *Commentaries on the Laws of England.* 1st ed., Vol. I. Oxford, England: Clarendon Press, 1765.

BLATT, B., and F. GARFUNKEL. A field demonstration of the effects of non-automated environments on the intellectual and social competence of educable mentally retarded children. Boston: Boston University (Co-Operative Research Project No. D–014), 1965.

BLATT, B., and F. KAPLAN. *Christmas in Purgatory.* Boston: Allyn and Bacon, Inc., 1966.

BOBROFF, A. Economic adjustment of 121 adults, formerly students in classes for mental retardates. *American Journal of Mental Deficiency,* 1956a, *60,* 525–535.

BOBROFF, A. A survey of social and civic participation of adults formerly in classes for the mentally retarded. *American Journal of Mental Deficiency,* 1956b, *61,* 127–133.

BORING, E. G. The psychology of controversy. *Psychological Review,* 1929, *36,* 97–121.

BORTNER, M., and H. BIRCH. Perceptual and perceptual-motor dissociation in brain-damaged patients. *Journal of Nervous and Mental Disease,* 1960, *130,* 49–53.

BOURNE, H. Protophrenia, a study of perverted rearing and mental dwarfism. *Lancet,* 1955, *2,* 1156–1163.

BRABNER, G. The myth of mental retardation. *The Training School Bulletin,* 1967, *63,* 149–152.

BRADLEY, C. Organic factors in the psychopathology of childhood. In P. H. Hoch and J. Zubin (Eds.), *Psychopathology of Childhood.* New York: Grune & Stratton, 1955.

BRAMWELL, D. M. Changing concepts of residential care. In I. Philips (Ed.), *Prevention and Treatment of Mental Retardation.* New York: Basic Books, 1966.

BRIGHAM, CARL C. *A Study of American Intelligence.* Princeton: Princeton University Press, 1923.

BRIGHAM, CARL C. Intelligence tests of immigrant groups. *Psychological Review,* 1930, *37,* 158–165.

BUCK, J. N. The sage: an unusual mongoloid. In A. Burton and R. E. Harris, *Clinical Studies of Personality.* Harper & Row, 1955. Pp. 455–481.

BURT, C. *The Backward Child.* London: University of London Press, 1937. (3rd edition reprint 1950–1951, 4th edition 1958.)

BUTTERFIELD, E. C. The role of environmental factors in the treatment of institutionalized mental retardates. In I. A. Baumeister (Ed), *Mental Retardation: Selected Problems in Appraisal and Treatment.* Chicago: Aldine, 1967.

BUTTERFIELD, E. C., and E. ZIGLER. The effects of differing institutional social climates on the effectiveness of social reinforcement in the mentally retarded. *American Journal of Mental Deficiency,* 1965a, 70, 48–56.

BUTTERFIELD, E. C., and E. ZIGLER. The effects of success and failure upon the discrimination learning of normal and mentally retarded children. *Journal of Abnormal Psychology,* 1965b, 70, 25–31.

CAIN, L. F., and S. LEVINE. *A Study of the Effects of Community and Institutional School Classes for Trainable Mentally Retarded Children.* San Francisco: San Francisco State College, 1961.

CALDWELL, B. M., and S. B. GUZE. A study of the adjustment of parents and siblings of institutionalized and non-institutionalized retarded children. *American Journal of Mental Deficiency,* 1960, 64, 845–861.

CANCE, A. E., J. A. FIELD, R. DE C. WARD, and P. F. HALL. First report of the committee on immigration of the eugenics section. *American Breeders Magazine,* 1912, 3, 249–255.

CANNON, G. L., and A. J. ROSANOFF. Preliminary report of a study of heredity in insanity in the light of the Mendelian laws. *Eugenics Record Office Bulletin,* No. 3, 1911.

CARPENTER, G. G., V. H. AUERBACH, and A. M. DIGEORGE. Phenylalaninemia. *Pediatric Clinics of North America,* 1968, 15, 313–323.

CARVER, J. Reactions of parents of severely retarded children at a state training school. Unpublished dissertation, Yale University, 1956.

CASLER, L. Maternal deprivation: a critical review of the literature. *Monograph of the Society for Research in Child Development,* 1961, 26 (Serial No. 80).

CASSIDY, J. M., and J. E. STANTON. An investigation of factors involved in the educational placement of mentally retarded children. Columbus: Ohio State University, 1959.

CASTLE, W. E. The beginnings of Mendelism in America. In L. C. Dunn, *Genetics in the 20th Century.* New York: Macmillan, 1951.

CAUDLE, H. V. Phenylketonuria without mental retardation. *Journal of Pediatrics,* 1960, 26, 502.

CENTERWALL, W. R., and S. A. CENTERWALL. Phenylketonuria, Følling's Disease: the story of its discovery. *Journal of Historical Medicine,* 1961, 16, 292–296.

CHARLES, D. C. Ability and accomplishment of persons earlier judged mentally deficient. *Genetic Psychology Monographs,* 1953, 47, 3–71.

CHESTERTON, G. K. *Eugenics and other Evils.* London: Cassell, 1922.

CLARKE, A. D. B. Genetic and environmental studies of intelligence. In A. D. B. Clarke and A. M. Clarke (Eds.), *Mental Deficiency.* Glencoe, Illinois: Free Press, 1958.

CLARKE, A. D. B., and A. M. CLARKE. Cognitive changes in the feebleminded. *British Journal of Psychology,* 1954, 45, 173–179.

CLELAND, C. C. Selection and training of attendants: a review of research. *American Journal of Mental Deficiency,* 1962, 67, 205–210.

CLELAND, C. C. Locational variables in the establishment of institutions. *The Training School Bulletin,* 1963, 60, 123–129.

CLELAND, C. C. Natural versus systematic selection of attendants: intrainstitutional and administrative problems. *American Journal of Mental Deficiency,* 1964, 69, 354–359.

CLELAND, C. C., and R. F. PECK. Psychological determinants of tenure in institutional personnel. *American Journal of Mental Deficiency,* 1959, 63, 876–888.

COATES, S., A. P. NORMAN, and L. I. WOOLF. Phenylketonuria with normal intelligence and Gowers' Muscular Dystrophy. *Archives of Diseases in Childhood,* 1957, 32, 313–317.

COHEN, P., and P. KOZINN. Phenylpyruvic Oliogophrenia in a Jewish Child. *Journal of Pediatrics,* 1949, 34, 76–79.

CONANT, J. B. *On Understanding Science.* New Haven: Yale University Press, 1947.

CONKLIN, E. G.　Some biological aspects of immigration. *Scribner's Magazine,* 1921, *69,* 352–359.

CRANEFIELD, P.　Historical Perspectives in I. Philips (Ed.), *Prevention and Treatment of Mental Retardation.* New York: Basic Books, 1966.

CROTHERS, B., and R. S. PAINE.　*The Natural History of Cerebral Palsy.* Cambridge, Massachusetts: Harvard University Press, 1959.

CRUICKSHANK, W. M., H. V. BICE, and N. E. WALLIN.　*Perception and Cerebral Palsy.* Syracuse University Press, 1957.

DANIELSON, F. H., and C. B. DAVENPORT.　The hill folk: report on a rural community of hereditary defectives. *Memoir I.* Eugenics Record Office, 1912.

DARWIN, C.　*The Variation of Animals and Plants Under Domestication.* New York: Appleton, 1890, vol. II.

DARWIN, C.　*The Descent of Man.* 2nd ed. Philadelphia: McKay, 1874.

DAVENPORT, C. B.　*Heredity in Relation to Eugenics.* New York: Holt, 1911a.

DAVENPORT, C. B.　Report of committee on eugenics. *American Breeders Association,* 1911b, *6,* 90–94.

DAVENPORT, C. B., and D. WEEKS.　A first study of inheritance in epilepsy. *Eugenics Record Office Bulletin,* No. 4, 1911.

DAVENPORT, R. K., JR., and G. BERKSON.　Stereotyped movements of mental defectives: II. Effects of novel objects. *American Journal of Mental Deficiency,* 1963, *67,* 879–882.

DAVIES, S. P.　*Social Control of the Mentally Deficient.* New York: Crowell, 1930.

DAVIES, S. P.　*The Mentally Retarded in Society.* New York: Columbia, 1959.

DAY, R., and M. S. HAINES.　Intelligence quotients of children recovered from erthroblastosis fetalis since the introduction of exchange transfusion. *Pediatrics,* 1954, *13,* 333–338.

DEGROUCHY, J.　Chromosome 18: A topologic approach. *Journal of Pediatrics,* 1965, *66,* 414–431.

DILLER, L., and H. G. BIRCH.　Psychological evaluation of children with cerebral damage. In H. G. Birch, *Brain Damage in Children: The Biological and Social Aspects.* Baltimore: Williams & Wilkins, 1964.

DINGER, J. C.　Post-school adjustment of former educable retarded. *Exceptional Children,* 1961, *27,* 353–360.

DOLL, E. A.　Is mental deficiency curable? *American Journal of Mental Deficiency,* 1947, *51,* 420–428.

DORIS, J.　The evaluation of the intellect of the brain-damaged child. In A. J. Solnit and S. A. Provence, *Modern Perspectives in Child Development.* New York: International Universities Press, 1963.

DORIS, J., and A. J. SOLNIT.　Treatment of children with brain damage and associated school problems. *Journal of Child Psychiatry,* 1963, *2,* 618–635.

DOWN, J. L.　Observations on an ethnic classification of idiots. *London Hospital Reports,* 1866.

DUGDALE, R. L.　*The Jukes,* 4th ed. New York: Putnam, 1910.

DUNLOP, F. S.　*Subsequent Careers of Non-academic Boys.* Ottawa: National Printers Limited, 1935.

DUNN, L. C.　Cross-currents in the history of human genetics. *American Journal of Human Genetics,* 1962, *14,* 1–13.

DUNN, L. C.　*A Short History of Genetics.* New York: McGraw-Hill, 1965.

EAST, E. M.　*Heredity and Human Affairs.* New York: Scribner, 1927.

EATON, J. W., and R. J. WEIL.　*Culture and Mental Disorders: A Comparative Study of the Hutterites and Other Populations.* Glencoe, Illinois: Free Press, 1955.

EISENBERG, L.　Behavioral manifestations of cerebral damage in childhood. In H. G. Birch, *Brain Damage in Children: The Biological and Social Aspects.* Baltimore: Williams & Wilkins, 1964.

ELLIS, H.　*The Problem of Race Regeneration.* London: Cassell, 1911.

ELLIS, N. R.　*Handbook of Mental Deficiency.* New York: McGraw-Hill, 1963.

ELLIS, N. R. (Ed.).　*International review of research in mental retardation.* New York: Academic Press, 1966. Vols. I–II.

EMANUEL, I., S.-W. HUANG, and E.-K. YEH. Physical features of Chinese children with Down's syndrome. *American Journal of Diseases of Children,* 1968, *115,* 461–468.

ESQUIROL, E. *Treatise on Insanity.* Trans. E. K. Hunt. Philadelphia: Lea & Blanchard, 1845.

ESTABROOK, A. H. *The Jukes in* 1915. Washington. Carnegie Institution, 1916.

FAIRBANK, R. E. The subnormal child—seventeen years after. *Mental Hygiene,* 1933, *17,* 177–208.

FALEK, A., R. SCHMIDT, and G. A. JERVIS. Familial De Lange Syndrone with chromosome abnormalities. *Pediatrics,* 1966, 37, 92–101.

FARBER, B. Interaction with retarded siblings and life goals of children. *Marriage and Family Life,* 1963, 25, 96–98.

FARBER, B., and W. C. JENNE. Family organization and parent-child communication: parents and siblings of a retarded child. *Monographs of the Society for Research in Child Development,* 1963, 28 (serial no. 91).

FARBER, B. S., and D. B. RYCKMAN. Effects of severely mentally retarded children on family relationships. *Mental Retardation Abstracts,* 1965, 2, 1–17.

FARQUHAR, J. W., J. RICHMOND, and P. T. HALDANE. Phenylketonuria in pediatric practice. *Journal of Clinical Pediatrics,* 1963, 2, 504–516.

FERNALD, W. E. The burden of feeble-mindedness. *Journal of Psycho-asthenics,* 1912, *17,* 87–111.

FERNALD, W. E. A state program for the care of the mentally defective. *Mental Hygiene,* 1919, 3, 566–574.

FØLLING, A. The excretion of phenylpyruvic acid [ppa] in the urine—an anomaly of metabolism in connection with imbecility. In S. H. Boyer, *Papers on Human Genetics.* Englewood Cliffs, New Jersey: Prentice-Hall, 1963.

FORD, C. E., K. W. JONES, P. E. POLANI, J. C. DEALMEIDA, and J. H. BRIGGS. A sex-chromosome anomaly in a case of gonadal dysgenesis. *Lancet,* 1959, 1, 711–713.

FOURACRE, M. H., F. P. CONNOR, and I. I. GOLDBERG. *The Effects of a Preschool Program upon Young Educable Mentally Retarded Children. I. Measurable growth and development.* New York: Teachers College, Columbia University, 1962a.

FOURACRE, M. H., F. P. CONNOR, and I. I. GOLDBERG. *The Effects of a Preschool Program upon Young Educable Mentally Retarded Children. II. The Experimental Pre-School Program.* New York: Teachers College, Columbia University, 1962b.

FRANKL, G. Language and affective contact. *Nervous Child,* 1942–1943, 2, 251–262.

GALLAGHER, J. J. A comparison of brain injured and non-brain injured mentally retarded children on several psychological variables. *Monographs of the Society for Research in Child Development,* 1957, 22: 2, Serial No. 65.

GALTON, F. *Hereditary Genius.* London: Macmillan, 1869.

GALTON, F. Experiments in Pangenesis. *Proceedings of the Royal Society of London,* 1871, *19,* 393–410.

GALTON, F. *Inquiries into Human Faculty and Its Development.* London: Macmillan, 1883.

GALTON, F. *Hereditary Genius.* Second edition. London: Macmillan, 1892.

GALTON, F. *Memories of My Life.* New York: E. P. Dutton, 1909.

GARFIELD, S. L., and D. C. AFFLECK. A study of individuals committed to a state home for the retarded who were later released as not mentally defective. *American Journal of Mental Deficiency,* 1960, 64, 907–915.

GARFUNKEL, F. Probabilities and possibilities for modifying behavior of mentally retarded children: tactics for research. Boston University, *Journal of Education,* 1964, *147,* 45–52.

GARROD, A. E. The incidence of alkaptonuria: a study in chemical individuality, *Lancet,* 1902, 2, 1616–1620.

GARROD, A. E. Croonian Lectures to the Royal Academy of Medicine: Inborn errors of metabolism. *Lancet,* 1908, 2, 1–7, 73–79, 142–148, 214–220.

GESELL, A., and C. S. AMATRUDA. *Developmental Diagnosis.* New York: Hoeber, 1941.

GIFFORD, E. G., and H. H. GODDARD. Defective children in the juvenile court. *Training School Bulletin,* 1912, 8, 132–135.

GINZBERG, E., and D. W. BRAY. *The Uneducated.* New York: Columbia University Press, 1953.

GLADWIN, T. *Poverty USA.* New York: Little, Brown, 1967.

GLUECK, S., and E. GLUECK. *Unraveling Juvenile Delinquency.* New York: Commonwealth Fund, 1950.

GODDARD, H. H. Suggestions for a prognostical classification of mental defectives. *Journal of Psycho-asthenics,* 1909–1910, 48–54.

GODDARD, H. H. Heredity of feeble-mindedness. *American Breeders Magazine,* 1910, *1,* 165–178.

GODDARD, H. H. *The Kallikak Family. A Study in the Heredity of Feeble-mindedness.* New York: Macmillan, 1912.

GODDARD, H. H. The Binet tests in relation to immigration. *Journal of Psycho-asthenics,* 1913, *18,* 105–110.

GODDARD, H. H. *Feeble-mindedness: Its Causes and Consequences.* New York: Macmillan, 1914.

GODDARD, H. H. Mental tests and the immigrant. *Journal of Delinquency,* 1917, *2,* 243–277.

GODDARD, H. H. Feeble-mindedness: a question of definition. *Journal of Psycho-asthenics,* 1928, 33, 219–227.

GODDARD, H. H., and H. F. HILL. Delinquent girls tested by the Binet Scale. *Training School Bulletin,* 1911, 8, 50–56.

GOLDFARB, W. The effects of early care on adolescent personality. *Journal of Experimental Education,* 1943a, 12, 106–129.

GOLDFARB, W. Infant rearing and problem behavior. *American Journal of Orthpsychiatry,* 1943b, 13, 249–265.

GOLDFARB, W. The effects of early institutional care on adolescent personality. *American Journal of Orthopsychiatry,* 1944, 14, 441–447.

GOLDFARB, W. Effects of psychological deprivation in infancy and subsequent stimulation. *American Journal of Psychiatry,* 1945a, 102, 18–33.

GOLDFARB, W. Psychological privation in infancy and subsequent adjustment. *American Journal of Orthopsychiatry,* 1945b, 15, 247–255.

GOLDFARB, W. Variations in adolescent adjustment of institutionally-reared children. *American Journal of Orthopsychiatry,* 1947, 17, 449–457.

GOLDSTEIN, H., J. W. MOSS, and L. J. JORDAN. The efficacy of special class training on the development of mentally retarded children. Urbana, Illinois: Institute for Research on Exceptional Children, 1965 (Cooperative Research Project, No. 619).

GOLDSTEIN, K. *The Organism.* New York: American Book, 1939.

GOTKIN, L. G. A calendar curriculum for disadvantaged kindergarten children. *Teachers College Record,* 1967, 68, 406–417.

GOULD, C. W. *America—a Family Matter.* New York: Scribner, 1922.

GRALIKER, B. V., K. FISHLER, and R. KOCH. Teenage reaction to a mentally retarded sibling. *American Journal of Mental Deficiency,* 1962, 66, 838–843.

GRANT, M. *The Passing of the Great Race,* rev. ed. New York: Scribner, 1919.

GRUENBERG, E. M. Some epidemiological aspects of congenital brain damage. In H. G. Birch, *Brain Damage in Children: The Biological and Social Aspects.* Baltimore: Williams & Wilkins, 1964.

GUERTIN, W. H. Mental growth in pseudo-feeblemindedness. *Journal of Clinical Psychology,* 1949, 5, 414–418.

GUESS, D. The influence of visual and ambulation restrictions on stereotyped behavior. *American Journal of Mental Deficiency,* 1966, 70, 542–547.

GUILFORD, J. P. The structure of intellect. *Psychological Bulletin,* 1956, 53, 267–293.

HALLER, M. *Eugenics: Hereditarian Attitudes in American Thought.* New Brunswick, New Jersey: Rutgers University Press, 1963.

HARTER, S., and E. ZIGLER. The effectiveness of adult and peer reinforcement on the performance of institutionalized and noninstitutionalized retardates. *Journal of Abnormal Psychology* 1968, 73, 144–149.

HAUSCHKA, T. S., J. E. HASSON, M. N. GOLDSTEIN, G. F. KOEPF, and A. SANDBERG. An

XYY man with progeny indicating familial tendency to non-disjunction. *American Journal of Human Genetics*, 1962, *14*, 22–30.

HAYWOOD, H. C., and J. T. TAPP. Experience and the development of adaptive behavior. In N. R. Ellis (Ed.), *International Review of Research in Mental Retardation*. New York: Academic Press, 1966.

HEBB, D. O. Intelligence in man after large removals of cerebral tissue: report of four left frontal lobe cases. *Journal of General Psychology*, 1939, *21*, 73–87.

HEBB, D. O. The effect of early and late brain injury upon test scores, and the nature of normal adult intelligence. *American Philosophical Society*, 1942, 85 (3), 275–292.

HEBB, D. O. Man's frontal lobes. *Archives of Neurology and Psychiatry*, 1945, *54*, 10–24.

HEBB, D. O. *The Organization of Behavior*. New York: Wiley, 1949.

HEBB, D. O. Intelligence, brain function and the theory of mind. *Brain*, 1959, *82*, 260–275.

HEBER, R. (Ed.). A manual on terminology and classification in mental retardation. *American Journal on Mental Deficiency*, Monograph Supplement, 1959, *64*.

HEGGE, T. S. The occupational status of higher-grade mental defectives in the present emergency. A study of parolees from the Wayne County Training School at Northville, Michigan. *American Journal of Mental Deficiency*, 1944, *49*, 86–98.

HIGGINS, J. V., E. W. REED, and S. C. REED. Intelligence and family size: a paradox resolved. *Eugenics Quarterly*, 1962, *9*, 84–90.

HILL, K., and S. B. SARASON. The relation of test anxiety and defensiveness to test and school performance over the elementary school years. *Monographs of the Society for Research in Child Development*, 1966, *31* (2), Serial No. 104.

HOFSTADTER, R. *Social Darwinism in American Thought*, rev. ed. New York: Braziller, 1959.

HOLLIS, J. H. The effects of social and non-social stimuli on the behavior of profoundly retarded children, I & II. *American Journal of Mental Deficiency*, 1965, *69*, 755–789.

HOLT, S. B. New thoughts on fingerprints. *Journal of the Forensic Science Society*, 1963, *4*, 7–17.

HORNER, F. A., C. W. STRAMER, L. L. ALEJANDRINO, L. H. REED, and F. IBBOTT. Termination of dietary treatment of phenylketonuria. *New England Journal of Medicine*, 1962, *79*, 266.

HOWE, S. G. Report made to the Legislature of Massachusetts upon idiocy. Boston: Presented from the State Edition by Coolidge and Wiley, 1848a (Senate No. 51, February, 1848).

HOWE, S. G. The causes and prevention of idiocy. *Massachusetts Quarterly Review*, 1848b, 3 (June).

HOWE, S. G. *Training and Teaching Idiots*. A report to the Governor of Massachusetts. Published as Senate No. 38, Feb. 1850.

HSIA, D. Phenylketonuria: A study of human biochemical genetics. *Pediatrics*, 1966, *38*, 173–184.

HSIA, D. Y., K. W. DRISCOLL, W. TROLL, and W. E. KNOX. Detection by phenylalanine tolerance tests of heterozygous carriers of phenylketonuria. *Nature*, 1956, *178*, 1239.

HSIA, D. Y., W. E. KNOX, K. V. QUINN, and R. S. PAINE. A one-year, controlled study of the effect of low phenylalanine diet on phenylketonuria. *Journal of Pediatrics*, 1958, *21*, 178.

HUGHES, A. *A History of Cytology*. London: Abelard-Schuman, 1959.

HUNT, J. MCV. *Intelligence and Experience*. New York: Ronald Press, 1961.

HUNT, N. *The World of Nigel Hunt: the Diary of a Mongoloid Youth*. New York: Garrett, 1967.

HUXLEY, J. Genetics, evolution and human destiny. In L. C. Dunn, Genetics in the 20th Century. New York: Macmillan, 1951.

HUXLEY, J. The emergence of Darwinism. In S. Tax (Ed.), *Evolution after Darwin*. Chicago: University of Chicago Press, 1960. Vol. I.

ITARD, J. M. G. *The Wild Boy of Aveyron*. Trans. by G. and M. Humphrey. New York: Appleton-Century-Crofts, Inc., 1932.

JACOBS, P., and J. A. STRONG. A case of human intersexuality having a possible XXY sex-determining mechanism. *Nature,* 1959, *183,* 302–303.

JASTAK, J., H. M. MACPHEE, and M. WHITEMAN. *Mental Retardation: Its Nature and Incidence.* Newark, Delaware: University of Delaware Press, 1963.

JENNINGS, H. S. *Prometheus.* New York: É. P. Dutton, 1925.

JENSEN, A. R. Social class and verbal learning. In J. P. DeCecco (Ed.), *The Psychology of Language, Thought, and Instruction.* New York: Holt, Rhinehart & Winston, 1967.

JERVIS, G. A. A contribution to the study of the influence of heredity on mental deficiency. The genetics of phenylpyruvic oligophrenia. Proceedings of the American Association on Mental Deficiency. *Journal of Psycho-asthenics,* 1939, *64,* No. 2, 13–24.

JOHN, V. The intellectual development of slum children: some preliminary findings. *American Journal of Orthopsychiatry,* 1963, *33,* 813–822.

JOHN, V., and M. DEUTSCH. The role of language in the cognitive processes of middle-class and lower-class children. Presented at the annual meeting of the American Association for the Advancement of Science, New York, December 1960.

JOHNSON, G. O. A comparative study of the personal and social adjustment of mentally handicapped children placed in special classes with mentally handicapped children who remain in regular classes. Syracuse: Syracuse University Research Institute, 1961.

JONES, D., and S. A. CARR. The relation between intelligence and social status among orphan children. *British Journal of Psychology,* 1927, *17,* 343–364.

JORDAN, D. S. Report of the committee on eugenics. *American Breeders Association,* 1908, *4,* 201–208.

JOYCE, J. The Boarding House. From *Dubliners,* in *The Portable James Joyce.* New York: Viking Press, 1947.

KANNER, L. Autistic disturbances of affective contact. *The Nervous Child,* 1943, *2,* 217–250.

KANNER, L. Early infantile autism. *Journal of Pediatrics,* 1944, *25,* 211–217.

KANNER, L. Irrelevant and metaphorical language in early infantile autism. *American Journal of Psychiatry,* 1946, *103,* 242–246.

KANNER, L. A miniature textbook of feeblemindedness. *Child Care Monographs,* No. 1. New York: Child Care Publications, 1949.

KANNER, L. *Child psychiatry.* Springfield, Illinois: Charles C Thomas, 2nd ed., 1948; 3rd ed., 1957.

KAPLAN, F., and J. COLOMBATTO. Head Start Project for siblings of retarded children. *Mental Retardation,* 1966, *4* (6).

KAPLAN, F., and E. FOX. Siblings of the retardate: An adolescent group experience. *Community Mental Health Journal* (in press).

KAUFMAN, M. E., and H. LEVITT. A study of three stereotyped behaviors in institutionalized mental defectives. *American Journal of Mental Deficiency,* 1965, *69,* 467–473.

KELLER, J. E. The use of certain perceptual measures of brain injury with mentally retarded children. In E. P. Trapp and P. Himelstein, *Readings on the Exceptional Child.* New York: Appleton-Century-Crofts, 1962.

KELLOGG, R. M. A follow-up study of one hundred males who spent some time in the special classes in the public schools of Newton, Massachusetts. Unpublished master's thesis, Boston University, 1941.

KENNEDY, C., and L. S. RAMIREZ. Brain damage as a cause of behavior disturbance in children. In H. G. Birch, *Brain Damage in Children: The Biological and Social Aspects.* Baltimore: Williams & Wilkins, 1964.

KENNEDY, J. L., W. WERTELECKI, L. GATES, B. P. SPERRY, and V. M. CASS. The early treatment of phenylketonuria. *American Journal of Diseases of Children,* 1967, *113,* 16–21.

KENNEDY, R. J. R. The social adjustment of morons in a Connecticut city. Hartford: Mansfield-Southbury Training Schools (Office of Mental Retardation, State Office Building), 1948.

KESSLER, J. W.   Learning disorders in school age children. *Psychopathology of Childhood.* Englewood Cliffs, New Jersey: Prentice-Hall, 1966.

KEY, W. E.   *Feebleminded Citizens in Pennsylvania.* Philadelphia: Public Charities Association of Pennsylvania, 1915.

KIMBRELL, D. L., and L. G. BLANCHARD.   Some psycho-sociological determinants of employed and discharged ward attendants in institutions for mental defectives. *American Journal of Mental Deficiency,* 1964, 69, 220–224.

KINGSLEY, L. V., and R. M. HYDE.   The health and occupational adequacy of the mentally deficient. *Journal of Abnormal and Social Psychology,* 1945, 40, 37–46.

KIRK, S. A.   Experiments in the early training of the mentally retarded. *American Journal of Mental Deficiency,* 1952, 56, 692–700.

KIRK, S. A.   *Early Education of the Mentally Retarded.* Urbana: University of Illinois Press, 1958.

KIRMAN, B. H.   The patient with Down's syndrome in the community. *Lancet,* 1964, 2, 705–714.

KLABER, M. M.   Should a retarded child be institutionalized?—a question of ethics for the consultant psychologist. *Journal of Community Mental Health,* in press.

KLABER, M. M., and E. C. BUTTERFIELD.   Stereotyped rocking—a measure of institution and ward adequacy. *American Journal of Mental Deficiency,* in press.

KLABER, M. M., E. C. BUTTERFIELD, and L. J. GOULD.   Type of institutional care and responsiveness to social reinforcement among severely mentally retarded children. 1968. Unpublished manuscript.

KLAPPER, Z. S., and H. G. BIRCH.   A fourteen-year follow-up study of cerebral palsy: Intellectual change and stability. *American Journal of Orthopsychiatry,* 1967, 37, 540–547.

KNOBLOCH, H., and B. PASAMANICK.   Syndrome of minimal cerebral damage in infancy. *Journal of The American Medical Association,* 1959, 170, 1384–1387.

KNOBLOCH, H., and B. PASAMANICK.   Complications of pregnancy and mental deficiency. In P. W. Bowman and H. V. Mautner, *Mental Retardation.* New York: Grune & Stratton, 1960, pp. 182–193.

KNOBLOCH, H., and B. PASAMANICK.   Environmental factors affecting human development, before and after birth. *Pediatrics,* 1960, 26, 210–218.

KNOX, W. E.   Sir Archibald Garrod's "Inborn errors of metabolism." II. Alkaptonuria. *American Journal of Human Genetics,* 1958, 10, 95–124.

KNOX, W. E.   An evaluation of the treatment of phenylketonuria with diets low in phenylalanine. *Journal of Pediatrics,* 1960, 26, 1–11.

KOCH, R., P. ACOSTA, K. FISHLER, G. SCHAEFFLER, and A. WOHLERS.   Clinical observations on phenylketonuria. *American Journal of Diseases of Children,* 1967, 113, 6–15.

KUETHE, J. L.   Social schemas. *Journal of Abnormal and Social Psychology,* 1962, 64, 31–38.

KUGEL, R. B., A. FEDGE, J. TREMBATH, and H. HEIN.   An analysis of reasons for institutionalizing children with mongolism. *Journal of Pediatrics,* 1964, 64, 68–74.

KUHLMANN, F.   The Binet and Simon tests of intelligence in grading feeble-minded children. *Journal of Psycho-asthenics,* 1912, 16, 173–193.

LASHLEY, K. S.   *Brain Mechanisms and Intelligence.* Chicago, Illinois: University of Chicago Press, 1929.

LAUGHLIN, H. H.   Report of the committee to study and to report on the best practical means of cutting off the defective germ-plasm in the American population, *Eugenics Record Office Bulletin,* Nos. 10A and 10B, 1914.

LAUGHLIN, H. H.   *Eugenics Record Office, Report No. 1,* 1913.

LEJEUNE, J.   Les aberrations chromosomiques humaines. *Bruxelels-Médical,* 42ᵉ année, nᵒ 4, 1962, 107–122.

LEJEUNE, J., M. GAUTIER, and R. TURPIN.   Study of the somatic chromosomes of nine mongoloid idiot children, 1959. In S. H. Boyer, *Papers on Human Genetics.* Englewood Cliffs, New Jersey: Prentice-Hall, 1963.

LEMKAU, P. V., C. TIETZE, and M. COOPER.   Mental health problems in an urban district. *Mental Hygiene,* 1942, 26, 275–288.

LEONARD, S. A., and F. L. MCGUIRE. Phenylketonuria: An unusual case. *Journal of Pediatrics*, 1959, 54, 210–214.

LESSER, G. S., G. FIFER, and D. H. CLARK. Mental abilities of children from different social-class and cultural groups. *Monographs of the Society for Research in Child Development*, 1965, 30(4), Serial No. 102.

LEWIS, D. *La Vida*. New York: Random House, 1966.

LEWIS, E. D. Types of mental deficiency and their social significance. *Journal of Mental Science*, 1933, 79, 298–304.

LILIENFELD, A. M., and E. PARKHURST. Study of the association of factors of pregnancy and parturition with the development of cerebral palsy. *American Journal of Hygiene*, 1951, 53, 262–282.

LOCKE, J. *The Philosophical Works of John Locke*. J. A. St. John (Ed.), London: G. Bell, 1905, vol. 1.

LORD, E. E. *Children Handicapped by Cerebral Palsy*. New York: Commonwealth Fund, 1937.

LOWELL, J. E. Public relief and private charity. *Questions of the Day*. No. XIII. New York: Putnam, 1884.

LURIA, A. R. (Ed.). *The Mentally Retarded Child*. New York: Macmillan, 1963.

MCCORD, C. P. One hundred female offenders. *Journal of Criminal Law and Criminology*, 1915, 6, 385–407.

MCINTOSH, W. J. Follow-up study of one thousand non-academic boys. *Exceptional Children*, 1949, 15, 166–170.

MCKAY, B. E. A study of I.Q. changes in a group of girls paroled from a state school for mental defectives. *American Journal of Mental Deficiency*, 1942, 46, 496–500.

MCKEON, R. M. Mentally retarded boys in war time. *Mental Hygiene*, 1946, 30, 47–55.

MCNEMAR, Q. Lost: our intelligence? Why? *American Psychologist*, 1964, 19, 871–882.

MCPHERSON, G. Preliminary consideration of the heredity of mental deficiency. *Proceedings of the American Association on Mental Deficiency*, 1936–1937, 42, 124–131.

MALTHUS, T. R. *First Essay on Population 1798*. London: Macmillan, 1926.

MASLAND, R. L. The prevention of mental retardation. A survey of research. *Journal of Diseases of Childhood*, 1958, 95, No. 1, Part II, 3–111.

MASLAND, R. L., S. B. SARASON, and T. GLADWIN. *Mental Subnormality*. New York: Basic Books, 1958a.

MENOLASCINO, F. J. Psychiatric aspects of mongolism. *American Journal of Mental Deficiency*, 1965, 69, 653–660.

MEYER, E., and B. CROTHERS. Psychological and physical evaluation of patients with cerebral palsy studied for periods of ten years or more. *American Journal of Physical Medicine*, 1953, 32, 153–158.

MEYERS, C. E., and H. F. DINGMAN. Factor analytic and structure of intellect models in the study of mental retardation. *American Journal of Mental Deficiency*, monograph supplement, 1966, 70(4), 7–25.

MOORE, A. *The Feeble-Minded in New York*. New York: State Charities Aid Association, 1911.

MOREL, B. A. *Traité des Dégénérescences Physiques, Intéllectuelles et Morales de l'Espèce Humaine*. Paris: Baillière 1857.

MOREL, B. A. *Traité des Maladies Mentales*. Paris: Baillière 1860.

MUENCH, G. A. A follow-up of mental defectives after 18 years. *Journal of Abnormal and Social Psychology*, 1944, 39, 407–418.

MULLEN, F. A., and W. ITKIN. The value of special classes for the mentally handicapped. *Chicago Schools Journal*, May 1961, 353–363.

MYERSON, A. *The Inheritance of Mental Diseases*. Baltimore: Williams & Wilkins, 1925.

NATIONAL ASSOCIATION FOR RETARDED CHILDREN. *Voices in Chorus*. 420 Lexington Avenue, New York, New York. 1962.

NEW YORK STATE DEPARTMENT OF MENTAL HYGIENE. A special census of suspected referred mental retardation in Onondaga County, New York. New York: Community Mental Health Research, 1955.

NITOWSKY, H. M., N. SINDHVANANDA, U. R. KONIGSBERG, and T. WEINBERG. Partial 18 monosomy in the cyclops malformation. *Pediatrics,* 1966, 37, 260–269.

NYHAN, W. Genetic defects of amino acid metabolism. *Pediatric Clinics of North America,* 1963, 10, 339–368.

O'FLYNN, MARGARET E., and D. Y. HSIA. Some observations on the dietary treatment of phenylketonuria. *Journal of Pediatrics,* 1968, 72, 260–262.

OLBY, R. C. *The Origins of Mendelism.* London: Constable, 1966.

O'NEIL, J. Siblings of the retarded: Part 2—Individual counseling. *Children,* 1965, 12(6).

OSBORN, F. *Preface to Eugenics.* Rev. ed. New York: Harper & Row, 1951.

OSBORN, H. F. Preface to the revised edition [1917]. In M. Grant, *The Passing of the Great Race.* New York: Scribner, 1919.

PAINE, R. The variability in manifestations of untreated patients with phenylketonuria. *Pediatrics,* 1957, 20, 290–302.

PASTORE, N. *The Nature-Nurture Controversy.* New York: Columbia University, 1949.

PATAU, K. The identification of individual chromosomes, especially in man. *American Journal of Human Genetics,* 1960, 12, 250–276.

PATTERSON, D., and J. C. SPENCE. The aftereffects of epidemic encephalitis in children. *Lancet,* 1921, 2, 491–493.

PEARSON, K. *The Life, Letters and Labour of Francis Galton.* Cambridge: Cambridge University Press, 1914. Vol. I, 1930, Vol. IIIA.

PENROSE, L. S. Two cases of phenylpyruvic amentia. *Lancet,* 1935, 23–24.

PENROSE, L. S. Phenylketonuria. A problem in eugenics. *Lancet,* 1946, 1, 949–953.

PENROSE, L. S. Propagation of the unfit. *Lancet,* 1950, 2, 425–427.

PENROSE, L. S. *The Biology of Mental Defect.* Rev. ed. New York: Grune & Stratton, 1962.

PENROSE, L. S., and J. H. QUASTEL. Metabolic studies in phenylketonuria. *Biochemical Journal,* 1937, 31, 266–274.

PETERSON, J. *Early Conceptions and Tests of Intelligence.* Yonkers, New York: World Book Company, 1925.

PEVZNER, M. S. *Oligophrenia: Mental Deficiency in Children.* New York: Consultants Bureau, 1959.

PEVZNER, M. S. The clinical characteristics of mentally retarded children. Child-oligophrenics. In A. R. Luria (Ed.), *The Mentally Retarded Child.* New York: Macmillan, 1963.

PINEL, P. *A Treatise on Insanity.* London: Todd, 1806. Reprinted, New York: Hafner, 1962.

PINNEAU, S. R. The infantile disorders of hospitalism and anaclitic depression. *Psychological Bulletin,* 1955, 52, 429–453.

PINTNER, R. *Intelligence Testing.* New York: Holt, 1923.

POLANI, P. E. Chromosomal factors in certain types of educational subnormality. In P. W. Bowman and H. V. Mautner, *Mental Retardation.* New York: Grune & Stratton, 1960.

POLANI, P. E. Cytogenetics of Down's syndrome (mongolism). *Pediatric Clinics of North America,* 1963, 10, 423–448.

POPENOE, P., and R. JOHNSON. *Applied Eugenics.* New York: Macmillan, 1918.

PRESIDENT'S PANEL ON MENTAL RETARDATION. A proposed program for national action to combat mental retardation. Washington, D.C.: U.S. Government Printing Office, 1962.

PROVENCE, S., and R. C. LIPTON. *Infants in Institutions.* New York: International Universities Press, 1962.

PUNNETT, R. C. Early days of genetics. *Heredity,* 1950, 4, 1–11.

RAE-GRANT, Q. A., T. GLADWIN, and E. M. BOWER. Mental health, social competence, and the war on poverty. *American Journal of Orthopsychiatry,* 1966, 36, 652–664.

RANK, B. Adaptation of the psychoanalytic technique for the treatment of young children with atypical development. *American Journal of Orthopsychiatry,* 1949, 19,

130–139. Copyright, the American Orthopsychiatric Assoc., Inc., reproduced by permission.

RAY, I.   Hereditary insanity. *North American Review,* 1869, *109,* 1–29.

REED, E. W., and S. C. REED.   *Mental Retardation: A Family Study.* Philadelphia: Saunders, 1965.

REED, T. E., J. H. CHANDLER, E. M. HUGHES, and R. T. DAVIDSON.   Huntington's chorea in Michigan—demography and genetics. *American Journal of Human Genetics,* 1958, *10,* 201–225.

REISMAN, L. E., A. DARNELL, J. W. MURPHY, B. HALL, and S. KASAHARA.   A child with partial deletion of a G-group autosome. *American Journal of Diseases of Children,* 1967, *114,* 336–339.

Report of the Royal Commission on the Care and Control of the Feeble-minded. Vol. 1. London: Wyman and Sons, 1908.

Report of Committee on Classification of Feeble-minded.   *Journal of Psycho-asthenics,* 1910, *15,* 61–67.

Report of a Study Group.   A proposed standard system on nomenclature of human mitotic chromosomes. *American Journal of Human Genetics,* 1960, *12,* 384–388.

Report of the Committee on Eugenics.   *American Breeders Association,* 1908, *4,* 201–208.

RICHMOND, J. B.   Report from Project Head Start. *Children's House,* September/October 1966, 40–43.

RICHMOND, J. B., and S. LUSTMAN.   Autonomic function in the neonate. *Psychosomatic Medicine,* 1955, *17,* 269–274.

RIMLAND, B.   *Infantile Autism, the Syndrome and Its Implications for a Neural Theory of Behavior.* New York: Appleton-Century-Crofts, 1964. Copyright © 1964 by Meredith Publishing Co.

ROBERTS, A. D.   Some I.Q. changes on the Stanford-Binet, Form L. *American Journal of Mental Deficiency,* 1945, *50,* 134–136.

ROHDE, R. A., J. E. HODGMAN, and R. S. CLELAND.   Multiple congenital anomalies in the E_1-Trisomy (Group 16–18) syndrome. *Pediatrics,* 1964, *33,* 258–270.

ROSANOFF, A. J., and F. I. ORR.   A study of heredity in insanity in the light of Mendelian theory. *Eugenics Record Office Bulletin,* No. 5, 1911.

ROSENBERG, C. E.   Charles Benedict Davenport and the beginnings of human genetics. *Bulletin of the History of Medicine,* 1961, *35,* 266–276.

ROSENTHAL, R.   *Experimenter Effects in Behavioral Research.* New York: Appleton-Century-Crofts, 1966.

ROSS, A. D.   *The Exceptional Child in the Family.* New York: Grune & Stratton, 1964.

SARASON, S. B.   Projective techniques in mental deficiency. *Character and Personality,* 1945, *13,* 237–245.

SARASON, S. B.   The content of human problem solving. *Nebraska Symposium on Motivation.* 1961. Pp. 147–174.

SARASON, S. B.   Some aspects of the brain-behavior problem. *Boston University Journal of Education,* 1964, *47,* 53–61.

SARASON, S. B., and T. GLADWIN.   Psychological and cultural problems in mental subnormality: A review of research. *Genetic Psychology Monographs,* 1958, *57,* 3–290.

SARASON, S. B., K. T. HILL, and P. G. ZIMBARDO.   A longitudinal study of the relation of *Anxiety in Elementary School Children. A Report of Research.* New York: Wiley, 1960.

SARASON, S. B., K. T. HILL, and P. G. ZIMBARDO.   A longitudinal study of the relation of test anxiety to performance on intelligence and achievement tests. *Monographs of the Society for Research in Child Development,* 1964, vol. 29, no. 7, ser. no. 98.

SARASON, S. B., M. LEVINE, I. I. GOLDENBERG, D. L. CHERLIN, and E. M. BENNETT.   *Psychology in Community Settings: Clinical, Educational, Vocational, Social Aspects.* New York: Wiley, 1966.

SCHAEFER, E. S., and R. Q. BELL.   Development of a parental attitude research instrument. *Child Development,* 1958, *29,* 339–361.

SCHAEFER-SIMMERN, H. *The Unfolding of Artistic Activity.* Berkeley: University of California Press, 1948.

SCHEERER, M., E. ROTHMANN, and K. GOLDSTEIN. A case of "Idiot Savant": an experimental study of personality organization. *Psychological Monographs*, 1945, 58(4).

SCHONELL, F. E. *Educating Spastic Children*. Edinburgh: Oliver & Boyd, 1956.

SCHONELL, F. E. Intelligence testing. In R. S. Illingworth (Ed.), *Recent Advances in Cerebral Palsy*. London: Churchill, 1958.

SCHREIBER, M., and M. FEELEY. Siblings of the retarded: a guided group experience. *Children*, 1965, 12(6), 221–225.

SCHULTZ, H. F., and S. T. BUCKMAN. A study of visiting patterns of relatives. *Welfare Reporter*, 1965, 16, 72–75.

SCHULTZ, J. Innovators and Controversies, *Science*, 1967, 157, 296–301.

SEGUIN, E. *Idiocy: Its Treatment by the Physiological Method*. New York: William Wood, 1866.

SEMLER, I. J., and I. ISCOE. Comparative and developmental study of the learning abilities of negro and white children under four conditions. *Journal of Educational Psychology*, 1963, 54, 38–44.

SEMMES, J., S. WEINSTEIN, L. GHENT, and H. L. TEUBER. *Somatosensory Changes after Penetrating Brain Wounds in Man*. Cambridge: Commonwealth Fund, 1960.

SHAW, G. B. S. Comments on a paper read by Francis Galton before the Sociological Society in 1904 and appearing in Galton, Francis: Eugenics: Its definition and scope and aims. *Sociological Papers*, 1904. London: Macmillan, 1905. P. 45–79.

SHAW, M. W., M. M. COHEN, and H. M. HILDEBRANDT. A familial 4/5 reciprocal translocation resulting in partial trisomy B. *American Journal of Human Genetics*, 1965, 17, 54–70.

SHULMAN, H. M. Intelligence and delinquency. *Journal of Criminal Law and Criminology*, 1951, 41, 763–781.

SKEELS, H. M. Adult status of children with contrasting early life experiences. *Monographs of the Society for Research in Child Development*, 1966, vol. 31, no. 3, ser. no. 105.

SKEELS, H. M., and H. B. DYE. A study of the effects of differential stimulation on mentally retarded children. *Proceedings and Addresses of the American Association on Mental Deficiency*, 1939, 44(1), 114–136.

SMITH, D. W. The no. 18 trisomy and D₁ trisomy syndromes. *Pediatric Clinics of North America*, 1963, 10, 389–407.

SMITH, G. B. Cerebral accidents of childhood and their relationships to mental deficiency. *Welfare Magazine*, 1926, 17, 18–33.

SNYDER, L. L. *Race: A History of Modern Ethnic Theories*. New York: Longmans, 1939.

SOLOMONS, G., L. KELESKE, and E. OPITZ. Evaluation of the effects of terminating the diet in phenylketonuria. *Journal of Pediatrics*, 1966, 69, 596–602.

SOLOMONS, G., H. ZELLWEGER, P. J. JAHNKE, and E. OPITZ. Four common eye signs in mongolism. *American Journal of Diseases in Children*, 1965, 110, 1146.

SPAULDING, P. J. Retest-results on the Stanford-Binet, Form L, with mental defectives. *American Journal of Mental Deficiency*, 1946, 51, 35–42.

SPENCER, H. *Social Statistics*. London: John Chapman, 1851.

SPITZ, H. Discussion of paper by Meyers and Dingman. *American Journal of Mental Deficiency*, Monograph Supplement, 1960, 70(4), 26–28.

SPRADLIN, J. E., and F. L. GIRARDEAU. The behavior of moderately and severely retarded persons. In N. R. Ellis (Ed.), *International Review of Research in Mental Retardation*. New York: Academic Press, 1966.

STAVER, N. The child's learning difficulty as related to the emotional problem of the mother. *American Journal of Orthopsychiatry*, 1953, 23, 131–142.

STERN, C. *Principles of Human Genetics*, 2nd ed. San Francisco: Freeman, 1960.

STOLUROW, L. M. Research on mental deficiency at the Institute for Research on Exceptional Children. *The Training School Bulletin*, 1961, 58, 61–73.

STOTT, L. H., and R. S. BALL. Infant and preschool mental tests: review and evaluation. *Monographs of the Society for Research in Child Development*, 1965, vol. 30, no. 3, ser. no. 101.

STRAUSS, A. A., and N. C. KEPHART. *Psychopathology and Education of the Brain-Injured Child*. New York: Grune & Stratton, 1955. Vol. II.

STRAUSS, A. A., and L. E. LEHTINEN. *Psychopathology and Education of the Brain-Injured Child.* New York: Grune & Stratton, 1947.

STRAUSS, A. A., and H. WERNER. Disorders of conceptual thinking in the brain-injured child. *Journal of Nervous and Mental Disease,* 1942, 96, 153–172.

SUMNER, W. G. *What Social Classes Owe to Each Other.* New York: Harper, 1883.

SUTHERLAND, B., B. UMBARGER, and H. K. BERRY. The treatment of phenylketonuria: A decade of results. *American Journal of Diseases of Children,* 1966, 111, 505–523.

SUTHERLAND, E. Mental deficiency and crime. In Kimball Young (Ed.), *Social Attitudes.* New York: Henry Holt & Co., 1931.

SWEETSER, F. L. *Patterns of Change in the Social Ecology of Metropolitan Boston: 1950–60.* Boston: Department of Mental Health, Division of Mental Hygiene, 1962a.

SWEETSER, F. L. *The Social Ecology of Metropolitan Boston: 1960.* Boston: Department of Mental Health, Division of Mental Hygiene, 1962b.

TARTAKOW, I. J. The teratogenicity of maternal rubella. *Journal of Pediatrics,* 1965, 66, 380–391.

TAYLOR, E. M. *Psychological Appraisal of Children with Cerebral Defects.* Cambridge: Harvard University Press, 1959.

TERMAN, L. M. *The Measurement of Intelligence.* Boston: Houghton Mifflin, 1916.

TEUBER, H. L., W. S. BATTERSBY, and M. B. BENDER. *Visual Field Defects after Penetrating Missile Wounds of the Brain.* Cambridge: Harvard University Press, 1960.

THERMAN, E., K. PATAU, D. W. SMITH, and R. I. DEMARS. The D trisomy syndrome and XO gonadal dysgenesis in two sisters. *American Journal of Human Genetics,* 1961, 13, 193–204.

THORMAHLEN, P. W. A study of on-the-ward training of trainable mentally retarded children in a state institution. Unpublished doctoral dissertation, Colorado State College (Greeley), 1964.

THORMAHLEN, P. W. A study of on-the-ward training of trainable mentally retarded children in a state institution. *California Mental Health Research Monograph,* No. 4, 1965.

TJIO, J. H., and A. LEVAN. The chromosome number of man. *Hereditas,* 1956, 42, 1–6.

TOWN, C. H. *Familial Feeblemindedness.* Buffalo: Foster & Stewart, 1939.

TREDGOLD, A. F. *Mental Deficiency.* London: Baillière, Tindall and Cox, 1908.

TREDGOLD, A. F. The feebleminded. *The Contemporary Review,* June, 1910.

TREDGOLD, A. F. *Mental Deficiency.* New York: Wood, 1922.

TREDGOLD, R. F., and K. SODDY. *A Text-Book of Mental Deficiency.* London: Braillière, Tindall, and Cox, 1956.

TREDGOLD, R. F., and K. SODDY. *Tredgold's Text-Book of Mental Deficiency.* Baltimore: Williams & Wilkins, 1963.

TURNURE, J., and E. ZIGLER. Outer-directedness in the problem-solving of normal and retarded children. *Journal of Abnormal and Social Psychology,* 1964, 69, 427–436.

VROOM, V. H. *Work and Motivation.* New York: Wiley, 1964.

WALLIN, J. E. W. The concept of the feebleminded, especially the moron. *The Training School Bulletin,* 1920, 17, 41–54.

WALLIN, J. E. W. *The Odyssey of a Psychologist.* Wilmington, Delaware: Published by the author, 1955.

WEATHERWAX, J., and E. P. BENOIT. Concrete and abstract thinking in organic and non-organic mentally retarded children. *American Journal of Mental Deficiency,* 1957, 62, 548–553.

WEAVER, J. The effects of motivation-hygiene orientation and interpersonal reaction tendencies in intellectually sub-normal children. Ann Arbor, Michigan: University Microfilms, 1966.

WECHSLER, D. *The Measurement of Adult Intelligence.* 3rd ed. Baltimore: Williams & Wilkins, 1944.

WECHSLER, D. Cognitive, conative and non-intellective intelligence. *American Psychologist,* 1950, 5, 78–83.

WECHSLER, D. *The Measurement and Appraisal of Adult Intelligence.* Baltimore: Williams & Wilkins, 1958.

WEISMANN, A. *The Germ-Plasm: A Theory of Heredity.* New York: Scribner, 1892.

WERTHEIMER, M. *Productive Thinking*. New York: Harper & Row, 1945.

WIENER, G., R. V. RIDER, W. C. OPPEL, L. K. FISCHER, and P. A. HARPER. Correlates of low birth weight: psychological status at six to seven years of age. *Pediatrics*, 1965, 35, 434–444.

WILLIS, T. *Two Discourses Concerning the Soul of Brutes*. Trans. S. Pordage. London: T. Dring, 1683.

WITMER, E. R., and L. WITMER. Orthogenic cases. XVI—George: Mentally restored to normal but intellectually deficient. *Psychological Clinic*, 1928, 17, 153–169.

WITMER, L. The fifteen months training of a feebleminded child. *Psychological Clinic*, 1907–1908, 69–80.

WITMER, L. The treatment and cure of a case of mental and moral deficiency. *Psychological Clinic*, 1908–1909, 2, 153–179.

WITMER, L. A fettered mind. *Psychological Clinic*, 1916–1917, 10, 241–249.

WITMER, L. Orthogenic Cases. XIV—Don: A curable case of arrested development due to a fear psychosis the result of shock in a three-year-old infant. *Psychological Clinic*, 1919–1922, 13, 97–111.

WITMER, L., and M. AMBLER. Orthogenic cases. XVII—Jack: Feebleminded or normal. *Psychological Clinic*, 1928–1929, 17, 217–225.

WOLFENSBERGER, W. Administrative obstacles to behavioral research as perceived by administrators and research psychologists. *Mental Retardation*, 1965, 3, 7–12.

WOOLF, L. I., and D. G. VULLIAMY. Phenylketonuria with a study of the effect upon it of glutamic acid. *Archives of Diseases in Childhood*, 1951, 26, 487–494.

WORLD HEALTH ORGANIZATION. The mentally subnormal child. World Health Organization Technical Report Series, 1954, no. 75.

WRIGHT, S. W., R. W. DAY, H. MULLER, and R. WEINHOUSE. The frequency of trisomy and translocation in Down's syndrome. *Pediatrics*, 1967, 70, 420–424.

YARROW, L. J. *Maternal deprivation*: Toward an empirical and conceptual reevaluation. *Psychological Bulletin*, 1961, 58, 459–490.

YERKES, R. M. (Ed.). Psychological examining in the United States Army. *Memoirs of the National Academy of Science*, 1921, vol. XV.

ZEAMAN, D., and B. J. HOUSE. An attention theory of retardate discrimination learning. In N. R. Ellis (Ed.), *Handbook of Mental Deficiency*, 1963.

ZEAMAN, D., and B. J. HOUSE. The relation of I.Q. and learning. In R. M. Gagné (Ed.), *Learning and Individual Differences*. Columbus, Ohio: Merrill Books, 1966.

ZIGLER, E. Social deprivation and rigidity in the performance of feebleminded children. *Journal of Abnormal and Social Psychology*, 1961, 62, 413–421.

ZIGLER, E. Social reinforcement, environment and the child. *American Journal of Orthopsychiatry*, 1963a, 33, 614–623.

ZIGLER, E. Rigidity and social reinforcement effects in the performance of institutionalized and noninstitutionalized normal and retarded children. *Journal of Personality*, 1963b, 31, 258–269.

ZIGLER, E. The effect of social reinforcement on normal and socially deprived children. *Journal of Genetic Psychology*, 1964, 104, 235–242.

ZIGLER, E. Research in personality structure in the retardate. In N. R. Ellis (Ed.), *International Review of Research in Mental Retardation*. New York: Academic Press, 1966.

ZIGLER, E., and J. WILLIAMS. Institutionalization and the effectiveness of social reinforcement: A three-year follow-up study. *Journal of Abnormal and Social Psychology*, 1963, 66, 197–205.

ZIGLER, E., B. SANDERS, and E. C. BUTTERFIELD. The effects of nursery school experience upon standard and optimal IQ. Unpublished manuscript, Yale University, 1966.

ZIRKLE, C. *Death of a Science in Russia*. Philadelphia: University of Pennsylvania Press, 1949.

ZIRKLE, C. The knowledge of heredity before 1900. In L. C. Dunn, *Genetics in the 20th Century*. New York: Macmillan, 1951.

ZUELER, W. W. Mental retardation and neonatal jaundice. In P. W. Bowman, and H. V. Mautner, *Mental Retardation*. New York: Grune & Stratton, 1960. Pp. 375–384.

Indexes

Index
of names

Index
of subjects